Carol's Alzheimer's Journey

Carol's Alzheimer's Journey

Treat Them Like A Person Not A Patient

Donald H. Ford and Carol C. Ford

Copyright © 2013, Donald H. Ford

All rights reserved. No part of this book may be reproduced, stored, or transmitted by any means – whether auditory, graphic, mechanical or electronic – without written permission of both publisher and author, except in the case of brief excerpts used in critical articles and reviews. Unauthorized reproduction of any part of this work is illegal and punishable by law.

ISBN 978-1-300-80321-8

Acknowledgements

I have written a lot of successful scholarly books. I know how to do that and am good at it. When I sat down to write this book I quickly realized writing for a general audience was something I had never done and didn't know how to do. At 84, I needed a teacher to help me learn how to do it! Fortunately I have a niece who is a talented, creative writer, a successful authoress of several books, and a literary reviewer for a diversity of journals. I first knew her as a baby and cute "Shirley Temple" like little girl. Her name is Laurel Johnson (affectionately nicknamed "little Iodine.") I came to know her as a young woman who became a highly skilled and widely admired professional nurse. As our lives progressed she became a warm friend. And now she has become my colleague and teacher. What a versatile person! I couldn't have written *Carol's Alzheimer's Journey* without her gentle and patient guidance. Throughout her life she has lived the major theme of this book: "Treat everyone as a person, not a patient." I recommend to you two favorite books of hers if you want a charming and heartwarming read. *My Name Is Esther Clara* and *The Alley of Wishes.*

Carol had a deep commitment to help enrich the lives of others in need through caring actions, and through over $100,000 earned through her paintings and crafts work which she contributed to help a create community based, nonprofit health and human development programs. Through this book and all income it generates (which will go into a special fund to support projects implementing its ideas about elder care) Carol's commitment to help others continues to live.

Carol's Alzheimer's Journey

Who is Carol? Why this book?

Suppose that you, your mate, parents, or a family member develop Alzheimer's. How will you be cared for as the disease worsens? The conventional answer is a nursing home where a medically trained staff will care for your medical and health needs until you die. They will be caring and capable, but often understaffed, and guided by program schedules as much as by your immediate needs and desires. That is **the medical model of elder care.**

What would that experience be like? You will be bored with nothing to do or accomplish most of the time, and lonely as you find it difficult to interact with others. If you can walk, you may wander from place to place, investigate other people's rooms, or the outdoors to brighten your life, and may become confused about where you are. If you can't walk you will spend 24 hours a day in your bed or wheel chair in one spot unless someone is available to move you. You will be unable to go to the bathroom, no matter how urgent the need, until someone comes to assist you. If others can't understand your speech, your social isolation will be greatly amplified. You will feel helpless and lost in an unfamiliar environment and may not recognize people who come to see or help you. You are likely to be plagued by fear, anger and depression. Is that the way you would want your life, or that of your loved ones, to end?

It doesn't have to be that way!! That bleak life results largely from a dominant focus on the person's disease state (despite the fact it is incurable). **There is an alternative!** Keeping a person alive isn't the same thing as helping them have a good life. **Caregivers can learn to treat people with Alzheimer's disease as a person rather than just a patient, by focusing on helping them lead a satisfying life using capabilities they still have. No matter how severe a person's limitations, they always have something left!** That alternative approach is called the **developmental model of elder care.**

One caregiver contrasted the two approaches as follows: "I was so impressed with how much better Carol's life was compared to my sister's two Alzheimer's patients. They were helpless, in bed all the time, always had bed sores, and had no activity or people around them. In contrast, when I observed Carol, even to the last, I could hear and see her talking, laughing, sometimes singing, doing things and enjoying life." This book will briefly describe both the nature of that alternative and its scientific base, and will illustrate in rich detail how it was used to enhance the life of a woman afflicted by late onset Alzheimer's disease.

Carol's story is simultaneously a biography of what it was like for a woman to lead her life mostly in the amazing 20th century when women's lives changed so dramatically, a love story, and a simplified "care giver manual" about how to use a developmental model of elder care. It was her hope and mine that her story might encourage, inform and enlighten others seeking positive ways of helping loved ones, friends, and clients to complete their lives as persons rather than just as patients.

Visualize Carol as an 80 year old, wheel chair bound, helpless, silver haired woman with advanced Alzheimer's, unable to walk, talk, feed or care for herself or communicate normally. Is there any way she could lead a satisfying and even pleasurable life? This book will show you that what most people consider impossible is indeed possible. Carol did it.

I spent my life as her husband, a teacher, developmental psychologist and psychotherapist focused on understanding the dynamics of human development. I learned what you see outwardly in a person with Alzheimer's isn't all there is. Hiding inside Carol, for example, was the shy little girl who enjoyed childhood play, singing, dancing, and Mother Nature; the fun-loving pretty young woman with raven hair and dimpled smile sharing the excitement of her growing up years with close girlfriends; the caring friend of adult women who delighted in her family and dancing with her husband; the gifted musician, artist, and compassionate, helping community member. This book demonstrates how such satisfying patterns of past activities can still be activated to help a person with severe limitations – like Alzheimer's – gain pleasure and satisfaction in their current life. They just can't do it in the ways they used to. Throughout her illness, caregivers could still activate and use these patterns to daily produce experiences of pleasure, satisfaction and sometimes even joy for Carol within the limitations of Alzheimer's. Carol's Alzheimer's journey covered most of the last four decades of her life, beginning with the appearance of the disease in her mother, and the knowledge she too was vulnerable.

Developmental care is not a new idea. We use it with babies while they can't walk, talk, care for themselves or use words. We do the same for children and adults with significant limitations, such as children with birth defects and soldiers with debilitating war injuries. We can do the same for seniors with limitations **if our society changes its outdated beliefs and decides it's worthwhile to help them live a satisfying life despite their limitations.** This approach applies not just to Alzheimer's patients, but to any person with significant limitations, like stroke victims. A key idea is that *as a person's limitations increase, regardless of the causes, they always retain some capabilities and possibilities that can be used to help produce some life satisfaction through programs that treat them like a person, not just a patient.*

Carol's Journey – the Prelude

Linda called, "Don, Carol is ready to dance with you." I put on a recording of Glenn Miller's *String of Pearls*, one of our favorite big band melodies, and moved close, holding out my arms. With one hand on my shoulder and the other holding mine, Carol snuggled against me in the dance position so familiar to us both.

We started our daily before-lunch dance through the dining room past her piano, through the living room past our big stone fireplace, onto the wooden walkway through the entry garden Carol created when we built the house. We paused while Carol stepped down onto a flagstone walkway, danced over to the steps, went up them and twirled into our dinette at the edge of the entry garden. Linda had our lunch waiting. Carol smiled as Linda sat her at the table, said goodbye and left. We ate our tomato soup while I talked about the cardinal eating on the platform outside our garden window. I drove Carol's wheelchair to the bathroom, and helped her transfer to the stool to empty her tanks. Then we went to our bed for her afternoon nap. As usual, I lay with her until she drifted off to asleep.

I started a load of laundry and then returned to lie beside her and read a book while she slept. Carol lay there, lifeless, with one arm draped over a pillow. I thought, *Dear God, she isn't breathing!* I knew she was gone. Choking with tears, I said, "Oh my darling Carol – we're separated again as we were before we married."

Carol died quietly and unexpectedly during her nap on a Wednesday afternoon, after living the first 11 years of the 21st century with Alzheimer's disease. Overwhelmed with a jumble of emotions, I endured the days following her death in a kind of fog. Our family encompassing me with love and happy memories carried me through all the rituals that follow a death. Then they went home and I was alone.

I lay awake many nights thinking about Carol. She had slipped beyond my worldly reach, yet my heart was thankful that her life ended without pain, filled with family love and activities she enjoyed. I took comfort remembering how people admired Carol's participation in her specially designed home care program, often commenting they hoped to get that kind of care if needed. I relived the warm responses of people around the country after listening to Patty Satalia's short public radio story about the active and satisfying life Carol led despite having Alzheimer's disease, e.g., "The radio interview describing such a positive approach to Alzheimer's care brought tears to my eyes."

One night, I looked into the dark bedroom we had shared for so many years and said, "Carol, we talked about possibly sharing our home care approach if it might help other care receivers and providers have a better life." I lay in the silence, then spoke into the darkness, "Do you still think it's a good idea?"

The response I received was as clear as if Carol were beside me, and to the point like always, "You bet your boots, Buster!"

For several weeks I thought about Carol's story and tried to get started on it. Lots of ideas came to mind, but I struggled to find the place in our lives and the right words to begin the story. Carol often said that as a couple we had charmed lives. She believed with all her heart that "someone up there" watched over us and guided our path. I have to smile while writing that last sentence because, even in absentia, Carol's influence guides and encourages me. Finally, she set me on the path to a solution for my problem as she had so many other times in our life.

Since her death, I'd been sorting through a lifetime accumulation of files, papers, correspondence and reports in boxes, drawers and closets. For some reason, I'd avoided going through a small box sitting openly on the Victorian era bar in our downstairs family room. That room, with its large, used brick fireplace, walls paneled with the rich color of old walnut planks, and large windows looking out onto our lawn and mountain stream, had been one of Carol's favorite places to relax, knit or crochet, work on our picture albums, and watch TV. One evening I decided to check the contents of that box. I found several layers of letters from friends during Carol's high school and my Air Force years. I put some in our "letter notebooks" and mailed others to the still-living friends who wrote them over a half century ago during World War II.

In the bottom of the box I found a prize – a happy anniversary card, a valentine, and a happy birthday card with a note attached in Carol's handwriting: "Put in greeting card notebooks." I had never seen those notebooks, so began an excited search and found them in a box containing Carol's high school annuals and newspaper clippings about members of our family. She had saved only greeting cards we gave one another. Reading through those vintage messages to each other provided me with a classic "Ah Ha!" moment. Two letters I found there transported me back to a pivotal moment in our lives. She had guided me to the starting point for writing her story. I smiled, remembering, and started writing.

Table of Contents

Acknowledgements v
Carol's Alzheimer's Journey vii
Carol's Journey – the Prelude xi

Chapter 1	Happy Memories and Love Guides Plans for the Future 1
Chapter 2	The Astonishing 20th Century and Its Impact on Carol's Life 9
Chapter 3	Carol Meets Her Soul Mate 27
Chapter 4	Maturing Views of Herself and the World 41
Chapter 5	Carol's Pathway to College and Love 49
Chapter 6	Living the Realities of College and Courtship 65
Chapter 7	Building Her Life As a Married Woman 107
Chapter 8	Carol's Pathway to Motherhood and Family Life 133
Chapter 9	Beginning a New Adventure 155
Chapter 10	Settling Into Our First Happy Valley Home 167
Chapter 11	An Old Dream Comes True 195
Chapter 12	1955 and the Future Looks Bright 209
Chapter 13	Carol Tackles New Roles and Discovers New York City 221
Chapter 14	Carol Reaches Goals and Plans Her Pennsylvania Dream Home 233
Chapter 15	Carol Juggles Changes, Promotions and Fun 253

Chapter 16	Elaborating Family Life	269
Chapter 17	More Travels and a New Dream for Carol	283
Chapter 18	New Challenges and Old Friends	299
Chapter 19	Chaotic Times and Travels	315
Chapter 20	Changes and Losses	331
Chapter 21	Our First College Graduate and Wedding	345
Chapter 22	Old Doors Close, New Ones Open	351
Chapter 23	Carol Plans Another Dream Home	365
Chapter 24	New Pathways, New Lives	377
Chapter 25	Winifred's Health Problems Ending with Alzheimer's Disease	387
Chapter 26	Paradise and Pathos	397
Chapter 27	New Beginnings and Sad Losses	411
Chapter 28	All Carol's Travel Dreams Come True	429
Chapter 29	Trials, Joys, and Travels	441
Chapter 30	More Travels, More Milestones	455
Chapter 31	Alzheimer's Emerges	469
Chapter 32	Carol's Magic Man Devises a Plan	483
Chapter 33	Accentuate the Positive and Eliminate the Negative	503
Chapter 34	Carol's Home Care Plan in Action	517
Epilogue		543

Chapter One

Happy Memories and Love Guides Plans for the Future

Carol and I sat on our deck enjoying a balmy summer evening with a full moon and fireflies flickering from place to place. Our deck overlooks a spring fed pond surrounded by brightly colored flowers. We sat in comfortable silence, enjoying the music created by Slab Cabin Creek gurgling over stones as it rushed past our Happy Valley home.

Our thoughts that night focused on losses. Carol's father had lived next door to us for several years and died a few months ago. We buried him beside his wife, Winifred, in Minneapolis, Kansas where they were born as the 20th century began. Two months later, my 90-year-old mother died. We flew to Kansas and laid her to rest in the Marysville, Kansas cemetery beside Herbert, her husband of seven decades.

For the first time in two-thirds of a century, we had no parents with whom to share our holidays and lives. No more newsy letters would be exchanged and those beloved familiar voices would never again be heard on the other end of the phone. As an only child, Carol had no remaining family, so the loss of both parents left a big hole in her life. Our sons had started their own families, so our nest was empty. Many friends had died or moved away. We both floundered a bit after the two funerals in Kansas, sharing a burden of grief and loneliness we'd never experienced before.

Later, as we lay in bed, I hugged Carol tightly against me and was comforted by the feeling of her. Finally, Carol's soft voice brought light to that dark night, "Don, I've been thinking that we need to celebrate the life we shared with our parents instead of being lost in grief. When I was 16 and you 17, we met on a blind date and began exchanging letters about our lives. We were separated so much by distance, school, the war and college that letters were our primary way of being together almost daily until we finally married." Her mention of our letters warmed my heart.

"Awhile back I counted our letters. We saved more than 1000 of them. And we've saved maybe 1200 letters exchanged with our parents over 40 years. Our parents are still alive in our letters! Let's organize all of our letters in big notebooks. Then, from time to time, we can read them together and relive the memories there, replacing our grief with mostly happy thoughts."

A ray of pleasure replaced the sadness we'd been feeling. "Carol, what a wonderful idea! I have a lot of notebooks I used for my teaching and scholarly work, so I'll empty them out for this use." Many happy hours were spent together filling those notebooks with our memories.

Over a year later, we finished creating the last notebook, 21 in all. We were both a muddle of mixed emotions from finishing our library of memories. Carol had seemed lost in thought most of the day, but finally turned her dimpled smile my way. "Don, day after tomorrow is your birthday. I'd like to have one of our special dates that night to celebrate and share some of the feelings our letters aroused in me."

I grinned and said, "I hope this birthday celebration won't be like the one you and our sons gave me several years ago – remember?"

Carol laughed, "We all thought it was great fun to roast you like we did. I can be funny with a martini or two in me, and surprised everyone with my Erma Bombeck-like monologue. I thought one of my best shots was, 'Dad's main fault is that you can't argue with him. You have as much chance of winning an argument with him as you do with an umpire. The only thing that can cheat him out of the last word is an echo.'"

"Carol, your comment that I'm an expert at handing out baloney disguised as food for thought wasn't exactly kindly."

Carol grinned, "My favorite was, 'When he tries to translate his big ideas into action, your dad is a big pain in the neck – and some people have an even lower opinion of the pain. He's always embarking on vast projects with half-vast ideas.'" She kissed me and said, "This time instead of feeling the heat of a roast I hope you'll feel the gentle warmth of love."

Two nights later, on another beautiful evening, we sat on our deck sipping martinis and nibbling snacks to begin our celebration. A small vase on the coffee table held a pink Alpha Xi rose nestled with a red Tau Kappa Epsilon carnation. Carol was gorgeous in an emerald green and white dress and her elegant silver hair glowing in the sunset. She seemed excited, yet nervous, with a little tremble in her voice.

"Spending the past year assembling and rereading some of our half a century of letters has reminded me what an extraordinary love I have with you. My birthday gift to you tonight is a letter in which I give you my love and my heart." She handed me a birthday card with her hand written letter. I read it aloud:

My Dearest Don. I love watching you sometimes when you don't know I'm looking. As I watch you doing any of a hundred different things, feelings of love and pride well up inside me. I'm so poor at putting my thoughts and feelings for you into words. You're so good to me and I know I don't show you enough how much that means to me (unfortunately, I think that much more often than I express it). So, I'll tell you my thoughts and feelings in a letter as I used to do before we married. I wish there was some big splashy way I could tell you and show you how much I love you! You are to me as precious as life itself, and when I stop to think of all you mean to me I get all filled up inside with deep emotion. I just wish you could be inside me for a moment to experience the feelings of love, respect and admiration I have for you. The best times for me are just being beside you (preferably alone) talking, eating, working, sitting looking at the scenery, touching and looking at one another. Then I feel whole. Haven't we been lucky to have had all these wonderful years together – even the sad days. You are my husband, lover, father of my children, playmate, best friend, confidant, cheerleader for my accomplishments, my safe harbor in troubled times, the healer of my self-doubts and wounded spirit when needed –you are my life! All I really want in the world is to be your wife, and for you to be happy and to love me as I cherish you – forever. Your Carol

I was so choked up with emotion I could barely finish reading her letter aloud. Tears trickled down my cheeks as I looked into

Carol's eyes. I usually hold my emotions in tight control, but that night I couldn't and didn't want to. Carol quickly moved from her chair to my lap. She kissed my teary cheeks, caressed my hair, and hummed a loving melody while I sniffled. Finally, I was able to say, "You lied when you said you couldn't put your thoughts and feelings into words. Your letter is a treasure beyond words."

We refreshed our martinis and talked about our letters and ourselves. Carol said, "We have my mother to thank for our letters. It was her suggestion to me that we save them as she and dad saved theirs from years in the Navy during WWI. I've read some of their teenage letters and in some ways ours sound like theirs. Dad told me he destroyed some of his because 'there was too much love mush in them'. It puzzles me why many men seem so uncomfortable or embarrassed by expressions of feelings. I'm glad you're not one of them."

"When we planned this celebration you said you hoped it would make me feel the tender warmth of love. Carol, you have succeeded. Your birthday letter to me is marvelous and there's also a special coincidence. Last May, while we were organizing our letters, I decided to renew our letter writing tradition and wrote a letter to you to include in your anniversary card. Then, we had a flood of children and grandchildren visit us over a period of weeks and I forgot to give it to you. So, let's also have a late celebration of our wedding anniversary tonight." I kissed her, handed her a card with my letter in it, and said, "Happy Anniversary!"

She said, "You read my letter aloud so I'll try to do the same with yours."

Dearest Carol – my best friend, my sweetheart, my inspiration, my wife, my lover, my companion, my life. Organizing our nearly half a century of letters reminds me of how wonderful it was to exchange letters with you in our lonely courtship years, particularly when we were separated by World War II. People frequently can say in letters things they find more difficult to express in person in spoken words. So, I have decided to write you a letter now to renew the tradition that brought us together originally, and that helped our love to flower into marriage. Over fifty years ago, I first met you on that fateful July day in 1943. I thought you were the prettiest girl I had ever seen (still do) and decided that I wanted to know you better. It took only a few times with you for me to realize that not only were you a beautiful young woman but also interesting, intelligent, fun to talk with and delightful to dance with. So, I set out in persistent pursuit as our 5 years of courtship by correspondence attests.

Finally, I graduated from college (courtesy of the GI Bill) and you became my wife. The fantasy we had created about ending our separation and being together always was fulfilled. What joy filled that first year as we began building a life together! And we have built well, haven't we. We have shared the happiness of the birth of children and the sorrow of the death of loved ones. We have pinched pennies to make ends meet – and found strength and deeper love in doing so. We built our first home with our own hands and that too strengthened us as a team. We shared the thrill and fears of new parents, and our combined strength, love and caring have brought our sons to manhood as people of whom we can be proud.

Through it all, you unselfishly encouraged and helped me as I completed my college degrees, created a new counseling service, a new college, taught students and wrote books. Despite giving so much of yourself to me and our sons, you continued to grow as your own person – as a community leader, a talented artist, craftswoman and musician, and a multitalented woman. You provided a widely admired role model for more young faculty wives and secretaries than you will ever know. Your humanitarian work has made a difference in the lives of many nameless people. The many health and human services you helped to launch and elaborate with funds you generated with your Personal Touch home studio will continue for a long time to improve the quality of life for others.

The young rosebud I first admired blossomed into a rose of everlasting beauty, and amazingly you are one of the few 'thornless' roses. That is a key reason other women feel so safe in confiding in you and in relationships with you. I admire and am deeply proud of your accomplishments and of you as a person. I feel greatly complimented when people recognize me as your husband rather than as Dean Ford (and that is happening a lot).

At that point Carol's emotions overwhelmed her ability to read. Tearfully, she said, "Oh Don, you can't know how pleased and thankful I am for the respect and admiration you've always shown me. You give me what I hoped for but never got from my father. You've been like a powerful antidote for my periodic bouts of self-doubt." Smiling through her tears, she continued reading:

We started life together, marrying and becoming one, initially focusing on doing only as we wished to please one another, to have fun and explore new experiences, without responsibilities for others. That soon changed, and for over 4 decades we spent much of our time serving the interests and needs of others. Our lives have now come full circle. Once again it is just you and me, sharing our daily lives, free to do what we wish without continuous responsibilities for others. In a way I feel like a newlywed. Only this time we have enough money to do what we wish – and I can do for you things I only dreamed of as a young bridegroom. We don't have the same physical capabilities but we do have the same love of and shared spirit for life.

So, how will we use this new freedom together? Whatever choices we make, I know that the underlying melody will continue to be that which we forged in our first years of marriage – joy in just being together day-by-day, quiet pleasure in sharing tasks, happy hour conversations about anything and everything, sharing the pleasure of music and dancing together, the competition of a gin rummy or cribbage game, and even an argument now and then (with the fun of making up). We can elaborate this melody with new adventures, pride in accomplishments by ourselves and our offspring, and unpredictable events. As we age, our limitations may grow in unpredictable ways. For example, since both your mother and aunt died in nursing homes with Alzheimer's disease, the fear it might eventually reach you has been present. Circulatory problems killed my father and could get me. We could be in an automobile accident.

But let's not focus on the bad things that might happen. Let's savor the good possibilities that lie before us and make them happen, as we have throughout our lives. We are two persons merged into one life by an enduring and undying love and that will continue into eternity. So, take my hand – come into my arms – and together we'll explore new patterns and pathways of living. I'll try to make living with me fun (though it may be a little challenging and unpredictable at times). I'll be your 'Bridge Over Troubled Waters' if and when troubles arise, as you are mine. When we first fell in love you told me that the song 'You'll Never Walk Alone' represented our relationship. I promise you that no matter what life brings us (Alzheimer's or anything else) we will live the rest of our lives together in our home that you designed, and I will try to bring to you every day the happiness I promised you when I asked you to marry me.   Just love me always.   Your Don

Carol stood facing me for a moment, looking deep into my eyes. Then she dropped her letter and flew into my arms. We hugged and cried happy tears until our legs gave out and we sagged into our deck chairs, holding hands.

Carol finally broke the silence, "Many times since we fell in love I've told you I always feel safe with you. That is particularly important to me tonight as we talk about our future together. I haven't said much to you about it, but I do occasionally have anxious thoughts about my family tendency to Alzheimer's. Of course, I hope it doesn't happen, but I know there is no cure if it does. What you said in your letter helps me immensely. I know that no matter what happens to me, if it can be fixed I can count on you to get it fixed, as you have throughout our lives. If it can't be fixed, I know with your love and creative mind you'll find ways to help us continue to live a meaningful life together. So, as you suggested in your letter, I'll join you in focusing on the good things our life offers, and try not to worry about the bad possibilities."

We both hated to see that wonderful evening of sharing our thoughts and emotions end. But the intensity of our feelings had exhausted both of us, so we went to bed to rest up for constructing the rest of our lives together while enjoying our memories of the life we had lived.

When I discovered those two cards and letters a year after Carol's death, I felt like she had guided me to them. Through our marriage, I frequently sought Carol's opinion while struggling with decisions about problems or potential pathways in my jobs or writing projects. She had the uncanny ability to cut through all the 'ifs, buts, and maybes' and focus on the essence of my problems. Carol didn't get bogged down in complicated scenarios like we scholars and professors tend to do. She looked beyond the chaos and focused on solutions. So, when I found that box and read our two letters, I could hear Carol's voice prodding me to action: "Stop messing around and get on with it, Buster!"

The rest of Carol's story describes not only real events and actions, but also reports a rich array of thoughts and feelings that occurred within them. How is that possible? From the time we met in 1943, we increasingly shared our most personal thoughts and feelings in our letters, conversations and behaviors throughout our lives. This is the first time they've been shared with others, although Carol's mother read some of our early letters.

As I began to write Carol's story, our letters served as what cognitive scientists call "retrieval cues", i.e., current events that selectively activate related memories. Because we were so open with one another about our private thoughts and feelings, the words in our letters often activated in me the thoughts and emotions we experienced and expressed in the events described. When strong emotions, particularly positive ones, are present in an episode for any person, the memories reactivated will be more extensive, elaborate, and powerful, as they were for me. Near the end of Carol's story I will tell you more about how the remembering process works.

Carol's story is presented with both our voices in two part harmony. It results from a combination of quotes from our letters and related memories and feelings, and memories of significant events in our lives with thoughts and feelings linked to them. Before writing each part of this book, I read and reread relevant letters written by us or our parents until memories surrounding those events blossomed both in thoughts and feelings. I did the same thing with relevant photographs, home movies, and special mementos.

The first part of the story is told in the form of flashbacks to our past to reveal how Carol's pleasurable pathways evolved to this pivotal point in our lives. Then, the rest of her story will be told in the form of episodes creating our future as we used our new freedoms to focus on new possibilities of pleasurable adventures. We seldom spent time worrying about potential bad things that might happen to us in the future, but did focus on dealing with new limitations as they arose. The story ends with descriptions of the progressive development of Alzheimer's disease and the ways we used Carol's history of activities that yielded pleasure for her to create her developmental care program to fill every day of the rest of her life with good times and feelings of accomplishment.

Chapter Two

The Astonishing 20th Century and Its Impact on Carol's Life

Every person's life is influenced by the possibilities and constraints provided by their general environment and specific life settings or contexts. Change those possibilities and constraints, and the opportunities for a person's behavior and development will change.

Every episode in a person's life is made possible by a specific context or framework. Therefore, a person's life cannot be understood without recognizing the nature of the framework in which it occurs. Much of what you read here occurred in different kinds of settings that existed before you were born or were a kid. Therefore, as you read about specific episodes in Carol's life, it's important to understand them in her contexts rather than interpreting them within circumstances you experienced personally.

For example, younger readers might wonder why Carol and I wrote so many letters. When we were teenagers and young adults, telephone service was quite limited, of poor quality, and expensive in contrast to present day cell phones and texting. Postal service was the only inexpensive, personal and private way people had of staying in close touch.

Why was it so hard for us to get together? One key reason was severely limited transportation possibilities. Cars weren't built during WWII so they were scarce during the war and postwar years. Buses and trains were still scarce, many nearly worn out prewar relics, limited in number and schedules, very crowded, and sorely in need of repair and replacement. Many soldiers and ex-GIs partially solved that problem with hitchhiking, but Carol and women in general couldn't do that safely.

While this is Carol's story, I provided many of the settings in which her pathways through life evolved. So, to understand her development it's necessary to know about our shared circumstances.

The 20th century produced more dramatic and rapid scientific, technological, economic, social and cultural changes than occurred in all of prior human history combined. Therefore, Carol's life span development evolved within those dynamically changing environments and contexts. For example:

Science Changed How People Decided What Knowledge to Trust and Use

During most of the 19th century, people relied primarily on religious, philosophical and political principles and leaders to guide their beliefs. *Scientific methods,* exploded into dominance in the 20th century. These new strategies and methods enabled people to *decide for themselves* what knowledge to trust and that process changed the world.

Science requires that knowledge and beliefs must be supported by evidence obtained by carefully observing real events, producing evidence available to everyone. That approach made sense because scientific methods are only a polished version of those everyone is born with called *curiosity, exploration, observation and learning from experience.* Those methods provide sound and useful answers to practical questions like "What is it?" "How does it work?" "How can I make it better?" "How can I make what I have imagined into something real and useful?"

For example, people no longer pray to gods to eliminate afflictions like Alzheimer's disease; they ask and support scientists to do it. Science did not replace the old guiding traditions. It simply clarified their roles in specifying reasons and values to guide choosing to pursue some goals and methods and not others.

Science and an increasing personal autonomy were catalysts for other astonishing changes in the 20th century. Here are key developments that significantly influenced Carol's life.

Transportation. From earliest history, people moved from place to place by walking, floating, or having animals carry them on their backs or pull them around in carts. The 20th century brought mass produced, affordable vehicles that gave people personal control over their transportation and therefore more control over their lives. They could go anywhere they wanted whenever they wanted to, at modest cost and in relatively short periods of time. In 1903 the Wright brothers showed humans they could fly. By the end of the 20th century anybody could fly to anywhere in the world in a matter of hours, allowing Carol to live her childhood dreams of exploring her country and world.

Communication. In ancient times humans communicated by making sounds or gestures face to face. Then they invented symbols – pictures or words – and ways of copying them to be shared. Then humans discovered how to code information on electric signals, send them through wires by telegraph and telephones. By the end of the 20th century humans replaced electric signals and wires with special "air waves" that could transport information everywhere through free space at very high speeds. That made it possible to use radio signals, cell phones, cyberspace, TV, and satellites to communicate with anyone, anytime, anywhere as often as we want with little cost.

The 20th Century Produced a Shrunken, Interdependent World. The world is still the same size, but functionally it has become much smaller. Human interactions and accomplishments have been dramatically increased by modern transportation and communication technologies. We can now interact with others elsewhere in the world as if we are neighbors, rather than distant strangers to be feared. Here are some examples of worldwide consequences that altered Carol's life and continue to influence people's lives everywhere:

Economic Interdependence. Commerce became an integrated system with countries relying on one another for food, materials, products and technologies. International rivalries and wars are being replaced by economic collaboration, competition and alliances. Markets in one country provide jobs in other countries. Isolated national economic policies are no longer feasible or functional.

Human Health Interdependence. Infectious diseases can travel around the world with the speed of transportation. This led to international cooperation whereby most infectious diseases have nearly disappeared worldwide, or are controlled with modern medical technologies that all countries share. Birth control is available worldwide. Effective preventive and remedial medical technologies for major health problems are widely available. Global life expectancy nearly doubled during the 20th century. World population grew from 1.6 billion to 6 billion.

Social Interdependence. By the end of the 20th century, the social taboo of sexism drastically declined around the world, and women now have rights more similar to men in most parts of the world. Most societies now accept equal rights for all races and backgrounds. The civil rights movement in the U.S. transformed society in many ways. Women won voting rights in 1920 as did African Americans in midcentury. Equal treatment in employment has grown with big strides. Colonialism ended allowing nearly a billion people in Africa to create their own nation states. People now use cell phones and small computers to organize rebellions in their country.

Cultural Interdependence. A multicultural view and development of social customs and the arts grew immensely in the 20th century. What young people like to eat, wear, do, and seek in their lives is highly influenced by their growing familiarity with other cultures.

Education. The 20th century brought transformations requiring different educational content, strategies and facilities to fit the needs of societies and economies worldwide for educating people who can work effectively within and lead modern technological societies. Most national governments lag seriously behind serving this growing need for modernizing education.

Development of Carol's life spanned most of the 20th century. As you experience the progression of her life you'll see how every new decade brought new possibilities. Chief among them was the great influence of declining restrictions and increasing possibilities for women's beliefs and activities. Carol and I led a life that was unimaginable for our parents' generation.

At Birth, A Person's Life Is A Book With Empty Pages Waiting For A Story To Be Written

Carol Clark was born October 8, 1927 in Topeka, the capitol of Kansas. But, she wasn't a city girl. Her roots and heart were in the beautiful prairies of Kansas. She often said, "People who imagine the plains to be flat and featureless don't know what they are missing." Carol loved the rolling hills and grasslands of Kansas and was fascinated with their history. The plains were once covered with a primordial ocean that supported luxuriant plant growth and wildlife, including dinosaurs. As that ancient ocean dried up, deep, soft deposits formed. The southern 2/3 of the ocean bottom became huge prairies with soil so rich that prairie grass often grew shoulder high. Before humans broke that antediluvian soil it was ten to twenty feet deep, laced with a network of sparkling rivers and streams teeming with fish, clams, frogs and other wildlife.

Carol's British and Scot ancestors were among the emigrants who settled in those prairies so lush for farming and raising animals, particularly cattle, near a new town named Minneapolis, Kansas. In that pioneer period, surviving and prospering in those sparsely settled prairie areas required close relationships and cooperation among those who lived there, so close, extended family relationships were a cornerstone of pioneer prairie life and survival. Carol's roots were deeply embedded in two such families.

Carol's parents, Winifred and Eugene, were born into that prairie life just before the beginning of the 20th century. A few U.S. statistics provide examples of what life was like in 1910 when they were in grade school. Only 14% of homes had a bathtub; 8% had a telephone; there were only about 8000 cars and 144 miles of paved roads in the U.S.; the average worker made $200-$400 a year; more than 95% of all births took place at home; 90% of all doctors had no college education; women often used Borax or egg yolks for shampooing their hair around once a month; formal schooling ended for most people with the 8th grade – only 6% graduated from high school. An 8th grade graduate was considered an adult and expected to do an adult's work. For example, at age 14, my father became a cowboy on a western Kansas ranch and could walk into any saloon for a shot of whiskey along with every other man.

Winifred and Eugene grew up and worked on their family farms. They walked or traveled by horse and buggy from their farms to Minneapolis (sometimes staying overnight with friends) so they could go to high school where they met and developed a warm friendship. Immediately after high school graduation, Eugene enlisted in the Navy and spent World War I escorting troop ships to Europe and chasing German submarines, while Winifred became a school teacher. Their friendship blossomed during the war with affectionate letters which they saved as a diary.

After the war, Eugene studied business at Kansas University and took an accounting job with Kansas Power and Light in Topeka, Kansas. They married, but had to keep it a secret until Winifred's teaching contract ended because under Kansas law if a teacher married she was fired. When the school year ended they announced their marriage and settled in Topeka.

In addition to his marriage and accounting job, Eugene took over the annual wheat planting and harvesting responsibilities on the family farm, so Carol spent part of her childhood and adolescent summers being a "farm girl", especially during wheat harvest time. After we met, Carol described to me her pleasure in those experiences:

"I came to love the fragrant prairie winds that carried scents of fresh turned earth, the wildflowers (particularly the big Kansas sunflowers), and the musical cries of meadow larks and other birds. It was exciting and fun to have Aunt Florence teach me how to care for the farm animals, and to sneak my hand under a hen to steal its eggs. The beauty and dramatic changes of the prairie skies and seasons fascinated me. I even loved the excitement of watching huge, dark, anvil shaped clouds towering higher and higher into the sky while flashing lightning, and running for the storm cellar when a tornado threatened. I called it *the land of the big sky!*"

Carol also told me of being with her maternal Scottish grandparents as a little girl, "They were both fun loving, enjoyed playing fiddle and piano music together, and were often asked to play for country dances. They were an early source of my music interests. I loved Grandma Campbell's needlework skill, and was delighted when she taught me to knit and crochet."

In 1929, Eugene became head accountant for the KP&L office in Marysville, Kansas. Two year old Carol moved to a pleasant and cozy home in a safe part of Marysville, high on a hill above the Blue River where flooding would not be a problem. It had a backyard perfect for children to play in, a small orchard, and a goldfish pond. North across the road was Billy Goat Hill, a place where gypsies sometimes camped as they traveled through the area, where children sledded in winter, flew kites, and played games throughout the year.

Marysville started as a frontier settlement providing ferry service across the Blue River, just a few miles south of the Nebraska state line. It became a major crossroads for wagon trains of settlers heading west, and a stopover for pioneers and military units moving between Fort Riley, Kansas and Fort Kearney, Nebraska. It became a home station for the Pony Express when that mail service developed. Eventually, it evolved as a major hub for the Union Pacific Railroad and a crossroads for east-west and north-south automobile and truck transportation.

Marysville flourished before and during the Civil War, with both Union and Confederate interests trying to control its transportation role. Eventually, the Southern sympathizers moved back south, but their influence on Marysville remained. When Carol lived there, Marysville's city ordinances permitted black people to travel through town but they could not live, eat there, or stay in hotels overnight. There were no African Americans or American Indians in Marysville when Carol and I lived there. It had become a vibrant community of four thousand people, and the seat of Marshall County government. It functioned as a shopping hub for the surrounding rural areas and a railroad hub with a round house for servicing engines and assembling trains. Churches of several faiths, two grade schools, one high school, and a variety of leisure activities made it an ideal, safe, small community in which Carol's abilities and interests could thrive.

What was life like there in 1929? The economic recovery after World War I was in full bloom. Factories and assembly lines flourished. The Model T Ford was a great new car. Fresh foods were typically available only during local growing seasons. Refrigeration technologies did not yet exist, so in most communities the "ice man" delivered blocks of ice that people stored in a sturdy wooden box to keep foods cold and fresh. The movie industry was in its infancy and talking pictures a recent innovation. Radio was slowly becoming a source of entertainment and news, but most people did not yet have them. After saving pennies for two years my father finally brought home a radio. We were the only ones in the neighborhood with one, so neighbors asked us to open our windows and turn up the volume so they could hear it too. The idea of airplanes as public transportation seemed like science fiction. Passenger trains were the only means by which people could travel any distance in a reasonable amount of time and sparked childhood fantasies.

Then the Great 1930s Depression struck. People were in great distress. A downward spiraling economy produced very high unemployment, poverty, plunging incomes, low agricultural and industrial production with subsequent loss of income and profits, hopelessness about the future, health problems and suicides. Eugene had a secure job with a steady income so the Clarks didn't experience serious financial stress, but they saw its effects all around them. For example, Eugene saw it at the KP&L where destitute people couldn't pay for water, gas and electric services. They taught Carol to understand and empathize with those in deep trouble.

For example, companies packaged feed for farm animals in cloth sacks with colorful patterns that women used to make clothes. Carol saw many boys and girls her age wearing feed sack shirts and dresses and not ashamed of it. Her parents taught Carol to admire and not criticize such clothing. People didn't have money so got what they needed and survived with the rationale of "make it, grow it, fix it, borrow it, or do without". It was a "fix it" rather than a "buy a new one" society back then.

Because of the railroad, Marysville had a steady flow of transient people in need. Winifred and Eugene taught Carol about hoboes who hitched rides on trains looking for work, camped around the railroad tracks while searching for food. Unlike tramps who only worked when forced to, or bums who didn't work at all, most hoboes were proud men, far from home, going door to door in search of work so they could support their families and themselves. Some were starving, not seeking handouts but hoping to trade work for a meal or a little money.

People in Marysville tried to help. Instead of just giving hoboes a handout, people like Carol's parents created small, temporary jobs for these men, such as chopping wood, raking a yard, fixing a screen door, or straightening bent nails so they could be used again. Instead of being treated like beggars, desperate men could earn a little money or a meal while maintaining a bit of their pride. Hoboes guided others to places they might find work and food with secret marks on telephone poles. These seeds of empathy and caring for those less fortunate, planted in Carol's early experiences, blossomed into significant ways of helping others in her adult years.

My parents moved from Nebraska to Marysville about a year before the Clarks arrived, so Carol and I experienced those same problems at the same time in the same town and learned many of the same lessons about the value of frugality. The railroad tracks were near my home so a playmate and I went there sometimes to visit with hoboes. We met former farmers, lawyers, plumbers, soldiers, professors, businessmen, and others, with wives and kids at home. I learned then never to "look down my nose" at anyone. Having limitations doesn't make a person unworthy of kindness and respect. Carol and I learned that lesson early in life.

My father also had a steady job but earned about half as much as Eugene, and we were a family of six. One of the ways we made ends meet was to grow much of our own food in a large back yard garden. Beginning at age six I helped plant and tend our garden and by age eight did most of the work myself. Then I'd make packages of garden produce like lettuce, spinach, carrots and radishes, put them in my bicycle basket and ride up on the hill "where the rich folks lived" and go door to door selling it to bring in a little extra money for the family. I also helped my mother can hundreds of quarts of fruits, vegetables and jams to see us through the winter.

Years later I learned from Carol that I first met her while selling my vegetables. Her mother was a customer, and Carol would peek around her mother's skirt to look at me when I came to the door. So, that was the first time the pretty little girl who lived "up on the hill" met the boy who lived on "the wrong side of the tracks". Those childhood lessons that we could make it no matter how tough our financial condition became stayed with us all our lives. We survived as struggling graduate students and newlyweds by applying that depression formula of *grow it, make it, borrow it, fix it or do without.*

People living in the Midwest suffered a "double whammy" during the 1930s. It was called "the Dust Bowl" or "Dirty Thirties" when a very severe, multiyear drought hit the prairie states from

Kansas through Texas. That, coupled with decades of faulty farming practices, left 100,000,000 acres of soil without natural anchors to keep it in place. So, it dried up and blew eastward in dark clouds as far as New York City, Washington DC, and ended up in the Atlantic Ocean. Hundreds of thousands of people were forced to leave their homes to migrate to other states seeking new shelter and work.

We experienced those immense dust storms in Marysville, sometimes called *"Black Blizzards"*. They often reduced visibility to a few feet, required covering your face so you could breathe, and produced so much static electricity they disrupted car engines. Grasshoppers sometimes descended in vast clouds seeking food and could destroy a garden in no time. They crunched under our feet as we walked home from school, emitting what looked like tobacco juice. We usually went barefoot in the summer, so that was a messy hazard.

Winifred and Eugene doted on their only daughter. Even though Marysville was a very safe environment, Winifred tended to overprotect Carol from situations and activities she thought had even the slightest potential of hurt and harm. For example, at the age of four Carol had a little difficulty maintaining her balance while playing. Winifred panicked and rushed Carol to the doctor, fearing she might have the dangerous and crippling disease of polio. The doctor thought that possibility was slight, but Winifred temporarily limited Carol's play with other children. The balance symptoms disappeared quickly, but Winifred's anxiety persisted. She taught Carol to stay away from homes that had signs with "quarantine" beside their door, because that meant they had an infectious disease she might catch. Different colored signs signaled different kinds of diseases (e.g., smallpox, mumps or measles).

In those days, transportation and communication for any distance were limited, so people in most communities had to create their own entertainment. So, Carol's childhood experiences occurred within a few miles of where she lived. Such entertainment consisted of games, contests, athletics, music, stage plays and dances produced by local talent of every age. Without money to buy toys, most kids had to invent or build toys and games for their entertainment.

I was eager to learn everything I could about Carol as a child so quizzed Carol and her parents at every opportunity after we started dating. On a Sunday picnic with her parents, I asked, "What was Carol like as a kid?"

Carol at any age was a topic her mother loved to talk about! "She was a cute, chubby baby with ringlets of dark hair and a strong voice. She was an only child, so I worried that she needed playmates and didn't want her wandering the streets to find them. I encouraged other kids to come play in our yard by planning theme parties with tasty refreshments in hopes of forming good friendships. Most kids like costume parties so for one fun party all the kids were invited to 'Come Dressed as a Gypsy.'"

Carol laughed, "I remember that one! I wore a bright red and yellow dress. Mom pinned several pretty scarves in my hair to flow onto my shoulders. I felt like the queen gypsy."

Winifred continued, "My plan worked. It produced lots of playmates for Carol and she began developing friendships."

Carol added, "Those friendships strengthened when I started grade school. Many of them, like Marceline, Mary Frances, Prudence, Mary Lou, Beverly, Kenny and Adriane endured into college and were remembered fondly by most of us for years."

Eugene added his two cents: "I tried to broaden Carol's horizons to include playing some sports and flying kites on Billy Goat Hill but that didn't work – she was all girl!"

Carol grinned, "Yes, I went along to please you, but preferred girl activities like making and playing with paper dolls."

Eugene nodded, "One activity we enjoyed as a family, and Carol particularly loved, was picnicking and boating on the Blue River. I had a motor boat so we putted up and down the river, fished a little, and stopped for a picnic on the river bank."

Carol remembered: "I liked being on the water but didn't care for fishing! I loved the music made by the water as it flowed around our boat. Kansas got very hot in the summer but it was pleasantly cool on the river. I liked the smell of its wet banks. It was fun to watch and listen to the birds and hear the wind's song as it rustled the trees, bushes and wildflowers on shore. I liked dragging my hand in the water and wanted to get in but Mom said it was too dangerous.

Our dog, Spufendyke, my pal and playmate, loved going boating with us. One weekend he got excited and jumped out of the boat. I screamed at Dad to get him, but we were near the dam where the current was quite strong and Spufendyke washed over the dam. We never found the little guy. My heart was broken; I felt I should have held on to him so he couldn't jump in." Spufendyke was Carol's first pet, but not her last. She loved animals and had cat and dog companions through most of her life, but dogs were her favorite.

The summer before the Army called me, I visited the Clarks in Topeka. One evening I picked up a photo album with pictures of Carol during her grade school years in Marysville. As I leafed through the pictures I watched Carol change from a shy toddler to a grinning eight year old hamming it up for a proud Dad's camera. In one picture she was demurely dressed as a ballerina with toe pointed just so. In another, she was dressed as a minstrel, flashing a mischievous smile and dancing to imaginary music.

I asked Carol, "Why the costumes?"

Carol examined the photos, remembering, "They were for dance routines. I began taking dancing lessons in the first grade with my friend Marceline. As we progressed, our teacher taught us to perform together. We became a popular song and dance team for shows on occasions like the Frankfort Opera House, Old Timers Annual Dinner Dance, The Starlight Follies of 1935 and the Municipal Band Show at the Liberty Theater. It was special because Dad played in the band. Our mothers made us costumes to fit our different dance performances and thought our performances were so much fun they started designing routines for us." Carol cocked her leg coquettishly and step-hopped making jazz hands in an exaggerated pantomime.

I laughed with delight and said, "So you were the Marysville version of the child star of the time, Shirley Temple – cute little girls in costumes singing and dancing your hearts out."

Carol smiled at the comparison, "I don't think we were quite that good but the local folks liked us. Some of our tap dance routines were *Big Bad Wolf, Indian Tap Dance, Military Tap to Stars and Stripes,* and *Apache Dance to Down by the Winegar Works.*

"It sounds like you had fun doing lots of programs"

"I stopped after a freak accident during a performance at the Liberty Theater. A flimsy stage setting had been built for the show. During a pause in our performance, I leaned against it and the whole thing fell down. The audience roared with laughter but I was so embarrassed and humiliated I decided never to perform like that again."

We stopped looking at the photos and went to a movie with Carol's friend since babyhood, Mary Lou. When we returned, Carol told me the rest of her Marysville story over a slice of Winifred's apple pie.

"What did you do after you quit dancing?"

"I played the piano. Mom played the piano and wanted me to learn so I started piano lessons before grade school. I soon developed some competence. So, after my dancing fiasco I shifted my emphasis to playing the piano. I loved music, loved playing the piano and really liked my teacher. The only problem was she told Mother I had musical skills beyond my years and they both insisted I perform in public recitals. I was shy and dreaded performing solo so hated that part of music lessons. In March 1936 when I was eight, I composed my first piece of music and named it *The Rainbow Waltz.* Piano playing replaced dancing."

"Your mother said you were creative and imaginative before you ever started school. When did you get interested in art?"

"I loved to color, draw and paint long before I started to school. I think my first big project was designing costumes for paper dolls."

Mary Lou had a mouthful of pie but jumped into the conversation anyway. "Carol introduced me to her paper dolls and the Montgomery Ward Catalog. She'd discovered that by cutting out the dresses and other clothes in the catalog, you could fit them right onto your paper doll creating many costumes. Carol's game provided us both lots of fun. We were both only children so created our playtime differently than those with siblings."

Carol added, "Later I made colored pictures of things I saw around me. I still have one of my earliest efforts. Chickens fascinated me and that picture was painted at the farm. It's of white chickens in front of a small red barn with a colorful sun setting behind the Kansas hills in the background."

Carol and her parents spent a week in Manhattan one summer while Eugene audited the KP&L books. For the rest of our lives we cherished memories of our long, personal conversations during that week. We learned a great deal about one another. Parked in her parents' car on top of a hill on the edge of the K-State campus one beautiful summer evening, Carol told me the rest of her grade school experiences. I learned her near-idyllic childhood ended when she was ten and KP&L transferred Eugene to their Salina, Kansas office. That transfer pleased him because Salina was only half an hour away from the family farm.

Carol wasn't pleased about that move at all and her strong feelings emerged when telling me about it. "I hated it! Everything changed except that I still lived with my parents. We lived in Salina a year and a half, lived in three different houses, and I attended three different schools. To make things worse, the family farm was only thirty miles away so we spent nearly every weekend there, eliminating possibilities for making new friends.

I was very lonesome, felt like a fish out of water and shed lots of tears. I struggled to adjust but never succeeded – felt tired most of the time, couldn't sleep, and had strange physical symptoms. Mother was convinced I had heart problems so restricted me from normal kid activities, which isolated me even more. My heart symptoms disappeared as soon as we moved away from Salina. I'm convinced I was just scared, angry and tired."

"Carol, that was a horrible experience so early in life! How did you endure it?"

"Music was my only source of confidence and comfort in Salina. I continued my piano lessons, had a good teacher and worked hard to learn. My only fond memory of Salina is when my piano teacher told me I had exceptional skill for my age, and that I *wowed* the audience at a recital with my perfect performance of Paderewski's *Minuet*.

Thank goodness Dad was transferred to the KP&L office in Hastings, Nebraska in 1939. The adjustment was not nearly as difficult as in Salina. It was a college town, I liked the new school, made new friends and quickly became involved in music activities. My music made this new adjustment easier and more satisfying. I resumed piano lessons with a faculty member at Hastings College and fell in love with the music of Grieg. In my recital I played Grieg's *March of the Dwarfs* and *The Butterfly*. While there, I attended a performance by the famous pianist, Sergei Rachmaninoff. The beauty of his music overwhelmed me. In Hastings I discovered the joy of singing choral music. I had no voice training, but was selected for the Hastings girls' symphonic choir. I came to love a kind of music I'd never experienced before!"

"It sounds like Hastings was an even better context for your interests than Marysville."

"It was and I began to make friends again, indicated by the kinds of things they wrote in my 7th grade autograph book, like:

Doesn't it beat the berries'	*May your life be long and sunny*
Doesn't it get your goat,	*And your husband fat and funny*
When you're in the bathtub	*With his pocket full of money*
And can't find the soap.	*To support his little honey.*
(Your best friend, I hope)	*(You are the prettiest girl in our school, Tootie)*

Just as I began to feel I belonged somewhere we moved again."

In the summer of 1941, Eugene was promoted to head auditor at KP&L's central office so they moved to Topeka. His new job required traveling around the state to periodically audit the books in every KP&L branch office. In his previous positions, Carol's dad was often home when she left for school, home for supper, and available for evening school and social activities. In his new job, he spent more time on the road than at home.

They settled into their Topeka home and then Carol and Winifred began the hard adjustment of living their everyday lives without Eugene. They'd been away from Topeka for twelve years so had no friends and had to relearn the city. Later Carol told me, "We started easing our loneliness by spending lots of time together in shared activities and grew closer than we had ever been. We both loved movies, particularly musicals, dramas and comedies, so we went to many. Movies couldn't replace Dad, but they helped us endure his absence."

Then Carol faced combining the transitions of early adolescence, which are difficult under the best of circumstances, with transition into another new school – Boswell Junior High. She discovered it was going to be nearly as bad as Salina, but in a different way.

Carol talked with her mother about the situation after several weeks of school. "A *popular clique* of girls at Boswell considers themselves to be more sophisticated and socially adept than everyone else and try to control all activities. If a newcomer doesn't conform to their rules they're shunned or treated badly. For example, the clique planned a dance and sent invitations to the *less popular* girls dictating which boy they should invite to the dance. Of course, the clique reserved the ones they thought were the best for themselves. I thought such lousy treatment of both boys and girls was offensive."

Winifred asked, "What do you plan to do about that lousy situation?"

Carol said, "Such snobbishness and cruelty hurt but it also made me very mad. I rejected their invitation and told them I wasn't going to play their games, so they shunned me for the rest of the year. I made three friends – Ada, Anne, and Mary – who were also new students and fellow outcasts. That helped ease my loneliness and loss of self-confidence a little."

Despite her pleasant demeanor and attractiveness, Carol suffered with shyness and self-doubts. She often felt lonely and socially insecure so was cautious about making new friends. She quit taking piano lessons because of her fear of performing in public, but continued to play for her own pleasure. She participated in fewer school activities, focused on her studies, and became an excellent student. She eventually graduated with honors from Topeka High School.

The summer before she became a freshman at Topeka High Carol told her mother she was looking for a part time job to have a little spending money. Her job as a restaurant waitress was short lived. She told her mother, "With my flat feet, after several hours on the job my feet and legs hurt so bad I decided to I quit. The result of that decision was good luck."

"How could losing your job be good luck?"

"I discovered a local photographer had a job opening that fit my artistic interests perfectly. As you know, colored film doesn't exist, so to get family portraits or wedding pictures with color they have to be tinted by skilled technicians. Realistic tinting requires skillful attention to detail and color sense to accurately capture hair, skin, eye and clothing color. He gave me a couple tests and decided to hire me on trial. He said that he'd train me and see how I did. If it wasn't good enough, I'd be fired. I took to it like a duck to water. He was delighted with my artistic judgment. It also enables me to enhance my artistic interests and abilities." That job provided Carol a steady income until she left for college. There are lots of tinted family pictures around Topeka, Kansas that are the result of her skill.

Winifred was pleased that Carol's job boosted her self-confidence a little. But, after worrying about Carol's social insecurity and wretched school experiences, she knew her over-protectiveness had contributed to Carol's shyness and self-doubt. She decided to revisit a method similar to the one that helped Carol create friendships as a little girl in Marysville.

She said, "Carol, you seem to be having a hard time making friends in your new school."

"Yes, I am. The only time I've ever thought I had real friends was in Marysville. I was just beginning to make some friends in Hastings when we moved."

"I have an idea about how you might make some new friends here if you'd like to try it."

"Tell me about it."

"One usually makes friends by spending time with people and doing fun things together. I'll bet other girls your age are sometimes lonely too. How about picking out someone you might like for a friend, invite them for a sleepover, and try to make it a fun night? Can you think of someone you'd like to try that with?"

After a thoughtful silence, Carol said, "How about Mary Lou Tutt. We've known each other for a long time but haven't been doing things together enough to become good friends."

Carol invited Mary Lou to a slumber party. They had great fun, so decided to do it again. Mary Lou asked if she could bring a friend to the next slumber party and all three girls had fun. They repeated that process several times. By the end of their freshman year a small group of classmates had become good friends and met frequently at each other's homes for slumber parties. Their circle included Carol, Mary Lou Tutt, Betty Grace, Lois Hedley, Jeanine Hill, Monna Lee Hutchinson, Mary Lou Kirk, Ada Seastrom and Karen Kennedy.

After we started dating Carol told me, "We don't slumber much, but we have lots of fun sharing secrets, eating tasty food, singing to popular records, teaching one another to dance, and helping each other weather the storms and savor the pleasures of growing up. We meet most often at my house because Mom knows how to help us have fun and to disappear when we want privacy. Having teenagers around brightens Mom's life with Dad gone so much. The girls like her, and she's a fountain of information and advice, even about touchy subjects like sex."

Later in life, Mary Lou wrote Carol about what those slumber parties meant to her:

"Your mother had been a teacher when she was younger and her apparent love of children was a boon for our 'gang' of girls. She provided a safe environment for us. She spent hours counseling us, laughing, giggling and throwing in a heap of good logic and common sense. Some evenings she played the piano while everyone gathered around to sing along. She encouraged me to bring my violin and play while you played the piano. It was fun being part of that scenario. In retrospect, I believe your mother was mentoring us how to interact with people. I think this influenced me to become a camp counselor for girls."

Chapter Three

Carol Meets Her Soul Mate

Winifred created another plan to help Carol increase her self-confidence and ease her shyness. She had no idea how successful it would be! The one place where Carol had been the happiest, had friends and felt she belonged was Marysville. Winifred thought perhaps a visit with old friends in Marysville might help Carol regain some self-confidence. So, she made a suggestion:

"Carol, how would you like to take the train this summer and make a trip by yourself to Marysville for a good visit with Marceline and some of your other old friends?"

Carol's shriek of excitement was Winifred's answer. "Oh Mom, I'd love it!" She was approaching sixteen that July of 1943, set to begin her junior year in high school. This would be the first trip she had ever taken by herself. Marceline greeted Carol with a delighted grin but said, "There's a little problem. My boyfriend, Benny, and I had planned on dating this weekend. Mom said I couldn't go out and leave you sitting home alone. Don't worry, Carol, Benny will get you date with one of his friends if that's OK with you."

I pitched for one of the teams in a summer softball league. We were playing a game at the town ball field when we saw two pretty girls in shorts and bright shirts walking towards the bleachers. We suspended play and gaped at them as they walked towards us. Everyone knew Marceline but who was her gorgeous friend? We resumed the game, but I was determined to meet that beautiful girl! I got a hit in the last inning and tried to stretch it into a double by sliding into second base and was out --- in more ways than one. The umpire called me out and the slide tore out the seat of my pants. No way could I meet a pretty girl with air caressing my bare bottom!

The next morning my friend Benny asked if I could help him out by going on a blind date with his girlfriend, Marceline's visitor. Her name was Carol Clark. I started to ask about the visitor and then the light dawned. "Benny, did they come to our ball game last night?"

"Yes." he said.

Grinning, I said, "Fate is on my side!"

We agreed to first meet casually and check each other out. I was seventeen in 1943, and head soda jerk at the Triangle drug store. Marceline thought that would be an ideal place for a casual meeting so scheduled it for the next morning. While walking to work that day I wondered about my potential blind date. Would she be nice as well as pretty? Would she like me or think I was a hick from the sticks? It was a typical hot Kansas summer morning. The asphalt paving felt soft under my feet so I knew lots of customers would come to the soda fountain for cold drinks and ice cream treats to escape the heat. I hurried to get organized for business so I'd be free for the "get acquainted" meeting.

When I saw Carol walk in, dressed in shorts and a brightly patterned summer blouse, I thought, *"WOW!!"* My heart pounded to see that beautiful girl up close, with her wavy brunette hair, long eyelashes, kind eyes, and dimpled, radiant smile. Oh yeah, and she had great legs! I thought, *How can a lowly soda jerk possibly impress such a pretty girl?* I guided them past the soda fountain with its high stools to the booth nearest my work station. After introductions and friendly greetings, I offered to fix them a special ice cream treat and they accepted.

They watched my creative efforts – one banana sliced length wise, three dips of vanilla ice cream, each covered with strawberry, chocolate or caramel syrup topped off with chopped nuts and a cherry. I lingered by their booth to talk, tease, and compliment them as they ate. My boss hid behind a rack of greeting cards, watching my every move, so I didn't dare sit down with them. Benny reported later, "Carol said, 'He's cute, funny, and makes a great banana split so I'll date him.'"

I nearly shouted with joy, "Alright!!"

We went to the Liberty Theater where we saw *Stormy Weather*. It starred a new singer, Lena Horne. We didn't realize then that the title song would later become a symbol of our growing relationship: *Don't know why there's no sun up in the sky – stormy weather, Since my gal and I ain't together, keeps rainin' all the time!* After the movie we went to a high school hangout for snacks and conversation. I learned that some of Carol's childhood friends were my friends now, and we both loved dancing and the great outdoors. We agreed our first date was a success so we planned another for the next day. Then, we took the girls home.

We took our time in the summer heat, talking and laughing as we meandered slowly towards Alcove Spring. I explained a bit of its history and Carol enjoyed imagining the pioneer wagon trains camping there because of its clear, cold water supply. She shivered at the part about the Donner party that camped there and later froze to death in the Rockies on their way to California. When Carol saw the shady, pristine beauty and quiet peace of the spring, she laughed with delight and said, "Look, there's watercress growing by that pool of clear, spring water. It's supposed to be tasty so let's try it." She picked some and we sat on a flat rock munching and talking while listening to bird songs, prairie sounds and wind stirring through the trees. Before long we were starving so ate our lunch and washed it down with clear spring water.

As we strolled along the dusty road back to Marysville, Carol confided, "These two days have been the first real dates I've ever had, and they've been great fun. I find it easy to be with girls, but around boys I'm usually shy and uneasy. This has been different."

Her confession prompted me to make one of my own, "I've never said this to anyone, but I feel the same way about girls. When I was a freshman in high school, I crossed to the other side of the street to keep from meeting or speaking to a girl coming towards me. But during my sophomore year, several girls decided to teach me to dance and to be less afraid around girls. For several weeks we met at the local teen dance spot. They took turns dancing and talking with me and teaching me dance steps until I had the hang of it. I've enjoyed dancing ever since and been more comfortable talking with girls."

Carol smiled at my story and said, "I've never danced with a boy. My girlfriends and I taught ourselves to dance and practiced at our slumber parties by dancing with each other."

There was only one answer a red-blooded American boy could say to that! "If you're still here tomorrow night, let's go dancing." So that's what the four of us did.

We made a great pair dancing together. Whether it was a two-step, waltz or Lindy, Carol and I didn't miss a beat. Other dancers started calling us "Fred and Ginger" for Fred Astaire and Ginger Rogers, the famed dance team. We both agreed that dancing together was special. That sealed the deal. After three dates we both really liked each other. After the dance, Benny parked his car in a quiet spot out in the country so he and Marceline could neck a little. Neither Carol nor I had ever necked and had no idea what to do so we spent that quiet time getting to know more about each other, our interests and activities.

Carol said, "I can't believe I've confided in you so much about my thoughts, feelings and shortcomings. I've never felt so at ease with anyone." I said I felt the same way and thought *She's holding my hand!* When I walked her to the door we kissed goodnight – a perfect ending to our first dates. I went home to bed and dreamed about her. Later in our relationship we laughed over that first kiss because we both thought at the time we needed more practice.

Back home with her parents, Carol's eyes sparkled and her cheeks flushed with happiness as she told them about the visit to Marysville, meeting me, and all the fun we had. She said, "We had so much fun! I really like him. It feels awful to think I may never see him again."

Winifred said, "Why don't you keep your communication channels open with him? It would be a socially appropriate gesture to send Don a thank you letter for making your visit so memorable."

So, that's what Carol did. My swift reply thrilled her, she responded immediately, and we became pen pals. In my next letter I said: "I'm sure glad you left Marysville when you did because you escaped the latest polio outbreak. It's nearly reached epidemic proportions here infecting people at the swimming pool, churches, movies, anywhere people congregate. So far, Marysville has 3 deaths, 9 active cases, and 100 people under observation."

From discussions about polio we progressed to sharing thoughts, opinions, feelings, reports of activities, likes and dislikes.

We were both hungry to share our private thoughts and feelings with someone, without embarrassment. We both discovered it was even easier to be honest in letters than it had been face to face, so quickly learned to trust each other. We tried to make our letters fun and interesting. For example, in one letter my dog Midget wrote to Carols' dog Micky with a special message. The letter said in part:

"Slug (that's what I call my master) got your mistress's letter yesterday. He is nuts. He read it twice before eating his dinner. He sure must enjoy them – reading them before he eats! He says to tell Carol not to worry about the polio, he couldn't catch it – he's too ornery."

Our letters played a very important developmental role for both of us. Up to that point, Carol had few opportunities to learn how to relate to males. She had an unexpressive father, no male siblings or relatives with whom to interact, and no male friends. Most males she had contact with were authority figures like her father, teachers and employer. Her shyness and insecurities only added to Carol's apprehension and difficulty relating to men. My limited relationships with girls had been very superficial, even though I had three older sisters. I had only dated a couple of times and didn't know how to relate personally to girls my age.

Through our letters we constructed a fantasy relationship in which we were both very much at ease. We expressed our thoughts and opinions freely, commented on current events, joked and teased, asked for advice, and sometimes complained about things in our lives. These were things we had never done, and still couldn't do face to face with other boys and girls. It was a wonderful, liberating experience for both of us!

That fall, Carol asked her parents if she could invite me to visit in September so we could attend the State Fair together. I was embarrassed to learn that Carol had let her mother read my letters, but it turned out to be a good thing. Her mother said, "He seems to be a sensible young man, and we can see that you've been much happier and more confident since meeting Don and corresponding with him. So, invite him to come and stay with us so we can meet him in person."

I was delighted with the invitation, but my boss refused to give me time off. I was smitten and knew this visit to Topeka was something I had to do, so I did the only thing possible. I quit my job and took the train to Topeka. I'd never been to a "big city" or a state fair so it was an adventure. Luckily, the polio outbreaks in Kansas stopped so the fair continued as scheduled.

The fair activities were exciting and fun. Her parents and I hit it off right away, and I even passed inspection with some of her slumber party gang. Carol's parents were pleased with her transformation since meeting me and told me, "In two months Carol has changed from a lonely, insecure teenager to a more confident, vibrant girl radiating happiness, all thanks to her budding relationship with you." You can imagine how good that made me feel!

My adventure had a happy ending. Back home, my boss took me for a ride and asked me to come back to work. He even gave me a raise!

Then, Carol began her junior year in high school and I my senior year. She approached school with new enthusiasm and confidence. Her slumber party gang provided an anchor she treasured. In her letters she often shared anecdotes about their "slumberless" activities:

"Last night we had so much fun at Monna's. We played ping-pong, danced and cobbed around. At midnight we were hungry so made grilled cheese sandwiches. Then I got a yen for a dish of peaches, Mary Lou craved baked beans and Monna drank a quart of tomato juice. We had a great time, but I'm afraid her folks didn't enjoy it as we didn't get to bed till 2:30."

After another slumber party at her house Carol wrote: "We had a lot of fun last night – it seems like we have more fun when the chaperones are away. But, it's a little dangerous as we found out. A few boys heard there was a party at my house so they generously invited themselves in – was I mad! I was afraid the neighbors would think I was awful because my parents were gone. So, we kicked them out as soon as we could and locked the doors. When Paul, Mary Lou, Vernon & Ada came in from their dates, we invited the two boys in and Paul entertained us with his imitations of Danny Kaye, President Roosevelt and others. He's really a good comedian. When the boys left, we played the piano and the Victrola, danced, ate and so forth. About 1:30 as we were singing at the piano the doorbell rang. I've never in my life gone up our stairs so fast – we all flew upstairs. I grabbed my robe, mustered up my courage, and went down to answer the door. Everybody's knees were shaking and my hands were trembling like I'd seen a ghost. I opened the door and there was Kirk just getting in from her date. We could have choked her. We all talked for quite a while and then finally went to our own beds to sleep. In the morning, the gang came tumbling downstairs to stuff themselves before they left."

I teased Carol with my reply: "I don't understand – when you grabbed your robe, why did you smear mustard on your courage?"

Mary Lou described how they taught each other new attitudes and skills: "Carol often played music on her record player and we'd dance in the living room. We taught ourselves the dance steps we saw in the movies. Carol loved classical music and on one occasion played *The Bolero* by Ravel. Paul, my boyfriend, and one of the girls tried to jitterbug to that music. It was fun to be part of the gang and Carol, in her own way, was introducing us to her beloved classical music. We also taught each other the value of inclusiveness, friendship, and shared fun. I thought Carol was one of the finest people I'd ever met. I wanted to spend time with her and be just like her. Carol and her mother were a godsend to me as that was a bad period for my Mom."

Carol became a trusted confidant to these friends who often shared tales of happiness and woe about their boyfriends. Her letters to me were filled with stories that demonstrated her intuitive understanding and thoughtfulness involving their breakups, reunions or new boyfriends. She sometimes helped initiate new relationships. For example, she introduced Ada and Vernon and later they married; she introduced Virginia and Earl and they too married.

As an only child, Carol learned much from the dynamics of her gang of friends. They were the siblings she never had. Throughout High School, Carol's self-confidence increased and she gained strength from friends who really cared about each other through good times and bad. It was here that she learned her sensitive skills for relating to and gabbing with other women. In a letter following Carol's death Monna wrote:

"I feel personally blessed to have had Carol in my life, especially in my impressive teen age years. Carol and I shared many thoughts and feelings. We loved the same music, & would listen (and sometimes cry) over music we both appreciated. We attended & loved many of the same movies – sometimes seeing the same one over and over again. My life was richer by far because Carol was in it."

Beginning with her childhood piano lessons, Carol loved classical music and that grew ever stronger through high school. For example she wrote me:

"I just got through listening to Tchaikovsky's *Romeo and Juliet* – that's the saddest, most romantic music I've ever heard. I want it played at my wedding (if I ever have one) and my funeral – morbid thought isn't it." She told me later my reply made her laugh out loud:

"So, you want *Romeo and Juliet* played at your wedding and funeral – do you mean your wedding or your funeral is a morbid thought?"

The love of participating in choral music that started in grade school in Hastings strengthened in high school. She participated in senior glee club for two years and enjoyed singing in the Presbyterian Church choir until she left for college. She was chosen to join a special group of Topeka musicians to perform Handel's *Messiah* at Easter. She fell in love with it and performed it every chance she had throughout her life. Carol had a beautiful voice, could sing several parts, and was always in key. It was a compliment to her singing ability when directors often placed less capable singers beside her to help improve their performance. Where Carol feared solo piano performances, she enjoyed performing choral works before audiences.

She learned to like popular music, partly because she loved to dance to it. They usually played and sang popular songs at their slumber parties. In one letter she made a prediction: "Today I heard a new singer named Frank Sinatra and told our gang to listen to him because he's going to be a big success."

Carol's pleasure and competence in doing arts and crafts also increased during High School. She took courses in making pottery and jewelry. A neighbor helped Carol polish her knitting skills. She and her girlfriends met periodically to learn sewing techniques and make their own clothes. Carol loved to sew and became skillful at making her own clothes.

We maintained our fantasy relationship for four months through letters. Then, Carol talked her mother into bringing her, Mary Lou and Paul to Marysville for a two day visit during the 1943 Christmas season. Happy, joyful smiles spread across Carol's face and mine when we saw one another! That night we went across the river to Marysville's Cahan dance hall, where Carol and I rediscovered the joy of dancing together. The night was perfection, with music and a ballroom glistening with Christmas lights creating the ideal ambience for puppy love. The next day when I said goodbye at their hotel, Carol kissed me in front of her mother – on the cheek!

Our letters continued through winter and spring. After graduating from high school I wrote Carol about my plans: "Earl Elliott and I have enlisted in the Army Air Corp aiming at flight training. We know it will be awhile before they call us to active duty, so we're starting college at K-State this summer until we're called. K-State is only 60 miles from Topeka. I have a part time janitor job to help pay for dates when I can hitchhike to Topeka to see you."

Carol replied: "That's fabulous! I hope they wait a long time to call you. Maybe I can come to Manhattan to see you some time. I have an idea." That comment intrigued me. In her next letter she gave me the good news. "Dad has to audit the Manhattan branch of KP&L this summer. I talked him into renting a small apartment for a week so Mom and I can come with him. We can spend time together for a whole week!"

Winifred knew our friendship was heating up, so tried to give Carol dating advice. One tidbit was how to keep a guy from necking with her by facing him with one leg cocked up on the seat so he couldn't get close enough to neck. The technique worked...when Carol wanted it to!

We spent every possible minute together, sometimes with her parents but mostly by ourselves. By avoiding double dates, we could be much more open about sharing our ideas, thoughts and feelings as we did in our letters. Many evenings I borrowed a buddy's car. We parked on top of a hill just past the campus where we had long, wonderful conversations. That week meant the world to both of us and became a cornerstone of our long term relationship. Later, when I was stationed at the Roswell, New Mexico air base Carol wrote about that week:

"Well, I've just spent a whole page telling you what a lousy mood I was in yesterday and why. I'm not sure you're interested in all this, but I like to spiel off to you. I only wish you were here to talk to in person. I'll never forget those good times we had talking at Manhattan last summer. Maybe some people would think that was dull, but it's my idea of real fun to talk to someone I can talk to who *listens and replies!*"

I replied: "I remember those talks too. During those delightful, long conversations I discovered what a really wonderful person you are. You're the only girl I ever met that really enjoyed conversations like that. In a sense, our exchange of letters is an extension of those conversations, except in written form."

At the end of that summer I wrote Carol: "The Air Corps hasn't called me up so I registered for the fall semester. Friends urged me to join their fraternity, Tau Kappa Epsilon – TKE. It provides housing, meals, and an active social life that can include you. It is a heck of a lot more fun than renting a room in a private home which is the only alternative at K-State."

Like most young folks in the 1940s, we enjoyed dancing to big band music. Meadow Acres was a large dance hall near the Air Force Base at Topeka and our favorite place to go dancing. Name bands of the era, such as Benny Goodman, Glenn Miller, and the Dorsey Brothers, often appeared there. Transportation to Topeka was a problem for me since I didn't have a car. When a popular band was scheduled, I found a friend who had a car and also enjoyed dancing. Then I asked Carol to find my friend a date. She seldom had a problem finding someone willing to date a friend, especially when big band dancing was on the agenda. We had several dance dates at Meadow Acres before the Air Force called me to active duty.

In October, near Carol's birthday, I wrote: "The TKEs are having a party and dance at our house next weekend. Could you come as my date?"

Carol gleefully replied: "Mom says we can stay at the hotel for the weekend. I'm scared and excited about going to a college fraternity party. What should I wear?"

My swift reply said: "It's not formal. Just wear whatever you'll feel good in." When I picked her up for the party she was lovely and anxious. Her anxiety quickly disappeared when everyone treated her like any other coed. It didn't hurt that she was beautiful and a great dancer!

After that big weekend, Carol told her mother, "It was fantastic fun! Don made me feel comfortable like I belonged there, so I wasn't the least bit nervous. Both the guys and gals made me feel like one of them. It really boosted my self-confidence!"

Several days later Carol wrote: "Going to a college fraternity party was a big deal to my high school gang. When I got home they immediately had a slumber party and made me tell all. What did you do? How did they treat you? How were the coeds dressed? Did you dance with anyone beside Don? I had fun reliving it with them through my answers."

When I was at Keesler Field air base I sent Carol some pictures of that TKE party. She responded: "You guys sure created funny skits – 'Shorty' dressed up as 'Francine Johnson' from Kansas City while he and you danced. When I saw the pictures you sent me I about died laughing. Oh yes & that delicate (?) pose of you two kissing!"

Later, I invited Carol to the TKE Sweetheart Ball where all the girls wore formal gowns and corsages. TKE friends arranged for Carol to stay at the Pi Phi sorority house to give her a preview of college life. She made a classic formal gown as a surprise for me. I'd never seen her in a formal and could hardly breathe, watching the beautiful young woman in her gorgeous emerald gown walking down the stairs towards me. Carol was no longer the shy, insecure girl I met at the drug store. It was a wonderful night and an exciting fall for both of us.

Carol told her mother, "It was so beautiful seeing that ball room full of women in gorgeous gowns gliding around the floor in the arms of their dates. I have never felt so wonderful and proud dancing with Don. I never wanted it to end. When the TKEs sang their sweetheart song to us as the evening ended, I cried with joy!"

During her high school senior year, Carol continued to develop into a gregarious talented person as doubts and shyness faded but never completely disappeared. Late that fall, Carol told her mother, "Everything in my life is going beautifully. I've never been happier!" Her joy continued until after Christmas, when I was called to active duty.

Carol's parents drove her to Marysville to say goodbye. She kissed me in front of her parents for the first time. Being apart would be brightened through shared memories and letters. Our letters now reflected a change from "pen pal" to "courtship" letters. In our letters, Carol vicariously experienced my Air Force adventures and took me with her as she finished high school and struggled with decisions about her next steps in life. We led two lives simultaneously. The first was our real life, full of activities and tasks – things to learn; decisions to make. The second was the fantasy life we lived through our letters and imaginations.

My first letter described my train trip through the south taking me to Air Force basic training at Keesler Field in Mississippi, and illustrates how I took Carol with me in my travels:

"Dear Carol: The army certainly believes in taking the long way around. We went from Kansas through Missouri, Oklahoma, Tennessee, Arkansas, Alabama, Mississippi and a touch of Florida. Some of it is pretty and some is poor. For example, in rural Arkansas we saw rundown shacks, a lot of them raised off the ground so hogs can get in the shade underneath. Almost everyone seemed to have at least one jackass and 10 kids. We've seen wooded hills, swamps, flat farm land, and cities caressed by rivers. A little while ago, everywhere I looked I saw cotton fields with black folks at work in them. Sometimes when we stopped, cute kids came train side to sing and dance, in hopes we'd throw them some money. Keesler Field is right on the gulf coast. We came down through swamp country and then suddenly it ended and we were right on the gulf. I wish you could have seen it, Carol, the sight was wonderful! I know you would have enjoyed the scene: Water stretches as far as you can see with an occasional boat on the horizon, with air fields filled with massive machines of war in the foreground."

Carol replied: "I loved your letter telling me about the trip. Oh, I wish I could have been with you too. I'll bet the country was beautiful. I envy you getting to travel and see other parts of the country and learning about new people, what they think and do. I've never been out of the middle part of Kansas. Someday I want to travel. Enclosed is a picture my parents had taken to honor my graduation. Through it I can travel with you where ever you go!

After you went off to war I've been feeling pretty blue so the gals decided to try to cheer me up. We got all dressed up, putting on the dog, and went out for a chicken dinner. By the time we got started, most places were full so we ended up at the Jayhawk Hotel. We had decided to be really mannerly and act like ladies, but I'm afraid when we all get together that little thing is impossible. But we had fun anyway, even if people did stare."

I replied: "If I had been there I certainly would have stared – mostly at you! Carol, when I unwrapped your picture it took my breath away and brought a few tears of joy! It will be the last thing I look at each night when I go to bed. Thank you – IT'S WONDERFUL!!!!!!! My buddies gathered around to exclaim over how beautiful you are, and wondered how an ugly runt like me got a girl like you. They had never seen a photo in color, so I explained how you used your artistic skills to tint pictures.

Chapter Four

Maturing Views of Herself and the World

By February 1945, we were communicating as partners. Carol's thoughts turned to the future. She wrote: "There are only 3 more months of high school. It seems almost impossible and I hate to think about college – it scares me to death! K-State doesn't have nursing, or decent programs in the arts or music so I wrote that I planned to take Home Economics. But I hope they don't go too much on that because I may change my mind. I hope we get those 'get acquainted' bids from sororities this spring. Are you permitted to tell me more about what your training involves?"

I replied: "Here's an example of yesterday. We fell out for roll call at 0500 (5a.m.). Then we washed, made our beds, swept and scrubbed the floor and cleaned the latrine, and I managed to do my laundry. At 0600 we marched to breakfast. Then we marched 4 miles out to the gas chamber. We had a lecture and smelled several gases – mustard, nitrogen mustard, Lewisite, phosgene, and one other I don't remember. Then we put on our gas masks and went into a gas chamber that had tear gas in it. Inside they had us take off our masks and stand there for about 30 seconds and then run out. That stuff is powerful! 'I Cried for You'! We frequently wear our masks as we march to learn to breathe differently in the mask. Finally, we participated in a sham battle. They used blank shells in the machine guns, rifles, etc. and they'd planted charges which exploded electrically as we moved through the battlefield. It was quite realistic.

I was suddenly struck by how differently our society views me now. A month ago I was an adolescent boy. Today, I'm viewed as a man capable of making important decisions and taking actions in battle to kill or save other men. I was sobered by the thought that basic training isn't a game – it says grow up and learn necessary skills fast; you have important, dangerous work to do, soon, and your life and that of others may depend on how well you do it.

While we were gone, officers made a surprise inspection of our barracks and it wasn't up to par so-o-o tonight we have a GI party. No, it's not like your slumber parties. We have to scrub down EVERYTHING in the barracks until it's spotless – floors, walls, roof beams, and all aspects of the latrine. If it doesn't pass another inspection, we have to do it all again. This isn't a form of punishment. With thousands of men living in close quarters, cleanliness is essential to prevent the development and rapid spread of infectious diseases."

Carol wrote: "Your sham battle sounds exciting and scary. What do you do in a sham battle besides avoiding getting shot? Are you learning to shoot guns and so forth, or can you tell me? Your thoughts about how society now views you moved me deeply. My view of you shifted suddenly to that of a man who may have to risk his life for mine. It scared me and made me think seriously about myself. I should also grow up quickly to become a responsible woman capable of helping deal with the impact of this war. Once again you have influenced my view of myself. When will the Air Force decide what they'll train you for? I wish you all the luck in your selection tests. Does it make you very nervous to take them?"

I replied: "We finished all the selection assessments. Early in the war, attrition during flight training was terrible; over half the trainees killed themselves or were seriously injured because of mistakes they made during flight training. The Air Force asked some psychologists to develop ways of identifying candidates who were more likely to fail in flight training.

So, in addition to standard mental and physical exams (including vision and hearing), we potential air cadets took the following: First we had to quickly turn square pegs around in their holes on a signal; next, we had to keep a pointer on an off-center dot on a turntable and at the same time switch lights; then, we had to keep a pointer on a dot by turning two handles in opposite directions at the same time. That was a little tough. Next we had to line green lights up with red lights by using a stick and rudder bar. Then we had to turn switches when certain lights flashed in certain positions. That was the hardest one for me. Finally, we had a little plane we moved from right to left by pushing a rudder bar and had to keep it lined up on a light that was on. The last was an amusing psychiatric interview. I'll let you know if they think I'm crazy."

Carol wrote: "This week has been full of wonderful music. Last weekend our community chorus performed the *Messiah*. It lasted 2½ hours and we had to stand all that time so it was tiring, but wonderful. It's hard to describe how exciting it is to sing that beautiful music with a group of 100 singers. Then last night I listened to the Kansas City Philharmonic. Oh, how I wish you were here – it was just beautiful! I saw the movie *Winged Victory* where they showed tests you took. I kept thinking that would drive me nuts. How do you think you came out?"

I replied: "I'm now classified as a PAC – pre-aviation cadet! My assessment was so good I qualified for everything – pilot, navigator and bombardier. Now you'll have to help me decide which to choose. Until the flight training fields have room for new trainees, we'll be assigned to participate at some U.S. airbase and learn how things work. I'll be shipped out soon, hopefully to the Topeka Air Base. I celebrated by carving your name on a chair in our recreation room, so now you're a permanent part of Keesler Field, the Riviera of the South."

With delight, Carol answered: "I'm so happy about your getting into the PACs – it's just wonderful!! Oh, I hope you get shipped someplace close by. I think choosing navigator might be good because you're so good in math and all that experience might be good after the war. Did going to that psychiatrist make you nervous? Tell me more about what he asked – we're studying psychology right now so all the gals are interested. This afternoon our gang went shopping for jeans, but couldn't find any that fit us. Men are built so funny!"

To offset gloomy times in our lives we frequently exchanged corny jokes. Carol wrote:

"I told him not to see me anymore and what did he do? He turned out the lights."

I asked: "If a buttercup is yellow, what color is a hiccup? Burple."

After lunch with her friend, Monna, who worked at a department store, Carol wrote: "It happened in a large department store during rush hour. The elevator was jammed and the cables groaned. The elevator rose slowly, and as it neared the third floor a piercing scream caused the operator to stop the car. All eyes focused on a large woman in a sealskin jacket who wore an injured expression. A small boy, not yet of school age, stood directly behind her. 'I did it' he said reluctantly. 'It was in my face so I bit it.'"

After a bull session in my barracks, I reported: "One of the guys said he asked his brother whether he liked bathing beauties, and his brother replied, 'I don't know – I never bathed one.'"

I wrote: "My interview officer told me today that my test scores were exceptionally high and that I could get into officer candidate school (OCS) if I wanted to. I might apply for Air Corps Administrative OCS. It wouldn't endanger my PAC status. They're taking men for preflight so very slowly now and wash out about 60% of them. What do you think?"

Carol replied: "I asked you to guess how many letters you've written me and you made a low guess. You've written 100 since we met 1½ years ago – can you believe it? I'm certainly proud of your high scores on those tests – I've been spouting all about you to the gang and they sigh and say, 'What a man.' You asked for my opinion about your choice. I've thought it over and think OCS would be best since you'd probably get furloughs more often and might qualify you for some jobs when you get out. Lately I've felt more tired and tense than usual. Mom fears I have a heart problem and insists I see an MD. I do have a heart problem, but not that kind."

I anxiously replied: "Carol, have you had your heart checked yet? I don't know what I'd do if you got sick while I was away! I didn't realize I'd written you so many letters."

Carol reassured me: "Our Dr. checked out my heart and said I was in perfect health but was doing too much and not getting enough rest. I'm relieved. Mom is such a worry wart. I told him a vacation in Mississippi would cure me. I didn't mention late night slumber parties. Our gang (some with dates) went to Meadow Acres last night for Glenn Gray's band. Isn't he a TKE? He had one little 5x5 man who played clarinet, sax and also sang. Gosh but I wish you had been here to take me dancing. Will you teach me to jitterbug some day? Is it a deal?"

Oh yes! It's a deal, I thought while penning my reply: "I remember our last dance – Stan Kenton! You're the smoothest dancer I've ever danced with, Carol. As for me teaching you how to jitterbug, all we have to do is to juice up the Lindy a little."

Carol wrote: "As an only child I've had no experience with babies. But, our apartment is rented to a couple with a little girl. Perhaps you remember meeting Jeannie. She's a cutie. We often have fun playing together on our porch, and I've discovered what a delight it would be to have a little girl. She's beside me now asking what I'm doing. I told her I was writing to Don and she keeps saying Don, Don. She always remembers you. She gave me a kiss to give to you so here it is (smack) – kinda sloppy but that's her technique. I missed something special not having a baby brother or sister.

This year our senior glee club has been performing at all the junior high schools. They seem to enjoy us. Yesterday our senior glee sang in assembly at our school and we wore our formals – first time I've had mine on since you were here. We gave a nice program but the students would have enjoyed more popular pieces. We had a community sing and they seemed to enjoy that. Afterwards we went to the Wagon Wheel, a teen center, to get something to eat. It's a place where it's not shameful for girls to dance together so that's a reason our gang like it."

I wrote: "We had three hours of instruction on 'booby traps' today. Three of us had to go together into a little room and try to find traps hidden there. We found a few and then several exploded. The charges weren't large but it really startles you to have one go off under your hand. It was fun and interesting, and I really didn't need that finger and those three toes."

Carol responded: "Weren't you scared with those booby traps? Will you still be able to dance without those three toes? Everybody in school is talking about going into service or entering college and it makes me realize that in 10 more weeks I'll be graduated – it just doesn't seem possible. I'm in a turmoil about what to do with my life. Have you ever had times when you just don't know what to do, which would be best to do and so on? It's awful isn't it.

We just got home from seeing this wonderful program put on by talent from the 7th Army Command. They had a string quartet and a concert pianist, a tenor and a comical master of ceremonies. Tonight they had a swing band, an impersonator from Hollywood and several others. We were thrilled to pieces and nearly clapped our hands numb."

I wrote: "Goodbye, Keesler Field!!! I've finished basic training and been shipped to online duty elsewhere. We went by troop train to a new B-29 training base at Roswell, New Mexico. The B-29 is a huge new bomber that they want in action in all war zones as soon as possible. We went through Texas. Eastern Texas isn't bad, but oh-h-h west Texas. You can see farther and see less than anyplace. It's mesquite, sage brush and flat as is New Mexico here.

We got the news of President Roosevelt's death about 1800 last night and were all shocked and sobered by this tragic event. I pray that President Truman and the other world leaders are farsighted and wise enough to frame a lasting peace so that the children of our generation will not have to go through the things our generation has."

Carol said: "Have you been able to listen to the radio since Roosevelt's death? They have beautiful music. Our rainy weather makes it seem the heavens are grieving the loss too."

I explained: "My work assignment is a key headquarters unit called classification. It keeps records about the competencies and service records of all personnel at the base and selects all personnel for job assignments here and overseas, so this unit could pick anyone they wanted to work for them. They picked my buddy, Les Allison, and me because we have the highest test scores on the base. The competencies of each person are identified with an MOS (military occupational specialty) code and each person's duty assignment is based on it. When headquarters receives battle zone requests for more personnel, we pull records of men whose MOS fits the requests and the classification officer chooses who will be shipped out. Some soldiers want to go and others don't, and some try to influence the decision. For example, the classification officer found a case of his favorite whiskey outside his door and he knew it was from a guy who wanted to ship out to the Pacific to get away from his wife. They asked me if I could use my shorthand skills to take minutes of the commanding officer's meetings. I declined, but said I knew a highly skilled pretty girl who could. Want to become a WAC?"

Carol replied: "If I took that WAC job would I get to sit on the general's lap? I'd prefer yours. Guess what! I'm really thrilled for I got to drive the car all by myself tonight. I must have caught

Dad in the right mood for he said right away I could take it to glee club. I nearly fell over ... It's really fun to get it by myself. Have you heard any rumors as to when you might get furlough? Maybe they won't be so strict, now that the war with Germany seems about over."

I wrote: "What do you want for graduation? Would you like one of Uncle Henry Ford's Mercury convertibles; would you rather have a mink coat; or are diamonds a girl's best friend?

I considered trying to change my job to fly in a B-29 as a put-put operator, but changed my mind. I've talked to a lot of crews and they call them 'flying coffins'. Most are trying to get out of them. The Army doesn't publish the fact, but they have a lot of wrecks as men try to learn to fly those huge planes. One wreck had funny results. The plane was on a training flight and didn't have enough fuel to get back to the field so they managed a noisy landing in a flat area of sage brush and mesquite. A farmer and his wife were awakened by loud noises, ran to the back door and looked out. There was the nose of that huge airplane towering above their back door! They were so scared they packed a suitcase, left, and never came back."

Carol responded: "What do I want for graduation? I want you, so save your money for a furlough!! Last night I went to hear Jose Iturbi, the pianist, and it was quite a thrill! He selected most of the pieces from movies in which he played. I succeeded in speaking with him and getting his autograph back stage. Every time he speaks he just beams, and you can imagine how thrilled I was. I envy you being so close to Carlsbad Caverns and so many other beautiful places. Go see Carlsbad and then tell me all about it for that is the place I want to see most in the U.S."

I replied: "So you want to see Carlsbad. Come on down and I'll show them to you if you don't mind all the bats flying around your hair as you climb out of the caverns. We had a USO show here last night, and the funniest part of it wasn't supposed to be in the show. They had a chorus of beautiful girls in scanty costumes and each time they made their entrance a big dog we call KP would dash up in front of the stage, sit down, and proceed to howl his head off. The effect was marvelous – typifying the wolfish spirit of the men confined at Roswell Air Base. I think I might be able to get a furlough in July. What would be a good time?"

Carol joyfully wrote: "The war in Europe is over – isn't that wonderful news!! This morning Dr. MacFarland made a great speech in assembly about VE day. He's a wonderful speaker and sometimes made us cry. You asked about my favorite songs. Right now *Dream* and *Laura* are mine. *Stormy Weather* will always have a place in my heart. Yesterday I bought Grieg's *Concerto in A minor* and just love it! What are your favorites?"

I responded: "I share your joy that the European war is over, but it's causing us a lot of work. We have a heavy focus in the Pacific because that war continues. In addition we're preparing discharges. Each person gets points for months in service, months overseas, combat service, and dependent kids (no mention of wives!). I guess I'll have to get married, have triplets, go overseas and get a decoration before I'll get out. They say the Air Corps is still too critically needed for the Pacific war to discharge many at this time. Carol, I don't know what comes next for me since they have also abolished our pre-aviation (PAC) status."

Carol wrote: "Yesterday I became a member of our Presbyterian Church (whose choir I've been singing in for over a year) along with six other girls in the glee club. Mary Lou and Karen were baptized and Dr. Zimmer made us all members. When we got back upstairs the rest of the girls told us several people were crying during the service – they probably thought the ruination of the church was coming since we joined."

I congratulated Carol: "It was wonderful to hear your voice when I called to honor your graduation. There are many things I'd planned to say but when I heard your voice, all I could think of was how far away you were. I could see your eyes sparkle when you laughed just as if you were right here beside me. Tomorrow night will be your big night. I'll be thinking of you and be as close to you as thoughts can bring me."

Carol wrote: "Well, the big day is over! It was really thrilling to walk up the aisle and receive our diplomas. I'm kind of sorry it's over. I feel a little lost and sad."

I replied: "Your commencement really sounded swell. I know what you mean about feeling lost and sad. I felt the same way until I started college. I see by your program that Miss Carol Clark graduated with honors. She must be a smart little wench."

Chapter Five

Carol's Pathway to College and Love

During the summer of 1945, our letters focused on Carol's summer job, my unsuccessful attempts to get a furlough, the impending changes in our lives, historic events affecting everyone, and how we longed see each other.

Carol announced: "Well, I've started my summer job with KP&L. The first day I took five shorthand letters and did some typing. Today the boss gave me lots of typing – I'm really getting good at it. I enjoy being busy doing something I like. I now know I could be a pretty good secretary. This weekend Monna is having a slumber party at her house – I'll bet you think we're awful to have so many, but we never see each other if we don't, and pretty soon this part of our lives will come to an end. That will really be a sad time!"

I wrote, "Carol, I finally got preliminary approval from my sergeant and lieutenant for a furlough. As we have agreed I will spend half of it with my parents and half with you."

Then the brass turned it down. I applied again, got approvals, and was turned down again. Then our new base commandeer froze all furloughs and passes for OLTs. They began shipping my buddies out to technical schools at other air bases. I told Carol a furlough looked hopeless, then added, "My darling Carol – In a happier mood I wrote this poem for you:

Oh, when the angels fashioned you, my love
They took the fairest things to make you fair
They found two perfect sea shells for your ears
And gathered morning sun beams for your hair.
From Heaven came the stars which are your eyes,
The rose was robbed to paint your sweet mouth red

And then the Angels smiled – and from a bird
They stole the brain and put it in your head."

Carol replied: "It must have been a blue bird, because this was blue Friday for me after reading the news about no furlough. I've planned on it for so long it seems, and now as you say, we haven't much to look forward to. Hurry and send me your picture – that might help a little. Don, I know what a terrible disappointment this is to you. My heart aches because of that too."

I replied: "I decided to follow your example and listen to some music to improve my mood. I'm in the record room listening while I write you. Right now I'm listening to Ravel's *Bolero*. I've already played Grieg's *Concerto in A minor* (I like that very much), the *Nutcracker Suite*, and Tchaikovsky's *Concerto #1 in B flat*. Enjoyment of classical music (& music in general) is a special gift you brought into my life. There was very little music in our home. No one played an instrument and my sisters played only a little popular music on the radio. Through you and with you I've discovered a source of beauty I didn't know existed."

Carol wrote: "I came home today and noticed nothing different. Mother told me to go out and come in again and to look toward the mantle. I did and just about fell over – I had the strangest feeling that you were right in the room with me. That picture, Don, is just wonderful – it looks as if you could step right out and start talking to me – if only you could. I've tinted it and have been taking it everywhere with me – to work, to show my friends, and here to the farm while we harvest wheat. Hey, I'm a real farmer now! I just got home from hauling a load of wheat to town. Mother taught me how to dump a load yesterday so now she and I can alternate. Betty came with me for harvest this year. We've been trying to get a tan. We go up on a big hill where no one can see us, get naked, and soak up the sun. It's a fun way to get an even tan. But Betty lay with her bottom side up too long, and now has trouble sitting down."

I wrote: "So you tinted my picture huh? Well, they say a good coat of paint will make anything look good. You said you were having trouble with your eyes. I hope they're better. I miss your letters. I'll shoot the guy who tries to steal that little moonbeam that peeks out of your eyes every time you smile or laugh."

Carol replied: "I'm sorry you missed my letters (oh yeah! I'm tickled as all heck) but I had to rest my eyes. The doc said it might be the wheat dust plus eye strain. He gave me dope to put in my eyes night and morning. I'm far sighted and have a little astigmatism in one eye. The doc said I had to wear my new glasses all the time except on parties and dates (what's a date?)"

Sorority rush week worried Carol all summer. Several sororities invited her to summer Coke dates and parties, but she got more and more anxious. Finally she wrote: "Mary Lou & I have both received sorority rush week invitations. I'm very thankful but worried about what to wear and how to behave. I wish you were here to talk to and help me choose one."

I replied: "Personally I wouldn't care whether you were Greek, independent, moronic or just an imbecile. I'd love you just the same. You asked what I'd like you to be. I would like you to be Miss Carol Clark – very pretty, very sweet, and very lovable. Other than that I don't care whether you're an 'I Beta Buck' or 'I Eta Pi'. Don't be scared; relax and enjoy the experience. My friends there have girl friends in most of the sororities and they guarantee you'll get an offer from Alpha Xi and that Pi Phi and Kappa Kappa Gamma will also try to get you, and probably others. Many of them remember you from the parties you came to with me. Your only problem will be which to choose – any of those three would be good.

The war news looks pretty good, doesn't it. The new bomb will probably end it. Les and I now realize we probably saw the first successful nuclear test bomb explosion in history. On July 16 we got up at 0500 and started off to breakfast and were surprised to see a big, very bright glow in the southwestern sky where the atomic bomb research site is located. Later, Los Alamos announced the Trinity test had occurred at 0537 that morning. Three weeks later, August 8, the first bomb was dropped on Japan. It's astonishing the military was able to move that fast!

Frankly, I'm not too enthusiastic about this atomic bomb. My physics professor at K-State said there is a possibility that if the process of atomic disintegration gets out of control it could destroy the whole world."

Carol replied: "I feel exactly as you do about the new atom bomb. We certainly can be thankful that we have it first, but I'm afraid it won't be long before our enemies think of something as bad. I don't think we should accept their peace offer unless they agree to get rid of their emperor. When the war ends, what do you think they'll do with you?"

I replied: "The decision about where to send me will be a big relief. We have been expecting the news for more than a week. When it ends I'll probably be in for another year."

Carol wrote: "Dad took me from work to go home to listen to the 6 p.m. news. I'm so nervous I can hardly write. Don, you have won a steak dinner from me!! Oh, thank God this hell of a war is over – I'm so excited I'm crying. I just can't believe it's over – it's just wonderful!! I'm celebrating with a glass of wine – boy is it delicious. If you get dead drunk tonight I won't blame you one bit. If you were only here!! I miss you more than I can say!!!"

I wrote: "Isn't it wonderful!! Peace on August 15 – what a birthday present for me! It's a wonderful, glorious feeling to be in a peacetime army! I thought there was nothing I wanted more than to be on furlough with you, but I believe this is the one and only thing that could be better than that. It seems almost impossible that the whole thing is over after so long. It seems strange not to hear 24/7 the constant roar of B-29s in training flights over the base."

After the VJ day celebrations, Carol wrote: "You said you might try to get a furlough the first week in September – that would be stupendous!!! Dad has even bought you a ticket to the fair thinking by some good fortune you would get to come. Remember, we shared the last two state fairs – you just have to come. Tell them your great aunt died or something."

I replied: "My dear sick aunt; Are you feeling better auntie dear? You said to tell the Lt. I had a sick aunt, so I did. He laughed and said he'd think it over. Last night every squadron on the field was frozen for an indefinite time – except ours! I want so much to be with you, to talk with you, to dance with you and just to look at you. I don't know when I've wanted anything so much. Here is another of my poems to share my feelings about you.

> *I know I ain't no beauty, My face, it ain't no star!*
> *But I don't mind it Cause I'm behind it*
> *It's the gal out front that gets the Jar!"*

Finally, I wrote the news we'd both been dreaming of: "Carol, I didn't get the furlough, but this is a great day for this private – we're being shipped out to Chanute Field, Illinois **with a fourteen day delay enroute!!** That means we'll be able to use those fair tickets. The Lt. was really swell to Les and I – let us take our pick of all the tech schools offered to the OLTs. We chose the weather observer school at Chanute. As we've agreed, I'll spend half of my leave in Marysville and half with you. This will probably be the last letter you get before I see you – if so, darling, keep the home fires burning."

At this point our letters stopped for a little over two weeks – except for one. My two brother-in-law soldiers also came home, one from Europe and the other from the Pacific. My parents asked me to stay over the weekend for a family reunion. With regret, I called Carol to tell her of the delay. That resulted in the following letter from her: "I guess I knew what you'd tell me over the phone, but I still had hopes you might come. You don't know what a terrible let down this is. I wanted mother to drive me to Marysville today, but she says I have no pride and if you wanted to come bad enough you'd find a way. I couldn't get to sleep last night and I've cried until I have no tears left. I guess I'm selfish, but after all you did say you were coming and we had our plans all made – I don't know what to do. Also, our fair tickets are for Saturday or Monday nights. I don't know whether to go with my folks or wait for you. I don't know if I can depend on you coming even Tuesday. I wish I could change all my plans to go to K-State now. The only reason I chose it was so we could go together, but I have no heart for it now.

All the time you've been in the service you've written how you longed to see me, dance with me in your arms, etc. and now that the time has actually come and you have the chance, you don't take it. I understand how your folks feel, but youth should have its chance too and we've been together so little. If you really wanted to come to Topeka, I don't see how anyone could have the heart to deny you happiness on your furlough. I know you will think I'm terribly selfish, and I'm even going to drive down to the motor and see that this gets on it so you get it Saturday. I'm selfish where you're concerned and guess I want to hurt you a little as you've hurt me. This weekend is going to be endless. Yours, Carol."

Carol's letter distressed me greatly and clearly showed her depth of feelings for me and mine for her. So, as I did two years before when my boss wouldn't give me time off work to visit Carol, I kissed my parents goodbye, got on the train and went to Topeka. I fought knots in my stomach and fear in my heart all the way, thinking I might have lost my Carol. Carol said that same kind of fear she might be losing me motivated her letter.

That visit of a few days transformed our lives! We did all the things we'd dreamed of in our letters – went big band dancing at Meadow Acres, went to the fair, and picnicked with Carol's gang. But most of all we spent glorious time alone together, transforming the fantasy relationship we'd created through letters into a real life relationship, sharing our thoughts and deepest feelings, hopes and dreams. Until this furlough, we'd stored our greatest fears, hopes and vulnerabilities behind a dam constructed to protect us from rejection. Now we allowed that dam to crumble, flooding us both with raw, honest emotions stronger than any we'd ever experienced. In the past, we'd always signed our letters with "Love" but didn't fully realize how powerful love could be when two people became one in thoughts and emotions. In our letters after that, we tried to capture our discovery in words. Carol was eighteen and I was nineteen when we embarked on the journey that would endure for a lifetime.

Winifred, accompanied by Mary Lou and Paul, drove us to Kansas City to catch my train to Chanute Field. She stopped at a restaurant and let us drive to the station so we could be alone. After farewells, I ran to catch my train at the last minute. I arrived at Chanute field at midnight and immediately wrote Carol describing my trip, then added: "My real reason for writing is very selfish – I want to get your letters as soon as possible. I couldn't sleep after leaving you at the station, darling. I just lay there in the dark, reliving the few short but wonderful hours we had together. I realized that during two years of exchanging letters, we've both gradually changed our view of life from 'you and me' to 'US'!! That makes me gloriously happy and yet so sad – thrilled with our dream and the beautiful life ahead of us – and yet it seems so cruel to dream of us as one – a dream so beautiful and full of promise – only to be separated again, and for how long we don't know. I no longer think of my goals and your goals, but OUR GOALS! For the rest of my life, that will be the primary focus of all my actions. I'm sorry I left you so abruptly last night darling, but I couldn't help it. My heart was so full of love for you and shared hopes for our future together that I was afraid it might spill over out of my eyes. My thoughts seem to have big sleepy places between them now so I'll stop. Goodnight Carol – I'll dream of you, and of our shared future together."

At the start of sorority rush week Carol wrote: "Oh, Don everything so far has turned out just perfect – Dad let me have the car and Mary Lou, Karen and I are in the same room which was beyond our highest hopes. I've felt so alone these last two days – sometimes I think I can't stand being away from you for so long. It was so terrible leaving the station – I'm afraid I was very bad company on the trip back to Topeka – I couldn't do anything but think about you and miss you terribly – I think I just about flooded the front seat of the car with my tears. I miss your letters and you more than I ever thought I could miss anyone. Every night I relive the few days we had together and marvel over the love we discovered in such a short time. I know it will last – it just has to. P.S. You know the song *We'll Never Walk Alone*? I think that song perfectly fits what we've found together."

A few days later, Carol wrote: "Almost all the houses recruited me! I narrowed my choice to Kappa Gamma and Alpha Xi. The Kappas have a lot of status and Mom hoped I would pledge them, but I remembered you said listen to your heart. So I chose Alpha Xi because they liked me, seemed my kind of people, and were the most fun. I share a study room with Mary Lou and Becky, who worked so hard to recruit me. We sit around drooling over our TKEs. At one rush tea they sang the TKE sweetheart song to me and was my face red – but I was proud!

My experience with my 'slumber party' gang prepared me well for living with a bunch of girls like this. Last night we were formally pledged. We were all dressed in white, and they gave us our pledge pins. I needed a bucket to catch my tears as usual."

The fall semester began, and Carol's letters were full of her new experiences in the sorority, developing friendships on campus, and fears about her academic work. Her old insecurities reared their ugly head again.

The Air Corps was having a hard time deciding what to do with me. The papers we signed when we made PAC said they couldn't send us to tech school. Several thousand OLTs around the country signed a petition to Congress to get us discharged immediately as was done with the Navy OLTs. One of them had a Daddy in the U.S. Senate who insisted on discharges. I wrote Carol: "All the information we can gather seems to indicate that we may get a discharge by December 1. Nothing is official yet, so don't count on anything until it happens!"

Carol responded: "Don, when I read about the good chance you might have of coming home I was so happy I could hardly contain myself! I keep thinking how wonderful it would be – both of us going to college together. Just think – you may be here for our Christmas formal and dance. What a way to celebrate your discharge!"

We OLTs had nothing to do but dodge KP duty while waiting for decisions about what to do with us. One day I got a nice, but unusual, letter from Carol's mother. She said: "I want to make you kids happy. If no other good ever came to me than to know Carol's and your future success and happiness were assured, that would be sufficient. Surely I couldn't feel so happy over your declarations of love for one another if it wasn't right. Let me tell you from my own experience, life can be so satisfactory, harmonious and beautiful if a couple starts out on the right track. I'm not saying that I did. I was a terrible prude, insanely jealous, and extremely selfish, but I have a patient husband who dealt kindly with me.

Anyway, I hope Carol will profit from my mistakes so she can be a good companion and helper some day. She is jealous, but not too much so, is probably selfish, but I think that can be overcome. Any way she isn't a prude – in fact, I'm afraid I have leaned over backwards in that respect, and as a result she may become too tolerant of some things. So, I am depending on you a great deal to use your influence to help her see the right."

I showed the letter to my closest buddy, Les, in confidence, and said, "What do you think she's trying to tell me?"

Les thought a bit and said, "She seems to be giving you strong approval about your relationship with Carol, so my guess is the primary message is about sex. She may be saying, 'Sex play is OK but please don't screw my daughter before you're married!'"

"That's what I guessed too. She also seems to be trying to gain some influence with me without Carol's knowledge. Carol wouldn't like that so I won't tell her about this letter."

Les said, "Could be trouble – smart move."

One week past Carol's 18th birthday I wrote her this joyful note: "This morning we saw the letter authorizing our discharge, so the rumor is <u>true</u>!!! We <u>will</u> be in college together next semester and we <u>will</u> celebrate at your December 14 Christmas formal. The discharge process will take a little time, but it <u>will</u> be soon."

Carol replied: "Oh Don I'm so happy it's true – I've been crying tears of joy since I read your letter!! Thoughts keep tumbling through my mind about what this dream means for us."

On October 30 Carol wrote: "I miss you so much – tomorrow is the last day of October – it's exactly one month until December 1 when you thought you'd be discharged. I can't wait!!!"

I hadn't written Carol I was discharged and planned to surprise her and my parents.

Carol wrote her parents about my surprise: "The afternoon of Halloween day a TKE came to the door and asked me to come with him to the TKE house to pick up a gift Don sent me. So, I went out to the car with him, opened the door, and out stepped Don!!! I nearly fainted – I screamed, jumped into his arms and started crying with joy. He'd been discharged over a week ago and came to see me for several days before going home. *It's a dream come true!!* We spent a little time hugging and kissing and then went inside where we could talk. He told me how it all happened. I tantalized him with the new peach satin formal I'd just bought for the Homecoming and Alpha Xi Christmas balls."

A few days later, Carol wrote her mother: "Last night we all went to the TKE house party. We girls had to dress in slacks, a man's shirt and a tie. The boys wore sweaters; we expected they would be padded with breasts but they weren't. I had a wonderful time – Don is as much fun as ever. A TKE and his girl announced their engagement so the girls and boys formed smooch lines. I'm usually too shy, but this time I decided to practice for my future. Don went to Marysville and really surprised his parents. He'll be back for the Homecoming Ball. When Don came to the State Fair in September, 1943, he bet me a steak dinner the war would be over in two years. Sunday he's going to collect. Sunday afternoon Tutt and I are taking Don and Paul on a picnic. That night I'm paying off my bet and buying Don a steak dinner.

My life is so wonderful now!! I find it hard to believe this is really happening. Don needs to earn some money before starting back to school so I won't see him except on weekends until February, but that's lot better than never seeing him."

I was in desperate need of clothes for college. I'd outgrown most of my old stuff and couldn't take Carol to formal dances in my army fatigues. During the war, clothing for civilians was rationed and in short supply. Now, with GIs flooding home from the military and all needing civilian clothes, 'civvies' were hard to find. Kenny, my brother-in-law and a Kansas City native, said he knew where to get clothes so I renewed my wardrobe at black market shops and used clothing stores in Kansas City.

On the way home we drove into an unexpected prairie blizzard. You have to live through one to believe it! Kenny piloted his car through the storm with me, my sister Maxine, and our cute little niece, Laurel (nicknamed Little Iodine) as white-knuckled passengers. Snow came fast, blown by howling winds, until the road disappeared. All we could see was a surface of white, and couldn't tell where the road ended and ditches began. We crept along slowly through the twilight, guided by the tops of occasional fence posts sticking up above the snow drifts. Kenny's shrapnel wounds started hurting severely and I was desperate to find a safe refuge.

As we approached Topeka, I suggested we stop and stay overnight with Carol's parents. They were delighted to see us. To ease

Kenny's pain, Winifred immediately put him under a machine she used to treat her arthritis. Then she served us all hot drinks and homemade cookies to raise our spirits. The Clarks were caring for two little nieces whose mother was crippled and in the hospital with polio. The kids hit it off right away, running around and playing noisily as kids will do. At breakfast, Winifred said, "It's wonderful to see you all, but I'm worried about how you can possibly make it to Marysville. Don, with this awful snow you may need to stay at home through the holiday. I hope not because we and Carol want you part of the time."

Kenny, a tough Irishman, said "I made it through the Battle of the Bulge in France in worse weather than this so I'll get us to Marysville." And that's exactly what he did!

It's impossible to describe the joy Carol and I felt at being reunited as we enjoyed the Homecoming and Alpha Xi Christmas balls. When I saw Carol in the new peach formal, my mouth dropped open and I stood and stared as she walked gracefully toward me with a big smile and sparkling eyes. My sweetheart had become an utterly gorgeous, delightful woman! The deep pleasure of dancing in each other's arms again was a dream fulfilled.

Carol and I longed for opportunities to have long talks as we used to, but there was no place we could have privacy to do that. Sunday morning after the Homecoming Ball we solved that problem. College students liked the young minister at Carol's Presbyterian Church. We went to his service and then I took Carol to Sunday dinner in the lovely dining room at the Wareham Hotel. We got a table in a private corner and spent several leisurely hours dining and talking. I started the conversation, "Carol, I'm impressed with how quickly your sorority sisters have come to like and admire you. One of the first things you did was to pursue your love of music by auditioning for K-State's admired choral group. Your sisters were astonished that you got in as a freshman."

"I'd met Luther Leavengood when he directed the *Messiah* with our Topeka choir, and that may have helped because he singled me out for praise then."

"Then, your pledge class elected you to represent them on the Interfraternity Council and your actives recognized your artistic, musical and performance talents by appointing you to their entertainment committee and chair of their decorating committee for all Alpha Xi Parties."

Carol blushed at the compliment, "That was probably my 'pledge mother' Becky's influence. I almost refused, but Becky told me it was time I showed some confidence in my abilities, so that's what I'm trying to do."

"Becky and Tutt tell me other pledges, and sometimes older sisters, often stop by your room to share interests or vent about troubles. Becky says you have an intuitive compassion and likeability that draws people to you like a magnet and Tutt says you're just continuing to play the role you did in your slumber party group."

Carol nodded, "I'm surprised and sad that so many young women have no one to confide in about their troubles and feelings. I'm lucky to have Mom, my slumber gang, and you."

"Carol, I wish you could see yourself as others see you. You are a new freshman and already a leader. I'm so very proud of you and agonizingly in love with you too."

With sparkling eyes, a big smile that deepened her dimples, and a flirty wink Carol said, "Right back at ya, Buster!!"

As we ate our delicious ham dinner, we talked about Carol's college experiences so far, and how things might change next semester when we were in college together. Over coffee Carol said, "Don, there's one aspect of my life I need to talk with you about. Maybe you can help me figure out how to deal with it."

"You needn't ask. From now on I'll always be here for you."

"My problem is money, my parents, and my feelings about it. Before college I earned my own money and decided how to spend it. Now I'm completely dependent on my parents for everything. They gave me permission to write checks on their account for my expenses, but every month I have to explain and justify every check, and they continually complain about them. I don't spend money foolishly. I feel guilty about spending their money, angry about their criticisms, and hurt that they don't seem to trust me. I told them I feel like a heel spending their money and will try to pay them back some day, but that's made no difference. What can I do?"

"Carol, since your birth, your parents have been responsible for your life and a bit overprotective of you. My guess is they're having a hard time giving you more freedom as you grow up, particularly you mother. It will take time, patience and some discomfort as both of you go through this change. Consider trying this: (1) tell them you're grateful they enabled you to go to college; (2) you're disappointed they don't seem to trust your judgment in spending the money they provide; (3) propose a specific monthly amount you'd like them to provide and ask they give you the freedom to decide how to spend it. Promise that if you run out of money before the month ends you'll do without until the next month. Even if they refuse your suggestion, you will have delivered a message. Then, ignore their complaints and use your judgment about how to spend whatever they provide. In your own mind, don't let them make you feel guilty or angry."

Carol nodded her agreement, "So you're saying I should feel confident setting my own rules about how to handle money as I have in the past, rather than simply conforming to theirs. You're right – I do want to be more independent, but have trouble standing up for myself."

"Carol, next semester I'll be here. The GI bill will pay K-State $500/year for my tuition, books, etc. My TKE board and room will be paid for by working as a kitchen boy. That will give me a lot of flexibility in using my GI bill small living allowance. I intend to pay for our entertainment expenses, like this dinner today. I can help you in other ways. For example, if you need transportation to or from a bus or train, I can borrow a buddy's car and provide it. If you need a small loan to finish out a month, I can be your banker. If you want to visit Carlsbad Caverns, I will take you. To quote one of your letters, from now on you'll never walk alone!"

Carol laughed at my Carlsbad comment, and her distress eased as I had hoped it would, "Don, I can't tell you how much it means to me to have someone I can talk with like this. We are going to make one hell of a team!" We strolled out into a sunny Sunday afternoon and enjoyed our time together until I had to catch my ride back to Marysville.

We split Christmas and New Year's holiday time between our families, half in Topeka and half in Marysville. After the holidays, I told Carol, "Mom talks about you a lot now, honey – she really likes you! She enjoyed your conversation Friday afternoon very much."

In January, the Alpha Xi pledge sneak occurred. Carol described it to her parents:

"The sneak began at noon. We snatched all the fuses in the house, greased the telephones and put syrup on all the 'Johnnie seats.'

(Marion Asher and several other actives sat flat on them – what a gooey mess!). Then we all spent the afternoon and evening in our suite in the Wareham Hotel down town eating and having a ball. Once in the afternoon and again in the evening we became a 20 voice chorus out on our balcony singing to the citizens of down town Manhattan.

College rules prohibit staying out overnight, so at ten p.m. we went back to the house. Waiting at the door were very vicious looking actives with candles in one hand and paddles in the other, ready to retaliate. They made us undress and put each of us through what is called the "fire drill". It is a series of distasteful tasks, all performed in the nude, like drinking what looked like pig slop but really was beer with old soaked up do-nuts in it. Their finale was to have each of us stand in the nude and give an assigned performance without laughing. I had to tell 'How to Make a Ford!' Everything I said they must have taken the wrong way for they just about split. It was rather embarrassing standing in front of everybody with nothing on."

The fall semester ended in January with the annual Royal Purple Ball. The Alpha XIs nominated Carol as their candidate for Royal Purple Queen. Carol wrote her parents: "My sorority sisters dolled me up in a borrowed gorgeous blue net formal (I wish it was mine). At the ball we candidates had to get up in front of everyone to be introduced. An hour later they announced the winner over the radio. I wasn't a bit disappointed that I didn't win, but it makes me feel good that dozens of people told me how great I looked and I should have won. Dancing there wasn't much fun, but the TKE Sweetheart Ball the next night was just wonderful! I was in the mood to dance and so was Don so we really went to town!"

I returned to K-State as a student the spring semester, 1946. Like most universities of the time, it was a place in transition. Most of the students were mature veterans of war, many married and some with children. Most of them struggled, trying to survive on the GI Bill with a little supplement from part time work. There were no residence halls for men. K-State hauled in and renovated former military barracks and travel trailers from nearby Ft. Riley to provide housing for the massive increase of students. Classrooms and labs were overcrowded.

Collectively the student veterans had experienced and learned to work with people in many different cultures, had trained in, used, and repaired new technologies, and had solved unique problems in combat conditions. Consequently, they found many of their classes uninteresting and outdated.

For example, I was taking an engineering class in electronics (an emerging specialty in 1945) taught by a professor whose text book was used in many universities. In one session he described a theory, explaining why certain kinds of things couldn't be done. In the middle of the lecture a veteran in the back row said, "Professor, your theory is wrong. During our battle on Okinawa, we had to rig up emergency communication arrangements and we did what your theory says is impossible." He talked with that veteran after class and a year and a half later published a revision of his book.

Veterans were also dissatisfied with the nonacademic environment. Many traditional student organizations didn't serve their interests. There were no facilities supporting leisure activities, such as a student union. Their bare bones GI Bill budgets had little money for recreational activities like movies, dates or costly parties. Curricula hadn't changed much since the late 1920s, due largely to stresses of the Great Depression and WWII. The student veterans had lived and worked with all kinds of military authorities and weren't in awe of faculty and academic administrators. They decided updated curricula were needed and asked student government to appoint a Student Planning Commission to explore ways of doing that. I was among the veterans asked to lead that task. Carol helped by encouraging her sorority sisters and their friends to support that push towards change.

The new K-State president, Milton Eisenhower, recognized the need for improvements, shared the students' concerns and supported their efforts. Later, after we became friends with him and his wife, Helen, he told Carol and me the back story about his appointment to K-State:

"In mid-1944, K-State sought to hire me as President. I was interested but we were still in the middle of a war and I thought it best to do my part in Washington until it was over. I talked with my brother, Ike, about it. He was in charge of the European front and said, 'Take the job! The European war will be over in a year.' So, I did, and it was. I found significant updating was needed in American universities like K-State.

As my starting point, I decided to focus on citizen roles and responsibilities in creating and maintaining a sound and vibrant democracy. When existing faculty opposed change, I tried to try to 'jump start' that change by creating an Institute for the Study of Citizenship, bringing in new faculty to lead it. When veterans started a movement for change, I jumped on board."

Between Milton Eisenhower's determination to update academia and his cooperative work with the Student Planning Commission, veterans at K-State helped make realistic and practical changes to curricula.

Chapter Six

Living the Realities of College and Courtship

Carol and I had dreamed of being in college together, but found it took some planning. We both had busy academic and activity schedules, so we devised a plan to see each other, study together, or talk on the phone every day, and to spend as much weekend time together as possible.

Carol wrote her parents: "Classes so far have been OK except for my teacher of Written Communications. Only 3 of the class are girls; he argues with the boys instead of teaching. My organic chemistry is so complicated. Don has agreed to study with me at the library tomorrow.

We went to a basketball game last weekend. I don't really enjoy the games much, but Don does and is so enthusiastic. For example, last night we played KU. It was an exciting, close game and Don started cheering, *Every Man A Wildcat!! Rock 'em Sock 'em, Beat KU!* After a while he had all the fans around us shouting *Every Man A Wildcat* to urge the team on. After the game the Wampus Cats president asked Don to join and to try out for cheer leader. Don explained he was a member from 1944 but wasn't interested in being a cheerleader."

Later she wrote her parents: "Last night I studied Written Communications with Don. We aren't supposed to do that, but Don can really teach me things in English – he's very good, especially in vocabulary which is what our test was over. He put definitions into simple English and it was much easier to learn."

During the winter it was hard for us to find quiet places where we could have some privacy. Most Sundays we went to church, then to the Wareham dining room for dinner and long leisurely conversations. We completed the day with a movie and holding hands, and a finale of kissing and hugging when I took her home.

Spring arrived at last. With the advent of warm weather, we could enjoy Mother Nature and each other in private. We explored the areas outside of Manhattan and discovered Wildcat Creek, which gurgled peacefully through a pristine meadow blooming with colorful wildflowers. Carol wore shorts with a matching halter top under her blouse so she could shed the blouse and start a tan. Such days were ours to hike, study together, wade in the creek, relax, and do as we pleased. We packed a lunch, drinks and a big picnic blanket and headed for our meadow. Usually we studied and talked, interspersed with hugging and kissing. One time, while sprawled out on our blanket sunbathing, a biology professor strolled by with his class on prairie wildlife. As they passed, we heard him say with a chuckle, "Not all meadows have that form of wildlife." After they were out of sight and earshot, Carol giggled, "Did you see the looks on their faces? The boys looked curious but the girls just smiled and looked envious."

One lovely April day in our meadow Carol said, "Don, ever since falling deeply in love during your leave, we've shared our hopes and dreams and agreed we would not get married until you graduated. I'm in the mood to make some tentative plans. Let's do that today."

"Carol, the thought of marrying you gets me all excited, but I'll calm down and think logically. After this semester, I'll have to finish in two more years because that's when my GI Bill money runs out. I promise you I'll graduate at the end of the 1948 spring semester."

Carol thought about possibilities for a while, and said, "The spring semester always ends the last part of May. We don't want to wait any longer than we must, so that's the soonest we could marry. Let's aim for June 1st. You'll have graduation ceremonies then too, but we can work around that. On June 1, 1948 we *will* become husband and wife." With a shout of delight, I grabbed and hugged her. We danced around our meadow pretending we were Mrs. and Mr. Ford. We agreed to keep our plan a secret, snuggled together, and dreamed of that happy future.

In early May we spent another afternoon in our meadow. Carol was unusually quiet. Her tense voice and body language told me she was troubled and fearful about something. After a hesitation, she said, "Don, I've been thinking a lot about what I want to do with my life between now and June 1, 1948. This is hard; please let me tell you my thoughts before you say anything."

Her thoughts came pouring out as if she felt she had to say them fast or break down. I was scared, anticipating what she might say.

"Four goals have guided my thoughts and actions this year. By far the most important is to begin our married life. So, I've been thinking how I can best prepare for that. I'd like to spend time making, gathering, and preparing all the things we'll need to make a nice home for us two years from now, and to create a nest egg of savings to help us get started.

My second priority is helping my parents develop and implement plans for their life when I marry and leave them. Dad's dream for decades has been to have his own farm. Mom insisted he couldn't do that until I graduated high school. They're now buying a farm 20 miles west of Topeka. They plan to renovate the buildings and I'd like to help them get ready to live there.

Third, I'm very concerned about Mom's periodic health and depression problems. I think her lonely daily life is one cause. She needs more goals, activities, and companionship from which she can get pleasure. I've been the primary source for that in her life so far. I'd like to help prepare Mother for the changes she'll face when I leave. She also faces a major upheaval of her life when they move to the farm and I'd like to help her with that.

The fourth has been to get a college education and degree. I can't finish a degree before we marry. I don't like my Home Ec major, and K-State has no good majors in the things I love, like music, arts and crafts and nursing. The only thing I really like about college is being with you. I enjoy my sorority relationships, but many activities are nonsense and restrict my freedom. I feel I'm wasting my time and money. I can do a lot of the things I like without a college degree.

The only reasonable solution I can think of is to forget college for now, move back home for two years to help my parents in this difficult time of transition for them, and get a good secretarial job in Topeka so I can save money and prepare to help launch our marriage in two years. We don't really have much time together during the week now, so it's weekends like this one we'd lose. We'd have to create ways of getting together on weekends because I'll never give up our weekends together. For these reasons I'm considering dropping out of college this summer. We've agreed to make shared decisions so please help me make this one!"

My heart dropped into my stomach! I wanted to shout what I was thinking, *We've dreamed for so long of being in college together, and just this past winter and spring have savored the joy of it. I don't want to lose our wonderful togetherness!!* The thought of another two years of loneliness without her, like the ones that had just ended, brought tears to my eyes. But, I was speechless. Carol was obviously fearful of my reaction because her own eyes filled with tears that poured down her cheeks as she stared at me, waiting.

I knew Winifred, had observed her difficulties first hand, and understood their closeness. I knew of Eugene's dream. I knew Carol loved our time together as I do, but also realized she didn't truly enjoy college. We'd talked many times about the personal goals she wanted to pursue and none of them required a college degree. She had obviously thought long, hard, and clearly about her goals. I decided to immediately support her plan to ease her fears about my reaction, and to make clear my deep commitment to our shared decision making.

I swallowed hard to keep my voice from trembling, "Spending the next two years this way will be hard for both of us, but..." I swallowed again and squeezed her hands, "...you've looked at our future with clarity so I just have to say, 'Follow your heart!' and I'll do everything I can to support your plan to reach our shared goals." By now my initial shock had eased so I could smile and mean it. "I'm an experienced hitchhiker and can easily cover forty miles to see you, and I'm confident you'll find time and ways to come and see me."

She drew a shaky breath of relief and moved into my arms, wiping tears and whispering soft words of love. Once again, our partnership for life was strengthened. We lay together on our blanket, savoring the silence of our beautiful meadow, and talking quietly about how to implement her plan. We agreed to keep her plan a secret until she went home for the summer, and to not share with others all her reasons for leaving college.

We had to enjoy our outings while we could before Carol left college. One of our favorite outings was climbing to the top of K-State Hill to soak up the sun and take in the beautiful rolling hills around Manhattan. One afternoon in late spring, we decided to picnic on the hill and stay to watch the sunset. We took hot dogs and marshmallows to roast over a campfire for our supper. At sunset, we sat on our blanket and held hands while watching the spectacular, multicolored show at the western horizon. As dusk fell, gentle breezes and night sounds accompanied softly spoken words. We felt so happy and in love, alone together in this private place. Finally, with just enough light left to see, I sighed and broke the spell by gathering wood for our fire. We roasted our supper and laughed while feeding each other marshmallows fixed just the way we liked them – crispy black on the outside and gooey on the inside. Later, we sat quietly by the fire, with a full moon and sky full of stars as our roof.

Carol nestled closer to my side and said, "When I'm in such a beautiful setting I hear music that expresses what I see and feel." Today, so many decades later, I can still see the dreamy look on her face as she said it.

"What music are you hearing now?"

"*Romeo and Juliet* because it's music full of love."

We snuggled together quietly for awhile, reminiscing about that moment we knew our love was for keeps, and how we felt about each other now. Carol enjoyed the sensual pleasures of touch as much as I did, so that night our kissing and touching took a natural progression. I couldn't tell whose heart was pounding harder as I gently unbuttoned her blouse and caressed her breasts. Her arousal matched mine as I removed her clothing piece-by-piece. Finally, she lay naked before me, her body gleaming with firelight and moonlight. I finally managed to choke out a few words, "Carol, I'm in awe of how beautiful your body is glowing in the moonlight."

She wasn't shy about lying on our blanket naked. In fact, she smiled! "Mother said I shouldn't let a man see me like this until we were married. I'm glad I didn't listen because it's heaven feeling like this while you look at me. But, I'm a little afraid of where this may lead us."

I fought to restrain myself and finally won, "My darling, I too struggle with desire but won't take us any further, so don't be afraid. Let's just enjoy this special experience together." We lay in each other's arms as desire cooled along with the night air and our campfire burnt to embers. Curfew time neared, I helped Carol dress and we went back to the Alpha Xi house, our hearts torn by a mixture of passionate love and anxious anticipation of being separated again.

Final exams for the spring semester were the first two weeks in May. Carol wrote her parents about a great party: "I'm so proud of Don for he was elected president of the Wampus Cats last Wednesday – that's the men's pep organization. Each spring they sponsor 'dandelion day' to get students to dig up dandelions on the campus lawns, followed by a dance that night. Don inherited that project, found no preparations had been made and they only had $8 in their treasury. Within a week he got it all organized, raised enough money to cover all expenses, hired Matt Benton's big band and ended up with a surplus of $150 in their treasury.

It was a 'Hobo Dance' so people came in costumes. Don looked so cute, he had a goofy lookin' hat on with jeans and a plaid shirt – I wore jeans and a plaid shirt. Doc Wempe looked so cute with old suspenders and a hobo hat. Matt's orchestra dressed as hobos and cut up while playing. I had more fun at this dance than I did at any all year – everybody did I think. I danced every dance – most of them with Don of course. President Eisenhower liked it so much he's going to give the Wampus Cats a whole day off to encourage other students to participate in dandelion day next year."

At the Alpha XI house after that happy night, Carol whispered "There was a touch of sadness for me when tonight ended as I realized it was my last party as a K-State student."

When the spring semester ended, Carol moved back home and returned to her old job at KP&L. Our courtship by mail began again. This time it lasted two years. Our first letters conveyed how hard it was for both of us to give up our dream of being in college together.

On May 20 I wrote: "I'm very lonely for you tonight, Carol. I treasure spending an afternoon alone with you like today. You looked so pretty. Whenever we go out together I feel so proud of you I could pop. Today was doubly important to me. It was the end of our time together when we could see each other anytime we wanted to. Being separated from you will seem almost unbearable for a while. Going to summer school is going to be pretty dull and unimportant to me I fear. My thoughts and heart will be elsewhere.

There's the whistle of the westbound streamliner. Let's get on it! We could go out to Carlsbad Caverns, down to old Mexico, over to California, and come back by way of Yellowstone, the Rocky Mountains, and Colorado. Darling, it would be so much fun with you. But then everything's fun when I do it with you: Dances like the one Friday night when we're all acting crazy and having a rowdy time; picnics like the ones we had at our meadow; and afternoons like this one. Such memories make it more and more difficult for me to be away from you. I leave you now darling, but I shall be dreaming of you because --- I'll love you, always!!

On May 20 Carol wrote: "Just as I told you I would, I'm sitting at the desk listening to our records – *Meadowland* is just finishing. Somehow they bring you closer to me. It was certainly hard leaving you all alone on the highway – as soon as I started down the road to the farm that feeling of emptiness came into my heart – it's there now and will be until we're together again. When I got to the farm we took our relatives to Gage Park to see the animals. We went to see the monkeys {by the way do you happen to have a twin brother rooming on monkey isle?} After playing the piano a little tonight I finally talked myself into going to bed. I kept thinking of how much fun we've had together this semester and this weekend, and how wonderful you are. I can't express my deep feelings well in words, but I think you know what I mean. Not being able to be with you is unbearable now – I'm going to have to get used to it."

I put my hitchhiking skills to good use and visited Carol before summer classes began. We established a pattern of me hitching rides to Topeka, Carol picking me up on the highway and taking me back to the highway when it was time to catch a ride home. Sometimes a fraternity brother or friend would be going to Topeka and took me with them. Hitchhiking was common then and produced some interesting experiences. When I couldn't hitchhike to see her, Carol either took the bus to Manhattan or rode with a friend.

I wrote: "Here's my summer class schedule. As you can see, I'm carrying 20 semester hours over 16 weeks this summer so I'll be busy. When I got into the car with those two guys last night, they turned to me with a long, loud BARF! and said, 'Why the hell couldn't she have been hitchhiking instead of you?' I replied, 'Fellas, that's preferred stock. Keep your eyes and hands off!' I watched out the back window until you faded out of sight. I confess – you discovered my secret. The little fellow you saw on monkey island is a son by my first wife. We decided he would have a better life there. How's he doing?"

Carol wrote: "I'm playing *Romeo and Juliet* tonight for I feel lonely for my one and only. I can't get over how fast you got a ride last night. I drove back to Topeka in a fog – since I had a ways to drive I released my emotions and let them pour down my cheeks. I seem to always cry when you leave me for it seems so strange and lonely not to have you beside me. I'll certainly be glad when the day comes when we'll be able to be together and won't have to put up with having to see each other off on cars, trains or buses!"

Such episodes reflect our summer of 1946. Every weekend possible I either hitchhiked to see Carol or she came to Manhattan to see me. When we couldn't be together, she went to movies with a friend and I buried myself in my studies. As we had when we were separated before, we turned to our letters as a means of being together in our fantasy life.

One letter described her greatest joy and biggest worry: "I received two letters today from the man I love so much I think I'll pop. When I read your letters I feel as if I'm sitting with your arm around me talking as if you were really here, and they help me endure Mom's periodic illnesses. Mom felt awfully sorry she wasn't able to be up when you boys were here – she enjoys having you around so much for it's lonely for her alone all day with Daddy gone. She's been in bed again for several days but beginning to feel a bit better now, for which I'm so grateful. It hurts me so much to see her suffer through these horrible arthritis attacks – they're so painful and nothing can cure it – that's what is so hopeless. If only Daddy understood she's in no condition to live alone and do the work of a farm."

I thought, *I wonder if Carol recognizes that her mom seems to get sick when Eugene leaves on one of his trips and gets better when he comes home?*

Carol wrote: "I've found a new love. I went sailing with Bill and Romana – our renter – and a friend. They each had sailboats. First I went on the big one. It was heavenly and very exciting when the boat would heel and we had to sit on one side to keep it from going over. Then the other one heeled over more because it was smaller. I've never had such an exciting and thrilling time without you. When I'm rich, a sailboat will be the first thing I'm gonna have."

After a visit I wrote: "I really enjoyed our talks. You can carry on an exciting conversation about so many more things than most girls I've met. But, I'll never be able to completely understand your mind, Carol. Just about the time I think I'm beginning to understand you pretty well – V R O O M!! – I'm right back where I started."

Carol replied: "So you don't think you'll ever be able to understand my mind – and since when have men been able to understand women completely? Sometimes we're a mystery, but usually there's a reason behind our actions and usually those reasons are men! Don, I love you so terribly and it makes me love you even more, if possible, when I think how hard you're working for us and our dreams of the future. I know what a grind it must be, but darling, when you get discouraged you always know I'm behind you, loving you, and some day this will be over and we'll be together forever."

I wrote: "This last weekend was great!! I'm kinda sorry we didn't get to go swimming Monday, but our poker game made up for it. Would you like to play again sometime?"

Carol replied: "I'm glad you didn't have trouble getting a ride back. I was kind of embarrassed when that young couple smiled while we were kissing goodbye, but was grateful when they turned around and picked you up. I'd love to play poker with you again, but my skill at the game is unlikely to improve for I'd rather lose."

That summer, Carol began implementing her plan to save money for our future. She wrote: "I've had fun sewing this summer and am getting good at it. I made a new skirt for $1.57; a new top for $1.43 and just finished a cute midriff for .39 cents. Pretty thrifty eh? I looked at new dresses but they all cost around $11. I can make one for $2, so that's my plan. I've found a new job!! I saw it advertised, interviewed for it and got it. I'm head (& only) secretary in the Kansas United Dry Forces office. (Your TKEs will sure kid me!) It pays a lot more, has excellent hours, and my boss, Dr. Farley, is a protestant preacher. I start next week."

My summer was packed with heavy class and study schedules, with a few extracurricular activities squeezed in. I kept Carol informed: "Last night the Student Planning Commission met. Your Alpha Xi, Jan Putnam, is also on the commission – she's sharp. We're planning a conference of about 100 campus leaders, Milton Eisenhower and all the Deans for 3 days starting Sept. 3 at Camp Wood – a 4H camp with barracks-like housing, a food service building, a large conference building, playing fields, and a small lake. We have a sizable agenda of proposals for improvements at K-State that will be debated and voted on, e.g. a detailed proposal for a student union, changes in general education requirements, some curriculum changes, and student membership on some University policy committees. Student committees have spent months collecting evidence in support of each proposal. Ex-GIs have had a lot of input. Each Dean will be living with about ten students. Milton Eisenhower hopes the Deans will learn something and be more supportive of student efforts. We have high hopes of bringing about changes.

Jan said she was sorry she missed you when you were here. She asked me to twist your arm to get you to come back to college. It's a fine compliment that they don't want to lose you!! I told her you had a mind of your own, and would bonk me if I tried to twist your arm."

Carol wrote: "I like my new job! Farley is very nice. We have a reception area and private offices next to each other. I do everything: take dictation; write letters; open and sort all mail; record all contributions and take them to the bank for deposit; keep up the files; greet and help visitors – I do everything because I'm the only one here! I like the responsibility. He knows about and gently teases me about us and about 'having my head in the clouds' all day. He's gone a lot and I'm in charge alone for several days at a time. Come up and see me some time!!"

Carol reported: "Don, I'm so happy with my life now. My folks are working together to get the farm ready to live in and Mom isn't sick so much. Mom and I go to the movies often like we used to years ago. I have a wonderful job I'm good at and a very nice boss; I go to movies with old friends frequently, and they want me to be part of their weddings when they marry. I'm saving money to help launch our life together, and I have the most wonderful man and lover in the world that I sometimes get to spend significant time with.

I had such a good time this weekend – the dinner at the TKE house was so much fun –even the embarrassment of that fake announcement of our engagement. I just don't see how it's possible for one person to make such a difference in another's feelings and emotions. When I'm with you, I'm so content and full of life and longing for you. But, when you're away from me, I feel as if the best portion of me has been cut away – I feel so empty and lonely."

One topic that irritated Carol was our discussions about smoking cigarettes. Her gang started smoking in high school and so did she. When our relationship changed from friendship to planning marriage, we talked openly about smoking and I asked her to quit. Finally, she did quit, to please me. Later, she discovered I occasionally smoked a pipe and didn't take the news well, as expressed in this letter: "Darling, I really don't mind if you smoke but it just hurt me a little that you ordered ME to stop smoking but it was OK for you. Let me get one thing straight, Don. I cannot tolerate any of this double standard stuff that so many boys seem to think is OK. Anything you do, I can do too, so if you smoke, I smoke. I confess that I love to smoke and it's hard to give up, but if you don't smoke, naturally I won't either. I love you, darling, but you can't run over me --- much!"

I replied: "You really gave me hell about smoking in today's letter. My ears are still burning! I apologize for my stupidity for not treating cigarette and pipe smoking the same. I guess I've been imitating my pipe smoking father. Smoking a pipe means nothing to me and I've quit! I'm glad you have guts enough to stand up and say what you think honestly and sincerely. I'm glad, too, you feel as you do about what you call double standards because I think you're right – for both men and women. I didn't know you enjoyed smoking so much, but I'm glad you're willing to give it up for me. It humbles me a bit, and makes me very proud of you."

Carol helped me understand she was part of a powerful post-WWII movement by women towards equality of all kinds. Before that war, our society generally viewed women's roles as cooking, sewing, keeping house, having babies and taking care of them, and pleasing their husband. (That was Eugene's view, and why he resisted spending money for Carol's college education.) During the war, women savored equality as they joined the work force to help with the war effort and to earn money to support the family while their men were at war. Carol's lecture to me was a small manifestation of women's post-WWII drive for equality.

Carol wrote: "Dr. Farley will be gone for a month to six weeks, and I'll have complete charge of the office. He really wants me to stay on this job and says he'll try to get me a raise. He wants to meet my 'fella'. I feel wonderful that he has so much confidence in me. The office will be lonely while he's gone. How about coming to my office to ease my loneliness while he's gone? Several of my high school friends and sorority sisters are getting married so I'm part of or singing at several weddings. It seems like all my friends are getting married – makes me eager."

Early marriages and fast courtships were common in those early post-WWII years when people were catching up with life delayed. Carol and I had the same urge, but we had seen the hardship and unhappiness in quick marriages so we endured the delay to help ensure that we got off to a good start. But, delaying living as man and wife created special stresses. Holding, kissing and caressing one another increasingly led to passionate arousal.

{Up until the 1960s, ways of preventing pregnancies were limited to (1) abstaining from intercourse, (2) abstaining during fertile parts of the menstrual cycle, called rhythm, or (3) blockage of semen by use of a diaphragm by the woman, or a condom by the man. The first birth control pill was approved by the FDA in 1960, but the first pills had serious health and life threatening side effects for many women. Modern, low dose pills without serious side effects became available in the 1980s. This opened an era of increased safety, freedom and convenience for women, and one in which the link between intercourse and interpersonal commitment was diminished, so that sex is often sought simply as a source of pleasure, sometimes called "recreational sex."}

We agreed to share responsibility for abstaining from intercourse until we married. Carol called it our "pact". She wrote "Darling, lets watch our pact this weekend – right now I could tell it to go to hell, but I know we mustn't let ourselves go or I would be very afraid for the future. When I write to you and play records, such as Beethoven's 5^{th,} every positive emotion in me is aroused and I feel very passionate – good thing you aren't here now!"

Later she wrote: "I had a farewell party with some of my old gang and their boyfriends before they went back to college. It's probably the last time we'll all be together – makes me sad to see that part of my life ending. Today when I came home, Mom was mad and started harping at me. Told me it was too late & I couldn't stay up to write you a letter. I really objected to that so she told me to go to my room. She's been griping at me for a couple days and I'm certainly not in the mood to take it. I'm in such a lonely mood tonight and thought for a minute what life would be like if I didn't have you. That made me feel awful."

In an attempt to improve her mood, I sought her advice: "Dear Dorothy Dix Clark – This is my problem: I'm in love with a beautiful, talented, intelligent young lady who also, I believe, is in love with me. She comes from a good home with wonderful parents and a fine background. In my lowly state of being, I don't feel I'm good enough for her. Should I ruin her life by marrying her, forcing her to live in degradation and poverty the rest of her life? Yours, Puzzled."

Dorothy Dix Clark replied: "Dear Mr. Puzzled – How are you tonight – still puzzled? Well, I'll try my best to straighten out your problem. So you feel you're a lowly being and not good enough for this girl – had you ever stopped to think just how important you are, especially to the one you say you love? Had you ever thought that she may be the one who is lowly, dumb, and ignorant and that you may be sorry that you ever thought about marrying her? I happen to know this girl you speak of quite well and my, my – she has some horrible faults! First is her incapacity to cook, one of the first things you must consider in the girl you plan to marry. She also is lazy, dumb, ugly and needs a bath! Her worst fault is that she'll plant her cold feet on you in bed unmercifully in the dead of winter. Think twice my good man – think of the mess you'll get yourself into. If you marry her she'll be getting the best of the deal. Yours truthfully, Dorothy Dix Clark"

I reported: "My old buddy, Earl Elliot, has been discharged and is back to college living in the TKE house!! He has a car. Let's get him a Topeka girlfriend so he can provide transportation to come to Topeka together – to visit our Topeka girlfriends!"

Carol and I resolved one bone of contention that summer. She dated another boy during her high school senior year. After he was drafted they continued the relationship through letters. She continued that correspondence after we fell in love. Near the end of our being in college together I asked her why. She said, "He's a nice guy and I hate to hurt him, but I will tell him."

On a summer date I said, "Carol, did you ever write to your high school boy friend? I must admit I *am* a little jealous that another man might think you were in love with him. I feel sorry for him because I can understand how he'd feel loving and losing you. Losing you would be like losing a part of myself, but I'd rather know than torture myself with false dreams. Telling him may hurt, but if you consider our love permanent he must know."

"I'll write him this week. I've avoided it because I didn't know how to tell him but you're right – he should know I'm deeply in love with you." In her next letter she said: "I wrote him a long letter today and told him we plan to be married when you graduate. I hope that will be the last I hear from him. Just four more days until you are again beside me – I can hardly wait!"

Carol wrote angrily: "Mother keeps telling me how she hates it that I quit school and all that sort of rot. I told her she should have told me all that before I made up my mind. She says she hates to see me not learning anything. I'm learning things in my job, but not what she wants me to learn. I do miss some (but not all) parts of school & have been quite sensitive about the subject every time she brings it up. I asked Dad if he thought I made the right choice and, of course, he thought it was just the thing for me to do. I'm a little mixed up and your opinion counts the most. Tell me honestly what you think. Am I doing what's best?"

I thought carefully about my answer: "My darling – you asked my opinion about going to college. Promise not to show this letter to your Mom because I don't want to hurt her feelings. First, I suggest we look at this from your mother's point of view. Since you were born, her life revolved around guiding your development and protecting your welfare. This role gave her much pleasure and was particularly important because of the loneliness caused by your father's frequent absences. You've often said she was somewhat over-protective. As a result, the two of you became close and interdependent. Now, you're no longer her little girl in need of protection. You're an intelligent and competent young woman with a mind of your own. You want to make your own decisions and guide your own life to reach your own goals. You love your mother and value her advice, but you want to be you. Meanwhile, she's having a hard time letting you move into adulthood because she cherishes her role as caregiver. My growing presence in your life has complicated the process because, in a sense, I've become a competitor for your attention and love, and her influence on you is being diluted by mine.

With that understanding, here are my thoughts. I'd love to have you back in college with me, but I think you should follow your heart and your goals. Have confidence in your own judgment. Be clear about what <u>you</u> want, listen to other's opinions about how best to accomplish that, and then make your decision. I think you've thought hard and well about your chosen pathway, and we've made sacrifices in our relationship so you could implement it. With love, I'll help you walk the pathway you choose to reach our shared goal of a life together, Don."

Carol answered: "Last weekend in Marysville with your parents meant so much to me that when I didn't hear anything from you but a hurried note, I thought maybe it meant very little to you. I'm afraid you gave me a tearful week. On top of that, mother and I didn't get along very well. Your wonderful letter Friday answering my request for advice made me ashamed for thinking you didn't care. Isn't it funny how a person in love has to be told over and over that her or his lover really loves them in order to keep satisfied? (understand?) I remember Saturday night in Marysville in each other's arms in the middle of that lonely road with a beautiful moon shining on us and the pleasure of our embrace. Our lips fit as if they are made for each other.

We are awfully lucky. Although we sometimes disagree we never have serious fights like so many people do and you are always so gentle with me. I know I must get on your nerves sometime but you're always so easy to get along with (and wonderful to make up with)."

The fall semester was well under way when Carol wrote: "Thank you very much for the *Collegian*. I'm very proud to see your name in it frequently. It helps me, knowing you're so active and popular." She didn't know those stories about my campus activities were the tip of an iceberg that would have a major influence on our lives. I was beginning to wonder if I really wanted to be an engineer. My grades were OK, but the courses were pure drudgery, and the nonacademic side of my college life much more interesting and rewarding. Dr. Wolff introduced me to the concept of extracurricular activities functioning as a form of leadership training for adult life. I discovered through my activities that I enjoyed and was good at working with other people to get things done.

I wrote Carol: "Honey, our SPC committee is working with Dr. Wolff preparing a formal proposal to Milton Eisenhower for a student union. He hopes our proposal will help him raise money for the plan. This weekend he is paying for my flight to visit the University of Wisconsin to see their student union first hand and collect helpful information and ideas from its Director. He's considered one of the best in the country. Wouldn't it be fun if we could go together!"

Carol wrote: "I'm adding choral music back into my life and rejoined the Presbyterian Church choir. The Topeka choirs are giving the *Messiah* this year sometime in the latter part of February so I can sing in it this year. It's a thrill to sing such beautiful music in a large group."

Despite my heavy load, we were able to spend time together many weekends during the semester, including the usual array of parties and proms. Sometimes my extracurricular responsibilities interfered with our together time. A biggie was Homecoming. I was responsible for much of the three day activity schedule. Carol really wanted to be there for Homecoming, but debated because she might not see much of me. I reassured her I would make time.

Carol wrote: I'm coming. I probably won't see you hardly at all, you'll be so busy, but at least I'll get a glimpse of you now and then." Later she wrote "It was heavenly dancing with you Friday night, and even though I didn't see you much Saturday it was fun. I feel guilty for making you lose so much sleep, but I want you with me every moment possible."

After another weekend Carol wrote: "Darling, forgive my foul moods like the one I was in Saturday night. Please don't take them seriously. I just sometimes get discouraged and when you're with me I always have to pour out everything that's on my mind. I got out of my foul mood when I saw your tears and wanted to take you in my arms and comfort you. I could kick myself for hurting you as I did, but you know I love you and nothing can or will change that."

Carol couldn't know that she'd inadvertently zeroed in on my discouragement and sense of futility about my major. Her comments brought tears because of doubts related to my private struggle about what to do with my life if I dropped engineering. I decided that required an US rather than a ME decision. We needed to discuss it. In my discouragement, I wrote "Carol, when you decided not to return to college we both knew it would be hard to be apart so long. It is much harder than I expected. School seems so futile! Sometimes my stomach ties itself into knots with longing for you, thinking 'will this waiting ever end'? I sometimes wonder if you won't get tired of waiting for me and find someone else. Life seems so empty without you."

Carol answered "Don, I understand your fearful discouragement. When we are apart so much I feel sometimes that you're nothing but a beautiful dream and I will never see you again. It is a terrible feeling—I get afraid! Please don't get so discourage that you think school is futile. I, too, sometimes feel this eternal wait will never end. Just remember, completing your education will end it because then we will marry."

During our lonely separation over Thanksgiving I remembered our favorite song during WWII – *Dream!* I wrote to Carol: "Today I've done nothing but think of you – of us – and dream. With dreams we can make our world just exactly what we want it to be. With dreams we can wipe away time and material things, leaving nothing but the life we wish were ours. With dreams we can sweep away the sadness of separation and replace it with the happiness of our companionship and love. A dream can do all of those things and yet when the dream ends, as all dreams must, I find myself more lonely and yet more in love with you than before."

After Thanksgiving came an annual party called the Gold Diggers Ball where the girls pay the fare. Carol came because she knew they planned a surprise announcement that I'd been elected

King of Pep. Afterwards she wrote: "I was so very proud of you Saturday night – everyone tells me how cute and swell you are and I just about pop with pride. Having the *Collegian* feature you as Man of the Week was icing on the cake. I sat your crown on the fireplace mantel, making a very pretty Christmas decoration with small candles and pine."

My reply was honest: "Carol, I considered it an honor we earned together, because you helped me plan many activities and we'd sacrificed precious time together to meet my responsibilities."

The final social event of the fall season, the Alpha Xi Christmas Ball, was always very special for us. While waiting for Carol in the reception area of the Alpha XI house, I heard someone say, "*O h h h h!*" and looked up the stairs. Carol appeared, dressed in a new, breathtaking, off-the-shoulder black formal, a dramatic new hairdo, glowing with pleasure as I watched her descend--a vision of loveliness. She knew she looked gorgeous. I took her hands, twirled her around and said, "You look stupendous and very sexy in your new gown!! You're more beautiful than I've ever seen you."

"You like? I made it special for you!" she said with a flirty smile. The evening only got better from there. That was our personal Christmas celebration because we didn't see one another again until New Year's week.

Carol went home from the Christmas Ball and wrote: "I'm still full of the joy of our Christmas Dance together. Tonight was a most sentimental evening because I decorated our Christmas tree, turned out all but the tree lights, lit the candles on the fireplace mantel, and played the record you gave me, W*hen You Trim Your Christmas Tree Let Me Be There Beside You.* You were there filling my emotions and thoughts with love."

We spent some of our New Year's week together with parties and dancing with friends. Most was spent alone enjoying simple activities like watching Carol bake a cake, listening to romantic music like *Romeo & Juliet,* doing 'filing' in Carol's office, and talking. I told her about my decision to leave Engineering and my search for a different goal and major. One possibility I'd considered was teaching math. She gave me her full support as always and told me as I'd been telling her, "Follow your heart, find what you like, and then we'll do it together."

I crossed my heart and kissed her cheek, "I promise you that whatever we choose together, I'll implement it so we can still marry by June 1, 1948."

When our holiday ended Carol wrote: "When you drove off with Earl last night, my heart and soul went with you and left me feeling lost and very alone. I went to my room because I wanted to be alone. I cried and thought of the meaning of love. I wrote this for you: 'Don, I'm overwhelmed with my love for you. I've learned that it's not the same as the excitement of sexual arousal. Love brings me deep feelings of joy and tenderness. It produces a sense of oneness, trust and safety with the one I love, and thoughts of wanting to help care for and protect you. I try to convey those feelings in my feeble letters. We'll never walk alone.'"

Our new year started on that high note as I returned to K-State to prepare for final exams and Carol resumed what had become an office management job. That high note faded for us as I buried myself in studying for final exams in several very difficult Engineering courses, finished some extracurricular responsibilities, performed my daily jobs as a houseboy, and decided what new educational pathway to pursue when I dropped Engineering.

For several years we'd written each other almost daily, and eagerly awaited our daily letters. As Carol put it: "Isn't it funny how our letters mean so much? I don't know what I'd do without your letters. Sometimes I think it's silly to write every day, but then when I don't get one I'm really disappointed. They make me feel much more a part of your life and you of mine."

During finals my daily letters to Carol became short and sweet or not at all since my workload almost overwhelmed me. That deeply disappointed and hurt her. On January 11 Carol wrote: "I'm glad you studied hard on that test and got a good grade on it, Don. Never mind writing me when you're busy. Honey, I wish you didn't have to cram so for your tests. I feel so terribly helpless and good-for-nothing when I know how much studying you do and how you have to slave away. I'm not only helpless but a hindrance to you. Sometimes I hate myself and wish I could go away somewhere, but I'd be even more lonely than I am now. I feel so awfully low today – in fact, I haven't been very high all week. I'm so damned nervous all the time. I don't know what's wrong with me, but I do know that if I were with you I'd be happy. I'm so pent up inside I think I'll bury myself under a chair or something and scream bloody murder – wonder if that would help? God, I miss you – You'll never know how much."

I wanted to hold her close, help resolve her jumbled thoughts and emotions, and reassure her with love, but I couldn't. So, I tried to work a bit of magic with words.

On February 4 she wrote: "Thank the boys for writing me a note with your letter. They wrote as nice and short a note as you did. Pee Wee says he wishes all girls were as true as I am – maybe that isn't too good – maybe I'm too true – because a certain young man seems to be getting awfully sure of himself. I probably demand too much attention but when I don't get it from you things happen inside of me that I can't explain. I'm in a foul mood, a horrible mood – I think I'll go have a good cry. I miss you terribly, but wonder if you really care about me as much as I thought. Sometimes I get an awful doubt in my mind. If you don't, please tell me. I never want to be a drag on you. P.S. All I need is you I guess; then I wouldn't feel this way."

Buried in final exams, I tried more reassuring words. On February 6 Carol wrote: "Please forgive me, honey for getting ruffled at you for not writing – it was terribly unreasonable of me and I'm sorry. I thought if you had time to play ping pong and go to shows etc. you had time to write me, but that was unreasonable. I know you worked awfully hard during these finals and need a little time to relax from them. Mother tells me its 'thwarted desire and sex.' She said she had some of the same feelings when she and Daddy were courting."

I was distressed by Carol's letters but glad she had enough confidence in me to pour out her thoughts and feelings freely and openly. I'd missed writing in the past and she'd never reacted this strongly. Most of my exams were finished so I had time to concentrate on what might be causing her distress. A possibility dawned on me! Eugene had been away from home much of Carol's life. He'd be home for brief periods and then be gone again. She'd told me how hard that was. I'd also noticed that her father was not demonstrative or complimentary and never expressed affection to Carol. Later in our life Carol told me, "My father never praised me for anything, but I learned he bragged a lot about me to others. As a little girl I hungered for his affection and praise, fearful of his leaving again. He once told me his strange idea that he didn't praise people for accomplishments because then they'd get self-satisfied and not work so hard."

I thought, *Maybe my not writing was like his leaving her and aroused those childhood fears.* One frequent dream she had about losing me made that idea more credible. For example: "Don, I dreamed last night that I came to the Roswell Air Base to see you and I couldn't find you. I asked for help but nobody knew where you were. I was so frightened and cried my heart out. I was so relieved to wake up and realize it was a dream." I had privately speculated that fearful anticipation of her husband's frequent leaving could be one cause of Winifred's periodic depression. Perhaps Carol's fears about losing me had similar roots. I vowed I would never give Carol cause to feel abandoned by me. I decided to apologize for not writing, give her lots of loving reassurance, and offer her an explanation for what we were feeling:

"My Dear Miss Clark: Please sit down in a nice chair and make yourself comfortable. I'm about to give you a good long lecture. But, first I want to tell you how pleased and proud of you I am for your willingness to talk to me honestly and openly about what you're thinking and feeling. I'm sorry now that I didn't write to you every day during finals. Honey, have you ever felt that everything was piling up on you? That nothing seems to go right – you make mistakes over and over and get so mad and discouraged you don't know what to do? That's the way I felt last week and my letters would have been just like that. I was in a very foul mood and the letters would have been lousy, but at least you would have known I was thinking about you.

Darling, I love you very much – don't ever forget that for a single moment. If I ever do anything that might make you think otherwise, please tell me and I will immediately prove you wrong. Carol, if you think I'm too sure of you, why do you think I get so damn jealous, as I was a week ago, when I saw that soldier's picture beside your bed and inferred it was one of your boyfriends. You and your mother had fun teasing me when you explained it was your air force uncle, and how stupid I was. So get that idea out of your mind before I get there Tuesday or I'll have to squeeze, hug and kiss it out of you!

Here's my explanation about what we both have been feeling. Your mother is all wet – it isn't 'thwarted desire and sex' (although we sometimes feel that don't we). It's lack of a loving, shared life we desperately want and planned for in those wonderful talks during our holiday together. Immediately after our New Year's love fest our partnership was temporarily disrupted. We didn't know what my professional future might be & I was so overwhelmed with demands that I let our open communications break down. It's very distressing to have goals you're failing to achieve, to be confused about what goals to seek, or not know how to share your partner's goals. As that happened, we became angry, afraid and discouraged. Thankfully there was enough left of our 'team' that we could talk (through our letters) openly about our feelings and concerns. In the next couple of weeks, I'll get the information we need to decide on an educational pathway for me. Then, let's get back to being good partners and travel that pathway to our wedding day."

Carol replied: "Your explanation has made a huge difference in my feelings. I've known you haven't liked your engineering pathway ever since you came back to college. When you're not happy, I'm not happy. So, let's pick a new pathway and get happy together again."

I immediately set out to remove the ambiguity about our future. After a week of extensive investigation I reported to Carol: "I've investigated becoming a math teacher. Everyone I talked with thought I'd be great at it and encouraged me to do it. Current salaries are between $2000 and $3000 a year, and have been going up every year. I already have most of the math I'd need, so I could easily graduate in time to marry you June 1, 1948. I've talked with the Dean of Engineering, Dean of Arts and Science, and head of the math department. They recommend I switch to Physical Science with a major in mathematics and minor in physics. They say job opportunities are good. I could use all my current credits and would only have to take 50 credits more to graduate, some of which could be psychology courses to explore counseling and student personnel work. To go into those fields, I'd have to go to graduate school. At 17 credits a semester that would be a much easier load than I've been carrying. What do you think?"

Carol wrote: "Don, I've observed the things that have given you the most excitement and satisfaction are your creative leadership accomplishments in extracurricular activities. Not only have you found it interesting and fun, but everyone says you're very good at it. You've often said to me 'listen to your heart'. Is that where your heart is? If so, let's go in that direction!"

My reply acknowledged her importance in my life and how much I valued her opinions: "Carol, you have a great way of cutting to the center of issues. You have a clearer view of me than I have of myself. I'll take your advice. I *will* graduate in the physical science major and *will* start down my new pathway in the spring semester."

Carol seemed much more satisfied with her life and her letters enthusiastically described new activities. She enjoyed rehearsals for singing the *Messiah* with the Topeka Chorus, especially since her friend Monna was also part of the chorus. On March 9 she reported: "I sang in the *Messiah* last night. I got goose pimples as usual, hearing and singing those beautiful choruses, especially the *Hallelujah* chorus."

Carol continued to sing in the church choir and increase her collection of music. She bought a portable radio so she could listen to music anywhere, especially on picnics with me. While thanking me for buying her a recording of *Hallelujah Chorus* and sheet music for *Blue Skies, More Than You Know,* and *Daybreak* she said, "Don, there's truly magic in music. It even brings me closer to you when we're apart. Remember the night we cuddled on the sofa listening to *Romeo and Juliet*? I thought I was in heaven. When I'm down, music is my therapy."

Two of Carol's high school buddies, Monna and Betty, still lived in Topeka so they went to movies together. Carol and Winifred also resumed their old pattern of going to movies to ease their loneliness or simply have fun together. Carol started knitting up a storm, including a beautiful sweater for me, and became quite good with informal instruction from a skilled neighbor. Each new creative accomplishment seemed to jump start another. After my sweater, Carol decided to make an afghan, and then painted decorative plates for Winifred to hang on the wall of their new farm home. She also sewed several articles of clothing for herself.

She reported many dreams about having a baby, including this interesting one: "I was about ready to have a baby and was with a doctor named Tommy Tucker. Well, I was going thru labor and by golly I had twins and they were boy twins. You can't imagine how proud I was – you of course were their father. Somehow, I was in the Alpha Xi house when I had the twins and all the girls raved over them. I felt so good. I woke up from the dream with a sort of hurting in my stomach and felt real weak – isn't that funny! I kind of wish we would have boy twins."

We went to all the traditional spring parties and proms, and the TKEs arranged a special dance at Meadow Acres. Glenn Gray, a former TKE, had a famous big band so many of the TKEs and our friends went to the dance. Neither Carol nor I knew that some friends sneaked vodka into Carol's Coke. What a night of dancing that produced!! Carol was so lively and gay. She said, "The special thing about dancing in each other's arms is that our movements have to be coordinated so we move as one – it's an icon of our future life together. I'm having so much fun, I don't want to dance with anyone else tonight. Let's just dance all night!!" A picture from that night shows Carol and I in the front row, glowing with happiness…and vodka.

A key focus in Carol's life that winter and spring was her parents repairing and renovating the buildings on their farm. They contracted out the major structural work, but Eugene, Winifred and sometimes Carol completed much of the interior finish. Carol wrote: "Sunday Daddy saw a couple boys and a dog get out of a car. The boys had guns and were going to shoot him, but the dog was too smart for them and ran off. Last night the dog came to Dad and he brought it home. He's a perfect farm dog. He has a face just like our old dog, Micki. Remember him and when your dog wrote a letter to him? I'm so happy to have a pet dog again."

Later she wrote: "Yesterday mother went into the barn for something and found a cat with four tiny kittens in a nest of hay. She called me in to see them. I picked a kitty for myself to cuddle and love. He's so cute and frisky, like you, so I named him Herbert after you."

In early May Carol wrote: "Dad sold our town house so we'll have to move to the farm in June. Could you help this 'farm girl' move? She would pay you *very* well!" One reason Carol dropped out of college was to help her mother have a better life, so seeing her folks enjoy shared labors on the farm pleased her no end. Their relationship returned to earlier, happier patterns.

I wrote: "Carol, I have to apologize because I went out on a date last night but it wasn't too good – it was a date with a potential fraternity pledge."

She responded to my teasing: "I was so disappointed that you had a date – how ghastly – how could you while I sit home every night with the baby slaving over dirty diapers. By the way, honey, when we do have a baby could I persuade you to wash the diapers, hmmmm?"

In the spring I handed over my Wampus Cats and SPC extracurricular activities to others and had more free time. But then the student political parties began asking me to run for student Council. Carol and I discussed it and agreed to say no. They kept asking and I kept saying no.

I was meeting frequently with Milton Eisenhower about how to implement SPC recommendations, like getting a Student Union. One day he asked why I wouldn't run for Student Council. We talked for over an hour. He told me effective Student Council leadership would help accomplish the goals students wanted. He finally talked me into running, if Carol agreed. She did agree, I ran for Student Council and won. Then, the Council elected me as Student Body President for my senior year. Carol said: "Now you have a bigger job than last year. I know there will be times when your student government activities (SGA) steal time from me. But, I'm so proud of you! I know you'll be good at it. I'll help you in any way I can."

Life produces unexpected twists and turns. That decision began a lifelong friendship between Carol and me and Milton and Helen Eisenhower, just as his brother, Ike, was becoming President of the United States. Milton became very fond of what he called "your beautiful Carol" and she of him, especially when his beloved wife Helen later died and left him devastated.

Carol's responsibilities were increasing too. In frustration Carol began bossing her boss around because of his inefficiencies. She wrote: "Yesterday my boss moaned all day because his financial report wouldn't balance. This morning I told him to stop moaning – I'd fix it. It took all day but I found all his errors. It was fun and I told him, 'You make too many mistakes so I'll do the books after this.' With a sheepish grin, he handed me the books and thanked me."

I replied: "Carol, I'm so impressed and proud of you! You are the chief financial officer since you handle all the money, keep track of how it's spent and prepare all financial reports."

She asked: "When we get married can I be your chief financial officer?"

My answer? "Yes – yes – yes – yes!!!"

My lifelong friend, Earl Elliott, and I needed to earn money that summer. I had wanted for a year to buy an engagement ring and formally ask Carol to marry me but had no money. There were no jobs in Marysville. In a cartoon strip called "Skeesix", two buddies named Wallett and Bobble couldn't find a job after they left the army so they started an odd job business. Their story was told in that cartoon. We decided to try that in Marysville. Our girlfriends, Carol and Ginny thought it was a clever idea, as long as we saved time for them. We moved home to Marysville, where we were both well known, and put an ad in the local paper:

WANTED
Let Us Do Your Dirty Work For YOU
ODD JOBS -- We'll Try Anything!!
DON FORD EARL ELLIOTT PHONE 155X

The response to our ad was amazing! It started as a trickle, evolved into a river, and ended up a flood. We trimmed trees, did yard work, hauled trash, cleaned a big old coal furnace, put up fences, scrubbed and waxed floors, washed and repaired windows, hung new doors, tarred bank and department store roofs in 110 degree weather, painted apartments, repaired plumbing, and painted four houses. We made the money we'd hoped for and more. It was hard work but some funny things happened along the way. For example:

A guy hired us to paint the outside of his house, locked the doors and went on vacation. Carol and Ginny were visiting us and helping paint trim in 100 degree weather. Suddenly Carol shouted, "Sounds like something just broke or exploded!" We all listened and sure enough, every so often we heard POW --- POW. Carol knelt by a basement window and said, "I think that sound is coming from the basement." For fear that something bad was happening, Earl got a basement window open and crawled in, then we heard another POW.

Earl shouted, "There's nothing wrong; he's bottled a batch of beer, it's hot down here, and the bottles are exploding!" Kansas was a dry state then, so making alcoholic beverages was illegal. Since it wasn't hurting anything, Earl crawled out, closed the window, and said, "He's gonna come home to a basement full of beer!" and we finished our painting.

Earl was an only child. He and his widowed mother lived in a small apartment in Marysville. Earl said he'd like to brighten it up for her, so we painted her bedroom a light yellow. I'd learned how to wallpaper as a kid helping my mother so I suggested we wallpaper her living room. Earl picked out a bright, multicolored floral pattern and we put it up, pleased with our accomplishment. Carol and Ginny were in town for another visit and came to admire our work. They walked in, stopped, look at each other and then with a grin, my artistic girlfriend said, "That's very pretty, and you've done a beautiful job putting it up, but you got the pattern upside down!" After we all laughed at our stupidity, we got more paper and did it over.

Earl had an old car and we missed our ladies, so occasionally after working hard for six days, we'd drive the 120 miles to Topeka on Sunday morning to visit the girls. We stayed as long as possible and drove home in the early morning hours so we could work on Monday. One time after driving about 70 miles, Earl said, "Uh oh!! We forgot to buy gas before starting back and the gauge reads EMPTY!" Well, at 2:30 a.m. in rural Kansas we knew no gas stations would be open. What to do? We drove slowly and turned the engine off when we could coast downhill. We stopped at every gas station, lifted each tank hose and drained the wee bit of gas left in the hose into our tank. We got maybe a couple of pints of gas each time, just enough to make it home before running out of gas. Our girls had fun razzing us about it, but we told them it was their fault for getting us so befuddled with their lovin'.

Three friends – Betty, Monna, and Tutt – were in Topeka that summer. Carol wrote: "We thought this would probably be the last summer we'd ever have as a group, so we've been spending as much time together as possible. I usually share lunch with at least one of them. We all enjoy movies so we're seeing at least two a week. Good friends are a joy!"

Carol enjoyed socializing with friends, but didn't lose focus on her main goal. She wrote me proudly of her progress: "As you know, I've been saving money every month to build up funds we can use to start our life together. By July I'll have $1000 in the bank." (She had every right to be proud! That would be the equivalent of over $10,000 in 2012.)

One major event changed Carol's life that summer: The Clarks sold their home in Topeka and moved to their new farm. Carol wrote: "I love the fresh, clean air, the sounds, the scents and the sunsets. I love watching the dog and cats frolicking, the cattle and wild animals doing their thing, and especially the chickens. Since I was a little girl I've wanted to raise chickens. The big sky and sunsets are beautiful, but the storms scare me when winds screech through the trees and rattle the house, thunder roars and echoes, and the terrific lightning flashes and cracks.

There are two beautiful, private places on our farm. One has a delicious spring feeding a small pond surrounded by lush green grass. The other is a small meadow filled with wild flowers, butterflies, bees and other pretty bugs. In the middle of it is a huge elm tree providing lots of shade. Can't you imagine all the picnics and blanket parties we can have there? *[We particularly enjoyed the meadow with the elm tree where we could lie on our blanket and watch the moon and stars in the big Kansas sky.]* Unfortunately it's a 20 mile commute to work and I can only get there and home with Dad because he has the car. That means I can usually no longer go places and do things with my friends in the evenings, so I'll have a somewhat lonelier life."

Earl and I closed our business, packed our stuff, and moved back to campus. No one, including Earl, knew I'd bought the prettiest engagement ring I could afford. I planned to ask Carol to marry me, and put my ring on her finger as soon as possible. Near bursting with excitement, I rode back to Manhattan with Earl to start my senior year at K-State.

I wrote Carol: "The first thing I have to do as SGA president is to help plan the Homecoming celebration. It will be the biggest K-State has ever had because General Eisenhower will be here and we're really planning things on a big scale. Today I had meetings with Milton Eisenhower about overall plans, Luther Leavengood (your Messiah director) about music, Dean Woolf to plan for student events, Thorton Edwards and H.W. Davis about housing and facilities. Honey, you must come for that celebration, PLEASE!"

I wanted to propose marriage before the fall social season started so it wouldn't outshine the important event of our engagement. I asked Carol to visit the weekend of September 18. Arrangements for visits had been going smoothly for the past year so Carol's reply shocked me:

"Honey, I'm afraid I can't come for the game next weekend. The one and only reason is that Mom won't let me. It makes me sick. Please don't be mad but I guess I should obey Mom."

I felt like screaming, *But I want to ask you to marry me!!* Instead, I wrote: "I'm very disappointed that you can't come to Manhattan this weekend. I had hoped it would be a very important weekend for us, but I realize you're doing what you believe is best." So, I tried again: "Carol, do you think it possible to come to Manhattan a week from this weekend? I'll send you the money for your bus ticket to Manhattan and make arrangements to get you back to the farm if you can come. There are a great many things I'd like to discuss with you and we won't have much opportunity on Homecoming weekend. Those are primary reasons. Besides, I miss you so damn much and Homecoming is too far away."

While waiting for her reply I wrote in my depressed state: "This weekend won't be at all like I had hoped. I've been doing a lot of thinking and wonder if I may have made a mistake in some of my guiding values. One we've talked about is the focus on economic security that guided our decision to delay our marriage. More than possessions, money, material wealth or high social status, I want and need for us to be together, forever. No matter what we face, no matter what we're called upon to endure, I will always be deeply in love with you. Our relationship is the only solid thing to me in this topsy turvy world."

Carol replied: "Yes darling, I understand what you mean. I too want to be secure, but I've never worried too much about it, maybe because I always had someone who provided most of the things I wanted and never had to be totally responsible for my own economic welfare, or for someone else. That comes from being an only child, I guess, but you've helped me realize it's time I grow up. I wish we didn't have to wait, but I believe our decision to do so is wise. I wish I knew whether I can come this weekend or not, then I'd know whether to look forward to Friday or dread it as the beginning of an empty long weekend."

The next day she wrote: "My folks still haven't come back. That means I still don't know if they'll let me come or not. I'll call you long distance tomorrow noon if I can't come." She didn't come but wrote: "I'm writing to apologize for not coming this weekend. I should have told you on the phone today that I couldn't come, but when I heard your voice, I thought I'd just have to. Mom is adamant. She will not let me come to see you until you visit me here first."

The next morning Carol wrote: "I got out of bed at 4:30 and started pleading again with my folks, but they were both firm and couldn't be moved. Such heartless souls."

I responded: "This has been a very lonely weekend. I had hopes you would come until about 5 o'clock in the afternoon. In fact, I sat on the porch most of the afternoon waiting. I had planned a weekend I hoped would make your trip worthwhile. I didn't tell you that over the phone because I didn't want you to come primarily for that reason." *(What I'd been thinking was: "This is a struggle between you and your mother over who is going to run your life.")*

My theory was confirmed when Carol wrote: "I'd like to come and see you, but my folks have laid down the law. It's an order that I cannot go to Manhattan before Homecoming unless you've visited me here. They have the old fashioned idea that a boy should court a girl at her home once in a while. Their arguments make me mad! So I guess it's up to you."

I wanted to reply, *No it isn't honey, it's up to you* but instead I sat down to think. My heart ached for her. After a little thought I extended an invitation again:

"I hope you will at least reconsider my invitation to come to Manhattan the weekend of Oct. 17, 18, 19. Would you think of it as you courting me by accepting an invitation to Manhattan? Please come Carol – it's important! It isn't that I don't want to come to the farm. In addition to doing my school work so I can graduate in May, I've accepted a major responsibility that is particularly important and demanding at this time. My failure to meet it will affect a lot of people badly, including us. I don't think I should shirk that responsibility. Idealistic? Perhaps, but that's a part of my beliefs. Since you don't have a phone at the farm I will call you at your office so we can try solve this problem together."

After our phone conversation, Carol wrote: "It was so good to hear your voice! As I tried to explain, it really isn't a problem for you and me to worry about. It just boils down to this – you can't get away to come here, and my folks won't let me do all the visiting. I think it's silly, you think it's silly, but that's the way they feel, You know, this whole damn situation was all my fault I guess, for not coming down weekend before last. My folks wouldn't have liked it if I had gone, but it certainly would have made things much better as far as we are concerned. I feel like a leaf caught between two tides…or something. Only one thing is clear to me and that is I love you and can hardly stand to see you feeling the way you do."

I replied: "As you proposed, I'll write a letter to your parents and try to resolve our difficulties. That way I can try to get you out of the middle of this argument."

Carol wrote: "After thinking the situation over I've decided to come to Manhattan this Friday despite my parents' orders. Probably I shouldn't, but if it will make you happy and end this feeling you have, it will be worth it. I may have to find a room in Topeka in the future." Then her parents got my letter, prompting this from Carol: "I was so happy when you called yesterday and we got things settled. It was beginning to get me down. I explained to mother and she understands so we needn't worry about my parents interfering with us after we're married."

Carol came to Manhattan, and on a beautiful moonlit night on K-State hill, I formally proposed, she happily accepted, and I joyfully slipped the ring on her finger. It took a little while to finish the hugging and kissing. She finally understood my efforts to get her to come without revealing why, and said, "Don, I'm sorry I fouled up your wonderful plan – I feel like such a stup. But, I've learned something important and it won't happen again."

We agreed to keep our engagement secret until we could announce it to our Alpha Xi and TKE sisters and brothers. We knew they'd been expecting it for at least a year. I wrote: "Some people were a little confused because of what we <u>didn't</u> do this weekend, Carol. It's so hard to keep our secret – I want to shout to the skies and tell everyone I see about it."

Carol wrote: "The folks met my bus. I didn't tell them about the ring. I wanted to see their reaction when they discovered it, which didn't happen until we got home. They reacted with real delight. They thought the ring was beautiful and are very happy about it, just as I am. I look at it constantly, dreaming of the future it promises!"

Carol's mother wrote a long, defensive letter in response to mine, not knowing at that same time I was proposing to her daughter. After learning of our engagement, she changed the whole tone of her letter by closing with these comments: "What are mothers supposed to say when their children become engaged? Congratulations? That's nice? Not me. All I want to say to you is, 'My Son!' and plant a big kiss on that sweet face. You are my little boy now, you know, and talk about a possessive mother – that's me! Woof!!"

Carol's act of independence and our formal engagement resolved the whole issue. They never again gave Carol orders, but Winifred continued to tell her how she should behave.

With a broader understanding of the different life Winifred faced on the farm, Carol shared with me her plan to help with the transition: "I learned our local country school was having a program so I took Mom at 8 p.m. The program started right off with all the little kids reciting poems, singing songs and so forth. Afterwards we had pumpkin pie and coffee. I'm very glad we went because Mom met a lot of her new neighbors and was invited to their monthly social where they sew and gab. Mom was delighted because life gets pretty lonely on a farm with no friends. Mom asked me to go with her to the first social so I did. She fit right in."

I wrote: "Dearest Carol. When I attempt to write to you, my thoughts run away with my mind and leave my pen incoherent. I wish I could analyze my feelings. I feel frustrated, tense and anxious. I'm succeeding in everything I try to do and yet there's a big gap. I'm earning recognition, success and influence, and yet I feel an anxious unhappiness. If only you knew how much I have come to depend on you, how much I need your companionship, your encouragement, your advice, your love. All I have to offer you is my adoration and admiration, and a tremendous desire to make you happy."

Carol decided our ability to spend time together would be greatly improved if she had her own car, so she started a search. An old family friend was helping her and found a possibility. She decided to wait. Then she wrote: "Now I must tell you some important news, honey. You will no doubt think I'm crazy – but you know it's a woman's privilege to change her mind. I thoroughly believed yesterday that I wouldn't buy a car. But I decided the one Jay found for me was just too good to pass up. I called two relatives who sell cars and they agreed. Even Mom agrees. It's a 1939 Oldsmobile 4-door sedan. It only has 36,000 miles on it and was owned by Don Rae, the Olds dealer. He sold it new to an 80-year-old man who stopped driving it because of gas rationing during WWII. Don bought it back from him for his wife to drive to work. It has a clock, a great $100 radio, and a wonderful heater. It cost me $1050, which I had in our savings account, with no tax because it was a private sale. I would have liked your advice, but it was such a good deal I was afraid someone else might buy it. I'm so excited to have our own car!!"

I replied: "Carol, you don't need to ask my advice. I'm so proud of you for getting such a good deal and making your own decision. I view it as a kind of declaration of independence, because it enables you to go wherever and whenever you want to without needing anyone's advice, approval or help." As we neared Christmas, I wrote Carol: "Darling, I had a long meeting today with Milton Eisenhower about our SGA projects. He thanked me for helping make the Homecoming celebration a big success. He said Ike really enjoyed it. Our current top priority is a student union. He told me that while he seeks funding to build a new one, he has a commitment for a temporary student union to be placed beside the Home Ec building in what is now a block square parking lot below the Engineering building. It's been an enlisted men's lounge and recreation center at Ft. Riley. They're giving it to K-State so we'll have a temporary student union, after renovations. He already has the money for a program budget. It will be a great addition, particularly for money-poor veterans and their families.

Milton congratulated me on my leadership, talked with me about you and our future plans, and offered his help if he could be useful. He said, 'People tell me your beautiful Carol is pretty special. I would like to meet her sometime.'"

Carol replied: "I'm so proud of my husband-to-be. I'm eager to hear what he said about us. Don, I've noticed something – our recent letters are longer with more interesting information and ideas, they seem free of stress, and they're more light-hearted."

I answered: "I agree. It's as if getting engaged and clearing things up with your parents has somehow destroyed our worries and freed us to feel more confident. We can share everything and stop knuckling under to others' opinions. We're truly partners now so can be more open and less defensive. It's a wonderful feeling to be US!!!"

We wanted to celebrate Christmas together this year for the first time. The Clark's tradition was to open presents Christmas Eve while the Ford's did that Christmas Day. So we agreed I should go to the Clark farm when K-State closed for the holidays, celebrate with the Clarks through Christmas Eve, and then drive to Marysville early in the morning for the Ford celebration. Everyone was delighted with that arrangement, especially Carol and me.

It was the Clark's first Christmas on their farm so celebrating together was special to us all. The entire experience thrilled Carol, who shared her feelings with me later, "I was both relaxed and full of love and joy. Spending evenings in front of their Christmas tree with a big fire in the fireplace after a delicious meal prepared by Mom and me together was wonderful. Even my bah humbug father enjoyed exchanging Christmas gifts." When that celebration ended we said goodnight. Carol went to her bedroom and I went to the attic.

On Christmas Day we left the farm about 4 a.m. and headed for Marysville. The morning was crisp and cold, but our car heater kept us cozy. Still, I'd nicknamed Carol "my li'l heater" whenever we were parked and smooching, so that morning I asked her to snuggle close and keep my heart warm! (This was before seat belts eliminated that pleasure.) A bright full moon lighted our way through glistening snow-covered fields dotted with farm homes and barns. We marveled at the beautiful winter tapestry along our rural roadway.

I could almost feel Carol's excitement in the air around me that morning as she bubbled with joy and love, "Oh Don, I'm breathless with what I feel and see! After being apart for so long, we're celebrating our first Christmas together! I feel like I'm already your wife. We're the only ones here, alone in this sea of beauty. I feel surrounded by music!"

"Can you actually hear music? Tell me about it."

"Yes, my brain plays the music for me. Right now it's *You'll Never Walk Alone*. I feel like singing it for you." She laid her head on my shoulder and sang in a clear sweet voice while I drove. I can't remember many moments in my life when I felt such a happy peace. After awhile, she said, "These fields are so peaceful. See the snow glistening in moonlight, with soft shadows tracing patterns on the contours of those fields? It's like a master artist painting a beautiful picture for us. Someday I'd like to learn how to paint such beauty."

After a long period of silence, she suddenly said, "Oh look, Don! Lights just came on in that farmhouse. I bet they're just getting up for Christmas. Can you imagine the parents lighting the Christmas tree, their children tumbling downstairs full of excitement, and their dog barking and wagging his tail?"

We laughed at the magic of that idea and watched for lights coming on in farmhouses, imagining each family's excitement as we drove through the early morning darkness. Finally, the excitement, joy, and love we felt overwhelmed us so we stopped in a roadside park and held each other close, kissing and whispering our feelings until dawn. As morning sun streaked the sky with shades of rose, we continued our Christmas journey to join the Ford family celebration.

And what a celebration it was! As we parked in front of my parents' small house, the cheery blinking lights of their Christmas tree welcomed us through the front window. In their home, the living and dining area were combined into one large room. As we walked through the door, a bunch of Fords shouted, "Merry Christmas!" Waiting to start the Christmas celebration were nine adults, three small children, and two babies who filled my parents' modest home to overflowing. We were part of the post-WWII population explosion, a family that loved to tease each other and laugh uproariously while everyone talked at once. It was chaos, happy chaos.

As an only child, Carol had never experienced anything like this. My family treated her as if she were my wife and kidded her about what married life would be like with me. Between rounds of jokes and hugs, Mom and her three daughters produced a great dinner with a variety of food to satisfy the special fancies of all participants. Once Carol caught her breath, she eagerly joined into the spirited exchanges. She told me later, "I hope we have a large family. It's so much more fun than being an only child!"

I laughed, "You'd better be careful what you wish for!" That Christmas experience became the blueprint for how Carol organized our future Christmases.

After four happy days in Marysville, we had to return to our everyday lives. We packed up the car and headed for Manhattan so I could begin my last semester before graduation. That was a big deal because no one in my family or ancestry had ever graduated from college. I would be the first.

We went to the TKE house first, where Carol helped me unload my stuff. We hated to see this special episode of our life end. We ate a light lunch and talked about the fact that in five months we'd be married, then Carol drove off alone to the farm. Later she wrote: "When I left you at the TKE house, I felt like a little puppy thrown out into the cold."

Within the next five months, Carol had to work at her full time job, get her summer wardrobe ready, finish making treasures for her hope chest, make some clothes she needed, plan our wedding, arrange for flowers, recruit her friends for the wedding party, get a wedding dress and something special for our honeymoon, make dresses for her bridesmaids, arrange with her preacher to marry us, make plans for a reception, take the required physical exams, apply for a job at K-State, get a marriage license, and figure out how to pay for it all.

I had to complete my last six courses and meet graduation requirements, complete several major SGA projects for which I was responsible, continue my TKE kitchen boy responsibilities, find a job to start in June, find an apartment, recruit friends for my wedding party, arrange for a honeymoon, take the required physical exam, get a marriage license, and try to sleep a little. Most important of all, we had to figure out some way of spending treasured time together that semester, because that was the reason for everything else. Moreover, coordinating our efforts was difficult because the Clark's had no phone at the farm.

We had to immediately confirm a wedding date and time so our family and friends could make their plans. We decided on Sunday, May 30 – Memorial Day – because K-State friends would still be in Manhattan and could come. It was a Sunday, so people's jobs wouldn't interfere. Then we learned graduation would be that Sunday. Other possibilities had problems so we decided, what the heck, we'll have them both on May 30. We planned our wedding ceremony after church services at 3 p.m. in Carol's church, followed by an afternoon reception in her aunt's big home. After the reception we'd change clothes, drive sixty miles to K-State for the graduation at 8 p.m. Then we'd leave for our honeymoon.

Carol knew she had to pay for the wedding because her parents were in the hole after buying and renovating their farm. My GI support ended so I only had a little dough from summer earnings to pay for our honeymoon. She wrote: "Planning wouldn't be bad if I just knew what kind of wedding I could afford." She kept firmly in mind the old motto from depression days of the 1930s: *If you can't grow it, make it, fix it, or borrow it – do without.*

Both Carol's mother and grandmother were skillful with a needle. Winifred wanted to make Carol's wedding dress, and said she'd also make the dresses for Carol's attendants. They worked as a team remodeling Carol's old wardrobe to fit current styles. (Carol said the dresses were stylish, pretty and saved her lots of money.) They both created those little niceties that make a house a home by making rag rugs, embroidered pillow cases, decorative crocheted doilies and throws for Carol's hope chest. The crocheted items were special because Carol had learned that art from her grandmother as a child.

Carol put her skills to work too. She finished a tufted rug and a variety of knitted items. In one of her letters she said: "I needed some new clothes but don't have the money to buy them so I started sewing. I bought different kinds of material and made several new dresses, skirts, a bolero jacket and two blouses." She added pretty nightgowns to her trousseau – for me she said – and embroidered dish towels. Instead of paying 80 cents apiece for the cloth, she asked me to buy ten larger and stronger pieces in Marysville, made of former feed sacks, for $1.70. The six bucks she saved so proudly doesn't sound like much, but in today's economy that would be the equivalent of saving at least sixty dollars!

I teased her: "People who hear of all you've made are calling you 'Old needle fingers Clark'." She also typed three reports to help me with my courses.

In mid-April Carol wrote: "It's getting on my nerves to live around my folks. I can't keep Mom out of the kitchen when I try to cook or bake something. They still boss, nag, and try to tell me what I can and can't do. It's Hell! There, I've exploded and feel better."

I responded: "I'm frustrated too. Everything is going well – my course work, my campus work, my search for a job. Yet I've lost my enthusiasm for all I'm doing. I have a cold, lonely, incomplete feeling that can't be displaced of late. I know I'm run down physically, but that can't account for it. I need you! It's a need as real as the need for food, for sleep, or for exercise."

Carol replied: "Oh Don, I know just how you feel! I, too, have that lonely, frustrated feeling. I feel like crying, knowing you feel much as I do when we're apart. Sometimes I had the feeling that you didn't miss me very much. To help you when I can, to love you and make you happy, to give you children, to share my road of life with you are my reasons for living."

We weren't the only ones feeling the stress. Carol wrote: "We had an unhappy time at our house last night. The carpenters were supposed to finish their job, but didn't. The whole thing got Mother down and she had a big crying spell. Mom has been feeling low since Grandma left, and this on top of that made her break down. She was feeling sorry for herself, I think. It's hard for Daddy to have Mom act up like that – he just doesn't understand women very well."

I wrote to Carol: "My heart goes out to your Mom because I suspect the primary reason for her tears is that her daughter is about to leave home for good, the daughter who has been her main source of happiness and social support for the last twenty years. While Winifred's mother was with her every day, working on your wedding, it probably helped your Mom cope with her impending loss. She's been working like a fiend helping you get ready for the wedding, and I think that helped control her feelings of loss, but it finally caught up with her."

I updated Carol on job possibilities: "As we agreed, I've been telling everyone I talk to about jobs that I plan to start work on a master degree in psychology. Two job offers have emerged. Dr. Wolff has offered me a job in his office. It includes opportunities to become familiar with counseling staff and the methods and tests they use. That fits well with my proposed graduate work. Dr. Baker, head of the Psychology Department, has offered me a graduate assistantship beginning in the fall to financially support my graduate studies. He took me for a cup of coffee and spent 1½ hours talking about our future plans. He's trying hard to get me to accept his offer."

Carol replied: "How wonderful, Don! Both sound good but we'll need a summer income. I've taken the state civil service test for various levels of secretarial work to qualify for positions at K-State. I passed all levels so now I can apply for K-State jobs!"

I replied: "Hi smarty pants!! You're one smart lady! I knew you could pass all those tests. Don't worry. If no one at K-State will hire you, I will. In fact, I'll give you a good steady job, guaranteed! You can sit on my lap while you work as you have on occasion in your office. Speaking of your office, have you told them yet you'll be leaving?"

She replied: "No, but when he gets back in town I'll give him the good news!"

I reported to Carol: "All the apartments we looked at are gone. But the apartment of Jules Funston, the one we really liked, is ours. You remember, it's on the corner just before Aggieville, only two blocks from campus. You enter off the front porch into a nice but a slightly small living room. From there a small hallway leads to that nice large eat-in kitchen. To the left of the kitchen is a nice bedroom. The bathroom is on the hall. There's a small back porch off the kitchen and a place to hang laundry in the back yard. It's completely furnished. Nobody knows he's leaving so we have no competition. He talked with the landlady and her husband, recommending us highly. I made a deal with the landlady. She'll confirm it Wednesday."

Carol wrote: "I'm so excited!! All our problems are solved except getting married. We have a home; you have a job and I've applied for one; we have a wedding license, a church, preacher, and organist. My aunt has asked for the privilege of hosting our reception in her beautiful house; the cake and flowers are ordered; the girls' dresses are ready; my wedding dress is eager to march down the aisle. We just have to get the church by 3 pm May 30."

I wrote: "You forgot I have to finish my final exams."

Carol's swift reply was: "Look, Buster, pass or fail, we're getting married May 30!!!"

I told Carol of the last project I worked on with Milton Eisenhower: "This spring He sought my help in implementing his plan to integrate intercollegiate athletics in our 7-university conference. He asked me to mobilize student support at K-State and others in our conference to support this integrative effort. I've been working at that all spring.

A few days later, I wrote: "Today the new student government officials took office and I am free at last!!! All my responsibilities are finished."

"No they aren't! I have elected you to a new responsibility --- as my husband!!!"

My classes were over. I was ready to marry Carol and start the next chapter of our lives, so I went around campus saying goodbye to people I had worked with closely like Milton Eisenhower, Provost Al Pugsley, and Dr. Wolff. I was stunned! I had no idea they saw me in such a positive light. I wrote Carol about it and said: "Please get a sharp pin to burst my inflated ego when things like this occur."

She replied: "I won't use no little pin -- I'll use my rolling pin!!"

We married at 3 p.m. Sunday May 30th, 1948. Carol was stunningly beautiful, escorted by her old slumber party friends. I was so excited I could hardly talk, supported by my old friend Earl Elliott, and in awe that Carol was finally my wife. We had a lovely reception at Carol's aunt's little mansion with lots of family and dear friends. Then, Carol changed to her special honeymoon suit, I traded my used Kansas City tux for a new suit my parents gave me, and we headed to Manhattan with my folks for graduation. We stopped at a little restaurant for a bite to eat and to relive the day's happy experiences. Then we went to graduation ceremonies.

Milton Eisenhower handed me my first college degree. Carol and Mom shed a few tears, Dad put on his 'grin and bear it' demeanor, and I heaved a huge sigh of relief. They left for Marysville and we headed for a brief honeymoon. We had very little money for honeymooning. We'd heard that 'everything is up to date in Kansas City', so that's where we went for three days. Carol had said, "I don't care where we go. After all our years of agony being separated, I don't want to do anything but experience the excitement and happiness of our life together."

We stayed at a small but charming, inexpensive old hotel across the street from the best hotel in the city. One sunny day, we went to a nearby park and rented a small canoe. We spent the afternoon floating around the lake, soaking in the beauty of Mother Nature, savoring the sight, sound, and touch of each other. I said, "Do you hear any music?"

Dreamily, she said, "Oh yes!"

"Tell me."

With shining eyes and a happy smile, she said, "*Romeo and Juliet.*"

"You told me once you wanted that played at your wedding."

"This is better because it's just for you and me!"

On our final day, Carol got out her travel iron to press a special dress for our last night. Most of our limited money had been set aside for one special night of dining and dancing at the fancy hotel across the street. The iron made strange crackling noises and quit working. We learned that our hotel was so old it still used direct current rather than modern alternating current electricity, and modern appliances only worked on alternating current.

We spent that last afternoon sipping wine a friend had given us while Carol sang love songs to me, making love, and napping. Finally, we showered and dressed, she in her beautiful new dress and I in my new suit. We walked across the street to the high class hotel, pretending we were rich for a night. The dining room was beautiful, glowing with candlelight, and the romantic big band music great for dancing. We ordered our food, danced until it came, savored eating it, then danced and talked until nearly midnight. Our waiter kindly brought us a free dessert of mint ice cream covered with chocolate. Absorbed in the pleasure of our night, we strolled arm-in-arm to the hotel. We made love and slept nude through the night with our arms around each other.

The next morning we showered, with a bit of frolicking and newlywed fooling around, dressed, and checked out. We had just enough money left to pay our bill. In a mellow mood, we drove to Manhattan, happy to begin our life together forever.

Chapter Seven

Building Her Life As a Married Woman

We started our life together by cleaning and moving into our first home. Since our little apartment was completely furnished, moving in was a simple task. One day drinking iced tea in our kitchen, I said, "Several times this last year you expressed frustration over living with your parents. Now you have your own place, so what do you think?"

"This isn't just my own place – It's *our home!* It's a wonderful sense of freedom, being completely in control of our lives. Look out world – Here We Come!!"

Since we no longer wrote letters to each other, we wrote our parents more frequently. Carol wrote: "Dear Mom and Dad. To celebrate moving into our first home we gave one another gifts. I gave Don a dish drainer because I knew after doing dishes twice a day 7 days a week for three years to help pay his college bills he'd be delighted to escape from that chore. I was surprised to discover how often I needed scissors, so that's what he gave me. He also bought me ice cream and a single rose. Being married is wonderful!

Don was offered a new and permanent job today with a very nice salary!! Dr. Wolff and vice president Pugsley recommended to Milton Eisenhower that Don be appointed Director of the Temporary Student Union. He'll be responsible for all facilities and programs, including food service. He'll also be on Dr. Wolff's staff and learn about counseling. He meets Friday with Eisenhower to seal the deal. Apparently that's what Eisenhower meant when he said at graduation, 'I look forward to seeing more of you.' The temporary union was a WWII enlisted men's recreation building at Ft. Riley. Don says it almost feels like home because he spent lots of lonely hours with his air force buddies and wrote lots of letters to me in buildings like it. He plans to hire as staff part time students, preferably veterans, in need of money as he has been. I too have a new job! The College of Agriculture hired me as a secretary – I start Monday. We've escaped from student poverty into an income 4 times greater than anything we've dreamed of."

Carol's parents were the first visitors to our new home. Carol had nothing to read in our apartment except my text books, so they changed her magazine subscription addresses, brought legal papers like insurance, and FOOD!! Carol's mother brought Sunday dinner and her father lots of eggs. They had a big flock of chickens so we ate lots of eggs! Carol was both disappointed and relieved that she didn't have to cook dinner for them. She said, "I need more practice so I can impress them with their first home cooked meal in my home."

One evening after dinner I said, "Carol, summer session is starting and I need to create some programs for students, veterans and their wives who have no money for recreation. Would you help me brainstorm about possibilities?"

Carol grinned and said, "I was hoping you'd ask. I've been thinking our lives designed us for this role! The years I spent with my slumber party gang taught me how hard it is for young women to find ways of having fun without money or dates. In college, most of the parties and dances are private parties held for small numbers of students, like our fraternity and sorority parties. Girls need ways to have fun, not only with dates but with each other."

I nodded, "I've known and worked with lots of students who had no organizational memberships, most lived in private homes, were short of money and often lonely. In my friendships with veterans, some with wives and babies, I listened to their stories about how hard life was for them. Through my student activities, I know how K-State works and how to get things done here. And as a team we can use our experiences to make this union work."

After kicking ideas around for a while, Carol said, "You should start with free movies. Almost everyone likes movies. You can see them alone, with friends or with a date, and with your kids if you have some. A movie is long enough to enjoy, but not too long if you have kids."

"That's a great idea! We can entertain a lot of people with little cost. We could have one every week end. Will you recommend movies from the catalogs of those available?"

"I think each time you should show both a movie and a comedy, so there'll be something for kids, or those who are still kids at heart, but avoid movies that are too gory or scary for kids."

I got approval to use campus facilities on Saturday nights, hired a student engineer who understood the equipment, and got my *Collegian* editor-friend to write a good story about it. Carol's first pick was *Jacre* plus two comedies. The second was *Night Song* with one comedy. The word spread around campus fast and weekend movie night was a big success.

As happens frequently in life, an unexpected consequence developed. Milton Eisenhower heard of the movies and asked if it might be possible for his family to view them before I mailed them back. Each rental was for a weekend, so we arranged it. Every Sunday for two years, Carol and I delivered the movie to their house, then his secretary mailed it back Monday morning. Frequently, Milton and his wife Helen invited us in for a chat, and sometimes coffee.

Carol said, "At first I was scared because they're so famous, but was delighted to find they were our kind of 'down home folks'. The stories they tell are so interesting, and both Helen and I like talking together. She's very interested in what life is like for young women now."

Impulsively, I invented a word we used frequently throughout our lives, "Yes, they're not afflicted with the disease of *'Bigshotitis'* like a few people we know." We learned an important lesson from Milton and Helen. Carol had an intuitive way of seeing below the surface of people. (A gift that was invaluable to me later in my career.) After one of our visits, Carol said, "When I talk with Helen I get the feeling she's lonely. She has lots of acquaintants but seems to have few close friends, and shows a gentle envy or sadness when she talks about people who do."

I had similar thoughts about Milton. Later in life we learned (and experienced) the fact that loneliness is fairly common for a person at the top of an organization. It's hard to form warm and enduring friendships with employees and their families for several reasons. For example, if an employee is seen as being close to the boss, jealous co-workers may label them 'brown noser', or relationships with others may become strained because they fear tales may be shared with the boss. For the boss, such friends may inadvertently (or intentionally) "leak" information that produces problems. Making decisions negatively affecting friends is difficult. Friendship with us was safe because, in the eyes of others, we were just two insignificant kids. Lifelong friendships emerged from those Sunday conversations.

One Sunday after delivering the movie, we relaxed and talked about the success of our movie program. Carol said, "Don, I have another idea. There's no place on campus for dancing but the gym, and the basketball coach limits that use to very special dances. Could outdoor evening dances be held on the concrete tennis courts beside the Union? They're smooth and should be easy to dance on, and they won't get muddy if it rains."

"Carol, that's a creative idea, and I've missed dancing with you. Let's try it. I'll meet with the building and grounds guys to get the OK, and work out a plan for using the courts. We'll need some lights. Your old slumber party pal Betty's hubby, Vaughn Bolton, has a pretty good band. Could you find out from Betty if he might help us give it a try? If it works, we could probably hire him for some more." So we scheduled the dance and advertised it. On a warm moonlit evening, the dance attracted a big crowd and some parents brought their kids to enjoy the music and even danced holding them.

Students began looking forward to the dances so we scheduled them every week during warm weather. While planning the last dance of the season, Carol said, "Why don't you make the last one a big celebration to end the summer session? I'll work with your student committee to decorate the place while you plan the dance." Later, Carol came to me with the committee plans, "Can you get us a couple hundred big multicolored balloons? The students want to fasten lots of balloons to the tennis court fences. Get purple and white ones since that combination is K-State colors. I'm helping them plan pretty patterns among the balloons with crepe paper streamers. The students want to tie balloons to sticks to give any little kids that parents bring. And they want to put up some signs like, 'Goodbye Summer', 'So Long Profs' and 'Let's Dance.' They'll place forty folding chairs in small groups around the courts where people can rest and watch. Could the Union create a refreshment stand with snacks and cold drinks?"

"Yes, but we can't provide free refreshments. Matt Benton will play for three hours."

"Terrific!" Carol said. "He has the best big band orchestra in the area. The students asked if they'll get to see us dance. I told them we'd dance the light fantastic, and they laughed."

We had a huge crowd that night and even Milton Eisenhower and his wife came for a while. More people arrived when the free movie was over. Matt planned to stop playing at 11 p.m. but the dancers didn't want the music to stop and shouted, "More!", "More!" But even the best of fun must end eventually. Matt played one more set and then the music and dance ended. Carol's dancing on the tennis courts idea became a summer tradition.

We'd been ignoring our friends while treasuring our newlywed status. Finally, we decided it was time to rejoin society. Carol said, "Let's start by inviting Bea and Al to dinner. They kindly invited us to their home on several occasions while we were single."

Later, Carol described her first dinner party to her mother: "I was a little nervous. For one thing I was rushed, so I'll correct that next time. I served a roast, parsley potatoes, frozen peas, rolls, tomato salad, coffee and lemon pie. I cooked the roast in the pressure cooker and boy, was it ever tender and good! It was fun to see them again and they enjoyed my dinner."

A few days after that first dinner party, Carol came home from work and bragged, "Don, the College of Agriculture transferred me to a new job in the marketing office! A week ago I took another civil service test to qualify for a higher secretarial rank and just learned I passed it and guess what – I got a $26 a month raise. Yippee!"

Carol and I both believed in keeping our nose to the grindstone to accomplish home and work related tasks, but we also liked to relax and unwind. With increasing frequency, those summer blanket parties along Wildcat Creek in our courting days became topics of conversation. We decided we deserved a 'vacation', so we packed a lunch and drove outside town to a secluded area near the Kansas River. We hiked through a corn field and followed a long strip of sandy beach along the river. The sun was shining, birds singing, and wild flowers buzzing with bees. Carol said, "Oh, I've missed being outdoors like this! The river is singing such a merry song I just have to join in. Remember? My mother named her baby goat *Lambsy Divey* from this song:

Mairsey doates and dosey doates and little lambsy divey, A kiddleet divey too, wouldn't you?" We walked along the edge of the river squishing sand between our toes, laughing with pleasure while Carol sang. After a rollicking rendition of *Mairsey Doates*, she said, "I sang this song to my fishies in the office: *Down in the meadow in a little bitty pool swam three little fishies and a mama fishie too. "Swim" said the mama fishie, "swim if you can" and they swam and they swam all over the dam. "Stop" said the mama fishie, "or you will get lost". The three little fishies didn't wanna be bossed. The three little fishies went off on a spree and they swam and they swam right out to the sea."*

As she sang, we rounded a curve and discovered a pretty, sheltered sanctuary. I said, "We're in a big watermelon patch! Let's pick one and put it in the river to cool while we rest."

We spent a few minutes thumping watermelons to find the ripest one, then laid it in the shallows. I straightened up from watermelon detail and turned to see Carol's mischievous grin. "Let's go skinny dipping. It's private here, I'm hot, and I'd like to see your birthday suit!"

So, we shucked our clothes and waded naked into the water with our happy laughter echoing up and down the river. We splashed and dunked each other, floated with the current, and tried to smooch a bit while floating. Turned out, that's hard to do! Carol floated into a deeper spot and swam a little. She said, "I love to swim!" Finally we waded out, flopped down on our blanket and let the sun dry us off. We smooched a little, and then Carol said, "I'm hungry so let's eat. I'll get our sandwiches and Cokes while you get the watermelon." Everything was delicious – especially being together in that carefree place for a while.

Near the end of the summer session Carol wrote: "Dear Mom. Thank you for bringing the sewing machine. I've missed my sewing and want to make a summer dress. By the way, when we had our marriage physicals the Dr. told me a fib. He said 'married life' would make menstrual cramps easier – another myth created by males. I just looked over at my husband and he has a book in one hand but a heck of a lot of good he's getting out of it – he's dead asleep! Poor boy, he's tired so guess I'd better put him to bed. This semester is almost over and I don't see how he does it. He has a big, new full time job, successfully carries a full load of graduate courses in psychology, helps with the housework and shopping, and most important of all, he keeps me happy. I hope he doesn't have to study so much at night this fall."

Planning for opening the Student Union in the fall, I hired a friend and fellow TKE named Bob Pearson as my business manager. He was smart, majored in business, and fun to work with. That took a big load off me. In addition to running the Union, I worked in the counseling office learning those skills. Carol, my artist-in-residence, made cartoon-like pictures of food and drink for advertising on the service counter. We'd hired staff and were ready to go. Beginning Monday of the fall semester, we'd be open from 7 a.m. to 10 p.m. seven days a week.

As always, a rapid increase in college social life accompanied the beginning of the fall semester, but this year was different for us. As Carol wrote her mother: "Don and I feel like we're living in two different worlds. On the one hand, we're students again, enjoying the parties and dances with our student friends. For example, a week ago we double dated on Friday night with Earl and Ginny to a college mixer (dance). Saturday we wore our picnic clothes to a TKE picnic on a big river sand bar in wonderful weather. They had a huge log fire going when we got there and the crowd circled around the fire to keep nice and warm. They had 4 huge roasts that were barbequed to a T. Boy did they come out delicious!

Sunday we went bowling with Paul and Tutt. This Friday, we went on a steak fry with Ginny and Earl and another married couple. They took us to the campus trailer park for ex-GIs and showed us their little trailer & I do mean little – only 9' by 14'! I just don't see how kids can live in them. The one thing I would object to most strongly is the community bath!

On the other hand, we've suddenly become members of the adult academic community. For example, Dr. Woolf invited us to a staff dinner at his home with all the professional people that work for him. I dreaded to go, but we went with Bob and Alice Pearson and after we were introduced, it wasn't half bad. Alice and I helped Mrs. Woolf with the dinner – she's so nice, just like a little girl. The psychologists who work in the counseling service were fairly young and interesting to me, particularly because that's a career direction Don may head.

Don and I feel like we're slowly walking through a door from one big room into a much larger room we haven't seen before, leaving our youth behind. We're now experiencing the great benefits. As college students we enjoyed the party and then went back to our lonely rooms. As married adults we go home together, and don't have to go to parties to have fun! I find it both kind of scary and kind of exciting, as long as I'm with Don. By next year, all our close friends will have graduated and I'm sure we'll begin to feel a little out of place with the sorority and fraternity crowd (but I hope we can still go to their formal balls)."

Over dinner one evening I said, "Carol, the Student Union has been running full blast for several weeks without a hitch. Quite a few people – students and faculty – come first thing in the morning to get something to replace the breakfasts they'd missed. After a brief lull, the midmorning storm of a couple hundred people continues until about 11 a.m. One of the things I like best is that we see an increase in students and faculty enjoying sitting and talking together. The lunch group was smaller, often arriving in pairs, eating, talking and sometimes playing games like chess or cribbage, or catching a cat nap. A similar pattern occurs in the afternoon until about four. Then there's a little burst of arrivals from 7 to 9 p.m. with students and occasionally faculty who'd been on campus for evening classes and activities."

Carol said, "That sounds like a fun place. I'd lots rather eat lunch and enjoy that activity with you than eat with the girls in the office. It would only take a few minutes to walk down the hill to the Union so we could enjoy our lunch hour together."

"Truth is I miss you during the day so a routine of eating lunch together would be great." We did more than eat. Sometimes people stopped to sit with us and talk awhile. We exchanged news of our day and funny stories, discussed future plans, and played games together.

Often Carol grabbed a cribbage board and said something like, "OK Buster. I'm gonna beat the socks off you today," and I accepted the challenge with typical macho bravado, like, "In your dreams!" Cribbage and lunch became a routine for us. It was wonderfully relaxing and made our afternoon work more pleasant, even when Carol beat the socks off me at cribbage!

Several weeks later Carol said, "Our lunch routine helps me feel a part of what you're doing. It's fun to meet people you know and work with."

"Since you feel a part of it, maybe you can help me solve a problem we've been having. We sell lots of coffee every day but get many complaints about how bad it is. I've tried everything I could think of, e.g., gave the coffee machine a special cleaning or tried different brands of coffee, but about three weeks after changing to a different coffee, complaints began again. You know more about cooking than I do – any suggestions?"

Carol thought awhile: "You say each time you tell people you're trying a new coffee, complaints stop for a few weeks? That sounds like the problem isn't in the coffee but in their heads. Try this. Buy a can of several of the best known and highest selling brands of coffee. Continue using your regular coffee. When the complaints become frequent, put one of the cans you bought on the counter by the coffee machine and let people assume you're trying that brand, but keep on using the same coffee. Whenever complaints increase, put up a different can but continue using the same coffee. I'll bet they won't know the difference."

Several weeks later I told Carol, "You were right about our coffee complaints. YOU are one smart lady!!"

Carol's 21st birthday, her first as a married woman, was a major milestone so I thought the day should be special. Carol gave her mother the highlights in a letter: "Don gave me a wonderful birthday surprise. After work Friday as we walked into our apartment the place was all dark. In the middle of the living room was a table set with our crystal and silver gleaming in candlelight. He had roses in that centerpiece Pearl gave us and it looked beautiful. Then he served a cocktail, soup, steak and French fries (a little too done, but delicious anyway) and peaches with cookies and a pretty salad. Then we took in a good show at the Sosna Theater. Every day I'm more amazed at the wonderful man I married. We're so happy!"

What a difference a year makes. Last year Carol had trouble getting away from home to visit me. This year the reverse was true. Carol wrote: "Dear Mom and Dad. I don't know when the heck we'll be able to get home since every weekend from now until Homecoming (which is Oct. 30) is full. Don has to be here every Sunday for the things he's sponsoring at the Union – one is a diaper derby for the married kids with babies. I teased him with, 'Are you hinting?' Earl and Ginny announced their engagement Sunday. We're having them over for dinner tomorrow night to celebrate."

Perfect fall weather drew us to the beautiful outdoors. Carol wrote her Mom and Dad: "When we sniffed that crisp, fresh air we just had to get out in it. We hiked a good 5 or 6 miles and climbed a real steep hill. We could see clear across the valley. I can't describe how beautiful it was – even the huge coyote we scared up. It felt so good to get some exercise."

We relaxed on top of a hill and talked. We'd been trying to save money and stay within a strict budget, but it wasn't working. I decided one of our brainstorming sessions was in order. "Carol, our current saving strategy has failed. We've tried keeping records but that didn't help, so I propose we try a new strategy. Each month let's immediately put a chunk of our checks in our savings account where it can't be touched, and then we'll have to live on what's left."

"I like that idea. That way we won't have to debate whether to spend or save during each month. Let's start with our next paychecks. And since we're talking about money I have another idea. Remember one time you commented my expanding job responsibilities made me the chief financial officer (CFO) for my employer. I asked if I could be our CFO when we got married and you enthusiastically said yes. Let's implement that agreement. I like keeping business records. Dad can advise us about our income tax reports since he does that for KP&L."

"Madam CFO - I love that idea!!" I gave her a big hug and kiss to seal the deal.

With a sly smile Carol said, "Does that mean you'll need my approval to buy things?"

"If you say so, except for when I want to buy you a present!" She laughed happily. That plan, hatched when we were newlyweds, operated through most of our married life.

Since our marriage, Carol had almost no music in her life except for listening to the radio in our car, and it was the first time she didn't have a piano to play since she was five-years-old! Winifred knew Carol really missed music, so told her they had an early Christmas present – a combination radio and record player that automatically played several records at a time, and she no longer had to use cactus needles to play her records. Listening to her favorite music on that radio-record player thrilled Carol so much that she rarely turned it off. She wrote her mother: "Listening to beautiful music again made me want to resume singing so a friend and I joined the community choir here. When Dr. Leavengood found out we'd been in a'cappella he said, 'You don't have to try out – that's good enough for me.' I'm going to enjoy choir a lot!"

We were excited to celebrate our first Christmas as a married couple. She told her mom: "We went shopping last Saturday and bought so many packages that poor Don looked like Dagwood Bumstead. I guess we looked so much like the typical Christmas shoppers that people stared and laughed. It was lots of fun! Christmas got me interested in knitting and crocheting again, so I'm making some Christmas presents.

We decided to have a little Christmas party at the Student Union for all the Union staff plus wives, husbands, and dates. I really looked forward to getting to know all of them. It feels funny to be the boss's wife. They drew names and Don and I got a baby doll that wets its diapers and a potty chair. No one would admit who gave it to us – did we get kidded! They all seem to think he's a great Boss. Boy, am I proud of my man!"

The following Saturday when I came home from work, Carol met me with sparkling eyes and a big smile, "This afternoon I took care of our neighbor's two month old cute-as-a-bug baby. I've never babysat a new baby and wanted him to wake up so bad so I could cuddle and feed him! It was a wonderful, special feeling holding a new baby at Christmas time."

We continued our holiday tradition of going to the TKE sweetheart formal. Carol wore her black, lacy off-the-shoulders formal I liked so well. She told me, "You better polish your dancing shoes because we're gonna dance the night away like old times." The TKEs welcomed us newlyweds back with lots of teasing and we had a great time.

Carol said "As a final holiday celebration let's invite some friends to our little apartment for dinner, and then go a local dive to see if we can act young and dance." We enjoyed letting our hair down and acting like fools again. About midnight, we all went back to our apartment, and lit the lights on our tiny tree. We were all starving so we fried hamburgers and ate them around the tree, savoring the pleasure of sharing Christmas with special friends in our own home.

That night Carol snuggled into my arms in bed and said, "Don, my family's Christmas celebration was only a brief gift exchange. Sometimes we had Christmas dinner with a handful of relatives. I had no idea how joyful celebrating Christmas could be until now, our first holiday in our own home. I want all our future Christmas celebrations with friends and the children I hope we'll have to be as joy-filled as this first one has been."

We repeated last year's holiday schedule by spending Christmas Eve at the Clark's farm and Christmas day with the Ford clan. It was very pleasant, but we both agreed that never again would we experience the intense joy of last year, traveling alone together through the darkness and beauty of our first early Christmas morning together.

We started the New Year talking about our future. I said, "Carol, this year I'll complete my Master's degree in Psychology. I'm tired of going to school. You're growing into your new life as a member of the academic community while maintaining contact with your old friends. But, our little apartment is inadequate for the kind of life we're leading now. Since it looks like we'll be here for several more years, what would you think about finding a larger apartment?"

Carol laughed, "Great, but Manhattan is so crowded it may not be possible. It would be fun to look around though."

Our social life in Manhattan was enjoyable, but mostly based on couples activities. Carol missed having girlfriends to 'cat around with' like she had with her high school gang and sorority sisters. She started participating in activities that might help fill that small hole in her life. She described two activities to her mother: "Monday night was Civic Choir practice. Did I tell you we're singing with the a'cappella choir for this Arts' Festival? The performance is Feb. 6. Not only do I love the music, but I enjoy gabbing with several women friends in the choir.

I was co-hostess at Becky's for the Alpha Xi alumnae meeting. I had fun talking with the girls, especially those at the house when I was there. I got home at midnight. Poor Don had to wait up for me as I had him drive me up and back – I was scared I'd get stuck in the snow."

Winter driving in Kansas in 1949 could be a real challenge. In that era, most places didn't have equipment to remove snow from streets and highways, so one had to drive through drifted, or snow packed, icy streets and highways. I worried about Carol's snow driving inexperience, so asked her if she'd like a few pointers. She said, "Yes, but it kind of scares me."

"Don't worry. Just trust me to keep you safe." I took her to a paved, snow packed road outside of town and demonstrated how to steer and brake if she started to skid. Then, I had her drive slowly down the road and suddenly hit the brakes to make the car slide. At first it scared her, but after half an hour of practice she was steering out of skids with skill and confidence. Next, we tackled starting and stopping in deep snow. I deliberately stuck the car in a drift and showed her how to get out of it. After more practice, she was doing winter driving like a pro. There's nothing like success to boost confidence! I complimented her and said: "You're set, so we can go back home now." As she slowly drove back towards town on the snow packed road, I surprised her by hitting the brakes again. Without thinking, she automatically made the right moves and kept control of the car. I enthusiastically cheered and said, "You've graduated from the Don Ford Winter Driving Course!" That was a good investment because, from that day forward, Carol was a skilled, confident driver on slick roads.

Carol was usually a reasonable, even-tempered person, but when something riled her, look out!! I couldn't help but smile as she shared a troubling incident at work. "I had a little trouble at the office. You remember how sick I was with my period and cramps last Monday and came home and went to bed. The next day was a holiday, so I didn't go back until today. I turned in my sick leave and the girl who handles sick leaves said my bosses were wondering about the truthfulness of my being sick since I take off about once a month. I was furious at being called a liar!! I told one of my bosses if they had complaints to bring them to me and not blab around the whole department about it. I also told him about the facts of life! Now we all understand each other and things are back to normal, but boy, was I mad – I was about ready to quit! They sure treat me nice now. All a person has to do is stand up for their rights I guess."

Our Student Union activities were time consuming, but rewarding. Carol wrote her parents: "Don and I spent last Thursday night at the Union. Don wanted to make sure everything was running smoothly because Milton Eisenhower was bringing some legislators over after the game to see what kind of Student Union K-State had. The place was jammed after the game, and if that didn't convince the legislators that we need a permanent Union, I don't know what will. Milton got their support and the following week appointed a committee, including Don, to develop a plan for a permanent Student Union. We were excited and delighted. We'd been working towards that objective with veterans, sororities and fraternities, the Student Planning Commission and student government for three years, giving up some of our treasured time together in the process, and we'd finally succeeded."

To enrich Carol's musical experience and provide entertainment for both of us, I bought season tickets to the artists' series. The first performance we saw was a marvelous troupe of comic ballet dancers. The concept enthralled Carol and she raved about it afterwards on the way home, "How amazing to see classical dancing used to satirize the circus, sports, newsreels, Carnegie Hall and other phases of our American culture! I enjoyed it thoroughly. Thank you so much for buying us those artist series tickets!"

After another experience with the artists' series, Carol wrote her parents: "The TKEs invited us to dinner Sunday noon. The food was so good! Our performance of the *Requiem* was that afternoon. My neighbor, Pat Hales, is an outstanding soprano soloist and had a solo in the *Requiem*. Her voice is every bit as good as Jane Powell's. It's too bad her folks can't afford to send her to a good music school. The artist series performance that evening was a Negro men's group called 'The Infantry Chorus'. They were terrific! I've never heard a chorus that could stay together so well and yet have so many outstanding solo voices. It was a wonderful day for me!"

Sunday night snuggling in bed Carol said, "I need the car to go to choral practice Monday night. We've started working on the *Messiah* now and it sounds beautiful. We'll perform on Palm Sunday with Leavengood directing. This will be the fourth time I've performed the *Messiah* and I never tire of it. It's wonderful to be a part of such glorious music! The Alpha Xi and TKE formals are this month. Let's go to the farm next weekend so my Mommy can help me make a new formal so I can be beautiful for my lover. You better be ready for me, Buster."

Carol could interact comfortably with other women in any situation, but was often self-conscious and apprehensive in her dealings with men. She often relived these concerns through letters to her mother: "Last Tuesday we went to Dr. Woolf's surprise birthday party. There were many people there I didn't know. After the meal was over we sat around talking and most folks left early, but we stayed until 10:30 and were about the last to leave. I talked with some of the women while Don got tied up talking shop with his counseling colleagues. I'm trying my best to get over my uneasiness in such situations, and trying to be a better conversationalist. It's an awfully hard thing to conquer, but I think with practice, I'll improve. I know it will be a long time before I can really enjoy a party with older and more intelligent people. Don says I'm doing fine." (Note: In Carol-speak, *older and more intelligent people = men.*)

After another more intimidating gathering, Carol wrote: "Saturday night we were invited over to Dr. Woolf's house for a dinner party and to meet his twin sister. Don and I felt a little out of place as the other guests were older and quite outstanding people. One man from Sweden was such a dynamic and interesting person, my eyes fairly bugged out of my head. Another guy was a famous novelist and works alongside Milton Eisenhower with UNESCO. Naturally, I felt somewhat insignificant. But, it was an unusual evening to say the least."

Carol and I discussed it that night. I told her, "I have such feelings too sometimes."

She seemed astonished by my confession, "I can't believe it!"

I nodded, reliving those childhood pangs, "As a little kid, I learned my family was considered to be in the lower echelon of Marysville society. I was the skinny kid from 'below the tracks' who went around hawking vegetables. One girl even said her parents wouldn't let her play with me because I came from a poor family. That hurt my feelings and made me mad, but even worse, I felt very self-conscious. Here's one trick I learned that you might try. If I have to talk with a person, I ask questions so they have to talk – most people like to talk about themselves. I listen to what they say to find something I can feel comfortable talking about. Then I talk a little. Sometimes, that starts a conversation on my topic. If not, I ask another question. As Winifred taught you about necking, if you get a guy talking you're safe.

And as I get older, I'm learning another lesson. Under each person's public persona there's often another story. For example, the 'famous author' at that dinner wrote only one of the many biographies about Ike. After that, nothing he wrote got published. Milton gave him a temporary job while that author tries to renew his reputation. He's just another guy, struggling to overcome troubles while trying to present a favorable view of himself to the world."

I was always pleased and amused to witness the one setting in which my bride exuded confidence. When she dolled up, Carol knew both men and women thought she was beautiful. Her beauty was guileless and natural, not something she had to cultivate or brag about. She was also an excellent dancer and knew people admired her grace and rhythm on the dance floor. Those two attributes together created a winning combination for the TKE and Alpha Xi formal dances. The weekend before the TKE formal, Carol and Winifred designed and made a new formal gown for her. When I led her into the ballroom, she drew many admiring stares and compliments all evening. She gave Winifred a full report after the dance: "We had so much fun and danced like mad – didn't sit out a single dance. We hadn't been to a dance for so long and both felt good, which makes a lot of difference. We double dated with Earl and Ginny. She was rather nervous to be a candidate for this year's TKE sweetheart. We knew she'd been elected but let her and Earl stew with anticipation a little. I was so glad she got it. Earl was even more excited than Ginny, I think. I had a little trouble with my straps showing, but pinned them down good for dancing. Earl and Ginny and 3 other couples came to our apartment and we fried egg sandwiches to top off the evening. I don't know when Don and I have had so much fun at a dance and I felt gorgeous in the formal we made. Thanks!"

The semester ended and Carol told her parents about her celebration party: "Saturday I planned a big dinner for eight of our friends to celebrate the end of the semester – Bob and Alice, Tutt and Paul, Betty and Vaughn, and Earl and Ginny. (Can you visualize that crowd in our tiny apartment?) We really put on the dog. We served highballs and 'horse de overs' when the company first arrived. Later we ate ham, potato salad, baked beans, all sorts of relishes, hot rolls (which I made with my own dainty fingers) and for dessert, strawberry shortcake with whipped cream right from your cow Blackie. Don fixed our card tables up so nice (we served buffet style) and I must say he's quite a decorator. It was a lot of fun cooking.

For students, Don arranged a semester end party in the Union where people could come and go as they pleased. Periodically they had entertainment. One was a men's barbershop quartet. Their harmonies were marvelous! I was standing fairly close and could almost feel their music. I wanted to sing with them. I've fallen in love with another form of singing."

Our first wedding anniversary approached and all my graduate courses were completed. After dinner I grabbed Carol in a big hug and said, "Let's celebrate!"

She kissed me and said "I'm ready!" She shared our excitement with her parents: "Just one year ago Don and I finally achieved our years' long dreams of spending our lives together, forever. In all my dreams I couldn't have imagined our first year of marriage would be this wonderful! Don knows I've dreamed of traveling, so he planned a little trip to the Ozarks to celebrate. We'll start full time work again when we get back."

On a beautiful, warm early summer day, as we drove past Kansas City into the Missouri Ozarks, Carol said, "I've never gone anywhere. I remember the excitement I felt reading your wonderful letter about your train trip to Keesler Field. I've so much wanted to travel!"

I grinned at her excitement and said, "Let's consider this little trip a start. Before we're through, let's travel through the whole U.S. and other countries, like England – the home of your ancestors."

A friend had given me a map to guide us into an area of public lands. The road wound through rolling hills, valleys, woods and meadows, past streams and small lakes. Carol's head swiveled side-to-side as she pointed out native birds and wildlife. I drove slowly so we could enjoy the scenery, otherwise we might have missed the narrow lane leading into the woods.

Intrigued, we decided to follow the lane wherever it might take us. It meandered along the edge of overgrown woods to reveal a small meadow with a picturesque stream running through it. We got out of the car and walked slowly to the stream, taking in the lovely scene around us. Carol laughed to see a couple chipmunks dash across a log, chattering as if telling us to stay away from their stream. The clear, shallow stream gurgled languidly over small, colored stones, sand and gravel. We couldn't resist the invitation, so took off our shoes and waded in the stream towards a little pond, watching tiny silverfish scooting past our feet. A sweet, spicy fragrance permeated the sun-warmed air. We looked around and spied the small bush producing that perfume. Light pink blossoms edged with dark rose covered the bush. Butterflies fluttered from flower to flower, feeding on the blossoms. We stood in silence for several seconds, hand in hand, absorbing the idyllic sights and scents. Carol finally broke the silence, "There's no sign of other humans around here. It's as if we're alone in Mother Nature's own beautiful garden."

We sat in the grass by the pond, savoring the pleasures surrounding us and tossing pebbles into the water to watch the ripples spread. I said "Carol, I feel like a kid at play – I can feel the tension seeping out of me. I haven't been relaxed like this for months."

She smiled and wrapped one arm around my waist. "That's what I hoped we'd find here."

When the sun sank into the western horizon, I said, "It's getting late. We better go find someplace to stay." Reluctantly, we headed back to our car with Carol investigating the meadow as we went.

As we neared the car, Carol suddenly pointed and said, "Look, Honey, doesn't that look like little strawberries?" We'd stumbled onto a large patch of wild strawberries! We tasted one, and then kept tasting. They were sweeter and tastier than any strawberries we'd ever had.

Dusk was rapidly approaching so I said we should leave soon, but Carol had other ideas. She looked at me with that dimpled smile and those twinkling eyes and said, "Why don't we stay here tonight? It's so beautiful here, and there's no one else around. We could sleep in our car and lock the doors for safety. We have a picnic basket full of sandwiches, cheese, crunchies, cans of soda and fruit, and now we have sweet wild strawberries!"

I said, "What a delicious idea!" So that's what we did. We spread a blanket on the grass beside the car with pillows to lean on, and sat there eating our picnic dinner. Later, with our tummies pleasantly full, we snuggled together and watched moonlight spread across the meadow until it touched the treetops.

Carol finally broke our relaxed period of silence, "Someday I'll learn how to paint pictures of beautiful scenes like this."

I thought she might have dozed off until she starting humming a tune and I asked, "What's that from?"

She answered in a whisper, *"Romeo and Juliet."* A little later she murmured in my ear, "I want to make love with you." So, we made a little of our own night music, there in Mother Nature's garden. We stayed there one more night and then reluctantly started home with a small box of wild strawberries in our picnic basket.

Back from the glories of the Ozarks to our too-small apartment, we talked about plans for the summer. Carol said, "Beyond doing our jobs there are two major things we need to do. You need to finish your Master's thesis so you can graduate at the end of the summer, and we need to help Ginny and Earl get hitched."

I reluctantly tackled my thesis research. For two months I busted my butt collecting and analyzing the data Dr. Wolff required, with Carol's help. I finally realized he didn't know much about designing good research and decided my thesis was lousy. I was fed up and discouraged with the whole thing. Carol said, "Let's take a break and finish the thesis this fall."

On our little vacation we'd talked about the stress of Carol's job. I'd told her, "Honey, if you'd like to quit your job, do it. I'm making enough now to take care of us."

"I'd like to keep earning a little to help build our savings. Perhaps I could work half time." She set out to implement that plan. All K-State secretaries were hired under state civil service policies. Carol's test scores gave her the highest possible rating in the clerk-stenographer category, so her bosses were eager to keep her. At lunch Carol told me, "The state office ruled that, despite my high rating, I can't go on half time unless I go off civil service and on a student basis. What would that mean? A huge cut in pay! So I told them phooey, I QUIT!!"

I cheered, gave her a big hug and said "Now relax and enjoy life with me!"

A few days later while eating dinner she said, "I've decided to sign up for fall semester courses. Instead of doing something for the University, I'm going to do something for myself."

The determined tone in her voice surprised and delighted me, "That's my girl!! Now we both have some free time for the rest of the semester. Let's enjoy it."

Over cribbage and lunch at the Union, Carol said, "The last of my old friends finally graduated and are moving elsewhere, most are married, and some have babies, so we'll have less social activity this year. I'm gonna miss them. Tomorrow night I'm having a little farewell supper for Tutt before she moves. It'll be just four of our old slumber party gang – Karen, Betty, Tutt and I. We'll have fun gabbing together. It's been a long time since we've done that."

In August Carol wrote her parents: "Yesterday we helped Ginny and Earl get married. Don was best man & I Maid of Honor. It meant a lot to Don because they've been buddies forever. Don's parents came to the wedding because, ever since Earl's father died the summer Earl and Don started college, Don's parents have included Earl and his mother in family gatherings such as Thanksgiving and Christmas, and invited her to dinner at other times. I was proud because I started it all by getting Earl a 'blind date' with Ginny."

While we ate a favorite dinner of ham, sweet potatoes, fresh fruit salad and Carol's delectable homemade rolls, Carol reported with a big smile, "The last few days have been spent visiting friends and their babies. Verla let me hold and bathe her ten day old baby. Ann has a 7 pound girl named Janis. Carlotte's Steven is 2 months old. Karen's 5 pound Jimmy just came home from the hospital. It's an epidemic – babies, babies, babies everywhere!! New mothers tell me there are so many babies in town they have trouble keeping things like baby clothes and equipment in stock." (No wonder decades later they called our children the baby boomers!)

I laughed and said, "Companies making diapers must be getting rich."

"Don, I registered for Family Health and General Psychology this fall. I'm a little scared. I know I'm probably not as smart as others but they look interesting so maybe I can do OK."

"Carol, you don't believe me when I say you're a very smart gal. Our counselors use several tests to measure how smart people are. Would you be willing to take a couple so we can find out whether you're right about being dumb or I'm right about you being smart?" She accepted my challenge so I gave her the Stanford Binet and Wechsler. The results came as no surprise to me. "Carol, compared with people in general, your IQ score is in the top 10% on both tests. Compared with K-State students, your score is in the top 15%. That means you have more native intelligence than most students in your classes. Just relax and you'll do well."

I laughed out loud at her reply, "Must be something wrong with your tests."

A few weeks later she reported, "We got our mid-semester exams back today. I got the highest score in my psych class and the second highest in Family Health. It about made me fall over!! How different from when I was in classes before."

Carol discovered that an Alpha Xi friend was interested in arts and crafts and told me, "Rosie Kerns is teaching me how to make pictures out of a sheet of soft copper. It's easy and fun. First you design a picture. I've created a lily and an abstract design. You copy the design onto an appropriate sized sheet of copper and use a wooden tool to press the copper surface into a three dimensional design. Then you paint a colorless chemical on the copper surface. It interacts with the copper producing highlights and shadows on the design, and also seals and protects the surface. It's a little 'smelly' but produces a beautiful result. I've almost completed the lily design for Lois's bridal shower. Rosie will teach me textile painting. This is really fun!" Later, Carol reported the outcome of her first copper creation, "When Lois unwrapped my framed copper lily, everyone raved over it and wanted to buy one. Boy was I pleased!"

One fall Saturday, Kenny Rowland and his wife Phyl visited us to share the traditional Homecoming parties and ball. Our relationship with Kenny was unusual. He and Carol became friends in second grade in Marysville (he always did have an eye for pretty girls). In high school, we became good friends. He was talented and funny and got most of the leads in our theater productions. At the ball I said, "Carol, you are *really* beautiful! I'm so impressed that you can design and make something as gorgeous as your formal in only three days." She stepped into my arms and we had a great evening dancing and greeting 'old timers'.

Driving home, Carol drowsily said, "It's wonderful to see our old friends. I miss them!"

That Sunday was a gorgeous fall day. I hugged Carol and said, "Let's forget everything else and take a hike to enjoy the fall colors." We hiked through gently rolling hills out in the Deep

Creek area, north of Manhattan along the Blue River. The air was crisp and fragrant.

Carol said, "I love these fall colors! Help me gather some pretty stems with seed pods, graceful fall grasses, and branches from bushes with multicolored leaves to take home to make a fall arrangement." For the next couple months, I watched her create one breathtaking arrangement after another, born of an artistic imagination that surprised even me. Carol's fall creations decorated our home, and the homes of friends and family for decades.

Carol couldn't wait for the Christmas season and the activities we shared. That year, she wrapped both arms around me in a bear hug and kissed me soundly on the cheek, "Saturday night we'll celebrate our second Christmas together as husband and wife at the Alpha Xi Christmas ball. This has such special meaning for me, because it was our first dance after your discharge from the air force. We'd fallen in love and started college life together as we'd dreamed of for so long. Once I had you in my arms, I hung on tight so you couldn't get away!"

January 1 Carol shared our excitement with her parents: "What a great way to start 1950 – Don's thesis has been approved!! He'll receive his Master's degree at graduation two weeks from Friday in the morning. Don has agreed to be best man in Hardy Berry's wedding on that same day. Sound familiar? Graduation and wedding on the same day? Both were discharged from the army and started at K-State at the same time. They became friends while working with other veterans to try and change K-State for the better. He and his wife Ann are journalists."

Later, Carol briefed her parents about graduation: "I sat among the proud parents at graduation to watch my husband receive his diploma. I had a good share in it too because we worked so hard together to earn it. You should have seen him in his cap and gown and yellow hood around his neck signifying his Master's degree. Don said that as Milton handed him the degree he said, 'That's two. Care to try for three?' We got home about noon, ate lunch with Hardy (I was glad to help the nervous groom), and dressed for the wedding.

Enrollment starts this week and I'm taking Abnormal Psychology and piano lessons. I don't know what good it will do because I won't have my own piano for some time, but I miss it and both Don and I think I should try it, so I will. I got my grades from last semester and got straight As. Maybe I'm not as dumb as I thought I was.

The big news is Eisenhower's resignation. For nearly two years we've been delivering the Saturday night free movie to him Sunday morning for his family viewing. The Sunday before the news was out, we delivered the movie and he invited us in. He told us all about his decision and what Penn State was like. He says leaving here is like cutting off his right arm, but the offer was just too good to turn down. The salary is much better and the University is larger. They'll be near Helen's folks, who are getting pretty old, and Milton will be near Ike in Washington. Helen was pleased about it too. With a broad smile she said, 'The president's home is beautiful, next to a golf course, and best of all they don't have chiggers!!'" (Every Kansan despises those tiny, itchy, biting bugs!)

Our friendship with Milton and Helen enriched our lives as we started our marriage. We admired and shared many of their values. As we left their Manhattan home that night for the last time, he said, "I hope I can find some young people like you two at Penn State!" Carol and I dreaded losing the Eisenhower's presence in our daily lives. Later, after they'd moved to Penn State, we discovered Helen was half right about the college president's home. Chiggers were thankfully absent, but the president's home was an old semi-Victorian house tucked behind College of Engineering buildings. The beautiful home she remembered next to the golf course was a lovely, small, on-campus hotel called The Nittany Lion Inn.

Life went on at K-State without Milton Eisenhower. I told Carol, "I'm being put on a lot of committees for some reason. One is a very important committee developing the proposal for a permanent Student Union – what it should provide and how the building should be organized. If we get that union building I'll feel that you and I helped accomplish something of essential long term value for students. We're making great progress in the planning. I'm being sent to the University of Nebraska for a Student Union conference. I'm hoping to tap into experience and knowledge of those who have permanent unions, about what works best for them."

Carol's plan to renew her musical interest through piano lessons turned out to be a dismal failure. She said, "Don, I'm getting more and more disgusted with my piano teacher. She wastes my time with her blah blah blah and rubs me the wrong way!! I haven't learned a single new thing!–GRR!! Carol liked her abnormal psych course: "It has helped me better understand some of Mom's difficulties." She added, "I'm having fun knitting little things for a little thing. I've finished booties and a cap, and started a sweater. Now don't get excited, I'm not that way. It's just that so many of my friends are having babies. I just wanted to tease you a little.

I'm having nice visits with my old friends. The relationships among our high school 'gang' are interesting. When we graduated from high school I assumed we would go separate ways, but we haven't. Most of us live in Manhattan or Topeka and stay connected. We helped each other through high school, boyfriends, jobs and college. Now we talk together about pregnancies and babies. I laughed at the look on your face when you found four here, two pregnant, one with a new baby, and Tutt with a kid who had my strawberry jam all over his face. It ain't like the old days is it! We need a larger apartment for a mob like that."

Something about Carol attracted little kids. Maybe it was her nurturing nature, or they just sensed she genuinely liked them. One day I came home from work after Carol had spent the day with 'Little Iodine', aka our cute niece, Laurel. She was still smiling and a little winded from the exciting activities. "This afternoon I took Laurel and two little playmates to the park to play. All three kids kept fighting over who was going to hold my hands while walking over there. Such popularity – I'm not used to it, but I do love watching and playing with little kids!"

Later in life, Laurel described how important that relationship was in her formative years:

"When my dad came home from war his violent rages and shouted criticisms scared me. Carol was always quite gentle with me – soft voice, soft touch – as if she knew instinctively that I needed such an approach. I remember listening to *Scheherazade* by Rimsky-Korsakov with Carol while she told me the story behind the music and showed me the beautiful artwork on a foldout in the album. That was my first introduction to music that was not associated with Sunday School or radio. Music transformed my life back then, with Carol's help."

One day Carol came into the living room just as I hung up from a phone call. "I think I may have found a larger apartment. Let's go look at it."

She'd waited a long time to hear that and crossed her fingers, "I hope! I hope! I hope!" We went to a large but nice brick house in an older part of town. It had been built following a huge flood in the 1880s, by a wealthy man who chose his home site on a small hill in the flatlands a few blocks from the Blue River. The first floor was built four inches above that high flood level, on the assumption no future flood would get that high. It was on a large lot with mature shade trees, about eight blocks from down town. Carol said, "That looks like it would be cool on a hot day."

We crossed a large porch and the owner, an elderly woman, took us inside. Carol breathed, "O-o-o-o-h, this is really nice!" The entry hall was spacious, with stairs on the left leading to the second floor where there were three large bedrooms and two full baths. The large carpeted living room had a fireplace, and beside it was an equally large unfurnished dining room. Beyond that was a modest sized bedroom with closet. To the left was a large kitchen, an enclosed porch with a door that opened on a back yard and a long clothes line.

I could see Carol was ready to say YES! YES! But I said, "Where's the bathroom?"

The landlady said, "Upstairs." and I saw Carol's jaw drop. There was a basement, but it was full of stored stuff. The deal was, she wanted to rent the bedrooms separately to young women for $35 each, and the downstairs to a couple for $75 a month furnished She would provide heat, electric and water and take care of keeping the second floor clean. We'd be expected to monitor the renters' behavior. For each room rented, she'd reduce our rent by $10 a month. That meant if all three were rented we would only pay $45!

Carol whispered in my ear, "Let's take it! For something this nice I'm willing to walk upstairs to the bathroom, and I've had plenty of experience in my gang with handling girls." So, we moved in, and the first night there Carol spread her arms and sang, "Space, space, space at last!" The first thing we did was purchase a used sofa that opened up into a bed for guests.

After we moved in Carol said, "Let's go to a movie to celebrate our new home," After the movie, I drove in a different direction than home. Puzzled, Carol said, "Where are you going?"

"On this beautiful moonlit night I thought we'd park on the hill where we became engaged"

With a wicked grin, Carol murmured, "Oooh, I like that way of celebrating!" We parked and smooched in the moonlight just like old times and got home much later than we planned.

One evening our friends, Ann and Hardy, came to admire our new home. Ann said, "My Dad works in Washington and wants us to visit them this summer. We'd like to go, but don't have any way to get there. Carol, you keep talking about wanting to travel. How about the four of us make the trip together? You have a car and we could pay for the gas. In August, we could camp on the way to save money. In Washington, we can stay with my folks and see the city and visit their little ranch in the Virginia mountains. If you want to, you guys could take off by yourselves for a few days to see the ocean and New York City. Driving time out and back would be eight or nine days, and we could spend another eight or nine days sightseeing."

I could see the excitement sparkling in Carol's eyes. Her cheeks flushed pink and she whispered, "Oh please – can we?" She'd been dreaming of travels like this from the time our letters began. How could I say no to a chance to live her dream? The four of us spent the evening planning. We decided to leave the second week in August and return the end of August.

Carol wrote her parents: "The last tennis court dance to celebrate the end of summer session and welcome K-State's new president, Dr. McCain, will be tomorrow night, weather permitting. The student committee is trying to make the courts look like a night club. There'll be hostesses to dance with shy stag men, cigarette girls to give the place atmosphere. Matt Benton's orchestra will play and some local dancing talent will put on a short show. I'm going later with some other girls whose husbands will be busy seeing that the thing is a success. It will be the first peep at McCain for me and lots of other folks. Don wonders how he'll change things."

Chapter Eight

Carol's Pathway to Motherhood and Family Life

I came home about 4 p.m. one day and shouted, "I'm home, Honey!" Silence greeted me so I walked through the dining room, calling out a little anxiously this time, "Where are you, Carol?"

The sudden noise of our bedroom door opening startled me. Carol stepped out wearing a big ornery grin and a maternity dress with a huge, bulging tummy under it. "SURPRISE!!!"

After the initial shock, I shouted with joy and ran to hug her, "Is that what I think it is?"

"No, that's a pillow, silly. You'll have to wait six more months to see our new Ford." We hugged and laughed and cried with joy! Carol had told me she'd missed a period, but then hadn't said more so I assumed nothing was happening. She said, "I wanted to surprise you!"

I wiped happy tears from my face and managed to choke out, "Well, you sure did a terrific job of it!" We sat on the couch together so she could tell me everything about her visit to the doctor.

"Dr. Bascom, my doctor, is considered the best in town. He will take over the seventh month. Until then, Dr. Belle Little, a woman doctor, takes care of me. She's very good and a specialist in maternity cases. I like going to a woman doctor because I feel so relaxed around her. The predicted delivery date is March 3, 1951. Dr. Little gave me a thorough examination and said I'm in excellent condition and my measurements perfectly OK. She's adding an iron supplement to my daily vitamins during pregnancy. She doesn't want any of her moms-to-be to gain more than fifteen pounds, and gave me a list of do's and don'ts. I was afraid I'd have to give up our trip, but she says if I take it fairly easy and get plenty of sleep at night I should be OK.

I can hardly believe I'm pregnant and don't feel a bit different – in fact I feel so good! Oh Don, I could hardly wait for you to get home so I could tell you! I'm bubbling over with excitement, happiness and love for you and our little Ford."

I sat with both arms around her, planting happy kisses on her smiling face. We talked about our future plans. We decided to keep our secret until we got back from the trip, but would have to tell Dr. Woolf, a couple of colleagues on campus for business reasons, and Hardy and Ann so they'd understand why we had to be so careful in driving and getting adequate sleep. We were so engrossed in planning and sharing our joy that we both forgot to eat dinner.

When the day finally arrived to leave on our trip, we loaded the tent, navy wool blankets, cooking utensils and clothes we'd need. It was a good thing we had that large, four door Olds or we wouldn't have had room for everything! We had our route laid out in detail from Manhattan, through Missouri, Tennessee, and Virginia to Washington sightseeing along the way.

Carol was so excited, we'd covered a hundred miles before she calmed down. Crossing the Ozarks brought back memories of wild strawberries. At the end of our first day, we parked in the yard of a rural school house. After supper we put up our tent and went to sleep. About midnight, rain poured down so hard and fast that water ran into our tent. We made a mad dash through the rain to the Olds and slept the rest of the night in our car. Ah, the joys of camping!

The next morning dawned clear and sunny so while the gals fixed breakfast, Hardy and I examined our tent. We'd set it on a slope and hadn't ditched the sides to control drainage. Everything in the tent was soaked. When Dad's navy wool blankets dried, they shrank to half their size. Lesson learned. The gals teased us about our ignorance as we started our second day.

We passed through southern Missouri where Carol's compassionate heart was touched by the poverty we saw. We crossed the mighty Mississippi on a high, long bridge from which we saw a steamboat and loaded barges moving downriver towards New Orleans. We camped during a beautiful night and drove into grey, misty weather in Tennessee the next day. Carol said, "Let's stop mid-afternoon and camp at Reel Foot Lake. Our travel guide says it's a shallow lake with swamps and clumps of bard cypress trees that are homes for nesting pairs of Bald Eagles."

The guide didn't say anything about mosquitoes! They were huge and hungry for our blood – nearly as big as our P26 fighter planes in WWII. We set up our tent near the lake. Ann described that episode in a later letter. "We spent a couple of hours battling mosquitoes in that miserable, cramped little pup tent on the muggy shore of Reel Foot lake. Don and I said we should get out of there and find a motel. Hardy was adamant that we should save our money and stay there. A heated debate resulted. Shortly, our young, gentle, pregnant Carol announced forcefully, 'This is a democracy, the vote is 3 to 1 against you Hardy, the majority rules against staying here and continuing to be eaten alive.' Presto! We were out of that tent hunting a motel."

As we drove through Tennessee early in the morning, Carol viewed the beautiful scenery with a sense of wonder. These were rugged vistas far different than our Kansas prairies! "The early morning mists spreading over mountains and fields is like a fairy land we'd see in movies. Oh, I wish I could paint scenes like this."

We took the winding roads through Virginia at a leisurely pace so we could enjoy the spectacular scenery. Carol said, "I'm fascinated by those road side stands selling locally handcrafted items. Please stop so I can admire their work. I want to buy something to remember this trip." She picked a small walnut footstool with a top of woven reeds.

After reaching Washington and sightseeing, Carol wrote her parents: "We found Ann's folks to be very hospitable. We spent 2½ days trying to see everything – the Capitol, the memorials and historic sights. We saw the House of Representatives in action, and had lunch with Kansas Senator Cole in the Senate dining room. The last night we took the Thackerys to see the play *Kiss Me Kate*. The boys liked the political stuff, but that play was my biggest thrill."

When we left on our side trip, Carol said, "The Berrys are great, but we have so much fun when we're alone together. I'm so excited to see these historic places and the ocean with you!"

Carol described our side trip to her parents: "We toured Mt. Vernon, and the historic sites of Jamestown and Williamsburg.

Actors really made us feel like we were back in colonial times. We took the ferry from Point Comfort to Cape Charles and spent a day loafing, picnicking and swimming in the surf of the ocean. Gee it was fun!!"

In New York we felt like a couple of ants among those huge buildings. We spent a day sightseeing. Carol said, "Before we leave I'd love to see Chinatown if we can. We drove slowly in typical New York traffic through several distinct parts of town so Carol could enjoy the Big Apple's cultural diversity. Then I inched my way towards the Holland Tunnel and Washington DC. I stopped for a red light and discovered I was in the lane that required me to cross that famous bridge to Brooklyn.

I probably had a horrified look on my face while trying to figure a way out of our quandary because the guy in a truck next to me said, "What's wrong, buddy?"

I said, "We don't want to go to Brooklyn! We have to go through the Holland Tunnel so we can go home."

I'm not sure whether it was my hysteria or the Kansas license that amused him, but he laughed while saying, "When the light changes you stay here until you hear a cop's whistle and then go straight ahead fast." The light changed, the helpful New Yorker drove into the intersection and stalled his truck, the cop directing traffic ran towards him blowing his whistle, and we took off like two bats out of hell heading for the Holland Tunnel exit.

Carol waved at our savior and told me, "He grinned as we passed him. Now I don't believe all those stories about New Yorkers being unfriendly."

After returning safely from our side trip, we spent one more day at the Thackery cabin in the Blue Ridge Mountains. Carol described it as "the most picturesque place you can imagine, with blueberries, blackberries, grapes, and apples growing wildly and profusely." The next day we four Musketeers left and reached home four days later. That night, in our own bed, Carol snuggled up to me and said, "Traveling with you like that was beyond my wildest dreams. Thank you for such a wonderful experience. Somehow I'm becoming a different person. My view of the world has expanded greatly. That taste of seeing new places makes me want more. But now I want to enjoy our home and create a beautiful baby for us. I love you dearly!"

We did our usual work-related tasks that fall, but our thoughts focused primarily on the new addition to our family. Every chance she had, Carol talked with friends who had babies or were expecting babies, seeking information like, "What are the best kind of diapers to use?" and, "Where are the best places to buy them?" She had to assemble a maternity wardrobe. She evaluated baby bottles, and got bargains on baby stuff at Rexall's one cent sale. She bragged, "I bought six nursing bottles at 2 for 36 cents. They're much nicer than Even-flo. These have a rubber cap to fit over the nipple and there's so much less handling. Of course, I'm hoping I can nurse the baby, but the bottles will be used later or for supplemental feedings. Tutt and I went to the matinee to see the latest movie with the new tenor, Mario Lanza. He's the best tenor I've ever heard. The music was so beautiful I felt like singing with him."

She went to a social gathering with the new K-State President's wife and spent all her time comparing ideas and suggestions with three other pregnant women there. On October 8, her birthday, Carol squealed, "Don, I feel life for the first time." Each new pregnancy-related experience thrilled her more, and I delighted in watching her enjoyment.

Friends and family wanted to be a part of our pregnancy experience so visited us often, but we cut way back on entertaining. At a small party with close friends she asked them to write down potential baby names. Then she had each person read their suggestions and explain why they recommended it. That was a game full of fun and good humor. One evening over a cup of hot chocolate, Carol reported, "We've reduced all the ideas and suggestions about a name down to this short list: Boys – Steven, Russell, Dennis, Douglas, Roger, & Duane; Girls – Marilee, Kathleen, Janet, Leslie, Sandra and Michelle. How will we ever choose?"

The baby was getting more and more active. At the farm on Christmas Eve Carol told her mother, "Your future grandchild is doing flip flops to amuse itself tonight – the stinker."

One wintry day Carol greeted me at the door with a hug and kiss when I came home from work. We sat in front of the fireplace with a cup of hot coffee to talk about our day. Carol said, "This morning when I went to see Dr. Bascom, Manhattan was a fairyland. Sun glistened off the icy trees and bushes like diamonds

Even the weeds were glorified. He says I'm getting along perfectly. He located the head – poor kid is upside down. I told him I'm feeling good and sleep well until my back starts hurting and the baby starts kicking – the little monster. Here's a letter for you from your old army buddy, Fred Feldhausen. I remember meeting him and his wife as students at a Nebraska football game in Lincoln."

I laughed at Freddie's letter. "He's working at a DuPont plant in Niagara Falls. They've been married three years and just had their third boy! She hardly pauses between pregnancies."

Our place had been jumping since Christmas with relatives and friends wanting to see Carol. One evening when I dragged in late from work, Carol shared the excitement of her day. "Anne, Lorraine and Ted came to visit. You weren't home so they took me to a movie. Walking down the sidewalk after the show, I suddenly found myself flat on the ground! I tripped on a rough sidewalk. The only thing I hurt was my dignity. I went down on one knee and caught most of the fall with my hands so 'Junior' didn't get much of a jolt. It scared us all though."

Carol decided to deliver our new Ford three weeks early, and on February 10, 1951 Russell Clark Ford was born. All went well. Carol returned home from the hospital after three days and her mother came to help out for four days.

Naturally, Russell waited until after Grandma left to develop colic and cry continuously in pain. The sound of his crying broke Carol's heart and she was in tears herself, "Oh Don, what can we do – there must be something!"

I searched my mind for anything anyone had ever said about treating colic, "I'll try a little heat by lying with him on my bare tummy with a blanket over him." It worked! Both Russell and Carol slept to his next feeding. I'd intended to stay awake but the sand man also found me for two hours. After a couple more nights of fitful sleep, I called my oldest sister Maxine – an experienced professional nurse who had years of working with infants in hospitals, and with three children of her own – and told her our problem.

She said, "Try brandy, not for you, for the baby! It's a frequent problem. When we couldn't control severe colic, we gave the baby a couple drops of brandy mixed in warm sugar water and it worked every time." I was ready to try anything so mixed Russell his colic cocktail and it worked. That was a great benefit for Carol, because she desperately needed sleep.

Over the next several weeks, like all first time parents, we treasured all the new learning involved. Beginning with breast feeding and changing diapers, things evolve: like feelings of pleasure when they cuddle in your arms; cleaning up the mess when diaper content leaks on your clothes; enjoying their contented sounds; trying to decipher reasons for their complaints; watching them look at you and smile; reaching for and holding things in their hand; seeing them start to watch the world around them; watching them learn to control their body and sit up; feeling gratitude when they sleep through the night; watching their reaction and then pleasure at being bathed in a tub of water; their reactions when introduced to solid food; and how they deal with all the friends and family who want to hold them; on and on.

Putting all the activities together, you get a picture like Carol described to her parents: "I have the baby beside me on the divan propped up on a pillow now – he was getting dissatisfied in his bed. He's just cooing and laughing at me, but he certainly lets me know if I'm not paying enough attention to him – spoiled brat! He's getting so he laughs and 'talks' back every time we say something to him – that is, if he's feeling good."

Like every new parent, we scrambled to combine our adult lives with baby care and discovered the world of baby sitters and dealing with post pregnancy life. For example, anticipating summer activities, Carol worried about fitting into a wardrobe that did not include roomy maternity clothes. She tried on her pre-pregnancy clothes and was pleasantly surprised at the result, "My figure is surprising me all to heck. My waist must be smaller and I know my tummy is flatter than it's ever been. I actually fit in my wedding suit pretty good now and I could hardly get it around me before I got pregnant!"

Eventually, parents want or need to go places without their baby. Carol told her mother: "In the beginning, our good friends volunteered to baby sit when needed. Then, I made deals with friends with babies to trade babysitting services. Finally, I discovered an older friend with lots of experience in hiring baby sitters who had a roster of good ones she'd used. Before Russell was 6 months old that list became very useful to me."

Carol loved being outdoors and now she had a baby to share it with. After Russ was three months old, they put a lot of miles on his buggy, walking for exercise with friends, going visiting, shopping down town, walking through the park. She said, "Russ loves lying on a blanket outdoors. He seems to have a sense of freedom he doesn't have in the house or his crib."

For me, having a new baby gave me *two* excuses to rush home from work – a sweetheart *and* a cooing son. Carol commented and smiled, "Russell loves his play time when you come home from work. Nights when meetings keep you on campus he's restless and seems irritated."

I nodded, "Yeah, I love giving him his morning bath on weekends. He gets kinda foxy, laughing, kicking and splashing water out of the tub. He's gonna like swimming like his mom."

"Don, it's fun to watch you two play. The other day you were holding him on your knees facing you while he held onto your fingers when all of a sudden he stood right up. You were so flabbergasted I laughed out loud. Now Russell thinks that's the best thing he ever did. When he pulls himself up and stands on your lap he shouts with joy."

One Friday night at the end of a grueling work week, Carol quietly said, "You look awfully tired and down tonight, Honey. Is anything wrong?"

I tried to play down my tension, "Oh, it's just stuff at work."

Old eagle-eye Carol wasn't that easily fooled, "Don't try to hide things from me. I know you too well. Something's wrong. We're partners, so let's talk about it."

I needed her comforting help and advice, so I talked. "The Counseling Center and Dean Woolf's office are in turmoil with all the changes President McCain is making. People are being fired and resigning right and left. This is very confidential – McCain plans to remove Dr. Woolf from his Dean of Students position because he hasn't been producing. I'll be working in the Counseling Bureau next fall on a nine-month contract. I'll like that, but the pay will be a little less because of working three months less, but I don't have to run the Union. I hope we'll get a clear idea soon what he intends to do at K-State."

"Don, You don't need that kind of stress! Just enjoy your job, learn what you can, and if you don't like his plans you can quit and we'll implement our plan for you to get your PhD."

"As always, you cut through to the heart of things. Thank you, Partner. I love you!"

Spring and summer rains soon gave us something different than college politics to worry about. The Kansas River flows through the prairies from west to east at the south edge of Manhattan heading towards the Missouri River. The Blue River flows from Nebraska south to join the Kansas River at Manhattan. It had been a very rainy spring and summer so the land in both river basins was saturated. Late June brought heavy rains producing flood levels in both basins. When they combined at Manhattan, serious flood conditions resulted. Water rose rapidly in the low southeast quarter of Manhattan; all but two roads out of town were closed. Carol and I watched water creeping up the street, nearing our house. Carol was fearful and crying for the safety of our baby and us, "I'm afraid – it'll be up to our house soon! What are we going to do?"

I replied in a voice calmer than I felt in hopes of soothing her fears, "Trust me, Honey, as you always have. I have our car waiting at the curb beside the house. If the water in the street reaches the front of our house, we'll get in our car and leave." The rain stopped and flood waters receded, but not for long. Heavy rains began again in both basins. The weather predictors said it would be much worse than two weeks ago. I said, "Let's play it safe and prepare for the worst."

Carol said, "Last time flooding threatened us I talked to Lorraine Volsky about staying with them if we got flooded, so I'll call her and tell her we're on our way. I'll pack two suitcases with the clothing we need and everything needed for Russell." While she did that, I stacked everything as best I could to protect it if water got into the house. Finally, I turned off the electricity, gas and water and we moved to the Volsky's.

The president's office notified me that the Student Union was designated emergency flood headquarters for the Army Corp of Engineers and directed me to get it ready. Two-thirds of Manhattan was flooded. We housed more than two thousand people on campus in gyms, lounges and other facilities, and many more were cared for in private homes above the flooded areas. On-campus food service and restroom facilities were arranged. All commercial communication capabilities had been wiped out, so we set up emergency communications on campus and in the Union. To help ease fears, we arranged for people (like Carol) to go on air to broadcast they were safe in hopes family elsewhere might hear their message and be reassured. Since many children were on campus, we organized student volunteers to create play and recreational opportunities to keep them entertained and less frightened.

An emergency medical center was created and they began giving everyone, including Carol, Russell and me, typhoid shots as a preventive measure. The only road open was Highway 24 going west out of town. The water came up so fast that many workers were trapped in the business district and had to be rescued by boat. Two didn't get out, and all they had to eat for four days was cat food. The lower quarter of town sits on sand and an underground lake, so manholes in the street were blown into the air by water pressure, basement walls cracked, some buildings, roads and bridges collapsed, plus many homes and some businesses were a total loss. No deaths were reported, but a few folks were still missing. Thank God K-State was there for those who needed food and shelter or the flood would have been a major human disaster.

When the water began receding, I waded down to check on our house because Carol was quite anxious about it. Then I waded back to the Volskys to reassure Carol, "The prediction by the guy who built our house in the 1880s was accurate. The water got to within four inches of going into our first floor! The basement is full of water, but there is no damage or mud in our house. All the houses around ours were hit hard." Carol cried with relief. The flooding began July 11th and we moved back into our house July 18th.

Carol settled us back in our home, and then wrote her parent describing our experiences: "We're home at last, and does it ever feel good to be here! Don got the KP&L to check our electricity and gas yesterday noon so I high tailed it for home as soon as I could pack up our stuff. We were lucky! Don is helping Charles Glotzback (a Counseling Bureau colleague) clean up his place in our neighborhood this p.m. Water got about a foot over their first floor. They have 2 small kids and a very new baby. Charles is pretty discouraged, but he's lucky compared to many who had several feet of water in their homes."

The town was a mess. Streets had to be cleared of debris and repaired before people and equipment could move around. Utility workers from all over worked day and night to restore essential services. Some businessmen lost everything. Homes that survived needed to be cleaned up and lots of now-useless furnishings had to be hauled away. Men, women and children formed bucket brigades to help friends and neighbors clean up their homes to make them sanitary and livable again. Outside of town, farmland had been transformed into miles of sand dunes! Amidst all the destruction and despair, Carol focused on one positive point. "People helping each other is the great story here. Times like this confirm my belief in the goodness of most people."

"Carol, you and Russell won't be able to leave the house, probably for a week. I have our washing machine on the back porch and cleaned up the yard under the clothes lines so you can catch up on laundry. Almost all the food supplies in town have to be replaced and made accessible to people. Make a list of anything you need and I'll try to get it for you." My staff and I got the Student Union cleaned, resupplied and up and running in two days because both students and faculty needed that resource.

Carol had trouble sleeping and had been tense and teary eyed ever since the flood, because of what had happened and what might happen in the future. At dinner the third night we were back in our home, Carol said, "Don, we have to find some way to get out of here. I'm afraid and anxious all the time with our baby here. We have to do something!"

I thought for several seconds and said, "The areas north and west of the campus are the only ones truly safe from floods. The roads up there are open so tomorrow, when Russell is awake, let's drive around those areas and see if we can find any possibilities."

Carol breathed a long sigh of relief and said, "We have to try!"

We discovered lots of people were out looking for housing in those areas, but nothing was available, so I said, "Let's drive west on highway 24 and see if there might be something within commuting distance."

About two miles from the corner of campus we found an area with trees, meadows and a small stream, and a sign beside a farm house that said **"Building Lot for Sale"**. We looked at each other and, without saying a word, turned into the driveway to investigate. If we couldn't find an apartment, maybe we could build a house. We met the owners, Mr. and Mrs. Beard, who were in their early 60s. They were down-to-earth really nice people. She was a warm-hearted, grandmotherly type. He was a six-foot, muscular man with a pot belly and skin well-baked by the sun. They had a small farm and were thinking of subdividing some of it for houses.

Like a lot of farmers, he was a good craftsman and builder. Their plan was for him to build the houses for people who bought lots. They had decided to try out the idea by selling an acre on HIghway 24 between their home and the woods and stream owned by another farmer. It was a lovely piece of land, with a huge old walnut tree at the front-center of it. The back part was flat, rich soil for a great garden, flanked by a few blooming bushes and mature trees.

We hit it off right away. He reminded me of my father; Mrs. Beard and Carol quickly became friends. She treated Carol like a good grandma should. The place fit Carol's love of Mother Nature perfectly. By the time we left we had a deal, assuming we could get financing.

That evening after dinner we talked while Carol sketched out a floor plan, "Don, I've been thinking about what's happened to us since we got married. You had trouble finding a job as we prepared for marriage, and at the last minute K-State give you a good job. We couldn't find an apartment and suddenly a TKE brother decided to leave town and privately arranged with his landlord for us to have his apartment one week before we became newlyweds. Later, we looked and looked without success for a larger apartment to fit what we hoped would be a larger family and were pretty discouraged. Just before the fall semester began, one of your secretaries told us she and her husband were leaving their very nice apartment, and got the landlady to rent it to us before it was advertised. Then, when finding housing after the flood seemed hopeless, we drove into a stranger's yard and drove away with plans to build a house. All that good luck can't be by chance. The good Lord must be looking after us."

Carol sketched a rectangular one story house with a kitchen, a large open area containing both living and dining room, three bedrooms and a bath, with a big picture window facing south towards that beautiful walnut tree. Carol was particularly excited about the picture window because, as she said, "That will bring the beautiful outdoors indoors to us every day."

The next day I gave her sketch to Beard so he could prepare formal plans. Then I searched for a mortgage. We had accumulated sizeable savings produced by Carol's frugality and role as our family finance officer. All lenders turned me down because they were either still recovering from the flood themselves, or were focusing all their lending on businesses and homeowners recovering from the flood. Two days later I went back to Manhattan Federal Savings and Loan, who had just reopened, and they approved our loan. Carol jubilantly wrote her parents: "Whoopee!! Our loan and building plan have been approved, thanks to you for helping us with the down payment. Mr. Beard and Don are down there right now completing the final contract. We'll sign it, and tomorrow Mr. Beard will start to work.

This is our agreement designed to save us money. He'll do all the building, and install the utilities. Don and I (and friends who have volunteered to help) will do the interior finish (under Beard's supervision and teaching) and help with the outside finish work. It's amazing. Just three weeks after the flood we're building our new home!!"

One morning, I heard Carol telling Lindsay, one of the upstairs renters, about our activities with the new house. "Don works on the house almost every night and weekend, when he isn't helping me. He, Earl and Ted have built a culvert and drive so we can cross the ditch from the highway to our building site. Don will help Beard pour cement footers this weekend. He couldn't work Sunday afternoon because we continue to have a flood of visitors viewing flood damage. Sunday morning the Fords came – Mom and Dad, Lois and Jerome, and Verla and her baby Roger. Don came home at noon so we could have a picnic together. They left and here came Mary Lou and Paul. They'd been looking all over for us. We fed them ice cream and cake, a friend came to drive back to Topeka with them, and then here came Ginny and Earl. All I had left to serve them was lemonade and cookies. They finally left, and we wilted."

After hearing about our crowded agenda, Lindsay said, "If it would help you, I can baby sit sometimes so you can go out to help Don with the house." Carol gave her a thank you hug.

A month later, after working on our house all day, I came home to a delicious dinner of roast beef, fried potatoes and onions, green beans and carrots. Russell sat at the table in his new metal high chair to eat dinner. Carol said, "Russell loves to sit in his new chair and pound on the tray. He looks like a pompous old man, pounding on a table yelling 'Service – I want service!' He's on three meals a day so it's a lot easier to feed him in the chair. How's the house coming?"

"Great. All the cement work is completed and he's nearly finished with the framing. Right now there's nothing we can do, but the framing will be done and he may have the roof on by next weekend, so the house will be completely enclosed. Then we could start doing our inside work. This weekend I plan to work at home on that old desk."

The old country school near the Clark farm had been closed for good so they auctioned off the contents. Carol's mother bought two things for us. The first was the teacher's bell. It was fairly large and attached to a wooden handle. When the kids were outside and the teacher wanted them, she'd ring her bell and they came running. It had a loud musical ring to it. (Later when our kids were small Carol used that bell to call them in from wherever they were playing.)

The second thing was a teacher's desk. I didn't want the desk, but as Carol often did in life, she saw beauty where others didn't. She said, "That's a beautiful piece of wood that represents the special history of country schools. We need a coffee table for our new house. Could we make one out of that?" We'd successfully accomplished many tasks we'd never done before, so agreed we could make a coffee table out of a school desk.

I cleaned and sanded the wood smooth. Carol raved about the finished product, "Isn't the golden color and grain of that old seasoned oak gorgeous! Will the legs look like that?"

"Yes," I said, "here they are." I'd created four legs from the sides of the desk. I assembled our new coffee table, she sealed it with a clear finish, and then we stood back to survey our accomplishment.

Carol laughed "It's splendiferous!"

The fall semester started. I told Carol, "I like my counseling work, and most of my nights are free so we can work on our house, which I like very much. My only other work is another building project – helping to plan the permanent student union. The architect told us there isn't enough money to build everything we want. So we divided what we want into two lists: (1) Everything we want right away; and (2) Things that could be delayed. We asked the architect to design a three-story building, putting as much as possible of what we want in the first two floors, leaving the top floor unfinished, significantly reducing building costs. The director of the Wisconsin Union told us that in his experience, once that unfinished space exists, the college will find money to finish it within two years, so that's our final plan."

We'd been working like mad to finish painting the house exterior. Carol described our work to her parents: "I finally got all the windows painted so they're ready to set in. Recent evenings have been so beautiful that we've worked until 11 o'clock. Russell loves to go out there. We put him to sleep in his car bed and he's been very good. Wednesday evening just Don and I painted under the roof overhang along the front of the house. Then last evening Ted and Lorraine came along and Lorraine and I painted under the roof overhang on the back side of the house while Don and Ted shingled. I took out a picnic lunch for us to save time. We worked until near dark, ate, and then hooked up flood lights and finished our work.

As we were driving home Don said, 'I think you may be working too hard; perhaps you should slow down.' I asked him why he thought that and he said, 'Because your hair is turning white!' I discovered I had white paint in my hair, so bonked him for his joke, and went to the beauty parlor the next day. It's surprising how a trip to the beauty parlor lifts one's morale."

We didn't work at the new house for a couple of days to give Carol time away from those labors. The first thing she did was go shopping for Russell. Over a dinner of fried chicken, mashed potatoes, and a salad, Carol brought me up to date, "I decided it was time for Russell's first pair of shoes, so we went shopping. The shoe store got his fit and showed us some shoes. The cheapest pair was $5. I refused to pay that much for shoes he would probably only wear for three months. So we went to the dime store and got him a pair of Wee Walkers for $2. I got a size larger than his foot measurement to make them last longer. He has the longest foot I ever saw on a baby! When I put shoes on him I had to laugh – they looked like clown shoes.

Last night, Betty had a farewell party for Karen who's leaving for Chicago. I had a lot of fun gabbing with the girls. I hadn't been to a girl party for a long time, and I really enjoyed it."

"What did you gab about?"

"Mostly babies. There'll be a lot of baby gifts this fall – there's Wilma, Lois, Tutt, Betty, Karen, Ginny and Monna Lee. The baby epidemic continues."

We resumed labor on our house and had nearly finished sheet rocking the ceiling and walls. Carol's parents got a laugh out of her description of the work. "As the boys put sheet rock on the ceiling, I laid the insulation bats on top of it. You should see me swinging from the rafters and walking on narrow 2 by 4s. At first it was kinda scary, but I'm used to it now. But then I discovered it was all upside down, so I had to crawl in the attic and turn it all over. The boys and Lorraine didn't tease me…much. I'm sure doing a lot of things I never thought I could do and probably will do lots more before we're done. It's fun, though, to work on a place of our own."

Work progressed quickly, once we started the interior finish work. One evening while I hung kitchen cabinets, Carol sat cross legged on the floor to write to her parents: "Russell has learned how to scoot around in his new walker-stroller. He was so funny this past week. We were finishing laying our beautiful oak floor. We put down a strip of tongue and groove flooring, wedged it tight in place so no open seam existed, and then drove nails into the edge to hold it tight in place. So, there was a lot of hammering accompanied by an occasional 'OUCH!' or 'DAMN!' Russell was in his walker-stroller scooting around behind us. He was curious about the hammering, so scooted up behind me and watched me work. I pushed him back and he just scooted up under our nose again. I think he thought it was a game; push away–come back, push away–come back. Finally, I gave up. He watched for the longest time.

We put his snowsuit on him on cold evenings and if he doesn't look cute in it! Last weekend we sanded and sealed the floor. It looks fantastic! I'm so pleased. All our appliances are in, so when Don finishes the kitchen we can move into our new home."

On day I found Carol frazzled and stressed out. I asked, "What's wrong, Honey?"

"Russell's what's been wrong all day! His smallpox shot finally took, he has a cold, his teeth may be bothering him, and he keeps yanking on my skirt, crying and complaining, trying to get me to hold and cuddle him."

I said, "I've been watching him while we talk. He keeps making funny faces, rubbing his jaws, and chewing hard on his fist."

Carol stuck her finger in his mouth and yelled, "YIPPEE!! He's got a tooth! You can feel the little rough edge just as plain as can be – it's a lower tooth and the one right beside it is almost through too. Golly, I was beginning to think there was no hope for him."

Friends and co-workers helped us move into our new but not quite finished house. That evening we cuddled on pillows with snacks and martinis in front of us on the new school desk turned coffee table, and looked out our picture window at the big walnut tree. Carol said, "Four and a half months ago our home was surrounded by flood water, I was scared, and thought our future looked pretty bleak. Now, here we are in a wonderful new home, much of which we built ourselves, in a lovely rural setting, enjoying Mother Nature's beauty. It's too incredible to believe. I'm so proud of us! I'm only 24 years old and have my own new house. I'm beginning to think there's nothing the two of us can't accomplish together. We make one hell of a team!"

So many people had helped us, we decided to thank them with the first big party in our new home. Afterwards, Carol described it to her parents: "We invited friends who were in town, the Counseling Bureau staff, and the new head of the Psychology department so everyone could meet him. Remember, I told you that our friends Vic Beneventi and Mary Taylor got engaged, so we decided to celebrate that also. I prepared a buffet dinner and baked an angel food cake (with Mrs. Beard's help). I made a couple of little dolls out of pipe cleaners, marshmallows and scraps of material to represent Vic and Mary. I sat them on the cake in a loving position and put a sign on a toothpick pointing toward the hole in the middle of the cake saying 'Fatal Step Gulch'. I hid the cake, then after dinner was over and guests were relaxing in the living room I brought it out for dessert. They got a big kick out of it."

We'd been to so many parties with academics that bored us to death – and probably bored the academics as well – because all they did was sit around and talk, talk and sometimes brag. So we decided that in our future parties we'd try replacing talk-talk with interesting activities. For our first venture, Carol created a try-out-that-idea party. She explained it to our first guinea pigs: "Here's a blank sheet of paper fastened to a board for each of you, along with a brush and some water colors. While I play music on our record player, we want each of you to paint a picture of what you imagine or feel as you listen to the music."

After about half an hour the music ended and Carol announced, "Don will hold up each painting and asked that 'artist' to explain what their painting expressed." Bob Wilson had secretly recorded the discussions, and later played them back to us. That gave the crowd plenty of laughs. They must have had fun because they stayed until 12:30 a.m.

We still had some interior details to finish. One was wallpapering the bedrooms and bathroom. My mother had decades of wall papering experience and was so good other people sought her to paper their houses. As a little kid, I'd helped her and learned a little, but our screw up when Earl and I papered his mother's living room upside down demonstrated I needed help. Carol called my mother, "Mom, your son is standing here, trembling with fear, as he faces wall papering some of our rooms. He's whining, 'I need my Momma!' Could you come visit and teach stupid us how to do it?"

She laughed, delighted we asked her help, and said, "Sure, if you feed me good." The first day, we got the ceiling and the east wall, kitchen and hallway papered. Mom taught us a lot. We hung most of it under her supervision. We were proud because it looked perfect. The next morning Mom hung the bedroom ceilings for us, with our help. We laughed because she could do in three hours what would take us two days to do. Over lunch, she handed us a piece of paper that said, "This Certifies That You Have Successfully Passed All Tests and Are Certified as Graduates of The Esther Clara Sophia Sanow Ford Professional School of Paper Hanging." We laughed, hugged her with gratitude and affection, and she went back to Marysville.

Frugal Carol had found a used chair and sofa she bought real cheap for our new living room, so we loaded Russell in the car and went to get it. He had a cold and cough. On the way home he cried hard continuously. Carol said "I feel so bad because I can't seem to sooth Russ."

I suggested, "You have a lovely voice – why don't you sing to him. It works for me when you sing me love songs." So Carol held him close and sang to him in a gentle voice, Russell stopped crying immediately, looked at Carol and smiled before drifting off to sleep.

Carol said, "I've told you music is my therapy. It looks like it works for Russ too."

Carol continuously astonished me with her ability to transform ugly junk into a thing of beauty. And when doing something like that, she seemed fearless. She took that old, beat up sofa and chair apart, retied all the springs to provide a stable comfortable base for the seats, reassembled them, bought some beautiful material, designed and made slip covers for the sofa and chair, and like magic we had a lovely sofa and chair set that visitors regularly admired. I wouldn't have known where to begin. I asked, "Have you ever done anything like this before?"

"No," she said, "but I've made a lot of clothing for myself, and figured if I could make something to fit me I could make something to fit a sofa." I roared with laughter at her reasoning.

When Carol had momentum in tasks requiring her artistic and creative instincts, she just kept going. She selected materials and made draperies and curtains for all the windows in the house, then reupholstered our old dining table chairs. It wore me out watching her.

One day when I came home about four o'clock I found Carol lying on our sofa with a damp small cloth over her eyes. I said, "What's wrong honey?"

"About two hours ago, after I put Russell down for his nap, I suddenly felt light headed, had blurred vision and bright flashes of light followed by a throbbing headache on the right side. I lay down here with this cloth over my eyes and it's easing up now."

"You continue to lie here with your eyes closed. I'll take care of Russ while you rest."

After two more hours Carol sat up and said "I feel a lot better now. The headache and other symptoms are nearly gone. That was a new experience and it scared me a little."

"Do you feel like eating?"

"Yes."

"You sit here with Russell and I'll get supper."

Later when we went to bed she felt normal and had a good sleep that night. The next day our doctor examined her and said Carol was very healthy. He told us the symptoms sounded like a migraine headache. They often begin to appear in early adulthood. Throughout the rest of Carol's life she occasionally had similar attacks but the headaches became more severe.

That evening Carol felt fine and told me with delight, "At our party Saturday for your Counseling Bureau colleagues two of the wives said to me, 'Our husbands make twice as much money as Don, and yet you guys have a large new home, beautifully decorated, while we have trouble making ends meet. How do you do it?' I laughed and told them, 'We don't eat fancy, wear old clothes, and use our imagination, skills, and hard work to make old stuff look like new, and enjoy doing it together.' They said, 'We need to take lessons from you!'" At age 24 Carol was already becoming an admired role model for other women.

One snowy evening I asked Carol to join me on our beautiful new sofa with a glass of wine for a serious discussion. I opened the discussion with, "My colleagues and I are disillusioned with the direction things are heading with the new President and Dean of Students. We've emphasized improving the quality of life for students, particularly veterans, and on using student activities to cultivate social, problem solving and leadership knowledge and skills. What we worked so hard to build is rapidly eroding. Several are thinking of leaving. Bob and Julie Wilson have already made arrangements. We succeeded here beyond my expectations when we married, but I'm not sure I can develop the kind of career I want in this current environment."

Carol nodded, "I've hear about these problems during get-togethers with the wives of our Counseling Bureau friends. They say Milton Eisenhower and Dr. Woolf were a student-oriented and the new guys aren't. You've worked hard to make K-State a better place for students."

"Thinking of leaving would have been easier last year, but we've just begun to enjoy our new home and I find it hard to think of leaving it." I expected Carol to express strong emotions at thoughts of leaving, but as she often did in our lives, she surprised me.

"Remember in our courting years how strongly we felt about wanting to be an US rather than a ME or a YOU? I feel even more strongly about that, now that we've been married four years. If you're not happy, *I'm* not happy and I know the same is true for you. My satisfaction doesn't lie in material things unless they feed our joy and love in being a family. I feel even more strongly about that now that we have Russ. So, if you think it's time to find a new path for our lives, I say let's do it! Let's think of it as an adventure, full of new, interesting things to see and do. It'll be fun to learn what the world is like outside the state of Kansas."

I felt great relief that night as I squeezed Carol in a happy bear hug. I whispered, "Thank you for helping clear away the fog obscuring our future." People saw the charming, talented but quiet Carol, but few discovered the clear values and wisdom beneath that persona.

We did not anticipate the family storm that resulted among Carol's relatives. Married cousin Charlotte and Carol had been friends for years. In a visit after making our decision, Charlotte asked Carol about possible activities next year. Without thinking, Carol said we'd be leaving before then. Charlotte passed the word to her mother that Don was being 'let go' by K-State. That juicy gossip spread like wildfire through the clan in Minneapolis. Winifred had bragged a lot about us there, and I had once spoken in Minneapolis about UNESCO at a public meeting, so we were sort of family 'celebrities', making the gossip even juicier. Winifred 'blew her stack' to Carol because she was the last to know I was 'being let go'. She wrote a diatribe about our failure to inform her and finished with: "I know you two may think this is pretty asinine, but it's different for us. Minneapolis is our home and it's full of friends and relatives."

That exchange was 'the straw that broke the camel's back' for Carol. Since our marriage, Winifred had persisted in 'advising' Carol how she should do or manage everything, including how to properly care for Russell. This latest turmoil, where Winifred treated Carol like she was incompetent and devious, angered and upset my normally mild mannered wife! She swallowed it, however, because she realized her mother had psychological problems.

Carol knew her own temper and tolerance limits, so asked me to intervene, "Don, I'm so mad I can't talk to Mom right now.

Would you write an explanation to my parents? Coming from you, that will end Mom's fussing, plus Dad won't condone any further fuss from her."

I drafted the letter and gave it to Carol for approval. Carol added her own post script: "I hope Don's facts clear up this tempest in a teapot. I want to clear up a couple of other things. I don't like being made to feel I'm incompetent and untruthful. I'm disappointed you thought I was hiding something from you. We certainly weren't avoiding the subject Sunday. You can raise any subject with us you want. We believe in being honest with each other and our families. I love you and Daddy dearly and do my best to show it, and to earn your love and respect."

The discussion ended with this heart breaking note from Winifred: "I feel so tied down here at times that I want to start screaming. I like people and want to be where they are occasionally, so at times I feel so thwarted. Guess I'm not the 'martyr' type. When you guys leave I'll scream like hell, yet I'll want you to go for your sakes. I'm a mess!! But I love you so. Mother."

Chapter Nine
Beginning a New Adventure

After celebrating our son's first birthday, Carol wrote: "Dear Mom and Dad. To Russell, his birthday was just another day, but his mama and daddy had fun celebrating the miracle that happened to us a year ago. How we do love our little boy – sometimes my heart is so full of love for my wonderful husband and son, I could just pop! Don and I have such a perfect love and understanding for each other that makes us completely happy as long as we can be together. Whenever I look for someone to thank for my happiness I always look to you. You made me what I am today – a very happy person. I love you very much!"

Spring would begin to spring soon, so Carol and I made our 'to do list':

1. Decide where to go for my PhD, and get admitted there with financial aid.
2. Sell our house.
3. New transportation (our old Olds isn't safe for taking our baby to his new home.)
4. Once we know where we're going, find out about housing.
5. Have fun while we still live here.
6. Finish Don's job at K-State.

We agreed that I would tackle 1, 3, 5 and 6 while Carol focused on 2 and 5. #4 could be put on hold for the time being. We went to work on our immediate goals.

Goal #1 I had a general idea about my graduate study. I wanted to focus on ways of helping people develop in positive ways and succeed in pursuing what they wanted out of life. While that included helping them solve life problems along the way, I didn't want to specialize on psychopathology. I was convinced of two things: First, current theory and practice in counseling and psychotherapy lagged behind advancing scientific knowledge about humans. I wanted a program on the cutting edge of scientific advances and sound theory-based approaches. Second, human behavior is largely the result of what people learn, so I wanted a program on the cutting edge of learning theory. After extensive research I selected the University of Minnesota; The Pennsylvania State University; and Oklahoma State University. I contacted people to serve as references and applied to all three.

Goal #2 Carol contacted friends to glean information about reputations of local realtors. She talked with finance faculty in the College of Agriculture to get their ideas. They outlined the good and bad practices to look for. I sought opinions from the V.P. for finance in the President's office. Carol selected two realtors and interviewed them in their offices. She thought both looked OK, but particularly liked the personal style of one. We invited both to look at our house and give us their views so we could size them up. They thought we'd have many potential buyers because it was new, very nice, and a beautiful site. They estimated it would sell between $15,500 and $16,500. I concurred with Carol's choice. She listed with her, and we waited for potential buyers. Carol said "Their estimated sale is twice what we have invested in it. I can't believe it!! If we get that much we can buy a new car and have a lot left over for future use."

Goal #3 Neither of us knew much about automobiles. I talked with faculty on campus and business leaders I knew. Most recommended the new Ford sedan, because of its mechanical excellence but also because it had introduced a new body style created from research about the effects of air flow over the car body. We looked at it and took a sample drive. Carol loved it, we ordered one, and the dealer said he'd have it for us in three weeks.

Goal #4 We enjoyed being outside gardening. Carol agreed to pick out vegetable and flower seeds and I started thinking about landscaping to enhance the appearance of our house.

Friends often dropped in to visit and sometimes eat with us, so I suggested to Carol, "We have a big lawn and it would take a long time for us to get it all planted. How about having a 'lawn planting party'? We could invite our old college and 'slumber party' friends and our friends from the Counseling Bureau. They could bring their kids and their rakes if they want to. With that many people we could get it done in a day."

Carol said, "That could be fun! In the evening we could have a wiener roast picnic in the area at the back of our lot, with sticks for everyone to roast their wieners and marshmallows over the fire, potato salad, baked beans, lemonade and cookies. I'll bet the kids would love it."

Carol did the inviting and I had the ground rototilled in preparation for planting. On a beautiful spring day they all showed up, including a bunch of kids. We set up teams. One raked the ground and got it ready for planting. A second cleared rocks and planted the grass. The third, composed largely of kids who were old enough, covered the seeds with straw. Even little ones thought that was fun. Teams one and two periodically exchanged duties because raking was the hardest work. Our rambunctious crew worked hard at their labors, accompanied by mischievous teasing and joking. Carol maintained a supply of lemonade for thirsty people.

One of the gals came for a drink and took Carol aside, "Carol, are you pregnant again?"

That took Carol by surprise, "My goodness, why do you ask me that?"

"Someone saw you at your doctor's office the other day, and assumed that probably meant you were pregnant. If people see young women like us at the doctor these days with all the ex-GIs back, they automatically assume it means we're pregnant."

Carol burst out laughing and said, "I was just there for a physical checkup, but I know so many pregnant women I can understand why people might jump to that conclusion."

Our labor force finished the lawn near dusk and everyone was starving. Carol and I carried out the food, gave everyone a stick for wiener and marshmallow roasting, and the mad dash to eat began. When everyone finished eating only two wieners and a spoonful of baked beans remained. As we all lounged around on blankets, tired and full, Carol impulsively started singing. One by one, our friend's voices joined Carol's in the moonlight. The sound of those blended voices was beautiful, like the friendships they represented.

When we crawled into bed that night, Carol said wistfully, "Wasn't that wonderful! It won't be long before we probably won't see most of those nice people ever again."

I hugged her close, knowing how she felt. "That will be a loss that hurts won't it."

Potential buyers started coming by and hopes of selling our property went up and down. We checked about our car and the dealer said it hadn't come in yet. Each hitch discouraged us.

I got an offer of admission to Penn State with a graduate assistantship paying $122 a month for twelve months, plus tuition and other fees. We had hoped for a little more. An offer came from Minnesota with a graduate assistantship about the same. Oklahoma also sent an offer with no aid. Gilbert Wrenn, a famous psychologist at Minnesota, recruited me aggressively.

It was decision time. We sat on Carol's beautiful sofa, with cocktails and snacks on our 'school marm' coffee table, and discussed this important decision. I said, "Carol, assuming that academically all the programs are equal, in which part of the country would you rather live?"

Without hesitation, she said, "Pennsylvania. I loved the east when we were there with Hardy and Ann. Not only was it beautiful in the mountains and on the sea shore, but also there's so much to see and do. We'd be close to New York City with all of its music, art, theater and other activities. Philadelphia is nearby, and historic New England where some of my ancestors are buried is in easy driving distance, and the ocean is only about 200 miles away."

I said, "Then that's where we'll go! I think their PhD program is by far the best for my purposes, with the added bonus that Milton Eisenhower is there."

We hugged, laughing like two kids on Christmas morning, then Carol raised her glass and shouted, "HERE WE COME, PENNSYLVANIA!!"

The decision was made, but several weeks of hard work lay ahead of us. I said, "I have to start at Penn State September 1st, so let's plan to leave here about August 15th so we can make it a sightseeing vacation trip on the way." We immediately wrote our parents of the decision.

That weekend we visited Marysville. My dad, who was well known and respected by area farmers, put an ad in the paper for a trailer we could use to move our stuff. Dad said, "Even before the ad came out, I got a call about a trailer that sounded good. It was built by a farmer's son as a high school project. It's well built, in good shape, and has extra strong springs, big enough to carry everything you want to take east with you." We bought it for $37.50.

We checked on our car and were again told it wasn't in yet. I decided we were getting the run around from the dealer because he had more buyers than cars. I got mad because time was running out, so in desperation I wrote a heart rending letter to the President of Ford Motor Company. I told him of our little baby whose life we couldn't jeopardize using our old beat up Olds, of the urgency of getting to Penn State or I'd lose my financial support, and asked for his help as a fellow member of the Ford clan. I mailed it special delivery so I'd know when he received it. Five days later I got a call from our dealer, "I don't know how the hell you did it, but I got orders to give you a car immediately and have one here for you. Come and get it."

Carol wrote her parents the good news: "We heard from the Ford Motor Company in Detroit and I nearly dropped over as I didn't think they'd pay a bit of attention to Don's letter. They instructed their Kansas City distributor to get us a car immediately. I'm astonished!! I'm learning never to underestimate my lovin' hubby's ability to get things done. Our new Ford is a pretty light green, four door sedan with a large trunk. The radio has beautiful sound and the heater could keep a car twice that size warm. All we have left to do is sell our house."

Two days later a man from Salina showed up and bought our house! It turned out that our old friend Kenny Rowland, who had visited us in our new house with his wife, had told a friend of his how great it was. That's why he came and bought it. Only goal four was left. We decided to wait until we reached Pennsylvania to explore the housing situation.

That night we celebrated again by sitting together on Carol's beautiful sofa, perhaps for the last time, with martinis and delicious cheese spread on small crackers served on our school teacher coffee table. Looking out the picture window at our beautiful tree, we toasted our success. I said, "Many of the friends we've shared life with here are like us, going to a new place to start a new life: the Berry's to Maine; the Volsky's to Minnesota, and the Wilsons to Hawaii. While we cherish old friendships, we now have the opportunity to make new ones."

Carol said, "Once again our big problems have been solved at the last minute, strengthening my belief that someone up there is looking after us. I don't believe in the Bible verbatim, but I do believe many of Christ's teachings and his basic philosophy makes sense. The preachers who stand pounding on their pulpit, shouting that we must do what the Bible says or we'll be punished, aren't talking about *my* God. My God is a good God, not a vindictive one. I think it's wrong to lay the responsibility for our lives on God. We must accept responsibility for our own behavior and changing ourselves for the better. I do think that belief in God can give people the courage and will to fight for happiness and learn to accept things that must be. Right now I'm so happy sharing life with you and Russell that I have no need to question much. I'm truly excited about the life we'll build together in Pennsylvania. What an adventure we face!"

We packed the trailer with everything we wanted to take with us and sold or gave away the rest. Finally, we covered our earthly possessions with a heavy tarp and anchored it firmly with ropes. The last remaining act was saying our goodbyes. Carol called friends and I went to campus to say goodbye to colleagues. I especially wanted to say goodbye to Vice President Al Pugsley and thank him for the wonderful letters he'd written supporting my applications.

We visited Marysville to bid fond farewells to that part of our life and returned to Manhattan the next morning. After hitching the trailer to our new car we headed for the Clark farm. Our lives had involved Manhattan for eight wonderful years, so we left with lots of happy memories and hearts tinged with sadness. We spent a day and night with Carol's parents, thanking them for everything they'd done for us. The next morning, after a big breakfast and a travel lunch prepared by Winifred, we all three hugged and kissed them goodbye, promised to try to visit at Christmastime, climbed in our new Ford and headed east. We didn't look back.

We'd arranged the back seat as a combination play pen and bed. Carol wanted to hold Russell as we drove towards Missouri so we all began our trip together, hoping to make our boy feel secure for the long drive. We planned to reach St. Louis by nightfall because our friends, Bob and Alice Pearson, lived there and wanted to show us the sights before we continued east.

We drove quietly for a while, then Carol said, "Don, I've been sitting here thinking about this being the fourth time in my life I've had to leave an old life completely behind and go to a strange town, live in a strange house, and meet strange new people in strange new places. Each time before, I felt frightened and insecure. Two of those moves were terrible experiences. This time I don't feel any of that. I think I've become quite a different person. I believe making this move together will be exciting, fun, and open a bright new future for us. I've modified that old saying when we were kids – '4th time's a charm'!"

Bob and Alice seemed delighted to see us. While Bob and I got updated and discussed his plans for our visit, Alice said, "Carol, bring Russell into the living room to see our TV." Later Carol wrote her parents: "We were astonished how good the TV picture was. Russell was fascinated. When Topeka has a strong signal I hope you'll get one. I'm sure you'll enjoy it."

We spent most of the next day at the Forest Park Zoo. It was free, huge and fantastic. Seeing all the animals excited and delighted Russell. That evening we left our kids with Bob's sister while we went to the outdoor municipal opera in another part of Forest Park. Warm summer air became the perfect backdrop to a divine performance. Carol gushed about the experience, "If I lived here I'd want to see every opera!"

The next day Bob sprung a surprise on Carol, "We know how much you love music and dancing, so tonight we're taking you for a night cruise on a Mississippi luxury ship that's a floating night club." Carol could barely contain her excitement as we dropped the kids off with Bob's sister and headed for the riverboat. She couldn't wait to describe the experience to her parents: "It was a beautiful large riverboat with a dining room and comfortable lounges on the first deck. The second deck was a huge ballroom with tables around the edges so we could look out on the river. We hadn't danced for a long time and never in such luxurious surroundings. On the cruise back, we watched the lights of the city from the top deck as we floated towards port."

The next morning we thanked Alice and Bob profusely for their hospitality and crossed the Missouri border heading east. Carol enjoyed driving so took her turn at the wheel to give me a break. The next day we stopped in Dayton, Ohio for a short visit with the Vogels, who were Clark's neighbors during WWII. Carol had often played with their little girl, Genie. The next day we drove through Wheeling, West Virginia and turned north towards Pennsylvania.

The terrain changed, along with the living conditions. We were both shocked at what we saw. Carol said, "This is *horrible* – everything is so dirty, with thousands of houses jammed together. How can people live that way? We've just entered Pennsylvania and it still looks like that. Why is it so bad? I hope it's not like that where we're going!"

"This region is probably packed with coal, iron and steel industries." I tried to sound convincing while thinking, *If State College looks like this, we won't be able to stay.* "Coal mining is a dirty business as are the furnaces used to make iron and steel. The people living in those places are probably poorly paid. I'm sure most of Pennsylvania won't be like this."

We followed our travel map east away from the Pittsburgh area and then turned north into the mountains. We saw few people and passed through only a couple of small villages as the road wound through pristine forest and mountain vistas. I said to Carol, "According to our AAA instructions we must be almost there." We topped one last mountain and parked in a small roadside rest area. A picturesque valley, surrounded by mountains, lay like a Currier and Ives postcard below us. "There's our new home, Carol. The town in that valley is State College."

Carol was speechless for a moment, taking in the breathtaking mountains and valley, then said, "Don, it's beautiful! Beautiful fields surrounded by tree covered mountains. I can't believe that's where we get to live!" The fatigue, tension and anxiety she'd been holding in broke loose and she started crying with relief. I gave her a moment to collect herself and carried Russell to the edge of the parking area so he could look into the valley. Finally Carol came and put her arms around us and, as a family, we stared in silence for a while at our beautiful new home.

Finally, she said, "It's so pretty!" and Russell mimicked, "Preeety." We laughed in delight at his imitation of Carol while piling into our car, then drove down the mountain to embrace our new adventure. We were all worn out from our travels, and hungry for a sit down meal. We found a motel with cabins and a restaurant. We ate a huge meal and retired to our rented cabin where we slept soundly. The next morning, over a hearty breakfast, locals told us they called this place "Happy Valley." That seemed the ideal name for our new home.

We were there, but didn't know what 'there' was like, so we drove around State College and discovered it was a small town. We went on campus to touch base with my new boss and to get information from Penn State's housing office. My new colleagues received us warmly, and Russell was a big hit. They couldn't give us real estate leads, but we got a list from the housing office and a few options from the local newspaper. Carol described our search to her parents: "We started looking in earnest, and what did we find? – nuttin!! Everything is so high, furnished places are as scarce as hens' teeth. Some were horrible. To save money we decided to stay that night in a tourist home. We found a lovely one and the people who ran it were wonderful to us. When we told them our housing problem they started calling everyone they knew but didn't have any luck. They referred us to a recently widowed lady a few houses away to see if she could help us. She really took us under her wing. We rented a room with her for the night while she checked all her sources with no luck. She sympathized with our financial problems. She had a little trailer in the country they used for camping purposes when they wanted to get-away, but was unused since her husband's recent death. She rented it to us for a week for $5.

What we're doing is camping out in the mountains and if I weren't so anxious to get settled I'd really enjoy it. We have a hot plate, ice box, and a comfortable bed but no running water or john. I remember your parent's houses where every bedroom had a container under the bed to be used during the night and emptied in the morning. There's a wooded gully next to us where such stuff can be disposed of. It's bedtime for 3 Kansas campers. Good night."

Several days later our luck changed, as Carol told her parents: "After 3 days of looking, finding nothing, and getting more and more desperate, we began to ask everyone we met if they knew of any apartment for rent. Well, on Wednesday p.m. we went to get some groceries and found all the stores in State College are closed every Wednesday afternoon (a dumb custom). So, we headed for Lemont, a small historic village 3 miles east of State College. John Boal's little corner grocery store was open so we went in to get our groceries. Then, as we'd been doing everywhere, we asked if he knew of any apartments. He said, 'Matter of fact I have two. I just bought an old brick two story house just two blocks from here. I'm redecorating an apartment on each floor. Don, do you know how to stoke a coal furnace?' Don said, 'That's what I grew up with.' Boal said, 'You're the kind of guy I need as a renter.' He jumped into our car, and took us to see his apartments."

When we pulled up in front of the house, Carol said, "The first floor would be best with our baby." The big red brick house sat on a large lot similar to the one we rented in Manhattan. Its location was perfect, at the base of a mountain called Mt. Nittany. We admired the large porch and front door. Like most old homes, the house sat at the front of the lot so the land behind it could be used for other purposes.

John said, "We don't want the upstairs renters to use the front entrance because it would interrupt the privacy of the down stairs renters. Everyone will use the back entry stairs we've created." So, we parked at the rear entrance.

Carol gave the exterior a swift once over, "Look, the entire yard is enclosed with an attractive iron fence. Kids can't get out of that big grassy yard and animals can't get in. Wouldn't that be a wonderful safe place for Russell to play! And see that big garden spot between the house and barn? That could save us money on our food bill."

Carol's eyes lit up as we entered the back door into a spacious kitchen and dining area. This house had been built in the era when kitchens were the heart of a home. She approved of the large sink and built-in cabinets, and smiled to see a half bath off the kitchen. The attached enclosed porch would make an ideal laundry room. A short hallway off the kitchen led to a sizeable entry hall and front door. "That area could be made into a nice little bedroom for Russell." Carol said. Through another door we discovered a room bright with light from big bay windows and an exit to a side porch.

From the doorway to that room I pointed to the left corner and said, "Carol, there's the perfect place for your piano!"

She smiled, imagining a piano standing there, "There must be a good used piano around here someplace!"

From there we passed into an even larger room that must have been the original owner's front parlor. Large floor to ceiling windows opened onto a front porch and side porch and another door connected this room to the entry hall. Carol was hooked by everything she'd seen, "What a lovely big bedroom this would make! All it needs is closet space and a bed."

John took us down to the furnace room, where I fiddled around with the furnace a little and made small talk until he could see I did, indeed, know how to stoke a furnace. Back upstairs we asked about bathing and he said he planned to put in a shower. The apartment had steam heat and was unfurnished but we were pros at furnishing our homes with used stuff so felt confident we could handle that. The other limitation was that only the kitchen and entry hall had ceiling lights. The other rooms would need electric lamps.

He offered to rent the property to us for $50 a month, all utilities paid if I'd tend the furnace. Carol nodded her approval so we made the deal and asked when we could move in. John said, "It'll take me 3-4 days to finish the redecorating, but you can move stuff in any time."

That evening, relaxing on a blanket beside our temporary trailer home, looking at the beauty around us, I pointed across the valley to Mt. Nittany and said, "Carol, that guardian angel you keep talking about has done it again! In my wildest dreams I never imagined we'd find a place to live so perfect for our purposes, and yet so cheap. There in Lemont is our first Pennsylvania home. Now, building our new life begins!"

She rolled over and snuggled into my arms with a kiss, *"I'm ready!"*

"Right now we're strangers in a new land. No one here knows us except Milton Eisenhower so it's truly a new beginning for us. We don't know yet what life will be like here, but it'll be built on the same foundation of love and trust we've created together. I think a part of our new lifestyle should be aimed at protecting and continuing that foundation. During our courtship and married life in Kansas, one special part was the fun and happiness we experienced in the many dances we shared. But, some were very special – ones like the Alpha Xi Christmas Ball and the TKE Sweetheart Ball – where you tried to please me by dressing in a beautiful gown and I tried to make you feel beautiful and desirable to create a special experience for one night.

In our life here, I'd like to create a new tradition – one where we dress up for a special night of fun as a couple and share our intimate thoughts and feelings about each other. We can discuss our hopes, plans and future goals and call such evenings a date. When either of us wants such a night, we can ask the other for a date. What do you think?"

Carol took my both my hands in hers. I could see her eyes glimmering in the darkness. "What a marvelous idea! I never doubt that you love me, but there are times when I crave that special closeness, like when we drove down that moonlit road in Kansas on our first Christmas morning together. Our dates here need to recreate the closeness we felt that early Christmas morning. Here's a kiss to seal the deal." She took my head in her hands and kissed my eyelids, then pressed a lingering kiss to my mouth while Mother Nature and a sky full of stars watched.

Chapter Ten
Settling Into Our First Happy Valley Home

We woke up to a sunny but pleasant August morning, noting how different August felt in the mountains as compared to Kansas. I suggested we drive to the campus after breakfast. "I'll ask my boss for a couple days off so we can unload the trailer into our new home. Then we can park it until we need it again. Would you mind waiting in the car with Russell while I do that?"

"Sounds good to me." she said. "I'm eager to get everything unloaded and see whether anything is broken." I parked on College Avenue where the view overlooked a low stone wall, across a manicured expanse of lawn to Old Main, campus headquarters. Wide sidewalks framed Old Main, running from College Avenue into the middle of campus, with academic buildings on the other side. Massive, old growth elm trees shaded both walkways. "This is much prettier than K-State! Aren't those rows of trees marching up the hill magnificent!" Carol got Russell out of the car to look around. "We'll wait for you here on this stone wall."

I went to The Division of Intermediate Registration (DIR) and told my new colleagues about our home. Their response as a group was wishing they could find something that nice. The boss gave me a week off to move and get settled. I went to give Carol the good news and saw two girls waving at her as they walked away. I said, "How did you hook up with them?"

"I was holding Russell's hand so he could walk on the wall and as they approached, Russ grinned and said 'Hi'. They said Hi back and Russ said 'Preeety'. They thought he was just adorable and said, 'Is this cutie your little boy?' I told them yes, that we were waiting for his daddy. They're freshmen and had nothing but high praise for Penn State."

"Carol, you amaze me! I remember when your mother worried about how shy you were. Now you walk onto a strange campus where no one knows us and immediately start connecting with other women. I saw that happen when you met the DIR secretaries."

Carol smiled, "Aw shucks, 'taint nothin! It's Russell, our little good will ambassador."

We drove to Lemont and parked our trailer by a gate leading to the back entrance. Carol carried Russell with her to unlock the back door. I was taking the tarp off the trailer when a car drove up and two men got out. One said, "Need a helping hand?" It was two of my new colleagues, Jeff Ashby and Fred Ball. Our boss gave them permission to come help us unload. From that helpful beginning, both men and their wives would become close friends.

Jeff and I were in the same graduate program. He came from Illinois with a new bride, nicknamed Spurge. Fred, a full time counselor, was a veteran who worked in military personnel during the war. His wife, Marge, was a secretary in the Department of Psychology.

I thanked them for their offer to help and reminded Carol who they were. She showed them our new home while I went out to start the unloading process. With three men playing 'fetch and carry' and Carol telling us where to put things, we finished unloading in three hours. Looking around our living room after we finished, I pointed to one corner and said, "Carol loves to play the piano and as soon as we can find a used one we can afford, that's where it goes."

Fred said with a big grin, "I love to play the piano too. How long have you played?"

Carol casually said, "Oh, since I was 5 years old. How about you?"

Fred chuckled, "You must be good!" and told us his story. "When I was a little boy my grandfather was a really good piano player and provided music for burlesque and vaudeville shows in a Scranton PA theater. I used to sneak in to listen to him play, and sometimes watched the girls and comics. I wanted to learn to play, but my folks couldn't afford piano lessons. While serving in

WWII, I read an ad in the enlisted men's service club offering 'learn by mail' piano lessons. I bought the lessons and taught myself to play. It took me three years to learn to play good enough to play for fun, so I've been playing for about 4 years now."

Carol said, "Fred, I can't provide burlesque girls for you, but you can come and play my piano when I get it." That brought a good laugh.

Fred and Jeff returned to work while we ate lunch and planned a search for used appliances and furniture that would put the finishing touches on our new home. It would be two or three weeks before we got the rest of our money from the sale of the house.

I said, "Carol, based on our experience in Manhattan with ways to save money, we decided to put money in savings at the beginning of each month and live on what was left. That worked. I suggest we do that with the remainder of our home sale profits. That money can serve as an emergency fund to cover things like major health care costs if needed. That would mean after furnishing our new home, we'd have to live on what we earn each month."

Carol had already been thinking about our money situation. "If you get me a new typewriter so I can work at home earning money by typing, I think we can do that. Let's give it a try!" We toasted each other with our Cokes while Carol grinned and said, "Look out folks – the frugal Fords are back in business!" We went shopping for used appliances and bought a Frigidaire refrigerator, a Hotpoint stove, and an ABC washer. We couldn't find any decent used furniture so we ordered unfinished furniture from Sears for our kitchen and bedroom. Later we would splurge on some nice living room furniture. We used our trailer to pick up the appliances, and John Boal helped us unload and install them. It had been a long day and we were pooped, so we locked up our new home and returned to the little trailer.

After putting Russell to sleep, we sat outside on a blanket to enjoy the beauty of a starry sky accompanied by Pennsylvania night sounds. Carol said, "I've enjoyed this wonderful day. I met two nice guys who are your new colleagues, plus we got all our possessions unloaded and in our new home. We bought and installed all the appliances and ordered most of the other things we need. Our baby has been terrific. We can move in immediately when John Boal says go. I'm surprised to learn there are so many villages and small towns outside State College. People clearly don't mind commuting to work. Our commute will only be 3 miles."

I said, "There's nothing more we can do while waiting to move in or until our Sears orders arrive, so what would you like to do tomorrow?"

"Let's explore Happy Valley. I'm eager to learn about this place we now call home."

I thought a bit and said, "How about this. In the morning while it's not so hot, let's explore the villages and towns in our valley. Then, let's have a picnic lunch and hike through the meadows along Spring Creek in the afternoon. I think Russell would like that."

After breakfast the next morning, I said, "Bellefonte is the county seat; let's start there."

Carol read from a brochure as we drove down the highway. "Bellefonte has an interesting history. French explorers named it for the beautiful, large spring located there. In its early history, many wealthy industrialists in Pittsburgh and Philadelphia chose to build big, Victorian style summer homes in Bellefonte. Those homes are still there. Collectively, they were a powerful group and started collaborating to use their power politically. For example, when it came time to elect a new governor, they sat together by the big spring, smoking cigars and sipping their whiskey, deciding who should be the next governor and how to get him elected. As a result, many governors of that era were residents of Bellefonte.

President Lincoln's administration passed legislation to establish a new college for the common man in every state, and funded each by giving the states a chunk of federally owned land, so they became known as 'Land Grant Colleges'. The powerful men in Bellefonte decided Pennsylvania's college should be located in Centre County, and that's how The Pennsylvania State College and the town of State College were born."

Our first sight as we entered town was the big spring. Carol said, "That's beautiful with the park they built around it. I love the ducks playing in the water! It must put out a huge amount of water because look at the big stream that originates at the spring."

Past the spring, I turned right, went up a hill and the road dead ended at the county courthouse. Carol said "That's the prettiest county courthouse I've ever seen. It's kinda like a smaller version of the Kansas State Capital." I turned left and within two blocks we entered the section with all the beautiful Victorian homes built a century ago. We were both fascinated and Carol said, "I'd like to look inside these homes some day. Do you suppose that's possible?"

We returned to Lemont and Carol read, "The Village of Lemont, nestled at the foot of Nittany Mountain, started before the college was established because, in addition to agriculture, that area was an early source of iron. A railroad was extended from Bellefonte to Lemont to serve commercial and agricultural interests, and a large bank was established. People coming to the new college could reach Lemont by train and get a buggy ride to the college."

She read silently for a few seconds, and then continued with growing excitement in her voice. I smiled, knowing Carol already loved our new location. "A large mountain stream with trout runs through the middle of the village. The main street runs parallel to Spring Creek, past the front of our house through the middle of the town. One of the churches is across the street from our home, and the branch railroad is a half block behind our barn. Some people still raise farm animals in their back yards. Across the street from our house is 'The Band Hall'. The community band practices there about once a week so, if we wanted to, we could sit on our porch and listen to them practice. My dad would have loved to be part of that when he was young!

The street beside our house goes on up to the base of Mt. Nittany and that's where that mountain ridge ends. They say in winter our road provides great sledding, except that occasionally deer came down off the mountain and bother the sledders. Oh, here's the explanation of the post office being in Boal's store. There are two small grocery stores in town. One belongs to John Boal, a Republican, and the second on the other side of street belongs to a Democrat. The only way to get your mail is to go to the store. The post office is clear in the back to tempt you to buy something as you walk back for your mail. The owner of the store is also the postmaster. If a Republican is president, the post office is in the Republican store; if a Democrat, it moves across the street to the Democrat store. Boy, that is about as local as patronage can get! What a delightful, historic little village!"

I asked, "Isn't there a village named Boalsburg nearby?"

"According to this little chamber of commerce map, Boalsburg is in the valley south of ours. You have to drive south around the base of Mt. Nittany to get there."

We passed a large cemetery, turned into Boalsburg and passed two big brick churches across the road from each other and a large cemetery. I said, "Those churches and the cemetery look like they've been here a long time."

Carol nodded. "The brochure claims this cemetery is where the idea of Memorial Day was created. On the next corner there's a place called *Duffey's Tavern* where stage coach and horseback travelers could stop for refreshments or stay overnight. Boal was a wealthy military man who wanted to own all the land he could see from his porch. Boalsburg was built on his land. Oh, here's something interesting! Boal had ancestral roots in Spain, allegedly linked to Columbus. They brought his private chapel to Boalsburg and it sits near the Boal mansion."

Russell, sitting on mama's lap, said, "*H u n g g y!*", so we drove back to Spring Creek and parked by a meadow. We got out our blanket and lunch, hiked through the meadow to a nice spot by the water, spread our blanket and dug into our food. In Kansas, which once was at the bottom of a big inland sea, the top soil is very deep. As streams form and flow south and east they cut deep trenches. Usually, to get to the water, we had to climb down muddy banks. The banks of mountain streams here ran right up to the edge of the water, weedless and mudless.

After resting, we walked along Spring Creek listening to the sounds of water and birds. Carol said, "Look at Russell – he's having the time of his life running wild in the meadow and along the stream. Whenever he sees the creek he shouts, 'Oh – wattoo!!' Sometimes he throws a stick or pebble in the water. He keeps saying 'fitch', do you know what he's trying to say?"

I replied, "He probably heard us talking about seeing fish in the stream and he's trying to say 'fish.' He's gonna sleep good tonight."

Along both sides of the stream we saw driftwood caught on rocks or scattered along the shore. Where I saw simply bits of broken wood, Carol's creative eye saw treasure. "Let's look for odd shapes of driftwood that we might be able to make lamp bases out of." Soon, she spied one she thought had potential. "Oh look, this piece has lots of curves and projections. It's perfect!" We took it home with us, a bit of Nature's broken beauty.

We decided to take Russell to our trailer for a nap. Along the way we stopped to check with John Boal about progress and he gave us the good news that we could move in tomorrow! All of our stuff was already in the new home, including the unfinished furniture we ordered, so all we had to do was park the car, walk through the door, and arrange the furnishings to suit ourselves. Another banner day for the Pennsylvania Fords!

I looked at the mountain views around us and said, "Carol, we ain't in Kansas anymore!"

The next morning we moved into our new home. Carol wrote her parents: "We've enjoyed 4 delicious nights of sleep on our comfortable mattress. Russell is snug in his own bedroom. In our back yard we have fruit trees, and ripe tomatoes. My Hotpoint stove works like a top. Don offered to peel the apples, so I baked a good apple pie in the oven last night.

We took a shopping trip to Altoona about 40 miles south of State College. It's a big railroad town and has a good array of stores for shopping. We splurged and bought a modern, 2 piece sectional divan with textured brown upholstery. I think it's beautiful and brings our new living room to life. We agreed that would be our birthday and Christmas presents this year. I think our home is ready now for making and entertaining new friends."

Carol tried to write a long letter to her parents at least once a week. One day while Russell was napping, she wrote: "I'll continue answering your last letter (the questionnaire). Until recently, any Penn State student who failed to come up to the grade requirement was automatically flunked out. A distinguished psychologist (and one of Don's new professors) convinced the faculty senate and President that most of those students weren't stupid – they just got off to a bad start which could probably be corrected. Milton funded the creation of the program to test Bernreuter's idea. It's called The Division of Intermediate Registration. (DIR)

Don's assistantship will consist mostly of counseling such students – he has a load of 53 counselees already assigned to him –

not counting what will come in during the year. His job is to try to help the student figure out if they're really incapable of college work, or if there's some problem interfering with their work. The student can enroll in DIR for 2 semesters. Then, if he or she still hasn't brought their grade average up they're expelled from college. If they have, they can transfer to a regular major and go on to graduate. The theory behind the DIR seems to be very sound. Over the past two years, about 85% of the DIR students have been helped to recover and proceed successfully. Without DIR they'd all have been kicked out of college.

This kind of counseling is essentially what Don did his last two years at K-State so, unlike most of the other graduate students with similar assistantships, he already has the relevant knowledge, skills and experience and won't have a lot of new learning. The majority of staff are also doctoral students majoring in psychology so it may easily lead to some new friends."

Our social life began anew with the Penn State fall semester. Carol shared the high and low points in another letter to her folks: "DIR had a farewell party for one of the staff, so we needed a baby sitter but knew no one. I discovered our elderly neighbors had a daughter and granddaughter (Patty) living with them. Patty agreed to baby sit Russell with the grandmother checking occasionally. The grandmother is a lulu. She's the nosiest old poker I ever saw! What she doesn't know by observing herself, she asks. Every morning on her jaunt to the outdoor john she cranes her neck to see what those strange people from Kansas are having for breakfast.

She says her husband is hard of hearing. Oh Yeah! Don was doing fall cleanup on our yard the other day and her hubby was doing the same. While they worked about 15 feet from each other, they talked quietly across the fence. She came out on their back porch about 25 ft. away and called for him. He didn't answer. She yelled louder and louder, but he didn't answer 'because he's hard of hearing.' So she gave up.

I enjoyed the DIR party. I'd met many of the guys so concentrated on meeting the wives. Graduate school here is much different than at K-State because the students are from all over the country (I should say world, because there are many from other countries.)

We are the only ones among Don's graduate student colleagues who have a car, so we picked up Mary and John Cogswell. John is an orphan who grew up on one of the farms for such children in Hershey PA. They have a dozen kids on each farm who do all the farm chores (without pay so the Hershey interests get free labor). John has a lot of negative feelings about his history and avoids talking about it. They've had a hard time financially. Mary said for a while they had to eat on only $7 a week and John lost weight something awful. They have a daughter, Vicki, who is only a couple of months older than Russell so they might be good playmates. At the party, I met Jeff Ashby's wife, Spurge. They're paying for their living costs by serving as night managers in a local motel. I met Fred Ball's wife, Marge. We hit it off well with all of them, and I think we may have the beginning of some good friendships."

Since Milton Eisenhower was at Penn State, I wanted to at least check in with him and share our plans. The evening after our meeting, I told Carol, "I had a hello visit with Milton. He's as warm and friendly as ever. He shared some of the problems he's dealing with right now, like Senator McCarthy's demand that all faculty sign loyalty oaths. He says helping Ike with his presidential campaign takes a lot of time and energy. He looks pretty tired. I told him I wasn't telling anyone of our friendship because I don't want anyone attributing any success I might have to his influence. He said, 'That decision sounds like the Don Ford I knew in Kansas.'"

In our bedroom and living room we had old pine floors that were newly sanded and varnished so they didn't look bad, but we could see through the cracks. Those cracks produced a funny story Carol described to her parents: "Last night (I have to laugh now) Don woke up, yelled something, and dashed down to the basement like a bolt of lightning – he saw an orange light coming up from the basement thru the cracks in the floor and thought the place was on fire. He remembered that my grandparents' farm house burned down from a furnace fire. He had forgotten to turn out the light, the stup! He's still learning to control the heat with that furnace."

In my spare time I worked for several days cleaning up the piece of driftwood we found at Spring Creek. It turned out to be a root from a wild cherry tree. That elaborate root structure was what caught Carol's eye. As I sanded it, a beautiful light orangey red color emerged. I said, "Carol, I'm ready to shape this pretty driftwood, but I need my artist wife to tell me what to do."

She held it up to the light, slowly rotated it in different directions, and finally said, "I think we might be able to trim it in a way to look kind of like a Disney caricature of a person sitting down and waving both arms." She told me where to cut and magically the wood sculpture emerged as she envisioned it.

She said, "Now if you can drill a hole down the middle of its torso for an electric cord we can make a lamp for our living room." I didn't have any drill bits that long. Luckily, a guy from the phone company was in the kitchen installing our phone and he had all kinds of drill bits. I asked if he would do it for us and he said, 'Sure'. After an hour he said, "This wood is so tough I'm having a hard time getting through It."

I said, "I'm sorry to use so much of your time when you must have other jobs this morning, but thanks for trying."

But he wasn't ready to give up! "I won't quit until I get this damn thing done!" And forty five minutes later he declared victory.

Later, Carol carried it down town to find a lamp shade. She returned, excited to report her experience. "As I walked down town carrying our driftwood lamp I got lots of stares and smiles. One man stopped me, said 'That's beautiful!' and told me a friend had made something similar and sold it for $40!" Our new driftwood lamp was, indeed, beautiful, and Carol's creation was admired by many visitors over the years.

So, our new home was furnished, my classes and counseling work settled into a routine, and we enjoyed our new life. Carol decided it was time to expand our social horizons. "Maybe we should entertain a little to see if we can build some good friendships. What do you think?"

I nodded my agreement, "Good friends evolve from having good times together, so some entertaining would be a good place to start." We didn't have much money for entertaining, but Carol was a master at serving tasty meals with the simplest of foods. I suppose young couples today would be horrified at the thought of serving waffles or egg sandwiches to guests, but back then, college students were just grateful for a bite to eat!

We had enjoyed the Cogswells at the DIR party, so invited them and their daughter Vicki to dinner. First we took them for a car ride (they didn't have a vehicle), and then Carol fixed waffles with pineapple and sausage for dinner, followed by sherbet and cake. Vicki and Russell played well together and we enjoyed our first evening of entertaining friends in Pennsylvania.

The next night Carol answered an 11:30 p.m. phone call. It was one of my new colleagues, Hal Segal, calling to say his wife had just had a baby. Carol said, "I swear I've never heard a more excited father!" We lent emotional support over lunch the next day, and then Carol drove him to the hospital to visit his wife. Carol told me, "She seems a lovely and lively person."

A week later Carol said, "Let's invite Jeff and Spurge Ashby to dinner – I enjoyed her at the DIR party. I learned Spurge is a nickname made from her last name." We took them for a car ride to look at the homecoming decorations. Then we brought them to our home for a waffle supper and dessert. We enjoyed their company and they ate their weight in Carol's tasty waffles. Carol said, "They're the nicest couple we've met yet."

The next Friday they invited us for supper. She had fried chicken – considerably fancier than the waffle supper we served them. We played bridge and visited. Russell slept so we had a very enjoyable evening. As we cuddled in bed that night, Carol said, "They're so natural acting – no pretense about them – so it's easy to feel relaxed with them."

Carol gave her parents an update: "A neighbor gave me some quart jars for canning pears from our tree. I got 19 quarts. I'm not too fond of pears, but these are good. I think I can save us a lot of money by canning fruits, so I'm going to do that next summer.

Russell eats like a hog – shows it too. I put extensions on all his pants but he's outgrown them. When Don gets home in the evening, Russ climbs on his lap facing him so his daddy can't read or pay attention to anything else and then tells him about the days happenings. He blabs on and on – the funniest thing you ever heard. Wish we could understand all he says."

In late October I suggested to Carol that we plan a Presidential election eve party. She jumped on that idea like a dog on a piece of steak and set out immediately to plan a fun party. She decorated our living room with pictures of the candidates, cartoons and slogans. I made a cake and she put flags on it representing the campaign issues. Her final touch was pinning an 'Ike Likes Me" cardboard button on Russell's front and a banner across his diapers saying, 'It's Time for a Change!' We invited the Ashbys, Cogswells and Balls to an election night poker party. Carol said, "I thought all this might break down the formality and reserve. Of course it takes time to get acquainted but I get impatient."

As the party began I asked each person to predict who would win and why. I thought Carol's rationale was priceless. "If candidates were elected solely on the quality of their voices or their ability to orate, Stevenson would win by an overwhelming majority. No wonder he's had proposals of marriage from women in his TV and radio audiences! I don't know where they're getting all the mud they sling. Guess that's something the drought hasn't affected."

Everyone stayed up playing poker, eating and drinking until the whole thing was over so we didn't get to bed 'til after 3 a.m. Over breakfast the next morning, Carol said, "I feel like the roof caved in on me this morning, but after all, presidents aren't elected too often so guess we can afford to lose some shut-eye over it. It was pretty exciting waiting for election returns on the radio last night and I'm happy Ike won by a good majority."

"Carol, I got a kick out of Russell going on and on about the political decorations you had up yesterday. 'Oh pretty – blah blah.' He all of a sudden came out with this 'pretty' stuff."

"He has good judgment too, Don. I laughed when he pointed to your fancy print rayon shorts this a.m. and said 'Ohhh-pre-tee.' You looked flabbergasted."

Carol decided it was time to get serious about typing theses to earn some extra money. She found exactly the kind of typewriter she wanted in the Sears catalogue. One morning DIR needed some secretarial help. The boss asked if Carol might be able to help, so I called her and she said OK. She called Spurge, who said she'd baby sit, so Carol took Russell to her house and reported for work. As she walked in, I sang *I'm Back in the Saddle Again.*

On the way home she said, "I did a little typing and other stuff. It was fun for a change and I wasn't as rusty as I expected. I'm disgusted with Sears' delay in delivering my typewriter."

The DIR staff asked Carol to buy a baby gift for the Segal's baby from the department. I was delighted because it was a sign they respected and liked her. She told her parents: "I've had a craving for pumpkin pie lately so I made one and we took it over to Jeff and Spurge to eat. They were very glad to see us and the pie. We left the rest as a gift. The next day Jeff told me they forgot and left it out, their cat ate it, and told them to tell me it was delicious. I was mad at the cat, so consoled myself by making us another one.

Harrah!!! As you can see, my typewriter just came today. I'm very pleased with it. The touch is very different on these noiseless typewriters so I'll have to get used to it.

Last Monday afternoon Russell and I went to visit Spurge. I just barely got my coat off before she told me she's pregnant. Naturally our conversation for the whole time was on that subject. I couldn't be more excited if it were one of my old friends having a baby. I like Spurge so much as she's so genuine. Don and I feel they consider us good friends as we're the first ones to know of their 'secret'. Jeff told Don the same afternoon. Poor kids don't have normal families so haven't told them and were just dying to tell someone.

That evening after supper Don & I decorated up the chocolate cake we'd made Sunday, even though it had a couple pieces eaten out of it, and took it over to the motel to celebrate. We made a clothes line with diapers, etc. across the cake and I put a stork made out of a safety pin on top of one of the clothes line poles. They got a big kick out of it."

I thought, *This is typical Carol. When a friend has a special moment in their life – good or bad – she senses a need for supportive attention and provides it.*

One evening after Russ was in bed, I said, "Carol, even though we'll be in Kansas on Christmas, let's put up a tree here – our first Christmas in our new home and the first one Russell is old enough to enjoy."

John Boal told me we could cut our own tree cheap at the nearby Nixon potato farm, so we went there. Our mouths dropped open when we saw the variety of trees. After growing up with scrawny cedar trees in Kansas, those glorious, perfectly shaped fir and blue spruce trees were an amazing sight. We cut a six-foot Douglas fir and set it up in the corner of our living room. We invited Jeff and Spurge for dinner so they could help decorate the tree that evening. A large part of our enjoyment was helping Russell put ornaments on the tree.

Later, we admired our handiwork. Then, I turned off the living room light and at the count of three, signaled Jeff to turn on the tree lights so I could take a picture. Russell froze for a moment as his eyes took in the colored lights, then he turned to me and said, "W-o-w!"

Carol laughed with joy and I was so surprised I almost forgot to take the picture. Carol said, "In my twenty-five years of life I've never seen such a glorious Christmas tree!" and she started singing *O Christmas Tree*.

Carol made most of the Christmas presents for our families that year to save money and had some last minute work to do. I knew she needed a break so asked her for a date the next night after Russell was asleep. I wanted to look handsome for our date, so dressed in my best suit and prettiest tie. While Carol fussed with her hair and makeup, I decorated our coffee table with a single red carnation – the TKE sweetheart flower – two red crystal goblets with martinis in them, two white glowing candles, and a few cracker and cheese snacks. Other than the candles, our only lights were from the Christmas tree, casting a gentle glow around the living room. I played the record I'd given her several Christmases ago when we couldn't be together, *When You Trim Your Christmas Tree Let Me Be There Beside You*.

When she stepped out of our bedroom, my heart skipped a beat and happy tears stung my eyes. My Carol was so beautiful! To surprise me, she had secretly made a new dress of emerald green with a tiny pattern of subdued red and gold colors. The material was thin and light and floated gracefully around her curves as she walked towards me. *Tantalizing!* was the thought that came to mind. I started to say a jaunty "Merry Christmas!" but what popped out was an emotional, "I love you with all my heart!" I grabbed Carol's hands and twirled her in a circle to see the dress float gracefully around her, and then we settled onto our new sectional 'Christmas present' sofa. I had my composure back so we picked up our goblets, took a sip of martini, and I toasted, "To my perfect wife who has given me a wonderful son – Merry Christmas!"

Carol's eyes sparkled with joy as she smiled and said. "For several years I dreamed of being married to you, but none of my dreams even came close to the wonder of being your wife. I didn't realize men like you existed. You're gentle, very loving and fun with me. Yet, when needed, as in getting our new car, you have great strength and that makes me feel very secure. I can't find words to tell you how deeply I love you and *We'll Never Walk Alone."*

We embraced, kissed gently and just hugged each other to enjoy the moment, then we sipped our martinis and talked about all the things we'd been through this year. Finally, I said, "Carol, it's been too long since we danced together. May I have this dance?"

We selected some records, set the sound to soft music so we wouldn't wake Russell, and spent the next hour dancing in each other's arms in a room filled with the beauty and joy of Christmas. Neither of us wanted the evening to end, but knew it had to because we had a long trip ahead of us. So we went to bed, and I drifted off to sleep holding Carol close.

We left early morning December 20. Jeff and Spurge rode with us to their home in Illinois. As we drove through the mountains Carol said, "It's fascinating to watch morning dawn as rays of sun erase shadows on the mountains. People seldom see the beauty of sunrise." We discovered riding through the mountains terrified Spurge. She actually got down on the floor of the back seat to control her fear. Once we were out of the mountains she was OK.

Carol's father had had surgery to remove a collapsed spinal disc a week before our trip and we hoped he'd be back to the farm for Christmas. We were happy to find Eugene at home, recovering nicely. It was a special time for them, seeing their baby grandson transformed into a little boy who could walk, talk a little, play games with them and admire their animals.

The second half of the trip was spent with the mob in Marysville. Carol was thrilled to see my mother's obvious delight with the pair of tooled-copper floral designs created especially for her. The warmth between Russell and my folks touched us both. As experienced grandparents, they were skillful at recognizing the nuances of Russell's moods and whether to be playful or soothing. My dad loved to tease and play with kids and Russell scrambled all over him seeking that attention. Of course, it goes without saying that we ate a lot!

As we headed home, Carol said, "It felt good to come back to our Kansas roots, and see our parents enjoying their grandson, but somehow it's not the same. Maybe it's because I feel so happy and complete in our own family those old ties now take second place."

In February, Carol wrote her parents about a wonderful change in our lives: "We finally have a functioning shower!!! It took John Boal five months to <u>finally</u> put in the shower he promised us five months ago. We haven't been able to take a real bath in our home until now!

I have my new typewriter, a Smith-Corona with elite type. I've placed ads around campus for typing theses. It'll probably take awhile before I get any business."

February arrived and when I came home from campus Carol said, "It doesn't seem two years since Russell was born. I baked a cake and put two candles on it so we can celebrate after dinner." After enjoying the birthday cake, we gave him his toy John Deere tractor. He told us about it in his own lingo for 15 minutes.

As he played, I said, "Think he liked it?"

Carol laughed, "It looks like he may have a little Kansas farmer in him. It was priceless to watch him blow out the candles – of course, we had to light and relight them for he has just learned to blow so wants to repeat this great accomplishment as much as he can."

"Carol, when he got his nose so close to the candles before he blew I thought he'd burn it. Then the closer he got to the flame the more cross eyed he'd look."

As another birthday gift for Russ, Carol went to work on her New Year's goal of finding more playmates his age. She said, "Don, beginning this Sunday I'm going to church with Russell so he can be around more kids. If he likes it, I'll do that as often as possible so he can be around kids a least once a week. I know you have to study for finals, so Spurge is glad to go with me. She goes to the Methodist church so that's where we'll go."

Later she described the results, "We took him to the nursery, stood around a little, and then left. When we went to get him a little girl, just a little bigger than Russell, insisted on helping me put on his snow suit. She was a regular little mother and Russ just stood so quietly while she zipped him into his suit." That became a routine almost every Sunday until summer.

Several nights later, over a tasty spaghetti dinner, Carol reported stage two of her goal. "A boy about Russell's age lives two blocks from here so I went down and introduced myself to his mother whose name is Freida. She had the same concern about playmates. Her son's name is Mark. We plan for them to play at each other's home twice a week. We had a good time talking and I really liked her, so maybe I've found a potential friend, too."

By springtime, Carol had found Russ several play mates and we often had several little kids playing in our back yard because we had the only yard with a fence around it for safety.

Spring was in full flower when I got a special work assignment, "Carol, how would you like to take a little trip to see Lake Erie this weekend?"

She said, "I'm in no mood for joking around!"

"I really mean it. Too many students are flunking out of the area hospital-based nursing education programs. Penn State created a selection process to reduce that costly attrition rate so we'll be testing nursing applicants Saturday at our Behrend Center. I'll give the tests and teach you how to score them. We'll be paid and reimbursed for all our expenses."

Carol said, "I'd love to do that! I thought of taking nursing in college. It would be fun to see that part of Pennsylvania. Can we take Russell?" The answer was yes, so Friday morning we got into our trusty Ford and headed north, stayed in a hotel two days, and drove home Sunday.

Carol described the adventure to her parents: "Saturday, while Don was giving the tests, I met Mrs. Ferguson, wife of the Center Head. She looked after Russell while I worked with Don. The Behrend family owns the Hammermill Paper Co. and is as filthy rich as they come. They gave their country estate to Penn State to create an educational center there. All the buildings, including a luxurious large home and a huge beautiful barn, have been turned into classrooms, laboratories and a library. We looked at the lake and then came home."

Carol's home typing business got off to a rousing start. Like my old odd job business, it started as a trickle, grew to a creek, and soon became a river flowing so fast she had to turn some jobs down. One quiet evening she briefed me on the work she'd been doing, "A thesis typically requires an original and four carbon copies, so if I make a typing mistake the error must be erased on five pages and it can't be smudged or the graduate school won't accept it. I've typed four doctoral dissertations, two Masters' theses, and two term papers in two months. I can type a 100-page dissertation with few errors in two to three days if there aren't too many interruptions. I just added it up and discovered to my surprise I've earned $465 in the past 75 days!"

"Carol, I'm astonished at your speed and skill. I've never heard of anyone who could type a hundred pages with almost no errors. The psych department head told faculty and grad students 'That's the best dissertation typing I've ever seen.' I'm proud of my typing tornado!"

I was fed up with studying and lonely for time with my sweetheart so asked Carol for a Saturday night date. We got a baby sitter, duded up, and I took her to an uncrowded restaurant near the top of a mountain looking down on a small town called Centre Hall. It was a starlit night with a full moon and we got a table beside a window looking out over the valley. I said, "Carol, do you remember when we were in Kansas City on our honeymoon, we went to that picturesque little bar to listen to the piano player? We'd never had a cocktail so asked the waiter for a suggestion. He thought a minute and suggested … what?"

Laughing, Carol said, "I remember it was delicious, but I don't remember the name."

"Think of the name of a famous city in Russia."

"Oh yes – order me a *Moscow Mule!* You told me it was made with vodka, ginger beer and lime juice."

We ordered our drinks and looked at the menu. "This restaurant has a special that friends on campus tell me is delicious, called *Stuffed Filet of Beef with Bordelaise Sauce.* It's beef tenderloin slices stuffed with a mixture of chopped onions, ham, and other stuff, covered with beef gravy with mushrooms and dry red wine. May I order it for you?"

"Sounds yummy!"

We sipped our Moscow Mules and I said, "Tonight we're celebrating an anniversary. In July, ten years ago, we met on a blind date. Just think of all the things we've experienced and done together since then! If you hadn't written me your thank you letter, none of that would have happened and our lives would have followed different pathways. Isn't it amazing how one simple act can snowball into such a complicated and wonderful life. Here's a toast to the 'snowball' you started with your first letter to me."

We clinked our glasses and took another sip. Carol savored the taste for a second, then smiled, "I did hope the little snowball we started would keep rolling. It was my mother who suggested that letter. I wish I knew what I said in that letter that triggered your response."

I grinned, thinking back to that letter. "It didn't take much to encourage me. I was praying you'd answer. Remember when we were courting how much we enjoyed parking somewhere secluded so we could have long, private conversations? We both stay so busy that our private talks have slipped away from us. I miss them."

"I've missed those talks too. Sometimes, when you're so busy studying and working, I feel some of the loneliness I felt before we married and were kept apart by distance. I'm glad you're following through with your idea about dates when we first moved here. Let's talk."

"OK. When we established our home here last September we agreed to try to live on my $120 a month assistantship and the small reserve we had in our checking account to protect our savings for future needs. Our rent is $50 a month, leaving $70 plus a little from our checking and savings for everything else. I can't tell you how grateful and proud I am of the way you've managed our budget for seven months, partly because you helped us have fun while doing it.

I'm thinking, for example, how much Russell and I look forward to our once-a-week shopping trips to the Bellefonte supermarket where you frugally choose the cheapest yet tastiest meals for the next week. I remember a debate over eating beef heart. It cost less than half as much other meats. You convinced me it was very nutritious and there were several ways it could be made tasty. We all came to like it, and that one stuffing you used was great."

Carol laughed, "I remember one shopping trip Russell and I filled up our cart and checked out. Then I discovered I'd forgotten my check book. I was so embarrassed, apologized for my stupidity and started to return our purchases. The manager came to the register with a big smile and said, 'Mrs. Ford, you're a good customer here. Just take your stuff home and pay us the next time you come in. We trust you!' I felt like kissing him with gratitude – but restrained myself."

"Well, things have changed for the better. Your typing business is a whiz-bang success! You've earned more per month this last three months than my monthly income of $120. You won't earn that much year round, but you get $100 for one long thesis so it looks like with the reputation you've earned, you might easily average $100 a month. That would nearly double our income. Let's loosen our purse strings a little. What would you like to buy?"

Without hesitation, Carol said, "Clothes! Russell is rapidly outgrowing everything he has, I need some summer clothes, and you need new trousers." We agreed to make a list so she could buy what we wanted or needed over the next few months. Our dinner arrived and Carol sampled the beef, "I've never tasted anything like this! I wish I could learn how to make it."

We continued our conversation as we ate. We discussed what to name a puppy when we got one and decided on *POGO*, a comic strip character, because that would be easy for Russell to say. We considered what to grow in our 15' x 60' garden. Our list included a spring garden of lettuce, onions and radishes, a summer garden of peas, green beans and tomatoes, a fall garden of big slicing onions, sweet corn, and pumpkins, and replanting the spring garden. And of course, we discussed the progress of our first born son.

"Don, Russell talks a blue streak now and is developing a sense of humor. He teases me by talking in falsetto or basso, loves to pull jokes, or to think he's put something over on us."

I nodded, "To get me to play with him, he tricks me. For example, he offered me his favorite car to play with him. Shortly after we started he replaced it with a smaller car saying I'd like that one better. He was pretty good at finding the little Easter egg nests you hid."

Carol replied, "I got a kick out of the way he unloaded each small nest into the big nest on the coffee table before he looked for another."

Carol had lost all her Kansas women friendships. I knew how important women friends were to her and needed to know her feelings. "How are you doing making friends?"

"I'm making progress, but you have to spend time together to become close friends, and we've been here less than a year. The parties we've had and have gone to have helped me meet people, and in general I think we're involved with very nice people. Spurge Ashby has become a terrific friend. We hit it off wonderfully. We like a lot of the same things, and she's always up front and open with me. I always know where she stands. Some aren't my cup of tea.

Mary is always so bored with everything. She can't see how I stand it 'way out here in the sticks' or how Spurge stands it 'so tied down'. She and I see the world differently, but with my Kansas friends I learned no one is perfect and try to focus on what I liked about them and ignore the rest. We 'gad about' some, visit each other's homes, and have lunch together. I like socializing with Marge Ball, but she works full time so we can only be acquaintances. I really liked the psych graduate school couple I met at our last party, Louise and Bernie Guerney. They're on internship right now but I think we might enjoy them as friends when they get back.

I have casual friendships with two neighbors who are mothers of Russell's playmates. Occasionally, Frieda – Mark's mother – joins me on our front porch and we spend a little time yacking. Robbie's mother, Angela, invited me to be a substitute at her bridge party Thursday night. I had a very good time with her and her bridge group. They might blossom into real friendships. Spurge and I are talking about the possibility of starting our own bridge group. I'm not lonely like I was when we first got here. Besides, you are my best friend!!!

Funny thing, all of these women are pregnant! It's like the baby epidemic we were part of in Manhattan. I'm really into Spurge's pregnancy, ever since we were the first to know. Maybe I'm so wrapped up in her expectations because I'm anxious to get pregnant myself. You've convinced me we need to wait until we get closer to your PhD. Maybe by summer I can talk you into it?"

I grinned and said, "Honey, used to be you dreamed about having babies. Now that you've had one, you have an appetite for the real thing. How many do you want?"

"More than one but less than ten."

"WOW! You have high hopes, or is it a lively sense of humor?"

I paid the check, and with contented hearts we drove slowly home to our bed and made leisurely love before falling happily asleep.

The Cogswell's baby boy and the Ashby's baby girl arrived the same week. Was Carol ever busy! We were the only grad students with a car. She hauled both families to and from the Bellefonte hospital, fed both husbands lunch twice, visited both mothers when their hubbies couldn't, baby sat Vicki, and worked at getting ready for my parents' visit. She said, "Recently time has slipped through my fingers like water through a sieve. Mothers are so different. Mary stayed in the hospital as long as she could, ten days, and Spurge pushed to go home as early as possible, five days. Once they got home, my load drastically eased."

When my parents arrived from Kansas, we showed them the sights in the valleys and mountains around us. They had never been out of the prairies so were fascinated with everything they saw, but the experience they enjoyed most was the personal appointment I arranged for them, alone with Milton Eisenhower. Afterwards, they could hardly stop talking about it. "He was so warmed hearted, interested in us, and seemed to love talking about his Kansas childhood. He treated us like we were just as important as anyone else he talked about." They were so proud and couldn't believe they now knew the brother of the President of the U.S.

I told Carol, "I bet they couldn't wait to get back to Marysville to tell everyone about it!"

Between tending to new mothers and entertaining my parents, we also canned fruits and vegetables. Carol couldn't help but brag a bit in a letter to her folks: "We've been a couple of canning fools this summer. Everything but peaches and plums came from our back yard. Here is the result: Sweet white and red cherries – 47 qts; black raspberries – 8 pints; pears – 10 quarts; golden jubilee peaches – 43 qts.; green beans – 51 pints; tomatoes – 42 qts; and quite a few small jars of peach and cherry jams. That's over 100 quarts of fruit and about 25 quarts of vegetables. I'm so proud of our larder since this is the first time I've ever canned so extensively and it will enrich our nutrition and really help our food budget. This summer Don has been home in the p.m. so we canned most of this together. Kinda fun."

We started enjoying swimming again in nearby lakes. Carol swam on her back with the beauty of Esther Williams, an Olympic swimmer and movie star. When I tried to float on my back I sank and she laughed at me. We played tennis with Russell chasing our balls.

We ended the summer by adding a new source of joy for all three of us. My boss's cleaning lady lived way out in the woods, called the Barrens, where wild life abounded. Her full bred beagle had five pups she wanted to give away. Carol said with excitement, "Don, both of us had dogs as kids and loved them. Let's go get one for Russ."

We rushed out to the Barrens where Carol and Russell picked out the cutest little female. While her husband was getting the puppy ready for us, she took us riding through some of the wildest country back of her house where they hunted rabbits, deer, wild turkey, and other game. Russell's eyes sparkled with excitement to see so many wild critters. Back at the car, Russell got in the back seat with Carol beside him holding the shoebox bed and puppy. She laid the shoebox in his lap and said, "Russell, here's your puppy. Her name is POGO." He gently touched his new pet and said, "Pooogoo." Our summer ended on that happy note.

Carol hadn't had a piano to play since we were married. I'd been searching for a used piano with no results. Then, the Assistant Dean of the College of Agriculture called me. We had worked together on some student problems. He said, "Don, I heard through the grapevine you want a piano for your wife. We're remodeling our house and need to get rid of our upright piano. I'll give it to you for Carol if you want it."

My heart did a flip flop of excitement! Fred Ball went with me to check it out. It looked and sounded beautiful. I arranged to pick it up Saturday afternoon. Surprising Carol was my goal, so Jeff got Spurge to take Carol to a movie while I baby sat. Jeff, John, and Fred joined me to load the piano on our trailer. Jeff brought a large dolly from his motel to expedite the move.

As we rolled it into the corner reserved for a piano, we felt like kids at a carnival, excited with our accomplishment and eager to see Carol's response to her beautiful upright! While I sat a lamp on top, Fred raved that its cast iron sounding board produced an unusually rich sound. Fred had brought some of his sheet music and I found more in the bench so pulled out a book of Chopin and one of popular music. I sat out champagne and snacks, then hung a sign that said *Early Happy Birthday*. I held Russell in my arms so he could see. When Carol opened the back door, Fred played a Glenn Miller piece. Carol said "Don must have bought a new record."

Just as she entered the living room, we all applauded and shouted, "Happy Birthday!" First, she looked at everyone in the room with surprise, then she spied the piano. Her mouth dropped open into a big, speechless **O O O H!!** I took her by the arm and sat her at the bench. "Here's the piano you've dreamed of for five years."

She said "I can't believe this is mine!"

Jeff popped the champagne cork and poured a little for each of us. We toasted Carol and her piano, then everyone left to give Carol privacy exploring her gift, and I sat Russell on the bench beside her. She still seemed dazed and overwhelmed, but played a little tune for him. A few moments later, she slid from the piano bench and threw both arms around me, crying with joy on my shoulder. Finally, I led her to the couch where we shared drinks and snacks while I told her how we got her piano, accompanied by Russell's tuneless plunking at the keys.

Later, calmed by champagne, snacks, and small talk, she couldn't wait to try out her new piano. I said, "Come on Russell – let's get dinner while your mama makes music."

As our house resounded with Chopin, I shed happy tears. I'd finally filled that hole in her life. Russell, always observant, tugged on my pant leg, "Why are you crying Daddy?"

I wrapped him in a reassuring hug, "Because I'm so happy to hear mama play her piano."

Supper was a simple offering that night – tomato soup, cheese sandwiches and a glass of milk. I couldn't wait to hear what she thought about her piano, "So what's the verdict?"

"The action is very nice – I don't have to pound the keys to get the sound I want. The sound is unusually good for an upright. I can't tell you how much this means to me! Not only do I love music, but the piano has always been my therapy."

I sent Carol back to her piano while Russell 'helped' wash dishes and clean the kitchen. Just before putting him to bed for the night, I sat him on the bench beside her to say goodnight. She used his little hands to play a simple melody. He said, "That's peerty."

She kissed him goodnight and I put him to bed, then put on my pj's and read while Carol played.

I'd dozed off when Carol snuggled up to me and said, "Thank you for being my magic man – somehow you always seem to make things come out right for me. Words can't express what I feel right now." and she sang, *"Good night sweetheart 'til we wake tomorrow."*

Carol's parents visited in the fall. Carol and Winifred had a great time playing duets on the piano. Both parents were delighted that Carol's life had been enriched with a piano, and they thanked me profusely. After their return to Kansas Carol wrote; "The let down from you leaving didn't come until this weekend. But, I perked myself up by playing the piano. I played thru all the songs in the book you gave me and all of Fred's pieces and didn't do too badly. Playing my piano is great therapy when I'm feeling low."

Later she wrote: "Russell's birthday gift to me is a book full of *Songs Children Like to Sing,* which I love to play and sing for him, and he tries to sing with me. He is an 'indian giver' cause he keeps telling me it's his. The fly leaf is so cute where he's signed it helped by his Daddy, of course, and his hand print in ink is there too. The second box of my music arrived today – thanks so much. There are lots of pieces I especially like in this bunch.

Fred came over last night to play for the second time. We do enjoy him and Marge and it's fun to see Fred getting such a kick out of playing. Our upstairs neighbors have complained about Fred's loud playing, so I wait till they're gone to play pieces I really want to pound – then I do have fun! I'm pleasantly surprised at how quick I'm picking up what I knew. I think all my typing has helped my fingering action. This piano has the nicest tone – I Love It!!"

Carol's piano not only brought the pleasure of music back to her life, it enriched our social life. No one else in our crowd had a piano. Gatherings at our house eventually led to singing around Carol's piano. Friends like Fred Ball, who had no piano, sometimes arranged with Carol to drop by and play a little. Getting that piano for Carol enriched all our lives!

Fall semester was under way, and suddenly I was offered a new job. After Russell was in bed that evening I said, "Carol, we have a decision to make – I've been offered a different job and here's the background. For years, the College of Liberal Arts has had a major called Commerce and Finance. Some 'intellectuals' on campus unfairly called it a place for dummies. The real problem was that the College of Liberal Arts gave that field of study little support.

Milton Eisenhower considers business a fundamental component of a free society so he decided to create a College of Business Administration. He hired a new Dean to create it, the Dean hired the initial faculty group who designed a new curriculum, and they've begun admitting students. He recognized they had a negative reputation about quality of students `to overcome and assigned three faculty members as part time special advisers.

He went to the psychology department and asked if they could recommend a doctoral student to lead in the creation of that program, and they recommended me. I'm pleased the psych faculty thinks that highly of me. Working conditions in DIR keep getting worse because of the boss's treatment of staff. If I take this opportunity, I'll no longer be as close to our DIR friends. All grad assistants are paid the same so my pay wouldn't change. What do you think?"

As she often did for me, Carol blew away the fog clouding a decision. "I've been aware this summer that you're not only dissatisfied with working in DIR, but you're bored. You've been doing that kind of work for over three years now, counting your time at K-State. I know you started your PhD to prepare for much more than that. You've always been stimulated by new challenges, and you sound intrigued by this one. Together, you and I are good at new challenges. So, as you've often said to me, I say 'Follow your heart.'"

So, I took the new job offer and ran with it! It was fun. My experience planning and managing the K-State Student Union helped me understand their business curriculum.

After a few weeks, I decided it was time for one of our conversation dates so I combined it with celebrating Carol's birthday. Over a delicious dinner of pork chops, homemade apple sauce, peas and baked potato, I said, "Madam, it would be my pleasure if you could join me for a dinner date at the Tavern Restaurant on Thursday, October 8 at 6 p.m."

Her reply came with a smile and fluttering lashes for added emphasis, "My dear sir, I never turn down dinner with a handsome man, as long as he pays for it."

The Tavern decor is what the name implies, traditionally a favorite eatery of university students, across the street from campus, decorated in rustic style with photos and mementos of Penn State's history. We ordered gin and tonic with a slice of lime. I raised my glass and toasted, "To my beautiful wife, the light of my life – *Happy Birthday!*"

She said, "This is a kind of anniversary too – this is the tenth year you've wished me a happy birthday, and the fifth year you've done so in person. May there be many, many more!" Our waitress appeared so Carol said, "What's your opinion about the lasagna?"

"My mother is Italian and she eats here whenever she visits."

"That's good enough for me!" and Carol ordered lasagna, a tossed salad with Italian dressing, and crusty Italian bread.

My mouth was watering, so I said, "Make it two." We walked around checking out the wall exhibits until our food arrived.

I wanted to save my big topic till last, so I said, "Speaking of friends, how are things going with your gal friends?"

"Well, it reminds me of Manhattan – babies, babies everywhere. Spurge and Mary both have babies. Frieda, Mark's mother, will deliver any day now, and Angela, Robby's mother, is about six months along. So, when I visit them it's all 'baby talk'. It's kind of fun – I might as well join them.

The bad part is that both Mary and Spurge have changed drastically. Mary is so obsessed with her baby that visiting her is no fun anymore. Spurge is a different person since Kathy was born. They've spoiled their baby terribly and fight a lot. They seem disinterested in socializing. My last visit, Russell touched Kathy's hand and Spurge jumped all over him and pushed him so hard he nearly fell down. I was so angry, but controlled myself, said goodbye and left. My best friend has become a completely different person. On a positive note, I'm really enjoying my Dames bridge group. We play a little bridge and gab a lot."

I said, "I liked playing bridge at the TKE house. Maybe we could create a couples' bridge group?" I took a big bite of bread while coming up with more small talk. "I get a kick out of Pogo now. You were smart to tie a stick around her neck so she can't squeeze through the fence and get hit in the road again. She and Russ have become great playmates. They chase each other around and play tug-o-war with a stick. If Russ gets too rough, Pogo grabs his arm with her mouth and holds it firmly without biting too hard and Russ stops."

"They're fun to watch." Carol said. "They're awfully jealous of each other too, Pogo more so than Russ. It really is amazing sometimes how human a dog can be. I wish you could have seen them play in that recent big snow. Russell looked like a cuddly ol' bear in his snow suit. The snow was so deep, Pogo would disappear into a snow drift, then jump up and disappear again. We made Russ's first snow man and was he ever excited!"

OK, enough small talk. On to the big topic. "Carol, I like everything about my job in the new College of Business. It's refreshing to work with these business people for a change. My psychology colleagues tend to beat around the bush over issues. These guys don't mess around; They define a problem, obstacles to overcome, get to work and get the job done. Best of all, I'm in complete control of my schedule. The huge benefit of that is that I no longer have to organize our family life around my job. I can organize my job to support our family life. I've completed my language requirements, and will finish my remaining courses by spring. Comprehensive exams are scheduled for May 15 so by May 16 the end of my PhD tunnel will be in sight!

So, I offer you this birthday present. If you still want to, we could consider creating a sister or brother for Russell."

Carol gasped and dropped her fork, "Do you really mean that?"

"With all my heart."

Her voice trembled with emotion, but she smiled her happiness, "Oh, I want to jump up and down and shout with joy! I want to kiss you 'til you can hardly breathe! I don't know whether to laugh or cry, I'm so happy! But most of all, Magic Man, I want to go home and get started!" I certainly didn't want to disappoint my sweetie so that's exactly what we did!

Chapter Eleven
An Old Dream Comes True

We both stayed very busy from October to Christmas. Carol typed three dissertations and a manuscript for a local publisher. With my flexible schedule I could take care of Russ while she met a typing deadline. That reduced Carol's stress and gave me more time to enjoy my son.

Workwise, I had to teach the business faculty how to use their new counseling program and still had studying to do and papers to write. Our friends, Hardy and Ann Berry, drove down from Maine to spend Thanksgiving with us.

Then the Christmas season began. December 1st we cut and decorated our Christmas tree so we could enjoy it longer before heading to Kansas. Russ was old enough to celebrate with us, adding to our holiday joy. Carol played Christmas songs, smiling as Russ and I tried to sing along with her. Christmas shopping in Altoona that year was especially fun, watching Russ's delight when he talked to Santa in three different department stores.

We celebrated Christmas with friends. Carol taught Marge how to make copper pictures to give as Christmas gifts while Fred played the piano and I invented black walnut taffy – new and delicious!

The Balls, Ashby's and Fords celebrated with a pot luck dinner at our house. Carol had planned to make a large Christmas candle for each as a Christmas present. I suggested teaching them how to make their own as a Christmas present instead and Carol liked the idea. After dinner, she explained the plan. Then step by step she helped each of them make their candle. Marge made hers all white while Spurge mixed colors together and got a kind of greenish grey.

Carol said, "Now, sprinkle these gold sparkles all over your candles." She put all three on a tray, turned out the kitchen light, and each lit her candle with accompanying 'ooos and ahhhs'. The joy and satisfaction of creating their candles turned out to be the ideal gift and our guests went home radiating Christmas spirit.

Two days before we were to leave for Kansas, we put Russell to bed so we could celebrate alone. We sat lighted candles on the piano and lit our Christmas tree, with instrumental Christmas music playing softly in the background. Carol said, "Don, I have a special Christmas present for you. Will you fix our refreshments while I get your present ready?" I mixed martinis and sat them with crunchies on our coffee table, then settled in to await my Christmas surprise.

After a few minutes, our bedroom door opened and Carol sashayed out wrapped in Christmas paper with a red ribbon circling her waist and a big decorative bow at the front. I laughed with delight and said, "All Christmas presents belong under the tree!"

She shot me a broad wink and said, "You have to unwrap your Christmas present first." I thought, *Boy, she's in a sexy mood tonight!*

She stood before me smiling mysteriously as I slowly unwrapped my present – first the big bow, then the wrapping with winged angels from around her breasts, and finally the wrapping with tiny angels from around her hips. I expected to see sexy lingerie, but what I saw was my lovely wife in a pregnancy smock with a diaper hanging on one side and a pacifier on the other. Her eyes twinkled happily as she said, "Merry Christmas, Daddy!"

I was speechless, but only for a moment. "YOU'RE PREGNANT!"

Carol nodded, laughing, "That's what Dr. Light said!"

I wrapped her in a bear hug and gave her a big smack on the mouth. "I had no clue! Tell me the whole story."

After sipping her martini and sampling a snack she said, "I missed my period last month but didn't want to say anything because it might be a false alarm. But when I missed this month I asked for an appointment with Dr. Light immediately because we plan to leave town. I saw him yesterday. I like him a lot. He's a very gentle, sympathetic person and put me completely at ease. He confirmed my pregnancy, examined me thoroughly, said everything looks good, and that I'm probably about two months along. He figured I'm due around August 20. I jokingly asked if he could arrange it for August 15 since that's the birth date of both my husband and his mother. Oh, Don, I feel so good and I'm so happy I could burst!!"

I said, "Let's burst together and scatter our happiness all over Christmas. Won't it be fun to surprise our parents with this news during our Christmas visit?" I finished unwrapping my present and we celebrated our joy with gusto! Two days later we left for a Kansas Christmas.

We had a wonderful Christmas and took a lot of good natured razzing about our new Ford. On our way home, Russell demonstrated his newfound knowledge of farm animals. At a gas station in Ohio, Carol took Russ to the john so they could both empty their crankcase. As Carol was doing her duty, 'Dennis the Menace' watched closely and finally said, "Mommy you peepee just like a cow!"

When we got home we learned that the Dames graduate student wives club had scheduled a formal dance the next Saturday. A formal dance was rare at Penn State. We went to dance, taking our 'new Ford' along for the ride. Carol described our evening to her parents: "I wore my black formal strapless with lace mitts and bought some black lace to make a stole, so with the 'diamonds' you gave me I looked pretty decent. Don and I had great fun dancing – the rest of them were a bunch of duds, but we went to have us some fun and that's what we had. We let our hair down and jitterbugged."

One Saturday, Carol told me, "We have new renters upstairs – Nancy and Bud Boal. He's our landlord's son. They're the age we were when we got married. Nancy is real nice and pregnant – baby's due in about three weeks."

Perfect timing, I thought. "Yes, Bud Boal asked if we'd be interested in paying half to buy a new Apex washer jointly. Our share would be $100. We could probably raise most of that by selling our trailer. What do you think?"

Carol smiled, relieved at my suggestion, "Oh, yes! With new babies and Russ in the house an automatic washing machine would be a godsend! It would it be lot less work, and get laundry a lot cleaner and drier. Let's do it!"

Carol wrote her mother with a pregnancy update: "I'm 4 months pregnant and getting big. Visualize me dancing with Don on a crowded dance floor. We did that Saturday night at a Dames dance. I had to collect money at the door, but then Don and I had a good time dancing to a pretty good band. I could hardly pour myself into my formal and I hardly dared take a deep breath. My view is, you don't have to stop having fun just because you're pregnant.

My friends are pushing me to have a girl with statements like 'think pink' and 'buy girlie clothes'. I tell them a girl might be fun, but all I'm praying for is a healthy, happy baby."

Carol and I sometimes discussed the psychological theories and their applications I was studying. On our Christmas drive back from Kansas we had a long talk about motivation and that there is always a reason for a child's behavior. One evening, as we ate sausage and pineapple waffles for supper, Carol proudly related how she had used those ideas with Russ.

"I've been working hard every day to get my typing orders done. Yesterday I was particularly busy and tried to get Russell to stop pestering me. Late morning, Russell went into our bedroom, closed the door and soaked his pants. He did the same thing mid-afternoon and I got pretty mad. Instead of scolding him, I took him on my lap and asked why he did that. He didn't look at me or answer. I said, 'What's the matter, honey, isn't Mommy paying enough attention to you?' He said 'NO!' 'You don't like Mommy to type so much, do you?' Again he said, 'NO', but added 'Daddy's have to go to work to earn money, but Mommies shouldn't have to work to earn money'. He had just turned four and I was bowled over at his insight. I explained why Mommy had to help out while Daddy was going to school, etc. We were both pleased about our talk, and he hasn't hid and wet his pants since."

Carol's pregnancy seemed to be going OK but she was bigger than she had been with Russell, so we were eager for her next exam. "Dr. Light gave me a thorough check up today and said I'm in excellent shape. I said friends are kidding me about having twins because I'm so big. He said that's typical of second pregnancies. He doubts if I'm having twins, but said nothing would surprise him. He usually delivers one set a year and so far this year there've been five! As I stood up to leave he said with a twinkle in his eye,

'Everything's just fine so far, all you have to do is to stay healthy, keep the weight down, and watch for any signs of twins."

Carol's instinctive approach to people always impressed me. I smiled when she described talking with Russ about a baby. "This morning I introduced the idea of having a baby to Russell. I started by telling him he used to be a tiny baby and showed him how I held him and a little bit how we took care of him. Then I asked him if he thought it would be nice if we had a little baby around here to take care of. He said 'Yes!' quite enthusiastically, so I told him maybe we could manage that next summer. That's why he told you that we're getting a baby next summer."

I said, "You're one smart lady! Sure wish I could have had you in psych clinic last year to pass along some of your wisdom to parents who had screwed up their families."

As the summer progressed, Carol grew increasingly larger and more uncomfortable, making a good night's sleep difficult. She was a good sport, though and kept on typing. I did everything possible to reduce her household work and distract her with interesting activities, even though I was on the home stretch of preparing for comprehensive exams in July.

She always enjoyed a good movie and communing with Mother Nature, so I tried to take her on leisurely side trips. We took Russell to a little carnival in Boalsburg and Carol enjoyed her favorite ride, the Ferris wheel. One lovely Sunday we took our picnic lunch to a small state park. We relaxed and ate by a peaceful lake while watching beautiful white geese and swans gliding across the water. Carol made her usual comment when viewing Nature's beauty, "This is so beautiful. Someday I'm going to learn how to paint beautiful scenes like this."

Carol needed a break, so when I was hired for another nursing testing job at Bradford PA, I took her and Russ along for a little vacation. Bradford was a wealthy oil town near the New York border, one of the places where the oil industry began. She told her mother about the trip:

"We stayed at a nice hotel, had a wonderful breakfast, and while Don tested the nurses, Russell and I went shopping. I went nuts over the wonderful materials in one store so I bought some to use later for baby clothes. I bought Russell a cute sport suit, tie and new shoes for his Easter outfit and a pink Easter bonnet for me.

Russell was wonderful company for me. Around 3 p.m. we picked up Don and headed home. I had a great time!"

Carol's checkups increased to every three weeks and still no twins in evidence. "Dr. Light probed around and listened to my belly and said, 'I've never missed twins yet. I feel just one baby and hear just one heartbeat so I don't think twins are possible.' I told him the way it kicks and rolls, this baby feels like a whole litter! He's scheduled his summer vacation in July so he can be back in time." By the time of that exam, Carol was so big that her arms were barely long enough to reach the typewriter, but she had a dissertation to finish so she kept going.

Dean MacKenzie asked me to come to his home for a private talk. He told me, "Milton Eisenhower, the head of the psych department, and I have been trying to find a way to increase your income this next year to support your growing family. We can't increase your assistantship but Milton has five scholarships he gives out each year. Next year you'll get one in addition to your assistantship. That will increase your income to about $1800. We hope that will enable you to stay here this next year." That news came as a relief to Carol and me! All we needed to complete our bright future was for me to pass my comps and Carol to deliver our baby.

My astonishing wife reminded me of the prairie pioneer women who worked in the fields until the day their babies came. In late June, Carol was typing yet another thesis. On three separate evenings she had people for dinner and another was scheduled including guests she hadn't met. She sewed a shirt for Russell, a smock for herself, and had plans for other sewing projects in the works. She canned forty two quarts of sweet cherries from our trees and was preparing to can green beans. She took care of Russell, insisted on helping me clean the house, cooked most of the meals, helped entertain guests, and still found time to play the piano. And have I mentioned that she was big as a baby elephant?

She drove herself to near exhaustion and refused to rest or take an afternoon nap. I helped as much as I could, as did Russell, but was also studying for and taking comprehensive exams covering all of psychology to determine whether I qualified for my PhD, so I was gone from home half of each day and studied at night. Somehow, we did manage to sleep, once in a while.

Then the bomb dropped! Carol went for her regular checkup with Dr. Light on Wednesday, June 13th. I could see she was excited when I got home. She gave me the news, "As soon as he had me on the table and examined me he said, 'I think you're having twins.' He sent me to the college infirmary for an x-ray. The technician was kind enough to develop it immediately and removed all doubt. I saw two heads and a mess of arms and legs.

Dr. Light called and confirmed it! I'm supposed to take it easy and not bounce around any so that my water doesn't break too soon. I don't know whether it's the power of suggestion, but I sure feel more incapacitated since hearing about twins. I move like a snail. I told Russell there would be two babies in our house and he said, 'That's great. You can have one and I can have one and Daddy will have to borrow.'

Don, the word we're having twins swept through Lemont in two days. Half a dozen women neighbors have offered help in all kinds of ways from lending bassinets to helping care for Russell, and lots of people call or drop by with congratulations."

Carol informed her parents about the news, and ended by saying: "After the initial shock, Don and I are thrilled about the whole thing. I can hardly wait till they get here. I really am tickled over prospects of having twins and Don is as proud as he can be, but he laid down the law – no more typing and I must lay down for a rest every afternoon! I'm obeying – he's cute when he gets firm with me."

Carol had another check-up July 9 and Dr. Light said everything looked great and the biological signs didn't suggest an early delivery. I said, "Carol, remember while I was stationed at Roswell you kept dreaming of having a baby, and once you dreamed you had twin boys? You wrote me and said you'd like that. Well, seven years later your dream is coming true."

Amidst our happiness and joy there was a deep sadness. Milton Eisenhower's wife, Helen, died of breast cancer. We had known her since our K-State days, where Helen and Carol were fond of each other. I told Carol about Helen's death and added, "I know this is an agonizing time for Milton because he loved Helen as deeply as I love you."

The afternoon of July 22, I met with the committee for my Doctoral orals. They spent more than two hours throwing questions at me, sent me out and let me sweat for twenty minutes. Finally, they called me back and congratulated me. I passed! I felt like a ton of bricks had been lifted off me. My chairman, Bob Bernreuter, waited until the others were gone to personally congratulate me, saying, "You didn't do as well as I thought you would. Is something wrong?"

I said, "No, I just had something more important on my mind. My wife is in the early stages of labor to produce twins."

He laughed and gave me a hug, "I'm surprised you didn't do worse! I would have in your shoes." (Later I learned they had adopted to get a child.)

The day following my oral exams, I took Carol to the hospital in labor and healthy twin boys were born at 7 a.m. the following morning. Everything went well with our babies but not with Carol. A couple of hours post-delivery her vital signs went haywire and she started convulsing. They put her in an intensive care room for close monitoring and I tried everything possible to sooth her. They taught me how to keep her tongue from obstructing her airway during seizures, a horrifying possibility that left me numb with fright. I loved Carol so intensely and was terrified I might lose her. I fought to appear calm and reassuring to ease her anxiety, while inside I trembled with fear and prayed for help.

They raised my hopes by taking her away for tests, like brain scans, and destroyed them each time they returned with no answers. I murmured quiet reassurances while caressing her hair and cheeks and holding her hands. My heart nearly broke when her eyes searched my face as if pleading for help. The doctors ran out of ideas about what to do, and I began to run out of hope.

Finally, a consulting M.D. told them to take her off all medications. In a couple of hours the convulsions ended. In a day her vitals were back to normal and joy replaced my terror. It's no wonder she got so big! The twins weighed twelve pounds! In five days, I took Carol home.

I sought an accurate explanation for the seizures. While helping care for Carol, they told me during treatment that they didn't know what caused her problem. Yet, in the official record they listed as the diagnosis 'Postpartum Eclampsia'.

Dr. Light talked with the doctor in Kansas who cared for Carol with Russell. He said they had observed a milder version of the same pattern and stopped it by discontinuing Ergotrate, a medication used to reduce bleeding following delivery. He said that was a well-known, frequent side effect in the Midwest so they had discontinued use of that medication for that purpose. The conclusion was that Carol should avoid Ergotrate the rest of her life.

Because of her convulsion ordeal, Carol was much weaker than she had been with Russell. As she put it, "I'm still groggy, my mind is fuzzy and I have a little difficulty concentrating." Those feelings passed in a couple days.

Russell helped me make preparations to care for Carol and the babies when she returned home. I arranged to do everything for at least a week, with back up help from upstairs tenants, Nancy and Bud Boal, who helped with laundry and other chores. Two of Carol's friends were available to oversee Russell during the day when I couldn't. We had to bottle feed immediately.

When I opened our refrigerator door, ten full baby bottles stared me in the face every day.

How could I feed two babies at once? I propped one beside me on a pillow in the corner of our divan, sat beside him, crossed my legs and rested the second baby in the nest that created. Success! I held a bottle in each hand and the twins nursed like little pigs. I wasn't able to burp them simultaneously of course. After that first day Carol was able to help feed, so we each fed one then alternated so each of us could feed both boys a couple times a day. During night time feedings, I fed both simultaneously so Carol could have an uninterrupted night's sleep.

Carol and Russell had missed each other terribly so Russ stayed close to her and was interested in the babies. The newness soon wore off and he went back to being a boy who wanted his playmates. A visitor asked Russ what he thought of his brothers and he said, "Oh they're all right. All they do is sleep and poopy their pants." Carol got a big laugh out of that.

Providing for twins was a daunting job! About eighty diapers a week had to be laundered, gallons of formula made, and about seventy bottles washed.

Despite her ordeal and caring for twins, Carol's thoughts had been with Milton Eisenhower's loss. One evening while we sat together feeding the babies, I told her about visiting Milton, "I made it a point to check on Milton today. This will be his first Christmas without Helen and I wanted to console him with a friendly visit. He's very lonely and beginning the struggle of rebuilding his life without her. When I left he gave me a hug and thanked me for coming. My heart weeps for him."

So many people wanted to see the twins that I had to restrict visitations to twice a day for one hour until Carol got her strength back. Everyone we knew seemed fascinated by the idea of twins. Carol had visits from girl friends in the neighborhood, husbands and wives from DIR, and members of DAMES – the graduate student wives club. Both sets of grandparents could hardly wait to visit and we didn't have the heart to ask them to wait, so we had my parents for a week at the end of August and Carol's parents for a week in early September.

Things finally slowed down. One morning we shared a relaxing breakfast while the twins slept and Russell was out playing, Carol said, "At last we finally have some private conversation time together! That's been an important part of our lives and I've missed that terribly. I was pleased that so many people wanted to see me and the twins, and seeing the joy of both sets of grandparents was gratifying. But, having twins is quite a demanding and special experience and having both sets of grandparents descend on us within a month after their birth made our lives so hectic. After a few weeks' time, I began wishing for our old routine of having relaxed private time together, and getting acquainted with our babies.

The outpouring of friendship and affection honoring our twins' arrival makes me aware of something important. I live in a nice neighborhood and have a circle of friends and acquaintances who genuinely like us and help us whenever we need it. I have gals I can gab and socialize with, and I'm respected for my skills. Suddenly I've realized I love living here!"

"Carol you've always underestimated your personal worth. You've developed such warm relationships with so many different women in your life because something special draws them to you. You're an interesting, attractive, talented person, but more important than that, you listen to others with an understanding and caring heart. Despite their differences, you find something about them you can like and show it in your actions so they don't have to keep their guard up around you. You show other women who you are and let them be who they are. That's a wonderful gift to give others!"

"Don, I know the foundation for all this is our love, and the security I feel knowing you're always here for me and will keep me safe no matter what difficulties occur. When I went through that terrible time after our babies were born, your voice speaking softly to me and the feel of your hand holding mine or caressing my face eased my fears and reassured me things would be OK. I never experience fear about our future because I know it's safe in your hands. You're not a self-centered man."

"And I feel the same security with you. It's almost unbelievable to me how you've made possible this difficult three years of PhD study. You've helped me selflessly, and brought security to our family doing it."

Carol's smile deepened her dimples but she raised both hands as if to ward off my praise, "We're a *team* – one *hell* of a team! Think back over everything you've done for me! While I was helpless you took good care me, kept my morale up, refused to allow me to do too much too soon, cooked all the meals, made formula for our babies, washed dishes, cleaned house, took care of the kids and the dog, learned to feed two babies simultaneously, changed diapers, and have been continually sweet and loving to us all. On top of that, you make my life fun and interesting. And I'd gladly do the same for you when you need it. The only thing you couldn't do was play the piano for me."

"When I paid our medical bill, Jack Light told me a story that fits this discussion of people helping each other. His bill was so unreasonably tiny that I questioned it, saying it should be more because he had to make a living. He replied with this story:

'I was a star wrestler at Penn State as an undergraduate. They didn't have athletic scholarships then, and I had almost no money. Kind people in State College took me under their wings and made sure I had enough money to stay in school. Without that help at that specific moment in my life I would never have become an M.D. I decided to pass that help on to others when they needed it. I'm passing it along to Carol and you because you need it at this moment in your lives. I hope that later you'll be able to pass that help along to others when they need it."

` Hearing that story about her doctor, Carol's eyes filled with tears, "What a lovely man and what a wonderful idea! I hope we *will* be able to help others as he's helping us."

"Since we're talking about money, Carol, let's talk about how to finance this final year of graduate school. By next year I'll have a regular job with a good income. With the scholarship Milton gave us and my assistantship in Business, we're guaranteed $150 a month this year. That's not enough. We stuffed part of the profits from our Kansas house in savings so we'd have it for backup as necessary. Now we need it. So, I sold our AT&T stock and that will provide another $50 a month for the next 12 months, yielding a total of $200 a month to live on, which is more than we've had this last year with my assistantship and your typing. So, you won't need to continue your typing business. You can use your time caring for and enjoying our family and for pursuing your personal interests."

Carol replied, "That's wonderful. Do we have any savings left?"

"Yes, we started a year and a half ago with $2000. We have $1600 left as a nest egg to start our new life when I have my PhD. Essentially we're using the profit we've made to help cover our living costs this year."

Carol said, "Unless I'm overwhelmed with caring for Douglas and Martin, I might like to still do some typing to make some 'fun money' to spend. Would that be alright with you?"

"Of course," I said, "if that would please you."

Baby noises and twins needing attention interrupted our conversation so I hurried to make my final point, "I have some good news. The joint research proposal for the dissertations of Bernie, Louise, Jeff and me has been approved by our advisors. I'm shooting for a June graduation but unexpected things might push graduation to August. But, in less than a year I should be Mr. PhD Ford. We're getting close, partner!"

Carol felt like her old self in time for Christmas. Shopping for baby gifts really added to our Christmas spirit. We chose another gorgeous Douglas fir Christmas tree and this time Russell hung a lot of the ornaments. He was in a jolly mood and added to the festivities by singing *Here Comes Santa Claus* as he worked. The twins sat smiling and cooing, watching Russ's every move, then kicked their legs with delight when he turned on the tree lights. Carol wrote her parents: "How I do love this season, and it seems more this year than ever I've felt the love and kindness toward my fellow man that should be the true Christmas spirit. Perhaps this is because we've received lovely cards from so many people – fellow graduate students, old and new friends, faculty and colleagues, and our families.

We got a big surprise yesterday – a package from the Penn State Creamery and we couldn't imagine why. It was a lovely box of different kinds of cheese from Milton Eisenhower with an affectionate personal card. For him to take time in his very busy life to send us a gift just amazed us. Don says he thinks the Prexy is pretty lonely, and that a thank you note from me would be especially pleasing to him because he's quite fond of me. I tried to make it special."

It wouldn't be Christmas at the Fords without one of Carol's great holiday parties. Carol described it and another event to her parents: "We invited several friends and neighbors, had drinks and a self-serve light dinner. Then I took the gals into the kitchen and helped each one make a Christmas candle. The guys played Christmas poker while Fred played the piano. The gals placed their candles on top of the piano, lit them, and while enjoying their glowing beauty we sang Christmas carols around my piano. It was fun and joyful. They must have had a great time since people didn't go home until 2 a.m.!

We had a special new Christmas experience. For over a year, Russell has been attending the kids' Sunday school at the little church across the street from us. This is the first time we've been in town for their Christmas services. Russell had a verse to say in their kids program: *A very little boy am I, as you can see, and when old Santa makes his rounds, I hope he won't miss me!* He learned it with little effort and has been saying it to everyone who would listen.

We dressed the twins for Christmas and all went to the program. Russell walked on the stage with the other kids and sang 2 little songs. Later he walked on the stage again and started saying his piece but very softly. One of the teachers told him to start again and speak louder and he said it perfectly. Mother, I'm sure you know how proud that makes a young mother like me feel. Don remembers having to be in Church Christmas programs like that as a kid."

On Christmas Eve, with our sons asleep dreaming of Santa Claus, Carol dressed in the beautiful nightgown and I in the fancy pajamas which were our Christmas gifts last year. By Christmas tree and candle light, we enjoyed the warmth of our bodies touching, sipping martinis.

I said, "Carol, words can't express my feelings having you here with me. When you were having convulsions and they didn't know why, I was terrified and desperate that I might lose you forever. I said to whatever higher power there is, 'It's not fair– we've only had six years together, we've only begun creating the life we dreamed of – You can't have her yet!' I felt helpless and loved you as hard as I could to keep you with me. When you came back to me, I was overwhelmed with a joy unlike anything I've ever experienced! I feel like the God Christmas celebrates has given me back your life as a gift. I promise to shelter it with all my love."

"I wasn't unconscious during that difficult period. I knew things weren't right – I could hear you and feel your touch – and I did feel sheltered by you. I thought, *Don is my magic man and he will make this come out all right.* When I recovered and they brought our babes for us to hold together, I thought, *Here's my gift to you my love – look at the power of our partnership.* My love for you is so strong that it will let nothing separate us. You're stuck with me forever!"

We lay in each other's arms while listening to Christmas music and admiring our Christmas tree, with hearts full of gratitude and joy for the gifts of life 1954 brought to us.

Our first Christmas day with Russell, and the twin boys Carol had in her dreams nine years ago, was full of joy, fun, food, and love. Carol's special version of homemade cinnamon rolls were so delicious that they became a family Christmas morning tradition.

Chapter Twelve

1955 and the Future Looks Bright

After the holidays, Carol wrote her parents: "It's a new and very important year for us. 1955 is the year Don will complete his PhD. I'm afraid it will be a lonely time for me. He works on it from morning to night, usually with Jeff, Bernie and Louise. I've hardly seen Don enough lately to say more than a few sentences to him during the day. Since way before Christmas I've been working 15 hours a day caring for my babies, my family, my home, and typing my last thesis.

Sometimes my stomach gets so knotted up it hurts. I just can't take it anymore! I will not take any more typing for a long time. I'm going to take it easier, enjoy taking care of my babies, play with Russell, keep up my housework, do some sewing for my boys and myself, gossip over coffee with my lady friends, and maybe arrange a few nights out with them."

That is what she did for the next six months, with very limited time for companionship and fun with me and occasional conversations about the antics of our boys. Somehow, I had to find time to help care for and enjoy my wife and three sons. Sometimes I could work at home and care for our kids while Carol went out with friends to see a movie or just gab. Occasionally, we managed to enjoy a special outing. Carol described one such outing to her parents: "Don and I had us a fling last weekend! We were invited to 2 formal dances and went to both.

I borrowed from my neighbor, Sue, a beautiful ballerina length formal – black with white lace over it and strapless. I didn't tell Don anything about it. Then Friday night when we were dressing I made an excuse to go up to Nancy's and she helped me into the dress. When I walked in our door with this Saks 5th Ave.

original on, Don stared and said, 'Pardon me lady – you've got the wrong place – I'm waiting for my wife!' It was more fun surprising him and though he is always pretty complimentary he really drooled over me in that get up. The dance Friday night wasn't much fun. It was mostly faculty members and Deans, and we didn't know very many there. One couple complimented us highly on how well we dance – I often wonder if we look graceful or look like fools on the dance floor, especially when we dance to fast pieces.

Saturday night was our Dames dance. The place was fixed up like a Cabaret – tables with red checked cloths and candles sticking out of beer bottles. A small band furnished music and believe it or not, Don and I danced a samba. It was fantastic fun for both of us with memories to keep us going when we have to be apart."

To keep me in the family loop during long hours of study, Carol collected anecdotes about our sons and shared them with me when we could be together:

"Douglas stands up in his Teeterbabe and crows like a hoarse rooster. He thinks he's so big when he does that. Martin grins over anything – except when you want to take his picture."

"I gave Russ money to buy Mark's birthday party present, and said 'Here's a penny for tax.' 'What's taxes?' 'Well taxes…er…um…it's money we send to the governor so he can build roads, schools, etc.' A minute elapses, 'I know taxes, Mommy. They're something like nails.'"

"I had a horrible scare with Martin yesterday. He has a violent temper when he gets riled up and stiffens himself and holds his breath until he nearly passes out. He and Douglas were playing with the play gym and it bonked Martin lightly on the head. He started yelling so I went in to see what the trouble was. Then I saw his head sagging down to his feet so I picked him up real fast and he looked like he was going to pass out. The thought that he was dying flashed thru my mind and I got panicky. I yelled and following my instinct dashed some cold water on his face. After that he looked perfectly all right and grinned at me. I sat him down and cried with relief, but I was so shaken and that's why I cried all over your nice clean suit when you came home."

"Douglas is getting to be quite the clown and jabbers a blue streak. Says 'MaMaMa' and 'DaDaDa' or variations on such sounds and loves to give everybody the 'raspberries.' This is murder when he has a mouthful of food!"

Carol wrote her parents: "I'm alone again tonight and believe me it gets on my nerves. The last 4 or 5 weeks it's been most every night that 'the experts' have to work, but Don and Jeff made it a rule that now they're taking one night a week and Saturday night and Sunday all day to be with their families. It's hard on both Don and I for we love our family life too much.

I took Russell to Dr. Light yesterday to check on an inflamed eye. Then I said, 'I'm so tired and tense all the time. Is something wrong?' He examined me and said, 'Biologically everything is fine. You just have too much to do and not enough time to do it. Any fights with your husband?' I said, 'I couldn't have a better husband!' He smiled, 'I can believe that.' I told him it was just graduate school and he knows how that is. So he said, 'Here are some pills for nerves and some to take when you feel tired and really want to get zooped up.'

I took a nerve pill this morning as my stomach was in a knot again and it sure did help. I think I've gotten myself in the habit of getting tensed up when I get up in the morning and think of all the things I want to get accomplished during the day. I told the doc that I never used to get nervous or tense and he said, 'Yes, but you've never had twins before either.' He's so right!"

One evening, snuggling in bed, Carol said, "I've acquired two little helpers, Barbie and Judy from across the street. They come over about 4:30 p.m. and ask, 'Mrs. Ford, do you have any dirty work for us to do?' I can't help laughing because they don't do that at home. They entertain the babes, and feed them now and then. They'll peel potatoes, do the dishes, and even empty dirty diapers when they change the kids. Neighbors say, 'How do you stand those pests?' But I enjoy them, especially Judy, for she's one of the sweetest little girls I've ever known. I wish she were mine." That statement brought tears to my eyes. I knew Carol cherished her sons but she would also dearly love to have a daughter.

I pulled her close and kissed her cheek, "Your daily life is full of males so it must be great to have little girls around to add spice to your life."

We decided it was time to get a twin stroller so went shopping in Altoona. Carol said, "Nobody seems to make twin strollers. Now what can we do?"

I put two strollers side-by-side like we were each pushing one and a light dawned! "Honey, I could tie these two together with straps so one of us could push both, but we could also use them separately and that would be good when they can each use theirs as a walker." She liked the idea so we bought two. Later our solution drew lots of attention as we strolled with the boys in them.

I'd had my nose to the collegiate grindstone too long and had news so decided a date was in order. "My dear Mrs. Ford, would you honor me by sharing dinner tomorrow night in our favorite mountain top restaurant to celebrate the bright future we face together?"

"I'd be delighted to dine with a man who is almost a PhD if you don't talk that psychology stuff to me."

It was a lovely June evening with the forests leafed out and wild flowers in bloom. The night air was so warm that we took a table on the deck where we could see village lights in the valley and the starry sky as night fell. We decided on Moscow Mules again with a small sirloin steak, tossed salad, and French fries. As we sipped our cocktail, Carol said, "What's this bright future we're celebrating? Do you have your dissertation finished?"

"No, it's better than that. How would you like to earn $4800 dollars a year with a two month summer vacation and all university holidays as well?"

She choked on her Moscow Mule, "You're kidding, right?"

"Nope. No joke. The Penn State Department of Psychology has offered me an assistant professorship beginning September 1. My job would be to supervise the department's training clinic and teach a course in personality theory."

She said, "That's fantastic! I can't imagine earning that much money after the poverty we've lived in for three years. That's more than twice as much as we've ever earned! I thought universities didn't hire their own graduates to avoid inbreeding."

"You're right," I said, "but the faculty voted unanimously to make an exception to hire me. Your Uncle Carroll told us the best we could expect in the Midwest would be a 12 month instructor appointment. So, this would be an exceptionally good start for us! How do you vote, Madam?"

"I vote AYE Mr. PhD Assistant Professor!"

I raised my glass to clink with hers, "But, we won't be able to finish our dissertations by the end of August, because most of our faculty won't be here then. So, how would you like to show our new sons Kansas for a couple weeks in August?"

She chuckled at the thought. "Only crazy Kansans like us would visit Kansas when it's so hot the asphalt in the streets starts to melt. Let's go!!"

"OK." I said, "You work out a schedule with your folks and mine and organize what we have to take on our trip. I'll make travel plans."

The twins were baptized in Minneapolis, Kansas and Carol's mother got to brag about them with all the relatives. As usual, Carol's Mom got 'sick' in anticipation of our leaving them and going to Marysville, but Carol didn't let that ploy get to her.

We had some much-needed fun and relaxation in Marysville. My parents loved keeping the babies while Carol and I went swimming, played tennis and visited old friends. Russ loved visiting the Lueers farm, the home where my sister Lois's husband had been born and raised.

We enjoyed the change of pace vacation in Kansas but agreed that returning to our Pennsylvania home and friends felt good. I immediately worked to finish my dissertation. Over morning coffee, Carol told our upstairs neighbor, Nancy, "Don is doing his writing at home. He writes during the day and then relaxes in the evening with me. It seems like heaven.

The twins are a real handful now, running around loose and getting into mischief every time they're out of my sight. The extent of their damage yesterday was pulling my one and only blooming African violet off the radio and breaking the pot all to pieces – the violet wasn't hurt too much, thank goodness. When I came back with my dry clothes off the line I found Don chasing Martin who was emptying the Bisquick box all over the living room. Martin is climbing on things the most so he's the biggest trouble maker."

Nancy said, "How do you keep up with 3 kids? I have trouble keeping up with Colleen."

"It is a challenge! You never saw such curious kids and they can travel from one thing to another so fast I can't keep up with them. Sometimes, they're great fun though, like a couple of days ago they both climbed up on the piano bench and played duets. Russell is becoming a big help. I noticed when we got home from the trip he seemed interested in helping around the place and asked for things to do. He empties the trash, picks up the scattered toys and many other things that save me a lot of stooping and steps. I'm amazed at his patience."

One evening I said to Carol, "Russell desperately wants an air rifle he saw at Boal's store that costs $2.50." We agreed to offer him a nickel a day for helping so he could save for it.

Eventually, he emptied his dog bank on the counter and Bud Boal handed him the gun. Carol said, "All his stored hope turned into the biggest gusher of happiness I ever saw in a boy." (As an adult, his favorite movie featured a boy who desperately wanted a BB gun for Christmas.)

My new salary began September 1, 1955. Carol said, "For three years we've pinched pennies to get by. We've finally escape from graduate student poverty." Her relief was short lived. Our check was delayed because they hadn't received my physical exam. Carol angrily chewed me out about the delay. We had to borrow from a friend to get through the month.

In typical Carol fashion, she funneled her frustration into constructive action and spent all day on the phone talking to various offices and authorities. Within three days we had the check, she paid our bills and repaid the loan from our friend. People in general saw my wife as a gentle and quiet person. Few knew how effectively assertive she could be when she got her dander up!

One evening after the boys were in bed we relaxed over hot chocolate at our kitchen table. Carol was eager to share her new plans. "Don, I'm excited about pursuing some personal interests now. I've enrolled in a continuing education course on sewing children's clothing and accepted chairmanship of the DAMES interest group on seasonal decorations. I'll help them learn how to make floral arrangements and other decorations to fit different seasons."

I was grinning, planning my response to that news when she blurted out her biggest plan, "You know for years I've wanted to learn how to paint. I've joined with five other people in an art group, and a fellow has agreed to be our teacher. He's starting with oil painting. I'm the only one who has no previous training so I may seem stupid, but I don't care, I want to learn."

"Carol, I'll never forget that first Christmas morning we spent together driving to Marysville and how you admired the moonlit scenes and wished you could paint them. Nature has been your muse for so many years, I'm delighted you can finally pursue your dream."

We decided the first purchase with our increased income should be a TV for our family. Dave McKinley in the College of Business was a friend with cutting edge knowledge about TV development in 1956. He got us a big Setchell-Carlson TV at wholesale price and installed it Saturday, November 12. That brought a new dimension of enjoyment to our lives.

On December 1st Carol proudly said, "Today I typed the last page of your dissertation, so it's ready for you to submit. I know how difficult Louise's life has been on your four person research team with her full time job, finishing her PhD, taking care of her home and hubby, and being pregnant all at the same time so I called today and said I'd type her final thesis as a gift for their baby. She was dumbfounded and delighted. I got Polly to type Bernie's. I really want to do this for I think a lot of them. Louise will babysit whenever I want while I'm typing hers."

When Carol died, Louise wrote, *"Thoughts of Carol have been running through my head, accompanied by occasional tears. I still feel close to her. She was a saint to me in typing my dissertation when I was exhausted. When I think back on how tough a job that was over 50 years ago, with all of those carbons and onion skin copies and white-out, I realize how great a saint she really was. She was always good humored and sweet, but quiet and unassuming about all of her many talents and achievements, and so low key about her many contributions to others. I remember how relieved and grateful I was when she gave a contribution for the dental work of a mother I was counseling who could not pay for it. Her family problems were horrendous."*

Carol, Russell and I put up our annual seven-foot Christmas tree and adorned it with the traditional decorations, with Douglas and Martin as our audience. We played Christmas carols while decorating, sometimes singing along. When we turned out the living room lights and Russell lit the Christmas tree, Martin and Douglas bounced their Teeterbabes up and down as hard as they could and laughed with excitement.

Carol and I repeated our Christmas Eve tradition of putting our sons to bed and having some time just for us. We were both pooped from the hard drive during the fall to meet our dissertation deadlines. I made Bloody Marys, sat a plate of small crackers with cheeses on our school teacher coffee table, and lit Carol's homemade candles. The night was very cold so we cuddled on the sofa, dressed in matching PJs Carol made, warm slippers, and cozy robes.

We touched our glasses, sipped our drink and relaxed in the Christmas ambience. I said, "Carol, we've spent three hard years together here and have accomplished our goal. We'll begin the New Year with the PhD we earned together. You've made a lot of sacrifices, worked very hard to make it all possible, and postponed pursuing most of your own interests like art and music. Buried under all that work is the core of love that brought us to this point, together.

Beginning this next year it's your turn. Let me work to support your interests and talents – something too long delayed. Let me be your assistant as you've been mine. I promise from now on there will always be enough money to make a good life possible. In my loneliness while I was in the Air Force, I dreamed of life with you, but the life you brought me makes those dreams pale by comparison. Thank you for all you are and all you've given me. I drink a toast to my extraordinary, beautiful Carol, the music in my life." I took a generous gulp of my Bloody Mary to wet my whistle after that big speech.

After a short silence, Carol replied, "My heart is so full of love and happiness right now that words are hard to find. You've already given me a life far beyond those my married friends talk about. It *has* been hard at times, but it's also produced lots of fun, happiness and love with wondrous results like our three sons. I feel like something is ending and we face a new beginning. I had that same feeling when we got married. It's exciting to face an unknown future, but I know what we're capable of as partners, so have no anxiety about it. There *is* one thing I don't want to change and that's the love we've shared since your 1945 furlough. So, here's to the wondrous man who's been transforming my life into something beautiful ever since we met when I was sweet 16 and hoping to be kissed!"

We snuggled together, drowsily listening to music, with my arm around her and Carol's sleepy head drooping on my shoulder.

Resisting sleep was futile in our state of exhaustion, so we dragged off to bed to rest up for Christmas morning.

We had a joyful and relaxing Christmas day. For the first time in our life we had a comfortable income, so went a little overboard with gifts. We lavished the boys with cowboy gear and laughed out loud at their noisy antics.

After three hard years, graduation day arrived! Carol described it to her parents: "While Don and I dressed for graduation, a huge red carnation corsage was delivered to our door. I thought it was from Don, but the card really got me. It was from Don's parents. They've been generous in their praise of what I've done to help Don. I'm lucky they love and accept me.

Russ and I wish you could have seen the graduation ceremony and watched Don get his diploma. I was so thrilled and proud when he walked across the stage, shook Milton's hand and had his yellow and blue hood draped over his shoulders. Milton said, "Don, this is one of the nicest things that's ever happened to me at one of these ceremonies – you are the only person to whom I've awarded all three degrees!'

We and the Ashbys took our kids to the Student Union for supper to celebrate and the kids behaved beautifully. Several faculty members stopped to congratulate us and admire the kids, which was more fun than eating the delicious food. To end our special day, all of Don's new PhD team and their wives went to the Tavern to slop up beer and eat pizza. We yapped about the past, present and future, and then went home exhausted but happy. Six close friends, sharing life's hardships and accomplishments, is a wondrous, never to be forgotten, experience.

A few days after graduation, friends gathered at our house to celebrate our success. It was a heartwarming event. We hadn't quite realized how many people liked us as we like them. We felt like a real part of the community. That's another reward from three years of hard work.

A week later Carol wrote her parents: "I've started building a new life style. This week I've done more loafing than since we had kids. I've played the piano and don't sound so rusty now. I've taken naps, had coffee with the girls, etc. My house is nice and clean with no pressing work. Don and I have been together a lot between semesters. We found a young couple to play bridge with –

she's in my decorating interest group and he's a psych graduate student. I'm so relaxed and see my daily activities as pleasure rather than a burden. It's a wonderful feeling!!

I feel much more at ease and enjoy watching our kids' antics. When major goofs happen I no longer get so upset. For example, one day I smelled something awful and dashed to the oven. Guess what was in there smoldering away? Douglas and Martin had put one of their shoes in the oven without me realizing it and they were pretty well cooked by the time I got them out. I told Don and he stood like an idiot laughing his head off. I had to admit it was funny.

You can read what it's like around here in Don's description of **one hour** of child care in our home: Don grades papers; Carol irons; Russell decides to play with a neighbor boy, puts on coat & hat, can't get shirt tucked in; Carol says he's a crybaby, that makes him mad so he takes off coat and says he isn't going; Don tells Russ to call Carol a name back; Russ thinks this is a good idea, puts on coat, hat, guns, calls Carol fatty pants and runs out; Don continues grading papers; Carol still ironing; Martin and Douglas play with blocks; Pogo sleeps by the radiator.

Carol puts pork in pressure cooker; chases Martin and Douglas away from kitchen drawer; tells Don to turn pork over in a little while; goes upstairs to wake Colleen to babysit for neighbor; Don grading papers; Martin and Doug pushing noisy toys; Pogo sleeps by radiator; Don hears Martin and Doug laughing and splashing, realizes it must be the toilet; washes toys; goes back to grading papers; Martin and Doug on chairs looking out window; Don hears bell ringing, wonders who's at door, remembers we have no doorbell, goes to kitchen and finds Martin pounding phone on floor; chases Martin away and restores phone to original position.

Smells smoke, realizes smoke is in kitchen, remembers pork, turns pork over; hears ironing board shaking, arrives in time to keep iron from flattening Doug's head; returns to grading papers; Martin and Doug have a pushing fight; Don hears Doug talking in an excited tone, finds Doug poured liquid detergent on floor, Martin and Doug in middle of the mess; tries to wash their hands, gets nothing but suds, decides it will dry and quits washing; tries to wipe up floor, gets nothing but suds; wonder what the hell to do;

puts rug over spot; Martin and Doug tearing pages out of magazine; Pogo sleeping by the radiator.

Don smells smoke again, remembers pork, turns it over, adds water and puts on lid; notices things are ominously quiet; goes looking for Martin and Doug; finds them sitting quietly by toy shelves thinking; decides better turn on TV before they think too much; Mickey Mouse club starts; Martin and Douglas come running; Carol comes back downstairs; Don goes back to grading papers; twins watch TV; Pogo sleeping by the radiator. Thank God for TV!

Now, you can see why we look forward to getting away by ourselves for some fun. For example, my Dames had their spring formal dance last weekend. I put on the fancy cocktail dress Don gave me for Christmas and we had a lot of fun kicking up our heels. It had been a year since we went to a dance. This week we gals got together for a bridge party and I had a great time, partly because I played well, but mostly because we had such a good time gabbing.

Many of our friends complain of having a hard time getting their kids to sleep. It's their fault; little kids can be trained to sleep when it's time. Don did that with Douglas and Martin. We put them to bed; if they wanted up we refused and we never got them up to show them off to visitors. Don laid them down and put the blanket over their heads so they couldn't see anything. He stood by their bed and if they moved around he slapped them lightly on their butt. He did that until they went to sleep, then he uncovered their head. After eight days, we could lay them in bed, cover their head and in a few minutes they'd be asleep. They've slept wells ever since."

Chapter Thirteen

Carol Tackles New Roles and Discovers New York City

On September 1, 1955, Carol and I were suddenly transformed from being graduate students to members of the faculty at Penn State. I had worked in the Psych Clinic for two years so it was easy to become coordinator of all its training activities and participate in faculty responsibilities. It was much more difficult for Carol to suddenly shift from the role of *graduate student wife* to that of *Professor Ford's wife,* and to begin participating in the social circles of faculty couples.

Despite her many talents and accomplishments, Carol's new roles reactivated some of her old self-doubts, which she shared with her parents: "Don is training three young women to do intake interviewing at the psych clinic. We had them to dinner to help them feel more at ease in their new roles. For some reason, I was uncomfortable about preparing a meal for three strange females and trying to converse with girl PhD candidates. All they and Don talked about was psychology, their careers, or things pertaining to the Clinic, so I was pretty much left out.

This was more my fault than theirs, for I just sat there like a bump on a log not offering any other subjects for conversation. I've overcome my social fears a lot, but still am unable to converse freely in a group, especially one I feel is intellectually superior. I exasperate Don and he keeps reminding me of my high IQ etc. and does so much to build me up.

I sure am gonna do my best to fight this dumb feeling. In contrast, we went to a late party of grad students and psych clinic faculty Saturday, and there I had a wonderful time, chatting freely with the wives and some of the men too. I went from group to group not feeling the least bit self-conscious. I sure don't understand myself."

Fortunately that difficult transition to a faculty culture didn't last long because I was offered a much better job. Bob Bernreuter, one of my mentors, sold Milton Eisenhower on a new idea which I explained to Carol, "Dr. Bernreuter told Eisenhower, 'We've demonstrated with DIR that most students who initially fail in college do so for reasons that can be fixed. Since we know what causes students to initially fail, why don't we prevent it in the first place?'

Milton liked the idea and asked for a proposal about how that could be done. Bernreuter asked me to help prepare it. Milton liked the proposal and submitted it to the Faculty Senate and Board of Trustees for approval. They also liked and formally approved it.

The program is to be implemented through a new unit called *The Division of Counseling (DOC)*. Dr. Bernreuter has accepted appointment as Director with the responsibility for creating and implementing the new program. He offered me the appointment of Assistant Director to help build the program. The old DIR program will become part of the new DOC.

If I accept the appointment, we'll have a larger salary, I'd be in control of my work schedule and continue to have faculty status in Psychology. It means our primary work relationships would change from academic to professional psychologists, similar to DIR. We're a team and always make decisions like this together. Should we do it?"

With a big grin, Carol said, "YES! I've enjoyed our relationships with your professional colleagues more than the psychological theorists. It would be a permanent job and I really like living here. Most important, I've watched how you love creating things and you're very good at it. I won't be happy unless you're happy, so if you like the challenge, do it!!" So we did.

Bernreuter and his wife Shirley invited the initial staff to a get acquainted dinner. Carol said, "I know he's a big shot at Penn State, and his wife was a very successful artist in Chicago. Students who met her are in awe of her. My knees are shaking in anticipation of this evening."

That night as we got ready for bed Carol said, "My knees stopped shaking almost as soon as we got there. They were so nice and quite common. Shirley inquired about my interest in art, shared her interests and a bit of her history with me, and set me at ease all evening. I'll enjoy knowing them. They certainly aren't afflicted with bigshotitis!"

In addition to responsibilities at the main campus in State College, my new job entailed traveling to Penn State's twenty branch campuses around the state. Most of them came into existence during the Depression years so students could save money by living at home while doing college studies. I explained the gist of my duties to Carol, "Most of them are located on former elaborate estates donated to Penn State by rich owners, like the Behrend center we visited at Erie. They're not like a junior college, but are an integral part of Penn State. Students can start on a branch campus and later transfer to the main campus to complete a degree if they wish. That's a unique arrangement and why Penn State is called one university, geographically dispersed. I'll be responsible for the counseling programs on all campuses.

Bernreuter wants me to visit each campus regularly so I'll be familiar with the locations and staff. He suggested I start by introducing myself to staff at the three campuses located in the southeast corner of the state: Hazelton, Pottsville, and Ogontz near Philadelphia."

Knowing how hard it was on Carol and Winifred when Eugene left them home alone over half the time each year, I'd promised myself a pattern like that would not happen in our marriage. Our pattern would be one of shared trips, whenever Carol was willing or able.

I suggested my plan to Carol, "Let's make this a kind of vacation trip. You can visit the campuses with me to experience that part of Pennsylvania and the people. Then, since we'd be so close, we could visit New York City for a long weekend before returning home. Expenses would be paid except for our NYC visit, so it wouldn't cost much. The two girls you liked at the clinic have volunteered to stay with the kids while we're gone."

"You know how much I've longed to travel! As long as our kids are safe I'd love to travel with you. I'd like to meet the people you work with, see how the centers work, and how they fit into the rest of Penn State. Then, look out New York City – Here we Come!"

"Great! We'll visit the campuses first, check into our New York City hotel Friday night to get a good night sleep and spend Saturday and Sunday exploring the city."

That Saturday morning we went shopping. Later Carol wrote her friend, Ginny Elliott: "We spent most of Saturday in all kinds of dress and big department stores. Don bought me a present of a beautiful cocktail dress made with beige lace, princess style with a huge flared skirt. I'm eager to go dancing in it. We found a street with nothing but big fabric stores. I went crazy – I've never seen so much beautiful material. I bought an assortment to make clothes for me and the boys. By midafternoon I was pooped, so we went to our hotel to rest.

Then we went to the Julie Harris play *The Lark*. It was a wonderful experience – there's an intangible rapport between an actor and audience that just isn't felt in movies."

Afterwards we strolled up Times Square on sidewalks packed with people, and then took a cab to Asti's. It's a small Italian restaurant on the edge of Greenwich Village recommended by our musical friend, Dave McKinley. He said singers from the metropolitan opera often went to Asti's to eat after a performance and while waiting to eat, they gambled to see which of them would have to sing for their supper. That became a popular but unpredictable happening, so Asti's hired aspiring opera singers as bartenders, waitresses and waiters who sing while they work. Dave thought and I *knew* that a singer like Carol would love Asti's.

The place was packed, but we got a table for two by the back wall. The walls were covered with signed pictures of opera stars. While sipping our cocktails and enjoying our entrée we absorbed the atmosphere and the music. Suddenly a group of waiters burst out with an aria from *La Boheme*. Then, a woman wandered among the tables singing various opera pieces. After a little pause, the bartenders and waiters played the *Anvil Chorus* on bar bottles and cash registers. That was so much fun we both laughed until our bellies ached! After a break, another woman wandered among the tables singing. The beautiful voices and happy atmosphere left Carol breathless. We'd finished our meal but just couldn't bring ourselves to leave.

One of the female singers sat down to rest at a table beside us. Carol spoke to her. "You have a beautiful voice and your singing is marvelous. How did you get into opera singing?"

She smiled at the compliment, "My father insisted I go to college so I completed a Master's degree in psychology at a southern university while I also worked towards becoming an opera singer. When I finished my degree I came to New York to pursue my dream of singing in the Met. I was lucky to get this singing job because wealthy lovers of music patronize Asti's and sometimes finance an opera career for a performer they like. It's hard to break into the Met without such a sponsor."

Carol said, "Hearing this singing makes me hunger to get back into some choral group." As if they'd known each other for years, the opera singer and Carol talked about their favorite choral works. Then the woman started singing a work familiar to Carol. Singers at the tables around us stood and sang with her. She beckoned Carol to join them. My formerly shy, self-conscious wife happily joined in and sang joyfully! When the singing ended, Carol glowed with happiness, "What a fantastic experience! For me, this is the highlight of our wonderful visit to New York City. I'll never forget it. You sure know how to make a girl happy!"

We took a cab back to the hotel, both worn out from our first day in NYC. In bed she nestled in my arms, too excited to sleep, and whispered, "You're my magic man."

We toured the city Sunday morning. The Circle Line Tour on the Hudson River was impressive and included the Statue of Liberty. A tour of the United Nations, made us think of Milton Eisenhower. At St. Patrick's Cathedral, Carol said, "I love beauty in all its forms, but this Cathedral is so huge and ornate I think the simplicity of Christ is completely lost in it."

We slept like a log that night and left early Monday morning to visit the Ogontz Center. We got home late that afternoon to a boisterous welcome from three boys overjoyed to see us and we felt the same. NYC was wonderful, but we'd much rather live in Lemont, PA.

That week Eisenhower shocked Penn State by announcing his resignation. Carol said, "I feel so sad. He's been our friend since we got married. Do you know why he's leaving?"

"The one-word answer is loneliness. He's lost the love of his life, his son is in the military, and his daughter is starting college elsewhere. He doesn't want to be rattling around all alone in the President's home. My guess is he'll come to roost near Ike, who owns an historic farmette near Washington DC. He once told me he'd like to do some writing. Just because he's leaving here doesn't mean we'll lose his friendship. He wants that to continue much as we do."

Carol said, "I was so scared of him when we first met. He and Helen set me at ease, but my weak self-confidence still troubles me. I think our trip to NYC has helped boost my confidence a little. Remember when we had to join other faculty and their wives at Dr. Snyder's home last week to meet a job candidate? Well, I usually hate such things but every time I've gone so far this year I've had an enjoyable time. Usually the women and men talk in separate groups, but this time I found myself talking with groups of two or three men and found it rather nice for a change. I've always been so shy where men were concerned, but I'm slowly realizing they aren't ogres and most are easy to talk with."

I chuckled at the word *ogres,* "Carol, you have a special advantage because most men are eager to talk with a beautiful woman like you."

As we sat in our back yard on a warm, sunny afternoon watching our kids play I broached a ticklish subject, "I know your mom is pushing hard for us to fly out there for a visit. Unfortunately, I can't go this summer because of my new job, but I'm willing to help make it possible and suffer the loneliness if you want to take the kids and fly out there on your own."

Carol grimaced, "I *might* have had the courage if not for that awful plane crash killing seventy four people! The idea is both scary and exciting. It *would* be hard because we've never been separated for that long since we were married, but it would mean a great deal to Mom."

Finally she decided to do it, so she flew out to Kansas and back with three little kids in tow! They had fun and I was lonesome, but very proud of Carol's confident accomplishment.

The next weekend, Carol said, "Don, I've decided to pursue some additional interests. I've joined the League of Women Voters and the Lemont Women's Club. I have registered for an advanced adult education class on oil painting and am eager to get started. I also recruited and started a two-table bridge group of gals I like."

"You're really rolling, Carol. Sounds like fun. It will give you more friends to gab with and provide relief from your all male family."

One sunny Sunday as we watched our kids play in the back yard, Carol said, "We've agreed that we need a new home and discussed possibly building another house. You've been so busy with the pressures of your new job we haven't gotten beyond the talking phase. I'm fed up with living here, so if it's OK with you I'd like to start looking around for possibilities."

"I'd be happy for you to do that because I'd like to get out of here too."

A week later during a happy hour before dinner she said, "I've talked with realtors, looked at houses and building lots, and got information about prices. It's discouraging. I found nothing worthwhile and prices are way too high. But, I'm not giving up."

One day when I came home from work, Carol said, "Get in the car and I'll show you where we'll build our new house!" I thought, *She really has a head of steam up.*

Carol drove toward State College on Branch Road about a mile, pulled into a private, crushed rock lane, and parked by a big apple tree. She said, "This is it! Follow me."

We walked across a sloping meadow to the woods, down a steep hill through the trees until we reached a mountain stream. I was astonished by the beautiful site and had no idea it existed. Carol gave me a moment to absorb our surroundings, then told me the story:

"This stream is called Slab Cabin Run, a good trout stream. A couple years ago a professor named Whitacer retired from the College of Agriculture. He and his wife, Miriam, bought this farmette, planning to start a small truck garden business. Two years later he died suddenly and Miriam was alone. She needs money so decided to subdivide some of her land for homes. I learned about it from her at a Lemont Women's Club meeting. She's very nice. Where we parked is the end of her little development. I told her I thought we'd buy those two lots and reserve the right to buy the two adjoining lots that go down to the stream, if you agreed. They're not expensive, so we can afford them. What do you think?"

I almost choked. "What do I think? I think *you* are *MY* magic woman – this is fantastic! There's nothing like it anywhere around here. What a wonderful place for our boys to grow up! The private lane is safe from car traffic and there's plenty space for a lawn where the house would be for them to play. Just think of the fun they could have playing around the stream when they're a little older. And, what a great picnic spot down by the stream! That stream would be a wonderful challenge for your growing painting skills. You've found one of Mother Nature's gardens. You're wonderful!" I swung Carol around in the air while kissing her smiling mouth. "Wow, Honey, when you take charge you do wonderful things!"

She replied, "Aw shucks – I'm just a poor Kansas farm girl who knows a good thing when she sees it. That's how I got you." We stopped at Miriam Whitacer's house at the head of the lane and paid a deposit to hold the land until our purchase was finalized. On the way home, Carol said with a satisfied smile, "This is another of our dreams come true."

After one of our favorite dinners of ham, potatoes and green beans, I said, "Carol, the Christmas season is upon us. Shall we cut our Christmas tree Saturday?"

She laughed, "First comes the Christmas tree then comes the Christmas shopping!"

With a groan I added, "Then comes Christmas bills."

At the Christmas tree farm I said, "You and Russell choose the tree while I keep Douglas and Martin busy." Pogo and the twins had great fun running through the trees.

Russell called, "Mom and I found a beauty!"

The twins chattered excitedly about the tree as I cut it down and tied it on top of our car. After supper, as Carol and the twins relaxed in the living room, Russ and I brought the tree into the kitchen. Carol and I laughed at the twins' screams of delight as Russell dragged our tree into the living room, singing *Jingle Bells* at the top of his lungs. After we decorated the tree, Carol sat at the piano with Douglas and Martin beside her and Russell and I standing behind them. She played Christmas carols and led the singing. She managed to play on, even when the twins' rendition of *Jingle Bells* drove Russ and me into fits of hysterical laughter.

Later that night, Carol said, "We have such fun at Christmas with our boys. Growing up as an only child with a bah humbug father, we hardly celebrated. It wasn't until we married that I discovered what I'd been missing. Now it's truly a time of excitement, fun and joy for me!

And it's becoming a busy social season for us. Friday night we have the annual candle making party for our friends, and will probably sing around the piano. Saturday night we're invited to dinner and a formal Christmas dance. I'm excited because I'll get to wear the new cocktail dress we bought in NYC. We haven't been to a dance for a long time so I'm ready to dance your feet off and have a ball. Some friends have invited us to an open house Sunday."

Then, Carol's Christmas spirit was bruised. When I came home from work she greeted me with, "I need a drink!" I thought, *OOPS something's wrong!* While the boys watched TV, I mixed two cranberry juice cocktails, filled a small bowl with nuts and we sat at the kitchen table.

I said, "OK, what's wrong, Honey?"

She sipped her drink and swallowed nervously several times before the day's happenings poured out of her. "The twins were into everything this morning while I worked. I was at my wits end and finally paddled them and sent them to our bedroom to play. Then I was out of bread so told Russ to watch the little devils while I ran down to Boal's store. When I got back the twins were looking mighty guilty and Russ was pointing to my violet plants. They'd broken off every leaf, leaving nothing but bare stems! I saw red, green, blue, purple and black! I paddled their butts good and then sat down and bawled like a baby. The boys shut up in a hurry because they've never seen me cry and crying is one thing they understand.

When I finally was able to make lunch, Russell locked himself in our bedroom and told me not to disturb him 'cause he was making me something'. He came out with some stick stems with green construction paper leaves pasted on them sticking in a bottle. He gave them to me and said he'd made them because the babies had ruined my real plants. I was touched and started bawling again. The twins sat in front of me and held my hands." I hugged Carol while she smiled through her tears and said, "When kids do things like Russ did it fills your heart with love, and you forget all the trouble they are at times."

Finally, *Twas the Night Before Christmas* ...and the boys were asleep, time for our private celebration! I told Carol to dude herself up cause we had lots to celebrate. In keeping with the Christmas season, I mixed cranberry-vodka cocktails and grabbed a few snacks. Carol's special candles and the Christmas tree lights cast a warm glow in an otherwise dark house. Carol looked delectable in the special emerald green dress with delicate gold and red pattern she'd made for our first Christmas in grad school. I didn't look too bad myself in the blue tweed sport coat with grey trousers Carol had given me for my birthday.

I passed Carol her cocktail and said, "Let's start with a toast – *Here's to a successful first year on our new pathway in life, and to the surprises and accomplishments the New Year holds for us."* We drank our toast and shared a gentle kiss. "Carol, what was the greatest highlight of this year for you?"

Without hesitation she said, "It was when Milton Eisenhower handed you your PhD and congratulated you. For me, that symbolized everything we enjoyed, accomplished and suffered through together since we've been married. It was the brass ring in our carnival of life."

"I agree, but that's much brighter than a highlight – it's more like the final big, colorful explosion in a 4th of July fireworks show! What would be your biggest personal highlight?"

After a little thought she said, "I think it's that I've finally started working towards my dream of becoming a painter. Painting, like music, is a special way of capturing beauty. Music isn't just a series of notes, it comes from the blending of those notes into patterns of glorious sound. For example, when I'm in a large chorus singing the *Messiah* I'm only one note, but when my voice merges with other voices, I'm part of the glorious sound made by all of us.

I think the experience of painting a picture may be like that. Each spot of color is like a note. When colors blend they collectively become a picture that, when viewed by a person, merges with their memories and thoughts to create a personal experience. I've only begun, but so far I'm quite pleased with my oil painting class. Last Tuesday I drew my charcoal sketch on canvas so I'm ready to start slopping on the paint!"

"I've never heard music or art described that way. I find your way of thinking exciting."

"OK, what would be your personal highlight?" I was still thinking about music and color blending, so sipped my cocktail thoughtfully before answering.

"It's one thing to pass courses, make grades and get degrees and quite another to gain respect for applying what you've learned to improve the lives of others. When the faculty voted unanimously to appoint me as assistant professor because they thought me capable of running their psych clinic, that was a very special evaluation. What's your goal for this year?"

She laughed and almost shouted, "I WANT TO MOVE INTO MY NEW HOME!!!"

"Next year we'll celebrate before a warm fire in our new fireplace in our new home. We've come this far in our dance of life. Will my musical artist dance with me into our future?"

Carol selected some romantic music, came into my arms, and we glided around the living room, two notes merging into our own melody, until we floated off to bed to share our love.

Chapter Fourteen

Carol Reaches Goals and Plans Her Pennsylvania Dream Home

I came home from my first day of work in the New Year and Carol said, "Milton Eisenhower has written us as personal friends to report that he's now president of John's Hopkins University in Baltimore, so he's close to his brother, Ike, in the White House. I'll read you the last paragraph of his letter because I'm quite proud of it: 'I'll always be interested in your prospective plans and your personal feelings and accomplishments so do keep in touch with me. Of all the students I have known in 14 years you are my favorites in every way. So you know I have a deep affection for you and want your pursuit of happiness to be completely successful.'"

A few days later, Milton called and invited us to visit. We agreed on January 11-12. As we drove down, Carol said, "I'm excited and a little nervous about our visit. I'm thrilled and honored he wants us to spend this time with him. He's such a busy person, it seems amazing to me he'd take time out to have us come to his home, but I know he's always thought a lot of us."

"Carol, I suspect he's lonely on weekends like this when Ruth has gone back to school. Important and powerful people like Milton have few people they can safely confide in. With a brother who is President of the U.S., it must be particularly difficult. He enjoys our company and trusts us to keep our mouths shut."

Carol wrote her parents about the visit: "We had a lovely trip down and back for the weather was perfect, arriving after lunch. While they build his new house on campus, he's living in a big old stone house built in the 1920s. We had a nice large bedroom on the second floor with a private bathroom. We spent the afternoon watching the North-South football game and chatting. He told us about his 18 year old daughter, Ruth, and the social whirl she had this year 'coming out' in Baltimore society. He laughed when he said it was quite an experience for him trying to see she did all the proper things, going with her to buy clothes, etc. He said Helen (his wife) would have been in her glory doing all this. He showed us pictures of his Latin-American tour last year for Ike. Ruth went with him as his official hostess. Can you imagine an 18 year old girl hobnobbing with presidents of countries and all sorts of high officials? She's a beautiful girl – and so poised – looks a lot like her mother.

He has an African-American couple helping him; Mary does the cooking and cleaning – Charles looks after Milton and everything else. I got a kick out of that. For example, Milton likes a happy hour before dinner so he said, 'Charles would you make us some martinis.' 'Charles, will you close the drapes.' 'Charles, will you turn up the lights.' Charles waited on us hand and foot and I found it nice for a while.

During and after dinner we got down to serious business and had a short course on everything from foreign affairs to domestic policies. At one point Don started complaining about John Foster Dulles (Secretary of State) letting the Russians take over the reconstruction of the Suez Canal for Egypt. Milton attentively let Don express his view and then explained: 'The best way to prevent war isn't with armies; it's to get countries like Russia into economic partnerships with so many other countries that they're so constrained by those partnerships they can't go to war.' What Milton wanted to talk with Don about was the crisis in education. While they talked, I listened and played his Hammond organ for an hour. Boy is it tricky to play two keyboards and foot pedals all at the same time.

It's strenuous and exhausting just to listen to a person like Milton – he's so well informed and brilliant. It's a blessing we have people like him helping our government. Both Don and I were so stimulated by his conversation we had a hard time sleeping. We had a leisurely breakfast and left at noon. As we left he hugged and thanked us for a wonderful time.

Don has never used our friendship with Milton for personal gain and wants it to remain a private, purely personal relationship. That's why we don't tell others about things like this trip."

Later that week we talked about our visit over steaming cups of hot chocolate. Carol asked, "Don, would you be my Charles? Then I could say 'Don, would you close the drapes? Don, would you take out the trash? Don, would you give me a kiss?" I laughed at her humor, of course, and willingly agreed to be her Charles.

Later that evening, after a dinner of left over ham, macaroni and cheese – which our sons love – and homemade applesauce, Carol and I relaxed over coffee and I said, "I talked with Bob Bernreuter who, as Director of the Division of Counseling, is my boss. I told him we had to get out of this old apartment, would like to build a house, but couldn't make such an important decision without a clearer perspective on whether we could afford it. He told me that we would receive a substantial raise July 1, and that I was being groomed to take over his job. Our future looks bright here for as long as we want to stay. Are you ready to build a new house?"

Carol replied, "I'm kind of overwhelmed with things moving so fast. Just 18 months ago we were poor graduate students surviving month to month, and now you tell me you'll be the big boss of this whole new enterprise in another year. I'm very proud of you – of us – but it *is* a little scary to think of being the big boss's wife like Shirley Bernreuter."

I laughed at that analogy, "Don't try to be like Shirley Bernreuter – just be that beautiful, talented, down to earth Kansas girl – just be you!"

Carol bonked me gently on the arm to punctuate her point, "OK, but you can't be a 'big boss' without a house to live in, so I'll find us an architect to help us create a plan for building our new house."

We met with Phil Halleck, an architecture professor. Locals considered Phil to be one of the more creative designers in the area. We signed a contract and Carol explained her ideas:

"Our lots slope down from the lane to the woods. I imagine a two-story house sitting in the middle of our land. The second floor would be at ground level on the lane side while the first floor would be ground level on the stream side. Three bedrooms would be in the first floor. The kitchen and living areas would be on the second floor and kind of flowing into one another. I'd like big windows in the second floor side facing the stream to sort of bring the outside inside."

As we drove home Carol said, "I like him and the way he talked about possibilities."

The winter-spring semester was under way. One evening after the kids were in bed we had a planning session about our schedules. Carol said, "I'll have three outside activities. I've registered for an adult education course in upholstery. That class meets Monday evenings. My bridge group meets on Thursdays once or twice a month. My painting class meets on Tuesday evenings, and that's the activity I look forward to the most. My painting teacher complimented me on my work and said she's really thrilled with me. I was so proud and inspired!"

I said, "The only night I have a regular commitment is Wednesday, working on research with Hugh, so I'll be home all the nights you have scheduled."

In the weekly letter to her parents Carol shared our latest activities: "Friday night we were invited over to Hugh and Nat Urban's – he and Don are working together on a research project with Dr. Snyder. We knew them a few years back when Hugh was a grad student and worked in DIR. They'll have their second baby any day now. They're nice and interesting people and we enjoyed the evening. They're the kind of folks I'd like to have for friends."

Dr. Bernreuter had a get-acquainted party at his home for the current staff. Carol described it to Nat Urban: "It really was a nice party and I enjoyed myself a lot. Don wanted me to circulate and talk to most of the men who work for him – the thought had me quaking, but as he said, I'm now the boss's wife and have to do such things. As it turned out it was much easier than I anticipated – in fact sometimes men are more fun to talk with than women. After dinner, a group of them wanted to sing down in the rec room and wanted me to play the piano. Luckily they had some music I'm familiar with. That always livens up a party."

Nat said "Carol, how do you find the time and energy to be the boss's wife while taking care of your house and boys, and pursuing your personal interests, activities and friendships?"

"It does keep me busy, but I'm enjoying it! Douglas and Martin get in less trouble now and are fun to have around. They're in our bedroom now having a lively conversation. If you listen carefully you can understand some of it. I was really surprised to hear Douglas sing a couple bars of *Jingle Bells* yesterday. Martin has become quite the lover of late. He'll come up and crawl on our laps and loves to be cuddled and often asks for a 'tish'. In the mornings when Don leaves for work it takes him about 5 minutes to get everyone soundly kissed – reminds me of Dagwood. Someday he'll forget and kiss Pogo too for she's usually also in the lineup."

After moving to Pennsylvania, letters to our parents were supplemented by annual two week visits to Kansas, half spent with each family. The 1957 visit surfaced a fundamental problem in Carol's relationship with her mother. It had been simmering for over a decade. Each year, Winifred tried to get more time out of the week spent with my family. During our current visit, she tried by various means to convince us to spend the last two days of our trip with her. Carol held firm and told Winifred it would not be fair to cut our time with my family.

After our return to Pennsylvania, Carol got an angry letter from her mother about that decision. Carol responded with tough love in the form of truth: "I was afraid you'd be hurt by my decision and it was MY decision. I did not tell Don or his parents about it. I was very hurt about how resentful you seemed. I know you wanted to see more of us and you know I'd like to spend more time with you too, but there are others to consider. While I'm getting things off my chest, every time I'm visiting you I feel guilty about spending time with friends alone in Topeka or even going to town for fear it hurts you. You've made comments that indicate you resent my doing this. Whenever things don't go as you would like them, you seem to resent me or Don and this is so hard for me to take. I don't feel free to make my own decisions when I'm home for fear I'll do something to hurt you. I risk telling you all of this because I'm desperately trying to help you understand how I feel. I know you have a consuming need to love and be loved, but when we do things opposite your wishes, don't interpret that to mean we don't love you."

A week later, Carol got a scalding diatribe from her mother. Again, Carol's response was carefully crafted, but honest: "Whew!! I shall try to pick myself up off the floor and answer your letter. You say my letter reflects my guilt feelings. For as long as I can remember I've felt guilty when I think I'm not doing things as you want me to. Why do you suppose that happens?

You don't seem to be able to enjoy us when we all come – you were very happy when Don wasn't with us last summer. Maybe I'm wrong, but I think Don is the reason. He feels no resentment or jealousy of you, but he does feel your resentment and jealousy and feels left out in our family circle. This makes me sick for I love him very much and want my family to love him too. He is not your competitor – I have more than enough love for both of you.

What really tees me off is your saying my not wanting to go see relatives when we're there is Don's fault. That's not true, but I don't expect you to believe that – once you make up your mind, you're like a Missouri mule. Last summer you dragged me and the boys around to see all kinds of relatives – some of whom I don't know and some I don't like. Please realize that to come 1200 miles with three little kids to see you is exhausting, and when we get there we don't want to go traveling – we just want to relax and enjoy you.

I make my own decisions in matters that concern myself – if they concern Don too, then we confer and sometimes we decide his way and sometimes my way. I think one of the reasons we have such a happy marriage is that we do consider each other's feelings and respect each other's arguments when we have decisions to make. You say I'm losing my identity – then I'm glad I have a good man to identify with. I don't see how you can say I show dislike toward you or rejection. If getting married and having to move so far away is rejection, then I'm guilty. If trying to live my own life as I see fit and according to my beliefs and needs is rejection, I'm guilty. I'm a woman almost 30 years old, not a child anymore. I want an adult relationship with my parents – I not only want it, I need it. To be accused of rejecting you and not loving you is too much. I could understand this if I never wrote to you, never came to see you, never paid any attention to you whatsoever, but surely I've not been that bad.

I'm not showing Don this letter – haven't decided yet whether I'll show him yours, but at least you'll know *these are my own thoughts and no one else's*!!"

They resumed their correspondence and after a couple of months, Carol wrote: "I'm ready to kiss and make up whenever you are." To my knowledge it was never talked about again, but Carol's feelings of guilt about her mother declined significantly.

The major focus of our activities during the rest of the summer was on trying to get construction started on our house. Final plans were produced for potential builders' bids. Government approvals were obtained for things like a septic system. Bids were evaluated and a contractor selected. The stumbling block was finding a favorable mortgage loan. Losing summer weather for construction was discouraging.

We did have a good bit of fun during the summer. Carol finished her first painting and wrote her folks: 'Van Gogh Ford's masterpiece was hung on exhibit at the new student union building. Ahem! I didn't win a prize, but Miss Ziegler, our teacher, says I have a very charming, luminous way of painting – sure made me feel good and inspires me to take more lessons."

I left Carol a note on her pillow: "Madam Van Gogh, I would be honored to purchase your masterpiece to hang on the wall behind the desk in my new office." She sold it to me for $1 and it beautified my office for years.

Our major source of summer activity and fun, while waiting for house construction to start, was the picnic spot by our own mountain stream. We worked on it as a family, sometimes with friends, and took breaks from our labors to wade, splash, or picnic. I manned the ax and saw while Carol hacked away with a little hatchet as we cut and cleared bushes and small trees to make a path from our house site down to the stream. Then we cleared out brush, shrubs and small trees down to our blue grass picnic spot beside our beautiful stream – about fifteen feet wide, shallow enough for wading, with sparkling clear water gurgling over smooth stones.

One afternoon we waded in the stream with a cool drink in our hand, watching the boys throw rocks in the water. Carol said, "I keep pinching myself to make sure I'm awake. I can't believe this is really ours. Not in my wildest dreams did I imagine us living in such a beautiful place! And just listen to the music of that water flowing over rocks accompanied by the laughter of our children."

I threw one arm around her shoulders in a hug, "Carol, if it wasn't for you and the friendships you've formed in Lemont through the Women's Club, we never would have found this place before someone else snatched it up. I love it, but my feet are getting cold and I'm getting out!" She laughed and waded to the bank with me.

A couple of weekends later we were all lying on a blanket at our picnic spot under a big oak tree. Suddenly a branch broke off the tree and fell into our midst. Carol screamed, grabbed the twins and ran yelling, "Bees!!Bees!!Bees!!" Russ and I ran after her. As a little girl, Carol developed a great fear of bees. There was a big hive of bees in that tree. In the warm spring air they had come out onto the branches and their weight had caused the branch to break.

While sitting outdoors on a pleasant spring afternoon watching the kids play, Carol said, "Next weekend is our wedding anniversary. To celebrate, how about inviting some friends to a picnic at our stream next Sunday?"

"That's a great idea! Let's invite Nat and Hugh Urban and their kids. Hugh just finished his post-doc in the psych department. I hired him in DOC. We've decided to write a book about psychotherapy, so they'll be around awhile."

Carol said, "I'm glad, I really like them. Let's invite Nancy and Bud Boal too – our kids play well together."

So, on a beautiful, sunny, warm May 30th, the Urbans, Boals and their kids joined us at our picnic spot for a celebration. We spread blankets over the bluegrass, stripped the kids to their underpants, and then waded into the water. The bigger kids had water fights and explored the stream. The little kids cruised the stream on floats with their parents' help. Adults took turns floating lazily in two inflated inner tubes. We shared an afternoon of fun, laughter and an occasional tear when a little one got hurt. What a treat – a burbling stream reflecting a sky full of sunshine, the air filled with happy shouts and laughter of children and their parents. After a while we dried everyone off and rested on our blankets with a cool drink and some pretzels.

Finally, Carol stood up and said, "I'm hungry – is anyone else?"

As one voice we all shouted back, "LET'S EAT!!" While the mothers assembled hot dogs, buns, marshmallows and other goodies, the older kids and fathers gathered twigs and wood to build a fire in the fire pit we'd created. We'd cut twenty wiener sticks the previous week. We all ate like horses. The sun was setting when everyone decided to call it a day. Driving to Lemont, Carol murmured happily, "What a great 9th anniversary celebration!"

I said, "Maybe we can continue the celebration after the kids are in bed."

The summer ended on a positive note as Carol described it to her parents: "Saturday night we had a delightful time going to see a play at Standing Stone Playhouse. This is an old barn renovated into a performance theater in the mountains south of State College. You park under trees, walk across a rustic bridge over a mountain stream into the theater with the stage in the middle of a circle of seats. The plot was about a girl who disrobed when she had two glasses of champagne and the psychologist who tried to treat her. The dialogue was terrific and loaded with double meanings. Our hubby/psychologist dates fairly rolled in the aisles.

Our nosey poker neighbors bought a new used car and we bought their 1934 Chevy 4-door car with bucket seats and curtains on the rear window for $30. Don will drive it back and forth to work and I'll have our car all the time. That will give me a lot more freedom."

October came and I said, "Carol, I have to visit the branch campuses so how about joining me and we'll end it by celebrating your 30th birthday in New York City."

She was all for my plan! "A weekend in the city carousing with you would be delicious."

We visited the York, Allentown and Ogontz campuses. Carol sat in on my test interpretation lecture to new students and said later, "Don, I was very interested in your talk and fascinated by the questions they asked. It was fun being your assistant."

We checked into our hotel in the city about 3 p.m. and rested for a while. Carol put on the cocktail dress I bought her the last time we were in the city. We tried to get tickets to the play *My Fair Lady* but it was sold out for months, so we saw Ethel Merman in *Happy Hunting*.

Then we went to a ritzy night club – the Copacabana. Their floor show included The Copa Girls (wow), a great quartet, Steve Lawrence and Martha Ray. Snuggling in bed that night, Carol was still savoring the evening. "Steve Lawrence was fantastic – I think better than Frank Sinatra. It was exciting when famous people started coming in from Mike Todd's 'little private party' in Madison Square Garden (18,000 attended), people like Steve Allen and his wife Jayne Meadows. I was bug-eyed looking at all the people and gorgeous dresses – it was quite a thrill."

The next day we found the Manhattan location of a major yard goods stores and Carol bought lots for sewing later. I smiled to see her drool over a beautiful off-white material with silver thread running through it. Carol said she needed such dressy material like a hole in the head, but I envisioned how beautiful she'd look in it so insisted she get some for her birthday.

As we drove toward Happy Valley and home, Carol said, "What a wonderful way to become 30 years old – we grown-ups do have fun, don't we Don!"

Carol's use of her time changed drastically through the year. The time she'd spent typing to help boost our income two years ago could now be used to pursue her personal interests. In addition to being a leader in the Lemont Women's Club, she created a new singing interest group. First they sang only for Women's Club occasions, but as their competence and reputation grew, other organizations like Kiwanis asked them to entertain. Along with singing popular melodies, they choreographed humorous song and dance routines. I knew then that Carol was recreating the kinds of things she did as a little girl in Marysville, reprising that happy time.

I was amazed at her energy and creativity. She led fundraising drives for a variety of worthy causes, and participated in the League for Women Voters. At the request of Women's Club friends, Carol created another interest group focused on arts and crafts. She taught them how to make decorative creations which they sold at fund raisers to benefit school projects.

Carol was liked and admired for her many talents and herself. She really enjoyed her eight gal bridge (or gabbing) group, and had me help create a couples bridge club we both enjoyed. But her primary focus was still her family. She collaborated with Russ's teachers to closely monitor and personally guide his development. She hosted children in the neighborhood on play dates for Martin and Douglas, while teaching socialization tasks like fair play, sharing and toilet training. She involved our sons in helping with simple household tasks. And always, play time and cuddle time were an integral part of her day with the twins.

We enjoyed spending time together as a family, entertaining friends in our home or visiting the homes of others. Carol was a congenial, fantastic hostess! But, the times we treasured most as a couple are what we called 'US' times, with the focus on shared pleasures, like learning to square dance, traveling together to branch campuses, or our date nights.

We discovered a special new activity we hoped would become a permanent part of our lives. Social dancing was very popular in the 1940s. After the war, when veterans returned to Happy Valley, there was no place to dance so a group of friends created a dance club. There were three criteria: The number of members was limited to fit the size of places that could be rented for dancing; half of the members had to be people working in town, and half working at the university – thus the name Town and Gown; and members met in each other's homes for cocktails and dinner before the dance to facilitate becoming acquainted. In addition, they had dance cards to encourage dancing with members other than a spouse. Members could invite guests to a dance, and if any guest wanted to join they signed up on a waiting list until a vacancy occurred. Friends who were members invited us.

We were excited about meeting this dancing group. Carol said, "I'm pulling out all the stops and made a gown out of that white material with silver thread we bought in New York. It drapes real pretty so I'm just cinching a belt around the waist, pinning the top at the middle front and draping the excess across my shoulder and down the back. It looks Grecian and may be a bit too sophisticated for this place. Oh, what if the darn thing comes apart while we're dancing!!" She shrugged and took a deep breath, "Well, if I wear it and lose it on the dance floor you'll never hear from me again – I'll die of embarrassment. I'm going to the beauty parlor Friday to get my hair cut and styled in hopes they can make me look like something."

Carol didn't lose her dress and didn't have to die of embarrassment. Over coffee she told a friend: "We enjoyed our dance last Friday and my dress was quite striking and drew compliments – I didn't feel self-conscious at all. We're eager to join as soon as a vacancy occurs. It's great fun making new friends and being with people who like to dance."

Throughout that fall, our biggest frustration was difficulty getting a decent loan, not because of our eligibility but because loan money was scarce and interest rates very high. In early winter, the builder we selected said he'd have to reschedule construction until spring. So, we continued our loan search through the winter.

We wrapped Christmas presents while the boys were sleeping. Carol said, "Our Christmas social life is much busier. Every weekend we're invited to several occasions – more than we can or want to attend. Just two years ago, we celebrated with graduate students. Now they're with faculty and townspeople. It's interesting to see typical faculty homes, but most don't seem to have as much fun in their nice homes as we have in our decrepit apartment."

I nodded, "With our graduate student friends, life was simpler. Because we all had so little, special times meant so much more. Having more often doesn't bring more happiness."

Carol replied, "The social whirl is fun for a little while, but when life moves too fast there isn't enough time to recognize and savor the pleasure of it."

On Christmas Eve we gathered round the piano and sang Christmas songs while Carol played. Later, while Carol put the boys to bed, I fixed martinis and canapés stuffed with cream cheese and chopped ham. While waiting for my sweetheart, I chose soft instrumental music to accompany the glow of candles and Christmas tree lights.

Carol exited our bedroom smiling, unexpectedly wearing the white and silver Grecian gown she'd created for Town and Gown, with silver combs in her hair. She looked exquisite. Reflections of silver threads shimmered in the candlelight as she moved towards me. Her beauty left me speechless! With teasing voice and twinkling eyes, she said, "I'd sure enjoy a martini."

I finally found my voice, "On Christmas Eve I'll give a Grecian Goddess anything she asks of me!" I pressed a soft kiss to Carol's cheek while seating her on the sofa.

She lifted her glass in a toast, "Here's to us."

"And here's to beauty – especially in the form of a goddess named Carol."

She chuckled at that flattery. "You're a hunk – I'm glad your poison ivy is gone."

I laughed at her reference to the poison ivy outbreak that kept us celibate for too long, then said, "Do you realize we're celebrating a tenth anniversary?"

Puzzled, she thought a moment, "It can't be our wedding anniversary because that was nine years ago."

"Think of Christmas ten years ago."

With a big smile she said, "I remember now! You mean the Christmas before we married, the first Christmas we spent together. We drove along snow covered Kansas roads in the moonlight about 4 o'clock on Christmas morning, watching lights come on in farm houses, and imagining children tumbling down the stairs to see if Santa had come. We pulled into a little roadside park and watched dawn chase the stars away. The ecstasy I felt that night, imagining spending every Christmas of my life as your wife, was more spiritual than sexual. The only comparison I can think of is being bathed in an endless universe of beauty while singing the *Messiah* in a chorus of more than a hundred people."

I raised my glass to her, "I toast the first time I believed we'd share the dream of being together forever." We kissed each other in memory of that night ten years earlier.

I said, "I can't tell you how much it means to see you freed from the shackles of your typewriter this year, and pursuing activities that give you pleasure – pleasure in your companionship with other women, in painting, in creative crafts, and in community leadership roles. I'm particularly glad to see you enjoying your choral group. I remember the joy you experienced from singing in the past, and that disappeared for a while after we got married. I also want to thank you for visiting branch campuses with me. Sharing aspects of my work life with you is a special delight. I don't like being separated from you."

Carol nodded her agreement, "Fewer demands on my time and energy bring a thrilling sense of freedom! Someday soon I hope to join a large group singing major choral works. I'm proud to have a voice good enough to contribute to such groups. And what you said about the branch campuses is true for me, as well. It's a special treat to share in your professional experiences. I felt that way when I typed your dissertation, but on our trips to branch campuses I feel more like a participant, a partner of yours.

Nothing I do would be much fun if they weren't anchored in my family – a wonderful, loving, considerate, creative, sexy husband and our three healthy, noisy but delightful boys full of potential for their future. My life would be near perfect if we could get our house built."

I chose a Glenn Miller record and asked my Grecian Goddess for a dance. We both felt giddy with happiness as we moved in sync with the music. After a couple of tunes, Carol twirled away from me and laughed as her Grecian gown dropped to the floor. Delighted and breathless, I admired her nude beauty. "I'm happier than you are that my poison ivy is gone!" *Merry Christmas to me!!* I took her into my arms and we danced to our bed to finish celebrating.

I started the new work year with nagging concerns about workplace morale. I couldn't quite put my finger on the problem so finally discussed my worries with Carol, knowing she would see the situation from a different angle. She taught me an important lesson, based on observations of people and situations during her work as a secretary:

"Bosses like to make decisions, and faculty like to write down ideas, but they're typically careless or less competent about implementing details – those usually get placed in the hands of other people, often secretaries like me. For example, working in the marketing department at K-State I never typed a report, lengthy letter, or scholarly manuscript that didn't have grammatical, spelling, punctuation or factual mistakes. A good secretary fixes all such errors and hands back a typed product that won't embarrass the writers with errors. We often had to remind those we served of deadlines to be met, like when grades, reports, or manuscripts were due. We were responsible for making sure all the supplies needed were always available.

Other staff played similarly important supporting roles. What would a place be without good janitors? How many people would be alienated by ineffective receptionists? The supporting staff is what quietly keeps an organization running effectively day-to-day, but their efficiency is often taken for granted and seldom openly praised."

Lesson learned! From that day forward, during decades of being a little or big boss, Carol helped me give employees special attention. For example, Carol said, "The DOC is a new program where treating students and their families well is essential. Your secretaries are on the front line because they're the first faces clients see when they come to your offices for help. And, secretaries play the key role in keeping your records accurate and up to date. Let's invite them and their spouses or boyfriends to dinner in our home. It's hard for some to understand how valued a person in the lower echelons feels when given special attention by its top dogs."

"Thanks for your guidance, honey, let's do it."

Carol was already making plans. "Find out if they could all come next Friday night"

She prepared a buffet supper because we didn't have a large dining table in our apartment. She had lasagna, a tossed salad, Italian bread, homemade sweet cherry jam, with beer, wine or water as a beverage.

During supper, Carol told of her experiences as a secretary and of typing dissertations, including a couple fun examples of errors by those she served. Remembering her own self-confidence problems, she tried to ease their apprehension about socializing with the boss by asking each guest to share similar stories. Their examples brought lots of laughs, including one about a goof of mine. We ended the evening gathered around the piano singing popular songs.

The result of Carol's plan delighted me. The atmosphere in the DOC offices was much warmer and more relaxed. That next week, workers had fun talking and kidding about the experience, and their pride in doing a good job was obvious. Stories of that evening quickly spread to other Old Main offices, giving DOC secretaries a special status among their associates.

Each Christmas after that, no matter what position I held, Carol made a little gift for each of my secretaries. And because of what I learned from Carol, I gave personal attention to a variety of employees, such as, occasionally taking a janitor out for a lunch of a hamburger and a beer. The full impact of Carol's thoughtful gifts surfaced nearly six decades later in messages from former secretaries. For example, Mary Rice Royer wrote:

"I remember Carol so well. She made a poinsettia pin and earrings from tiny sea shells for all the secretaries in the Division of Counseling one Christmas. I still have mine and have always loved wearing them for the holidays."

Micki Pharo, my secretary in the College of Health and Human Development, wrote:

"Carol, I still have the gifts you made for me over the years – a big, musical Christmas ornament, a golden angel, an oil painting of flowers, a little stone owl on a tree branch. Your family inherited your thoughtfulness – your son Russell and his wife gave me the special gift of blood I needed during my brain surgery at Hershey Medical Centre. I have worked for a lot of Deans over the years, and you and Don were the best by far!"

Carol continued to hone her leadership skills through the Lemont Women's Club. The singing group she started had grown to a dozen women who enjoyed creating innovative programs. They'd been working on a variety show, similar to old Vaudeville skits and routines. Carol described their success to her parents: "Today was the day for our 'big show' and I had butterflies in my stomach. Everything went over without a hitch. I had a good partner for the 'Winegar Woiks' routine and it worked out very well. You should have seen us dressed in our garb – we were gruesome. Our hobo routine went over real good. I surprised myself by not being scared to death in front of the crowd. I was pleased the program was pretty successful.

I had one small problem – most of the ladies wanted to wear formals. One, who didn't have a formal, said she would drop out of the performance. I told her she was more important to the group than wearing formals and got everyone to agree. Sometimes I feel like a producer working with temperamental primadonnas."

One evening after supper, over coffee, Carol said, "I'm going to apply for membership in the State College Community Choral Society. All the singers in it are very good, so I probably won't get in, but I miss classical choral music so I plan to try out."

"Carol, if you don't get in the director has rocks in his head! Few people have perfect pitch and can sing more than one part. I'm delighted you'll be singing choral music again."

She was accepted, the Chorus had four performances, and they were terrific. So far, so good with all Carol's goals and plans. Now if only her new house was underway!

Construction of our house finally began in June, but it was a very wet year so there were seemingly endless delays. We hoped it would be done by mid-fall, but weren't able to move in until December 19. Carol shared our frustration with her parents: "To save a little money and get in before Christmas we agreed to clean up ourselves. It was a mess. I never realized a new house could have so much dirt – sawdust, plaster, linoleum paste, etc. Some of our friends helped with the cleanup and our builder used his big truck to move stuff over from our apartment.

Today, Dec. 23rd, Don laid carpet in the living room. We'll try to put up a Christmas tree tomorrow. This house is our Christmas present except for the boys. Don brought home 4 bar stools so we can eat off the breakfast counter now. Most things are unpacked and stored away in cupboards and closets. We're dead tired and there's still lots to do."

On Christmas Eve we decorated the tree, Ate a grilled cheese sandwich supper, and put the boys to bed. While tucking them in bed, Russ said, "We each have our own bedrooms for the first time in our lives!"

I kissed Carol goodnight and said, "Last Christmas we vowed to celebrate Christmas this year in our new home, and here we are, but too pooped to celebrate. I'm sorry it took so long to get you this new home."

Carol kissed me and said, "Old home – new home – any home is OK as long you love me and keep me warm!" She stuck her cold feet on my warm legs and we went to sleep knowing we'd finally reached another of our goals.

Christmas day we laughed to see the boys enjoying their new home. They played with their gifts in the living room, using the slightly elevated stone hearth for their cars and trucks. When that activity bored them, they raced down stairs and played in their rooms awhile before tearing back upstairs to slide and wrestle on the dining area's slick linoleum. What a hubbub! We spent the day finishing our clean up.

The next morning, Carol started on drapes while I designed and built bunk beds for the twins' room. One evening after they were all hung I admired the drapes and said "Carol, your skills are amazing! You've never made drapes before. Yet, in a week, you have turned 70 yards of different kinds of material into beautiful drapes for our entire house." She grinned. "I'm quite proud of my creations! I did my own pleating with buckram and found it does a much better job than pleating tape. Our home is finally complete. I haven't seen any of my friends for weeks, so I'm taking a break and going out on the town with three gals."

As we prepared for bed the next night I asked "How was your night out with the girls?" "We went to a movie and then to the

Tavern for beer and pizza. It was pleasant, but I get tired of listening to women complain about their husbands all the time. I sometimes wonder if these gals aren't at fault too, for some of them are awfully selfish."

Carol's mother wrote a New Year's Day letter. Carol read it and said, "It looks like my frank comments to mom and my invitation to 'kiss and make up' is bearing fruit." She writes: 'You kids have what few married folks have – understanding and the ability to iron out your problems. You can listen to each other and are interested in each other's work, hobbies and play. Also you both enjoy your boys and love simple family living. Please stay that way. You each have *somebody!*' Then she writes about what we suspect is the core of her problems. 'I'm alone here on our farm all day five days a week. I have to take care of the animals in all kinds of weather, let them in and out of the barn each day, feed them grain and green hay and provide water. I get so tired, lonely, discouraged and sometimes afraid. It would be easier to take if when Daddy comes home he'd express appreciation and affection for what I do, as Don does for you.'"

I felt sadness for Winifred and concern for Carol so I said, "Professionally, I understand her emotional turmoil, but my heart aches because I can't help her and thereby ease the distress it causes you. I tried once to talk with your dad about it, but ran into a brick wall."

"I've lived with this problem most of my life. I've blamed myself, puzzled over the causes of her illnesses, and suffered along with her. But in the past few years, I've come to understand her situation and accept that I can't change it, so that has helped me a great deal."

Carol continued her efforts to build an adult relationship with her parents and showed me part of a letter she had just written to them: "Mom, I hope your depression has improved – it's really hard to pick yourself up and be interested in anything when you're down in the glooms. You and Dad both need to learn to sit down and have heart to heart talks with each other and really open up – a wonderful understanding can develop.

Don has always been a great one to listen and understand me – I cannot say the same for myself. Only until recently has Don unburdened on me and it made me realize that I've been quite self-centered in not realizing that he 'feels' too. I've been so dependent on him, visualizing him as being so strong, capable and adjusted. Well, he is all those things, but occasionally he has spells of discouragement and needs to blow off steam and lately he's learned to turn to me for this release. It makes me so happy, for now I feel I know him like I never have before and it makes me feel good that I'm so needed by him.

But, and I do mean but, it has to be a 2-way street – you both have to accept criticism from each other and if it is a legitimate criticism try to do something about it. I know how stubborn you can be Pop, but I hope you can open up to Mother and in turn sense her needs and respond with understanding. I love you so much and want you to be happy together."

My voice trembled with emotion as I said, "Carol, you're an amazing woman! You express your wisdom so sensitively, and you have a lot of guts to relate to your parents that way. I do treasure the way you strengthen me with your thoughtfulness and love when I need it."

That year Douglas and Martin started kindergarten. Russell was in the third grade. With the boys in school, Carol had mornings free to pursue her art, music and community interests. She registered for a water color painting course at Penn State. Weekly rehearsals continued with the State College Choral Society and they performed the second part of the *Messiah* and Mozart's *Messa Brevis* in Lewistown and State College. She served as Vice President of the County Federation of Women's Clubs, and agreed to be President of the Lemont Women's Club. She said, "I hesitated, but decided being President would do wonders to help me grow."

The Lemont Women's Club chorus of thirteen women sang on an average of once a week at various churches and organizations. Her new small crafts interest group met once a week and produced copper tooled pictures, shell jewelry and other small decorative items, the prettiest being heritage wreaths made from pine cones and nuts. She stayed knee deep in activities involving all the things she loved – her children, her women friends, painting, music, crafts, community activities, and her husband.

Chapter Fifteen

Carol Juggles Changes, Promotions and Fun

While we lived in Lemont, Carol had several friends living within a block of her and they visited each other frequently for gab sessions. Since our move, contact with those friends required a car and none of them had one. Knowing that companionship with other women was a fundamental need of Carol's, I asked "Carol, are you finding it lonely here?"

"A little, but I still have a good bit of interaction with my women's club friends. Three women live above us on Branch Road and I've had them in for coffee. But I've been thinking it might be nice to spend Christmas in Kansas to escape work pressures and please our parents."

"OK, but we can't take the risk of traveling that far in our nine year old Ford." So, our family Christmas present that year was a bright red, nine-passenger Plymouth station wagon that had enough room to sleep the whole family. The boys opened their presents a week before Christmas. Then we loaded up and took turns driving to Kansas in two days. Both visits went smoothly and we also saw old friends in Topeka and Marysville. As we started back, a winter storm with freezing rain and snow was behind us moving east. We couldn't risk stopping overnight, so took turns driving and sleeping until we made it safely home to Happy Valley.

A few weeks later, snuggling lazily by a crackling fire, I said "Carol, I promised we'd have a delayed Christmas Eve party. I'd be honored if you'd dude up for a celebration and be my guest Saturday night for dinner at eight in my Slab Cabin Chateau."

She fluttered her long eyelashes at me with a smile, "I thought you'd never ask!"

I set the mood with cozy fire and four of Carol's pillar candles placed strategically around the living room. Our card table with a deep blue table cloth in front of a pretty fire looked quite festive with champagne on ice beside it. I'd gussied up in a soft white shirt and dark blue slacks, so all I had to do was set the music playing and wait.

At precisely 8 p.m. I heard Carol coming up the stairs from our bedroom. I held my breath with anticipation as she walked into the room wearing ….. an old paint stained flowered dress?? Dismayed, I blurted out, "This is not what I expected!"

She curtsied demurely and said, "My mistress sent me to apologize for being a little late – she will be here soon." After a pause to give the full effect of her dress, she turned and left. Ten minutes later she reappeared in one of her creations – a lovely, off the shoulders burgundy gown with a full slit skirt allowing tantalizing glimpses of a dancer's leg. She wore tiny rose earrings dangling on fine gold chains. With a teasing smile she said, "Is this better?"

I'm guilty of ogling her like a randy high school kid, but finally said, "Thank God that first outfit was just a bad dream!"

"Oh, Don, you should have seen your face!"

I twirled her around to admire the gown and growled "You'll pay for that before this night is over!"

She laughed, "I hope so!"

We danced awhile, enjoying the music. Finally, I said, "Maybe we should stop dancing and start talking before holding you close makes me forget about dinner."

We sat at our fireside table, quietly sipping champagne, "Sometimes in our daily life I forget how beautiful my wife is, and then on a night like this you reappear to compete with movie stars like Ginger Rogers, Betty Grable and Marilyn Monroe for most popular pin up among soldiers and sailors. You always manage to raise my heart rate to a boogie woogie beat!"

She replied, "That was my intent!"

I said, "In mid-April the Eastern Psychological Association is having their annual meeting in Atlantic City. Will you please come with me so we can stroll down the board walk together and I can show off my gorgeous companion to colleagues and friends?"

An excited smile signaled her answer. "What a terrific idea! I've heard about Atlantic City since I was a kid but never thought I'd get to go there. There was a time I would have been scared pea green to meet important people like your colleagues, but I've changed a lot since we hauled our little trailer and two-year-old son over the mountains into Happy Valley.

Getting completely away from family and friends and old habits of behavior helped me grow in confidence. Since people here didn't know me, I could start fresh, dare to be more outgoing, and I had your love to reassure me. My life now is much more interesting and fun."

"Carol, when we had our first date in 1943, you were a rose bud, like your pretty little ear rings, and I was a neophyte gardener in Mother Nature's garden of girls. A decade and a half later we've both changed. The rose bud opened into a lovely Alpha Xi rose, increasingly admired by others. I grew into a more accomplished gardener, attracted you for my private flower garden, and together we created our family garden of rapidly growing seedlings that sometimes seem like weeds! Unlike some, we haven't wilted in bad weather.

With your music, art, and love you brought beauty to a garden that was barren of those delights without you. So here's a toast to the people we've become! I'll find someone to take care of our seedlings while we hit the boardwalk together for fun and frolic!" We clinked glasses and sipped our bubbly. "Some of our friends, like Nat and Hugh, are also going so you gals can have fun together while we do our psychologist thing."

Carol said, "What should I wear to this conference?"

I replied, "While you think about that, I'll serve dinner."

I'd purchased a light dinner of shrimp, fruit salad, chocolate-dipped strawberries, and delicate cookies. While we ate, Carol told me some of her ideas for the Lemont Women's Club.

"I'll need to meet occasionally with some members to plan projects. Would it be OK to use our house for those meetings?"

"Yes, so long as they don't interfere with our dates."

I poured the last of our champagne and said, "I have a surprise to share with you. Yesterday, Dr. Bernreuter informed me that at this weekend's Board of Trustees meeting he'll be appointed Special Assistant to the President for Student Affairs and I'll be appointed to replace him as Director of the Division of Counseling."

"WOW! Congratulations! It isn't unexpected because he'd warned you a year ago you were being groomed for the job, but it's still exciting and a little scary for me. Three years ago we'd just finished graduate school and now all of a sudden we're part of Penn State's 'upperarchy'. What does it mean, exactly?"

"One consequence should please you. It means a significant increase in our pay check so will make that part of our life easier. We'll probably have more involvement in University level activities, but we're already partly involved in that through our visits to the branch campuses."

She sighed, "Well, guess I've been groomed for the last couple years to be a 'big shot's' wife. But it'll take a little getting used to."

The conversation was over. I held out my hand and said, "May I have this dance with the loveliest flower in Mother Nature's garden of women?"

We held each other close, dancing in flickering firelight. Carol nuzzled my shoulder and sang to me softly as we danced. Smiling, I pulled the dress down around her waist and she unbuttoned my shirt so we could dance skin to skin. Finally, I danced her from the living room to our bedroom where, as promised, she paid for the paint-stained dress trick she'd pulled on me.

Three weeks later we went to Atlantic City with three other couples. While Hugh presented a paper and I held recruiting interviews, the four wives explored the board walk. Carol wrote her parents: "It was a lark!! We wandered on the boardwalk, exploring little shops, watching people on the beach, and commenting on what other women were wearing. We had one mishap. One of the gals always dresses up and was wearing high heels on the boardwalk while the rest of us were casually dressed. Suddenly Nat said, 'Where's Mary?' We found her a few paces behind us standing still and pulling on something. The heel on one of her spiked heel shoes was stuck between boards and she couldn't get it out. We finally freed it, but the heel was loose. We went to the hotel for different shoes. She took a good bit of teasing about that.

One night the guys took us to a casino to see how the high rollers live. The last night, the conference had a dinner dance. Several psychologists came to our table to talk with Don and Hugh (I learned they were developing quite a good reputation). Of course Don introduced me (with considerable flattery I'm pleased to say).

I was delighted that I felt completely at ease and actually enjoyed talking with his colleagues."

The dancing was great and in bed that night Carol said, "Don, being married to you has expanded my life in ways I never imagined possible, even in my adolescent fantasies. My self-confidence keeps growing, as does my love for you."

Two weeks later Carol wrote her parents: "I'm down with the mumps of all things!!! I must have been exposed in Atlantic City. I've been in perfect misery since last Thursday. I had no idea how painful they could be and have no effective pain killers. I've been in bed for 3 days waited on by my faithful nursemaid husband. He's a perfect jewel. He and the boys are so thoughtful. I'd give anything for a solid meal but salivating is agony and chewing nigh impossible. The whole family is exposed so by the time I'm well the twins may have it."

Thankfully, our boys didn't get the mumps.

By late May, Carol had recovered from her mumps so I asked if she could squeeze me into her busy schedule. "I have to visit Branch Campuses in the Pittsburgh area. Come join me and we can celebrate our wedding anniversary with a date in Pittsburgh."

She jumped at the chance. We visited the campuses during the day Friday, checked into our motel and rested a little, and then went to a night club I'd heard about. The place had a happy atmosphere and we got a table on the edge of the dance floor. Carol said, "Look at the couple dancing over there. They're excellent dancers and I love that music. Let's watch them to see if we can figure out their moves. Then, when we've finished eating, let's try it."

We discovered the basic pattern was simple and that made variations fairly easy to create. Learning new dance steps is second nature for Carol, so she guided me through the basic steps. Once we caught on, both the music and the dancing were so much fun it was hard to stop to get some sleep. We learned that new dance was called 'The Cha Cha'.

As we snuggled in our motel bed that night Carol kissed my cheek and said, "That was a marvelous anniversary celebration – I love learning new dance steps with my hubby!!"

We loved outdoor activities in the summer, such as gardening, landscaping and loafing. Spending time at our picnic spot by the stream on a warm, sunny day was Carol's form of relaxation, which she described to her parents: "I'm writing this letter down by the stream while soaking up some sun. I have quite a tan on my back so am trying to even it up on the front which I find hard to do since I hate to just lay and do nothing. It's so lovely and peaceful down here – the stream is nice and full and fascinating to watch as it babbles and tumbles over the rocks. When I get too hot in the sun I just stick a toe in the water to cool off. It's a perfect day – low humidity, the sun warm and the air cool – makes a person glad to be alive.

Sunday we invited the Urbans over for a picnic. It was a lovely day, and the kids had more fun in the water and so did us grownups, except for Nat who is 8 months pregnant. Don and Hugh worked at moving some rocks around to open up the water flow and to make wading nicer. They worked on trying to lift one big rock high enough so it could be a 'sitting rock' in the middle of the stream. Suddenly we heard a big splash and yell. Both of them were putting all the leverage they could on a 5-foot long pry bar, suddenly it slipped and tossed both of them in the stream. They both sat there soaked, laughing and splashing water on each other. We got everyone out of the stream, lay in the sun drying off, and ate potato salad, baked beans and fried chicken. What a wonderful afternoon with dear friends!"

Carol was a huge help to me throughout my professional life creating pleasurable social events for recruits, colleagues and professional visitors in our home, partly because DOC budgets were so tight we didn't have money for high cost venues. Nothing was catered. It was hard work because she prepared everything herself and sometimes had her sons help serve. She was a warm, charming and skilled hostess.

For example, Carol had visited most of the branch campuses with me and knew that people there felt they were treated as 'second class citizens' by the main campus. That troubled her so she came up with a plan, "Let's host an informal reception at our place for all DOC staff from all campuses so they can get acquainted and feel part of the same team. Let them bring their kids if they want to. Our woods and stream would provide the ideal spot for such a get-together." The reception and Carol were a huge success, and invaluable to my efforts to create a first rate program. Once again, her old adage bore fruit: "We make a terrific team!"

In my spare time between university-related tasks and working on a new book, I tackled projects around our new home. One of our landscaping projects was to create a dining and lounging terrace shaded by trees on the edge of our woods. The area lay a little lower than our lawn so I was building a low rock wall to hold up the bank. Carol said, "Wish I could be out here with you but I have to finish typing your book chapter so you can meet the deadline."

I thought a minute and said, "I'll be right back." In a few minutes I returned carrying her typing table and typewriter and placed them on the terrace where she could supervise me.

She laughed and said, "What a marvelous idea! Being in this beautiful setting with you makes typing almost seem like fun." We had a delightful afternoon, stopping sometimes to drink some iced tea and gab. By late afternoon, she'd finished her typing and I'd completed the wall.

One evening we all sat at the picnic table on our new terrace, eating beef sandwiches, macaroni and cheese, and fruit salad. I said, "Remember last fall we drove around in the mountains north of us admiring the fall foliage and saw a lovely abandoned stone bridge with a nice stream running under it?" They remembered, so I asked if they recalled what Carol said.

"Sure, she said she wished she could paint it."

I grinned at Carol, "OK, tomorrow is supposed to be a hot day so I suggest we head for the mountains where it'll be cooler Saturday morning. We can take a picnic lunch and play in the stream while Mom sketches the bridge to make a start toward painting it."

Carol's eyes sparkled with delight at the thought, "How about it boys?"

They shouted, "Yeah!" So that evening, we males prepared a picnic lunch of hot dogs, potato chips and sweet grapes while Carol packed supplies for a morning of art work.

The day dawned cloudless and warm. I had to explore a little bit to find the place but we did and Carol said, "It's even prettier than I remembered it. I can hardly wait to get started!"

We carried everything to a shaded sandy beach and spread a blanket where Carol could sit and work while we played. She concentrated on her sketching and forgot all about us. We played in the shallows by the beach for a while, then waded slowly downstream, throwing rocks and trying to catch little fish. We found a spot about three feet deep so played in it and splashed water at each other to cool off. As noon approached, we worked our way back towards Carol, collecting wiener sticks and small pieces of wood for a fire.

Back at the beach we built a small fire and unpacked the food while Carol put her supplies away. The food disappeared fast! We were all enjoying the day so I suggested we explore the area before heading home. We put out our fire, packed everything into the car, then hiked upstream further into the mountains. We discovered wild raspberries so snacked on them as we walked. Around a curve in the stream we came upon a lovely area of wild bluegrass free of bushes. Here, the stream tumbled over a little waterfall to form a quiet pool. Carol and I looked at each other and I said, "Does this remind you of a spot we visited in the Ozarks?"

With a broad smile she said, "Oh yes! A place where we made memories."

That night in bed, snuggled with Carol in my arms, I said, "You know what I thought when we discovered that beautiful spot on the stream?"

She said, "Let me see if I can read your mind … Hmmm. Were you possibly thinking it would be a nice place to go on one of our dates?"

I said, "You're good!"

She kissed my cheek and said, "I'm not good – at least not if you knew what I imagined about going back there with you as we drove home!"

I said, "I like your imagination!"

The summer wasn't all play. Carol and a friend started working as volunteers at the hospital. Carol had a lifelong interest in helping people as a nurse, so she decided to experience hospital work through volunteering. She had several planning meetings with her Women's Club committees, and made crafts to sell at the school carnival. As school time neared, I said, "Carol, let's give the boys one more adventure before school begins. They're baseball fans. Let's take them to see the Pittsburgh Pirates and St. Louis Cardinals play?"

Carol poked me "As a kid you were a big Cardinal fan. Pleasing the boys is just an excuse so you can see them play. It would be the highlight of the summer for them."

Russ took his new baseball and left it at the hotel where they promised to get Stan Musial, the Cardinal star, to sign it. After the game, both the team and Russ's ball were gone. Tearfully, he expressed to the hotel management his anger and disappointment about losing his new ball. After we got home, I helped Russ write a letter to the Cardinal's in St. Louis telling them his sad story and asking for his new ball back. One month later Russ got a package from St. Louis. It contained a new ball signed by the entire Cardinal team. He still has that treasure.

That fall of 1960, Carol assumed responsibilities as President of the Lemont Women's Club and had to give a speech at their first meeting about plans for the year. She told me, "It's only three days until I have to get up in front of the Women's Club and make a darned fool of myself and the closer it gets, the weaker I get. I've got cold feet, a butterfly stomach, a sick headache and nervous fingers – not to mention weak knees. Anybody got a tranquilizer? Maybe I'll have a slug of vodka to get me through it. Oh, for a hole to crawl into."

I waited up for her with crossed fingers and a slug of vodka in a coke. She came home, sat with me and her slug of vodka and told me with relief that the meeting had been a big success. Once she started talking, her fear disappeared. After hearing her report I held her close, hugged her hard and nibbled her ear, "I'm very proud of you, Madam President. You have demonstrated again your skill in gaining respect and working with other women. Your description of how the fear eased once you started talking sounds like actresses describing their feelings just before a performance. How would you like to see how a real actress handles it?"

"What do you mean?"

"About a year ago when we went to the theater in New York, we saw an advertisement for *The Sound of Music* scheduled to open in a year. It sounded terrific, so we gambled and bought tickets a year ahead of its scheduled opening. Our tickets are for the opening week, that's next week. So we're going to New York with our year old tickets to see it."

Carol gasped, "That's fantastic!!!"

We checked into our hotel Saturday afternoon, took a nap, and then dressed for the theater. While standing outside the theater watching the crowd arrive, Carol said, "I love looking at all the gorgeous gowns, and many men are wearing tuxedos. New Yorkers must consider this opening very special. We're hobnobbing with high society tonight." We had very good seats, and Carol took a big breath as the lights dimmed and the curtain opened. It was great!! The audience was enthusiastic and gave the cast a standing ovation when the play ended.

Outside, Carol grabbed me, danced on the sidewalk, and after a huge hug and kiss said, "Don, that was a thrill beyond words!! The music was heartwarming and beautiful. Thank you for daring to buy those tickets a year ago because I heard it's already sold out for a year. I'm still flying high from the show – let's top off the evening with dinner and music at Asti's!"

I grabbed a taxi, and after a quick trip got a table with a bunch of opera lovers. The waiters and waitresses thrilled us with a flow of beautiful music, and Carol was so entranced she could hardly eat. The sparkle in her eyes and joy on her face said she wished she could sing too. Suddenly, everyone at our table stood up and joined in the singing. Once again at Asti's, my formerly shy and self-conscious wife joined them and sang her heart out!

She returned to her chair a little breathless, but flushed with joy, "I never dreamed I would have such an exciting singing experience."

I replied, "I envy you! I'm like 'Johnny One Note' only worse – I'm Donald No Note."

Carol laughed, "But you love music and are a great dancer!"

That night Carol cuddled up to me, still too high to sleep. She hummed a little music, kissed my cheeks and lips, and whispered, "Don, since we met I've had lots of fantasies about things we might do and enjoy together, and we've lived a lot of them. None of those fantasies even came close to tonight. You make my life wonderful – you are my magical music man!!"

We enjoyed a beautiful fall, filled with friendship, tailgating, football, Carol's creative activities, and my work. Then the holiday season began. The Thanksgiving tradition I grew up with included a family gathering and a great dinner. In Pennsylvania we had no family for such a celebration, nor did most of our close friends. So, we became an 'extended family' for Thanksgiving. Carol announced, "This year for our Thanksgiving feast we'll have six adults and six children. I'm fixing the turkey, dressing and mashed potatoes, Nat is bringing two vegetables and the relishes, and Jean the rolls and pumpkin pies."

We had a beautiful eight-inch snow, so the kids had a great time sledding on our hill. Dinner was a feast of delicious food and happy conversation. As we prepared for bed, Carol said, "What a wonderful day – good friends, good food, and good kids."

Early in December we put up our tree and Carol began the process of decorating our home. This year she added a "kissing ring" made out of an embroidery hoop, covered with red velvet, with one part inside the other and mistletoe hanging in the middle. She hung it in the entrance by the front door. During the Christmas season Carol got quite a few kisses there. I teasingly told her, "Now I know why you made that kissing ring. Save some kisses for me!"

I had to deliver five completed chapters of my book to the publisher so I said, "Carol, let's do an overnight trip, see NYC in its Christmas finery and do some Christmas shopping."

On the way home Carol raved, "The artistry of all the decorations is astonishing. I loved the musical, *The Unsinkable Molly Brown*. It's one of the happiest shows we've ever seen. Some trips the city seems ugly to me, but not this time." We got three bicycles from a NY Santa to deliver to Slab Cabin boys for Christmas.

Carol's music group gave a lovely Christmas program for the Women's Club. She proudly noted, "There were lots of non-members who said they came because of our program."

As always, our Christmas season was packed with parties, but we reserved Christmas Eve for just us. We put our sons to bed and prepared to celebrate our personal Christmas Eve by practicing dancing to some Latin-American records. We hadn't danced in a long time. I wore a bright floral print sports shirt with grey trousers and a fake mustache. I made vodka Collins and cheese snacks, thinking we'd need a tall drink for the thirst we'd develop dancing. Carol made a full skirt of rich red material with a delicate green leaf design that swirled around her when she moved. She surprised me by wearing the white, lacy, off-the-shoulder blouse I'd purchased for her years ago in Mexico when she was a senior in high school and I was in the Air Force in New Mexico. With it, she wore colorful jewelry and dramatic makeup.

I gave her a wolfish whistle and said, "May I offer my sensational senorita a cool drink before we begin an evening of exciting dancing?"

She said, "I'll accept your offer if you start with a kiss." I happily granted her wish and served our drinks. She said, "I want to make the first toast. This is the first year since we've been married that we haven't had to struggle dealing with some unpredictable change. In the past we've had changes in jobs, in where and how we lived, in life style and friendships, and by adding babies to our lives. Sometimes I felt I was on a hard-to-steer raft floating down a flooding river, wondering what was around the bend. This year has been pleasantly different.

So, I drink to being part of a nice community, financial security, three sons who make me proud, and my marvelous magic man who regularly surprises me with new adventures and the security and excitement of his love." We touched our glasses, sipped our drink, and looked into each other's eyes seeing nearly two decades of sharing ups and downs.

I replied, "I'm glad our life has stabilized, but it certainly isn't boring! I need no variability in women because you bring all the variety to my life any man could want! You're the woman I love dearly. And you frequently surprise and entertain me with all the different personalities hiding within you. So, I drink to the stability our love provides and the variability our imaginations and talents create." I stood, bowed, and held out both hands, "Would my beautiful senorita help me perform her exciting dances?"

She took my hand with a merry laugh and led me to our private dance floor. She'd purchased a booklet of Latin American dance steps to guide us. We started with the Cha Cha, and quickly polished what we knew. We both felt happy and full of energy, so allowed the Latin beat to move us and really shook a mean leg or two. We practiced a couple other steps, like the Samba, then rested with a cool drink and snack. Carol said "Let's end our dancing evening by learning the Tango." So we went to work. After about an hour Carol said, "I think we've got it. I love its grace and sensuality. It's one of the most fun dances there is."

I turned off the music and whispered in her ear, "Let's transfer that sensual Latin dance of love to our bedroom."

"Si, Senor. I've been waiting to do just that."

We relaxed Christmas day with a fire in the fireplace, taking turns unwrapping presents and showing our gifts to each other. One gift for the boys was called 'buster blocks'. These were 3"x5" cardboard boxes simulating bricks, strong enough to stand on and painted orange with brown stripes. They could be used to build all kinds of things. As an adult, Russ described one use to illustrate Carol's patience with her brood of boys:

"Mom was not a yeller. We invented a game in which one of us had the blocks at the top of the stairs leading down to our bedrooms and the brothers were at the bottom. The game was for those at the bottom to try to come up the stairs while the person at the top bombarded them with buster blocks. If they made it to the top they won. Sometimes the blocks hit the wall of the stairs and left orange marks. Mom was not happy about that, but she never prohibited the game. She let the consequences teach us to be more careful, like having to clean off the marks.

After our traditional Christmas morning cinnamon rolls and beverages, we could see the boys were a little disappointed with so few gifts. I went to the front door, pretended to look out, and yelled, "Santa left some presents out here – apparently he couldn't get them down the chimney." The boys stampeded out to discover their new bicycles, and we saw disappointment transformed into animated joy. They spent the morning washing and polishing their new wheels.

The medical community started the tradition of an annual 'Charity Ball' to raise money for hospital needs at the beginning of every New Year. We bought tickets and were invited for cocktails before the dance by a local physician I'd worked with. We enjoyed dancing to a good orchestra. That night as we lay in bed, Carol said, "It was interesting seeing all those Docs in civvies and their wives in fancy gowns that Docs can afford. In general, the people I met were nice and not 'putting on airs'. I was upset about the senior surgeon from Bellefonte. He was drunk and had surgery scheduled for 7 a.m. the next morning – that's scary!"

Most activities slow down in mid-winter. Carol used the time to renovate and redecorate our house, work on her oil painting and crafts, and to play her piano. One cold night, as we cuddled before a crackling fire, Carol said, "I started teaching Martin the piano this week. He seems to like it and I'm surprised at how quickly he's picking it up." She introduced our sons to music by teaching them the basis of piano playing. Then she encouraged each to choose an instrument and learn to play it. Martin chose the piano, Doug the clarinet, and Russ the guitar.

As spring approached, Carol's Women's Club, music, arts, crafts and community activities increased. One evening, talking about her activities, she said, "I like my extracurricular activities as long as it's not too much and doesn't take away from my family life. I feel, however, that some outside activities help make me a better wife and mother by broadening my interests and giving me the feeling that I'm an individual too. Also, it won't leave me at such a loss when the kids grow up if I have a variety of interests and activities to fall back on."

I said, "I like being your assistant when I can help. It broadens my life too, and it's fun watching you skillfully manage the conflicts and skirmishes among the women you work with."

Carol laughed, "Honestly, between Steve and Jean I have my hands full – they can get more people upset in less time than any other members in the club! Jean is domineering and Steve is good hearted but bungling in handling people. They're my best friends, but my worst enemies at times. That's life in the old Women's Club!"

We were delighted to finally be invited into the membership of the Town and Gown dance club. The next morning Carol said, "I'm excited by this dance club. I liked the people we met and it's a treat to go to a dance where people really enjoy and know how to dance. Two men asked me for a dance last night and in contrast to most men dancers they were quite good."

Spring came and we focused on cultivating, improving, and enjoying our gardens. The previous year Carol had planted bulbs in the woods and by the stream. One morning she stopped about half way down the path to our stream, stretched out her arms and said, "Don, this is glorious! I'm smack in the middle of Mother Nature's spring blossoms, her canopy of green leaves and rays of sunshine, while our stream sings happy melodies as it flows across the rocks. It makes me want to laugh, cry, paint what I see, and sing the *Hallelujah Chorus* all at once!"

Affection warmed my heart and I thought, *Carol doesn't just look at beauty – she lives it.*

In mid-summer we had a surprise visit from Milton Eisenhower after he visited some friends in Bellefonte and Helen's grave. Carol wrote her parents: "Dr. E. looks good even though he just spent 6 weeks in a body cast and then had to sleep in it for 3 months (slipped disc). My, he's full of nervous energy, his conversation is like quick silver, and he's interested in everything around him. He said that since Ike finished his presidency, he's pleased to now be able to freely express his own ideas. He's taking up oil painting (how in the world he has time for it I'll never know). He's an accomplished water color painter – also can play a mean 2 keyboard Hammond organ (which I tried to play on our last visit). He asked who painted the picture over our divans and I nervously said, 'I did'. He was quite impressed with it, so that made me feel great and increased my motivation for painting."

Carol loved our family life, and decided we should celebrate our sons' accomplishments. At that age, Russell was our athlete, Douglas our social guy, and Martin our project guy, always collecting or manipulating something. Their grades were excellent.

One hot late summer morning we took the boys and Russ's little league baseball buddy Johnny, to play baseball. The boys got a kick out of seeing their mother try to play. We headed home, a hot and sweaty bunch, and cooled off by splashing around in Slab Cabin Run. We rested awhile, ate sandwiches, then went to the PSU creamery for big ice cream cones – usually a Sunday afternoon tradition. Then we went to a matinee of the Disney movie, *The Parent Trap* and rounded out the afternoon by invading a new miniature golf course.

We got home around 7 p.m. so I sent the boys to build a camp fire by the stream. I cooked hamburgers while Carol made the supporting goodies, and we all ate beside the camp fire. Later, at dusk, the boys pretended they were cowboys searching along the stream for rustlers while Carol and I snuggled contentedly by the fire. Carol said, "What a wonderful day! I can't remember ever having so much fun with our boys. They're smart, funny, have confidence in themselves, enjoy teasing each other and us, and today treated us as one of the gang rather than parents. It's so cozy and peaceful sitting here with you, listening to them play in the dark. What a joy it is to have a family like us!"

Beginning with her slumber party gang, Carol had an innate talent for understanding a person's feelings and how to help that person cope. People sensed that in her. For example, women friends struggling with problems with parents, husbands, or children often talked with Carol to share their concerns. One young wife ran away and no one could find her, except Carol. She listened to her, comforted her, and the woman finally decided to return home.

Our sons all remember examples of Carol's sympathetic heart. Here's one from Russ: *"I had a paper route every day after school and rode my bike to deliver papers. One day, when I was 8 or 9, I was riding down Branch Road and saw a dog lying by the roadside. It was Pogo – my first pet and playmate from when I was about 3 years old. I fought back my tears, parked my bike by the side of the road, picked up Pogo and gently carried her home. Mom came out, saw my distress, controlled her own tears, gently put her arm around my shoulder and said, 'I think we should have a nice funeral for Pogo.' She found a good box, placed Pogo in it, picked some flowers and we scattered petals over Pogo. Then Mom, my twin brothers and I carried the box down by our stream and Mom brought a shovel. We found a nice spot, Mom dug the grave, and we created a little ceremony to say goodbye. Mom had a talent for knowing what to do and say when she saw we each needed some loving support to cope with distress.'*

Carol wrote her parents: "This year we started a new fall tradition. A group of friends bought season football tickets to sit together at games. We meet before the game for refreshments, called 'tailgating' because people gather around their cars, share refreshments, and then go to the game. After the game we have a potluck dinner at someone's home.

This game it was our turn. We created decorations for the hearth: Don made goalposts at opposite ends of the hearth and we used the boy's footballs. Russell's old beat up one with bandages and a woe-begone expression for Syracuse, and the twins new football with a happy look for Penn State. We put helmets on the balls and they really looked cute. Pennants added color. My lasagna was a hit at the pot lock and we all stuffed ourselves. We ended the evening by playing 'Password' which everyone enjoyed. It was a wonderful day!"

Chapter Sixteen
Elaborating Family Life

As president, Carol chaired the Women's Club Christmas meeting. Afterwards, while having hot chocolate by the fireplace, I said, "Carol, I remember you were a bit scared when you became President but told me you did so to put new life into the organization and also test yourself. You've certainly accomplished your goals, illustrated by this meeting today. The arts and crafts program resulted from the interest group you created, and the musical program was produced by the singing group you created. The unusually large attendance is evidence of renewed interest in the organization. It has blossomed under your leadership. Now that your term of office is coming to an end you should be very, very proud of what you've accomplished."

Carol nodded, "It's been hard work and I did doubt my competence to do it, but must admit I'm very proud of the results. The club now has more interest, energy, creativity and membership than it had when I joined. It has filled my life with good women friends."

"And it's added fun to my life watching your creativity and skill at work with the ladies."

"I do sometimes wonder how I'll use my time when this ends. I now have enough confidence in myself to believe I can make other contributions, and already started on two new endeavors. I value my volunteer work at the hospital, and serving on the Board of Directors of the new Community Counseling Service excites me because there's such a need for it in this area. But for now I want to focus on our Christmas."

Over a delicious Italian dinner the following weekend, Carol said, "Yesterday I felt so Christmassy I spent the day in the kitchen baking cookies. When the boys came home we formed a 'cookie team' and had great fun making Christmas cookies for our family and to take to school. Then they pleaded with me to make Christmas candles for them to give their teachers. I was delighted with their pride in my creations so we made candles.

We've been invited to more occasions than we can manage or want. I suggest we focus primarily on celebrating Christmas with close friends and your work colleagues."

Carol wrote her parents after the Christmas rush: "After the excitement of Christmas morning, we ate a delicious dinner, if I do say so myself, and then played Christmas gift games with our boys. Sunday we all went to a church we've admired from outside, and discovered a beautiful gothic interior. They were having an all music service and it was lovely.

The day after Christmas I worked at the hospital and when I see some of these poor souls who had to spend Christmas in the hospital I'm most grateful for all the blessings we have. My emotions are bubbling with a special kind of excitement as I feel encompassed by the love of my family. I'm so happy I sometimes want to sing and laugh all at the same time. I can't imagine how my life could be any more wonderful than it has been this Christmas."

1962 got off to a scary start! Douglas woke Carol up at 3 a.m. with pains in his stomach. Later, Carol woke and briefed me, "I poked around and from the way the pain was located and the fact that it was not moving or didn't come and go made me suspect the appendix right away. Then Doug vomited and I found his temperature only a little above normal. I called Dr. Light then and he didn't get very excited. He told me to give him a low enema and call him back in an hour. I followed his instructions and by 5 a.m. his temperature rose to 101 degrees.

I called the doctor again. He still didn't get concerned and said to call back in an hour if the pain persisted. Well, Doug has rested fairly well until now. His temperature has gone down a degree, but the pain is just as bad and localizing in the lower right side. I'll take you to work and then call the doctor before he has time to go out on calls."

About 8:30 a.m. Carol called and said, "I'm at the hospital with Doug. He may have surgery. Doug and I both need you!"

With a stomach full of fear I had a colleague rush me to the hospital. Carol briefed me, "When I called the doctor he thought since the temperature had gone down that Doug was getting better. I said, 'Well then how come this stomach pain persists, doesn't move around and doesn't come and go?' He listed some other things it could be and said to come in at 1 p.m. I was sure my diagnosis was right and scared because I knew if it was, it could be urgent, so I said I'd feel much better if he'd see him right away. His wife called back shortly and said to bring Doug in at 9:30 a.m.

As soon as Light examined Doug he said, 'Go to the hospital immediately for a blood count.' and asked who I wanted for a surgeon. I said, 'You pick the best.'"

We went to Doug who was clearly scared and had big tears in his eyes. I hugged him and said, "Hang tough – your Mom and I won't let anything bad happen to you!"

The surgeon confirmed Carol's diagnosis and nurses prepared Douglas for surgery.

The surgeon came out and told us an hour later that everything went beautifully. He also said it was an acute gangrenous appendix – a real red hot one – and we were lucky to have caught it in time.

We knew how lucky indeed when we saw the little boy in the bed beside Doug whose appendix had ruptured because their doctor didn't have time to see him on New Year's day. They almost lost him, and his little body was struggling to survive. Through tears, Carol said, "Boy, we don't fully realize how precious our kids are until something like this happens!"

Doug did so well they let him come home 48 hours after surgery. That evening after our boys were in bed, I took Carol into my arms and said, "You're a very special mother; with your knowledge and insistence on immediate attention you may have saved Doug's life! Thank you!"

Our tension and anxiety finally broke loose and we cried in each other's arms for a while. After drying our tears Carol said, "I'm enjoying nursing Dougie since he's home. I'm spoiling him, but it's such fun. He's getting his old sparkle back and his main problem now is trying not to laugh at the antics of his brothers as it hurts his stitches."

A week later, as we were cuddling in bed, Carol said, "Don, I'm lonely for you. It's been a long time since we've had a date. Would you join me for dinner at nine Saturday evening?"

I replied, "I accept with delight dinner with my magnificent wife."

She whispered, "Let's have Moscow Mules for cocktails."

Carol set up a card table for an intimate, candle lit dinner before an open fire with only shadows surrounding our pool of soft light. Our Christmas present was a new hi fi sound system so she played her favorite *Romeo and Juliet* for romantic background music. I wore the royal blue pajamas she gave me for Christmas and Carol wore the black lace peignoir and gown I'd given her. I handed her a Moscow Mule in a small rose colored goblet and said, "You're stunning in black lace with glimpses of enticing skin peeking through!"

She teasingly said, "That's all part of my plan for topics to be discussed later."

She sipped her drink, obviously a little discouraged. "I really need this date because I feel so isolated with this midwinter heavy snow. No one ever comes to see me or call and I get down in the dumps. I sometimes wonder if there's something wrong with me – B.O., halitosis or some such thing that even my best friends won't tell me. In my more objective moments, I realize many of my friends have lovely babies that keep them home. You're so busy since Christmas we have little time together. I shouldn't feel sorry for myself, but I get lonely."

I nodded, feeling guilty, "I hate myself for neglecting you, even as my heart longs to be with you. The primary reason I've been so busy since Christmas, the *Systems of Psychotherapy* book I've been writing, will be gone soon. It's done, but the publisher made editorial suggestions for improving it. The final manuscript will be sent to Wiley's this next week."

A joyful shout of, "Thank God!" was her response.

"I've accepted an exciting new assignment from President Walker, but it will only take about two evenings a month. He asked all the Deans and VPs to each give him the name of a visionary thinker on their faculty. Bernreuter recommended me. The group is very diverse – e.g., a historian, a biochemist, a meteorologist, an electrical engineer, a biophysicist, an artist, and a psychologist. We met in his home around a tub of cold beer and he said, "The primary role of universities is not focusing on the present but on opening doors towards the future. You've been selected because current Penn State leaders think you're imaginative thinkers about possible futures. Here is what I ask you to do. Look ahead twenty years to 1980 and tell me what you think are the new frontiers this university should be exploring by then. That sounded like fun, so we all accepted and will meet about twice a month.

I've hired eight new DOC staff, so we start this year with a full staff of very good people. I won't have to spend time recruiting more staff so that reduces my workload. So, by March I'll be able to spend much more time with the love of my life."

Carol's eyes sparkled and her smile couldn't have been bigger, "That's great because I have in mind some interesting new ways of using that time. For now, please refresh my Moscow Mule while I serve us dinner."

On two antique plates, she served thin slices of chicken with a wine and sour cream gravy and fresh mushrooms, half a baked potato with sour cream and chopped chives, and small asparagus spears. She lifted her glass and toasted, "Here's to the man of my dreams. It's said the best way to a man's heart is through his stomach so I hope this works."

While we ate, Carol said, "Our Town and Gown dance is coming up. Now that we're members, let's invite some other members here for dinner before the dance."

Through a mouthful of delicious chicken I said, "Good idea."

Carol said, "Let's invite the Anthonys, Guthries, Whaleys, and Gentry's. You haven't met Frieda and Bob Gentry yet. He's a veterinarian from K-State. I enjoy Frieda very much and would like to cultivate her friendship. She's interested in learning to paint too."

"A biologist, veterinarian, 3 psychologists, two painters, and a nutritionist sounds like an intriguing stew of interests. I wonder if Bob knew any of my veterinary buddies at K-State."

We polished off our dinner and I said, "That was a wonderful dinner my delectable cook. May I have a dance before we continue our conversation?"

She selected a big band romantic melody, came into my arms and we danced dreamily around our dining room dance floor, our bodies moving as one with the music. When the music ended, Carol looked into my eyes, "I have one more thing to discuss with you." She pressed a sweet kiss to my lips and led me back to our candle lit table.

We drank the rest of our cocktail, and with a little sigh Carol said, "When we started our evening and you admired my revealing black lace peignoir, I told you it was part of my plan for a later topic. This is it." The sound of her voice let me know the topic would be serious.

"I'm surrounded by friends with new babies, as I was in Manhattan. For several months I've been fantasizing about the wonderful feeling of cuddling a new baby in my arms and hearing them coo. I'm now a healthy 35-year-old woman, and I'd like to give life and love to one more baby. I've been wondering what you'd think about that."

She watched anxiously as my mouth fell open with surprise and out came "***WOW!!***" I reached across the table and grabbed her hands, "What a stupendous proposal! I confess I've secretly entertained such thoughts. Remember the slogan you introduced early in our life together – 'We make one hell of a team!' That goes double when applied to our baby-making."

Her eyes spilled with tears so I pulled her close, "Why the tears?"

I listened closely to her muffled words as she sniffled against my shoulder. "I've been struggling alone with this for a while and I'm so happy and relieved that you think about it as I do. I confess I'm a little afraid because of the trouble I had with the twins."

"Don't worry about that. I was dissatisfied with the hospital's explanation of what happened to you so Jack Light investigated with the doctor in Manhattan who delivered Russ. He learned your problem was a frequent reaction to ergotrate, a medication used to stop bleeding after delivery. He said you could safely have another pregnancy if that medication wasn't used."

I kissed her gently, then more firmly, to signal my joy. "Our decision deserves a celebration! Pick out happy music and let's dance in anticipation of the new Ford to be created."

I twirled her around the floor with such energy that Carol started giggling so I swatted her on the bottom with a mock scowl and asked what she found so funny.

"I was remembering dancing at a ball with you when, as you so delicately put it, I was as big as a baby elephant with the twins."

I laughed at that memory and said, "The more we talk about this the more excited I get."

Carol giggled again and started unbuttoning my pajama top. "Then, let's stop talking and do something about it!" We scooted down to our bedroom, threw our clothes on the floor, and began the most delightful manufacturing process in existence. As a Ford manufacturing team, Carol and I were efficient. Our production process quickly produced a new pregnancy!

On June 10th Carol turned over responsibility for the Lemont Women's Club to a new president. I was waiting at home to hear all about it. "I've been so keyed up yesterday and today over our Banquet; yesterday it was the anticipation and today it was excitement. We had a wonderful time and the music was superb. I really went out of office in a 'blaze of glory'."

I responded, "Congratulations, Mrs. Ex-President. Now you can use all your energy on developing our new model Ford."

"With another child we need more room. Could we build an addition to our house?" "Let's do it before the baby arrives!"

So, during the rest of the summer and fall we constructed an addition – another bedroom and bathroom down stairs and a large combination family/arts and crafts room upstairs.

A couple of weeks later, while eating Carol's fried chicken specialty, one of our sons' favorite dinners, Carol told us a sad story about Felix, a cat we had raised from a kitten. "I was driving down Branch Road coming home from shopping and saw Felix lying beside the road apparently hit by a car. I stopped, placed poor Felix in the car, and drove home crying. I decided to save you boys the distress of seeing Felix dead. With tears pouring down my face, I got a little box and shovel, took Felix down to our pet cemetery, and buried her beside Pogo. I trudged up the rough stone steps from the stream to our house, crying all the way, put the shovel in the shed and walked around to the front entrance to our house. To my astonishment, there stood Felix meowing to get into the house! I finally realized it wasn't a resurrection and my tears turned to relieved laughter. I'd buried someone else's cat!" We all roared with laughter.

In late July, my parents came for a visit. We decided to take them on a tour of places we knew they'd enjoy. We borrowed a big tent and camped along the way while lodging them in motels. First we visited Gettysburg. Then we took them to Amish country at Lancaster, PA. They were excited to buy cup cheese – something they hadn't had since childhood. Then we showed them historic Philadelphia which they both enjoyed.

Our final stop was on the beach at a New Jersey state park. We were both touched to see my father standing bare legged in the surf, smiling with joy as tears rolled down his cheeks, saying, "I've dreamed of this but I never thought I'd get to see the ocean." We had a luncheon picnic on the beach, stayed overnight and returned home.

The day before they left for Kansas we had the annual DOC summer picnic on our lawn and my parents were so proud to meet the people who worked for their son.

We were pooped from our travels so didn't do much but loaf by the stream that weekend after my folks left. I stretched lazily and said, "I think we did our parents a great favor by moving out here. Because they had to come here to see us, we opened a whole new chapter in their lives. They're enjoying adventures they would not have had otherwise, like the one my parents just had. In addition, I think it helped your parents grow closer to each other

Carol agreed: "It makes me happy knowing we helped bring a little fun into their lives."

All summer, Carol's friends had been offering their help in a variety of ways. One night Carol told me, "I'll never be able to face anyone if I don't have a girl! Boy, do I ever get the remarks like, 'I hope it's a girl.' or 'Are you thinking pink?' or 'Now don't disappoint us – have a girl.' etc. I tell them all a girl would be a new experience, but all I'm hoping for is a <u>baby</u> – one that's whole and healthy. Right now the gender doesn't concern me much."

Our new Ford arrived early again, and Carol shared the big news with her parents: "Dr. Light's prediction missed by about 3 weeks. Don stayed with me until they took me into the delivery room. I asked him afterwards if he was black and blue, I grabbed on to him so hard. Cameron Michael is special beyond words. I feel so relaxed with this baby and it's pure pleasure to feed him, then snuggle him up to my side and snooze together.

I guess it's my 'old age' but I'm so thrilled with motherhood this time. I probably felt the same the other times but have just forgotten how wonderful it is. There's nothing so fulfilling.

Here's a funny story about Don my nurse told me. 'I went running out of the delivery room to where Don was waiting yelling, 'Well it's four boys!' and Don nearly passed out. When I revived him I explained I meant four <u>including</u> the ones he already had.'"

Having a baby didn't slow Carol down. She and the boys decorated the tree and house for Christmas. She made a new formal gown and enjoyed a special Christmas dance. She enjoyed making preparations for and hosting the annual DOC senior staff Christmas party.

She wrote her parents: "Early one evening the boys called me in to look at some decorations they'd made. I went to praise them and found them giggling and pointing to the Christmas tree. They had rolled Cameron in his blanket and placed him under the tree with a sign saying, 'All Christmas presents belong under the Christmas tree until it's time to unwrap them.' I burst out laughing, sat down and thought, *Those boys are gonna have a lot of fun with their kid brother.*

Last year I didn't see how my life could be much more wonderful, but this Christmas it is! What a special Christmas this was for our family! A babe in the house after 8 years is wonderful and the boys get such a kick out of him. Russell is old enough to take care of him and does so when I'm busy. They all like to hold him when he's quiet. The boys gave Cam a cute stocking hat. Mom & Dad's Christmas presents were a brand new Ford and new space to house him in. It all started with the seed you planted by sending me on a visit to Marysville in July 1943. So, with hearts full of love we say Thank You and Merry Christmas!!"

1963 started with a very cold, snowy winter. At its worst, we had a snowfall of two feet with a temperature of twenty degrees below zero! Sometimes it took two days to dig ourselves out. Carol loved the beauty (she didn't have to shovel it!) and being isolated with her new baby.

She said things like, "I'm enjoying Cam beyond words!", "He's such a doll!", "Cuddling him while he nurses is a pleasure impossible to describe!", and "I swear he gets cuter every day!" Pleasure with her baby only increased as winter moved towards spring.

She reorganized the house so we could use its new addition. She moved us into the new bedroom, the twins into our old bedroom, and Cameron into the twins' old room. That meant repainting, redecorating and refurnishing all those rooms, and reorganizing closet space.

Then she turned her attention to the new family room she particularly loved. She had told the builders she'd like the walls to be finished with barn wood to give it a rustic appearance. One said he could buy some cheap that his grandpa had stored for years in the attic of a shed on his farm. I discovered it was clean, seasoned black walnut which, when sanded, was stunning on the walls. Carol's face glowed with delight to see the results. "Do I ever like my bay window looking to the south! My plants like it too. The window's red brick floor goes beautifully with the richness of the walnut walls and the three kerosene-style copper pull lamps add just the right touch. I want it to look as if it was part of a turn of the century prairie ranch." It provided a play room for the boys, an art and crafts studio for Carol, and a lovely room for entertaining guests.

With a big family and house, Carol had continual housekeeping, laundry, ironing and cooking activities that required major time. Periodically entertaining job candidates had to be squeezed in. Usually, by night time, Carol was pooped. Then, she attacked spring cleaning and added repainting most of the upstairs. I suggested she slow down and spread the tasks out more.

She responded, "When I start something I stick to it till it's done!"

I decided it was time for a date. One evening when we were relaxing after the boys were in bed, I said, "I'd like to invite this lovely and charming woman sitting beside me to join me on a picnic date this Saturday afternoon. It's supposed to be near eighty degrees so I thought it would be nice to spend some time together enjoying one of Mother Nature's gardens."

Carol grinned, "I haven't been asked on a date in some time. You know I have children?"

"Yes – that's one of the things I find attractive about you, and they *are* great lads. But, I don't want them to accompany us this time, so I'll arrange for a reliable baby sitter."

Her dimples deepened as she smiled and batted her lashes flirtatiously, "I can't turn down such a distinguished and handsome psychologist."

I said, "Great – it'll be a sunny day so dress for sunbathing."

I prepared a lunch of small sandwiches, grapes, rum and Coke, and rolled up small pillows in a large picnic blanket. On a cloudless May day we headed north into the mountains. While admiring the scenery, Carol said, "Mother Nature is wearing her prettiest spring garments today. Where are we going?"

"Guess."

She looked around at the landscape, "It reminds me of something."

I smiled. "Here's a hint. You were here once before."

"There's a pretty mountain stream – Oh, I remember now! You're taking me to that pretty bluegrass glen beside that small waterfall and pond. Marvelous! I've imagined being here with you more than once since we discovered it."

I parked behind a big grove of fir trees and collected our supplies. Hand in hand, we followed the stream until we found our private glen with the bluegrass carpet. Scatterings of wildflowers and the rush of a small waterfall welcomed us. Carol danced a little jig, jumped into my arms with a big hug and kiss. "It's a dream come true!" We spread our blanket on the grass beside a small slope holding our pillows. Carol stripped to her shorts and halter, I took off my shirt, poured some rum and coke, and we stretched out in sunshine to enjoy our drinks in silence.

Finally, Carol said, "I didn't realize how tense, anxious and grouchy I've been, trying to accomplish so much this spring. Sitting here in the sun with you, surrounded by this lovely place, I can feel all that tension flowing out of me and floating away in that pretty stream. Thank you so much for knowing I needed this and for arranging with Mother Nature for this super-duper date." She sighed with contentment and sipped her drink before continuing.

"My life hasn't been all work. Each day starts with the joy of feeding our baby. The mid-winter Town and Gown dance was great fun having you all to myself, and our winter Women's Club program was a big success. Our chorus performed better than ever, my guitar folk song routine came off beautifully, and so did our barber shop quartet."

"I wish we husbands could have enjoyed the show. When your crafts group met the other day several of them told me how great you were, and I puffed up with pride. Let me refill our drinks and we can talk some more while we eat lunch."

I popped a grape into my mouth and savored the sweetness while thinking how best to word my concerns. "Carol, I've added to your burdens by seeking your help in recruiting a new head of Penn State's placement service. Arranging for luncheons and having receptions for them in our home has been very helpful to me, but on top of everything else you have to do I think that's unfair. I hate to see you so tired when you go to bed at night."

"I *have* felt overwhelmed sometimes. Each morning I get up with a 'to do' list in my head. But, I usually end up short of accomplishing everything I need to – it's frustrating. I seldom have time for my personal interests like learning to paint or even playing my piano."

"Darling, I don't want you to be just a drudge and housekeeper for me, always tired out with taking care of our home and family. I want you free to pursue your personal interests and to just be my wife sometimes. Since we've been married, I've cherished the way our love and closeness have anchored us through good times and bad, and I don't want that to weaken."

"I feel the same way, and – Oh Don! I just realized this is May 30 and we were married 15 years ago today! You asked me for a date to celebrate and I've been so busy I forgot!" Carol moved into my arms and cried on my shoulder.

I caressed her hair and whispered reassurances in her ear until she stopped crying. "Together we've solved every one of our problems in the past, so let's solve this one. Name one or two kinds of weekly tasks you dislike the most."

"That's easy – cleaning the house and washing and ironing clothes."

"Both of those tasks have grown a lot. I don't see how you keep up with it."

"Sometimes I don't and it makes me feel lousy."

We sat quietly sipping our drinks in that peaceful place with the waterfall as background music. Finally, I said, "Carol, I suggest we give each other a special anniversary gift. We'll hire a cleaning woman to come in once a week to clean the house under your supervision. Then, all you'll have to do would be a little touch up during the week and our sons could help with that."

"Can we afford doing that?"

"The way your life is going we can't afford not to!"

I couldn't help but smile to hear a relieved tremble in her voice, "What a <u>huge</u> difference that would make for me, and you'll get your wife back!"

"Now about the laundry – I've heard you talking with your girl friends about how much work the new clothes dryers save in drying and ironing the wash. Is that true?"

"They all rave about theirs."

"OK, then lets buy a dryer – and, yes, we can afford it."

With a joyful "WHOOOPEEE!" Carol jumped up and pulled me to my feet while dancing a jig in the grass singing, *"Oh what a beautiful morning, Oh what a beautiful day! I've got a beautiful feeling everything's going my way!!!"* She gave me a big kiss, stripped to her birthday suit, threw our clothes in the pond and jumped in. I stripped and jumped in with her.

What fun! We splashed in the pond and waterfall. After frolicking in the water, we chased each other around the grass, wrestled on the blanket, and made exultant love. I gathered our clothes from the pond and spread them on bushes to dry. We lay together peacefully until Carol raised up on one elbow and smiled, "Being married to you is an adventure! You can be delightfully unpredictable, and yet you're always there for me. You *are* my magic man!"

I said, "I have one more present for you before we leave this love nest." I handed her a small package wrapped in blue paper with silver stars on it.

Puzzled, she unwrapped it slowly, then shouted, "It's your *Systems of Psychotherapy* BOOK!! Oh Don, I'm so proud of you!"

"It's OUR book! Without your help in preparing the manuscript and simplifying our sometimes turgid prose, we'd never have finished it. Your name should be on it as a co-author."

With that last bit of celebrating, we dressed and drove home, with Carol humming '*Oh what a beautiful morning*' and other happy tunes all the way.

A few weeks later, Carol wrote her parents: "My cleaning lady is about done with her chores this a.m. – the house looks so nice. Boy, I feel like Lady Astor with someone like her doing my work for me. But, it surely has made a difference in the way I feel. I'm so much more relaxed – not as grouchy to live with and have more free time for my family and my own interests. And, my dryer saves a lot of time not having to hang up clothes and everything is very soft and fluffy. And best of all, much of the stuff I used to iron no longer needs ironing."

We made a quick drive to Kansas to visit family and have Cameron baptized in Marysville. On the way back we stopped at Proctor and Gamble in Cincinnati to try to recruit a head for our placement service. P&G provided a baby sitter and gave Carol a very interesting tour of their research department. They showed her a new product to be on the market soon – disposable diapers! They gave Carol a case to try at home with a request to send them her opinion about the product. She said, "Those disposable diapers made the trip worthwhile! What a great invention" It erased a business that picked up dirty diapers, washed and returned them.

One lovely Sunday afternoon we sat on our deck, sipping iced tea and basking in the beauty of Slab Cabin Run. I said, "As acting director of Penn State's placement service, I've met and won the respect of college student recruiters for companies all over the country. They're having a conference at Poland Springs, Maine this fall to discuss their recruiting problems and asked me to listen to their discussions and critique their ideas. You're invited too – want to go?"

"Are you kidding? Maine at the height of fall colors would be a treat for any artist."

So, we flew to Boston and drove to Poland Springs. While I attended conference sessions, Carol spent time with other wives. She told me, "These gals are very down to earth and fun to talk with. We had one interesting experience. As you know Poland Springs water is a big seller on the east coast and in Europe's fancy bars, and is always on the tables when we eat here. We laughed when we found two little elderly men sitting in a shed, bottling water as it came through a small pipe from underground springs. Someone must have been a great salesman!"

We took one day to explore the Maine coast and enjoy the colorful fall foliage. The rugged coastline, gorgeous fall colors, and sparkling ocean reflecting blue sky threw Carol's artistic imagination into overdrive. As we flew home, Carol said, "You're certainly fulfilling my adolescent dreams of traveling with you. I've seen much of the East coast, but remember, you promised to show me Carlsbad Caverns."

"Carol, we've only just begun our travels."

Chapter Seventeen

More Travels and a New Dream for Carol

Christmas 1963 was busy like always, as Carol described the season to her parents: "We had four couples for dinner before our Town and Gown Christmas formal. I made a new, kind of sexy, formal gown and told Don to put his fangs away when he saw me in it!! It was a special night because we get to dance so seldom. Watching Cam experience his first Christmas was great fun. His eyes were big and his mouth hung open when his brothers turned on the Christmas tree lights. Christmas morning his brothers adored introducing him to Santa's generosity. The New Year began with twenty-eight inches of snow and bitter cold winds. It took three days to open roads and driveways so people could get to work and shop again."

One evening, while we were snow bound and the boys sleeping, Carol and I relaxed, enjoying the beauty and warmth of a crackling fire. I asked, "Do you have any plans for 1964?"

Carol winked and said, "Yeah – to spend more times like this with you."

I grinned, "Want to make a schedule?"

"No, but I'll try to make sure whatever you schedule will be worth your while!"

She snuggled closer to me and shared her goals for the New Year. "You know that for years I've wanted is to learn to paint well. This year I'll get serious about it. Freida Gentry has the same goal so we've decided to spend one morning a week painting together. Painting together makes it fun and keeps us motivated. Our new room is perfect for an art studio. Three of us who like to swim decided to swim once a week in the women's pool on campus to promote our health and have some fun."

"Wish I could join you."

"No men allowed, but what would you think about buying a family ticket for the community pool this summer?"

"Great idea! We all like to swim."

We got a cup of hot chocolate and a cookie and Carol asked, "What are your plans?"

"The Division of Counseling and Placement Office are running smoothly now with excellent staffs, but Bernreuter has tossed me a new one. Foreign students are rapidly increasing at Penn State. He wants me to reorganize that office to be more effective and then hire someone to run it. It's a small office, so that's not a big task. Would you like to meet some foreign students?"

"Sure. That could be fun."

"Carol, we've never taken a vacation with our children. Would you like that idea?

"Terrific! I always wanted to see the places you described while stationed in New Mexico, like Carlsbad Caverns, and our boys could learn from new experiences."

"I'll participate in the American Psychological Association annual meeting in Los Angeles this August. We might link a family vacation to that."

Carol shivered at the sound of wind howling around the house, kissed me and said, "Let's go to our warm bed and dream about it."

As spring approached, Carol said, "Interest in our Women's Club seems to be declining but our choral group is still providing me singing pleasure. We're in dress rehearsal with a Hawaiian themed program. I'm playing a guitar for a couple of numbers, which I'm enjoying. We also have a 'Ku-Ku-Nuts' satire on the Beatles. We'll wear coconuts for bra's. Our first performance will be April 2 for the Lions Club."

"That sounds like a hoot!" I cleared my throat, signaling a serious change of subject. "Carol, I'm worried about Mrs. Whitacre. Twice within the last week I found her car sitting in the lane with a door open – once the motor was still running. Both times I went to the door and she didn't remember her car was there."

Carol nodded, "Several times either I or some other neighbor found her wandering down the lane feeling lost and we walked her home. She could be developing scrious problems."

We decided I should talk to her son. He was grateful, feared that she appeared to be developing Alzheimer's, and confided he was trying to decide what to do. I said "We'll organize the neighbors to watch out for her." Shortly thereafter he moved her to a nursing home.

A few weeks later, Ben Whitacre called me and said he had to sell her land to raise money for her care and offered to sell it to us. Someone had offered to buy the land for a development of little 'cracker box' houses, but he hated to see the area ruined with that kind of development. He gave us forty eight hours to decide.

Carol didn't hesitate. "That would destroy the beautiful setting of our home and significantly lower its value. Development is exploding all around us because of Penn State's rapid growth, so that beautiful property will increase rapidly in value."

Our lender rewrote our mortgage to provide enough money to buy five more acres of land. This purchase gave us ownership of both sides of the stream. Carol said, "Our share of Mother Nature's garden has become even more beautiful."

In March, Town and Gown had a formal dance. We decided to flaunt tradition by not dancing with others because we wanted it to be an *US* evening. We had cocktails with our sons who said, "**WOW!!**" when they saw their mom. Carol was ravishing in a slinky blue gown with light blue net overlay and a fancy hair do with her long hair swirled strikingly atop her head.

Carol said, "Russ, what kind of dancing is popular now with your friends?"

"The popular one now is *'the jerk and tromp'.*"

She teased, "Ours is called *'the swing and sway'*." We put the younger boys to bed, assigned Russ as baby sitter, and went off to have fun swinging and swaying. Carol received many admiring glances and compliments as we glided smoothly and floated around the floor. Several men tried to cut in and laughed when she said, "Sorry, but tonight my arms and dancing are only for my husband."

We'd promised Russ to be home by midnight and made our curfew, then thanked our built in baby sitter and sent him off to bed. We were in a mellow mood, sitting on the sofa sipping hot chocolate. Carol said, "Don, when you're away I get a kind of anxious and lonely feeling – it's terrible being so dependent on you but it's also kind of wonderful."

"I don't like the empty feeling when we're apart either, but the way you make me feel when I come home is wonderful. How would you like to be with me continually for 21 days?"

"That sounds delicious; what do you have in mind?"

"You remember our K-State friends, Lorraine and Ted Volsky? Ted asked me to speak at a conference in Estes Park, Colorado the third week of August. The APA convention is in Los Angeles the next week. We could take our family on a camping vacation through the southwest and up the Rockies to the conference. Then we could go west through Utah and Yosemite National Park, turn south to Los Angeles for the conference, and then come home."

"You mean I could see Carlsbad Caverns, Mexico, the Grand Canyon, Indian settlements, those big sequoia trees, the Pacific Ocean and *everything*?"

"That's right."

"That would be another dream come true. I feel excited and scared – let's do it!!"

Carol pulled me over onto her lap and kissed my face all over. I felt a tear on my face and said, "Why are you crying?"

She sobbed, "Those are tears of joy, you Stup!"

"OK, I'll agree to give that speech. Tomorrow is Sunday so let's tell the boys tomorrow and have everyone make lists of what they'd like to see. Your list, of course, will take priority."

After a little smooching, I sat up and said, "I have another piece of good news. Our *Systems of Psychotherapy* book has been adopted by the Behavioral Science Book Club as their main selection this fall. They've been flooded with requests and predict sales will reach thirty to forty thousand copies. That's astonishing! The royalties will pay for our vacation. That book made us national figures in our field. Publishers are already offering us contracts for the next book even though we haven't written a word. As you often say, 'We make one hell of a team!'"

Thoughtfully, Carol said, "There are so many wonderful things happening in our life together. It's like being in a casino, where every time we place a bet we win. Why us? I don't think it's chance. As I've said before, it's as if someone is looking after us."

I replied, "When I was a kid, my parents frequently said, 'The good Lord helps those who help themselves.' We've worked hard to accomplish our goals and to be considerate of others, But I agree that our parents and maybe even the good Lord have helped make it all possible."

"Don, I feel so humble in the face of our good fortune, that I think it's time to start fulfilling Dr. Light's request. I plan to do some thinking about how to 'pass it on'."

On that note we put away our party clothes. I snuggled in behind Carol and held her close. We drifted off to sleep feeling the peaceful joy that comes of being deeply in love.

In early July, Carol's parents showed up in a neat little Volkswagen camper van for a visit. It was the beginning of a long vacation trip that took them to the world fair in New York, through New England seeing the sights and visiting old friends, through eastern Canada down to Michigan and then back to Kansas. As we sat watching our boys playing in the stream on a hot July afternoon, Carol said, "Another of my dreams has come true. I desperately wanted to transform my parent-child relationship into a mature, loving adult relationship. You and I went through some difficult times with them, ending in my confrontation with Mom. It has finally happened. We now have a very close, loving relationship in which I feel like my mother's best friend. My father now communicates more openly with me, and shows respect for my abilities and judgment. They're happier than I've ever seen them.

I couldn't have gone through my struggle for adult independence without your patience, loving support, and knowledge about such things. My mother no longer sees you as a competitor and has a high regard for – as she puts it – 'the marvelous man you married'. Because of you, I'm free to be who I am, and want to be only with you. You'll always be my magic man."

I struggled with my emotions while trying to respond to such deeply meaningful thoughts. I finally said, "Thank you, Honey. I'm honored and moved by your belief in and love for me. But, always remember the dancer's adage – it takes two to tango! Our love and happiness together provide the music for our dance through life together."

A car full of camping gear, provisions and six excited people headed west one August morning. Our first vacation stop was Carlsbad Caverns which Carol had dreamed of seeing since 1945. After touring the caverns, we camped near the entrance and in the evening dusk watched bats stream out of them like a column of black smoke. Carol said, "This was an even more astonishing experience than I had imagined. You've made another of my dreams come true. Our sons were excited and awed at being in such a huge cave."

Then came Juarez, Mexico and the experience of a different culture. The boys and Carol enjoyed the new game of negotiating a price for purchases. Then we explored the southwest and ancient Indian cultures. Carol especially enjoyed historic Santa Fe, an early Indian center and now also a community of artists. We visited an Indian woodcarver widely praised in the New York Times but had to find an isolated, ancient Indian village surrounded by a wall to do so.

As we drove to another Indian village searching for a man famous for creating silver and turquoise jewelry we saw women washing clothing in a river. Carol said, "I'm astonished that ancient practice still exists."

He wasn't home so Carol put her skill with women to good use and conversed with the silversmith's wife while we waited for her husband's return. She openly talked of her anger at his wasting all the money he made on whiskey. We finally met him, admired his craftsmanship, bought a small piece of jewelry, and continued our tour. We discovered fascinating historical facts about ancient and current Indian life and the history of the southwest. At Gallup, we saw El Morro, the Indian festival and colorful dances. We toured both the south and north rims of the fantastic Grand Canyon, visited an ancient cliff dwelling village, and many other special sites. At an old mining town, we toured a gold mine and saw a fun old-fashioned melodrama in their fancy historic hotel. That leg of our adventure ended at Estes Park for the conference and we all enjoyed several days of comfort in a very nice motel.

Then we headed west to Salt Lake City. Carol loved listening to recordings of the Mormon Tabernacle Choir so was eager to see their Tabernacle. To her delight, the evening we were there, the choir was rehearsing Beethoven's *9th Symphony* for a concert with the Philadelphia Orchestra. They also practiced some light numbers, like *Deep River* and *Shenandoah*. Carol said, "This has been the most wonderful experience I could have imagined. The acoustics in the Tabernacle are astonishing and their arrangements were out of this world. This will be the highest point of the whole trip for me!"

Our next stop was Yosemite National Park which we entered from the east across mountains and left by the west exit. The boys said, "This is awesome!" They had a great time hiking up a stream to the base of a towering waterfall.

As we left Yosemite, Carol said, "I'll never see any place more beautiful ever again!! It's more spectacular than the Rockies." (Later she did an oil painting of a Yosemite scene).

After Los Angeles, Disneyland and Marineland, we drove to San Diego to visit Mary Lou Allgire and her husband Paul. It was wonderful seeing these dear friends from Carol's 'slumber party' days. It was a fantastic family experience, but we were all happy to get back home.

Our recovery time was brief because the boys had to get ready for school. Carol faced Women's Club responsibilities and projects with her painting buddy, and work awaited me.

Before we knew it, another holiday season was upon us. We hosted our annual Christmas party for my staff, and danced with delight at the Town and Gown Christmas formal. At our Christmas gathering for old friends we shared our travel pictures. Then we hid presents in the new family room and locked the door until Christmas morning.

On Christmas Eve I built a fire in the fireplace and each person unwrapped one present from Kansas to warm up for Christmas day. With the boys safely in bed, Carol and I dressed for our traditional Christmas Eve date. We'd lost a bag of dirty laundry that included our warm pajamas while sightseeing in Arizona's Petrified Forest. We bought unusual replacements at the Grand Canyon; I became a papa bear and Carol a mama bear with bear feet on our new PJs. I fixed martinis and a cheese dip with crackers, positioned chairs facing each other by the fireplace, and laid refreshments on the hearth while Christmas melodies played.

As we relaxed and sipped our martinis, I said, "I've never had a date with a mama bear before." We laughed and I added, "The last six months have been the busiest, wildest, and most unusual we've ever had. It feels so great to relax with you on one of our private dates."

Carol said, "I'm so proud of our sons. They all earn excellent grades, study without being pushed, are well liked by their school mates, and they all delight in their little brother."

"Carol, I was thinking today, as I listened to the activity in our house, how you've filled it with music. Russell plays the guitar, Douglas his clarinet, Martin the piano, and you sing and play everything but the clarinet. What will Cameron play?"

"He's my angel so will have to play the harp!" We both laughed at that imagery.

"Are you still enjoying your singing group?"

With a touch of anger, Carol said, "That singing group is all that's worth anything in the Women's Club anymore! Nobody wants to take any responsibility, plus participation in meetings and activities keep going down. I've been considering giving it up. After the fiasco of our Christmas meeting I've had it! I'm saying to *hell* with the Women's Club and finding other ways to have fun! Maybe I'll stay with the singing group for another year."

"I've thought for two years that you were the last president that gave that organization any pizzazz. You've enjoyed some nice friendships within it though."

We ate some dip and finished our martinis. Carol fiddled nervously with her glass, and didn't look at me. I said, "You seem to have something on your mind – want to talk about it?"

She looked at me with a little smile, "I love that you know me so well. As I considered quitting the club, I thought about how I might use that free time. I want your opinion on an idea. I've always loved making pretty and useful things and crafting creations to be sold at school carnivals and club bazaars to benefit good causes. People seem to like and want to buy my creations. Sometimes they ask me privately to buy certain items, like my copper pictures. So, I thought instead of selling them through the club, why not sell them myself? I tried that idea out this fall in a friend's beauty shop. It didn't work.

I think we need an actual arts and crafts shop that people could visit, so here's my idea. For a year I've been using space in our new addition as my studio and displaying things I made until club sales. I thought I might use that space as a combination studio, workshop, and arts and crafts shop. Do you think that's a crazy idea?"

I raised my glass and said, "Here's to your crazy, wonderful idea – I think it's fabulous!"

She flashed me a relieved smile, "Do you really think so?"

"I've heard women ask my secretaries who made the wonderful jewelry they wear, like the poinsettias you made of shells. Your creations are unique and I think there's a market for your work. The Women's Club sales demonstrate the interest in your creations. Our walnut clad room is a beautiful place to display your work and is perfectly designed to also serve as a shop. From our front door, customers can turn to the right and enter your studio/shop without having to go through the house. It might take a little while to spread the word, but we can put our heads together on that. Merry Christmas my crafty creative Carol! I hereby volunteer as your uncreative but willing assistant!" Carol's eyes twinkled as she laughed in delight.

Basking in the warm glow of a fire and the martinis in her tummy, Carol shot me a playful smile, "Mama Bear would like Papa Bear to come keep her warm as we hibernate together."

Papa Bear growled, "Guide me to your cave!"

Cam's excitement tickled us all pink on Christmas morning. He caught on quickly to opening presents, but wanted to stop and play after the first few. When everyone had opened their presents, we brought out Cam's trike. That excited him again.

After our traditional cinnamon rolls and beverages I said, "Follow me!"

The boys looked puzzled, as they followed us to our family room. When we revealed a new pool table, gasps and shouts of excitement were quickly followed by grabbing pool cues for a rousing game. Watching the fun, Carol said, "At first I was very much against getting a pool table, thinking it most extravagant. Now I have to agree with your argument that the more interesting things there are at home, the less our kids will want to go somewhere else." Later we got a ping pong table to lay on top of it and doubled the fun.

After Christmas we went to a cocktail party where there were many people we knew and liked. Provost Rackley and his wife (former Oklahomans) asked us and two other couples to join them for dinner. Snuggling in bed that night Carol said, "I suddenly realized I'm no longer intimidated by 'big shots'. When they let their hair down they can be a lot of fun and have had very interesting experiences. When our psychiatrist friend and his wife invited us to dinner at the Holiday Inn before the annual Charity

Ball I had the same feeling when I discovered it was a buffet for the entire medical society. When I met one guy I said, 'I've met you before. I was having twins and you were so good and kind as my anesthetist, I thought you were an angel.' He grinned, 'You needed one then.' They're a close knit group and I enjoyed meeting their wives who were dressed quite exquisitely. I'll bet I was the only one there who made her own gown."

We both started the New Year with a resolution to keep ourselves in good shape through exercising at home. After a couple of weeks, Carol reported, "I'm so much more limber and I can actually see the difference. I'm also swimming on campus with friends Tuesday and Thursday for an hour. I hope I can keep it up – it feels wonderful."

One evening after dinner Carol sat down beside me and said, "Well, I just put two-ton to bed. It's quite a chore bathing Cam and dressing him for bed as he's so heavy to lift. But, he sure is a cutie and I make it a routine to read him a story or two while he drinks his milk. It's a nice little interlude. Boy, I sure do hate to see him get out of his baby years. Caring for my wonderful baby is one of the most precious experiences in life."

"I wish every child had a mother as good as you. Our kids are blessed."

"Don, this year, in addition to our usual family, social and entertaining activities, I want to focus more on my personal interests. Freida and I agreed to meet every Wednesday morning to work on our painting. We really enjoy each other and share a love for painting. I still get a lot of pleasure singing with the Lemont Women's club choral group. The State College Choral Society is doing *The Messiah* this year and I'm eager to be part of that. Martin seems to be losing interest in the piano. It's hard to keep him practicing."

"Is it possible he might be a little bored with it? All his lessons focus on classical music, but friends his age are interested in popular music and performers."

"Maybe, but I don't know what to do about it."

"I have a suggestion. Remember last Sunday when Fred Ball was here playing his jazzy piano? Martin watched his every move and seemed interested. Ask Martin if he'd like to learn to play like that. Fred would be willing to teach him."

Martin decided to try it. During dinner a few weeks later, Carol said, "Martin, you seem to enjoy playing the way Fred taught you."

Martin replied enthusiastically, "Until Fred showed me his technique, I didn't realize how fundamental chord structure really is. Practicing classical piano lessons is like reciting something someone else composed. By manipulating chord structures, I can do more than just recite on the piano. That's so much more fun!" (Eventually, he discovered a connection between the two, renewing his interest in classical music and leading him to compose his own music)

As we proceeded through winter, a small glitch appeared on our horizon when the highway department announced they were studying alternate routes for a highway bypass around State College. Carol said, "One proposed route would go right through our living room, but it will be a long time before they make a decision. They have yet to find a source of funding."

One Sunday evening while relaxing by our fireplace, I said, "Carol, I have two pieces of news for you. First, I got rid of a small work load this week. The '1980 committee' turned in its report. The new Provost, Paul Althouse, and I had the task of writing it. There are two major recommendations. The first stresses that the next scientific breakthroughs that will have a major impact on humans will occur in the biological sciences, and recommends a major expansion of Penn State's efforts in those fields. The second recommends creating a new kind of professional college, a College of Health and Human Development, to focus on the human and social problems that will be fundamental issues in the rest of the 20th century."

"What will he do with it?"

"We don't know – he hasn't read it yet. The second piece of news is I got a job application from an old friend for a DOC position on a branch campus."

"By old do you mean Kansas friends?"

"Yes."

"How old?"

"Very!"

"Quit teasing me – who is it?"

"Earl Elliott is finishing his EdD in counseling and student personnel work at Kansas University and is looking for a job outside of Kansas."

"You really did mean old, didn't you! You've known him since 1st grade and I've known Ginny since high school. We helped them get hitched. Does he have a chance?"

"I invited him to visit. His academic and teaching credentials qualify him, so it depends on the campus director's evaluation."

"It would be wonderful to have them close enough to renew our friendship."

They came for interviews and our wives were delighted to reconnect. Earl got the job at our Mt. Alto campus, formerly a facility owned by the State Department of Forestry.

Our life flowed smoothly into spring and then bad news hit. I hurried home to tell Carol.

"Paul Althouse had a heart attack last night! He's in the hospital but I understand it wasn't a major one." Three weeks later Paul was back at work.

Then, President Walker asked to see me. "Don, I want to protect Paul from too much stress while he's recovering. I need someone who could do some of the work I'd ordinarily have him do. But, I don't want him to know that's what I'm doing because it might upset him. So, I'm offering you a temporary job on my staff with the title of Special Assistant to the President for Federal Affairs. My public explanation will be that the position is needed because of new federal legislation regarding funding we might need for new programs."

I said, "I'm not interested in that kind of career pathway, but I might consider it temporarily because Paul is a good friend. I'll talk with Carol and give you my answer later."

That evening, when the boys were in their rooms, I explained the proposition to Carol. "This isn't my cup of tea, Carol. It would require more out of town travel to places like DC and that would interfere with the kind of family life you and I want, so I'm inclined to say no. But I do care about Paul's recovery. I feel like I'm between a rock and a hard place."

"What do you want to do here in the long haul, Don?"

"My heart is in the academic and student life parts of University activity. I think of myself as a counselor, teacher and scholar – not a university administrator."

"That's what I hoped and thought you'd say. Would you retain your regular job?"

"Yes, I'd just take a leave and arrange to have my lieutenants run things while I'm gone."

"Then it seems to me the question boils down to whether we're willing to make some short term sacrifice to help protect a friend's health. The main focus of your work so far has been on helping people with troubles. I've admired that in you and shared in your efforts when I could, so I'm willing to sacrifice if that's your decision on Paul's behalf."

With Carol's blessing, I accepted the appointment, but only for one year.

A major task in my temporary job was to represent Penn State with the State Council for Higher Education in preparing a new state master plan for future developments in higher education. I ended up co-authoring it with the President of Temple University in Philadelphia. In addition to trips to Philadelphia, I had to make a variety of trips to Washington, New York, Maryland and Harrisburg on University business. Even though they were only one to three day trips, Carol suffered with loneliness and anxiety during those trips (as did I). We were both unhappy about being separated so much and I didn't find the work fun.

I told President Walker my weekends didn't belong to him – they belong to my family. So, we did manage to have some fun family times and a social life. Carol suggested we take the kids to the New York World Fair since it ended that year. We combined it with a camping trip to a New Jersey State Park with the nice beach. We made it an end of summer vacation.

Summer and fall flew by and the holiday season loomed. One cold, snowy night we had one of our dates. Lounging by the fireplace sipping a drink, I said, "Your singing group's program this year was the best ever. That satire of a reducing dude ranch was hilarious!!"

"Our singing wasn't as good as usual, but the performance was the most fun we've had."

"How's your painting coming?"

"Freida and I have really enjoyed painting together this year. We learn from each other, make suggestions about our work, and have fun with girl talk. I finished two painting of scenes, one of which was from that colored slide you took of that beautiful Yosemite stream. I'm trying something new now – let me show you."

She came back with two samples. "I typically paint on canvas, but I've been puzzling over how to get a richer background. I decided to create a new surface by gluing burlap onto a thin piece of plywood, then painting the burlap as a background, like this." She held a 15 x 20 inch board covered with rough burlap and painted a rich turquoise. The texture of the weave produced interesting variations in shading.

"Then, instead of using a brush, I use a pallet knife to apply the paint in different colors and thicknesses to create the picture, like this!" She showed me a completed and framed painting of orange, white and deep blue flowers with lots of green leaves in a graceful white basket with a round handle. The picture jumped out with a three dimensional effect.

"Oh, Carol, that is *beautiful*! I love hearing why and how you do your art work."

"Painting with the pallet knife is special because it gives me a freedom in applying paint I can't get with a brush. People seem to like it – already two people asked if they could buy one."

The art lesson ended and she asked, "How's your temporary new job going?"

"I have no contact with students. While my administrative tasks are important, they have no direct connections with the teaching and research activity of the university. The only thing I find interesting is watching the power dynamics of people in the 'upperarchy'. Most but not all people in leadership positions worry about protecting their turf, and try to pump me for information because my role was made intentionally unclear by President Walker. I'm eager to get back to doing my own thing. Thank God I have you in my life – otherwise I'd be miserable"

I wrapped both arms around her in a bear hug and whispered, "Let's go love our loneliness away."

She giggled, "That may take awhile!"

The Christmas season arrived again so we went to Seven Mountains Christmas Tree Farm to choose our tree. We started to leave but couldn't find Cam! Carol and I about died of fear that he was lost in the mountains. We five spread out looking and frantically calling his name. Finally, he came wandering out from behind a clump of trees and said, "Hi." Carol scooped him up in her arms ready to scold him, but controlled herself so as not to scare him, hugged him and quietly explained the importance of not wandering off by himself.

We enjoyed the parties, receptions and dances leading up to Christmas, but our fondest recollections were the activities we shared as a family: singing Christmas carols around the piano with Martin playing; opening a Kansas present on Christmas Eve; and sending the boys to bed so Carol and I could have our traditional Christmas Eve date.

I built a merry fire in the fireplace, stirred up a Christmas punch of frozen lemonade, cranberry juice and blended whiskey, and sat out chocolates that a friend gave us for Christmas. Dressed in our Christmas finery, we sat by the fire and talked. Carol said, "You look quite dashing in your new tuxedo – we're in a social context now where you need one occasionally."

I countered with, "You look good enough to eat in that delectable blue brocade formal."

"I made it this summer to attend the dedication of the Art's Building with Freida. It got so many compliments I decided to wear it to that posh formal Christmas dance at the Vice President of Finance's home. Among all those big wigs I felt a little out of place, but we had fun dancing and talking with the few younger people who were there. Can you imagine people having enough money to throw a party with fancy refreshments for a hundred people?"

"Paul and Ginny Althouse commented that you fit in nicely and seemed at ease with that 'bunch'. And President Walker whispered to me, 'Carol is the most beautiful woman here.' Was it fun to see how the other half lives?"

Carol laughed and said, "It was fun to visit but I wouldn't want to live there."

I said, "I get a charge out of Cam's talking, mixing his own jargon with regular words and varying intonations. He does so much of it sometimes I wish he'd shut up!"

Carol chuckled, "The older boys play with Cam and tease him when they aren't busy. Cam loves to be with 'The Guys' as he calls them. One of his speech problems is a little embarrassing in public. When he tries to say 'truck' it comes out with an 'f' rather than a 'tr'."

I roared with laughter, poured some more punch and stole a kiss. Carol said, "This has been the year of the music lesson for the three older boys. Russ finally succeeded in talking us into getting him an electric guitar and has made the transition from folk to electric guitar."

"Carol, when he hooks it up to our two twelve-inch speakers, this house really rocks!"

"Douglas is in his second year with the clarinet and doing very well. He hopes to make the Junior High band next year. Martin has a bonafide teacher of piano now and what a difference it has made! I gave him lessons for two years, but with a good teacher he's very motivated and practices regularly every day. They could have quite a combo in a few years."

"Carol, we've been celebrating Christmas together for two decades, but they're never the same. We always have new and exciting things to discuss. One thing never changes – my awe that such a beautiful, smart, creative and fun loving woman chose to spend her life with me!"

"At 16 I wondered if dreams ever came true. You and I together are proof that they can."

We raised our glasses in a Christmas toast and I asked, "May I have a Christmas Eve dance?" We put on a romantic record, held each other close, and savored the pleasure of our bodies moving together to the same music.

Carol smiled mischievously "How about changing your suit – from tuxedo to birthday."

I laughed out loud, "Your wish is my command!" We turned off the record player and went to bed to make our own music.

Chapter Eighteen
New Challenges and Old Friends

A peaceful January was a relief after the busy holidays. Carol wrote her parents: "You must be in Texas now with Uncle David, enjoying the first winter vacation of your life. We look forward to hearing of your adventures. I'm really enjoying a kind of hibernation with my hubby and our sons. Cam is such a sweetie and comes up with cute comments. For example, he now says to Don and I, 'You are my friends.' and doesn't call anyone else that. His brothers were talking about someone having little girls and he piped up with, 'I have a big girl – her name is Mom.' My selfish heart says I wish he would stay 4 years old.

 I'm constantly amazed at how much fun the boys have with him and how he likes to be with them. He loves to have them play their records for him. On weekend mornings he crawls in bed with Doug who then takes him upstairs to watch TV. I get up and see Doug with his arm around Cam and Cam snuggled up against him while they watch *The Cisco Kid* on TV– it's such a cute picture. Martin would rather entertain him by playing records, reading to him or just acting kookie. Russ is the big tease, but also my young man and sometimes I really depend on him. I'm so lucky to have four such wonderful sons!

 I finished my painting of the Clark farm for Uncle Frank. I was so pleased when he wrote, 'Your painting surpassed my wildest expectations. I can even tell it's late spring and can almost taste a drink from the pump. It will give me many hours of happy memories.' To my astonishment, he sent me a $100 check! I returned it to him with thanks, saying that painting it also brought many happy memories back to me and that was all the payment I wanted.

 We have some new friends that I like very much – Virginia and Paul Althouse. The friendship grew this past year as Don worked in Old Main with Paul who is now the Provost. Paul and Ginny both grew up in Pennsylvania Dutch country east of Lancaster. They're ten years older than we are, but are our kind of 'down home folks' and although Paul is second in command at Penn State they display no signs of 'bigshotitis'.

I'm still exercising at home and swimming every week to stay healthy and feeling good, except when we have 2 ft of snow like we had last week. I'm getting a little lonesome for my gal friends. I met a new gal at lunch today with some neighbors. Judy Hobbs is such a dynamic, talented gal – a big red head. She has an artistic flair and is a crafting nut like me, so we hit it off great. Some of my friends have moved away so it is nice to have some new ones."

Milton Eisenhower had become a dedicated fan of gymnastics while at Penn State because of consistently championship-caliber teams. A national championship meet was scheduled so he decided to come. He invited us to join him for dinner and then asked us to sit with him to watch the meet, along with all the 'Brass'. That night in bed, Carol said, "It was great to see him again. It's amazing – he doesn't seem to age. He always looks and acts the same. I've never seen gymnastics so didn't know what to expect. It was beautiful – so graceful and powerful – almost like a ballet."

One evening after I returned from Harrisburg meetings, Carol and I exchanged news. "Carol, the state higher education master planning activity is over. That will drastically reduce my travels and work load."

"Don, that will be a huge relief for me. I've been chronically anxious and lonely with all your traveling, particularly in the bad fall and winter weather. Does that mean you'll be able to go back to DOC soon?"

"I committed to a year; that ends in early fall, and Paul's health seems to be good. The other interesting news is that the President has distributed the 1980 committee report to the Board of Trustees and all Deans and vice presidents for review and suggestions. He says the reactions are generally positive so far, particularly for the two major ones about biological science expansion and a new kind of professional college. That pleases Paul and me because we initiated them in the committee. Have your activities picked up momentum?"

"I'm really enjoying my singing groups. There are only four more Monday night rehearsals for the Choral society. Then the weekend of the performance we rehearse Friday night, Saturday afternoon and the performance is on Sunday night. You know *The Messiah* in its entirety is three hours long – ugh! This is why it's seldom done in its entirety. Our Women's Club group is practicing a program for the June club meeting. I'm to sing *My Lovely Valentine,* but you know me – I'm leery of solos."

"Carol, Hugh and I are going to a professional meeting in New York in a couple of weeks. We wondered if you and Nat might like to enjoy a weekend of city life."

"Yes – it would be fun to get away for a while."

NYC was a welcome respite for the four of us. Between meetings we enjoyed a new play, *Luv*, browsed through art galleries, and went to a night club, The Upstairs at the Downstairs, where we saw a hilariously funny satirical revue.

Back in Happy Valley, Carol described her plans for my birthday to her parents: "It's sort of a shock to think this is Don's 40th birthday and I'm only one year behind him. They say time flies when you're having fun, but I think it's flying much too fast. We spent the day getting packed up for a 4-day camping trip and birthday celebration at the ocean. We're going to leave tomorrow a.m. and stay at Cheaskequake State Park in New Jersey. It's only 20 minutes from Sandy Hook State Park which has a very nice beach. We're going in the middle of the week in hopes it won't be so crowded. We're taking Johnny Crouse along with us so Russ will have a buddy. Don and I are looking forward to finally getting to swim this summer."

One sunny morning as we watched Cam play on the beach, Carol said, "Cam and I are at home a lot while the rest of you are at work or in school, so we've become companions. He's so cute. He'll climb up on the bar stool and talk with me while I'm cooking. I'm kind of surprised how much fun I have talking with such a little kid, and it keeps me from becoming too lonely."

Cam also found that a special time as described in this memory:

"I would climb up on a bar stool (a thrill cause they were so high) and sit there watching mom cook and watching stuff in pans cooking and we both liked that. In conversations about social activities, it became apparent to me that the part of her social life she liked most was with family and friends. Instead of criticizing others she'd say, 'They're not bad people, just not my cup of tea.' I thought it was neat when she told me her bridge group had a rule that negative gossip about others behind their back was not allowed."

After celebrating my 40th, I suggested to Paul we take our wives out to dinner so they could get better acquainted. Over a steak dinner, Virginia told us funny stories about growing up with a doctor for a dad and what life was like in their Pennsylvania Dutch sub culture. They came to Penn State as a young married couple. Paul was a biochemist working on top secret military research during WWII, so he was exempt from the draft.

Carol told them of her involvements with music, arts and crafts. They invited us to their 25th wedding anniversary the following weekend. We all enjoyed the evening and each other's company. Carol said, "I feel so comfortable with them – like I've known them for a long time."

Later, Carol talked about the Althouse parties over lunch with her friend Jean Vallance: "We joined the Althouse friends and work colleagues, many of whom we knew, at their cocktail party. We secretly joined the others to honor them with a gift. They'd told us earlier that we were to stay after cocktails as they were taking a few of their special friends to dinner. We were honored to be in that category. It was a delightful evening and I really had a wonderful time. I told Don it seemed easier to be around people like the Deans, Vice Presidents and even Eric Walker himself than a lot of the faculty or staff of DOC. For some reason, people who have 'arrived' so to speak and are older seem content to just be themselves – more relaxed and gracious – real genuine people. It has taken me 20 years to appreciate that and be unafraid."

Jean said, "All those big shots are 10 or more years older than you and Don. I'm impressed that despite that age difference you can enjoy their company."

"I used to be uncomfortable with older people, particularly men, but Don and I now agree it's what a person is like, not how old they are, that's important. Don discovered that Paul and my birthdays were nearly the same – mine on the 8th, his on the 9th of October. So Ginny and Don decided to celebrate our birthdays together. Well, we went out to dinner and then came back to their house to find a surprise party in progress. Boy, were Paul and I dumbfounded! We had no idea. Ginny and Don really were sneaky. We got some joke gifts and among them were plaques – sort of certificates of merit. Paul's was for being a member of the 'Half Century Club' and mine for 'The Over 30 Club'. It stated my age as 39, so now I'll never be able to lie about my age! Well, it was lots of fun and something to remember."

Circumstances said one of our dates was in order, so I said, "Would my marvelous wife honor me by being my dinner guest at our mountainside restaurant Tuesday night at 7 p.m.?"

"The honor would be all mine. How did you know I needed a little lovin'?"

We drove through the autumn colors, were led to a table by a window looking out on the Centre Hall village in the valley below, and ordered vodka Martinis. We ordered seared filet mignon medallions and a tossed salad. As we reminisced about our year so far, I said, "Things started quietly this year but they've certainly been accelerating the past few months."

"That's true, and it's been full of special wonderful moments with old friends and new ones, traditional and unexpected experiences, and emerging capabilities of our children."

"Carol, it's hard to believe that only ten years ago we were graduate students without a job, facing an uncertain future. I was a little fearful, weren't you?"

"No! Every step in life, from the time we met, you've never let me down. No matter how dark or discouraging things looked we've somehow ended up with a positive step forward in our lives. I doubted myself, but never you."

Our dinner was served so I shifted the topic. "What a marvelous impact your Clark farm painting had on your uncle. Your dream of becoming a skilled artist is coming true."

"I do feel like I'm making progress. It's a great source of pleasure, like learning to sing a new choral work. It's helped a lot to paint with Freida every week. Not only does it keep me motivated, but we learn from each other."

"Of the paintings you've finished there are two I particularly like: the Yosemite stream and the dramatic sky behind the windmill. There's a lot of emotion in both."

I'd made all the small talk I could stand. I had a huge decision to make and needed Carol's wisdom as my guide.

"Carol, we face another decision. It's not public yet, but President Walker decided to create the new college the 1980 committee recommended, and the Trustees approved his decision. He wants to appoint me as founding Dean to create the college. His argument is that I created the idea, I'm a respected teacher, scholar and skilled administrator, and I know how Penn State works. He told me that under Dean Henderson's leadership, based on her personal recommendation, the College of Home Economics faculty voted to become part of the new college. I need to decide whether to accept this new appointment or go back to running DOC. Both are good jobs. I consider it a decision not just for me but for us. It's an important idea, but I'm not the only person who could do it. Help me examine the pros and cons?"

"Do you think you can do it?"

"Yes, I started the DOC from scratch and no one anywhere knows the nature of undergraduate education at Penn State better than me. If I get the financial and administrative support needed, I can do it. My only doubt is how good I could make it."

"Then why hesitate?"

"I don't want another year like this one. I've hated my extensive travel and missed you and our boys greatly. I feel I've hurt my family by leaving you alone so much. You and our sons are the heart and soul of my world and there are no 'do overs' in life. Once each day is used it's gone forever."

"Don, we agreed there would be temporary sacrifices this last year to help Paul. Would being Dean require continuation of that sacrifice?"

"Not if I could prevent it. As Dean I'd have complete control over the ways I use my time. I'd have staff and colleagues to do many things I've had to do myself. If Eric Walker can send colleagues like me on trips to do things for him, then I could do the same with my staff. But unpredictable things can happen. If we agreed on some 'rules of the game' about how to control college demands on my time and yours, we could probably protect our personal time."

"Don, I've watched you with love over two decades. I know you. You like to create things. Your ways of creating are different than mine in art and music, but they bring similar satisfactions. You'll never again have a creative opportunity this big or important. If you want to take a shot at it, then I say do it. We've had a lot of success collaborating as a team to make life work for us. It will have an impact on our life together, but it could be more good than bad."

Once again, one of our dates helped clear the fog away from our path forward. We drove home through a moonlit fall night, our heads full of thoughts about what we'd decided. We went to bed and held on to each other for dear life, feeling the security our love provided.

President Walker announced my appointment to be effective January 1, 1967. I privately agreed to the job for a minimum of five years – because getting a new college up and running would take at least that long – but not for more than ten because then new ideas are needed.

Carol wrote her parents: "Don has agreed to be Dean of the new College of Human Development. He'll tell you about it when we're there. I've had mixed feelings about all this. All my feelings of inadequacy come to the fore when I ponder being a Dean's wife and I keep wondering what it will mean as far as pressures and demands on both of us. I'm terribly proud of Don. It's quite an honor to be a Dean at his age and I think he'll do a wonderful job in making this college something unique and worthwhile, as he did with the DOC."

We and our sons flew to Kansas to celebrate my parents golden wedding anniversary, and to spend Christmas with Carol's parents. Before we left, Carol finished a very successful Christmas Bazaar for her Women's Club, we enjoyed the Town and Gown Christmas formal dance, and spent a weekend in New York with the Althouses celebrating Christmas together.

We got back from Kansas in time to co-host with the Althouses a Carol masterpiece of a New Year's Eve party which she described to her parents: "It was fun! We had all the guests play a get acquainted game first, then set people up in teams (not husband and wife) to play different games like ping pong, dice, racing cars, etc. and ended the evening with charades. We cleaned up and went to bed realizing when we got up in the morning we'd be Mr. & Mrs. Dean Ford – a thought both scary and exciting."

For both Carol and I, 1967 was a year focused on creating something new. For Carol it was an in-home arts and crafts shop, for me a new college. Carol had been making, teaching others how to make, and selling various kinds of crafts for a decade. The Women's Club crafty interest group she formed broadened her reputation and people started asking her to create items for them. A women's club friend, Jean, had learned crafting techniques from Carol, liked Carol's idea of opening a shop, and asked if she could participate. The more they talked the more excited they became about the idea. They named it *Carol Jean Crafts*.

For years Carol had been perfecting her painting techniques to be proficient in oils and watercolors. In recent years, friends had either bought her paintings or special-ordered work with themes meaningful to them. Last year she sold four paintings, so decided to display her work in the new shop. They created a diversity of craft products, displayed them on Carol's beautiful walnut walls along with several paintings, then announced the shop would be open every Thursday in Carol's home studio.

One day over a turkey sandwich lunch, Carol said, "I wish to invite your Deanship to join me for a dinner date at 8 p.m. in the Victorian Manor Restaurant in Lemont for one of our talks.

I replied, "Nothing would give me more pleasure than to sit close to an enchanting lady, sip a martini, and exchange ideas on a cold January night."

We sat at the corner table on their enclosed porch where we could look out the windows and watch cars passing by through a light shower of snowflakes. I raised my martini and said, "A toast – To a year of creative activity by an artistic woman and wordy man whose partnership has always produces awesome results."

Carol touched her glass to mine, smiled and said, "We've only begun. Let's order two Boeuf Bourguignon, with a slightly sweet red wine. Judy Hobbs tells me this is the best thing on their menu." Then she segued directly into her biggest concern.

"Don, I want to talk with you about *Carol Jean Crafts*. You've seen how much I love arts and crafts since we married, so actually having a shop to display and sell my creations is another dream come true for me. Since we've been open for business on Thursdays, we haven't done too badly. I've sold three paintings and have one on commission coming in if they ever produce the sketch of what they want me to do.

Most of the crafts on display have been purchased. I work all the time I can on our stuff, but so far Jean has been little help since she's been sick and only helps on Thursdays at best. But, I've done real well so far, and our crafts have been so well received that it's most gratifying. Freida is back painting with me one morning a week and that makes me more productive, as well as providing a companion for girl talk. Our combination family room and crafts shop functions beautifully! I'm so grateful for your encouragement and help. I have two questions for you now. First, do I need to collect state taxes, and pay income taxes on money we collect?"

"That probably depends on what you do with the money. For example, you've been making and selling stuff to raise money for school and community use through your Women's Club. The Club hasn't collected or paid taxes has it?"

"No."

"Then, the question is, what will you do with the money you earn?"

"I plan to do what Jack Light recommended when he helped us with the twins – pass it along to others in need. Jean has agreed. We started by providing support for a little boy named Joey through the Christian Children's fund."

"Then, assume it's OK. If a legal question comes up I'll talk to a lawyer, but doubt the Feds would go after such a charitable cause. Remember, when we talked about this a year ago I said I'd be your assistant and I mean that. Tell me when you want help and I'll do it."

"I believe in our partnership. As the Dean's wife there will be ways you need my help and I'll gladly give it, which brings me to my second question. Last fall, when we agreed you should accept the job, you spoke of creating 'rules of the game' to guide me in dealing with demands on my time. Can we do that now?"

"You read my mind! That's precisely what I wanted to talk about on this date. I'll summarize my basic plan for the college and then we can agree on how to manage your roles.

The new college will be called the College of Human Development. It will have four academic units, each focused on different aspects of human development. Each will have a multidisciplinary faculty, because finding solutions for human problems requires integrating knowledge across many disciplines. They'll be named Biological Health, Individual and Family Studies, Community Development, and Man Environment Relations. The first goal will be to hire someone to head each of those Divisions. When that's accomplished, all the departments and programs that asked to become part of the new college will be abolished, and each of those faculty appointed to one of the new units. I'll interview each person to decide which unit best fits their career plans. If their interests don't fit within any Division, I'll help them find another job somewhere or, if they wish, give them a one-year leave to gain the additional training needed to fit one of the divisions. All of that needs to be accomplished in a year.

The second goal is for each Division Director to provide leadership in creating the new programs: One, specify the kinds of new faculty needed, and provide leadership in recruiting new faculty; and two, organize their faculty to create a new curriculum to serve that Division's mission. I expect that to be completed in the second year. Once that's done, the new college will officially exist and its further development can proceed from there.

This first year will be the most demanding for both of us. Tearing everything apart and starting fresh will be an upsetting experience for those whose work life will be drastically changed in unpredictable ways. My job, with your help, will be to reassure them there's a bright future and guide them to it while keeping their morale up.

That will require a good bit of interaction with the Dean and his wife. I want you to feel free to decline any request when necessary. For example, since your shop is open every Thursday you should decline all invitations for that day. Simply tell me in advance when you plan to decline an invitation so I can make other plans.

I'll have to recruit seven key leaders – four division heads and three associate deans – and I'll need your help in accomplishing that this year. You've often emphasized two ideas to me: 'You don't just hire a person, you're always recruiting a family'; and 'Candidates are more at ease and impressed by being entertained in our home than public space.' You know what that's like because you've done a lot of that. I've already chosen one associate dean, although I haven't told anyone yet, including her. Louise Gentry and her staff created the focus I want for our undergraduate students. She'll be a superb Associate Dean for Undergraduate Students.

What I'd like to do is collaborate with you on planning and implementing recruitment of the other six. When we accomplish that, your role in recruitment will be drastically reduced. Does that help clarify how we can proceed?"

"Don, that's a mind-boggling vision! I'm overwhelmed with the scope of changes to be made and how fast you expect to make them. I'm astonished at your guts in attempting such a creation, but I have no doubt you'll accomplish it. We'll both have to work our butts off this first year! I can't imagine where and how you'll find the kinds of people you need and how you'll get everyone's cooperation. As we proceed, I'll probably need more guidelines."

"I just thought of another point – nothing will be permitted to interfere with attending every one of our Town and Gown dances!"

Carol laughed, "Pay the bill and let's dance home and into our future. It looks like it'll be one hell of a ride!"

Once she learned what her responsibilities would be with my new position, Carol focused on our home environment. She knew recruiting associate deans and their families would be quite different than simply entertaining friends or employees. Yes, she'd still provide the friendly, cordial atmosphere, but our home as it was needed some polishing. It looked a little worn and shabby from several years of wear and tear from four rambunctious boys and two busy parents.

One morning as they worked on their latest art project, Carol expressed her concerns to Freida, "I need to get myself and our house spiffed up for entertaining recruits for Don's new college. I don't know where to start. The TV is on the fritz, my dishwasher is waiting for a new part, the hot water valve on my washer isn't working, our tape recorder is busted, Russell's amplifier for his guitar keeps blowing fuses, several faucets drip, the toilet upstairs doesn't flush right, and our living room needs redecorating before we entertain a flood of guests. The ironing is piling up, I need to see the doctor about my sore shoulder, and one of my paintings was selected for exhibit at the Bellefonte Library show but I have to go get it."

Freida laughed, "I know you and Don have always had to pinch your pennies and do everything yourselves to get where you are now, but your responsibilities and income have expanded. Stop thinking you have to do everything yourself! Make a 'to do' list and write down beside each item how you plan to get it done and when. I'd start by getting a plumber in here. Don doesn't have time now to fix everything that breaks down."

"That's wise advice. Grandma used to say, 'It's time to stop stewin' and get to doin'.'"

One evening while the boys were doing homework, Carol said, "Dr. Light reported on my physical checkup today and says I'm fit as a fiddle so I'm organizing our home and my work load to help with recruiting and other official activities. I'd like to free up time from my household work by hiring someone to do my ironing. With four growing sons, a husband needing a clean shirt every day, and a woman who'll have to dress up as a Dean's wife, ironing is big weekly task and I hate it. Can we afford it?"

"Yes, that's a smart move – do it."

"Here's a bigger one. Our living and entertainment area is shabby and worn looking. We need to redecorate. That means new carpet, reupholstering or buying a new sofa and chairs, and new matching drapes. I can make the drapes but would need someone to help with the rest."

"I hadn't thought about that. Things do take a beating with four boys. We can pay for that with our next royalty check. Buy what you want and hire any help you need."

Carol said, "I have one more suggestion. This goes against my belief that entertaining should be in our home, but times have changed drastically here. We live practically next door to the country club. It has a golf course, a swimming pool and a lunch room. You and the boys could walk over and play golf any time, we could all use their swimming pool, and I could occasionally entertain candidate's wives and friends in the lunch room. Plus, you and I could both use some healthy exercise. Dr. Bernreuter offered to help us become members."

I grinned, imagining the hours of thought that went into her suggestion, "You're really on a roll tonight! I think that's a great idea and I'll arrange it."

Carol laughed and said, "Boy, it's easy to talk you into things tonight – how about buying me a mink coat?"

I wrapped her in a bear hug and planted a juicy kiss on her mouth, "Here's a down payment – I'll start saving in my piggy bank."

With her problems resolved, I shared an idea. "I've been evaluating the three buildings our College inherits and made a discovery. Right off the entrance to the main building is a large lounge with windows on three sides. The doors are often closed so I asked why and was told it was to keep students from loafing in there, putting their feet up on furniture, and taking naps.

I remembered how we helped students and faculty use the temporary union at K-State and said, 'Open the doors and leave them open. From now on we'll call this The Student Living Center. I want it to become a place where both students and faculty can take a break any time and talk informally with each other, hopefully with some food and beverages available for midmorning snacks. Evelyn Sauble on Dean Gentry's staff is a friend of students and we can make a little office for her there so she can be in charge of making it work.'"

I came home from work one spring evening and Carol greeted me with a huge hug and radiant smile. Her voice trembled with excitement, "I'm getting a wonderful piano! Mom has both an organ and a piano. She doesn't play her piano anymore and wants to give it to me to brighten my life. I've tried to talk her out of giving it up, but she insists with one requirement. She wants us to record Martin and me playing duets on it for her. Not only is it a wonderful piano, but also holds many happy memories for me."

It arrived two weeks later and Carol gave her old piano to our friend, Hugh Urban.

On a beautiful May Saturday we relaxed on the deck admiring our gardens, listening to the sounds of birds twittering and breezes stirring the trees. While sipping a cold root beer, Carol said, "The Choral society had its final rehearsal today for the Bach piece we've been working on. The performance is tomorrow afternoon."

"Carol, I'll take you and enjoy the concert."

The following Sunday afternoon we sat on our deck, nursing a Tom Collins and savoring memories of the performance. I said, "Your chorus filled the place with beautiful music."

"I'm surprised the auditorium was full. The Bach piece is a little unknown – more so than *The Messiah* at any rate. I thought we did well. Singing with a choral group is a joyful experience. But, it's hard work, so I'm glad I have my Monday nights free again for a while."

Carol wrote her parents: I hope you're enjoying your first vacation in Florida. I thought you might be interested in what it's like for your daughter to be a Dean's wife. This last weekend was a busy one. The College had an Arts and Home Economics conference plus an alumni spring weekend something or other. So, Friday a.m. I went to one of the lectures and looked at the exhibits and then had lunch with some women.

Then I had my hair done for the Town and Gown formal dance that evening. We had 12 guests at our home for refreshments and then took them to the dance. Saturday, Don spoke at a luncheon I attended so people could see the new Dean's wife. There was a dinner dance that night sponsored by the hotel and restaurant group. I made a fancy short dress with a chiffon tent over the sheath. We showed everyone the new Dean and his wife could dance up a storm!

We spent the week before recruiting Ted and Jean Vallance for Associate Dean for Research and Graduate Studies. He's currently Associate Director of The National Institute for Mental Health. Don recruited Ted, I recruited Jean, and Russ recruited their son. They all had a great time and accepted the job. I think they'll be good friends.

Recruiting is going well. News stories about all Don's new people led the VP for Research to say, 'It sure ain't the old college of Home Economics anymore!' Don said, 'That's what I want them to say.'"

Carol's music group prepared a great program for the annual club banquet composed of music and skits linked together with a story line. Carol had been teaching these ladies song and dance routines like those she and Marceline did as kids in Marysville. I told Carol this latest program was the best one yet.

Carol described it to Freida as they painted, "There were a lot of husbands there. I was a bundle of nerves with anticipation – all we gals were fighting for the bathroom with our jitters. You'd have thought we were performing on Broadway! My costume was a beat-up pair of bib overalls with red kerchiefs sticking out, an old plaid shirt, straw hat, a scroungy red wig and beard, round glasses to look over, with a blacked out tooth and a bucket of water to carry around.

I think we had a nice variety. The theme was 'Travel – See America First'. There's a soft shoe routine to *East Side, West Side* – we did a 1-2-3-4-5 routine that I made up from what I remembered from my old dancing days. Marilyn and Nancy did a cute take-off on *The St. Louie Woman*. Three gals did a Charleston to *Chicago*. I did a skit as a farmer singing *The Little Red Barn* and ended it by throwing my bucket of water at the audience – it was confetti instead of water but made them duck – and my black tooth fell out. That brought the house down.

The rest of the numbers *Alabama Bound, Oklahoma, Sentimental Journey, Donkey Serenade, Springtime in the Rockies, California Here I Come,* and *This Land is Your Land* were all done by the Chorus. Some of the numbers had beautiful colored slides behind them from our southwest trip last year. On our *California* number we about fell off our chairs when Evy Bierly did a 'walk on' as Phyllis Diller with the laugh and all. Russell handled the slides, lights, and played his guitar for *This is Your Land*. We're scheduled to do this two more times for other audiences and then we'll quit for the rest of the summer."

Our hectic pace slowed down for the summer, although recruiting continued. We all enjoyed swimming and golfing at the Country Club. Carol's flower gardens remained beautiful all summer with a little loving care. Her arts and crafts business grew so fast it was hard to keep a supply available. They created a new form of 'antiqued' silk flower bouquet shaded with gold paint that was a hit, with customers asking for more. We took a midsummer vacation with the Althouses to Myrtle Beach, South Carolina. That was our introduction to the historic south. And we hosted frequent picnics by our stream with friends and family.

Late summer, Carol and the boys brought home a replacement for our dog, POGO. They went to a small shopping center where Carol saw the boys huddled around a cage laughing. Inside was a Manchester terrier mix in shades of brown with the cutest little face. Long story short, Carol and the boys fell in love with her.

Carol said, "She's nearly full grown and partly trained, the kind you can tuck under your arm and take anywhere. We decided to call her Twiggy after the skinny British model. Camie loves her but doesn't exactly like all her wiggling when she's playful and excited."

That fall, Carol's last baby started kindergarten and she struggled briefly with turbulent emotions as he left babyhood, but like his older brothers he did well. One evening after work she said, "My heart really melted the other day when Cam said, 'I sure miss you when I'm at school, Mommy!' I've never seen such a demonstrative and loving child – he's a real delight. He even compliments my friends if he thinks they look nice. He should grow up to be a diplomat. I sure miss him – it was a lively place with Cam and his friends in and out all the time."

Later Cam remembered: *"There were lots of kids in our neighborhood and Mom let me freely go out and play with them without continually checking on me. The freedom she trusted me with made me feel real good about myself. When we were playing in the house, if things got a little too rambunctious, she'd get out her chocolate chip cookies and that worked to slow things down. There is one momism she only used once with me, but it really stuck in my memory. My friends and I came in the house and I was being pretty nasty to one trying to get him to do what I wanted. Mom was working in her craft room, overheard me, and said 'Cam, could I see you a minute?' I went in, she smiled at me and said, "You'll catch more flies with honey than you will with vinegar.' That memory has been usefully applied in my professional life."*

We arrived at the holiday season wondering where the year went so fast. Business at Carol's shop had been brisk, overrun by people looking for unique Christmas decorations and gifts. We made our annual pilgrimage to the mountains for a seven-foot blue spruce, with the added fun of towing the boys on their sleds behind the car up and back down the snow covered mountain road. Carol and I even joined in that frolic

Because of my new job we were overwhelmed with holiday invitations. We accepted a few, celebrated with a few close friends, and declined all the others. Carol looked gorgeous for the Town and Gown Christmas Ball in a new white brocade formal she made especially for that event. We went to bed Christmas Eve exhausted but feeling blessed with our life, our family and love for each other.

Chapter Nineteen
Chaotic Times and Travels

1968 got off to a bad start. Over coffee, Carol told her friend Judy Hobbs, "I've done nothing much this past week but run a bloomin' hospital. Cam came down with a fever of 103 last Sunday. Monday, Russ had a severe sore throat, headache and queasy stomach. Then Doug started vomiting Thursday a.m. and continued through most of the day. Thursday I got up with a severe sore throat and by Friday felt like I was getting bronchial pneumonia – an exaggeration but not much. With antibiotics, bed rest and careful diet we're all healthy again."

Judy asked: "How'd Carol Jean Crafts do over the Holidays?"

"I've been eager to get back to my craft work and painting. We didn't have much left in the shop after Christmas sales. Yesterday, we worked most of the day on our crafts. I'm real eager to start on my Folk Art painting. I painted with Freida this a.m. and got a lot done on the two canvasses I've started – boy, it's a good feeling to get in a work session like that! I hope the one turns out good because I'd like to give it to Paul Althouse for his Provost office. I really admire and respect him, and he makes me feel he respects and admires me also."

"Sounds like your new shop is a big success and keeps you busy."

"I save time for fun. I can hardly wait until Friday to get my hair cut and set so I can get duded up for Town and Gown! We're invited to dine before the dance with the Anthony's and Althouses. Don and I are eager to dance again – we really miss it. Socializing takes the edge off my anxiety about the Vietnam war. I'm hoping it will be over soon since Russ is near draft age."

One Monday evening in early spring, after Carol got home from choral society practice, we relaxed with a cup of hot chocolate and I asked, "How did practice go this evening?"

"We got off to a slow start but by the end of the evening things started coming together. For a while I was furious! Our director stopped practice and started yelling at a 70-year-old woman who still has a fine voice, criticizing her in brutal ways. When we began singing again, she got up and left in tears. She sits near me and didn't deserve such treatment! I felt like slugging him and leaving with her. He has the reputation of being nasty and arrogant. He's severely afflicted with bigshotitis! I'd hate to quit because our women's club singing group has folded. If I quit choral society I'd have no place to sing and I get much pleasure from singing."

"Don't let your director take that away from you. You'll only hurt yourself if you let him make you quit. Wait for a chance to get a new director."

"Don, having our dissertation team of Ashby, Ford, Guerney and Guerney together again last weekend, dear friends we've known since moving here sixteen years ago, was wonderful. You were talking with Bernie so missed the music when our sons came home. The men wanted Russ to show them guitar chords because they're trying to learn it. Russ made a hit playing and singing folk songs. Then, Martin, Doug and Russ played piano, guitar and clarinet. Everyone thought our kids were so talented so that made me feel very proud."

"Love of music is another important thing you brought into their lives as you did mine." I sipped my hot chocolate before changing the subject. "Are you having any success getting help from Dr. Light with your headaches?"

"No! I'm really getting tired of these 'time of the month' headaches and hate going off the pill seven days of the cycle. I don't know whether it's the pill or something else, like my vulnerability for migraine headaches. If I have an alcoholic drink during my period, I'm likely to get my one-sided headache. But, there are times I've gotten one without drinking. Nothing Dr. Light has given me for the pain helps. They can last anywhere from one to seven days.

He called me today and we had a 'heart to heart.' He says they're caused by vascular dilation and the classic treatment is ergotrate and caffeine. I can't use ergotrate since that's what caused the trouble when the twins were born. He suggests I go off the pill for two or three months to see if it's the culprit. I've always felt that the pill has improved my health, so I may be in for some bad days. I'll be worried and we'll have to be ultra careful."

"We can abstain, like we did before we married, while you conduct this test."

In April I flew to Detroit to speak at a professional meeting. That day Martin Luther King was assassinated. Detroit was shut down for fear of riots but I managed to fly home on the last flight out of the Detroit airport. Carol cried in relief when I arrived. I told her, "I was just preparing to give my speech when the announcement came with plans for controlling violence. I decided to leave immediately. I was heartsick over Dr. King's death, but that elevator ride down with a group of angry black men scared me, and the taxi ride to the airport with an enraged black driver worried me. Dr. King's assassination, combined with uprisings over the Viet Nam war, has torn apart the fabric of our society. Somehow, we have to figure out a way to mend it."

That weekend Carol showed me a letter she was sending her parents: "It was interesting to hear your comments on the King assassination, riots, etc. I don't agree with you about M. L. King as I feel he was a very great man doing what he could for his race in the right way. I don't believe he stirred up his people. They've been treated miserably with no respect as humans long before he appeared. They lived under such conditions longer than most could endure them. He represented the intelligent, thoughtful side of the civil rights movement. I hope his work isn't lost with him. If you could see the horrible conditions many of his people live with, you'd understand why hate, discontent and hopelessness exist. They deserve our sympathy and help."

After reading her letter, I looked at her in admiration, "Carol, you've often criticized yourself for an inability to express your thoughts well. This lucid letter from your heart shows you don't deserve that criticism. I'm proud of you for trying to enlighten your parents."

I came home one noon bringing pizza and fruit salad to have a surprise lunch with Carol while our sons were in school. She was working on a painting when I arrived and laughed with delight at my luncheon plan. We sat on our deck on a warm May Day, eating pizza, drinking iced tea, and enjoying the spring beauty of our "private park" on Slab Cabin Run.

I said, "I'm temporarily resigning for one day as Dean on Thursday so I can just be a fellow in love spending a day alone with his enticing artist sweetheart, enjoying Mother Nature in all her spring beauty. Can you fit me into your schedule?"

She smiled and took my hand, murmuring softly, "I haven't forgotten this time – Thursday is our 20th wedding anniversary! Can we go back to our mountain glen with its little waterfall to be just US for a day?"

I kissed her soundly and said, "That's what I had in mind."

On a warm May 30 morning, we drove north into the mountains under a cloudless sunny sky. We parked behind our grove of evergreens, collected our supplies, and walked leisurely along the stream through the forest. As we rounded a bend in the stream, Carol stopped and said,

"Oh Don, it's just as I remembered it – it makes me want to sing!"

We spread our blanket and sat our picnic basket in the grass. Carol picked a couple little blue blossoms, stuck them in her hair, and wrapped both arms around my neck. "I say this every anniversary, but honestly, I just can't imagine why a remarkable man like you chose me to love. While exchanging letters, I created fantasies about being your wife, including giving you babies. None of those fantasies even came close to the reality that began May 30, 1948. My heart is just bubbling over with happiness and love, not to mention delicious anticipation!" She took my face in her hands and pressed a sweet, lingering kiss to my mouth.

I said, "What a great way to say happy anniversary!"

She giggled, "All the way up here I've been rehearsing how to say that. I can paint beautiful pictures on canvas, but find saying it in words much harder."

"You're a creative, desirable gal! I worked for five years to win your heart and hand." In a reprise of the last visit to our special spot, I picked her up and whirled in a giddy dance, singing in my special off-tune style, *"Oh what a beautiful morning!"* Carol joined in, *"Oh what a beautiful day!"* We stopped our twirling dance and caught our breath for a few seconds.

Carol took my hand and said, "Let's follow the stream for a while to see what we can find."

After an hour of exploration we returned to our glen and settled on the blanket. We soaked up the sun in silence until I decided it was time to break out the drinks. "I combined a Moscow

Mule with Mint Julep for our drinks by adding a slice of lime and a touch of mint,"

She sipped it, savoring the flavors, "Mmmm! Let's name your invention a Mint Mule." We laughed, sipped our Mint Mules, and enjoyed the sun's warmth on our skin.

"Carol, have you thought about what we might do for fun the rest of this year?"

"I want to participate in the Arts Festival again this year. It was heartwarming that festival visitors loved my creations last year. I sold several of my paintings, a lot of our crafts, and commissioned two more paintings. Russ's musical group will perform again this year."

"When is it?"

"About the middle of July."

"I'll arrange my schedule to help you set up and enjoy it with you this year."

"That would be terrific! A dinner time happy hour with friends there might be fun."

"Paul Althouse asked if we'd like to vacation with them at Myrtle Beach again this year."

"We all enjoyed it last year, but a week is too long; cut it to four days plus travel time."

"OK, I'll give him that answer. Now, let's have lunch. I brought chicken salad sandwiches, cherry tomatoes, and cheese curls. And, of course, more Mint Mules!"

As we ate, Carol said, "Russ will graduate from high school next year and start college. This summer will likely be the last one our whole family can vacation together. I wish we'd dream up something special." We chewed and thought.

I said, "Russ, more than any of our other boys, has loved our camping trips. You've wanted to visit the northwest U.S. and Pacific Ocean. I bet Russ would love that."

"So would I, but not in a tent. Tent camping is OK in good weather, but it's miserable in rainy weather. Our old friend, Kenny Rowland, worked in Seattle and told us how rainy the northwest coast is. If we make such a trip, I'd want to buy or rent a travel trailer and let me expand on your idea. My parents have had a ball the last two years traveling all over the country in their camper.

They're in a camper's club. Maybe they could give us some advice about a travel trailer."

I replied with a grin, "Let me expand on your expansion. Let's invite your parents to join us. Our gang would consider that fun, and we could help each other if we had any trouble."

"What a fantastic idea! I bet they'd love it."

We agreed that Carol would write her folks and explore our idea with them.

She said: "That's enough planning, let's play. I'm hot and sweating from the sun so let's go skinny dipping and cool off." We repeated our antics from last year. We frolicked and wrestled like teenagers and I relished the vision of Carol standing naked in the waterfall. The sight of Carol's naked beauty always seemed to leave me dumbstruck!

I said, "I know we're abstaining from sex until you finish your headache experiment, but will you come and lie in my arms while the sun dries us off?"

"Yes indeed!"

I thought, *That's my Carol, always ready to snuggle!* So we lay together on our blanket, enjoying the pleasures of kisses and caresses. I helped Carol up, stole one final kiss and we surprised ourselves by simultaneously saying, "Happy Anniversary!"

We left for our Myrtle Beach trip immediately after graduation. Our daily rhythm was pleasant: breakfast together in the Althouse room; morning on the beach playing in the water, loafing under our umbrellas, talking, reading and watching our kids; lunch together in our rooms; naps while our older offspring went back to the beach; afternoon play in the enclosed swimming pool, Cam's favorite; cocktails on our balcony enjoying the ocean view; dinner in our rooms to save money; cards and other games; and then to bed.

The last night we all went to a restaurant for dinner. While we waited to be served, Martin started playing the restaurant piano. Customers obviously enjoyed his playing. When our dinners arrived and Martin rejoined us, one customer handed him a ten-dollar tip.

July and the Arts Festival arrived. The boys and I helped Carol organize and arrange her display. Russ attracted visitors by playing his guitar. She had a greater diversity of exhibits than other participants so immediately drew a rush of customers, some returnees from last year. People browsed, talked with Carol about her work, and nearly everyone bought something.

One piece she'd created for fun attracted the most attention. Throughout the year she'd saved different shapes of beef bones, bleached and arranged them in attractive designs on black velvet, and framed them. An orthopedic surgeon saw one, loved it, and bought it for his office. Carol said, "There's no reason why art can't be both beautiful and fun."

At sundown we packed things up so we could bring them back the next day. Carol said. "It's a lot of work, but also lots of fun meeting so many interesting people, and gratifying to have them like my work. I haven't had such a rewarding experience in a long time!"

Later in life Russell described his memories of the festival and his Mom:

"I vividly remember being with her at the central PA Festival of the Arts. I was very impressed and proud to watch and listen as lots of people examined, admired and bought her work. I'd eavesdrop on conversations like, 'I love the combinations of colors she used!' or 'How in the world did she do that?' Occasionally someone would commission a work, like the man who asked her to paint the scene where he proposed marriage to his girlfriend.

My dad, brothers, sometimes Mom's parents, and I would lounge in chairs, watch the people and help with customers. It was a special time together for our family, and one that was all about Mom. I bragged to my friends about what Mom made, felt very proud to be her son, and to this very day remembering her at the Arts festival is one of my favorite memories."

After the Arts Festival, we prepared for our camping trip to the Pacific Northwest. We bought a used travel trailer and joined up with Carol's parents in Kansas. From there our jolly caravan headed north to South Dakota and turned west.

We laughed at prairie dog villages with their lookouts, gaped in awe at huge buffalos, and admired the graceful beauty of wild horse herds. We visited the Mt. Rushmore memorial, studying the stone faces of Washington, Jefferson, Lincoln, and Roosevelt. The Crazy Horse Indian Memorial was magnificent, even though in the early stages of construction.

After that we spent three days at Yellowstone Park, a place so fabulous we couldn't find words adequate to describe it. Continual rain followed us across the northern Rockies to the Pacific. In Seattle I finally called the airport and asked how far south we'd have to go to get out of the rain. After a brief pause the answer was "San Diego!" So, we only spent one day exploring Seattle, and a day on the rocky coast collecting small gemstones Carol planned to polish to reveal their lovely colors. The Pacific shores displayed a varying array of natural wonders as we drove slowly south on coastal highways. The rain finally stopped and we camped about forty miles north of San Francisco, where Carol's parents left us to head back to Kansas.

We built a big bonfire on the beach and enjoyed a night of ocean sounds with a canopy of stars and a full moon overhead. The whole family relaxed around the fire while Russ played his guitar and sang folk songs with Carol. The rest of us chimed in when we knew the words. It was the sort of family closeness we'd always cherished, bound together with a nurturing affection. The experience created what our sons called an indelible memory.

The next day the family explored San Francisco while I attended professional meetings. Then we started our trek east, back to Pennsylvania. We spent a day boating on the gloriously blue Lake Tahoe. That evening, the boys played miniature golf while Carol and I enjoyed a dinner show at the Nevada Lodge casino. Later, sitting by our little campfire Carol said, "What a wondrously beautiful country we live in! My head is filled with scenes I'd like to paint. Spending two weeks enjoying my Ford men this way is an experience I'll cherish forever!"

Four days later we were back to our regular Pennsylvania lives. The boys returned to school, I resumed scrambling to solve a multitude of problems, and Carol was back to being an artist and party giving hostess. We were gobbled up by the fall social whirl of football, parties, receptions, and protocol occasions. Cuddling in bed one night, Carol said, "Let's go to New York and have a pre-Christmas fling. I'm fed up with this fall social upheaval and you need to get away from what I call your impossible job." She didn't have to ask me twice!

Carol gave her folks a rundown later: "We had such a nice weekend in NYC all by ourselves. We did some shopping, saw Pearl Bailey and Cab Calloway in *Hello Dolly* and an off-Broadway play – both really good. Then we took in an excellent revue at the Latin Quarter, danced 'go-go' style at one of the new discothèques, and had the time of our lives. On some trips the city looks ugly to me, but in its Christmas finery it's pretty."

Carol told her friend, Jean Vallance, "I bought my Ford men a new pool table as a Christmas surprise. My craft work had ruined the old one. They secretly delivered it and I hid it with my craft stuff so it looks like the old beat up one. It's driving me crazy for fear someone will discover it. It gives me lots of pleasure to actually give them something on my own."

But Cam discovered it. As he recalled:

"I was crawling around under the pool table while Mom was working and suddenly realized it was a different table. That was big news and I was the only one who knew it!!! I was the little kid looking for ways to get more attention and to temporarily be a 'big shot' to my brothers. This was a huge opportunity to do that, by revealing the BIG SECRET. So I did.

Mom was disappointed I had ruined her surprise, but she didn't get angry or yell at me about it. She talked about why it would have been nice to keep it a secret. She was always like that with me – trying to help me learn from my experiences."

Lying in each other's arms on Christmas night, Carol said, "Don, I've been pinching myself to make sure this incredible family is really mine. I'm surrounded by love and cherish all of you to the point that I'm overwhelmed sometimes."

"You've said from day one that we make one hell of a team, and the family we created is proof of that. One thing that makes you so special to me is the excitement you generate while living life to its fullest. You're incredible!"

Carol started the New Year with a letter to her parents: "The holidays are over, the boys are back in school, Don is meeting with his nursing faculty, and I'm hibernating. I hate the thought of going anywhere. I've been focusing on my painting and finished one a lady commissioned of the round red barn about six miles east of here. I think it's pretty good so hope she likes it. I've started two new oil paintings. One is based on an old photo of historic Lemont that the Beaver sisters (they were neighbors in Lemont) asked me to paint for their mother.

Choral society rehearsals also begin in two weeks. I've missed singing since the Women's club group disbanded, so decided to join the Presbyterian Choir in State College. I haven't sung in a church choir since high school. This one is pretty good.

Since Doug started clarinet two years ago he's doing very well. He's taking clarinet lessons from a teacher in the PSU music department. He wants to make 1st chair in the worst way. We agreed to pay for the lessons if he agreed to practice at least one hour every day."

Doug did win 1st chair, played in the high school orchestra and marching band, and played four years in Penn State's marching Blue Band, including playing in three football bowl games. So once again Carol's cultivation of her sons' talents paid off.

My college leadership team was complete except for an Associate Dean for Continuing Education. One morning, the deputy director of the Pennsylvania Dept. of Public Welfare brought a handsome African-American man to my office and said, "This guy applied to me for a job but I told him I thought he should come to work with you in your College of Human Development. His name is Ed Ellis and he has a doctorate in public health."

After getting acquainted, I thought, *Here is my Associate Dean*! His wife was one of the best librarians in the country and our librarian was eager to hire her. Carol arranged get-acquainted gatherings and asked our sons and their friends to show the Ellis kids the schools and help them enjoy the area. Ed and his wife accepted their job offers.

I burst through the door at home, grabbed Carol in a big hug and said "Thank You! Thank You! Thank You! We got the Ellises! No one is better at recruiting than my wife!"

Carol laughed, "I really like them and their kids. I hope this town treats them well."

Ed was a treasure in both competence and style, and the first African-American in a significant leadership position at Penn State.

After pleasing her sons with a superb fried chicken dinner, Carol told me, "You've hired so many new faculty this year I've decided to arrange a series of informal coffees in our home so I can get acquainted with the wives and they can get acquainted with each other, perhaps three or four people at a time. I'm keeping it very informal. I'll wear slacks and invite them to do likewise to feel at ease. I remember what I felt like when I was new here."

"Carol, that will be a big help in boosting morale for them and their spouses."

Then, student demonstrations against the Viet Nam war and other social concerns hit Penn State, as they had other universities. Eventually the peaceful demonstrations, protests and speeches mushroomed into physical disruptions and violence. I worried for my family.

"Carol, I want you and our sons to stay away from campus until this is over. The student group organizing all this is small, but trying to provoke violence, so current conditions are dangerous." I felt she had to hear the truth, regardless of how it might distress or frighten her.

"Students demonstrated at Old Main and staged a sit-in around the President's offices, refusing to leave unless carried out. They even threw bottle bombs against doors of the Human Development buildings at night but fortunately they were incompetently made and did little damage, but we've had to station people in the buildings at night. They also threw stones through the windows of President Walker's home while his wife was in it, so guards are necessary. And now the shooting of students by national guardsmen at Kent State has raised tensions higher. Classes have been canceled and meetings with students are on hold. I'm trying to organize the Deans to try and calm things down."

The next morning the campus had been transformed with color floating everywhere. The story was so great I had to call and share it with Carol. "When I arrived this morning, the campus was covered with a thousand helium-filled, brilliantly colored balloons floating above trees and bushes and tied to every immovable object with crepe paper streamers. Each balloon contained a message like, 'Think Spring', 'Say Hi to Someone', or 'Have Fun'.

Evelyn Sauble got a bunch of our students together and they spent all night blowing up balloons, making the messages and scattering them around campus before dawn. Her idea was to create a fun and happy atmosphere to offset the current negative one. No one knows yet who did it, so part of the fun is in seeking the answer, which shifts attention to this positive event.

Evelyn didn't tell me about it in advance so any policy violation wouldn't backfire on me. I hugged and thanked her for demonstrating the message of peaceful solutions to problems that we're trying to cultivate with our college."

Carol said "How wonderful! Evelyn is more understanding and sensitive working with students than anyone I've known, except for you. It sounds so beautiful I wish I could see it."

A few days later I explained to Carol how the Dean's stopped the uprising, "I met with Russ Larsen, Dean of Agriculture and said, 'Russ, the SDS (Students for a Democratic Society) is using a well-known strategy, probably encouraged by outsiders. They focus all issues on one public leader—the top one if possible. Here, that is Eric Walker. The way to defeat their strategy is to prevent zeroing in on one person. The major issue that enabled SDS to gain student support is curriculum reform. Most students supporting them are decent and smart. Take away that issue and I predict support for the SDS will rapidly disappear.

With Eric's approval I suggest we Deans invite interested students to meet with us in front of Old Main so we can deal with their concerns. Assemble the Council on the Old Main steps and you, physically our biggest dean, deliver a message like this:

'Your primary concerns all have to do with curriculum change. President Walker has no power to do that. That power rests with the Dean of each college. So, if you want your ideas to be considered, you need to discuss them with your Dean. All the Deans are here before you. Each of us will cooperate in considering and resolving your concerns.'

We did that and it worked. Demonstrations dwindled to a small group and then stopped altogether. It's safe now and our new colleague, Ed Ellis, was helpful in preventing the SDS strategy from spreading to students concerned with civil rights issues."

Carol said, "Don, you look and act worn out. Let's rest up on a camping vacation along the Mid-Atlantic shores. I'd like to see where my Dad was in the navy during WWI."

I agreed she was right, that I needed some stress relief. So, we headed for the Atlantic shore. As we drove Carol said, "Russell looked so grand in his high school graduation robes! The mob outside Recreation Hall, where the ceremony occurred, was something to behold. All the girls were weeping – everyone was hugging, kissing and congratulating each other. Russell was surrounded by friends. I shed a few tears myself."

We camped across the road from Jamestown Festival Park near Williamsburg. Sitting by a campfire that night, while the boys played cards, Carol sighed and said, "The only fly in the ointment is we don't have our big boy with us and we'll miss him. It was a hectic and emotional week with Russell's graduation. One night it hit me – he's grown up and such a bright and beautiful specimen, and he won't be going with us on our vacations any more. It's the first breaking of our family unit. As a friend of mine said, 'It's never the same again.'"

We all missed Russ as part of our family unit so threw ourselves into sightseeing to offset his absence. Colonial Williamsburg had a fascinating history and seemed like stepping back into the 18th century. The next day we drove down to Okracoke Island below Cape Hatteras and spent several days sunning ourselves, swimming and beach combing. The boys were eager to follow the coastline so we took the seven a.m. ferry, a two and a half hour voyage. We ate our breakfast in the trailer then lazed around on deck. Carol said, "It's like being on a luxury liner."

We spent several days in a nice campsite right next to the beach then took the ferry back to the North Carolina mainland and drove home.

The summer was packed with our usual activities. Carol's art festival was very successful. She sold four paintings and lots of craft items. At the end of the summer we sat on our deck drinking iced tea and Carol said, "We're now regularly making lots of money in my shop so I can implement Dr. Light's 'pass it on' tradition and make significant contributions every year. I'm considering ways of choosing recipients. I want to focus on individuals and health and human development programs here in Happy Valley. I'd like to support services using volunteers and use my contributions to attract more help from others."

"Those sound very good, Carol. Do you have any examples in mind?"

"One possibility is Meals On Wheels. If they had a big freezer and refrigerator, they could accept food contributions from farmers and others and store food until needed for meals."

"You might try seeking a newspaper story inviting people to make suggestions."

"That's a good idea. I think I'll buy Meals on Wheels their freezer this year."

With the holidays, a new experience emerged. Carol said, "Our boys are starting to socialize here with their friends. They come here after movies with dates to eat, talk, shoot pool, play table tennis and watch TV. That's cheaper than taking their girls to a restaurant! Russ plans to bring twenty college friends for a picnic by the stream. Now I realize what my mother put up with, having my slumber party friends and their dates around so much!"

One day when I came home from work, Carol said, "We have a big surprise. My parents are coming to spend Christmas with us for the first time. It's taken me three years to talk them into it. They'll be here to help with the decorations, Christmas shopping and everything! Mom may have fun helping in my shop. We better rearrange our social commitments."

I organized the boys to give our house a good cleaning so it would be spic and span when her parents arrived. Our first color TV arrived and we hurriedly set it up because part of the cost had been a cash gift from her parents the previous Christmas.

The weekend they arrived, Carol's folks helped us choose our Christmas tree. When decorated, the seven-foot blue spruce looked spectacular and Winifred raved, "Now *that's* a Christmas tree!" Accompanied by friendly banter and laughter, Eugene helped hang the greens and other decorations around our fireplace.

As we prepared for bed Carol said, "Mom told me, 'We never made much of Christmas but seeing the beauty, fun and joy you create in your home makes me regret that.' I think Mom will enjoy helping with customers in the shop and she'll want to help me with meals."

"I'll have your father help the boys stack firewood, then I'll take him across the stream and show him where we might build our house when the state takes this one for the new highway. I think they might like to meet some of our friends you write about."

"That's a good idea. Let's have the Urbans, Halls, and Balls for dessert Tuesday night because my parents have met them, and the Vallances and Althouses for dessert Friday night."

The shop was busy and Carol's mother proudly observed, helped and talked with customers. Eugene and I walked across our little bridge and I showed him where we might build a house. He liked the spot we chose. Before dinner, Carol and Winifred joyfully played duets on the piano. Martin gave them a piano concert while they cooked dinner.

That evening the Urbans, Halls, and Balls came for dessert. Carol asked Fred to play the piano the way his grandfather had for vaudeville and burlesque shows. He put on a jazzy performance that delighted Winifred as it brought back memories of music in her teen years. Russ was home for term break so he played guitar while he and Carol sang folk songs. To Carol's delight, Winifred joined in a couple times. The guests left and Winifred said, "Carol, what a wonderful evening. Your family really knows how to have fun together."

Friday night, we introduced the Clarks to the Althouses and Vallances. Over dessert, the Vallances told funny stories about their lives in congressional politics and the Althouses shared a fascinating rundown of their recent trip to Europe. Carol and Martin played a piano duet to end the evening. Carol and Winifred relaxed by playing duets before going to bed.

The next day they experienced our traditional Christmas morning, including Carol's cinnamon rolls, and even her bah humbug father was moved when each grandson gave him a present to open. We had a wonderful Christmas dinner prepared by a mother-daughter team. The boys and I then played pool with Grandpa while the girls talked and played the piano. After a day of rest, they left for Kansas with lots of hugs, kisses, happy words and a few tears.

After our traditional Sunday evening hamburgers, cooked by me, we all lounged by a pleasant fire to watch TV. Carol said to her four sons and me, "I want you to know how grateful I am for all the attention and fun you gave my parents. We're their only family and this year you added a lot of holiday happiness to their lives. It's the nicest Christmas present you could have given me. I dearly love all of you and I'm the proudest mother and wife in the world."

That night, Carol lay in my arms with her head on my chest and said, "After Christmas my Mother told me, 'Years ago I made unsound criticisms of Don and want you to know I now realize what a treasure he is as your husband and our son-in-law. Few women are lucky enough to have such a man in their lives.' My father hugged me and said, 'Don is quite a guy – you're a lucky girl.' You're my Magic Man – the husband I adore."

I whispered in her ear, "I owe them a huge debt because they gave me you – the treasure of beauty, music and love in my life."

Chapter Twenty

Changes and Losses

Early in February, Carol had a coffee gab session with neighbor gals and they asked if we'd heard anything from the highway department about their proposed bypass.

"No, but we've started exploring the possibility of building a house across the stream. The Mitchell farm owns the land above us over there. It's been legally subdivided and approved for housing development. It shows a planned road coming from the top of the hill to our property. We could get access by buying the lot at the end of that planned new road."

Mary said, "All five of us will probably have to move so maybe we should all start looking. Carol, do you have some more of those delicious chocolate cookies?"

Carol laughed, "You can eat them all because I'm going on a diet. Last weekend we went with friends to a gymnastic meet – Penn State vs. the Budapest team. It was a joy to watch. Budapest brought a women's demonstration team and they were glorious – beautiful young women performing complicated movements with astonishing ease and grace."

One Saturday afternoon we talked while Carol worked on a special order painting. She said, "I've been increasingly upset about my craft shop partner. She's done little for the shop since before Christmas. Business is booming and I have a hard time keeping up by myself, so I've had to suspend my painting. I finally got her to come over and had it out with her. I said she either had to get in our get out. She's been doing a lot more since then so I hope it lasts."

"Carol, I've watched you get more and more disgusted and it looks like the fun is leaking out of your crafts work. She's a dear friend but has become a poor work partner because of other pressures in her life. I'm glad you decided to do something about it."

From then to late summer Carol was busy with a steady stream of shoppers who bought her crafts and paintings. She said, "I'm enjoying unexpected side benefits of my shop. Visitors say, 'This is different and much nicer than shopping in a store. It's like visiting the artist in her studio, where we can talk with and watch her making things while shopping' They often ask questions about my work and sometimes I do a little 'teaching'. So, I have the pleasure of gabbing with lots of interesting people, some who are steady customers and good friends."

I helped set up her increasingly successful Arts Festival exhibit. As customers admired her work, my heart swelled with pride to see the multitalented woman my wife had become.

Relaxing on our deck a couple of weeks later, Carol said, "After the Arts Festival, just when I needed a distraction, I got to see two wonderful pianists perform. First, we saw the Pittsburgh Symphony Orchestra with that exceptional young black pianist. Both he and the orchestra were wonderful. Next we went to the concert by the outstanding pianist, Van Cliburn. Martin went to his reception afterwards to try to meet him but I was tired so we came home."

The rest of our fall was packed with the usual football and party weekends. December was big business for Carol's shop. She reported, "We sold most of our decorative and gift items. I ended up with orders for four paintings of local scenes, one from a lady in Chicago." I thought, *Her fame is spreading*!

Russ told us, "I applied for a summer apprenticeship job with the National Park Service and have an interview scheduled in Washington DC." So, we took our camping trailer for a three-day weekend of fun, frolic and Christmas shopping in our beautifully decorated Capitol. Russ said, "I think I had a good interview, but they make their decisions after the holidays."

In her Christmas card, Carol told her parents about two of her favorite holiday events: "Saturday and Sunday afternoons the Choral Society had dress rehearsals for Verdi's *Requiem*. Sunday night wasn't one of our best. We need a new director. Then we had the big Christmas Town and Gown formal dance. We had several couples over for drinks beforehand and it was a fun evening. The combo they had at the dance was a rather mild rock and roll group – something we've never had before, and it was really a lot of fun to dance to.

I wore a black crepe and chiffon pants formal and I surely received a lot of compliments on it. Russell's girlfriend whispered to me before we left for the dance, 'You look sexy!' I felt that was quite a compliment coming from a 19 year old."

With young men staying up till all hours in our home with their friends or dates hanging out, we had to abandon our tradition of private, romantic Christmas Eve parties just for us.

So far in 1971, Carol and I had very little personal time together and I missed her. So I decided it was time for a date. "Dear crafty lady, I've heard so much about your artistic and musical creativity that I'd like to learn more about you and your work over dinner for two at The Penn Belle Hotel and Restaurant in historic Bellefonte. Could you join me Friday at seven?"

"Sir, your timing is perfect! I have cabin fever from this long cold winter and would love to thaw out in the companionship of a charming man."

As we drove to Bellefonte, I explained, "It's a hotel with roots in Bellefonte's Victorian history, on the bank of the large stream fed by Bellefonte's big spring. The restaurant is at ground level looking out onto the stream. Friends say the menu is very good."

After we were seated and ordered martinis Carol said, "This place has an old world charm that creates a wonderful atmosphere for dining. Why haven't we heard of it before?"

"It's been closed, and only recently renovated and reopened." I toasted Carol, "Here's to my wife – a woman who never ceases to amaze, delight, tease and please me!"

Carol smiled seductively and replied, "Here's to our dates – each one full of fun and sometimes surprises ever since the first one we spent together at Alcove Spring in 1943." We laughed at the pleasure of that memory and sipped our martinis.

"Bring me up to date on your painting and crafts activities and plans."

"If you evaluate it in terms of people's appreciation of my work and the amount of our sales I'd say our shop is doing well.

But in terms of getting things done, it's going badly and I'm getting fed up. For example, my partner showed up last Thursday morning and did one little piddly job. I had to go to a luncheon that I couldn't gracefully avoid. She didn't even offer to keep the shop open. She's getting so negative anymore. It's really getting hard to talk with her."

"Carol, you're trying to work with an unhappy woman whose personal life is full of problems. You've treated her kindly and with compassion for her personal problems, and generally ignored her shop work behavior for two years, but instead of things getting better they're getting worse. It's time to accept the fact that no matter what you do, it won't get better."

"That's a dim view of my future with her, but I suspect you're right. What can I do?"

"Do you really want a suggestion?"

"Yes, I'm getting nowhere!"

"I'll suggest a starting point that took several years for me to learn. You're a kind and thoughtful person, a good and caring listener, a person other women trust in telling you about their troubles. Now, you have three friendships that initially evolved because of shared creative interests and activities. All three have now created a second kind of relationship with you. They've been confiding in you the most intimate unhappy details of their lives, using your kind and trustworthy ear to ease their troubles. They often use that second relationship as an excuse for inadequate and unpredictable work activities.

You have to learn to keep the two kinds of relationships separate. I learned to do that as a psychotherapist. For example, I once had a client who was also a student in one of my classes. Despite our therapy relationship, I had to treat him like any other student. In your work relationship with each your friends, you should expect and require them to meet their commitments as coworkers, despite their personal troubles. For example, when Freida agrees to regularly paint with you, she should be there despite her other troubles. When Jean wants to be a partner in your shop, she must do her share of the work despite her personal troubles. You have to learn to treat them differently in your work and personal relationships. That's easier said than done, but I learned to do it and so can you."

"Don, that makes a lot of sense, but how can I learn to do that?"

"A senior member of Penn State's Board of Trustees has a favorite saying: 'The most important word in the English language is START!' So, let's pick a starting point. You've mentioned difficulties about reaching agreement with your crafts partner about where to make your contribution this year. Is there a place you'd like to see the money go?"

"Yes! Last Saturday our college had an interesting symposium on 'Population Control'. We gave the local Family Planning Center money last year as matching funds for a Federal start up grant. Jean Vallance helped create the program and says it's been a real success so far and I feel we played a small part in that. I'd like to donate more of our craft money there this year but my craft partner disagrees with every contribution proposal I make."

"I suggest you take this first step. Tell her you realize she disagrees, but you've decided to make this year's contribution to the Family Planning Center. If she starts to argue with you, as she probably will, don't argue with her. Just say, 'I value your friendship, but when it comes to our relationship as coworkers I'll treat you as an equal in such decision making when you start playing an equal role with me in how much you make for sale in our shop,' If she continues to argue, walk away and go back to your work. Make the contribution and wait to see what she does. With that act you'll deliver the message that you won't accept her procrastination with shop work despite your friendship."

"Don, that's the kind of thing I've been wanting to say to her but now I understand how and why to do it. Thank you!"

While we ate, Carol talked about two of her other pleasures – piano music and swimming. "The other night Martin and I went to see the great pianist, Rubinstein, play. He was really tremendous and thrilled the audience with his faultless technique and strength. It's hard to imagine that he's 85-years-old. The whole second half of his program was Chopin and with two geniuses coupled together like that, I could hardly stand it! It inspired both Martin and I to go home and practice some Chopin.

And I really enjoyed going to the NIADS swim meet with the Elliotts the other night. I love to swim but hate for my head to be underwater. Guess that's why I swim on my back!"

As we finished our meal, the restaurant owner, an alumnus of our college's hotel/hospitality program, recognized me as his Dean, introduced himself and said our meal was on him. He paid our check and produced a bottle of his best dessert wine for us. I asked him to sit down and share it with us so we could get acquainted.

He told us a heartwarming personal story: "I grew up as a Bellefonte kid in a poor Italian family. I walked to school past this historic hotel, up the hill past the magnificent home of a rich man, and thought it must be wonderful to have a home like that. After graduating from Penn State, I spent ten years working for a national restaurant chain.

One summer I came back to visit my family. While walking around my old home town, a local banker came up to me and said, 'You're the guy we've been looking for. The old hotel went bankrupt and we have to do something with it. We remembered you had a degree in that field so wondered if you might be interested in bringing it back to life.' They offered me a fantastic financial deal so I decided to do it. The hotel was in terrible shape but we're bringing it back. Our new restaurant is pulling people in. I was asked by the borough to help plan renovations for the entire town. I bought and now live in the fancy house I walked by as a kid."

We thanked him for his hospitality and wonderful story and drove home. Carol said, "What a fascinating story! It reminds me of how wonderful this country is despite all the political mish mash. Here is a poor Italian boy, brought up in Bellefonte in a poor neighborhood by blue collar parents, coming back, making good, and helping to improve his hometown."

Snuggling in bed together that night, Carol gently brushed my cheek with her fingertips, "Tonight brought back wonderful memories of a summer in Manhattan, Kansas. We enjoyed talking for hours every evening that week about all kinds of things and continued it through our letters. That must have been the starting point for our dates like the one tonight. I started the evening with a troubled mind and heart and through our discussion ended with renewed confidence about myself and my shop. Thank you for another of our wonderful dates! Over the years, each one has had a surprise in it. Tonight it was an interesting new restaurant and a big-hearted new Italian friend. You sure know how to help a girl have a good time."

I whispered in her ear, "There are other methods I didn't use tonight." She giggled and kissed me goodnight.

Carol wrote her parents: "We just got back from a get acquainted brunch at the Nittany Lion Inn for the new College of Science Dean and his wife. I enjoyed it more than most such affairs because I was fortunate enough to sit by Charlie Hosler, an old friend of Don's, a meteorologist, and Dean of Earth and Mineral Sciences. He is one nice guy and a most entertaining conversationalist.

During lunch with her friends Nat and Nancy, Carol described a surprise party: "Don usually plans a little celebration for our wedding anniversary. I decided to turn the tables on him and arrange one this year with our whole gang. I asked Don to go camping with me and Cam at Kettle Creek State Park, about 50 miles east of State College. It's a very popular place so we drove up Friday to get ahead of the weekend crowd. There's a big stream coming out of the mountains that forms a sizeable lake, with a camp ground above the lake and another below it where another stream emerges from the lake. We camped in a shaded grassy spot right beside the stream where we could hear it sing to us as it flowed by.

Secretly, Russell helped get the rest of our clan organized. He brought Cindy and his folk music group – Russ, Jim, and Terry. Doug and Martin had their Jr. class prom Friday night. After taking their dates home they came to join us. When we got up Saturday morning we found them sound asleep in our Barracuda parked behind the trailer, with Russ and his friends' tent camping beside us. I got a big kick out of surprising Don for once rather than the reverse.

That night we sat around our camp fire, listening to the night sounds, and singing folk songs, with Russ and Jim playing their guitars. It was a wonderful weekend. I haven't seen Don so relaxed in a long time. I didn't want to go home. It was so pleasant there enjoying the stream's beauty and the companionship and fun of our wonderful boys and their friends. When we married 23 years ago, I thought I'd never be that happy again. I was wrong – now I have five wonderful guys to love, and do I ever!!"

Later that summer I picked up a pizza and root beers, hurried home, and asked Carol to suspend her creative crafting and join me on our deck for lunch. As we ate I said, "Carol, Paul Althouse will be serving as Acting President while Penn State's President recovers from his heart attack. You know Paul had a heart attack and is vulnerable to another. His doctor wants him to take a small vacation and rest up before he assumes that stressful burden. Ginny asked if we could join them for a Myrtle Beach vacation to help Paul relax. She's worried about him. If we do, we'd have to leave in a couple of days."

"Of course we'll help those dear friends in any way we can."

We spent four days at Myrtle Beach. The first afternoon Paul and I lounged on the beach while planning how to handle the job. I suggested he invent a team to help so he wouldn't have to carry the burden and stresses alone. He did so and named it The President's Advisory Council. It included the Acting Provost, Vice Presidents for Research and Graduate Studies and for Continuing Education, and the Chairman of the Council of Academic Deans.

Once he had that plan worked out, he focused on relaxing and having fun for a few days. He loved joking around and teasing Carol, so she was a big help keeping him and Ginny relaxed.

While the President was recovering, he asked me to come to his home for a consultation. He offered me a job as one of his Vice Presidents. I declined as gracefully as I could because I still needed his good will as a Dean. I went home and told Carol, "Some Board of Trustee members are trying to use his illness to get rid of the President. He's fighting back by trying to reorganize his office to win trustee support. He tried to sell me the idea that becoming a vice president with him would be great for my career. I told him I was sticking by my commitment to finish building our college."

Carol hugged me, "Thank you for that decision. I hated it when you were temporarily in the President's office, and I'd hate it worse if you worked for that guy."

"I've learned to trust your intuitions. Apparently I've become a hot item in the university president job market. During the past year, five universities have invited me to be interviewed for their presidency. I keep saying no. We've agreed that's not our cup of tea. When we finish building our college, I'll go back to being a teacher/scholar while sharing our life together."

With big kiss she joked "I'm glad I'm not married to a guy afflicted with bigshotitis!"

Thankfully, Paul survived the stresses of being acting President. Carol's shop had an excellent year, so her shop contributed to four more Happy Valley services.

This was Doug and Martin's senior year in high school. Their music interests and talents involved them in many activities and they both had multiple student leadership roles. They were having a ball and we joyfully shared in many of their experiences. Carol said, "I love having young people in our home working together on music and other projects, or just having fun with their girlfriends, watching TV, playing ping pong, pool and other games, eating and relaxing. It makes me feel so much more a part of their lives."

One bitterly cold, snowy January evening, the boys were in their rooms while Carol and I warmed our toes in front of a crackling fire. *Romeo and Juliet* played in the background as we enjoyed a steaming mug of hot chocolate. When the music ended I asked, "Did you see anything that interested you as we drove around town looking for homes when the bypass takes us?"

"Not really. Property and houses are just ridiculous in price. We have two choices – buy or build. I know you don't want to live in a house that's on a city size lot with no space around it. I'd be satisfied to buy a house – most any house – move in and be done with it. As long as I can do my crafty work, I'd be happy. Driving around looking at places like we did today drives me nuts. You're like Don Quixote with all your impossible dreams!"

I grinned at the Quixote reference. "I know you don't like the idea of building again, but don't tell me you'd rather live in a smaller house with no beautiful natural environment around you! You'd be cutting off your nose to spite your face. You've loved our flower and vegetable gardens, lawns, woods and stream for picnicking and play."

"That's true, but every time you talk about building I get into a cold sweat. It's hard to plan anything not knowing how much money we'll get for this property or the time table."

"Our neighbor called the highway department in Clearfield about timing and they said it would be at least eight months to a year before they can proceed because they've run into some legal problems. So, our making a decision is not urgent."

"Good. I'll be like Scarlet O'Hara in *Gone With the Wind* – I'll think about that tomorrow. Let's talk about something else."

"OK, are you getting used to the idea of having a son engaged?"

"I wasn't too surprised when they came in the other night all sparkly eyed and grinning to give us the news. I've been expecting it. On a less joyful note, I've started painting the very difficult canal street in Strasburg that Althouses photographed while they were in Germany and asked me to paint. I hope I can do it justice. Did you see the article about the Choral Society in our local Town and Gown magazine?"

"Yes, and it made me very proud of my wife!"

"I don't know how I deserved being singled out about my art work, but it was a nice plug. We have to rehearse tomorrow afternoon with the orchestra. Then, next week we rehearse Monday night, Wednesday night, Friday night, Saturday afternoon and do the concert Sunday night. I'll be glad such intensive practice is over. It's a thrill to sing this *Requiem,* now that I've learned it. It's truly a beautiful thing!"

"I've never heard it, so I'm looking forward to it!"

"I forgot to tell you about our Choral Society executive board meeting. I got myself into a job for next winter – chairman of the Elizabethan dinner that we're planning for the Christmas season. It's an event we hope will become a tradition. The plan is to sell tickets to a dinner served in an Old English tradition with madrigal-type singers in period costumes wandering among the tables singing period music – kind of like Asti's and opera singing in New York. It sounds good. I hope I can do it OK"

"Carol, you know you've never failed at anything you decided to create. It sounds like a beautiful idea. If you can use a fetch and carry guy, let me know."

I'd been meaning to compliment Carol on her hair so it seemed the ideal change of subject, "Your longer hair is so beautiful. Your 'do' during the holidays was wonderful."

"I know you like it long and I confess I kind of enjoy it for a change. I can wear it down or up in a French twist, which is quite easy to do. I've been going to Pietro's instead of Audrey. She's too hard to get in to and she'd never put up with my long hair anyway. This fellow can do a beautiful upswept hair do and use my wiglet in the style. One of my pleasures in life is to get my hair washed and a creative "do". It's an art form for skilled people like Pietro."

"Carol, my hot chocolate is gone, our fire is dying and it's getting late. How about coming to bed with me? If you treat me right I'll let you warm your cold feet on me."

"That's my kind of deal – let's go!"

A heart wrenching loss followed our holiday season. Carol wrote her parents: "We're in a state of shock and grief over the unexpected death of our dear friend, Paul Althouse. He died of a massive coronary at 6 p.m. Friday when he took his snow blower out in zero degree temperature to clean off his driveway. I just couldn't comprehend it and still can't. They were to be here this evening for hamburgers. Don has really been down about it all day. I've cried so much that I have one of those one-sided horribly painful headaches, so am doped up on aspirin and Darvon. Don has lost a big brother in Paul, a man with whom he shared ideas and worked very closely. Everything will be harder without Paul's support.

He was a very unusual man, so knowledgeable and with a rare ability to make a woman feel feminine. He made even a dumb-dumb like me feel important and special. I guess that's why I loved him more than any man-friend we've ever had. How we'll miss him! Don is a pall bearer and our boys are going with me to the funeral. My painting of their favorite Strasburg, Germany scene is almost finished. I told Ginny that was going to be my memorial to Paul."

It had been a tough year for us and we both needed relief. Semester break was the only time possible, so we packed our camping trailer, loaded up the boys, and headed to Washington DC. The next day we took the boys on a tour of the capitol.

The first stop was Washington's monument. The park service was handing out free kites so we joined the kite fliers. What a glorious sight! Imagine the long stretch of green grass between the Washington and Lincoln monuments and a brilliant blue sky with a few fluffy white clouds, then put hundreds of people in that scene, each with a brilliantly colored kite. Now, look up and see all those kites like spring blossoms floating in that big blue sky. Finally, add shouts and laughter and you have the beginning of our sons' tour of Washington.

We saw all the monuments, the capitol building and White House. We finished the day by visiting Washington's home at Mt. Vernon. The next day we drove to Williamsburg and found a great municipal park and campground near Newport News, Virginia. From there, we could visit all the historic places and the boys could golf at a nearby course, which was perfect because Martin planned to try out for the high school golf team that year.

Carol wrote her parents: "Dad, I remember you telling about shipping out of Newport News during your navy duty in WWI, so we dropped Martin off to play golf and went down to explore the place. It was too early for a harbor cruise so Don arranged a half hour plane trip over the area for me, Cam and Doug – the plane could only take 3 people.

It was great fun and a good way to learn the geography of the place. I imagined seeing your destroyer down in the Navy docks. Cam was a little scared when we banked to turn in that little plane (I must confess so was I) but we were really thrilled with our sightseeing flight."

Then, we had to get back to our Slab Cabin home so the twins could finish high school. They completed a wonderfully successful senior year, each with their own musical and leadership accomplishments. As we sat at their graduation ceremonies glowing with pride and warmed by the joy they obviously felt, we held hands and shed a few tears as we saw two more sons advance into the adult phase of their lives. They both planned to attend Penn State so would still be close to home, but it would be a time of transition for us.

When Russ returned from his summer job in Vermont he brought us a wonderful gift, an aluminum all-purpose canoe/boat. The people who had it weren't using it any more so sold it to him for $20. It was shaped like a canoe, but a little wider and one end was blunt for mounting a small motor. In the middle was a brace for attaching a sail rig. The aluminum seats were filled with buoyant material and sealed so the boat couldn't sink.

We bought a sail rig and a small motor and I mounted a boat rack on our station wagon that enabled us to carry it on top. Carol had fun boating on the Blue River as a little girl, and had been dreaming of owning a sail boat since she was a teenager. Much of our summer was spent learning how to row, sail and motor around nearby lakes in our boat.

Carol described one such day to her parents: "Last Friday, Don, Cam and I took our boat up to Lake Gallitzen where you had your national campvention a few years ago. The picture shows you what the canoe looks like with the sail; I'm at the tiller and Cam is in front of me. We motor boated all Saturday a.m., stopped to pick up driftwood along the shore, and got caught in a rain shower. After a late lunch we put on the sail, even though it was so calm we just sat or so it seemed. There must have been a very gentle breeze because we did sail across the lake.

Don decided the water looked so inviting he managed to 'fall in' and cool off. (Lake rules prohibit swimming off a boat.) Then he decided Cam should go in with the life preserver on so he'd know how to behave if he should get dunked. Cam (after he got over being a little scared) loved it and we could hardly get him back in the boat. I took my turn too, with the life preserver on, and I must say they really work and it was great fun swimming around so effortlessly. My only problem was I had a hard time climbing back in the boat from the water. One of the special things about this boat is that it can go into very shallow water. We'll have many years of enjoyment camping by a lake and rowing, sailing, motoring, and swimming off the boat by ourselves, or with family and friends, and finding driftwood for my crafts. It's so much fun!"

Carol had another very successful Arts Festival, but this one was special because her parents were visiting and eagerly participated. Later Carol said, "I was delighted with how much fun Mom had talking with people and helping sell my stuff. She's good at it."

I nodded, "I thought they'd pop with pride after watching how much people liked and bought your work. I'm glad we could take them out on our boat while they were here."

Family in Marysville planned a celebration to honor my father's 80th birthday. We scheduled a flight into Lincoln, Nebraska for the occasion and would fly back from there because it was easier access than Kansas City. We only had a few days in Kansas due to my work load.

Winifred worked behind the scenes, insisting they could pick us up and take us back to the Kansas City airport instead of Lincoln. I was unaware of that struggle until later. Carol stuck with our plan and we had a wonderful time celebrating Dad's birthday milestone.

Later, Carol told me of the problem and addressed it with her mother: "Dear Mom, There's another reason I wanted to fly this way this time, which I'd never mention to Don. He's exhausted, I can see it every night when he comes home that he's bone tired from the frustrations and demands that have piled on him lately, including preparing a major report for the Board of Trustees and a new master plan for Pennsylvania higher education requested by the Governor. So I think if he doesn't have to go through a tiring trip on top of everything else at this time, it will be best. There are too many men his age having heart attacks around here so I want him to get away and relax, which he can't do if he's driving or riding for 2 days."

When I learned how she'd protected me, I said, "I tried to hide my fatigue so you wouldn't worry, but guess I didn't do a very good job of it."

She smiled, gently bopped my nose and said, "You bet your boots buster – I know you too well – forget trying to hide things from me."

I gave her a big kiss and said, "Yes M'am!"

Carol's decorating team helped her create the setting for the Choral Society's Madrigal Dinner. She wrote her parents: "I wish you could see it. We worked one whole day making the table decorations (about 36 of them) and hanging balls. With red table cloths, banners hanging from the ceiling, and wreaths, garlands, etc. it will look most festive. The singers are marvelous and look great in the costumes I borrowed from our community theater. Two sold out presentations were a huge success both musically and financially, and the Madrigal dinner became an annual tradition for the Choral Society.

Chapter Twenty-One
Our First College Graduate and Wedding

One snowy evening as we relaxed before a sparkling fire, Carol said, "We need to start planning for Russ and Cindy's wedding this summer. I'd like to get a really nice dress for it. You haven't bought any clothes for so long you're looking a bit shabby, so you need a new suit and some trousers with sports coats. I need supplies for my shop. Let's make an overnight shopping trip to New York after the reception in our home next week for the College's alumni board, all 30 of them!"

A friend sent Carol to a store that had top quality women's wear at bargain prices. She found the perfect dress for the first wedding in our family. Then we found a high quality men's clothing store at outlet prices where Carol selected a new wardrobe for me.

Carol wrote her parents: "Enclosed is a copy of the Centre Daily Times story about *Carol Jean Crafts.* There was a short one in the Mirror too. They really stimulated the shop business. Every time we make a contribution to help some health and human development service, like Easter Seals recently, they do a story and picture. I'm embarrassed to be in the paper so often. I don't want people to think I have bigshotitis. Don says that's another kind of help for our recipients. The free publicity helps them attract other donors, so I guess it's OK.

Our Choral Society is doing my favorite choral work, the Messiah, this weekend. Last night we had a 3-hour rehearsal that was very tiring. It was the first day of my period too which didn't help. The chorus and orchestra rehearsals really sounded great.

I'm at Pietro's getting my hair done; gotta get gorgeous for the Choral Society concert tomorrow. This will be a busy (hectic really) day so I can use my hair do for several events. I go to rehearsal at 1:00, then right after we go to a reception to meet the new Dean of Business Administration. After that we go to a dinner-dance affair that our hotel and restaurant alumni put on periodically. We'll bow out early from that as I need to get to bed at a decent hour.

We've decided to have the rehearsal dinner for Russ and Cindy's wedding at home and have the 'Greeters' (our hotel and restaurant student organization) cater it. I'm determined to enjoy this wedding and if I have to get a dinner for 16-20 people the night before I won't."

Carol enjoyed gabbing over lunch with her good friend, Jean Vallance and couldn't wait to fill her in on the concert, "Our choral society concert came off well, in fact everyone raved about it, and I know we've never received such an ovation from an audience before. Everything seemed so well-balanced this year. The soloists and orchestra were both excellent and that makes a big difference. I was so enthused I gave Doug, our new director, a big smackeroo on the cheek after the concert. He deserved all the admiration he received last night. He's such a nice person as well as being an excellent musician and director. He's such a contrast to that ogre we had before. I really consider it an honor to belong to such an excellent group."

Jean teased, "You better be careful about kissing good looking men in public. People might start rumors about the Dean's wife!"

Carol laughed, "After the concert we went to Ginny Althouse's for a night cap. We've tried to help and support Ginny since Paul's death. She thanked us by presenting Don with the Nikon camera and lenses that the Board of Trustees gave Paul for the great job he did as acting President. She wrote a most touching note with it and we all had tears. I gave her the picture I'd painted for them as my memorial to Paul and that brought more tears."

It was nearing the end of the spring semester at Penn State. That meant it was graduation and wedding time for us. I made night caps for us and we sat on our deck enjoying an unusually warm May evening, looking out on our lovely piece of Mother Nature's beauty.

I said, "Carol I have marvelous news for you. You know Russ is graduating with two degrees, one in Health and Physical Education and the other in Human Development. In every college, the student with the highest grades in their graduating class is designated the Marshall for that college. The Marshall accepts the diploma for the entire class since classes are too large to hand out diplomas individually. Then, the President or Dean says something about that student. Russ has the highest grades in both colleges so he can be the Marshall in either. The other Dean and I agree Russ should choose. Do you want to ask him that question?"

"Are you kidding? I'll knock his head off if he doesn't choose you!!"

I laughed, "To keep the decision objective, I asked Louise Gentry, our Associate Dean for Undergraduate Instruction, to formally ask Russ the question. Russ already knows from the grape vine. He and I are both proud to be the first Dean and Marshall in Penn State history to also be father and son. That makes my struggles as a Dean worthwhile. I think you have more to do with his success than me, so you should get most of the credit."

The proud mom's eyes brimmed with happy tears, "Our first son to graduate from college, at the top of his class, and receiving his diploma from his father as Dean! That's a triple in baseball. And he's getting married right after graduation like his dad did. That makes it a home run!" We both laughed and raised our glasses in a toast to each other and Marshall Bridegroom College Graduate Russell Ford.

Carol said, "I have another little piece of news. You know I started Cam on the piano like the other boys. Martin picked it up from me and taught him some more. Now the school has asked him if he wants to learn an instrument. He said yes and chose a trumpet. So, we have two pianists, a guitar, a clarinet and now a trumpet in our family orchestra. I asked him why he chose trumpet. He said, 'Well, the trumpet plays the melody so they have to lead the band. That's better than struggling behind with a tuba. Besides, I like the sound.'"

I replied, "Here's another unexpected treat. Last Wednesday I answered Milton Eisenhower's recent letter and told him Russ was getting married. He responded immediately with a very sincere invitation for Russ and Cindy to stop in Baltimore on their way to

North Carolina, for dinner and to stay overnight. He said he wrote me right away so it wouldn't be too late for them to plan. Russ called Milton immediately and made arrangements to stay there next Saturday evening. Milton enjoys young people and in fact he has a former graduate student coming that same night so the kids are in for an interesting experience."

On May 25, 1973 our oldest son married Cindy. (He missed his parents wedding day by 5 days.) Carol described it to family and friends in our traditional Christmas letter: "The wedding was a beautiful, evening candlelight service with music performed by harpsichord and flute and written by the best man, Jim Hughes, who was Russ's buddy in the 'Good for You's' folk group. It had the flavor of an old English service in a gothic style church that is an exact duplicate of one somewhere in England. They're now in Chapel Hill, North Carolina where Cindy teaches art and Russ is a graduate student in city and regional planning."

Spring and summer progressed uneventfully until political turmoil surrounding President Nixon erupted shortly after Carol's birthday. She wrote to her parents: "Things are happening so fast in this old world it's hard to keep up. I feel like a fighter that's punch drunk. You think everything has happened that can, then WHAM, we're hit again! It's an incredible time we're living in. I hope these tapes show Nixon to be as clean as a hound's tooth. Then maybe my faith in people may be renewed. But, it's beginning to look like he's a liar, a crook and a jerk."

Through fall to Christmas, Carol's shop did a booming business. Christmas shopping for her creations had become a tradition in Happy Valley. They donated $1,000 to help start a new legal aid service for poor people, and additional money to family planning. During the fall and holiday season they accumulated another $2300. Carol said, "It's grown to about the maximum of what we can create for sale."

There were three traditional Christmas activities. First, the Madrigal Dinner. Carol said, "I'll be glad when this is over. I shouldn't have said yes to the Madrigal dinner a second year I suppose, but I do like being part of it and we do such a beautiful job, even if I do say so myself! I'm eager for you to see it. We scheduled it for three rather than two nights this year. Tickets are sold out and there's a waiting list. I'm proud that it's become an annual event."

The second was our annual open house for my administrative team – a party for eighteen couples. The third event was the annual Town and Gown formal Christmas dance.

We decided to really dude up for the dance. Carol wore her black crepe and chiffon pants formal in which she looked gorgeous and sexy, and I wore my tux. There was a very good band. We drank cocktails and got a little high to shake off the tiredness and sorrow of the past year. Dancing together was always a wonderful form of psychotherapy and sensual pleasure for us. All our sons were home for Christmas and provided music, fun, and games to help make it a happy time. It was another first for us: A Christmas with a married son and wife.

Carol's bridge group of eight women had their first gab fest of the New Year in our home. They started twenty years ago as wives of graduate students. Since then, they'd shared the experiences of childbirth, husbands taking new positions, relocation from tiny apartments to new houses, and occasional surgeries. They'd become close friends who shared each other's joys, struggles, likes, dislikes, hopes, fears and health issues. They usually met once a month at eight p.m. and went home after midnight. Early in their existence I commented to Carol: "You gals must really like the game, playing for several hours each meeting."

She laughed, "Typically, we only play two or three hands a night. The rest of our time is spent gabbing and eating. You guys go to work and are around people every day. Most of our daily lives are spent with kids and husbands, taking care of homes and families. We get lonely for some female companionship and our bridge group is a main way we get that. Our group has one cardinal rule that helps keep us close. We agreed not to gossip about each other behind our backs, which makes it easier and safer to share personal information."

Nat asked, "Have the bypass people talked with you about taking your house?"

"No, but most of the others on our lane have had their land taken and moved out, with most of their houses gone. You may have seen in the paper the picture and story about an Amish family dismembering a neighbor's house. It was amazing to watch! They worked so efficiently and it was completely gone in three days! They took everything including the nails. It's like when we first built here – nobody else around. I kinda like the beauty and privacy that way."

"Have you made plans for when they take your place?"

"No, but we're exploring the possibility of moving our house to the land we own across the stream. One neighbor moved their whole house. I didn't know they could do that."

While they had dessert and coffee, Carol asked, "Did any of you go to the gala opening of the new Milton Eisenhower auditorium?" No one had attended so they asked for a run down.

"It was a black tie affair, a pretty hoity-toity event for this town. The Deans all had tickets. The Pittsburgh Symphony and University Choir did *Beethoven's 9th Symphony*, and brought in a woman from Boston reputed to be a superb choir director. Doug is in the Choir and described the arrangement. The auditorium walls have excellent acoustics so the choir stood unseen behind those walls and sang from there. Hearing it that way was an awesome experience. I once sang *Beethoven's 9th* and wished I was behind the walls singing with Doug's choir."

Chapter Twenty Two
Old Doors Close, New Ones Open

It was Carol's 47th birthday so I left her a note asking for one of our special dates. "Dear Dr. Clark. I'm in need of some psychotherapy. Could you join me for that purpose (and others) on October 8 at 8 p.m. at the Toftrees restaurant and conference center?"

I chuckled at her reply because I could just see her ornery grin while writing it: "Dear Distressed Man. It would be my professional and personal pleasure to meet with you. I'm sure I can ease your distress."

We drove to the edge of State College, past a pretty golf course to an attractively designed lodge. I escorted Carol into the spacious, beautifully decorated dining room. On a platform above one corner we saw a small bar with several booths flanked by a dance floor and couple performing piano and vocal music. We chose a booth in that secluded section.

When our martinis arrived, I lifted my glass in a toast, "To a perfectly, permanently beautiful woman, the love of my life, and the custodian of our money!"

After a sip of martini I gave her a package. She opened it and pulled out a pumpkin-colored sweater set. She squealed with delight and held it up to admire the color, "I got dreamy over that set while looking through the new Alden's catalogue last week. How did you know?"

"I saw you go dreamy-eyed so sneaked a look when you went to the bathroom. You can wear it on Halloween as a pretty pumpkin, come to my door and you can have all my treats."

She lifted her martini, "Here's to the sneaky guy who lied when he said he didn't know how to pick pretty clothes."

I ordered our dinners and continued our conversation. "How is my crafty lady's shop doing this year?"

"We had our best art festival. I sold four paintings! Having a picture of my exhibit on the front page of the paper helped I think. Sales for the whole year will be even more than last year. Did I tell you we're making a contribution to the Centre Crest Nursing Home craft program this year? It was great fun seeing the woman who heads the program practically drop her teeth when we told her we had $1000 to donate. She's so grateful, as they need small equipment so badly and just have no funds. The activities room is in the new wing and it's beautiful. The gal running the program is truly gifted working with the residents. I've not felt this good about what our money can do for a long time. For example, Grandma Dobbs is 94-years-old, has to use a walker, but she's down there every day painting and crafting and just loves it." As we ate our lasagna and salad, Carol said, "What did you think of Milton Eisenhower's 75th birthday party?"

"Only a famous guy like Milton could have the outfield of the Baltimore Orioles major league baseball team for his birthday party. The game announcer said there were over six hundred people there. Milton seemed genuinely pleased that we drove down for it."

I savored another bite of salad, then added, "You picked up a lot of driftwood while we were boating this summer. For what crafty purpose are you using it?"

"I've been experimenting with making dried arrangements on pretty pieces of drift wood, using fall grasses, seed pods, small pine cones, and anything I think looks pretty. People seem to like them because they're selling like hot cakes. I need more materials. Would you take me on country roads this weekend to find some? I love the fall colors."

"Your wish is my command." *OK, now on to the main reason I brought Carol here tonight.* I squirmed a little because creativity was never my strong suit. "Carol, do you remember meeting Doug and Elaine the last time we were out here dancing to their music?"

"Oh yes, I love her voice!"

"Doug gave me the lyrics to one of their new compositions. It states how I feel about you. They'll play and sing it for us, and you can read the lyrics. Happy Birthday!"

When I was a child I had hopes and dreams
Of how the world would truly be.
Who would have guessed they would all come true
But they did on the day I met you
Nothing you can do about the way I feel
No one can change my mind.
Don't know how it ever came to be
That I was so lucky find
The love of a lifetime.
Our love is no ordinary love – It's something special
It's the best that can be, I want the whole world to see
That our love is no ordinary love!

Carol said, "I couldn't read all the lyrics because I had water in my eyes. My heart is so full of love and joy now I want to dance with you to that music." No one else was dancing so they played that song and several others for us before we had to go home. At home, our sons and their girlfriends shouted, "Happy Birthday!" when Carol walked in. We finished the evening with their surprise birthday party and gift of an FM stereo tuner to enjoy in her shop.

After their party ended, we said good night and went to our bedroom. I took Carol in my arms and pressed a lingering kiss to her mouth. "Thank you for the psychotherapy. I'm no longer distressed."

She chuckled, "Your therapy isn't over yet!" So, we went to bed and completed our therapy session.

The football season and usual parties came and went. We had a reception in our home for fifty college alumni. Carol's Choral society and a symphony orchestra gave another first rate performance. She barely kept up with creations in her shop, but somehow found time to make a beautiful caftan-style dress she wore to dinner with Penn State's President and distinguished guests from England, and more importantly wore it to the Town and Gown Christmas formal.

As we went to bed New Year's Eve, Carol said, "We've had another year in which happiness, stress and sadness were mixed together. I suppose as families grow older the negative parts are to be expected, but it's not something to look forward to."

The New Year began with news that Carol's parents had decided to sell their home in Topeka and move to Lawrence, Kansas.

They told us about Eugene's job as apartment complex manager at Kansas University and Carol responded: "I know decisions like this are hard to make, but we really think it's a most exciting and sensible possibility. I'll come and help if you do make the move – I'd enjoy it." I wanted to help too, but Carol was eager to get out there, so I said to go ahead and I'd come later with Cam, if I could get away.

While Carol was painting with her fellow artist, Frieda asked "When's the bypass taking your house?"

Carol grimaced at the question, "The bypass is breathing down our neck again, but we aren't holding our breath because we've heard this song before. Three highway persons came yesterday to assess the property. They process that and come up with a bid sometime in the future. They still say they don't have the money to build it yet."

One morning over breakfast Carol said, "I'm lonely for you – you're gone so much. This week you go to Philadelphia, then to Washington, and then to Harrisburg. We're becoming strangers that pass in the night. We have a free weekend coming up. How about having a picnic with me down by our stream Saturday so we can get reacquainted – that's always fun!"

"I'd be honored – you bring the food and I'll bring the drinks!"

On a warm summer day, with perennial flowers we'd planted years ago blooming around us, we sat on a blanket enjoying the sights, sounds and scents of our streamside garden. We sipped Mint Mules and breathed our loneliness for each other away into gentle summer air.

Carol said, "I generally like our busy life together, but periodically I need our dates to keep life in perspective, and to reinforce the oneness that provides the foundation for it all. Being alone like this does that, but sharing daily activities also enriches our relationship. Busy schedules sometimes can be a pain, but they can also provide interesting and fun experiences.

For example, yesterday we entertained a distinguished alumnus and his wife. I usually enjoy these affairs as we've met some interesting people from other walks of life. I really enjoyed this wife and vice versa. We hit it off right away."

"Carol, I'm grateful for all the ways you contribute to the activities of our college, especially when you're also busy with your own interests."

"Well, tomorrow evening you can watch me perform in our Choral Society concert. Next weekend the Human Development Building is being named and dedicated to your old colleague, Grace Henderson. Then we go to the Delaware campus where I get to hear you give a commencement address. After that, you get to help me investigate some craft shops down there. Experiencing, understanding and enjoying each other's activities maintains a sense of newness, anticipation and pride in each other."

"I understand what you mean. When I'm giving a speech and you're there, happy memories and thoughts about you sometimes disconnect my brain from my mouth."

We sipped our Mint Mules for a moment, enjoying the silence.

"Don, Martin was really disappointed that he missed being your college Marshall. His average was 3.89 but a girl had a 3.95. I know being your College Marshall would have pleased him and me, though some might have been suspicious about the Dean having two sons who were college Marshalls. He has every reason to be proud of himself, finishing his degree in three years with an almost perfect record and working on a research project so many hours a week."

"I'm still savoring the pleasure of handing another of our sons his diploma. It was great to see you, Doug, Cam, Sheri and her parents in the audience as Martin's cheering section. You produced a dinner worthy of an honored college graduate. It was a great occasion all around."

"Don, your idea of taking our whole family to Pittsburg Sunday to see the Pirates and Braves play was a neat idea to top off the celebration. I was sleepy all day but still had fun being with our gang, particularly Sheri and Martin on his special day."

"I have what I think you'll consider good news. As you know, Russ has been looking for a job now that he's finished his Master's degree. You remember meeting and helping entertain my friend, Helene Woglemuth, State Secretary of Public Welfare, at a football game last year?"

"Yes, I liked her and her Pittsburgh ex-football player husband."

"She's been looking around for job possibilities and found an opening in Harrisburg's Department of Recreation. Russ interviewed for it, liked it, and got the job, so Russ and Cindy will be living in Harrisburg! Helene said they found an apartment on the first floor of an older home that's real nice and she thinks they'll have fun fixing it up."

"WOW! It will be wonderful to have them so close! Another source of anxiety is erased."

Carol brought a light lunch of half a tuna salad sandwich, a few grapes, and three potato chips each. *THREE potato chips?* While we ate I asked, "How's your shop doing?"

"The paper featured a big article about our shop tonight, and there'll be another story in the morning paper so I hope that brings in more customers. I tried staying open three days this week and really enjoyed it. I wish I could stay open more, but my partner wouldn't like it. However, I take it with a grain of salt as I know how insecure she is and all that is her way of saying, 'See, I'm worthwhile too.'"

I was all out of news and so was Carol, so I said, "What should we do now?"

Carol rolled over against me and planted a big juicy kiss on my mouth, "I'd like to make love here in this beautiful place right now."

I started to answer but she put her fingers on my lips and smiled, "But privacy is too uncertain. Could I have a rain check?"

I pinched her bottom, and said, "There's your rain check – it expires at midnight."

We climbed the stone steps from our stream to the house to rejoin the world.

With fall came football and tailgating with friends. Russ and Cindy attending games added to the fun. The holiday season began with a nice newspaper story about Carol's shop.

One night I woke up for a bathroom visit and discovered Carol missing from her side of the bed. When I found her she said, "It's about 4 a.m. and I'm awake like an owl so decided to fix myself some hot chocolate and do something constructive. I wake up in the middle of the night often and have a hard time getting back to sleep. It's the age, so my menopausal women friends tell me. It's aggravating however."

"Come back to bed with me and maybe I can cuddle you back to sleep."

That weekend we relaxed in front of our fireplace with a cup of hot chocolate. I asked, "How did your shop do this Christmas season?"

"Even though my partner is in Florida this year, my shop has netted over $2000 since September. It's more than we've ever made, and I'm convinced my workday is more productive and relaxed without the tension of her erratic and stressful participation. I now realize that I've been dreading our work contacts without realizing the negative emotions linked to it.

I've finally made up my mind to close *Carol Jean Crafts* and sever the partnership that was never there except at rewarding times like the Arts Festival. This is the perfect time to do it in a diplomatic way while she's away this year. Outside the shop, I'm still fond of her. We've had good times together so I hope we can remain friends. I plan to continue my painting and craft work and will create an alternate way of making my work available to the public."

She seemed relaxed and not a bit anxious about her big decision to close the shop. I hugged her close and asked, "Do you know yet what your plans might be?"

It warmed my heart to see her mischievous grin, "Enjoy the holidays with my hubby and regroup for a while. I did a fun thing yesterday. I went to a sing-in of the Christmas portion of the *Messiah* at our new Eisenhower auditorium. Anyone could join in. There was an orchestra and soloists and it was directed by Raymond Brown, our former Choral Society director. I'll bet 500 people showed up. It was really thrilling. I hope they do it again next year." I thought, *I would give almost anything to be able to share singing such music with Carol. My inability to share that joy with her is a huge disappointment to me and must be to her.*

A few days after Christmas, Carol relaxed in my arms and said, "Christmas is quite different now, since everyone but Cam is an adult. We enjoyed more jokes and laughs with our adult kids than when they were younger. With our grown sons and their ladies at the table, it was one of the nicest Christmas dinners we've had."

I nodded, "It looks like we'll have more additions in the near future. Martin and Sheri are engaged, and Doug dashed off to Pittsburg after dinner to spend part of Christmas with his sweetie, Pamela Chesaro. I interpret his eager departure to be a sign of love in full bloom."

"No doubt about it! Cam continues to be a bright spot in our lives. He's always so good, a bit lazy but cheerful. He loves kidding around and seems to take life with a sense of humor. His grades are mediocre. His teacher told me he and a friend goof around in class and don't pay enough attention. Needless to say, I've sat on him good and hard about this and he's trying to rectify his mistake. It's not that he's dumb and doesn't get it. He just loves to horse around."

Carol began the New Year by filling me in on the latest about her shop. "Jean replied to my announcement about closing the shop saying she was all for it but still seems to think we'll be working together so she didn't take the hint. Today she called me, said she was homesick. I think she's curious how I felt about her letter and if I was still adamant about closing the shop. I'll have to make a public announcement about the closing, but need an alternate plan first."

"I'm glad you're rearranging your painting and crafts work so you can do what you want when you want without having to involve other people. I've scheduled a meeting with Russ Larson, the new provost, and a colleague and friend of mine for years. I'll inform him privately of my wish to retire as Dean and return to faculty status within a year. I'm eager to get back to being a teacher and scholar. Now, if I can just get my professional life rearranged, we can both do what we really like to do, get rid of a lot of stress, and have more time for each other."

"That sounds like a wonderful future!"

During a combination lunch and gab session, Carol's friend Jean Vallance asked if we'd heard anything from the highway department about our house.

"This thing is a mess. We have five leaks in our roof from snow melt. Some guys are supposed to do repair work this week. We need a new roof, but keep trying to avoid spending money on repairs because we know the highway department will take our home soon.

We've been frustrated with the delay, so two weeks ago I wrote the Secretary of the Highway Department, since he was new and recently appointed, and poured out our sad story to him. Tuesday Don got a call from the state Senator he'd talked to before, telling us the highway department plans to finish negotiations with us. Wish we'd tried political pressure sooner!"

"I'll bet that's a relief, Carol. What are you going to do about a place to live?"

"We'll build a new house across the stream. We found house plans we like and can get detailed building plans if we want them. Don has talked with Mrs. Mitchell about the road and utilities. Her plans for developing her land are approved. If we buy one of her lots for access to ours, she can use that money to put in the road and utilities.

We're hoping if the state doesn't have money to build the rest of the bypass for a number of years that we can buy our property back for $1000 and just stay here until the other house is built. Then we could move into it and sell our old house to the Amish to tear down. What a relief it will be to have this uncertainty and temporary feeling over."

June 1976 was an exciting and important month for our family. During one of their morning painting sessions, Carol told Freida, about it: "First Doug graduated with his BS in Community Development. His three brothers, his sweetie pie Pam and I were his proud cheering section. Don puffed up with pride when he handed our third son his diploma. Afterwards we enjoyed watching Doug and his friends congratulating each other. Pam threw her arms around Doug and congratulated him with a big kiss. Afterwards, we enjoyed a fried chicken dinner and I got a kick out of the teasing and joking around among the boys.

The second big event was Sheri and Martin's beautiful wedding. I bought a new dress – a long blue and green chiffon paisley print. They were married at the Eisenhower chapel on campus. Sheri wore a gorgeous white dress and her attendants each wore different colored gowns. The men all wore white tuxedos. After their honeymoon they'll move to Minnesota University where Martin will study for his PhD in their Institute for Child Development."

As we ate breakfast I said, "Carol, I've completed a new proposal to the Feds for funding a new building for our nursing program. The Feds turned down the proposal prepared by our faculty. I think it has a good chance of being funded so now I have to take it to Washington and sell it to the relevant bureaucracies. I'll probably be gone for about 5 days. I hate the thought of leaving you home alone for that long, but I'm the only person who can sell it."

Carol replied, "I'll miss you terribly, but if you can get that building for the nurses it will be a great way to end your Deanship."

The goodbye hug and kiss we shared was longer than usual as I left to spend a lonely time away from Carol. Leaving her for any reason didn't get easier with age!

In Washington, I had a message waiting at the hotel postponing my first meetings. Wasting time always frustrated me and I resented losing that day. To salve my irritation, I turned to the tried and true method of easing our feelings when apart by writing a letter: "Dear Carol, My meetings have been delayed a day so I'm sitting here stewing in my frustration and loneliness. I should probably go over my materials in preparation for tomorrow, but this song playing on the radio haunts my mind. It's music to you from my heart:

> *"You know I can't smile without you*
> *I can't laugh without you*
> *I can't laugh, I can't sing*
> *I'm finding it hard to do anything.*
> *I feel sad when you're sad*
> *I feel glad when you're glad*
> *If you only knew what I'm going through*
> *I just can't smile without you.*   Your Don"

Carol immediately tried to ease my loneliness with a return letter: "Building the new college has been important, but I'm looking forward to getting rid of all those outside demands and just focusing on being US, like we did when we were newlyweds. Here's the song running through my head and heart:

> *What are you doing the rest of your life*
> *North South East and West of your life*
> *I have only one request of your life*
> *That you spend it all with me.*
> *I want to see your face in every kind of light*
> *In fields of dawn and forests of the night*
> *And, when you stand before the candles on a cake*
> *Oh let me be the one to hear the silent wish you make.*
> *Through all of my life*

Summer, Winter, Spring and Fall of my life
All I ever will recall of my life
Is all of my life with you. Your Carol!"

I received Carol's letter the afternoon before my last meeting with the nursing officials whose approval I sought. As usual, her letter was a morale booster. I went into the meeting with renewed enthusiasm and confidence and left with their assurance that they would support our proposal. They acted on their promises by approving and funding the new building. I jumped into the car and hurried back to Happy Valley. On the way I planned a getaway for just the two of us to celebrate accomplishing my final big objective as Dean.

The next week Carol wrote her parents: "I've been in a kind of a daze all week, dreaming of the lovely romantic weekend Don and I spent down in the Lancaster area. We took off on a Friday morning and came home last Sunday night. It was so nice to get away from our responsibilities and do some sightseeing in that interesting section of PA. We went to some craft shops of various kinds and went antiquing. We got hooked on the antiquing and decided to start collecting pattern glass goblets since I have two of them to start with. Then Don got to looking for a chair that would fit in the narrow kneehole of the old walnut desk he built for his parents as a high school freshman.

That led us to a huge antique sale place north of Lancaster with hundreds of dealers open only on Sundays. We really had fun looking at all the stuff and ended up finding a chair to our liking. I fell in love with a beautiful, mirrored, solid walnut sideboard in a rather plain Victorian style. The dealer was from Philadelphia and showed us documentation that it had been handcrafted in the late 1800s to exactly fit in a wealthy Philadelphian's library. We decided then and there it would be much more fun, and a wise investment, to get antiques (if we find what we want) instead of all new furniture for our new house. We paid $300 for this gem. I remembered all the special things Grandma Clark lost when her farm house burned down. I used to sit in front of her china closet as a kid looking at all the pretty things in it."

One beautiful June evening we relaxed on our deck sipping lemonade, listening to Slab Cabin night sounds and watching a beautiful sunset. I said, "Carol, because it's the bicentennial year, how about having a real old fashioned 4th of July picnic with lots of old time games?"

"Our big lawn would be a great place for that kind of fun – let's do it! We can make it pot luck. I'll ask guests to bring a favorite summer dish and get a big, delicious, boneless ham."

We decorated the back yard with red, white, and blue crepe paper and flags and dragged chairs and benches to our shaded terrace and lawn. Over twenty people came! We organized everyone into teams and had a 3-legged race, sack race, a relay race balancing an egg on a fork (which turned into mayhem when the young bloods started throwing them at each other), a watermelon eating contest, and the usual volleyball. We all laughed so hard at the hilarious antics going on that our stomachs hurt. After everyone stuffed themselves with an intriguing variety of delicious food, the evening ended with our rather meager display of fireworks.

Everyone pitched in to take down decorations, clear the table and put away chairs. After the goodbyes, Carol and I sat alone on the deck, still too hyped up from the excitement to sleep. We marveled at bright stars in the night sky and watched fireflies flickering around a dark yard. Carol laughed and said, "I think the funniest thing I've seen in a long time occurred during that egg race. The other team was harassing Doug since he was the last one on our team and winning the race. Doug remained cool even when Martin cracked an egg on his shoulder and dropped it on his head like you would crack an egg into a bowl. It didn't faze Doug; he won and then took out after Martin's tail and started a free-for-all!" Finally my hostess with the mostest said, "Time for bed. I need to rest up because I have lots to do to get ready for the Arts Festival."

Carol completed preparations for the Art Festival by pricing, labeling and packing everything. She said, "This year I'm displaying categories, like tole painting, weaving, burlap painting, decoupage, oil painting, wood crafts, and driftwood fall arrangements. I think this way will make it easier for people to find the things that interest them." Her sons and their ladies provided the muscle needed to unload and arrange displays the way Carol wanted them.

When the festival ended, we brought the leftovers home and put them back in her shop. She asked for a night cap so I mixed her a cold rum and coke. She said "This was an excellent festival

– I think the best ever. I was particularly pleased because I sold an unusually large number of my paintings. I've been thinking about what to do in the future and decided to open a new shop on my own. What would you think of naming it *The Personal Touch*?"

"I think that's a fabulous name! It carries two meanings: Everything is personally made by you, and your original creations enable people to give their homes a personal touch."

"That's what I'll do then. I'm excited about starting over in a new shop."

As a result of interventions in Harrisburg, the highway negotiators came back to reevaluate their offer. They gave us broad hints about ways they could increase their offer within their guidelines. Our new proposal was several thousand dollars larger. They promised to call back the next week to advise us on wording a formal proposal for the 'big cheeses'.

Carol said, "Do you think we'll get it?"

"It's my impression they've been told by their bosses to make a deal. That's why they gave us so many hints. I bet it will go through. They won't quibble over a few thousand more dollars if they want to complete the deal."

Carol sighed, "Since Mrs. Mitchell is being cooperative with us on our road proposal, everything seems to be going well. We may finally be able to get started on our new home."

The University publicly announced I was "relinquishing my responsibilities as Dean to return to my teaching and research interests." I had announced my plans to the faculty earlier, telling them I'd be a lame duck for the last year, but not to think I was a *dead* duck. When we went to bed that night I said, "Carol, our first pathway together was as students; our second was creating and running programs to facilitate the success of undergraduate students with the student union at K-State and the Division of Counseling at Penn State; our third was creating and running the College of Human Development and providing an academic model that other universities have followed. All of that took a quarter of a century of our teamwork. Now we're creating a fourth pathway. The big positive change will be that for the first time in our lives we'll be pretty much in control of what we do and how we do it. We'll have more opportunities and time to do things together, you as an artist and me as a teacher and scholar."

Carol replied, "We did a good job for others in those first three pathways, so I think we've earned this new freedom to focus on our own interests and accomplishments."

Carol particularly enjoyed participating in the Choral Society and Presbyterian Church choirs during the holiday season. After church on a wintry Sunday, she said with a big grin, "Our bridge group had so much fun last night I stayed up too late. If the preacher hadn't shouted at us in his sermon, I'm sure I would have dozed off in church. I did enjoy singing our Christmas program though. I've been getting a lot more than I expected out of going to church. It lasts a couple days and then I go back to my miserable self again. Maybe I'll get the faith one of these days and live in a state of brotherly love all week long."

I asked, "Could that include husbandly love too?"

She grinned her answer to that and continued without missing a beat, "Don, I loved that ingenious Christmas gift from Russ and Cindy. They went to so much effort, going all over town taking pictures of all my paintings they could track down. I was so touched by their thoughtfulness. They asked if I could find others, but that would be hard. I've sold or given as gifts between 50 and 100 paintings and they're scattered all over the U.S."

Chapter Twenty Three

Carol Plans Another Dream Home

The New Year started with the Highway Department buying our property for the amount we requested. We promptly bought it back for $1000 so we could continue living in it while building our new home, with the understanding we'd be responsible for getting rid of it when the new house was completed. We signed a contract to buy a lot from Mrs. Mitchell to connect our land to her new road, Squirrel Drive. The next task was to find a contractor. Carol said, "We had a miserable time when we built this house because of an incompetent and untrustworthy builder. I don't want to go through that again, so let's be sure we get a good one this time."

  A friend was building a new home in State College and highly recommended his contractor. Carol and I decided to evaluate his work by going that Sunday to look at the house under construction. It was under roof and the internal wall structures were being built. Carol's first reaction was, "This is the cleanest construction site I've ever seen. You don't see a lot of crap lying around like scraps of wood, bent nails, mud and loose tools."

  I said, "Look here," and read a note attached to a 2x4 wall stud: 'This one is warped – replace it with a straight one.' Then I showed her a mathematical formula written on some steps being constructed, "He's used calculus to specify the slope and dimensions of these stairs."

  Carol said, "He doesn't seem like an ordinary 'wood butcher'. Let's talk to him."

  His name was Mike Green. As a Penn State undergraduate, he'd been a star on our gymnastics team. He loved to ski, explore caves and was about Russ's age. He graduated in architecture and took a job with an architectural firm. Mike turned out to be a master craftsman, a superb carpenter, stone mason, and structural engineer who got fed up and quit that firm because, to quote him, "Architects design things but many don't know enough about what it actually takes to build their designs, so plans often have to change during the building process." Disillusioned, he went into business for himself.

We showed Mike tentative plans we'd found in a magazine. He talked us through them, explaining the positive and negative aspects. Then he gave examples of design and structural changes that would make the building more attractive and functional in ways that served our life style, such as Carol's art and crafts interests. He loved the possibilities of our building site. After discussing what we wanted in a home, he offered to sketch a floor plan and exterior design to give us a basis for deciding whether to use his construction firm. We were delighted with his sketch and raised two other possibilities.

Carol said, "We entertain a lot and I hate it when people have to stand outdoors to get snow off their shoes or worry about wet umbrellas. Could this wall with the front door be moved out, with a large area of flagstone at the entry so people could come inside without worrying about snow and rain?" By simply moving that front wall, Mike created a 15 x 25 foot space designed to function as an entry garden. The base was dirt, just like outside. Around the front entry was the flagstone Carol suggested. Leading from that, a wooden walkway curved through the entry garden to the living room. He visualized a diversity of plants growing around the walkway that could easily be watered with a garden hose the same as outdoor plants. The outer wall was lined with windows. Skylights in the ceiling provided the right environment for living plants. It fit Carol's idea of bringing the outside inside, and she fell in love with Mike's plan.

I told Mike, "Carol will need more work, storage and display space for her shop. We don't need a two car garage, so could you convert one side into a self-contained art studio and shop? Located right next to the entry garden it would be convenient for visitors to her shop."

Mike agreed, "Sure, and we should add a large sink to make cleanup easy."

At home Carol said, "He's a gem! I'm so impressed with his creativity, competence, and personal qualities. I like him and trust him." We both had complete confidence in Mike, so signed a construction contract to build our new home. Mike became a treasured life time friend and later built two other imaginative homes for us on our private Slab Cabin Lane.

While painting and gabbing with her painting buddy, Freida, Carol said, "Doug's gal Pam graduated yesterday. Her mother, father, sister, Aunt Helen and Uncle Lisle were here to celebrate her accomplishment. I know her parents, but enjoyed meeting her aunt and uncle. I fixed a fried chicken, potato salad, relish plate lunch for them before the ceremony. Pam is a very talented young artist. She did a wonderful water color painting of what our new house will probably look like. I look at it and dream of our future in it. This was a kind of warm-up celebration for the big one this fall when they get married. Pam stayed with us this past week and I dearly love having her around. She seems to feel quite comfortable here."

"How's your *Personal Touch* shop coming, Carol?"

"I hope to open by Sept. 6 but may not make it until the following week. I've decided to endow a scholarship with the $2500 I made this year for a State College High School student with financial need and focused on the health or human development field. It's named for my parents: the Winifred and Eugene Clark Human Development Scholarship. It means a lot to me.

The Arts Festival is 'juried' this year. That means a committee of professional artists will decide whose work deserves to be exhibited. Each person is allowed only one art form – ceramics, oil painting, sculpting. That cuts me out because my creative juices produce multiple art forms, including decorative arts like my crafts work. 'Real artists' reject them as art forms but Mother Nature is a better artist than any humans. I don't want to concentrate on just one.

Originally, the festival's purpose was to provide an opportunity for central Pennsylvania artists to exhibit their work. The professional artists have essentially tossed out that idea and are trying to make it a national event. Bigshotitis raises its status head again."

Freida laughed at the idea of bigshotitis, then said, "Carol, people like your work. Festival visitors buy more of your paintings than of most other exhibitors. They also frequently ask you to do original paintings for them. It's a shame you won't be exhibiting anymore."

"My work is well known locally, and lots of people like it, so I'll find other outlets."

Her monthly bridge group gals asked for the latest about Carol's new house. She told them, "Construction is going well, Mike now has it all under roof. I thought it would be both beautiful and useful to have the walls of our entry garden and my shop made of weathered barn wood. Don and I have been driving around the countryside looking for possible sources.

Last week we found a farm with an old fallen down barn right by the road. When we explained how it would be used, the elderly farmer agreed to let us take as much as we wanted. We've been busy pulling the siding off that old barn and I think we about have enough for the walls of the entry garden and my studio/shop. Not only will its textured, weathered grey look great with the garden plants, but I can put nails in it anywhere to display stuff like my paintings. Mike also got two big, rough beams to use for both structural and beautification purposes down stairs. Downstairs walls will be covered with the walnut planks from our old house."

Ginny Elliott said, "It's wonderful you can keep that unique, beautiful walnut paneling."

My decade-long role as Dean ended in August. There were two celebrations. The first was a private weekend at an historic hotel at Bedford Springs in south central Pennsylvania, arranged by our executive team colleagues. We ate, swam, 'happy houred', teased, joked, and shared pride in what we had accomplished together at a closing dinner.

As we drove home, Carol said, "That was a happy and heartwarming time, but I feel sad because it's probably the last time we'll have such a close relationship with those people." Later, a card from one of them brought temporary tears:

"Thank you for everything: for instructive seminars on administration in Don's office; for lovely parties Carol hosted in your home; for 'The First Step' – it's so handsome and meaningful; and most of all, for being you – two people I admire and respect and love."

The second was a three-day, college-wide celebration of the first ten years' development of the new college, with eminent speakers discussing the societal importance and need for each of the program missions of our College. The 10th birthday celebration was quite a whoop-tee-doo for three days. Carol and I helped host a distinguished speaker and his wife most of the time. Our guest, Rene Dubos, was the father of antibiotics – 75 years old, born and raised in France, and came to the US in 1927. The story of his life would make a good book.

I thought while watching Carol entertaining them, *A person's potential for further development, no matter what their starting point in life, always amazes me. Here was a shy, insecure young woman, fearful of encounters with accomplished adults – particularly men. Now she spends a day with one of the most distinguished men in the country and his wife, with ease and skill and finds interest and pleasure in it.* Carol was the perfect example of my belief that we should focus less on a person's weaknesses and more on their potentials.

One evening relaxing after dinner I said, "Carol, I'm finding it strange not going to work every morning after doing that all my adult life. Are you getting used to having me around?"

Carol snorted her answer, "What do you mean all the time? You're across the stream most of the time, working with Mike on our new house. I'm happy if you're here to keep me company every evening and to go to bed with every night."

"Are you getting geared up to hand our third son over to another woman's care?"

"It's getting close. I'm honored that a fine artist like Pam asked me to design the flower arrangements for their wedding. She's coming up on the train Thursday. Doug and I will meet her in Altoona. Then I'll take her over to my wholesale flower place to pick out the dried and silk flowers she wants for her wedding arrangements. I'm making the sprays she and her attendants are carrying and a three-foot-long mantle arrangement. Hope I can do it justice. Ginny Althouse, Ginny Elliott and Jean Vallance are giving her a shower Sunday."

On November 12, 1977 we married off our third son at the Sacred Heart-Saint Peter's Catholic Church in Tarentum, Pennsylvania. Carol couldn't wait to tell her bridge group about it: "Pam and Doug are two loving, thoughtful people and their wedding reflected those qualities. Martin played an original composition, created for his twin brother's wedding, just before the bridal procession. It sounded great in that big church. The kids had lovely music played and sung by some of their musical friends. Remember Sheri Smith, the girl who played duo piano with Martin when they were in high school? She and her husband, Steve McCamley, combined flute, piano and singing, and Jeanne and Ron Byron combined piano, guitar and singing to surround the ceremony with lovely music. Afterwards there were cocktails, dinner and dancing at a Country Club and that was a happy time. Our other three handsome sons were ushers and we had some family fun there. Three sons down and one to go!"

Squirrel Drive was completed with its crushed rock base, providing access to our new house. Russ found a used 4-wheel drive Jeep with snow blade in Harrisburg because I needed to keep our lane and Squirrel Drive open through winter since paving wouldn't start until spring.

After a very successful first year in operation, *The Personal Touch* closed a week before Christmas so Carol could relax and enjoy the holiday. We attended only one party, the Town and Gown Christmas formal. We had a wonderful time with old friends and forgot day-to-day pressures as we danced the evening away in each other's arms. We were grateful to have our family together because this would be the last Christmas in the home where our sons grew up. Leaving it would be poignant because of the happy memories we all shared with such nostalgia.

The first half of the New Year was organized around finishing and moving into our new home, and helping Carol's father deal with Winifred's growing problems. We had hoped to move in by mid-January, but subcontractor delays and forty inches of snow made that impossible. Thank goodness I had the 4-wheel-drive Jeep with a blade! It enabled me to clear snow around our old house and the new one so construction crews could get to work every day.

Carol said, "Since we can't move yet I'm starting work on my New Year's resolutions. I'm going to diet and exercise to lose weight and feel better, practice my piano to polish competence and improve my mood, and continue to enjoy singing every chance I get. Pam and a friend have enrolled in a belly dancing class and urged me to join them. She says they guarantee a flat belly after taking the course. I said I should go; my belly would be a challenge to them. Making *my* belly flat would take a miracle!"

I laughed, "Belly dancing seems a strange way to exercise – can I watch?"

"I wrote dad about it. He said coeds at KU are making money performing it.

I've renewed my commitment to the church choir and the choral society. Some of my friends from our women's club music group have joined a women's barbershop group and are urging me to join. I've been interested in singing close harmony since I first heard it in the temporary union at K-State, so I'm joining them. They call themselves The Sweet Adeline's."

Carol, Cam and I finally moved into our new home just before Easter 1978. Cam had the spacious downstairs bedroom and the entire family room with a pool table to entertain his buddies. Our new bedroom opened onto a deck looking down on a pond we created to catch water from a natural spring, and beyond that was our stream and the graceful trees lining it.

One morning we woke up to a loud bird song. Carol opened the curtains and said, "There's a beautiful male cardinal sitting on the railing, calling for his mate." A few minutes later we watched a female cardinal walking back and forth on the balcony, preening for the male.

I said, "So, I'm not the only male that misses his pretty mate! That must be the same guy that's been attacking our house. He must see his image in the window because he keeps flying at the window, hitting it with his claws. We've probably invaded his territory."

Our weekend started out with about fifty of our friends and family throwing us a surprise house-warming and what a surprise it was! Carol shared our surprise in a letter to her parents: "Ginny Elliott and Nat Urban instigated the surprise with the help and intrigue of our sons (and wives) and they pulled it off to perfection. When I came down the stairs and saw all those people grinning at me I could not believe what I was seeing. They said I *really* looked surprised!! It was a gala evening, very heartwarming, and almost overwhelming to realize how many friends we have that care so much for us. We were up half the night, but it was worth getting tired for. Russ's replica of our house out of cake and frosting was quite a masterpiece.

The next day we went to an auction near Williamsport and found our Victorian bed. We were thrilled as it was in beautiful shape. So, at last we have our Victorian bedroom furnished."

Some of Carol's singing-group friends asked to see the house so she gave them a tour. It warmed my heart to hear her descriptions, knowing her ideas were behind its creation.

"We chose an exterior finish of burgundy brick and white stucco, and I thought the flagstone walk leading to the front door was the ideal complement to the setting. Mike did a beautiful job. We wanted the walls of this garden entry to be finished with grey weathered barn wood so I could display paintings and crafts. I love lots of natural light so the wall of windows and the skylights provide that, plus the skylights are lined with mirrors that reflect sunlight around the room as the sun moves. It makes a perfect environment for our indoor garden.

This wide flagstone walk leads to the kitchen. On the left is my shop with a section of wall I can open as a window to see the garden and people in it while I work. This wooden walkway leads through the garden to the living room. On your left is the small antique table and chairs where we can eat breakfast or lunch or have coffee with a couple of friends while we look into the garden and through the windows to trees outside. That beautiful stained glass window above the breakfast nook was once part of an old church."

I smiled to hear the occasional 'oohs and aahs' as Carol walked her friends through the house, and the flurry of compliments that came as she led them into the living and dining area.

"We wanted the living and dining area to be spacious for entertaining and bring the outside in. The ceiling slants from eight feet to twelve feet high. The wall of windows faces our back yard, pond, flower gardens, Slab Cabin Run and the woods beyond. The stairs lead to the lower level, and beyond the stair railing are three upper level bed rooms and a bath.

Our contractor built this ten foot wide floor-to-ceiling wall of horizontal gray-green stone strips containing a fireplace. Behind it is a U-shaped kitchen with a window looking east at a flower garden and woods. A door at the end of the dining area opens onto a covered deck with picnic table and the door at the far end of the living room leads out to a 'loafing' deck. Don and I plan to do a LOT of loafing from now on!

Downstairs has the same general layout with a used brick fireplace, rustic wood beams, walls paneled with black walnut planks, and an antique Victorian-era bar. A mechanical room is behind the fireplace. There's also a bedroom, bath, study and large laundry."

Then, Carol and her friends sat around our dining room table sharing coffee and snacks. I was their serving boy and smiled to hear Carol's final answer to their many questions. "This house and setting provides the beauty and openness I love. It brings outdoor beauty into our home. We plan to live the rest of our lives here on our private Slab Cabin Lane slice of heaven."

Carol loved her new barbershop singing group. They were asked to sing at the Arts Festival. She came home excited to share the experience with me, "We were scheduled to perform on the Arts festival outdoor stage, but were hit with a big rain and hail storm so we sang inside a tent. The tent was full, so we sang our hearts out. The audience loved it. Barbershop is such happy music! The close harmonies are different than anything I ever sang before."

In August, Carol wrote her parents: "Sunday evening we had our 'roast' on Don celebrating his 52nd birthday and it was one hilarious time! A 'roast' is when a group of people gang up on a friend and jokingly say lots of nasty things about them. Everyone in the family took a shot at him. Russ came up with a great slide show kidding Don about his picture taking and other foibles. I had them 'rolling in the aisles', especially Don, with an 'Erma Bombeck-like' monolog. I can be funny with a martini or 2 in me, but it's a side of me seldom seen so that's why it surprised the kids so much. Here the opening to my monolog:

For years and years you kids have been getting a distorted view of your father. That's because it was HIS view. That's the way Dad is – when he wants your opinion, he gives it to you. Well, tonight I'm going to give you the lowdown on what your father is REALLY like.

Now, it's not that he has that many faults, he just makes the most out of the ones he has.

Cindy baked and decorated a cake with 'King Dad' and a crown on it. I can't get over how clever the boys' are; all of them are funny in their own way."

Over breakfast Carol asked, "We've been so busy for the last several months that I've become lonely for personal time with my one and only. Would my ex-Dean lover be able to get 'duded up' and join me Saturday at 8 for our first private evening date in our new home?"

"It would be a delight to have my gorgeous wife all to myself for an entire evening!"

I put on my tuxedo, built a blazing fire in our fireplace, and prepared martinis with an olive and chips with Carol's favorite dip. I turned when I heard Carol, took a deep breath and said, "O-h-h-h!!" She was stunning in a slinky rich blue formal she'd made several years ago but had modified so it was now a tantalizing, subtly revealing strapless gown. She had an elaborate new hairdo with silver combs and delicate silver ear rings with azure blue stones.

I took her hands, twirled her around to see her loveliness from all sides, and said, "You look magnificent. You keep getting more and more beautiful!"

She smiled and curtsied, "Thank you sir – I seek to tease and please you. I'm ready for a martini." We sat down close together and I served my gorgeous date.

Our matching sofas faced each other before the fireplace, separated by matching coffee tables with walnut frames we'd made several years ago. The top of each featured a Carol creation of a large, tooled cooper, curving three-dimensional abstract design, with contrasting shades of copper and dark areas. They were covered with glass to protect them.

I said, "These table tops are my favorite work of art by you. With the firelight flickering across those copper designs their beauty is remarkable. They symbolize the creativity you brought to every Pennsylvania home we've shared. No wonder people want your creations."

"Your compliments provide encouragement I need right now. I've opened *The Personal Touch* and I keep feeling so anxious about it. I want it to be successful and am afraid people won't know I'm here and the shop is open. I've done well the first week – had orders and sales totaling around $300. Then I worry if I'm too busy and can't make enough creative and pretty things to fill the shop. Maybe I'm not cut out for the uncertainty of a business."

"Carol, it won't take long for customers to discover your new location. I'll bet a lot of them will be curious to see what your new place is like. Actually it will be a lot easier for them to come here because we have a paved driveway and lots of convenient private parking space."

While sipping martinis and nibbling snacks I could see Carol was tense and nervous about something. After a pause, she finally opened the main topic she wanted to discuss: "Don, after several debates with myself I need to share a decision I've made. I hope it's OK with you. As you know, for years I've been having my hair dyed to maintain its original color. Often the chemicals feel like they burn my scalp until it hurts. Recently I've noticed my hair getting dryer and more brittle. I don't want to start losing my hair the way your sister, Lois, has so I've decided to stop dying it. Since our courting days you've bragged about the beauty of my hair. I hope you won't be disappointed in the change."

I chuckled, "It *will* change one thing you've liked. You've been pleased with how often women said to you, 'Carol, you're too young to have four sons!' That won't happen anymore."

Before I could say more, tears poured down her cheeks as Carol blurted angrily, "I don't give a damn if you think I'm no longer beautiful. I'm going to do it whether you like it or not!"

Knowing I'd made a thoughtless response shocked and distressed me. She'd misinterpreted my comment. I should have said first thing that I supported her idea. Somehow, I had to dig my way out of that blunder!

"Oh Honey, I'm sorry my comment gave you the wrong idea. It's *you* I love – not the color of your hair! From comments you've made in the past, I've realized for some time you were fed up with having your hair dyed. I'm glad you made your decision and think it's a wise one." I watched her face as I tried to fast-talk my way out of the mess I'd created. "The famous movie star, Jean Harlow, had silver hair, called *platinum blonde,* and people rave over its beauty. With silver hair like your father's, you'll be just as gorgeous as Jean Harlow. And, your hair has the natural waviness women covet. Your hair is *beautiful* and I'll continue to enjoy running my hands through it and helping you wash it, whatever color it is. I won't stop loving you and hope you won't stop loving me as our hair loses its color. You could get knock kneed, cross eyed and bald and I'd still adore you. Please forgive my stupid comment!"

Relief washed over me to see her sweet smile return as she wiped away the last of her tears, "I don't know why I've been so worried about this. I guess I was kind of scared, thinking I couldn't stand it if you didn't love me anymore. Even when we both get grey we can still enjoy dancing together, so let's dance my fears away now."

We spent the rest of our date dancing and loving one another. (Carol did become a *platinum blonde* and received frequent compliments about how pretty her hair was.)

Doug, Pam, Cam, Carol and I decorated our new house for our first Christmas there. The corner of our large living room, next to Carol's piano, was a perfect spot for the tree. Carol wrapped an arm around me as we lit the tree lights, "During our bypass problems, I didn't let myself believe we'd end up with a beautiful place like this. Now I realize the bypass did us a huge favor. Thank you for refusing to buy just any house when I wanted to. Time after time we haven't found solutions for our problems until the last moment, and each time I said to you that someone up there is looking after us. Now we've done it again. What we share is never ordinary because you're still my magic man! I'm ready to live the rest of my life in this beautiful home with you."

Amidst the happy hubbub of Christmas, I sat quietly for awhile, watching Carol's face. Our entire family spent that holiday together in our new home, and the joy reflected in her face was the greatest gift anyone could have given me.

Chapter Twenty-Four
New Pathways, New Lives

We started another decade by creating a new pattern of life together. Carol had a large, efficiently organized space she used exclusively for her creative work. She no longer had to clean up and store supplies when she finished working, but could just walk away and pick up where she left off the next day. She had a large, beautiful display space on her barn wood walls and in her entry garden. Her new shop boasted its own telephone (a special convenience before cell phones) and a small combination TV/record player to entertain her while she worked. The kitchen was only a few steps away, convenient for monitoring cooking.

Another unanticipated benefit was her shop's comfortable, attractive setting for friends and customers to hang out and visit. People enjoyed laughing and talking with Carol while she worked. Since her high school days, she'd treasured gabbing with other women and a steady flow of such opportunities resulted from her new shop. Since I now spent most of my time at home, I often overheard conversations with customers. As an experienced psychotherapist, it astonished me that people who'd never met her before initiated intimate conversations about family and other problems while shopping with her.

When I commented on that, Carol said, "I meet many fascinating people and often learn of interesting events through such conversations. Old friends, neighbors, strangers and out-of-towners like to visit while they browse in my shop and watch me work. That's what makes it different than going to a store. I want *The Personal Touch* to stand for more than just shopping. It also means visitors get my personal attention and that's fun for me."

We began 1980 by welcoming two new members to our family. We'd known for a year that Russ and Cindy's marriage was in trouble. It finally ended in divorce. That was painful for Russ and us, but it led to a happy development later. Russ remarried just before Christmas. His second wife, Lois, was a lovely, dark-eyed Italian Catholic girl who taught special education in the Hershey schools. They had a small charming wedding in a historic Catholic church in Harrisburg, PA, where they continued to work and live.

The second addition came with the arrival of our first grandchild, Matthew Ryan Ford. Pam and Doug introduced him to the world on January 6. Holding a young baby had always been a great joy for Carol. She said, "I'm delighted and a bit awed, holding this wonderful wee little boy who's almost a carbon copy of his daddy twenty-six years ago. Since they live in town I'll get to watch him grow and explore life."

During our morning coffee break, a tradition started after my retirement as Dean, I said, "I love our new pathway. For the first time in our life together I feel nearly stress free, and enjoy being more involved in each other's daily routines."

Carol's dimples deepened with a happy smile, "Since that huge chunk of time we spent on University business and events is out of our lives, I feel great relief from that pressure. Now I seldom wake up at night or in the morning with an upset stomach or anxiety about the stuff I have to do that day. I *love* knowing you're around if I want or need to talk with you. Remember before our marriage we talked about wanting to be an 'US' rather than a 'You and Me'? During busy times in the past, I sometimes worried we were losing 'US'. Now I feel that closeness again and treasure it."

"Being in control of our own schedules rather than having to meet schedules created by others is a real treat. But won't you find it stressful having me around to pester you every day?"

"If I do I'll just tell you to skidoo! We do have some good stress in our lives that I enjoy, and that's watching and helping Cam grow into a young man. He's working harder now and seems more interested in his school work. He's much better on the trumpet and really enjoys the marching band and playing with his buddies for fun. After I told him about Grandpa Clark's band when he was young, Cam did a very nice thing for Dad. This latest letter from Dad shows clearly how he felt." Carol scanned through the letter until she found the part she wanted me to hear:

'Several days ago I received a tape of band music from Cam. I love band music, and this band had it. Anyone who can sit and listen to the *Star Spangled Banner* played like they did it and cannot feel a tingling go up his spine, has no spine. Likewise, any gob (like I was) who can listen to *Anchors Aweigh* played like that and not feel that same tingling has never marched before the Naval Station Commandant and Secretary of the Navy, or steered his ship through an Atlantic storm or chased a Nazi submarine. Cam's high school band can play with the best.'"

I said, "We'd better prepare for a bit more stress from that source soon, because Cam's excited about getting his driver's license soon."

Carol laughed, "That means we're entering another era of playing, 'Who forgot to put gas in the car?' He's a walking book of sports statistics; almost as much of a 'sports nut' as Martin."

"Cam is a better worker and complains less than his brothers did at his age. He built our storage shed for tools and did a great job. I got the materials and only helped a little.

Speaking of his work efforts, he told me a while back, 'I've got one cool Mom! I was splitting fireplace wood with a buddy and we cracked one big log but it didn't split apart so we pushed our big pry bar in the crack and pulled as hard as we could to split it. The bar slipped out and hit me high on the forehead. That hurt and when I touched my forehead my hand came away all bloody. My buddy yelled, 'Cam, you got blood all over your face!!' It scared hell out of me so I panicked and ran for the house screaming for Mom. When she came out I was astonished she wasn't scared. Instead of acting upset she quietly comforted me, took me into the house and cleaned off the blood so she could see the wound, saying reassuring things to me to calm me down, and then gave me the diagnosis: 'It's just a little scalp wound; they always bleed a lot. Let's go get a stitch or two so it won't leave a scar.' The doctor said it was good we came in so he could clean and stich it up. I really admired how she cared for me so calmly.'"

Carol said, "I was scared – I'd never seen so much blood! He needed calm strength then, not my fear. I love having him around – he's thoughtful, caring, responsible and so much fun!"

I knew her parents' well-being was a major source of concern for Carol. I wanted to help her work through those thoughts, emotions, and responsibilities so decided it was time for one of our special dates. While watching Carol work in her shop, I said, "Could I have the pleasure of a dinner date with my creative lady Friday night?"

Carol grinned, "I'd be delighted to dine with a famous scholar who is also a fine dancer."

We drove east to a small village near Lock Haven and a restaurant that was in an old, picturesque three-story house, owned and operated as a hobby by a local high school teacher. The first floor contained the restaurant, open only on weekends. The other two floors were a gift shop featuring items I knew Carol would enjoy seeing. When she saw the place her eyes sparkled with pleasure as she said, "What a wonderful place!"

I explained, "For many years the owner went to France and befriended some special chef he'd arranged to meet, then took his new chef friend to a bar and spent the evening getting acquainted. When the evening ended, he'd have that chef's favorite entrée recipe. Now, his menu offers a different selection each weekend from among his file of those entrees." We chatted with the owner to get acquainted and then asked him to choose our dinners for us. He served his favorite soup and beamed when Carol raved about the flavors in it. While waiting for our main course, he took us to the back yard and showed Carol his garden of fresh herbs, some of which he'd used to make our soup. As she questioned him about growing herbs I thought, *Looks like I may be helping Carol start her own herb garden.*

Our entrée was a special lamb dish. We'd never eaten lamb and found it delicious. Carol said, "At first I wasn't sure I could eat it because it reminded me of the pet lamb Mom had on the farm."

I nodded, "I remember 'Lambsy Divey'. She named it after that funny little song."

After we'd enjoyed our meal, I expressed my main concern, "I know your folks are always on your mind. What are your thoughts about trying to help them now?"

"Since I can't be with them most of the time, I'm using frequent letters in an effort to boost their morale, sharing our news and emphasizing how much I care for them. It may be working a little. I sent him a newspaper clipping of a donation I'd made and his reply really touched me. He said tears came to his eyes to think I'd accomplished so much and done so much good for people, and that he'd always admired me for my accomplishments, even though he hadn't encouraged me like you and Mom did.

Honestly, that was the first time he *ever* expressed positive emotions about me or said he was proud of me. He always believed people can be better motivated by criticism. I think that misguided attitude was a key problem in his relationship with Mom and me. It's probably the reason we never became close. Maybe now we can build a closer relationship."

"When would you like to go visit them again?"

"I'd like to see them twice this summer or fall."

"Then that's our plan."

After dinner I took Carol upstairs to browse the gift shop. She spent a delightful hour exploring and got some ideas for her own shop. Then we drove home on a warm, moonlit night.

Moonlight bathed our deck as we enjoyed listening to night sounds under the stars. As always, we were two people in love, sipping Drambuie and savoring the decades we'd shared together. Carol broke our companionable silence first, "Thank you for our date. Being introduced to a delightful new place by my loving companion reminds me of how interesting and pleasurable our life has always been together."

"Could we pursue that pleasure further?"

"I'd love to – give me a minute."

I put our glasses in the kitchen and headed for our bedroom where my sweetheart waited for me in bed. After a period of marital bliss, we lay relaxed beside each other and Carol said, "Do you remember the letter I wrote you before we were married, expressing my thoughts about the relationship between love and sex?"

"Yes, I thought it was quite eloquent!"

"Lying here after the happy evening we've had, I feel what those thoughts said. The sensual excitement of sharing our bodies is short lived, but through that sharing comes nurturing feelings of love and tenderness that make me so happy. Goodnight sweetheart!"

I replied, "I'll dream of you."

In March, Carol's dad had surgery to repair his hernia. She spent time caring for him and her mother while Cam and I stayed home tending our educational responsibilities. I wrote, "One of the Sweet Adelines called asking if you were going to the barber shop competition in Pittsburgh. They'll make a reservation for you, but you can cancel if you decide not to go.

As you suggested, I'm now a member of the Elks Club so we can go dancing and play golf there. This is a very lonely place without you. It seems like forever since I held you in my arms. We'll take a 'vacation' together this spring to recuperate!"

In May we took that vacation and celebrated our wedding anniversary camping and boating at Raystown Lake. She wrote her parents: "We simply said to heck with all our other duties and took off. All the camp sites were full when we got there but we lucked out. We saw a young couple leaving so swooped down on that site. We set up in about 45 minutes and are close to our boat. Yesterday we boated for a good portion of the day, hunted driftwood, took our lunch and went to one of our favorite coves to swim and fish. As usual we were fishing at the wrong time of day so caught nothing. You could see those big buggers swimming lazily back and forth just ignoring our worms and chicken livers. Some people showed us a big string of catfish and told us where they caught them. This p.m. we're taking our supper and heading there to try our luck. I'm not as patient as a fisherman needs to be, but I love being on the water in this big lake. Both of us forget all our cares while we're camping, swimming and boating here.

Matthew had his baptism Sunday and many of Pam's relatives came up for the short ceremony. They brought tons of food and the gathering afterwards was at our house. Pam was so nervous about it all, but it came off beautifully. Her kin all seemed to enjoy themselves. Kim, Pam's sister, was the godmother. We were touched when she tried to mark the sign of the cross on Matt's forehead. Her hand control is so limited she really couldn't do it so the godfather took her hand and traced it for her."

One evening while relaxing on our deck, Carol said, "I was both proud and kind of sad watching Cam graduate from High School. It was fun watching him celebrate with his band buddies, but I'll be lonely for him if he takes a job somewhere else."

"Carol, I wish we could have watched Martin and Sheri graduate with her BS and Martin's PhD at Minnesota. Martin has been discouraged with his interviewing for jobs without success. But, the Stanford University job he got is excellent. They'll live near San Francisco."

"That will give us a good reason to visit California! Our family is spreading out. Since Doug has been admitted to the Maxwell School of Public Administration for a Master's degree, they'll be moving to Syracuse, New York in January. It's probably the best school of its kind in the country, so is a fine opportunity. Cam is the only son still with us in Happy Valley."

"Do you remember Maude Peters who was in the Lemont Women's Club with you?"

Carol chuckled at the memory, "How could I forget her! She always expressed her opinions forcefully and upset the other members. She and her daughters sure didn't get along."

"In her will she left her property to her grandsons. The grandsons, who are also high school friends of our sons, no longer live here and have no access to the land so they can't use it. Their lawyer is a friend of mine and contacted me yesterday. They want $14,000 for a little over four acres. It includes both sides of the stream and goes from our property line east to the township park. Their only other alternative to get money out of it is to clear cut the land and sell the lumber."

"Don, that would be terrible! Clear cutting would destroy this lovely area and chase all the wild life away. We can't let that happen! Can we dig up enough money to buy it?"

"I agree – it would be a calamity. If you want to do it I'll find some way to finance it." So, we doubled our property to eight prime acres on a mountain stream, all within a ten minute drive of the campus, hospital, high school and two shopping centers. In a rapidly expanding community it looked like a good investment.

We had planned the annual visit to our Kansas families for mid-August. I asked, "Carol how would you like to add a visit to California to our Kansas trip?"

"That would be fantastic!"

"OK. I'll see what kind of connections we could make and how much it would cost." Later I reported: "We can make good connections but it would cost more than we can afford. We spent everything we had buying that land, and I can barely dig up enough to fly to Kansas."

Carol responded, "No! I can't stand not seeing those kids for over a year! I've saved some money from the shop so will add that to what we have to pay for the trip to California. It's a cost I won't mind a bit. To see people that mean the world to me I'd spend my last dollar!"

So, we visited our Kansas families and then flew to California. We went at a pretty fast pace while at Martin and Sheri's with lots to see and do for they hadn't seen much yet either.

Back home Carol wrote her parents: "I wish you could see it here today, everything is so beautiful, flowers blooming, the stream running fuller since the rains. The only blemish is that I'm unhappy with you out there and me here. I feel torn, wanting to be 2 places at once.

We decided we needed to get back in shape. I started exercising, dieting and working in the shop. Don is exercising too. Exercise makes all the difference in the world to me. I put on my leotards first thing and 'dance' to records until I'm sweating and out of breath, then take a shower. After that I'm really awake and rarin' to go.

Cam is now a Penn State freshman living in a dorm. He made the Blue Band as a freshman. That's quite a compliment because there's lots of competition for band membership. He's really looking forward to it because he saw how much fun Doug had in it. We gave him a surprise birthday party! We worked with his good friend, Brian, who invited the kids. We took Cam to the Elks Club for their Friday buffet, then returned home at 9 p.m. Doug and Pam were here to greet and organize the guests, so when we went downstairs and turned on the lights all of them rose up out of their hiding places and yelled 'Surprise!' It was fun! We had a casino party organized and I think the kids enjoyed it. We gave Cam his own checking account so he can enter the adult world of finance to pilot himself through college."

The year ended the way it started. We added another person to the Ford Family. In our annual Christmas letter Carol wrote about our new grandson: "He is Joshua Russell Ford, an alert 9 pounder with big, beautiful, almost hypnotic eyes. Grandma had the privilege of going to Harrisburg for 3 days to admire him and has gone plum coo-coo over Josh and Matt. Grandpa is also impressed and spouts great psychological wisdom at the new parents, which may or may not be taken with a grain of aspirin. Grand parenting is fun. Maybe this will be a next generation 'Baby Boomer' period for our family."

We started the New Year with an empty house. Three sons were married, two with babies and living elsewhere. Our youngest was at Penn State and living on campus. As we empty nesters ate breakfast together on a cold day with sunshine glittering off the latest snow, Carol said, "It's nice to start the morning this way. It reminds me of that special time when we were first married. After breakfast we each went off to our separate jobs somewhere on campus and reconnected after work. We do the same thing now, with one big difference. Our careers are now right here in our home. We can meet any time we want to share thoughts or plans or take a break. Occasionally, you have to go on campus or I have to go to town, but we spend most of our time here, in our own little world. It gives me such a secure and happy feeling."

I replied, "I love it too! But, many other people we care about are in our thoughts, influencing our activities. We often think and talk about how we might help our parents and bring pleasure to their lives. Each of our sons are building adult lives, each struggling with typical problems of that phase of life like getting jobs, having enough money, getting along with wives and having babies. We love them, want to see them and help when we can. Now that our family baby boom has begun, we're eager to know, hold and love those babies.

Earlier in our lives our time and activities revolved around work, social life, friends and colleagues. We're shifting much of that time now to interactions with our offspring and parents that produce both pleasure and stress. So in actuality, we're never really alone here."

Carol laughed and said, "Boy, when you put it that way it's a little scary, but true. For example, while dressing this morning I was thinking about my mother, then wondering when and how I might see our grand babies, Matt and Joshua, and then wondering how Pam is coming with her new pregnancy. I guess that's why some have called us 'The Sandwich Generation.'

I think a lot about our son's families as problems come up in their lives. For example, I miss Doug's family so much, especially baby Matthew, and it seems unreal they're living where we can't see them whenever we want to. It will take time to get used to it, like we're used to Martin and Sheri being so far away. It's different, however, when there are babies involved since they change so fast and it's hard for me to miss out on the cutest times of their lives."

"Carol, wasn't your Grandma's slogan, 'It's time to stop stewing and start doing'?"

She laughed and said, "You want me to stop complaining and go to work in my shop?"

Carol wrote her parents: "I'm on a Trailway bus on my way to Syracuse. Don, bless his heart, gave me a Valentine's Day gift of a 3-day visit with Doug, Pam and Matt. He sprung it on me at breakfast yesterday and at first I couldn't make up my mind to go – I'm chicken, I guess, I get all hyper. That's why he didn't want to give me much time to worry over the trip. I was to leave today and come back Thursday. So, I finally said OK and he drove me up to Williamsport to catch the bus because of good connections."

On the bus ride home she added a postscript: "It was all worth it when I saw the kids. They seemed so delighted I came up for a few days; that really made me feel good. I know they've been pretty down at times, especially Pam. She's had lots of nausea. Matt is perfectly darling, he hasn't changed much. What a mop of beautiful brown curly hair. He truly is a beautiful child and even if I wasn't his grandma I'd think so. He warmed up to me right away so I guess he remembered me a little bit."

Chapter Twenty-Five
Winifred's Health Problems Ending with Alzheimer's Disease

Winifred had a long history of health problems with which Carol had to cope from childhood. Knowing her mother's health history, its impact on Carol, and how it ended, will help you understand Carol's Alzheimer's journey. Instead of presenting Winifred's health history in small disconnected episodes scattered throughout this book, I'll summarize it here to provide a clearer picture of the overall pattern. Knowing Winifred's history and treatment plan will clarify and emphasize why Carol's life with Alzheimer's was different.

Winifred's health history ends with Alzheimer's disease and the pattern of care she received. This provides a simplified description of the illness and typical care provided for it, often called **the medical model of elder care.** At the end of Carol's story I'll describe the different kind of care she received for the same illness, which I call **the developmental model of elder care**. You can then compare the care each received which will reveal the dramatic difference between the two.

Winifred battled depression and other mental health problems most of her adult life. In that era (1920-1970), most doctors focused on physical symptoms and seldom considered or understood potential underlying mental conditions. When the Clarks finally moved from the farm to a house in Topeka, Winifred's psychological states improved. Carol was delighted at the change. Her parents seemed happy in their new home and Winifred's health problems gradually faded for a time. They bought a camper and joined a camping club where they made new friends, went to the World's Fair and toured the northeastern states where their ancestors had lived, visited friends around the country and spent some cold winters in Florida and Texas.

We gave them a golden wedding anniversary gift of their first airplane trip so they could spend the Christmas holidays with us. Despite past problems in Winifred's relationship with Carol, their visits with us were pleasant and joyful.

A few years after their move back to Topeka, I received a distressing call from Carol. The sound of her voice scared me so I rushed home. The day was pleasantly warm and life all around us was in full flower, but all I could see was my wife's red-rimmed eyes.

I said, "I can see you've been crying. What's happened?"

After some deep breaths, the concerns poured out of her. "I had a long phone conversation with Daddy this morning. As you know, Mother has had all kinds of illnesses and physical symptoms that came and went over decades. She's gone to different doctors and clinics, tried many kinds of treatment, but nothing really helped. Things have been getting worse again in recent months. Dad was desperate so took her to the Mayo Clinic in Minnesota to find some answers. They spent almost a week with all kinds of specialists going over Mom from every angle. Yesterday the doctors reported their diagnosis.

The group of doctors who examined Mom reported there was nothing biologically wrong with her. Their diagnosis is that all her physical symptoms result from psychological distress, and they recommended psychological treatment for both Mom and Dad. Dad asked them, 'You mean I've paid doctors all that money for all these years and there was nothing biologically wrong?' They said 'Yes' so he's furious about that and scared too. I suspect he's like most people and sees psychological conditions as something to be ashamed of.

Dad asked for my help in deciding what to do. You and I have thought for years that Mother's symptoms were mainly caused by emotional distress, but I had no idea *none* had a physical cause. I'm sure that diagnosis is a hard one to swallow, at least partly because of what their relatives might think. Please help me with this problem as you have with so many others!"

I had been holding her hands while she talked, so I gave one a gentle squeeze. "Of course, we'll deal with this as a team.

However, my first concern is for you. Do you feel in any way responsible for their difficulties?"

"I did once, but no longer. She's been a loving mother and I've tried to return that love. It took me a long time to see that Mom used her symptoms to manipulate me, as far back as when I was a kid in Marysville. I'm not the cause of her problems, so I feel no guilt. In fact maybe the love and attention I gave her over the years kept her from being worse earlier in life. But, I feel so sad that someone I love is so miserable!"

"Carol, no mother has a more devoted and loving daughter than you are. In that spirit let's consider how we can help them long distance. It's important that you and I agree that only by their own actions can these problems be eased or solved. All we can do is to help them accept that responsibility and make that commitment.

I suggest we focus on three goals: (1) help them understand and accept the diagnosis and the wisdom of spending money on it – Dad needs persuasion about the cost; (2) help ease their fears about negative reactions from others; and (3) provide sound information on which to base their decisions. Because of their deep love for you, you have the best chance of accomplishing one and two and I'll use my professional contacts to focus on three. Write your suggestions to them because then they can reread them any time they need reminding."

Carol immediately drafted a letter and asked me to read it. I said, "Your letter is excellent in both substance and style – it sounds like you. Your use of examples provides them hope for their future. I've recommended the Menninger clinic in Topeka to your Dad because they have a good reputation. I think Winifred will have more confidence in an MD, and only MDs can prescribe antidepressants which may be useful."

Two months later Carol wrote a follow up letter: "I yelped with joy when I read that you've not had to take a pain or sleeping pill for a week, Mom. You really had a heavy dose of Dr. Menninger there for a few days didn't you."

Their continuing correspondence indicated things were going better for them. After a few more uneventful years in Topeka, Winifred wrote: "We've decided to sell our home in Topeka and move to Lawrence where Kansas University is located. Your Dad's favorite brother and your favorite uncle, Carroll, has worked at KU for years. He retired there and moved to an on campus faculty apartment building. The manager of that apartment building left and your Dad has been appointed to that job."

Carol replied: "We're delighted with your decision. I think both of you will have fun keeping things humming at the apartment complex, meeting and making friends with people with common interests and problems. I'm excited about coming to see you and helping you make the move."

Carol flew out alone since Cam and I couldn't get away. She had fun helping with their auction, necessary because the new apartment was much smaller than their house. She helped with the move and with redecorating the apartment, and after a week's work flew home and reported her homecoming to her parents: "It was good to see my family again. Don met me with a big kiss and some beautiful roses. I'll bet people getting off the plane thought I was meeting a 'lover' and not a 26-years-married husband. Well, he *is* a lover and he and the boys have surely shown they missed and appreciate me. I'm beginning to realize how important a woman's contribution is in creating a happy family and home, which sometimes gets obscured in this day and age of women's lib."

We continued exchanging letters with her parents, but Carol had a great idea over breakfast one morning, "Don, I know it would help my mother's morale, and probably Dad's if they could hear us and their grandchildren talking with them. Doing so by phone is very expensive and not very effective. Let's buy a modern tape recorder for both our parents for Christmas presents. We could make tapes on which all of us could tell them of our activities. I could record myself playing the piano and singing or the boys playing their instruments. They could make tapes back to us when they felt like it."

"Carol, that's a terrific idea! We used the new recording technology in DOC." We followed through with the plan and Carol's parents really enjoyed it. Although my parents were great talkers, they were a little intimidated by the microphone. Winifred liked it so much she wanted to keep all the tapes rather than recording over old messages. On our first recording for our parents, Carol and the boys played and sang Christmas carols.

Winifred's life proceeded smoothly for awhile, until we noticed disturbing changes in her behaviors. One morning over breakfast, Carol voiced her concerns, "Mother has been going downhill. She's no longer answering my letters and seldom says anything on their tapes so I want to go out there and see what's going on. Ginny Elliott wants to go see her father so she suggested we fly out together."

"I wish I could go with you, but I can't right now. I know you're competent to go by yourself, but it'll be a safer journey if you and Ginny go together."

Carol's concerns were well founded. She filled me in; "Mom is getting more forgetful. She has trouble taking care of their apartment and getting meals. Sometimes she gets part way through a task, or something she's saying, and then gets confused. Sometimes she doesn't remember the name of someone she knows in their apartment building. She seems to stay consistently between discouraged and depressed. It's hard to tell whether her meds are helping and whether she takes them regularly or not. Thank goodness Dad is with her most of the time. I suggested hiring a cleaning lady and going for walks but couldn't persuade Dad. If Mom continues to get worse, they won't be able to continue living as they are now."

"I know how frustrated and helpless you feel, Carol. Keep communicating with your father and maybe he'll respond to some of your suggestions. If things keep going downhill we could both go out later this summer to size things up and discuss it with your father."

Several weeks later we got a heart breaking letter from Eugene: "I guess you could tell by Winifred's telephone conversation that she imagines things about having to move. She just seems lost, and does the queerest things. I know I lose my temper at times, and wish I could restrain myself, but she provokes me to no end and sometimes I just blow up at her. She often gets up early in the morning. Yesterday morning I discovered she'd started to cook something and then forgot it. I found it before it caught fire. People here tell me I should put her in the Presbyterian Manor, but I just can't bring myself to do that. She'd never forgive me for deserting her – she'd be so lost. No one seems to realize how much she depends on me, even though she might be better off without me."

Carol cried as I tried to comfort her, "I knew she was getting worse but kept praying she wouldn't get this bad. Don, I have to go out there immediately to help Dad decide what to do."

"Let's both go! We're partners and we'll deal with this problem together."

We saw immediately that the current situation couldn't continue. Winifred looked bewildered and frazzled, nothing like her usual self. And Eugene seemed agitated yet exhausted from trying to care for her. I said, "Carol, it isn't just Winifred's increasing problems, but also Eugene's inability to control his own frustration and anger. His frequent angry, negative reactions to her actions and inactions scare and anger her, and make her feel he no longer cares for her. That just makes things worse."

With great reluctance and sadness, Carol and her father arranged with the doctor to move Winifred to the Presbyterian Manor, a pleasant nursing home with a good reputation, near the edge of the KU campus. We stayed for another week, trying to ease both through the tough transitions. We spent most of our time with Winifred as caring companions, trying to help her adjust and find some pleasure in her new environment. We also tried to help Eugene understand the need to change his reactions to Winifred's atypical behaviors. The staff seemed kind and sympathetic, so we hoped for the best.

Back home in Happy Valley, Carol monitored Winifred's situation through frequent lengthy telephone conversations with her father and nursing home staff. They reported that Winifred wandered around a lot, frequently going into the rooms of other patients and sometimes taking things. One thing was clear from their reports: Winifred was not improving or adjusting well to her new environment and no one had a satisfying explanation why that might be.

Carol needed answers so several months later we flew back to Kansas for a visit. Carol said, "I want to talk with Mom's doctor to hear his views about how things are going and what caused her illness. If it *is* Alzheimer's, I need to know."

During our long conversation with him, the doctor said, "We haven't diagnosed your mother's illness as Alzheimer's. We suspect it resulted from other cumulative influences such as hardening of the arteries, or multiple infarct damage over the years. Her long history of uncontrolled self-medicating may also have had some influence. The only way to absolutely diagnose Alzheimer's is through brain autopsy after death."

Afterward Carol said, "His explanation is somewhat reassuring, but leaves me with a lurking fear I might have a genetic vulnerability."

I tried to reassure her, "Carol, research about genes and a potential genetic link to Alzheimer's has barely begun. So far there's no solid scientific evidence of genes causing Alzheimer's. There is some evidence that it occurs more frequently in some families than others, but that doesn't necessarily mean that's caused by genes. Families differ in lots of ways. For example, Winifred's mother didn't have Alzheimer's. You've lived a healthier and much different life than your mother, so there's good reason to be hopeful about your future."

On that visit, we concentrated on observing the nursing home staff at work, including their interactions with Winifred. We deliberately varied the hours we spent there so the timing would overlap shift changes. Winifred seemed less restless and confused when we were there. She walked or dozed peacefully, holding Carol's hand, and smiled when we arrived to visit.

After several days of monitoring, I said, "Carol, the staff's primary role is to care for the medical and health needs of their patients. Their care activity is shaped more by staff work schedules and workload than individual patient needs or desires. The staff is nice, caring and capable, but shifts are typically understaffed and over worked, with too many duties for too many patients, with almost no time to try to enrich their daily life.

Have you noticed that most of the time your mother is alone with nothing to do? When she has something interesting to do she perks up and enjoys it. We've seen three examples during our time here. When you play the piano and sing for her, she smiles, her eyes sparkle, and sometimes she laughs or waves her hands in rhythm. She likes sitting at the piano with you while you play. When I talk about the boys' families and show her pictures of them, she focuses and sometimes comments, smiles or points. When your Dad takes her in the car to get Kentucky Fried Chicken, she clearly enjoys it.

I'd be bored as hell with nothing to do or accomplish all day, unable to converse with people, and no one to interact with in a friendly way. I'd probably invent things to do to brighten my life, like Winifred wanders around from one place to another and investigates the rooms of other patients. Or who knows, maybe she believes in that moment that she's at home and thinks the things she takes are hers. It seems that most of the focus is on what these patients can no longer do. My decades of professional and scholarly experience have shown me that people with limitations of all ages have more capabilities and interests left than others usually realize."

During the flight home we both reluctantly agreed that there was no way we could change things for her parents now. We had to focus on making their lives as satisfying as possible within their current contexts and limitations. That day as we flew home, I made a silent vow to myself: *If Carol ever has Alzheimer's, she won't end up like Winifred. I'll invent ways of providing a meaningful and pleasurable life using capabilities she has left. And I'll see to it that she's treated like a person, not a patient!*

Carol phoned her father and talked with her mother's nurse several times a week. She tried to keep his morale up and to get his views about Winifred's condition. He reported she now spends all her time in bed. The nurse kept Carol informed about her mother's slow decline.

One day I came up from my study for our morning coffee break and found Carol sitting at our breakfast table crying. I got us both a cup of coffee and said, "What's wrong, Honey?"

She sobbed, "I just talked with Mom's nurse. She said Mom is fading fast and won't last longer than 2-3 weeks. I knew this was coming but it's so hard to think of her as gone."

I sat there quietly, gently holding Carol's hand while she gained control of her emotions. When she felt like talking, I got us each a piece of raspberry Danish which we ate with sips of coffee (eating something often helps a stressed person relax). I said, "Carol, this is the first time in our lives we've had to face such a loss. I share your grief and as we've always done in our marriage, we'll cope with it together."

With a big sigh Carol said, "I think I'd better begin making preparations for Mom's funeral so I'll be ready when the time comes. I want to plan for music I know Mom would like and I'll need your help finding the recordings I choose."

A week later she called her father and reported, "I'm creating a recording of beautiful and appropriate music I know Mom would like to be played at the funeral. What I've done is pick out a variety of Mormon Tabernacle Choir pieces to be played as people are gathering, ending with Tennessee Ernie's *The Old Rugged Cross* and *How Great Thou Art.*

Then words by the minister and others can be said. After that, as people are leaving, the other side of the tape can be played. There are two long choruses – two of my favorites that I've sung with our Choral society and that Mom liked. The first is from Bach's *St. Matthews Passion*, and the second from Brahm's *German Requiem*. Cam is recording all of this music for us. As soon as it's finished I'll mail you a copy of the tape so you can listen to it."

Carol's mother died September 6, 1981. Carol struggled to maintain her composure through all the rituals of a funeral, and the condolences of family and friends. In the privacy of our room after it was all over, I held her in my arms for a few hours as we grieved together. In a phone call home we learned Pam and Doug's baby girl was born on Winifred's birthday, September 7. That brightened our hearts. While flying back, Carol said, "Mom would be pleased to think her life on this earth was replaced by a new life in the form of a great-granddaughter. Mom's maiden name was Campbell so Pam and Doug named their daughter Lindsay Campbell Ford in her honor."

As soon as we got home, Carol went to help Pam for a few days. She wrote her father: "Lindsay is a good little thing. She's so tiny it's hard to believe, like a little bird. Pam's recuperating very fast; she feels a little stronger every day.

The hardest thing I've had to do since Mother went into the Manor was leaving you last Thursday. I wish I could have stayed awhile with you. I don't know if that would have helped you, but I would have felt better about it. My 'talents' are of use here as well. A new baby and a toddler are a lot of work and need lots of attention.

I've been slowly getting back to 'business as usual' – each day I feel more rested and not so weepy. We're eagerly waiting to hear when you can come out and visit for a while."

Chapter Twenty-Six
Paradise and Pathos

Eugene flew out and spent two weeks with us in October. His visit was good for all of us, but particularly for Carol and her father. Being together helped them adjust to their loss. After returning home, he wrote: "Gee, it was a beautiful flight yesterday, and a non-stop one from Pittsburgh to KC. They gave us lots to eat and seconds on coffee. Well, I can tell you and everyone I enjoyed my 17-day vacation in Pennsylvania and all the wondrous new things and people I saw. Bless you all, have fun, but don't spoil the little ones."

Carol replied: "Today is Mother's birthday and it seems odd to have it go by without sending a card or something. Sometimes it seems so unreal that she's not here anymore and there are times when I feel she's really very near me. She's always with me just as all my loved ones are, not physically, of course, but in my mind where I live."

Carol's father responded:

"Don's mother sent me this verse after Winifred died. I feel better each time I read it. Perhaps it will help you:

Along the golden streets a stranger walks tonight
  With wonder in her heart – Faith blossomed into sight.
She walks and stops and stares, and walks and stares again,
  Vistas of loveliness beyond the dreams of men.
She who was weak and feeble and shackled to a bed
  Now climbs eternal hills with light and easy tread.
She has escaped at last the cruel clutch of pain,
  Her lips shall never taste that bitter cup again.
Oh, never call her dead, this buoyant one and free,

> *Whose daily portion is delight and ecstasy.*
> *She bows in speechless joy before the feet of Him*
> *Whom seeing not, she loved while yet her sight was dim.*
> *Along the golden streets no stranger walks today,*
> *But one who long, long homesick is home at last to stay!"*

We had fun with the members of our family who were with us for Thanksgiving. We didn't have our traditional family gathering on Christmas day. Instead, we celebrated Christmas with each on the day they could be with us. The tight bonds of our family had weakened a little as each son built his own family. We'd recommended they establish their own holiday traditions because it's part of the glue that holds families together. We also told them we'd like to shift from being thought of simply as parents to also good friends.

Our sons had returned with their families to their own nests and Cam was with the Blue Band at the Bowl game, so we were alone on New Year's Eve. I decided to revive the custom we had years ago of a private party during the holiday season, so I said, "Carol, we're alone again at last! Would you join me in a private New Year's Eve party of fun and frolic?"

Carol replied, "Fun and frolic with you would be a great way to begin the New Year!"

"You always wanted to see Hawaii so let's dress Hawaiian and have a pretend party." "What a marvelous idea – I know just what to wear!"

While she devised her Hawaiian-style surprise, I donned a flowery shirt, built a cozy fire, sat our snacks on the coffee table and started music playing. Our traditional tailgating drink was a tasty mix of frozen lemonade, blended whisky and water, and that seemed kind of tropical.

Carol called, "Are you ready?"

"I'm eagerly waiting!"

She danced the hula from our bedroom wearing a fake grass skirt and a bra made of coconut halves. I nearly fell over laughing!! Years ago, her Women's Club singing group had included a skit in one of their shows using such costumes and Carol kept hers. She gave that hula skirt a workout as she swayed towards me, winked and said, "I could use a drink." She lifted her glass in a toast, "Here's to the warmth of Hawaii with my lover."

"And here's to snorkeling with my Hawaiian sweetheart, with or without her grass skirt."

We laughed and ate some snacks. We talked about the origin of her interest in Hawaii, mostly from movies featuring the swimming star Esther Williams, and what she imagined seeing and doing there. I knew better than anyone what a good imagination she had! I said, "If I play some Hawaiian music, will you demonstrate your hula dance?"

"I'd love to entertain you."

I started the music and watched her invent a routine from her long history of singing and dancing. She really made the skirt move and allowed an occasional tantalizing peek at shapely thighs. Finally, she swished her way to the couch, puffing a little, and I refilled our drinks.

I said, "Where did you learn to hula?"

"When our Women's Club group did that skit, a gal who'd been to Hawaii taught us."

I gave Carol an unopened Christmas card and said, "Here's a gift from Santa we missed." Curious, she opened it and discovered round-trip tickets for a two week vacation in Hawaii beginning at the end of January.

Her mouth dropped open with surprise, then she grabbed my neck and said, "Oh Don!!" while kissing my face all over.

We discussed our trip after she wiped the lipstick off my face. Then, I put on some Glenn Miller music and we danced together. After a few minutes, Carol said, "This darned coconut bra doesn't work very well for couple dancing." She took it off and sighed relief, "That's better!"

"Oh yeah," I said, "much better!!"

We'd always found that dancing was the best foreplay going, so we danced into our bedroom and topped off the New Year's celebration in our traditional way. As we snuggled together later, secure in our love, Carol said, "You've made another of my dreams come true."

Before drifting off to sleep, I murmured, "That's been my goal since I married you."

We began our Hawaiian vacation in February. It was both exciting and disturbing to see from the air what the Japanese saw when they bombed Pearl Harbor and brought America into WWII. When we checked into our Honolulu hotel, we found a bottle of champagne waiting for us courtesy of Doug and Pam. Carol said, "The first thing I want to do is to go to the beach, swim in the Pacific Ocean and snorkel." So that's the way we spent our first afternoon.

The beach was fine sand, the water perfectly clear and shallow for considerable distance. The diversity of small, colorful fish amazed us both. There were no waves to speak of so the water was perfect for swimming, snorkeling, and chasing each other. After an hour we lay on our blanket soaking up warmth from the sunny blue sky. Carol said, "It feels so good to finally be warm after the zero-degree temperatures we left at home. I've always been afraid to swim with my face in the water, but I can see why you like it because I love the colors and activity visible while snorkeling." After lazing on the beach, we snorkeled some more, dressed, ate a light supper and went to bed early, worn out from flying and frolicking in the ocean.

The next morning early we headed to a state park on the north coast of Oahu. We were so early the park wasn't officially open yet. There were no barriers so we went in and had the whole park to ourselves for two hours. It featured a great variety of beautiful tropical plants, flowers, birds, insects, sounds and smells. Carol said, "There's a path leading into the interior, let's follow it. Almost all these trees, plants and flowers are new to me. I'm in awe of Mother Nature's artistry here. She's created a wonderful tapestry of shapes and colors, and there's a small stream meandering through it! It makes my hands itch to paint what I see." After exploring for awhile, she said, "There's a waterfall ahead where the pathway curves to the right." It was fifteen or twenty feet high with a lovely, clear pool surrounded by pretty plants.

I said, "Carol, there's no one here so let's cool off in the pool."

She laughed and said, "I hope we don't get caught!" We stripped to our undies, swam over and stood under the waterfall. Carol said, "Being part of this beauty is like living a fairy tale. This moment will stick in my memory." Later, we dressed and returned to the entrance.

The park entrance area was officially open and had scheduled some small historic presentations to start the day. We watched a group of young Hawaiians perform the hula like it was before Christian ministers banned it. I nudged Carol and whispered, "I liked your New Year's Eve performance better." She bonked me in reply and pretended to ignore me.

The next morning we drove to a beach on the west coast of Oahu, known for its great snorkeling and varieties of beautiful fish. We were early birds again so the beach wasn't crowded. That beach wasn't as nice as the one in Honolulu, but the swimming and snorkeling were superb. While eating lunch, Carol said, "It's a glorious experience, swimming through schools of such beautiful fish and not scaring them away. The next time we camp at our lake I think I'll try snorkeling. What's next on our agenda?"

"We'll visit the Polynesian Cultural Center."

"I've read about that and suspect it'll be a highlight of our vacation."

Carol was right. The center was a memorable experience. The Polynesian culture and lifestyle had been reproduced in great detail. The demonstration I enjoyed most was when they invited volunteers from the audience to learn how to do the hula. I nudged Carol and she volunteered along with three other women. I was impressed because the movements aren't nearly as effortless as they look. The audience applauded enthusiastically and the volunteers grinned and bowed. Carol said, "WHEW! I might include that in my morning exercise routine."

That evening we enjoyed a buffet dinner, then watched an ancient ceremony using replicas of prehistoric boats transporting Hawaiian royalty to special occasions. Carol described our next stop to her father: "We boarded a small plane at Honolulu, made a stop at Maui (where we'll go last) to pick up passengers and then flew to Hilo (they call it the Big Island). Cousin DeEtta met us with beautiful real flower leis. It was fun visiting with her, Roy, and their multicultural adopted children. They're a fascinating family. The next day we drove up to the volcano which is a desolate, awesome experience. Today, when their family gets back from church, they're taking us to the Kona coast on the opposite side of the island which apparently is their version of farm land. Tomorrow we fly to Maui for the rest of our stay."

The first day at Maui we visited a picturesque village located on a small harbor. We bought a fresh pineapple, a chunk of cheese and some crackers, and then went to a good snorkeling spot about half way back to our apartment. After stripping to swim suits, we sat our lunch under a shade tree and went snorkeling. The water was too shallow for swimming but we floated around and snorkeled through an interesting terrain of rocks, sand, and marine life.

After half an hour of snorkeling, I heard Carol cry out. She was about fifteen yards from me, standing on a flat rock crying as if her heart were broken, tears pouring down both cheeks. "Oh Don, I've lost my wedding ring! I don't know how or where; I know I had it on when we got here. It must have come off when I reached under water to pick something up."

I looked around at the wild mixture of rocks and sand and thought, *There's no way we can possibly find that tiny thing.* But I had her point out the area where she'd been snorkeling and told her to stay on the rock so she wouldn't accidentally step on the ring. Then I slowly snorkeled through the area she identified. After ten minutes of searching, I spotted her ring resting on a tiny pile of sand. I couldn't believe my eyes! I retrieved the ring and gently slid it onto Carol's finger, where it had been for so many years. We both broke down and cried with relief. I said, "Carol, you always say after solving one of our problems at the last minute that someone up there must be looking after us. Now it's my turn to say that to you. Finding your ring in this mess is incredible!"

Drained from the excitement, we waded to the beach and settled on our blanket under the shade tree. I cut chunks of fresh, sweet pineapple and cheese and served them with crackers and ice cold Cokes. Carol was still a little tearful, "That experience has taken the fun out of snorkeling for now. I'd rather sit here with you and enjoy a quiet lunch in this beautiful place."

She nibbled a chunk of pineapple while staring at the ocean, "That wedding ring is my most important treasure. I'm astonished you found it, and so happy you did! You continue to be my magic man, working your miracles."

For our last day in Paradise, I planned what I hoped would be a nice finale. A road circles the outer edge of the island, but there are no roads into the mountainous interior. Because of the mountainous terrain, several high waterfalls empty into the ocean. We rented a car and drove to the other end of the island. A few miles from road's end I pulled over and said, "We'll need to hike to a special place the guy at the store told me about." I carried our blanket and lunch as we made our way up the rocky slope. After about twenty minutes we broke through the forest to face a high waterfall. Carol drew a deep breath and held it, speechless at the sight. Her eyes took in the mountain top waterfall and followed its path down to the ocean.

"I don't know which is more beautiful – water rushing down from the mountain, that tumbling stream and pool, or that second waterfall pouring into the ocean! The sound of it is Mother Nature's symphony!" I stood back watching her shining eyes absorb the view.

Finally, I led her to a flat ledge beside the pool and spread our blanket there. We threw our shoes aside and dangled our feet in the pool, relishing the flow of water over and around them. With a sudden burst of exultant laughter, Carol said, "I can't believe I'm seeing this! It's amazing, and I'm a part of it! What an astonishing experience!"

We took our cold feet out of the water and dried them briskly before slipping into our shoes, then sat in silence for a while, warming ourselves in the sun. Finally, I unpacked our lunch and a thermos of cold water. We ate and talked, accompanied by bird songs and water sounds before heading along the stream towards the upper falls. Reluctantly, we finally hiked back down to the road because we had a long, slow drive back to civilization. As we drove the winding road, we saw three more glorious waterfalls along the way.

We flew home to Pennsylvania and wintry weather the next day. On our first night back in our own bed, we snuggled against the chill and Carol summed up our trip, "It was a long, tiring trip to Hawaii and back, but worth it. We made memories that will last a lifetime."

The rest of the year followed our usual pattern of Carol working in her shop, my teaching and research, yard work, and communications with our sons. We enjoyed a few positive high spots, such as trips to Kansas to visit my family and Carol's dad. We bought Eugene a light blue jacket that looked stunning with his silver white hair, and took him to his high school class reunion. We had great fun watching *him* have fun! We enjoyed a long weekend camping at the Jersey shore with Russ's family, and relished that time with our grandson, Josh.

Carol wrote her father about other summer events: "We had what has become our traditional backyard 4th of July celebration. We had at least 50 people. Cam and his dance band buddies brought their instruments and played for the crowd before the games. Everyone brought covered dishes and we provided the rest. There was the usual volley ball, badminton, croquet, ping pong, and we had one competition race – carrying an egg on a fork relay. Many of our old friends are too decrepit to play the games and would rather sit and gab. It's fun to have the young folks around to liven things up.

We had a wonderful week of camping and boating at Raystown Lake, mostly by ourselves with occasional family visits. By dumb luck we got the best camp site in the whole darn campground this time. We're set off from the other campers – have a large expanse of mowed grass around 3 sides of us – the swimming beach is nearby and it's easy for Don to get the boat into the water on a sandy beach. I tried snorkeling but you can't see much in that water. I'd like you to come down here in October since we only have one home game that month."

Carol's father came by bus for a visit. He timed it to see Penn State's first football game of the season. Eugene clearly enjoyed his trips here and liked being around his grandsons. He played Mr. Fixit for Carol every time he visited and was an undemanding guest.

Carol had been having intense pain in her hips and back and riding in a car aggravated it a lot. She'd been through examinations with several MDs and a lot of physical therapy but nothing helped much. I'd been searching for a car that might be more comfortable for her. A friend told me of a nearly new Lincoln Continental for sale in Lemont by a woman whose husband bought it for his work travels and dropped dead of a heart attack less than a year later. I thought a bigger, heavier car might help Carol's back so I bought it. Carol wrote her father: "We picked up our Lincoln last week and what a beauty! I've driven it a couple times and it's so comfortable and quiet. Takes some getting used to managing such a 'boat'."

Our lives had been proceeding uneventfully when my father died suddenly at the age of ninety. A blood vessel exploded and he was dead in a matter of hours. The loss of a parent is always sad, but I was thankful his passing was fast and painless. We made a quick trip to Kansas for his funeral and to console Mom. They had lived together most of their lives and dealt with both triumphs and sorrows. We urged Mom to visit in the spring to meet her great grandchildren.

After our return from Kansas, Carol added another skill to her resume when she agreed to teach a college course. She told her dad: "Last Thursday I was on a panel in a class on 'Courtship and Marriage' that's being taught by one of Don's graduate students. She thinks I'm 'wonderful' and asked me to represent the 'traditional wife and mother' role in talking to approximately 40 students. I was pretty nervous about doing it, but wanted to help her out. It turned out to be fun and the students were very responsive, asking lots of questions."

Eugene told us he'd been watching old home movies from the years he and Winifred were together. Carol wrote her typically encouraging letter in response: "You're having a sentimental journey with the movies and old letters. It must make you nostalgic to see Mother back in the good old days. God, I miss her – never a day goes by I don't think about her and doubt if I'll ever get over the grief of losing her."

We had the usual run up to Christmas. *The Personal Touch* buzzed with customers and we had invitations to lots of parties but only had the endurance for a couple – the Town and Gown Christmas Ball which we still enjoyed, and our couples bridge group celebration that had been a long term pleasure. For the first time in a while, our entire family gathered together for Christmas day. That was a special treat and the boys seemed to enjoy each other.

We started the New Year with the joy of knowing Russ's wife, Lois, was pregnant with our fourth grandchild. Joy turned to ashes in mid-January when Russ called and asked if we could be with him for a medical exam Lois had scheduled. He was scared and needed emotional support, plus help with Josh. When they came out of the exam Russ told us Lois had cancer. As they clung to each other in tears, we took Josh outside to give them privacy in their grief.

That began a sorrowful, demanding and difficult period for Carol. For eight months she periodically spent several days in Harrisburg helping with Josh and Lois, and giving Russ emotional support. Sometimes we kept Josh in our home and I arranged for him to participate in the nursery school on campus. Lois rejected chemotherapy. She was willing to risk her life to protect her unborn baby. Surgery was deemed safe for the fetus so they removed a tumor the size of a small grapefruit. Lois recovered enough to go back to teaching but had to quit after a few weeks. Two months later a small tumor reappeared and was surgically removed. After one period of care in Harrisburg, Carol wrote her father: "I was very tired – emotionally wrung out from it all. It seems like this past month has been too hectic. I enjoyed Joshua and we became much closer. We did have fun and one day as we were playing he looked at me so seriously and said, 'I love you, Grandma'. Well, I just melted like a pan of hot butter."

From spring through early summer, the baby grew and the cancer spread. Finally, the doctors said the baby was big enough to survive if Lois and Russ wanted it delivered surgically. The Caesarean section in April produced a healthy son named Zachary Clark Ford. Russ took care of Lois and the baby at home with some support from home nurses and family.

Back home after one period of care, Carol told me, "Lois's illness is very hard for Joshua. One day he commented, 'I don't like my Mommy, she's sick.' I understood because I can remember how I felt when Mother was sick so much of the time when I was growing up."

One late July morning a tearful Russell called to say Lois was dying so could we come. We rushed down and were there with him when she passed. The funeral was held early in August. Russ was a widower with two baby boys to raise.

All of us needed recovery time, so we took Russell and his boys to the shore for a week. Carol wrote her Dad about it: "We're about to leave our vacation at Wildwood, NJ. We arrived tired and cranky after a long trip of trying to keep 2 babies content and occupied. Thank God for the Lincoln, it's comfort and air conditioning. We stayed in an old beach town double house, but spent most of the time on a nice beach. I'm really tired. The signs of depression are on me. I can't wait to get back to normal life again, but must help Russ while I'm able."

During this sad period, Carol tried to keep up with the rest of her life. When Pam and Doug told us that another grandchild was on the way, Carol focused her thoughts on when Pam might need help. Then she had three root canals and a tooth pulled, followed by a painful dry socket. And, she flew out to see and help her dad, who wrote after her trip: "You're gone and I'm missing you. I hope you had a nice trip to see Russ & Josh & Zach. Then on home to give your lonesome husband and Cam big slobbery kisses, as well as Scooter. Please take care of yourself. In a couple of years won't those two boys have fun!"

During lunch with Ginny Elliott Carol said, "Mother Nature has given me spring in our Slab Cabin paradise to brighten my spirits. At last the sun is shining – what a relief! Every day there's more green in the woods, more flowers blooming, and the stream is full and gushing. It's a lovely scene out our window."

Ginny said, "After what you have been through you need some pleasure in your life."

"I had my women's bridge group here last night. I think we ought to call it a 'therapy group' as the girls are not interested one bit in playing cards. It's getting to be a competition of who can butt in with their story or gripe first and more often. If it wasn't that I've known some of these gals for 30 years and it's the only time I see them, I'd quit.

We gave Don's mother a Christmas present of air fare to come for a visit, with Laurel as her companion, to help her adapt to the loss of her hubby of 65 years. This will be her first time on an airplane so it'll be fun to see how she takes it."

"I remember her. She's the kind of gal I bet will get a big kick out of it!"

"Don took me to Penn State's Hershey Medical Center for a general checkup to see if they could help ease my stress and sleep difficulties."

"Is everything OK?"

"They told me my difficulties were from life style rather than biological. They said, 'However, you have a gall bladder in bad shape, and it could blow up on you on one of your trips and you'd have to have emergency surgery so you'd be wise to have it taken out before that happens'. I remembered my Dad had his gallbladder removed, so maybe it runs in our family. I said, 'Let's do it!' They scheduled me for their earliest opening."

We decided to have our traditional July 4th back yard celebration. It was a big success, although we sweltered in the heat and humidity. We hosted more than fifty people, ranging in age from five months to eighty-two years. Among the activities was an old fashion egg toss that everyone but the smallest kids could play. After cleanup, Carol said, "Our friends look forward to our July 4th party. It's a lot of work, but a great way to enjoy old friends and family."

We gave ourselves an eight-day vacation of camping, boating and swimming at the lake. That was the only truly relaxing activity we had during the summer. But, we had one exciting night that Carol wrote her Dad about: "We had some storm excitement. Don put the sail on our boat and we went sailing across the lake. We saw clouds gathering and heard thunder so Don came about heading fast towards the shore with me protesting all the way; it scared me silly! Later, we were playing our usual gin rummy game when a huge storm hit. All of a sudden we saw this white wall of rain coming down out of the divide to the left of us and I could see down the lake 3 big motor boats hightailing it to land here. I saw one make it; I don't know what happened to the other two. The wind tore the awning loose on our camper.

There's a new baby boy in the family by the name of Ryan Douglas Ford. He took only 4 hours to get here. Pam hardly got to the hospital in time for this one. She came home the next day feeling great. So, at last some good news. We're eager to meet our 5th grandchild."

Fall began with Carol's gall bladder surgery at the Hershey Medical Center. Everything went well, with relatively little pain while she recovered. Visits at the hospital from the Hershey bunch and her curious, affectionate grandchildren really boosted her morale. The hospital stay was brief, partly because we had our easy-riding Lincoln to transport her home.

Several weeks later she wrote her father: "I'm feeling lots better this week. The miracle is that all my back pains are gone. For 2 years I've suffered because all my other docs had the wrong diagnosis. The pain came from my infected gall bladder, not problems with my back.

Getting back into my own life has helped and I sleep better. Tuesday I gave a $2000 donation to the new and struggling Infant Evaluation Program and that was satisfying. The newspaper took my picture with a mother and her Down's syndrome baby for an announcement of my donation. I got to hold him. He was 21 months old but very good and cuddly.

I feel so sorry for parents who have to cope with a handicapped child and realize how lucky Don and I have been. That article inspired people to bring me craft materials. One bonanza came from one of the stores downtown: A whole van load of goodies of all kinds."

Carol's father used the gift of an airplane ticket for a flight to visit us. He waited until fall to attend a football game. His presence helped Carol to return her life to a positive rhythm. Mr. Fixit did some repair jobs and helped in Carol's shop. After returning home, he wrote: "I want to thank you both for a wonderful time during my vacation. Couldn't have enjoyed it more. I was particularly delighted to be there for the big birthday celebration for Carol at your tailgate. It's been a long time since I celebrated her birthday with her."

Carol's reply: "Dear Mr. Handyman – Thank you for your many services while here. Please send the bill to my husband. Doug, Pam and their three kiddoes were here for a nice Thanksgiving vacation. Ryan is very alert for 3-months old. Doug and Pam drove down to Harrisburg to visit Russ and left the kids with us. It's amazing how much better behaved little kids seem to be when their folks aren't around. We had fun with them.

All our families except Martin's were with us during the holidays. The kids and grandkids together made quite a rowdy crowd but we enjoyed every minute of it. We had seven little ones here over night. What a zoo! But, they had fun and looked so cute playing together.

We gave ourselves a swimming pool for Christmas, thinking it would be healthy for us and fun for the grandkids. The same man who built our house agreed to build the pool and greenhouse enclosing it. That way we can swim in it year round with minimal maintenance."

Chapter Twenty-Seven
New Beginnings and Sad Losses

We started 1984 in California. Sheri and Martin picked us up at the Oakland airport and drove us to their new house. We Kansas-Pennsylvania folks were shocked at California's congested housing developments, with houses a few feet apart and hardly any yard. The packed subdivisions and highways boggled our minds. The first night, Carol said, "The traffic is scary to me but Martin is a good city driver – fast and sure. I just close my eyes and try to relax."

The first thing we did was go shopping with the kids to spend our Christmas gift of money to buy furnishings for their new home. We toured the Stanford campus and Martin's office, Sheri's workplace, and explored the sights and scenes of San Francisco. We spent most of the time gabbing about their work and what it was like to live there. They were doing well, enjoying their lives, and we happily fulfilled our role as proud parents.

On the flight home Carol said, "I'm eager to get home. All the holiday activities have been gratifying, but exhausting. I want to get our own lives back to a routine."

"I agree. We left our house in a mess, and have things to do. It's nice to share in our sons' lives, but we need to focus on leading and enjoying our own lives – your arts and crafts interests, my scholarly work, friends, fun at the lake, and new experiences yet to be explored."

"Don, we do have a big event to prepare for. I'm delighted Russ is moving forward after Lois's death. He gave Barbara an engagement ring for Christmas and she'll fit into our family nicely. She grew up in State College and was a classmate of Martin and Doug. We've known her parents for years as faculty colleagues but I never expected them to be in-laws. Russ will sell his current house and they'll buy Barb's house in Hershey. Their wedding is early spring."

"Carol, on top of that, we have two other big things to accomplish in the next six months: Build a swimming pool, and celebrate Cam's graduation from college."

"I'm both excited and a little sad about that last one. Cam has been kind of like an only child as we lived together after his three brothers left and married. That, and the fact he's my last baby, make him special to me and I'll be lonely without him."

"Maybe you won't be without him for a while. The College of Business Administration decided to experiment with accepting some of their best undergraduates into their graduate program. Two of his faculty honored Cam by asking his permission to nominate him for that opportunity and have him as one of their graduate students. Cam finds the possibility attractive, but is concerned because he has absolutely no work experience in the business field."

"That's fantastic! When does he have to decide?"

"If he opts to do this he'll start in the fall, so he'd have to decide by early summer. I'm sure he'll be talking with us about it."

It felt great to walk into our house and have it all to ourselves. We stood with our arms around each other, looking out the wall of windows at our little piece of Happy Valley heaven. Then we went to work. In a few days we'd restored our house to its usual clean and neat state. I wrapped Carol in a bear hug as we sat down for coffee break and said, "Working together like this brings back memories of our newly married lives together."

She laughed, "It *is* fun isn't it. But don't carry those memories too far right now. We still have work to do." So I kissed her and ate cookies dunked in coffee to keep my strength up.

Carol resumed her creative crafting and I resumed teaching, researching and writing. From that base of activity there were occasional variations in the melody of our daily lives. We went to a retirement party for our old friends, Jean and Ted Vallance, and helped launch them on their post-retirement trip to Mexico. We were invited to a special session of Town & Gown and learned it was honoring ex-presidents, including me. We enjoyed catching up with our dancing friends and savored dancing together, something we hadn't had a chance to do for a year.

As I'd predicted, Cam talked to us about his future. He was attracted to the idea of graduate school, but was also exploring possible summer jobs to replenish his bank account and get some business experience. I explained the process of applying for graduate school admission. Carol expressed her pride in him, regardless of what he decided to do.

An important theme underlying our winter and spring activities was preparation for the marriage. Carol accepted Russ and Barb's request that she plan and arrange the flowers for it. Since her shop had prepared flowers for many weddings, that was her cup of tea. I drove Carol to Hershey to deliver the wedding flowers and to touch base with them before the big weekend.

Their wedding was a beautiful and glorious affair, not just the union of man and wife, but also a merger of two cute little girls and two handsome little boys – the creation of a new family.

Carol laughed and said, "That's one way for us to get girls in this male dominated Ford family." We took the two boys home with us and the Guthrie's took the girls while the newlyweds honeymooned. We enjoyed our time with the boys but, as most grandparents would understand, we were happy to return them to Hershey and their parents.

Cam finally made his decision, "I've applied for admission to graduate school and the PhD program in business. I filled out all the forms, passed the Graduate Record Exam that all applicants have to take, and have been admitted. I won't know whether I'll have a graduate assistantship to help finance my studies until late summer, but I have the offer of a summer job with IBM north of New York City and that's the kind of business experience I need before starting graduate school. Now I can focus on final exams for my BS degree."

While Carol and I ate dinner she said, "I've had my nose in the shop for a week getting caught up on orders, but today I made a trip to Altoona for silk flowers. I really went nuts over the sale items so came home with a bundle. Now I'm working on orders and a huge wedding. Betty Coughlin went with me. She likes sewing so I took her to the Roaring River's fabric place and she went nuts right along with me, buying stuff. She told me Milton Eisenhower's daughter died recently of cancer; she was only in her 30s."

"I hadn't heard that. Her loss will be very hard on Milton. I'll write him immediately with our condolences." I thought back over our long history with Milton, planning what to say in a sympathy note, then switched our conversation to a happier topic: "Carol, we've both had our nose to the grindstone since we returned from

California. Would you care to join me on a long weekend date in Pennsylvania Dutch territory down by Lancaster? It's a little early, but we can celebrate our 38th wedding anniversary. Spring should be in full bloom there now."

"I'd *love* to have a springtime lark with my lovin' hubby! We've both felt so tied down and work-worn that this will be a lift. That area has so many craft shops, discount places, and interesting antique auctions – even a wholesale antique store for us to investigate."

I made reservations at a motel with an indoor pool, a place we'd been before. As we drove on a warm morning with a few fluffy clouds floating in a deep blue sky, Carol said, "What a beautiful morning with green fields, pastures with early wild flowers and cows grazing, wild dogwood blooming on the forest edge, and robins looking for a wormy treat. In all our years here, I've never been able to decide which is the prettiest season – spring with its renewing beauty, or fall with its blaze of color." "You left out winter."

She laughed and said, "I'll leave that for Eskimos to admire."

We checked into our motel and went crafting. Pennsylvania Dutch families have diverse ways of earning a buck. One is to create and sell handcrafted items typical of their culture, like quilts made with scraps of material put together in homemade designs. We explored towns named Mascot, Bird in Hand, Blueball, Bareville, Intercourse, and Paradise, stopping to browse at any shop that looked interesting to Carol. She understood and admired the skill needed to create every item. She loved talking to the women about their shops and bought something from each because she wanted to encourage their creativity.

At noon we had a snack at one shop and they told us of a nearby farm that offered Pennsylvania Dutch dinners served family style. We made a reservation for that evening. By mid-afternoon we were hot, sweaty and pooped so returned to our motel for a nap.

After napping, we put on our swim suits and the light cotton robes provided by the motel and went for a swim. We had the pool to ourselves and swam vigorously for a while to get our exercise fix. We stopped for a brief rest and Carol said, "This feels wonderful. Just think, by summer time we'll be swimming every day in our own pool."

"I'll love that as long as I can swim with my 'Esther Williams' wife."

We swam, paddled and flutter-kicked around the pool until we were both waterlogged, then returned to our room to sit relaxing in our robes. I opened a bottle of champagne and poured a glass for each of us, "A toast to my beautiful bride and thirty-eight years of sharing and exploring life as husband and wife!"

She touched my glass and we drank. "A toast to the man who, since our first date forty-three years ago, has made my exploration of life exciting, fun and full of love."

As we sipped champagne, Carol said, "As we drove through towns named Blueball, Bareville, Intercourse, and Paradise I wondered how they were named. I decided they either had a down to earth sense of humor or loved sex."

"Maybe it was both – like me!" She grinned as I gently tucked her into bed so we could celebrate our 38th wedding anniversary.

As we rested with her cheek on my chest she said, "We do make life fun don't we!"

Dinner at the Pennsylvania Dutch farm house reminded me of meals on the Iowa farm with my mother's German family when I was a kid. They went to work at 4 a.m., worked hard for three hours, ate a big breakfast, then worked like dogs until evening and had a huge supper.

Our Pennsylvania farm house dinner was served in a large room with six wooden picnic tables. Each table seated three on each side and one on each end. There were no menus and no waitresses, just plates, cups, glasses, flatware and napkins. After everyone was seated, our hosts sat platters and bowls of steaming food and baskets of fresh homemade bread on each table. Carol's eyes bugged out when she saw the variety – fried chicken, roast pork, salami, mashed potatoes, sauerkraut, cooked mixed vegetables and a few things we didn't recognize! We ate family style, passing bowls and platters around the table as everyone filled their plate. The food was excellent, but the best part was visiting with the people around us. We were all 'outsiders' as the locals called us. For dessert we had three kinds of homemade pie and good strong coffee. As we drove back to our motel Carol said, "There went my diet! I'm stuffed, but it was worth it. No wonder the local women are pudgy."

As we settled into bed, I kissed Carol and said, "Goodnight pudgy." She bonked me and drifted off to sleep.

The next day we went antiquing. Carol bought a couple more glasses for her collection, and some colorful teacups she'd started collecting for table settings at special dinners. We went back to the motel for a nap before another exercise session in the pool. As we sat on the edge of the pool with our feet dangling in the water, I said, "I've saved the best for last."

"I thought yesterday afternoon was pretty good."

"Not that kind of best; this is a night club kind of best. There's a huge, classy hotel near here where well-to-do folks from Philly, Baltimore and DC come to experience this subculture and entertainment. They have a night club where they serve dinner, followed by a variety of performers and comedians, kind of like a modern vaudeville show, and later they have dancing on the big stage used by the performers."

"That sounds great! Let's get dressed and go."

The food was good, the song and dance routines delightful, the comedians hilarious, and dancing to their band a thrill for us. The band preceded each set with an announcement of dance style, such as, big band, waltz, Latin American, so people could choose when to dance. We danced them all, commenting on those we needed to practice, and left when the band quit. We slept late the next morning, ate a big Pennsylvania Dutch breakfast, and headed back up the mountains to Happy Valley.

Our next adventure would be the new swimming pool and green house. Carol described our new pool and green house to her father and justified the expense: "We're making an investment in our health. We'd been toying with replacing our old car. In talking with our contractor, Mike Green, we found we could have an in ground swimming pool for as much as a new car would cost and since we both feel so much better when we do aerobic exercise, and the one we like best is swimming, we decided to put one in.

We'll enclose it in a greenhouse so we can use it all year. This has all happened so fast it makes my head swim (no pun intended). Mike, bless his heart, works for Landscape II who sells pools, so Mike can do the job. I wouldn't agree to it if Mike wasn't supervising the whole thing. He's wonderful to work with and a genius at building.

It will be 16' by 40' and from 3½' on one end to 5'deep on the other – strictly an exercise pool. The entrance will be at the edge of the small brick terrace next to the door into the lower level of our house. If the weather cooperates, Mike says we can have it in by the end of May. Our sons' families are all excited about it and it will be great for all our grandkids. We'll put little life preservers on them and throw them in.

We had a short but sweet visit with Milton Eisenhower last week. Adjusting to his daughter's death from cancer has been especially difficult since his wife died the same way. And now he has colon cancer, going downhill fast. He's been such a dear friend to us, and an important part of our lives since our K-State days."

"Was he the reason you came to Penn State for graduate study?"

"No. In fact, we didn't let him know about that until we arrived here.

We were both proud and teary eyed when Cam graduated with a degree in business the other day. He's such a good student that the faculty invited him to continue for a PhD here and he's doing that. He has a summer job with IBM near New York City.

I've been so stressed and anxious, getting Cam ready and adjusting to the idea of sending him out into the world on his lonesome! But he started his new job and called to say he's all excited about it, said his boss at IBM is great and treats him like an equal. He's having a wonderful experience, but it's hard for his mama to let go and not be anxious."

Carol wrote her Dad: "The swimming pool is done and full of water. We went in for our first dip and it was wonderful. However, we've had to wait until the greenhouse is finished. The end closest to the house has a door and two large windows. The other end has four larger windows. All the windows can be opened to let in fresh air. The roof has two layers of heavy plastic covering it. The two layers are kept apart with a fan constantly blowing air into the space and that provides insulation. It's air tight to keep dirt and bird poop out of the pool and animals from getting in, so keeping it clean will be simple.

We invited Ted and Jean Vallance over for a swim and they liked it. Jean has arthritis but is able to exercise painlessly in the water. We spent yesterday getting in the flower plants and cleaning up the flower beds. We sweat so much we were drenched. We got in the pool twice to cool off and twice more when Jean came over again. I was beginning to feel like a prune, but it's wonderful relief from this heat.

I hope you're seriously considering the idea we discussed of moving here and living near us. We have 8 acres of land and could build a house where you could live as our neighbor."

Her father flew out for a visit and checked out the property where we suggested building him a house. He enjoyed our pool, spent time with some of his great-grandchildren, boosted his daughter's morale, and flew back to Kansas without committing to a move. Carol wrote: "It was lonesome around here after you left and I felt pretty blue that day, in fact most of the week, until my routine took hold again. We enjoyed having you with us so much. We're eagerly waiting your decision."

He replied: "I've decided I'll spend my remaining days on 'Slab Cabin Creek', down where the big owl hoots, and the deer and the antelope play, as soon as you get that house you talked about built for me. My only negative thought is that I'd hate to be a burden to you."

Carol responded: "My concern isn't that you'll be any burden (maybe a loving burden like I was to you all the years you brought me up). But, I don't want you to get homesick for Kansas. However, we can always trek back if'n we're able.

We want you to be as independent as you can be. Every human has that need and I think this way of having you close by, yet in a place of your own, is the answer. The township has approved our plan, so designing the house can begin when Mike gets back from Maine."

One day, when I came home from teaching a class, Carol greeted me with, "Sheri and Martin have presented us with another grandson – Jason Patrick Ford! He missed being born on my birthday by ten days. Sheri's parents are flying out to help when Sheri comes home."

When they got back, Carol invited them for dinner and a report. We sat on the deck after they left and Carol said, "I fixed my delicious beef stroganoff with Caesar salad, green bean almandine and Dutch apple pie because I just had to outdo Betty. She's such a super homemaker! When Bob raved over it and ate like a Kansas hog, that made me feel great. It was nice of them to give us that wonderful picture of Jason and proud parents. I'm eager to see him."

One of the people I hired for the new college was a brilliant young man named John Nesselroade, with a wonderful wife named Carolyn. Over the years he and I found we shared scholarly interests and enjoyed each other socially. We spent many noon hours over lunch, talking about developmental theory and research methodologies, about our personal lives, and we also co-authored some scholarly work. John became an international leader in human development science with a special interest in aging. After I left the Deanship, Carol and Carolyn developed a close friendship. Carol said, "Carolyn is a wonderful gal, and we're alike in many of our ideas and feelings, like 'two peas in a pod.'"

Carol wrote her father: "Last night we took John and Carolyn Nesselroade to dinner at the Elks Club to celebrate their 25th wedding anniversary. John and Don work closely together and like each other and Carolyn and I enjoy each other a lot too. It's rather rare when you find friends where the wives and the husbands enjoy each other equally. They're about ten years younger than we are and have two bright, lovely daughters.

Since we're starting this little development, we thought it would be wonderful to have them as neighbors if they're interested in building a house. We've explored that idea with them and they've decided to do it. They will be your neighbors."

Mike Green agreed to design and build both houses, so the planning began. Of course, electric, water and sewer were prerequisites, so Mike and I arranged for those services to be available when construction actually started.

Our Italian daughter-in-law Pam gave Carol her secret recipe for great lasagna, and I enjoyed the results one night. Carol said, "How do you feel about having eight grandchildren?"

"I like it as long as it's in relatively short episodes. I've been imagining all eight of them in the pool at once – that'll be a hoot!"

"That's good because the list is still expanding. Russ and Barb informed me today that Barb is pregnant. That will make nine."

"That didn't take long! Apparently his boys and her girls weren't enough for them."

"They're calling their expanding brood his, hers, and ours."

I laughed, "Looks like we're on a schedule of adding one a year."

A late fall tradition for years had been driving around the countryside looking for grasses, seed pods, pine cones and similar things in fall colors for Carol to use in fall arrangements. In early November Carol said, "I've had a lot of orders this week. Some people from Delaware came to see my shop and bought $70 worth of stuff. I need more arrangements in fall colors so will you take me on our annual hunt for materials?

We came home with several baskets of nature's bounty. Carol, Cam and I went to the Elks Club for their Thanksgiving feast so Carol wouldn't have to cook.

All of our families came to celebrate Christmas – nine adults and 8½ grandchildren. Doug and Pam came mid-December so they could go to NYC for a Van Gogh art exhibit while we took care of their kids. Russ's brood stayed with us through Christmas day, then Martin's brood replaced them. We changed so many beds so often that we all began calling our place 'The Hot Bed Hotel'. Carol said, "Having all the little kids here together was a wonderful Christmas gift for me. They surely enjoyed each other and they're so cute together. They got a big kick out of swimming at Christmas time."

Carol wrote her father: "The highlight of our time with our adult kids was New Year's Eve at the Elks. Dancing to big band music, getting a little buzzed on champagne, teasing each other, seeing how high we could stack our empty champagne glasses, and finishing with a huge brunch at 1 a.m. made for a great evening. It's fun to have our kids look up to us as the best dancers on the floor! And they all have a great sense of humor."

Over breakfast on a sunny, below zero January morning, Carol said, "Getting that new house built and moving Dad out here from Kansas will take a lot of our time this year, but I don't want that to interfere with our other pleasurable activities. For example, I want to spend considerable time with our family of babies this year. I sure don't want to miss their babyhood because that's the time I enjoy most of all. But it takes a good bit of time to go see them or to have them here. We'll probably need to help a little when Barb has her baby.

Then there's my shop, your book and teaching, staying involved in our sons lives, keeping our home and gardens in good shape, sharing time with our friends, and having time just for us.

And time seems to go so fast each day. I sometimes feel a little overwhelmed and anxious thinking about it all. I think it would help me if we could set some priorities."

I nodded, "I know the feeling and agree with you. Let's take the biggy first – the house and moving Dad. All the legal things are done. Mike can't start building until the ground thaws so that means March or April. We can't do much until he gets it under roof and needs decisions about interior finish, appliances, floor coverings etc., and that probably won't be until July.

So, we should focus the next six months on other things. We should probably go see your father by early spring to help him get started on making the arrangements for moving. He has a lot to do. We might plan on a week of travel, working with him, and a visit with my mother."

"That makes sense. Maybe I should focus on building up a supply of materials for my shop and creating an inventory for sales during these cold months so I don't have to spend as much time on that later in the year."

"And I should use the first part of this year to finish my book. The editor wants the completed manuscript by July. Could you look into a flight schedule for a trip to Kansas around the end of February or early March?"

"Yes. And you could arrange a trip to the Lancaster area in early to mid-February so I can buy craft supplies, and we could also have some fun."

"I'd like that."

She wrote her Dad: "We took a 3-day weekend trip to the Lancaster-Reading area last weekend for a little break and to visit craft shops and outlets for ideas and supplies. I had fun and Don enjoyed it too. Sunday afternoon on the way home we stopped to see the Hershey kids. The little ones were excited to see us and we loved them to pieces. Barb is big as a barn and has a week to go. So, now I'm all excited and motivated to go gung-ho in the shop. I saw lots of ideas – now all I need is time, energy, and customers."

We flew out to Kansas the beginning of March to clean up Dad's apartment and help him make a list of everything he had to do before the move. We drove to Marysville for a brief visit and then back to Lawrence for discussing Eugene's legal arrangements. As we flew back, Carol said, "I feel a lot better about his move now. He'll stay busy the next few months and seems excited about it."

He wrote a few days later: "You're gone, yet your efforts linger on. I do appreciate all you did for me, from the toe-nail clipping, to organizing my planning for the move, to the delicious beef stew. What a difference you young folks make."

We'd been home from Kansas two weeks when Barb delivered a boy named Jordan Andrew. We took their kids while Barb recovered. Carol wrote her father: "We had fun with the kids last weekend and Barb and Russ really appreciated the quiet time. They had fun helping me with my 'sales' and swimming (we heated the pool for them). They're such loving kids.

We heated and opened our swimming pool April 7th and on sunny days it was pleasantly toasty in there, plus the exercise made us feel great. During a happy hour on our deck Carol said,

"I'm really busy in my shop, with lots of orders and walk-in customers. I do enjoy visiting with my customers while they shop. It keeps my life interesting. The old ones who've been coming back for years I know pretty well by now. Last year I created a new kind of gift by taking a wedding announcement, decorating it with pretty little flowers, and framing it. It's so popular, making them has become a manufacturing process. That's no fun so I've stopped making them."

Hearing that, I almost strangled on my drink from laughing, "Your decision to stop making something because too many people want to buy it reminds me of the time when we were in grad school and went to that old store on College Avenue to buy a garbage can. Our friends told us they were good and cheap. When we got there they didn't have any. You asked the old guy who owned the store when they would have some more. He replied, 'We've stopped handling them because people bought so many we couldn't keep them in stock.'"

Carol laughed at the memory and said, "I'm still making lots of money. I've made two contributions of $2000 each from my recent sales to support the start-up of two new programs. One is called *Second Wings*. They're helping retirees find part time jobs when their social security or meager incomes aren't covering their needs. My contribution will help them incorporate and get a tax number so they can apply for a grant. The second is *The Women's*

Resource Center's program focused on preventing child abuse and helping abused kids'"

To celebrate Mother's day, Cam and I took Carol to see *Amadeus*, the academy award winning movie about Mozart. She loved it. Afterwards we took her to the Elks Club for dinner. It was fun listening to Cam talk about his graduate work and tell funny stories about students.

Our swimming pool quickly became quite popular with friends. We had Helen and Evan Pattishall (my replacement as Dean) over for a swim followed by cocktails by the pool and dinner. Helen was Carol's down to earth kind of gal. They teased me mercilessly because Helen was taking one of my classes. The Vallances also came for a swim and hamburgers. Carol had encouraged Jean to swim frequently to ease her arthritis pains.

Then we got sad news. Carol wrote her father about the end of an era we treasured: "Don and I were so distressed and saddened to learn that Milton Eisenhower died. We've been friends for nearly 40 years. Then Penn State's Director for religious affairs, an old friend of Milton's and Don's, came to see Don. He explained that in anticipation of dying, Milton asked him to guide the arrangements for a memorial ceremony in State College after his death, and asked that Don give the eulogy. Don was speechless, honored and tearful.

Don's message was well received and President Jordan asked for a copy to be used with alumni. After the service we went to a small, private luncheon at President Jordan's home. I was pleased because I wanted to get to know Mrs. Jordon a little better."

By mid-summer we had to work on Dad's house. My job was to find and buy the kinds of appliances needed. Carol's job was to handle what I called 'decorating stuff' like choosing colors, fabrics and rugs for the interior finish. Even without furnishings, the house looked great. The top floor was designed specifically for Carol's father with entry off a deck. Inside to the left was his bedroom with a sink and full bath. To the right was a large 'great room' with a window wall looking out onto the stream and into the woods. We created a kitchenette, small dining area large living room, and another big room for his pool table, work bench and other activities. The lower level was a 3 bedroom apartment.

One autumn evening while enjoying lightning bugs dancing, Carol said, "Mike and I walked through the house today and talked about his timetable for finishing it so we could plan Dad's move. Mike said he could finish it soon so Dad he could move in the first week of October and live there while the lower level is finished. Can we manage that?"

"Dad says his packing is nearly done and he has a tentative agreement with a moving company. We'll have to go out and help him with finishing touches and loading. He wants the three of us to drive back here in his Subaru. I can arrange that in my schedule, can you?"

"Let's do it! I'll work out the schedule and other details with Dad on the phone."

Eugene moved into his new home the first week of October. A few weeks later Carol said, "Dad loves it! He really enjoyed the combined house warming and celebration of my 58th birthday with friends and family getting a tour of his pad. It didn't take him long to get acquainted at the Senior Center down town where he frequently eats lunch and has made new friends. I stifled a laugh when he described the widowed ladies seeking to sit beside him and offering him their desserts. I doubt if he realizes their intent."

I chuckled "As an ex-farmer, he loves using our tractor to mow and for other labors. He's gained a reputation as resident pool shark by regularly beating his son-in-law and grandsons at pool. Tailgate parties and football games with the family are high on his list of activities. In short, your Dad has quickly adjusted to life in Happy Valley and didn't miss a beat."

When the lower level of Dad's house was finished, we rented it to a delightful, newly married couple, Patty and Ed Satalia. Dad gushed, "Patty is the prettiest woman I've ever seen!!" I thought, *Look out Ed*!

We revived our old pattern of regular family gatherings for Thanksgiving and Christmas dinners. Grandpa enjoyed his grandsons' families. Since his parenting experience involved only one girl child, being part of our big bunch on a regular basis was a whole new ballgame.

Snuggling together in bed New Year's Eve, Carol said, "Our arrangements are working beautifully. Dad seems to like it and his being here has removed the continual burden of worry I carried while he was alone in Kansas. Feeding one more person at dinner is no extra work and he isn't picky about what he eats. He's really enjoyed socializing with our friends. Thank you, Don. Once again you've found a way to make my life happier."

With Carol's worry about her father gone, our lives entered a period of sailing on smooth waters. Eugene wove his presence into our lives in many satisfying ways. We enjoyed happy times with our friends, including periodic parties by my beautiful and skilled hostess. And always, we found delight in our private Slab Cabin home, its gardens and stream, while looking forward to relaxing periods boating at the lake. Our swimming pool had paid for itself many times over by providing fun for the two of us, and socializations with family and friends.

Most important of all, Carol and I were healthy and full of energy. We enjoyed our time together as two aging soul mates who were still happy and in love.

In the summer of 1988, Carol said, "You and your mother have the same birthday and this will be her 90th. I think we should fly out there and wish her a happy birthday because we haven't seen her in quite a while." I agreed so we flew to Kansas and did our best to spread a little happiness around. Mom was failing with age, but still feisty and full of vinegar.

After those happy years of smooth sailing, suddenly and unexpectedly a wave of sadness hit us when Eugene was diagnosed with colon cancer. Beginning when he was a teenager he'd been a heavy cigarette smoker. For decades he smoked two or more packs of Lucky Strike cigarettes a day. In his early fifties he read a frightening story about bowel cancer in the *Readers Digest*. It scared him so much he finally quit smoking cold turkey. His older brother, Carroll, had the same habit and died of colon cancer after several agonizing years. Carol said, "Dad has decided to have that part of his colon surgically removed, despite the fact that he's 89-years old. He remembers Uncle Carroll's agonizing illness. I'm scared but he wants to do it."

Surgery was performed at the end of November. Carol wrote to our sons: "It's been difficult for him, his recovery is slow, and he's still in the hospital. He's beginning to eat some food now, so we're hoping things will improve more rapidly for him."

Several weeks later Carol called them: "Your grandpa seemed to be recovering and then a blood clot produced cerebral damage. That complicated his recovery and caused some paralysis. He struggled for a month but his body finally couldn't take any more and he passed away January 3. He was 89½ years old."

Carol held together fairly well as we took care of necessary tasks but grief finally overwhelmed her when we'd gone to bed. I held her for hours, trying to give a bit of comfort as she sobbed in my arms, heartbroken with her father's death and the awful realization that she no longer had parents to turn to and care for. Over the next few days, friends and family surrounded her with love and attention to support Carol through her grieving.

We arranged for Eugene to be flown to Minneapolis, Kansas for burial. We flew out there and in the company of a few remaining relatives and old friends, we buried Eugene next to Winifred in the prairie community where they both grew up.

He was a WWI Navy veteran, so at the end they folded the flag and placed it in her arms. She held it a moment, gave it back to be used in future Memorial Day celebrations, and then broke down. We sat on a nearby bench where I held her until she stopped sobbing. Then I said, "Carol, we've lost your Mom and Dad, but we have a big, loving family waiting in Pennsylvania for us to come back to them."

She looked at me with a tentative effort at a smile and said, "Then let's go home to them."

As we flew home, Carol said, "I'm so happy Dad could live near us in Happy Valley for the last three years of his life. He told me so often that they were very happy years. But, we were with him daily so it will take quite a long time to adjust to his loss."

Then another blow hit. My mother's health went into a rapid decline and she died peacefully on October 13, 1989 at the age of 91. We flew out to Kansas and joined family and friends in laying Esther Clara to rest next to her husband Herbert Owen in their family plot.

Back home in the quiet beauty of our Slab Cabin home, sitting before a cozy fire, we struggled with our double loss. I reminisced, "We've visited the family home in Marysville every year for 40 years. When her mother died at age 90, Mom said,

'Now I no longer have a home to go home to.' Now I understand what she meant.

After your first Christmas in Marysville with my family, Mom said, 'The good lord surely smiled on you when he led you to Carol. She's very special and I love her dearly."

Carol said, "I never forgot the big red carnation corsage she sent me to wear at your PhD graduation. I came to love my wonderful mother–in–law. I'm so happy she was able to come see our new home. She was thrilled to fly in an airplane for the first time."

Relaxing before dinner I said "Carol, I had a private lunch today with our new President, Bryce Jordan." "I've met his wife, but not him. Why the meeting?"

He thinks the College of Health, Physical Education and Recreation is in bad shape and is considering phasing it out." "WOW, some of my friends husbands are on that faculty!" "I told him that would hurt a lot of people unnecessarily. I suggested 'The College of HDev has a successful history of transforming old programs in ways that fit emerging societal needs. Announce that you are creating a new college named The College of Health and Human Development by merging the two. That will give it a positive spin without criticism of the old college. Make the current HDev Dean head of the new college with the private understanding she is to build new interdisciplinary formats.' He liked the idea. My bet is he will probably do it.

"Don, that would finally make your dream of the integrative College of Health and Human Development originally proposed by the 1980 committee a reality. Knowing you I should have realized you would eventually find some way of making it happen!" I grinned "It is typical that new ideas can't be implemented until current conditions make it feasible. Let's Eat!"

Chapter Twenty-Eight
All Carol's Travel Dreams Come True

One Sunday a friend and colleague called and said he wanted to discuss something with us. Val Delissovoy was a senior professor in our college. He was born in Russia and his father was an officer in the Czar's army. After the revolution, they had to run for their lives for several years through several other countries, finally arriving safely in the United States. He and his wife, Charlotte, were delightful, interesting people we both liked very much.

We met at their home and Val wasted no time on small talk. "Penn State is sponsoring this summer a two and a half week tour of the USSR for alumni. Because of my Russian background, they asked me to participate to provide relevant information and interpretations of what they see and hear. I haven't been there since my family escaped so I'm eager to go. Charlotte and I thought the two of you might like to go and share the experience with us."

We were startled and speechless. Then I said, "Carol, since I was in the Air Force you often said it was a dream of yours to travel and see new places and people. We've done that in the U.S. and Caribbean. Here's a chance to expand that dream to other parts of the world!"

Carol's hand shook as she stirred her coffee, "The idea of traveling through Russia scares the hell out me, but I'd feel safe with Val beside us. I think it would be an astonishing, exciting experience, so I say let's do it!" Experiencing Russia was a fantastic opportunity at a time when it was seeing a dramatic shift away from Stalin's brutal dictatorial government. Carol said, "Let's keep a diary of this trip that we can share with our family when we get back."

"You'd better do the writing because your penmanship is much better than mine."

It was July and hot as blazes. We parked at Kennedy airport outside of NYC and flew to Moscow. It was our first time going through customs so we were a little anxious, and became even *more* anxious when two Russian officials snatched Val and took him away. Carol said, "Don, I'm scared! If they've arrested Val what will we do?"

"We'll stay with our tour group."

We finished customs, waited anxiously, and breathed a big sigh of relief when Val came back alone. Carol asked, "What happened, Val?"

"They keep track of everyone. They knew my Russian roots and interviewed me extensively about my history and why I'm here. You need to get used to the idea that anywhere we go some visible or hidden observers will be keeping track of us."

Our Russian 'tour guide' checked us into a modern hotel and we had our first view of shoddy workmanship while examining our room. Our group always ate and traveled together under the close supervision of 'tour guides'. That first night, Val and his wife visited our room.

He said, "Here are copies of two documents written by Gorbachov's new government. They're being distributed all over the country. They announce and describe two major policy changes aimed at de-Stalinizing the country. The first is named *Perestroika* which describes new and much more open economic and social reconstruction policies. The second is named *Glastnost* describing much greater freedom to openly criticize and communicate about government policies and programs. Their society is very inefficient and has a low standard of living and productivity because its regimentation and rigid controls provide no incentive for a creative work ethic. This is a first step towards trying to change those conditions. It will be interesting to see the people's reactions as we travel around the country."

After they left, Carol said, "We're lucky to be with Val, who can interpret and explain things to us as we go along. He'll give us the straight scoop!"

The goal of our tour guides was to impress us with their country, so we visited many historic and beautiful places like Red Square and the Kremlin, with a museum containing the fantastic jewelry owned by the Czars. As we admired St. Basil's Cathedral,

Carol said, "I've seen pictures of it, but the wonderful shapes and many bright colors of those diverse domes are even more awe inspiring close up. Do they have church services here?"

Val shook his head, "No. Stalin destroyed the power of religious institutions and took their wealth. Fortunately, he didn't destroy their architectural creations and couldn't destroy the religions. People continued to worship secretly."

Evenings we attended music and dance performances. Carol said, "These samples of their culture will be one of my favorite memories. I wish they had shown us some of their famous ballets."

One morning we toured their recently completed Moscow subway. Carol raved, "The beauty and cleanliness of their subway system is astonishing, particularly when compared with the dirty ones we have in the U.S. The architecture and art work in it are wonderful. No wonder they're so proud of it. It's such a contrast to the barrenness of the city in general. There are no skyscrapers but many tall, ugly concrete apartment buildings with lots of windows."

"Carol, I nearly laughed when you asked our guide who washed all those windows and he replied, 'The people who live there are all responsible for keeping them clean.' I thought, *When everyone is responsible no one is responsible. No wonder the windows are so dirty*!"

One evening before dinner we, Val and his wife took a private stroll near our hotel and saw a long line of people in front of a store. Val spoke with one of them and told us, "That store just got a new shipment of cabbages. Food shipments from collective farms are so unpredictable and limited that people rush to get in line when they hear of a new shipment."

The next day we flew south from Moscow to Rostov-on-the-Don near the Black Sea, a port on the Don River. Then we boarded a Russian cruise ship for a 9-day trip up the Don and Volga rivers. The trip covered over 1000 miles to the old city of Kazan east of Moscow.

Our first stop was Volgograd, a large industrial city and port where the Don and Volga rivers meet. German armies laid siege to it from 1942 to 1943, nearly destroying it but failing to conquer it. Around 1½ million people were killed and buried there, the greatest casualty figure in the history of warfare. Those victims are honored in three ways:

The first is a huge, beautiful statue standing vigil as the victor on a hill that changed hands eight times during the siege. The second is a garden-like memorial with a perpetual fire, guarded 24/7 by military guards. The third is an underground memorial museum with music playing continuously, a symbolic grave for everyone who died and were buried there.

Back on our boat, Carol said, "As we walked around that large underground circle looking at displays, tears came to my eyes thinking of the millions of people whose lives were destroyed there because of ruthless leaders. Having seen that, I have no doubt that ordinary Russian people are eager for a peaceful world. They know personally the hell of war because they lost over 20 million people and had massive destruction of their cities in WWII. Since the Germans caused the Volgograd slaughter, I was astonished to realize the beautiful music being played was *Brahms German Requiem,* music I sang with our choral society."

Carol had lived on a farm, so our next stop was an eye opener for her as we visited a collective farm and a home there. Val said, "Smell the fresh paint? They tried to 'dress up' this home to impress us, but most of their dwellings aren't this nice."

Carol responded, "Yes, but those women are proud of their home just like my friends in Happy Valley. I asked a couple of them to show me some of their favorite things and they were obviously pleased." I thought, *Even in Russia, women respond warmly to Carol.*

A colleague from Penn State's College of Agriculture was in our group and said, "They produce lots of good food in these collective farms, but because their infrastructure for storing and shipping to cities is very poor, much of it goes bad in storage and creates food shortages in the cities. Cabbage is the most durable crop in storage so it's the most available in the cities."

Carol's heart was warmed when we visited a *Young Pioneers* (children's) summer camp and played games with them on teams involving both children and us. Carol said, "They were adorable and like children everywhere, curious and friendly."

Much time was spent traveling on our ship where we slept and ate our meals. Evenings they had a good band playing big band music, so we often danced and talked with the young musicians who were eager to hear about life in America. They were particularly interested in cars and couldn't believe anyone could own one and that many people own two.

One evening while I talked with a crew member who was fishing, Carol saw a small elderly man sitting by himself. She thought he looked lonely so introduced herself and sat down to visit. Later she told me, "He's escorted on annual trips like this by his son and daughter-in-law. It turned out he'd been a 'big shot' in the movie industry, serving as head of two major studios during his career. His name is Charlie Prutzman. He personally knew all my favorite movie stars like Bette Davis, Ronald Reagan, Alfred Hitchcock, and Ginger Rogers.

He told interesting, funny, and sometimes sad stories about the movie industry and the people in it. He said, 'The toughest to work with was W.C. Fields. He was a pretty heavy drinker, an ornery guy. Abbott and Costello were also hard to work with but they were my personal favorites because of their ability to do funny movies. People in the entertainment industry can be a troublesome group. Tempers flare and disputes constantly threaten production. Massaging egos, smoothing ruffled feathers and settling disputes were all part of my job.'

I was flattered that he seemed interested in me and my arts and crafts work, and even more so that he considered me beautiful since he had worked with many movie beauties." During our cruise they often enjoyed each other's companionship. By the time it ended, Carol and Charlie Prutzman had become friends. They became 'pen pals' until he died at age 102.

We ended our trip in St. Petersburg, called Leningrad during Stalin's rule. It was built by Peter the Great to give Russia a far north military and commercial port. Most of the USSR (even the southern parts) is farther north than the U.S. St. Petersburg is near the Arctic Circle where there is always daylight during the time of year we visited.

We shopped in their 'best' department store and bought watercolor paintings from street vendors. Several times young Russians stopped us asking if they could buy our American clothes, especially jeans, so there was a tiny bit of free enterprise spirit operating there.

As we flew home, our final gift from Russia was food poisoning. We made the mistake of eating the meal provided on their plane. Its shabby and dirty interior should have been a clue.

When we arrived home, we stopped for a moment on top of Squirrel Drive. Carol breathed a sigh and said, "I realize more fully now what a treasure we have in our life here." We called our sons to check on their lives and share a couple of highlights from our trip. We got a nice surprise: Sheri was over 3 months along with our tenth grandchild!

For several weeks we loafed, worked on our gardens, and swam in the pool every day to relax and get back into shape. One evening, sitting on the deck sipping iced tea and watching lightning bugs dance above our lawn, Carol said, "I've missed being at the lake. Let's go camping for a few days. The weather will be nice all week. I'd like to find some small pieces of driftwood to make things in my shop. All my driftwood designs have been sold."

We spent a week boating, swimming, talking, and exploring for drift wood. Carol beat me four of six games of gin rummy, five of seven games of cribbage, and teased me unmercifully. Back home, relaxed and renewed, Carol said, "We haven't seen the Vallances for quite a while. Let's invite them over for a swim and a picnic."

That weekend, while relaxing with cocktails on our deck, Jean said, "Thanks for the swim; it really helps with my aches and pains. Carol, how's business in your shop since you've been back from Russia?"

"I've decided to cut back by eliminating special orders and being available to customers by appointment only. That will give me more freedom to create and more flexibility in use of my time."

Ted asked "Don, how's your book coming?"

"I finished it. *Humans as Self-Constructing Living Systems*, and the companion book edited by Martin, *Putting the Framework to Work,* were published last week."

Carol added, "Now he'll have more free time too. That will help us to enjoy more of our shared interests, like camping and boating at the lake."

We celebrated the holidays with a houseful of eight grandchildren, three sons, and two daughters-in-law. Sheri and Martin were home producing our tenth grandchild – Kevin Donald Ford. Carol said, "I'll dream of holding Kevin Donald until we get to see him."

I'd been saving a surprise for Carol, so I asked her for a date. "Carol, I'd like to entertain my beautiful wife with cocktails, dancing and dinner before our fireplace Saturday evening."

"I can't think of a nicer way to start the year than with my handsome hubby, and not having to cook dinner!"

Carol wore the rich blue cocktail dress I'd given her for Christmas and I wore my tuxedo. Sitting at a small table before a cozy fire with some big band music playing softly in the background, we sipped our Moscow Mules and I said, "You look like a queen in your gorgeous gown. Could this admiring Knight have the pleasure of a dance with your highness?"

"I guess so, if you hold me close and 'swing and sway' with me."

"I selected *Dream* for this dance because that was a favorite song I listened to while sitting in the enlisted men's club writing my daily letter to you."

"Don, those were fantasy dreams – now we're living them."

The song ended and we shared a gentle kiss before returning to the table. After a little reminiscing, I served dinner – rotisserie chicken, tossed salad and mixed fresh fruit with a small glass of white wine. While eating, we shared memories of our Russia trip. Carol said, "My friend, Charlie Prutzman, said in his annual Christmas card that his trip this year was to Brazil. He makes a trip with his son and daughter-in-law to a different country every year."

"Carol, if we did that, what would be the next country you'd choose to visit?"

"England! I've always been fascinated with its history and royalty, especially since my ancestors on both sides came from England and Scotland."

"Well, I have a surprise for you. My sabbatical leave has been approved. There's a scholar in Scotland doing work relevant to mine and I'd like to use my sabbatical to talk with him. How would you like to turn another of your dreams into reality? We could visit England and Scotland this summer to explore their histories and your family roots."

Carol squealed with excitement, "REALLY? I've fantasized about seeing those historic places but never expected to actually do it. I'd *love* to locate some ancestral homes. Dad had a book someone created about family history that might help us locate my ancestors. But, I wouldn't want to do this in a tour group like we did in Russia."

"I agree. I'd rather create an itinerary of what we'd like to see, make a list of bed and breakfasts where we might stay to get a feel for the folks who live there, and rent a car to explore on our own." So, we planned and created our own schedule and itinerary.

Our first stop was London. After checking into our bed and breakfast lodgings, we went to a local pub for a drink before dinner. The crowd was wall-to-wall, but we found a small table in the corner. I said, "Carol, you guard our table while I elbow my way to the bar for drinks."

I returned to find a man sitting on each side of a smiling Carol, deep in conversation. I thought, *No matter how old Carol gets, she's still a beauty who draws men like flies!* I sat our drinks on the table and said with a mock-frown, "We've just arrived in London, you've already been picked up by two natives, and seem to be enjoying it!"

The Londoners laughed and Carol flashed her dimples at me, "Yes I am! They just got off work to get a beer and this was the only table open."

They introduced themselves and said they were 'tailors'. I couldn't quite make out their accent. "You make suits?" They laughed and said they put down TIALS.

We finally deciphered their accent. They were 'tilers' who installed tile on floors and walls. After a lively hour of beer and conversation, we ate a light supper at our lodging and slept like logs after our long day and introduction to a London Pub.

We'd purchased a car-train package through AAA that turned out to be very convenient. Travelers picked up a car, toured an area, then dropped off the car at a train station, took a train to the next destination, and picked up another car. We repeated that procedure throughout England into Scotland and back through England to the airport. Carol said, "This is so convenient and easy and we don't have to make reservations in advance. I wish we had something like this back home."

We visited important historic sites in London and southwest England. The following is from the diary we kept: *One tour took us through an interesting old residential area. Our tour guide said, "In this house lived a man who became famous as a manufacturer of a new household appliance called a flush toilet. His name was Thomas Crapper and his name became a piece of slang, e.g., 'I have to go to the Crapper' or 'I am going to take a Crap.'"*

Another tour took us through an area of old cottages with thatched roofs. Inside the bedroom of one was an attractive bed with a canopy over it. One woman asked, "Why did they put canopies over their beds?"

"What would you guess?"

"Because the roof leaked?"

Everyone laughed and our guide said, "Thatched roofs provide a nice home for all kinds of insects and small varmints. Imagine yourself asleep in your bed and a mouse or little snake fell from the roof into your hair. Canopies protected the sleeper from such events."

We drove west from London to another bed and breakfast place and explored ancient cathedrals and Roman-built structures, like a Roman bath still existing in a town called Bath. Then we drove to Paignton, Devon, in the southwest corner of England because that had been the home of some of Carol's ancestors. We had written to the current head of a still functioning 12th century church there to schedule a visit with him.

When we arrived the minister was busy with a wedding. Since the old cemetery surrounding the church was empty, we decided to browse around looking for ancestral names like 'Chapin'. Suddenly a small, rotund man appeared from nowhere, introduced himself as a retired postman, and asked who we were looking for.

Carol said, "An ancestor named Samuel Chapin was baptized and married in this church before he emigrated to America in the 1600s."

When he heard the name, his face flushed with excitement and he said, "My hobby is studying the history of this place and recently I've been studying Samuel Chapin! He married Cicely Penny, the daughter of a local merchant. She lived about 2 blocks from here. Would you like to see her home?" He showed it to us, including the still-existing secret tunnel she used to sneak out and see Samuel.

Carol said, "Even then a girl in love found it hard to see her guy!"

The minister and his assistant were delighted to meet us because a century ago the American ancestors of Samuel Chapin had financed the carving of a beautiful reredos, a decorative screen placed behind the altar, from a flawless piece of bier stone. They showed it to us, discussed church history, showed us their ancient Bible, and gave us a tour of the church.

In the middle of one side was a dog door where dogs could enter and leave the church at will. They showed us a worn area of stone on an outside wall and explained that the law required all men to maintain skill shooting a bow and arrow so they'd be prepared if required to join the King's army. They sharpened their arrows on that wall as they practiced.

We thanked them, made a contribution to their church, and drove from Paignton towards Bath to catch a train north. As we drove Carol said, "Don, isn't it wonderful how this country preserves its history? In our country, we tear down our history to build something new. Someday I want to visit Deacon Samuel Chapin's statue in Springfield, Massachusetts. He and a friend started to build that town, the Indians burned it down and they rebuilt it."

We turned in our car and took a train to Stratford-on-Avon, Warwickshire, home of the Royal Shakespeare Company (RSC), touted as probably the most famous classical theatre company in the world. We drove a couple miles south to our bed and breakfast. It was a delightful surprise, a very old house still surrounded by an ancient but dry moat. Allegedly, Shakespeare occasionally stayed there with his friend, the owner. It was furnished with wonderful antique furniture. We were on the second floor where the floor slanted a bit but was safe. Talking with the owner while we ate was a treat. We drove around the area sightseeing, and attended a play in their theater. It was a charming old town, with the Avon River meandering through groves of ancient trees and clusters of old homes, some with thatched roofs.

The next day we took a train to Edinburg, Scotland. As we rode, looking at the scenery and fields of sheep in north rural England, Carol said, "I've never really enjoyed reading Shakespeare's stories or seeing movies made of them, but sitting in that theatre I was deeply moved by his play. I wish Doug and Pam could have been with us to see it."

We toured the great historic city of Edinburg, home for much of the long struggle for dominance between England and Scotland and Mary Queen of Scots. Then we drove northwest to meet the scholar who was the focus of my sabbatical. He and his wife had a picnic lunch with us on their back yard terrace. He and I talked the afternoon away and exchanged some of our work. While our wives had a good gab fest he showed me his on-campus office and gave me a package of his most recent papers.

After our Scotland experiences, we turned in our car and took the train south to York. It's an old walled town located north of London on the east side of England, once occupied by Norsemen around the 7th century. The old Norse town under the current York had been excavated and Carol was dying to see it with her own eyes. We took an elevator down to the ruins and rode a cart through an amazing underground museum.

Our main purpose there, however, was our search for Carol's Clark family roots, so we drove east to Beverly near the North Sea, once the 10th largest town in England, and one of the richest. It was also occupied by Norsemen at the same time as York.

We went there to look up the Clark history, but as we drove into town Carol said, "Look, Don, there's a beautiful cathedral, let's go see it!" We explored in hushed silence, impressed by the hand-hewn beauty and skill in evidence around us. Carol said, "Just look at these beautiful murals, carvings, and statues! The artwork is wonderful!" We saw a repairman working so asked him about its history. He enjoyed telling us:

"This town was full of rich people so they spared no expense in building their cathedral. But, later they got into a big fight with each other and split up. One faction went down to the other end of town and built their own cathedral, just as nice if not prettier."

We toured the other cathedral and agreed that he was right. Carol said with a chuckle, "Nasty arguments within church congregations must be a very old tradition!"

We had information that the Clark family church still existed and the name of a contact. We found the parsonage and talked with the minister and his wife. A scholar studying the history of that church had just recently left, so they gave us the following information:

In the 1600s, Rowley was a small community in the area for which Beverly had a governing role. The congregation of their small protestant church had concerns about the behavior of their minister. It ended in 1639 when Reverend Ezekiel Rogers and about twenty church families boarded a ship and sailed to the Massachusetts colony (some allege they took some of the church money with them). They established another town named Rowley there. Included in those families were Carol's ancestors.

We visited the old 11th century church (which is still used and never locked) and then went to the appropriate office in Beverly and asked to see the three and a half century old records. In a few moments they placed old, worn record books on our table. We spent two hours searching through hand written records for references to the Clark family, including public statements of intent to marry, records of marriages, births, and deaths. Carol said, "I'm astonished they casually gave us these historical records without protecting them, but

I'm moved to read about the lives of these ancient ancestors who carried my genes to the new world."

We drove south past London, turned in our car, and flew home. Carol seemed quieter than usual, staring out the window as we flew across the Atlantic. I said, "Are you OK, Honey?"

She turned to me with tears in her eyes and said, "I'm wonderful. Do you remember when we took your parents to the Atlantic shore and your father stood in the surf with tears in his eyes? He said, 'I dreamed of seeing the ocean but never thought it would happen.' That's the way I feel now about our trip to England. Your plan was perfect and worked so smoothly. I didn't have to worry about a thing because I was with you. You've made every single one of my dreams come true and I love you so much, my magic man!" Back home, we shared our adventures with family and friends and renewed our regular activities.

Then, my Dean called. We sat on the deck drinking ice tea while I told Carol the story, "The Department of Communication Sciences and Disorders moved from the College of Education to our College. Some faculty wanted this move when I started the College, but it was blocked by two senior faculty. Our Dean says it's a mess and begged me to act as temporary head to rebuild it for the future. I'm not interested in getting back into administration."

Carol said, "In your opinion, is it a good idea?"

I grimaced and nodded reluctantly, "Yes."

"Does the Dean have anyone else who could do it?"

"No, it needs a person with clinical training."

"How long would it take you to do it?"

I sighed. "Probably 6-9 months."

"You put a lot of effort into building the college so maybe it's worth another nine months to get this new part going." That response was typical Carol, thoughtful, clear, and to the point, so I agreed to the temporary appointment.

Chapter Twenty-Nine
Trials, Joys, and Travels

Then, the dire consequences of medical misdiagnosis and erroneous treatment hit Carol again. The year before she'd had a benign tumor removed from her leg. She'd never fully recovered and the tumor seemed to be returning. This was quite a blow for an active woman like Carol to absorb. The head of orthopedics at Penn State's Hershey Medical Center discovered the first tumor had not been removed. He explained, "It's true that you have a benign tumor, but it's actually an intramuscular lipoma. That means it has grown around and through the fibers of that large muscle on the front of your upper left leg. The only way to get rid of the tumor and keep it from spreading is to remove the whole muscle. The guy who worked on you before obviously misjudged what you had, so all he did was scrape off a little of the tumor and sew you up."

Carol was furious. "That son of a bitch lied to me! He told me he took care of it! If you take that muscle off will I be a cripple the rest of my life?"

"No. There's another muscle underneath, and with hard work in physical therapy you can strengthen it to take over the work of the removed muscle."

Carol looked to me for advice: "It looks like I don't have a choice. What do you think?"

Carol's temper rarely flared, but no one can say the same about mine! My anger exploded as visions flashed through my mind of Carol suffering pain and struggling to walk, Carol unable to dance. "First, I'd like to beat the living shit out of that quack!" I took a deep breath, "But you know I'll do whatever it takes to help build the strength of that smaller muscle so you can walk normally and we can dance together again. As you've often said, we're a terrific team and we'll deal with this problem like we have with others."

Carol had the surgery. It went as planned and she came home after four days. The doctor said, "I can arrange for a physical therapist but frankly, if you do what I tell you, you and Don can do it yourselves at home."

We agreed we'd rather do the therapy ourselves. The routine was for Carol to sit on the end of our dining room table with my help, and then do left leg lifts, lots of leg lifts! It was hard, painful work, but when Carol set her mind on something she was stubborn as a mule. Her friend and neighbor, Carolyn Nessleroade, had a wheelchair we could use whenever we needed it.

Celebrating a special milestone distracted us from Carol's rehab routine and brightened our lives. Cameron graduated with his PhD from the Penn State College of Business and got a job as assistant professor in the School of Business at Rutgers University. Carol said, "I'm so proud to see him launch his new life pathway but, in a sense, it is another loss because he's been here with us in State College since birth." Our Happy Valley nest was now empty, with just we old rooster and hen left at home. Luckily, Carol and I were old hands at entertaining ourselves.

As we approached the Christmas holidays, I said, "Carol you're one tough cookie! Despite your surgery you continue to create things in your shop, scooting around in your borrowed wheel chair and taking care of your customers and me."

She grinned, flashing those big dimples, "I still have the goal of throwing my crutches under the tree Christmas morning because I don't need them anymore."

On Christmas day, after everyone had opened all their presents, I pulled a box from behind the Christmas tree and gave it to Carol. She tore the wrappings off and laughed to find a cane inside. In grand, dramatic style, she braced herself on the new cane and laid both crutches under the Christmas tree. "NOW I'm ready for the new year!" We all cheered.

After recovering from a holiday full of laughter and fun with grandchildren and their parents, Carol invited her old friend, Ginny Elliott, to a Valentine's Day lunch. The day turned out cold and dreary, so she built a fire and sat a card table in front of the fireplace. Ginny said, "Oh, you're putting on the dog!" when Carol poured two glasses of wine.

Carol laughed, "No, it's just been so long since we visited that I wanted to celebrate the occasion. This wine was a Christmas gift."

Ginny sipped her wine and savored it, "What else did you get for Christmas?"

"My favorite gift came from Don; a computer-controlled bread maker. He thought it might help entertain me since I still can't go out much. It's really neat! You just toss the ingredients in, turn it on, and four hours later you're eating delicious homemade bread. I have two favorite recipes so far. One is a multigrain recipe. A hot slice of that covered with butter or strawberry-rhubarb jam is delicious! The one Don and the grandkids like best is banana bread."

"How's your rehab coming?"

"I've made a lot of progress. I can walk reasonably well with a cane and most of the time can walk without a cane around the house. There's still a lot of pain because of nerve damage when the muscle was removed, but I'm learning to handle that. I want to get stronger so still do leg lifts twice a day. When weather permits, we'll warm up the pool and I'll swim every day again. Those water exercises help leg strength and coordination and make me feel good too."

Carol served a tasty lunch of homemade chili, milk, and warm just-baked bread with butter and jam. "I started this multigrain bread about 8:30 and it just finished baking."

Ginny took a bite of jam-covered bread and said, "Yum yum!" Then, mumbled with her mouth full, "Are you able to work in your shop now?"

"I work there most days and sit in my wheelchair while I work. That way I can scoot around the shop to find what I need without having to get up and down so much. I'm trying to think of ideas for something new to make. My recent contribution of $2000 was to a local volunteer agency called 'On Drugs' to help finance their telephone hot line. Drugs are an increasing problem here in Happy Valley."

We passed the summer months with Carol crafting, me writing and gardening, and both of us swimming, and spending time with friends. We finally gave our combination canoe, sail and motor boat to friends because Carol couldn't climb in and out of it with her bum leg.

As October began, Carol said, "I have yet to hold the newest baby in our family. Could we go to California to see Martin, Sheri, Jason and Kevin?"

"Your birthday is October 8 so let's celebrate by flying to California."

Carol loved holding Kevin Donald. How could it be otherwise since he was named for her husband? One night in bed Carol said, "Sheri really enjoys performing with her choral groups. I told her how much I miss that pleasure."

"I lectured in Martin's class today about my Living Systems theory and we had a good discussion. Martin is a very good teacher."

We took a side trip for a couple days to explore area wineries. That was a kind of farming we'd never experienced. On Halloween, I was in the living room reading when Carol called, "Don, come here to see two cute kids!" I went to the family room and saw Jason and Kevin dressed up like crayons for trick and treating, with a doting grandma at their side.

We flew home into tailgating and football season. Carol said, "I'm looking forward to gabbing with our friends while tailgating, and I think I can climb the steps in the stadium with my cane and your support. Let's try it this game." She handled those steep stadium steps like a pro, so we went to the rest of the games.

Carol had her usual hectic holiday season in the shop, and we enjoyed the traditional Christmas gatherings with family and friends.

One quiet midwinter week Carol wrote to Mary Lou, a cherished childhood friend: "I love the beautiful hand crafted, unique cards you send us each year. You're a talented gal! I wish we could work together in my *Personal Touch* shop. Wouldn't that be a hoot! My customers would love your work. The shop continues to be popular, but I'm starting to cut back a little so I can have more time for other things. Many women have become long term customers and good friends, and I enjoy our gab sessions very much. Sometimes it reminds me of our high school gab sessions with our 'slumber party' group.

I continue to work hard to strengthen the remaining muscles in my left leg. I do leg lifts every day, and can't wait to get back into our swimming pool. I can now walk quite well without a cane, and can work in my shop without using my wheel chair. However, for extensive sightseeing or shopping the leg tires quickly so then I still use a cane or Don gives me thrilling rides in a wheel chair. Sometimes he teases me and I have to bonk him to slow him down.

He's published another book, *Developmental Systems Theory*, and is starting a new book about psychotherapy. He never runs out of new ideas or words.

Don is a 'pinch hitter' academic administrator again. The College has just created a new unit called *Biobehavioral Health (BBH)*. Don's friend, Gerry McClearn, was appointed head. Then, the President demanded Gerry become the College's next Dean. Gerry called Don: 'I just got BBH started and don't want it to fail. It's one of your old ideas so you know what its vision is about. Would you serve as acting head and finish building the graduate program I've started until I can hire a new head?' Don now spends about half of each week doing that."

We went shopping at post season sales in the largest mall in State College. One day the mall had a pontoon boat on display. Carol said, "Let's go check out that pontoon boat." The more she saw, the more enthused she became. Later, we stopped at a little eatery for a coffee break. As soon as we got our coffee, Carol grabbed my hand and said, "Let's get one! We both love swimming and boating at the lake, but haven't been able to do that for a couple years because of my darn leg. That boat would be easy to get on and off, and I could even drive it. And think how much fun it would be to take our grandkids on it!"

I laughed and said, "Slow down and drink some coffee while I digest your proposal. Such a boat would require storage at the lake, but Jim's marina has good dock space. I wonder if we'd have to get some kind of drivers' license?"

"I don't know, but if we did we could. Let's buy one!!" So, we did.

We found three used pontoon boats advertised for sale. The first two had no enclosure and looked in bad shape. But, the third one was parked at Jim's anchorage, was in great shape and had a white, waterproof enclosure that could be unzipped and opened on any or all sides when on the water. It also had an audio system and an electronic fish finder. Carol was so excited at our find, I feared she'd pee her pants because her cheeks flushed with happiness and she fidgeted like a kid waiting for Christmas morning.

The owner explained he bought his pontoon boat new and used it mostly for fishing. He had a trailer and had towed it to the Finger Lakes in New York State to fish. He needed cash because his business was in trouble, so that's why he was selling it at a bargain price.

He took us out for a short ride around the lake and let Carol drive. I'd never seen such a joyful smile on her face except when holding our new born babies. When we returned dockside, he demonstrated parking the boat and backing it out. Those maneuvers took more skill than I expected! I said, "Well, what do you think?"

Carol answered with a grin, "If you don't buy it I will!"

So we became the proud owners of a pontoon boat and arranged to transfer dock rental into our names. As soon as we officially owned the boat, we drove to the lake on a Monday morning because we knew it wouldn't be crowded then. At first I was nervous, but after pulling away from the dock successfully I felt like an old hand. I filled the tank with gas and off we went, slowly cruising the lake, exploring each cove and inlet as we went. After getting my 'sea legs', I turned it over to Carol and she took to captaining our ship like a duck takes to water.

After about two hours we discovered a private cove with its own beach. We set anchor, put on our suits and life vests and went swimming. A ladder attached to the deck made it easy to get in and out of the water. The water was shallow enough to stand in by the ladder, but several yards out it was over our heads, so swimming with life jackets was easier and safer. I can't adequately express the joy that pontoon brought into our lives. While I swam and checked the pontoons, Carol floated lazily on her back, singing like a happy bird.

After about an hour in the water, we climbed into the boat, took off our swimming suits and dried each other off with a fluffy towel. I wrapped my arms around Carol, surprised her with a juicy kiss, then spread our blankets on the deck. She looked puzzled, "What are you doing?"

I wondered if my grin was as wicked as I hoped, "I want to christen our boat."

"But you didn't bring any champagne."

"That's not the christening I had in mind."

Ah, the light dawned! "What a great idea! Sex in the great outdoors around water has always been one of my favorite pleasures." We did our best to make the christening a memorable one.

As we ate lunch, Carol reminisced, "Remember when you were in college and I was working in Topeka, our renter took his friends and me for a ride on his boat?"

"I remember how excited you were when you wrote me about it. You said when you got rich, a boat was the first thing you'd buy."

"Now you've made another of my dreams come true. Is there no end to your magic?"

"I don't know about magic, but can say for sure there's no end to my love for you."

Most of our free time was spent on the boat that summer and we decided to park our camping trailer at the lake so we could stay a week at a time. We explored the lake, searched for driftwood for Carol's shop, swam, fished, napped, played gin rummy or cribbage, and read.

Occasionally we took friends or family members with us and they loved it. Creating and maintaining friendships requires enjoying time together. Now we had a new way of doing that. We kept our boat in the water until mid-October so we could enjoy the fall colors in the forest surrounding the lake. Occasionally, we took the boat out on clear nights to bask in the glow of a full moon in a sky full of stars, creating patterns of light and shadow on water.

That summer we lost our special friends and neighbors, John and Carolyn Nesselroade, to the University of Virginia. As I had expected, John became an internationally respected scholar on the cutting edge of his field. Virginia enticed them away from Penn State with a prestigious and valuable endowed chair. Carol said, "I'm very lonely for them. I'm so fond of Carolyn because she's like a sister I never had. Could we go visit them?"

"I miss them too. I'll call John and see what we can arrange."

We went for a long weekend and refilled our cup of friendship. Their house sat above a wooded stream with a view somewhat like the one they had here on Slab Cabin Run.

One highlight of our trip to Virginia, other than seeing our friends, was visiting Thomas Jefferson's home and seeing all the unique inventions he used there. Carol said, "What a creative man he was! Our country was so fortunate to have men like him directing its creation. It's sad we don't seem to attract government leaders with that kind of creative vision today."

An important college-related issue came to a head so I decided it was time for one of our dates. I knew Carol loved the restaurant in the village of Mill Hall with its gift shop and herb garden so I said, "Would the beautiful lady with 'The Personal Touch' honor me by being my dinner guest at the Mill Hall gift shop Saturday night?"

She curtsied demurely, "It would be a privilege and pleasure to dine with such a distinguished scholar of human nature." I made a reservation and we drove east through a balmy early September evening to the village of Mill Hall. The owner welcomed us back with a hug for Carol and a back slap that nearly knocked me off my feet.

Carol said, "I'd like to browse in your gift shop before dinner. Would that be OK?" "Of course!"

As we meandered through the two floors of gift items, Carol said, "What a huge task it must be to keep all these treasures dusted and cleaned." She found a fragile antique tea cup for her collection and then we went to eat.

The owner said to Carol, "I remember you like my soup with fresh herbs. Would you like to start with that?"

"I'd love it!"

"My special this weekend is the French delicacy Boeuf Bourguignon."

My mouth watered just thinking of it, "That sounds delicious – we'll both have it."

As we ate I shared my news, "Carol, the State of Pennsylvania has created a special opportunity for us. As a part of their effort to balance the budget, they're suggesting that senior, well-paid employees retire early to free up their salary. To do that, they're offering a retirement bonus of four extra years. I'm eligible. If I retire now, my annual retirement income will be as high as it would be if I worked another four years through 1995. I'd like your opinion."

"How much would our annual income be?"

"I've worked for Penn State for forty years. The way their formula works, my annual retirement income would actually be a little more than our current income."

"Are you worrying about how I'll feel if you're around our house all the time?"

"Well, maybe a little."

A girlish giggle was her answer, "I say what's not to like! We make more money, I get more of my sweetheart's time, and we have more flexibility for traveling and other things."

"I think it's a good deal too! I'll have complete control of my time. OK, my retirement will begin January 1, 1992. For the first year or two, I'll co-teach a graduate seminar on *Humans as Living Systems* so I can continue to get graduate student feedback on my scholarly writing. When I want to do something with you, my co-teacher can pinch hit for me."

"Professor Ford, it sounds like you're arranging a kind of non-retirement retirement."

"It will put me in the same position you have with your shop; you do what you like to do when you want to do it and no one can dictate your agenda."

As we drove home Carol said, "The more I think about it the more I like it. This will be the beginning of yet another new pathway. We went from newlyweds and graduate students, to being parents and creating the Division of Counseling here, from DOC to creating a new College, then from that to being grandparents while you write and teach and I craft and paint. We no longer have children to raise, will both have complete control of our time and the resources to do whatever we choose. That sounds like a pretty good pathway to me!"

We still devoted time to crafting, writing, gardening, entertaining, tailgating and football, but in general nothing gave us as much pleasure as our new boat. As we went to bed after New Year's Eve, Carol said, "Come spoon me and warm up my feet, Mr. Retired Man, while I dream of fun and frolic on our boat come spring."

In a letter to old friends, Carol wrote: "Our life is changing. I'm now married to a retired psychologist (I should say semi-retired because he has another book to finish). We're planning how to use our new free time for fun and frolic. Our health is good, generally speaking, and we are now on Medicare (yikes!). We try to fight the battle of the bulge (not too successfully) and to get plenty of exercise through housekeeping, gardening, and swimming in our pool or from our boat. We joined our son Russ in buying a 27' RV for camping and sightseeing. After they get back from a vacation through the western U.S., we'll use it to camp and explore the country. Oh yes, we have a wonderful pontoon boat on a nearby lake. Come and see us and drive it."

In the spring Carol crafted while I got our vegetable and flower gardens growing so they could provide summer treats for us. We eagerly awaited the boating season, and immediately went down to check on the boat when the marina put it in our dock.

We serviced the motor, filled the tanks with gas and took it out for a spin to make sure everything was OK. It wasn't! As we drove, the motor threw a rod, which broke a piston, which meant we had to get a new motor. A friendly boater towed us to our dock. We pulled the motor and took it to Jim's service center, less than a mile from the lake, where the boat had been stored all winter. We bought a new motor and they installed and serviced it. I backed it out of the dock onto the lake and turned the wheel over to Captain Carol.

She said, "It's a lot smoother and has more power. Their service is wonderful and they didn't charge us a penny for bringing it to the lake and installing it. There are two campgrounds near the marina. Let's check them out." Each campground had several sites near the lake shore.

I said, "If we camp at one of those sites, we could park the boat at the shore while camping and wouldn't have to take it back to the dock each day. Let's write down the numbers of the best camp sites so we can pick one when we register." We stopped at the registration building as we left and reserved a site for the first week in June.

Carol said, "Our boat is absent a crucial element – a pot. Do they assume everyone will go into the woods to do their job?"

I laughed, "That can be dangerous! Remember our friend, Arnie Goldstein, told us he did that at a lake in Canada and got poison ivy all over his you-know-what."

"I think we better buy a port-a-potty. I want to protect my you-know-what!" So we added a port-a-potty to our boating and camping essentials.

What a wonderful week! Each morning we ate a leisurely breakfast, then packed a lunch and drink. We wore swimming suits under our clothes and cruised the lake with Casey, our dog. Casey loved our boating adventures as much as we did! Each new day started without a plan. We just explored and stopped when we saw something interesting. We often discussed our discoveries – abandoned campgrounds on remote islands or schools of fish glinting silver in the sunlight. Carol played tapes of her favorite music, and sometimes sang along. And we fished, but seldom caught anything big enough to eat.

When Carol spied a shoreline or cove with lots of driftwood, we stopped and searched for 'art objects'. Those searches sometimes yielded surprises. One day she stepped over a big piece of driftwood and nearly stepped on a huge turtle blocking her path. Another time an adult deer and her fawn came to the shore for a drink. We became amateur bird watchers, emphasis on amateur, because of the many different species of large and small birds inhabiting the lake.

When we got hot, we shucked our clothes and took a cooling swim. If Carol saw dried weeds she could use in her shop, we stopped and cut them. When hunger pangs set in, we pulled into a cove sheltered from the wake of other boats. Our routine was to swim awhile, then dry off in the sun as we ate lunch. And, we shared endless conversations about anything and everything – past, present and potential futures. Cell phones didn't exist to interrupt us.

One day Carol said, "I treasure being alone together like this, sharing our thoughts, feelings and hopes. Do you remember the first time we were together like this?"

Oh yes, Sweetheart, I remember! "It was a summer evening in 1944 in Manhattan, sitting in your parents' car on K-State hill. That's when I began to discover who you really were."

"Same here. In those few evenings we had, I talked about private thoughts, ideas, and beliefs I'd never shared with another person, including my mother. For the first time in my life I felt like someone really cared about _my_ ideas and _my_ beliefs. In my experience, most people were eager to talk about themselves rather than others. You weren't like most boys I knew. You never bragged about what you did or knew. When we argued, you treated me like an equal. Those conversations gave me a kind of freedom, and began changing the way I thought of myself. I loved our letters because you were the only person I felt completely free to say anything to without worrying how you'd react or respond. It was fun to tease you, and still is!"

"Somewhere, somehow early in my life, I learned that if I kept my mouth shut and listened to others I could learn a lot and they were more prone to like me."

Carol laughed and said, "Well, it sure worked with me."

After lunch we usually took a nap. Carol curled up on the sofa while I stretched out on an air mattress on the floor. Sometimes I read while Carol napped. After a nap, weather permitting, we took Casey for a walk. We always kept her on a leash because once she chased a critter into the forest and we spent an hour rounding her up. Frequently, we enjoyed another swim to refresh ourselves before returning to camp.

After dinner we often took a stroll and visited with other campers. On cool nights we built a campfire and sat mesmerized by the sight, sound, and smell of our fire. We did whatever appealed to us at any given time – read, play cribbage or other games, or just vegetate. Carol wasn't one to just sit and do nothing, so she had knitting or crochet projects to keep her hands busy. We felt comfortably tired after a day in the great outdoors, so went to bed at nine p.m. and slept soundly, unless we had noisy campers nearby.

We enjoyed outings like that several times during the summer, ranging from a weekend to a full week. Occasionally, we took another couple or some of our kids and grandkids with us. It was a wonderfully inexpensive way to pass a fun summer.

Late that summer, we used the new RV to explore New England and Carol's roots. We had two major destinations for our explorations. The first was in Massachusetts, the second in Vermont. In between the two we planned to enjoy the beauty and history of that region.

We started in the small town of Rowley, Massachusetts. That's where Rev. Rogers and twenty families from his congregation in Rowley, England landed in 1639 to begin their new life. We found a small center focused on community history. Records showed that Rev. Rogers owned a good bit of land, and a number of Clarks lived and died there. Rogers was chased out of the church in England because of his very rigid Puritan beliefs and we found evidence that some early settlers of Rowley, MA migrated elsewhere in New England to get away from him.

Next we went to Springfield, which Deacon Samuel Chapin helped create after emigrating from Paignton, England with his wife Cicely. Carol was eager to see his famous statue. It stands on a round pink granite base, stating he lived from 1595 to 1675 and was a founder of the city. His statue is often called *The Puritan.* Carol stood beside me, looking up at her ancestor.

"I'm awed by the power he conveys, with the Bible in one hand and reaching out beyond himself with the other. I can't help but shiver because I feel like he's reaching out for me!"

I helped her stand on the statue's base and then took several pictures of Carol looking up at his face. The effect was eerie, because past and present seemed to come together in that moment. Carol said, "He was a powerful man who lived for eighty years when the normal life span was half that, and was a major religious icon of his time, an important, trusted leader with the wisdom and skill to create a city."

From Springfield we went to Rochester, VT. An employee of their history center gave directions to a very old cemetery not far from town. We proceeded slowly through the cemetery while Carol made notes of what we found. Later, she read her notes as we drove: "We found several descendants of Richard Clark, who was in the group Rev. Ezekiel Rogers brought to America from Rowley, England in 1639. He helped create Rowley, MA and died there. Many of his descendants stayed in Rowley but some moved north. Timothy Clark's gravestone says he was fifth in line of descent from Richard Clark. His son, Jonathon Rogers Clark, died here in 1769. Note that Rogers was the last name of the minister who brought the original group from England, so Jonathon may have been named for him. Ebenezer Clark died in the Rochester area in 1716 at age 29. It's not clear how he relates to the others. Now, I wonder if my Clark family in Kansas is in any way descendants of these people."

Shortly after we got home, football season began. October 8th was Carol's 65th birthday. I thought that deserved a celebration, so planned a surprise birthday party while tailgating that weekend. Russ and Doug and families, Cam, and many of Carol's old friends planned to be there. As usual, we took the RV and set up for tailgating. Then the fun began. Pam and Doug came out of hiding shouting, "Happy birthday Mom!!" and dispensed hugs and kisses.

Carol said, "What a wonderful surprise, but where are the kids?"

The grandchildren had sneaked on top of the RV and jumped up holding signs, yelling, "HAPPY BIRTHDAY GRANDMA!" while throwing paper streamers at her.

Carol's eyes filled with happy tears, "I'm flabbergasted!! Come here and give me a hug!"

At home after the game, the grandchildren continued the celebration in our pool while the adults had 'Happy Hour' on the deck. Carol said, "You really surprised me and it was a great party, but the best part of all is spending time with my wonderful family."

Chapter Thirty

More Travels, More Milestones

After the holidays, we settled into our late winter routine – Carol in her craft shop and I in my study writing. One evening I served hot chocolate and couple of fresh-baked oatmeal raisin cookies, put on *Romeo and Juliet,* and we sat toasting our toes in front of the fireplace.

I said, "Carol, Martin and Sheri have decided they want to move back east. He says friends and colleagues think they're nuts to leave a prestigious place like Stanford, but he and Sheri think living conditions are getting intolerable in California. They don't want to raise their kids in the California culture. They'd also prefer being closer to family.

Carol said, "I'd love to have them closer so we could see them and their kids more than once or twice a year. I hate missing their childhood years. Martin is such a dedicated football fan so he'd love to be close enough to come to games. I hope it works."

We sat in silence for a while, sipping our hot chocolate. Then Carol said, "I really enjoyed using our RV to explore New England last year. It's so much easier and more comfortable than trailer camping. But, since Russ also uses it as a co-owner, we can't always use it and I'd like to do more traveling. We need to get one of our own so we could go anywhere, anytime and stay away as long as we wanted to."

"I like that idea. The place over towards Lock Haven where we took our trailer for servicing sells and services RVs. Let's look at their place first."

We waited until early spring to head out on our quest for a new RV. They had RVs of many makes and models, but most were larger than Carol wanted. But, after looking at a small Flair with twin beds, she said, "I've changed my mind. I think it would be a mistake to buy that little Flair. I don't like the idea of sleeping alone in single beds, and the walls are poorly insulated. With our beds against the walls and windows, it would be hard to stay warm when it's cold outside. The kitchen and bathroom are too small."

"I agree with everything you said, particularly sleeping alone and being cold at night. There are lots of RV dealers in the Harrisburg, York and Gettysburg area. Let's look there." At first we didn't have much luck. As we drove south past York towards the Maryland border we saw a smaller dealer with a 'BIG SALE' sign, so we stopped. He said, "I have a Sea View we've been using as a demo that sounds like what you want. I'd give you a good price with a full warranty." He left us alone to look it over.

Carol stood there with a big grin and sparkling eyes and I instantly knew we'd be buying it. She said, "Don, look at this terrific U shaped kitchen. It has a 4 burner stove, both a regular and microwave oven, a stainless steel double sink, a big refrigerator and lots of cabinet and drawer space. The dinette is right beside one of the kitchen counters which would make it easy to transfer food, and there's a big sofa across from the dinette. It's wonderful."

"Carol, come look at the driver seats."

She sat in one and said, "WOW! Look at the wonderful view through that huge windshield. The seat is fabulously comfortable; I could really enjoy the scenery riding in this."

The dealer came back to show us all the features. The big front seats could be rotated to face into the RV to provide more seating, and there was a big TV, radio and music system. Carol laughed with delight. "I could listen to my wonderful music while riding, working in the kitchen, or loafing; I could even sing along! Let's see the bedroom and bath. Look, it has a full bath with a combo tub and shower and a nice sink and mirror. That would make it easy to wash my hair. Ohhh, it has a queen size bed – no cold feet and chilly nights for me."

The dealer said, "In addition to this bed, the sofa and the dinette can each be turned into double beds, so it can sleep 6 people. Here are two special features. Often camp sites aren't level – push these buttons and you lower 4 jacks under the RV to level and stabilize it. Now, sit down in the dinette." We did, he pushed another button, and the whole dinette slid out the side of the RV making a much larger living area. We gasped with surprise and delight. Carol was in her *I can't stand still* mode of excitement, and gave me *The Look!*

We dug into our savings and bought it.

Carol said, "Let's drive it around for a day, live in it and use everything for a night. That way we can make sure everything is OK." We stayed two nights and a day in a campground near Gettysburg, had the dealer fix a few things and headed home. Carol said, "Don, this is fabulous! It's so comfortable, so efficient, so pretty and so good sleeping with you! It's a dream come true. I feel like a queen! I should have expected nothing less from my magic man!

Let's take our new RV on a trial run to Rochester to see Doug's family and one of their plays. All three of the children perform in their plays. Matt often plays the leading man, Lindsay has a beautiful voice, and they say Ryan comes alive with humor on stage. Pam designs the sets and Doug constructs them."

On the weekend we visited we saw *Sound of Music*. The play was terrific and their sets wonderful. Carol offered well-deserved praise, "Your set was as good as anything we've seen on Broadway. Your family makes a terrific team and we're so proud of you!"

Back home I said, "Carol, it's near our anniversary. Let's celebrate by camping in our SeaView and boating at the lake." We were excited to be back on the water again in our pontoon boat! Our first adventure was to explore the upper end of the lake. We discovered that what had been a public campground had become a privately owned resort. Carol said, "Let's stop at the resort for lunch on the way back and see what it's like."

It had a restaurant and motel-like lodge perched on the edge of a big bay. The food was surprisingly good. They had a tour boat and Skidoo rentals. They also had a water park.

"Our grandchildren would have fun here." Carol said.

We loved the lake because surprises waited in each cove. We pulled into a large cove with a sandy beach and a backdrop of blooming wild roses. Carol said, "This is beautiful! Let's stop and take a swim here."

The water was shallow enough to stand up on a sandy bottom, but deep enough to swim, so we swam without life preservers. We preferred swimming in coves because the water was warmer, sheltered from currents and wakes of boats speeding by. Casey joyfully joined us on our swim and frolicked around us in the water until nap time. As we headed back to our camp, Carol said, "Let's remember that cove – it's the nicest we've found so far."

Later that summer Martin informed us he'd accepted a new job as Associate Dean of The Graduate School of Education at George Mason University in Virginia, near Washington DC. They were searching for a home in that area and would then arrange to move.

Then, Cam announced his engagement to a lovely lady, Gricel Fernandez, and invited us to dinner to meet her parents. Over lunch, Carol told her friend Ginny Elliott: "In January our youngest son will marry. We're delighted! They were both born during the Cuban missile crisis, only Cam was here and Gricel was in Cuba. Her parents escaped Castro when Gricel was five-years old, settled near Newark NJ, and became U.S. citizens. We met her parents for the first time recently. Cam asked Gricel to marry him while riding in a horse drawn carriage. He gave her roses and a box of chocolates with the ring in a chocolate he knew she'd choose. She asked what he would have done if she'd swallowed it!"

Martin's family finally moved to Virginia so were close enough to share the Christmas holidays. Having our sons and their families with us for Christmas was a special treat. We loved watching our grandchildren play with each other and frolic in our swimming pool. Like our sons before them, our grandkids did have fun together.

After the holidays, Carol asked me to mix martinis while she fixed snacks to enjoy by the fireplace. Snuggled cozily on the couch in her jammies, she lifted her glass and said, "A toast. After a third of a century, I've decided to retire from my career as an artist and crafts person. Beginning January 1st *The Personal Touch* is closing for good."

Her announcement brought tears to my eyes because closing her shop would be the end of an era, but I managed to choke out, "A toast – to the creative woman who brought beauty to my life and that of many others, and who enriched our community with her generosity!" I sat my glass down and hugged her, whispering, "I'm so proud of you and love you so much."

Carol nibbled at a snack, planning what to say next, "I've been thinking about this for a year. The shop has been an important part of my life so is hard to give up. The high regard of friends and customers for my work, and what it helped me to do for the welfare of others, both made me feel worthwhile. But, it's too much stress at this stage of my life, and not really fun anymore. I'll still enjoy making things for our home and as gifts for people I love, but now I want to concentrate on organizing our photos into albums in historic order, as a record of how our family developed. And, I want to spend the rest of my life enjoying our companionship and exploring our world together as we have been."

"Sweetheart, I support that decision and share those goals with all my heart. May I add an idea? Let's use some of our retirement and my royalty income to continue your mission of making contributions to help others. We still make a terrific team!" We went to bed, having passed another milestone in our lives.

On a very cold January 8, 1994, Gricel and Cameron were married in New Jersey. On the road home, Carol said, "I thought their living room was the perfect setting for an intimate ceremony – so warm and personal. Gricel and her mother did a beautiful job of decorating. Wasn't it fun to see our boys welcoming Cam into the fraternity of husbands! They're all so ornery, teasing him like they did about when he might become a father. Gricel is a delight and I loved seeing our newlyweds together. Now I'll sit back and wait for our eleventh grandchild and hope we get a girl baby for me to hold."

We got our gardens started and then camped at the lake for several days. One afternoon as we cruised up the lake, Carol said, "That looks like fun!"

"What?"

"Those people have what looks like a big inner tube they're towing behind their boat with someone on it. I'll bet our grandkids would like that. Let's buy one."

I nodded, but my mind was on my growling stomach. "We're near the resort so let's stop there and have lunch."

As we ate, Carol said, "Four members of our family turn 40 this year – Pam, Doug, Martin and Barb. Why don't we have a birthday bash for all four. We could make it a kind of 'roast' where everyone including their kids could take a shot."

"That's a great idea. How about having it here at the resort? They have a motel, food service, a banquet room and a marina. We could have fun at the celebration and fun in the lake."

Don, that would be a great way to keep everyone together in the same place. Let's talk with the management about the possibilities." Management was enthused about the idea and very helpful. We made reservations for rooms for twenty people and for the banquet room, tentative until confirmed with our families.

In July, our twenty-member, three generation family gathered at the resort. On the first morning we boated with two tube floats tied behind so two people could be towed at the same time. That was hilarious, watching the riders try to knock each other off their floats. Everyone swam and sunned themselves on the resort's sandy beach. Later that afternoon, most of us rested, showered and dressed for the party while some decorated the banquet room. The party started with music, a happy hour, and conversations full of teasing and fun memories. Then the resort served a dinner we'd chosen to appeal to kids as well as adults. Occasionally someone proposed a toast to tease, needle or ridicule the birthday girls and boys while we ate.

Then the real fun began. Everyone, including children, had prepared presentations. Carol and I started it with a slide show portraying each of them from babyhood to teen years. The slides were accompanied by humorous commentary, mostly from Carol, with spontaneous remarks by others. Then we had skits, songs, parodies, and poems by different people. We ended with joke gifts. The grand kids, in particular, had great fun taking shots at their parents.

After breakfast the next morning we rented the resort's fleet of six Skidoos, which Carol called 'water motorcycles'. Each could carry two people at a time. No one in our gang had ridden a Skidoo so there were some funny learning experiences. We took turns so everyone who wanted to had the chance to zip around the lake. Our boat served as a safety stop.

We turned in the Skidoos, had lunch together, and everyone checked out and went their separate ways. As we watched them leave, Carol said, "That was a great success – particularly last night. Underneath all the fun there was a lot of affection. I think it was a memory maker."

We spent the spring and summer working in our flower and vegetable gardens and enjoying our usual pastimes. Carol worked on collating picture albums and I worked on my new psychotherapy book. We swam in our pool nearly every day and sometimes invited friends to join us in swimming, eating, playing bridge or having happy hour or some combination thereof. Carol's bridge group had been together more than three decades and was as comfortable with each other as a pair of old shoes. Our couples' bridge group was composed of long-time personal friends, some who had helped create our college.

Boating remained our favorite activity and Carol wrote Charlie Prutzman about it: "Periodically I'll say, 'Let's go to the lake!' We pack up our RV and go, sometimes alone and sometimes with friends. This summer we had at least six couples at the lake with us at different times. We even got some of them to take a tube ride. One day we were boating when a very severe storm hit. Don drove quickly into a cove, tied the boat to a big tree, and he and Jim Koontz stood inside hanging on to the roof of our boat to keep the top from blowing away until the storm ended. It was both scary and funny. Connie Koontz and I were happy to get back to the dock and out of the boat after that."

One late summer afternoon, Carol and I dried off, got dressed after swimming, and had a leisurely happy hour on our deck. We felt contented and relaxed as we drank our tailgater punch and munched our crunchy snack. Carol said, "How would you like to take a trip to Topeka?"

"Why would you want to do that?" Carol hadn't talked about Topeka in a long time!

"My high school graduating class is having a 50th year reunion"

"All these years I thought you didn't care about your graduating class or reunions."

"You're right, I usually care diddly about such things but all my slumber party gang will be there this time and I'd like to see them. I can't believe we're all nearing 70 years old."

"I'd like to see them too, so if you want we'll pack up our RV and go. But think about this: It's hard to have private time with old friends when you're at a crowded reunion. Are there any other classmates you'd like to see?"

"No!"

"Then why not set up your own private reunion with the old gang?"

"That's a great idea! How can we do it?"

"How about a private three-hour luncheon in some nice place?"

"Remembering how much they ate at our slumber parties, I bet they'd all like that, and we could gab to our heart's content."

"OK. I'll get on the internet and phone some contacts and see what I can work out."

Three days later we were on the deck again nursing a gin and tonic. I said, "Here's the deal. The Menninger Clinic no longer exists, and the Menninger home has become a piece of Topeka history available for meetings and social gatherings. It's possible to have a private luncheon with cocktails there for up to 30 people, prepared and served by them. I've tentatively reserved it from 12:30 to 3:30 p.m. on the date you gave me. Check and see if that works for your friends." They all enthusiastically approved of the idea so I confirmed the date and time.

Then Carol told me of her neat idea. "I'm going through all the letters I wrote you during my high school years, looking for anecdotes about each of them, like having troubles with a boyfriend or something stupid they did. I'll describe anecdotes for each of them. After lunch, I'll hand them out and have each person read theirs out loud. Their hubbies will hear some things they've never heard before! That should trigger a lot of fun memories and reactions."

My reaction was, "W-O-O-O-W!"

The private reunion went beautifully. People ordered cocktails as they arrived. After hugging, kissing, talking and laughing all around, we sat down. Carol told them this was our gift to them for old times' sake, so we were paying the bill. Each person ordered lunch and another cocktail if they wished, and we all ate and talked. After lunch, Carol gave each of the old gang their sheet of anecdotes and asked them not to look at it until their turn came. The results were hilarious! Even the husbands roared with laughter. When Carol's turn came, she said, "I don't have one – I was the authoress." So, the gang started telling stories about her and brought a blush or two to Carol's cheeks. Everyone had so much fun they didn't want to leave, but our reservation time had ended. So we all went outdoors and posed for lots of pictures. I was amazed at how close they still were, despite having little personal contact for forty-plus years.

Later, Carol said, "We became very close while sharing the trials and joys of moving from girlhood to womanhood. It was such a delightful experience to share that time today with people whose friendship meant so much to each of us. They're still a beautiful bunch." The enduring happiness of that luncheon was expressed in letters over the next ten years.

In her Christmas letter to friends Carol wrote: "On Thanksgiving day, Gricel and Cam brought home from the hospital our 11th grandchild, Celia Fernandez. She's a beautiful, dark haired little girl – a rarity in our family. I'm eager to hold her and love her in the New Year."

In keeping with our new tradition, we went to sunny Florida to escape Happy Valley's midwinter cold.

We both enjoyed the rides and shows at Disney World and Universal Studios theme parks, and discovered that pushing Carol around in her wheel chair had huge advantages! We didn't have to stand in long lines because they provided special access for people with limitations. That enabled both of us to have more fun without getting tired.

Back home we settled into a pleasant summer routine of gardening, swimming, boating, spending time with friends, and playing and swimming with grandchildren when they came to visit. Carol worked on creating our photo albums and I on finishing my latest book. Sometimes we'd walk together through the woods, stop beside the stream and rest at our private little bridge. Once, while sitting there, Carol said, "Sometimes when I'm feeling sad, confused or depressed I come here by myself, sit in this beauty, watch and listen to the water flowing over rocks and think. It helps me feel better. For me it's a little bit like going to church."

For our next wedding anniversary I secretly set up a card table with two chairs on our bridge, packed martinis and a light dinner in our picnic basket, and sat a TKE sweetheart red carnation and an Alpha XI pink rose together beside a white candle on the table. Then I took Carol for a walk. When we reached the bridge she stopped. "Ohhhh Don, this is heavenly!" She hugged and kissed me, "Being your wife is marvelous."

We sat in our special spot, sipping martinis and reminiscing about our pathway through life, such as college parties and dances, our first home together, and other happy episodes. At dusk, Carol lit the candle. We enjoyed its gentle flicker as we ate and laughed about past episodes, like when she put the insulation in upside down in our Kansas house, our first baby upchucking down my back while I was burping him, and skinny dipping in the Kaw River. The evening finally cooled to a crisp chill. We left our bridge and walked hand in hand back to the home we planned to share the rest of our lives, still very much in love.

One day at lunch, Carol was all smiles, "Here's great news! Cam accepted a faculty appointment in the School of Business at the University of Central Florida in Orlando. That's terrific! Now we can spend part of our Florida vacations playing with our grandchildren."

That next winter we drove our SeaView to southwest Florida where we'd spent Easter with our sons years ago. We visited old friends from our graduate school days, Spurge and Art Funke, who had retired there. They, too, had a pontoon boat and showed us the area by boat.

We lived in two different but nice campgrounds, took a boat ride through a big state park, went to a couple of auctions, browsed at a sidewalk art and crafts show, and loafed. Then we went to Orlando and spent a week with Cam, Gricel and Celia. Carol said, "Celia is such a pretty little girl, and smart. I love being with her at this age as she's changing from baby to little girl."

That spring our children invited us to a party. Our 50th wedding anniversary is May 30 and our offspring planned to honor us with a party in Orlando. The whole family, including one member still in the oven, gathered for three days of family fun. The boys reserved a suite of rooms in a nice hotel, and one room had a kitchen and large living-dining area. One day the males had their traditional golf tournament named "The Ford Open", while the women had a baby shower for Gricel who was carrying our 12th grandchild. Another day we went to Disneyland. Carol laughed and said, "It must be quite a sight to have the whole family lined up behind my wheel chair so they can get into all the rides and events easily."

The "Big Show" was on the last day. What a happy memory maker! It started with a delicious meal. The boys had contacted old friends and colleagues all over the country requesting pictures and memory letters, and presented us with a box full. Some were funny, some were serious, but all were heartwarming and elicited great memories. Barb, who teaches other people how to create beautiful photo albums, created a fabulous memory album representing our family. She organized them in picture chapters. As we looked through it, Carol commented on the chapters.

"It starts with a wonderful chart of our five-generation family, beginning with our parents. For each member, there's a baby picture paired with a current picture showing how each of us has changed. How blessed I was to hold and love all these babies!

The next chapter features each of our childhoods. There's our gang at Meadow Acres dancing. You're still in your air force uniform so that must have been when you were home on your only leave, and we fell head over heels in love. It ends with our marriage.

The next chapter is titled 'Starting A Family'. There's a section on each of our sons as babies and little boys. They were such cute little rascals! WOW, there's a picture of me shortly before I delivered the twins; I was as big as a buffalo! The next four chapters represent our sons families. There's a section on their family fun and a page about each of their offspring. Before we were married, I dreamed about having babies with you, Don, but I never imagined it would turn out like this, though I did once dream I had twins!

The last chapter is titled 'The Fords Have Fun'. There's a section on each kind of fun: Building Things (like houses); Growing Things (like vegetables and flowers); Loving Our Pets (more dogs than cats); Making Music Together (singing and playing the piano); Celebrating (like birthday party roasts and 4th of July); In The Pool (where grandchildren learned to swim and play games); At The Lake (where driving the boat, swimming and tubing thrived); Tailgating; The Ford Bowl (an annual football game involving our sons, friends, and some grandsons); and Christmasing."

I said, "Russ, during one family get together with children laughing and splashing in the pool, you said 'You know what you're doing here? You're making memories for all of us.' This wonderful album shows how right you were. Thanks for this treasure."

They gave us a list of things to visit on our travels: the Wicki Wacki Mermaids in Florida; the world's largest ball of string in Kansas; and the biggest colony of prairie dogs in South Dakota. There were funny skits and corny jokes. Several songs, with lyrics composed by family members summarizing our family history, were sung by combinations of family members and "The Ford Family Singers." Here is an example:

We Are The Ford Family

Christmas presents by the tree, Penn State football on TV, Sunday burgers, shooting pool, all the kids are out of school.

Climbing up the apple tree, ice cream at Penn State's creamery, Pogo, Twiggy, lots of love and loyalty.

Melting chocolate Easter eggs, Mom's delicious birthday cakes, hot dogs, big log, picnics by the stream.

Ford Bowl, Little League, Goode For You makes it big, playing golf at Centre Hills, lots of bowling alley thrills.

Sledding down the mountain side, slipping off the slippery slide, summertime vacation trips, crazy Kansas relatives.

Family trips that self-destruct, rainy days and bad luck, Kids fried, engine died, trailer falling on its side.

Cutting grass, raking leaves, washing cars and pulling weeds, septic tank, no thanks, hauling wood up from the stream.

Shoveling snow up to our knees, planting all those Christmas trees, everyday another chore, I can't take it any more!

Now its 1991 and we keep on having fun, Ford Open, tailgating, Personal Touch, trying to sell the LSF, academic BS.

Happy hour, take a swim, watching Nickelodeon, trap a groundhog, let 'em go, playing Super Mario

Walking on the Indian Trail, producing another show for sale, build a hotel, write a book, make a logo, how's it look?

Who knows what the Fords will do? (Billy Joel will probably sue), But we will always be the Ford Family!

We are the Ford Family, We can try to hide it, but we can't deny it. We will keep on going 'till the world stops growing

With a happy smile, Carol cut the wedding cake, we fed it to each other and then shared it with our family with great love and gratitude. The party ended, and we went our separate ways.

At home we sat on our deck, basking in the glories of Mother Nature and reminiscing. Carol said, "My heart is bursting with the many ways our family honored us. Growing up in the beauty, safety, fun and love of our Slab Cabin habitat has produced some very special people. Life has been very good to us."

I added, "And still is."

A few weeks later when I came in the door from lunch with a colleague, Carol shouted happily "We have number 12!!"

"Twelve what?"

"Twelve grandchildren – Gricel just added Corin Sebastion to their family."

"That's great! At our anniversary celebration Cam told me this baby would complete their family, so I guess we will have to wait for our grandchildren to produce another crop of Ford babies for us to enjoy."

Back in our normal routine, we enjoyed our usual summer and fall activities. Barb provided advice, tools and supplies so Carol could create her special photo albums, and she completed two more. I published my last book.

Then we and our good friends, Juanita and Alex Gregal, were invited to the New Year's Eve centennial gala being thrown by Russ's Hilton Hotel in Harrisburg. The transition from one millennium to another is an historic event so we looked forward to the celebration.

Russ provided us deluxe accommodations at the Hilton. Carol wore a beautiful new burgundy dress, I dug my tuxedo out of storage, and we both put on our dancing shoes to party our way into the new century. Carol's bum leg didn't keep her from dancing!

The Tommy Dorsey Band played our kind of music for a night of greeting, drinking champagne, eating, dancing, drinking champagne, dessert, dancing and drinking champagne. The party's handsome host, Carols' first born son, delighted her by dancing with his mother in celebration of the new millennium. As midnight approached, Russell took us to the penthouse terrace and we watched the crowd as they counted down to the magic moment. The crowd exploded with cheers, kissing and hugging as the new millennium arrived amidst a beautiful array of fireworks. Carol melted into my arms, and we looked into each other's eyes for a moment before sharing a long, lingering kiss. We stood there, bubbling with joy, love and champagne until the fireworks ended. Then we thanked our host and went to bed.

Chapter Thirty-One
Alzheimer's Emerges

Carol and I shared a leisurely breakfast the weekend after Russ's big centennial gala in Harrisburg, enjoying our memories. I said, "Carol it was wonderful to get all duded up for a formal dance again. We hadn't done that in quite a while. You were gorgeous in your glittering burgundy gown, and dancing with you in my arms was a delight!"

"After a little champagne I felt like dancing all night. It was a special treat when Russ danced with me, but he isn't as good as his dad! I thought of ten years ago when we sat on our deck reading our letters to one another and agreeing that we were going to emphasize the good things in our life in the future. I never dreamed one of those 'good things' would be to dance our way into a new century as guests of our oldest son at his fancy New Year's Gala!"

"It was a 'once in a lifetime event' to celebrate being alive in two different centuries. Russ learned from his mother how to throw a great party."

I said, "Have you seen my car keys? My biggest irritation is not remembering where I left them."

"I think I saw them yesterday in our bedroom on the dresser. Don, I had trouble remembering a couple of names at the Gala and felt uneasy about that."

I laughed, "You know that's been a problem for me since high school."

"Yes, and you were lucky to have me next to you in reception lines after we married to whisper names you couldn't remember."

Recently I had noticed Carol's sharp memory fail her on a couple of occasions. Knowing Alzheimer's had been in the back of her mind since Winifred's death, I said nothing about it because such "senior moments" are common as people get older and I didn't want to unnecessarily worry her. However, we had always been very open with each other so I planned to encourage a discussion about her observations and thoughts on Alzheimer's whenever she brought up the subject.

"Don I know such memory slips are common in older people, but I've been thinking it might be helpful to me to have a general understanding of Alzheimer's symptom development. Could you help me with that?"

"I don't have detailed knowledge about that, but I can give you a general picture of early symptoms. There is no single pattern of symptom development – they can be quite different from one person to the next. The symptoms generally come on very slowly. Some kinds of short term memory disruptions are typically the first to appear, like temporarily not remembering names of people, places, things, or event schedules, where some object has been placed, directions to some one's home, or a shopping list. These kinds of forgetfulness are commonplace in older people and can be caused by lots of things besides Alzheimer's.

Such disruptions may slowly elaborate, such as occurring more frequently, beginning to include forgetfulness about how to use common appliances, how to carry out familiar procedures, forgetting one's address or phone number, or starting to carry out some task and then forgetting what they started to do. An increasing patterns of disruptions like that make the onset of Alzheimer's more likely.

Let's agree to talk with one another if we observe anything we think might be relevant. Let's deal with it as a team as we have other things in our lives."

"That helps, Don. I don't have any major concerns right now so let's talk about a winter vacation. I'm really happy that all our clan is back on the East coast because it's easier for us to get together. But, we're still spread from Pennsylvania to Florida. Celia and Corin are our only grandchildren still in childhood and I really enjoy kids when they're that age. Let's take our winter vacation in Florida and spend some time with them."

We packed up our RV and headed south February 4. We stopped in Virginia to visit our special friends, Carolyn and John Nesselroade. We caught up on their news and their offspring, enjoyed Carolyn's cooking, John's professional tales, and the companionship of both. We sorely missed them.

As we neared Florida, Carol said, "Don, it's years since we first visited St. Augustine. Let's explore its history and arts and crafts again." After enjoying a day in that historic atmosphere, we meandered down the east coast, stopping occasionally at an appealing beach. Carol couldn't walk in the sand, and I had an even harder time pushing a wheelchair through it. We made a discovery on one beach. Some creative person had invented a wheel chair with 'balloon tires' that was easy to push on the sand. Carol said, "This is great fun being pushed along the edge of the water!" In the Palm Beach area, we explored where the rich folks live and then went back north to Orlando and Cam's family.

We parked in their driveway and hooked up to their water and electricity so we could sleep in our RV. Celia and Corin called our RV 'the Bus' and they loved to be in it and pretend they were driving it somewhere. With their parents' permission we invited them to have dinner and a 'sleepover' in the Bus. What fun! When they came out for the night, Carol said, "Let's have a party! We'll have happy hour drinks and snacks like grown-ups do, and play card games of your choice." They chose games they were good at and had great fun beating us. Finally Carol said, "Time to eat – will you help me get dinner? Afterwards we can listen to music or play games or read stories or just talk."

At night Celia slept on the sofa bed and Corin on the table made into a bed. In our bed Carol said, "What a treasure to have this special time alone with them. They're wonderful kids and so much fun. I feel I know them much better now." The kids liked it too, and it gave their parents the possibility of a night out, so we had several 'sleep overs' while there.

One day Gricel and Cam took us shopping with them looking for a piano to buy for the kids. Cam said, "I remember how learning to play the piano from you, Mom, brought music into each of your son's lives in special ways. We hope it will do the same for Celia and Corin."

With delight, Carol said, "I'm so happy you're doing that! If you'd let us pay for their music lessons I'd feel like I was helping them achieve that result." We did that for several years and they both became quite good. Celia moved from piano to superior ability on the violin.

In March we went back to springtime in Happy Valley. We spent spring and summer gardening, swimming in our pool with family and friends, enjoying the beauty of our stream and woods, visiting friends, camping, boating and swimming at the lake with grandkids and friends. Football season, tailgating, and the holiday seasons were filled with friendship, family and fun.

As the year evolved, I noticed some slight increase in Carol's memory difficulties and slight changes in her voice. She began having sleeping problems and anxiety, so Dr. Guillard prescribed a small evening dose of Ativan. I thought, *If these symptoms continue to elaborate we will have to face the implications together in the New Year.*

On Saturday after Thanksgiving we had happy hour and a light supper before our living room fireplace and a blazing fire of wild cherry logs flaming with multiple colors. Carol said, "We got a letter from Barb today. She's planning a surprise 50th birthday party celebration for Russ on December 30 and combining it with the New Year's Eve party at his hotel where we will all stay overnight."

"That sounds like fun. We'll have to think up something to add to his birthday roast, like the story of Russ and his buddy nearly getting arrested in Canada on their high school graduation vacation." Early evening December 30th Barb took Russ to dinner at the hotel dining room before the New Year's Eve celebration that night. As they prepared to order, his hotel manager said, "Russ, we overbooked. Would you mind shifting to our overflow dining room so we can use this table?"

Russ said "That's fine!" They went to the other room, opened the door and walked in ….. to a room full of three generations of Fords!

As the room erupted with applause, jeers, and laughter, Carol whispered in my ear "He's dumbfounded! Barb really fooled him. This is the first time I've ever seen Russ speechless!"

In the Ford family tradition of adult birthdays, there were jokes, silly gifts, roasting speeches, songs and lots of laughter. It was a great success and Barb had pictures taken of each family group.

After the party we all went to the ballroom for the New Year's Eve celebration. Everyone danced, including the very young Celia and Corin who were attending their very first New Year's celebration. It was especially fun to see those two cavort on the dance floor. Carol and I showed them how we real dancers "cut a rug", and then danced with them. We finished the evening on the hotel top floor terrace to watch the crowd below welcome in January 1, 2001.

I took us a few weeks to recover from Russ's big 50th birthday party and to savor the fun we had with our entire family. Then we packed up our RV and headed for our now traditional February winter vacation in Florida.

We spent nearly two weeks with Cam and Gricel. Carol was delighted to listen to our grandchildren demonstrate the fruits of their year of piano lessons. We had fun with them in their personal playground in the back yard. One evening while we were having a sleepover in "the Bus" Carol said, "I'd like to see the Kennedy Space Center where they send people into space. How about you guys?" They responded enthusiastically and the next morning Gricel and Cam approved our plan. We spent a day there and all agreed it was a fantastic place, both as an active space travel center and a museum. A highlight of our day was when we all took turns sitting in one of the early space capsules.

That night as we cuddled in bed, Carol said, "Just think, when I was Corin's age, seeing a dinky little one wing, one engine airplane was so exciting. Sixty five years later we're sending people into space where they live for weeks. It's unbelievable!"

We went back to our Slab Cabin paradise to start our spring gardening and our typical summer activities. In late summer Carol began having abdominal pain that grew in frequency and intensity. In her annual physical exam, Dr. Guillard found her generally in good health and could find no explanation for her increasing pain. A CAT scan ruled out several possibilities. Her annual gynecological exam indicated those organs were OK, and diagnostic imaging found nothing wrong. That was followed by her every five years colonoscopy, which showed that everything was in good shape. After all this diagnostic activity, Carol ended up with chronic gut pain diagnosed as "irritable bowel syndrome". Translated that means "something is producing gut pain but we don't know what and so we don't know how to fix it". Darvocet was prescribed to reduce the pain but was not helpful.

Carol said, "Don, this feels like severe menstrual cramps, or colon cramps from something like diarrhea. I'm miserable and discouraged. Am I going to have to live with this the rest of my life?"

"Carol, what we've learned is that MDs don't have all the answers. We've solved a lot of problems together so let's see if we can solve this one. The pain seems to be coming from the gastrointestinal system but the docs all say those organs look OK, so the pain isn't from structural damage. You say it feels like 'cramps' which implies smooth muscle spasms. The pain seems to be coming from organs like the stomach, intestines, uterus, or other smooth muscles that contract and relax to move stuff around inside them. If your pain is coming from those smooth muscles and we can find ways of getting those muscles to relax, then your pain should decrease. Does that make sense to you?"

"It fits my experience. For example, when I go to bed at night my gut hurts, but after I go to sleep and then wake up, I'm much more relaxed and usually feel less pain. Your theory suggests that the cramping, pain producing muscles relax when I'm sleeping and that reduces my pain experiences."

We developed a plan to try behavioral and psychological methods to relax smooth muscles in the gastrointestinal organ systems. This included drinking glasses of hot water or warm milk periodically, soaking in a hot bath before going to bed, wearing a brace to support and prevent movement of her belly, and eating lighter meals with more frequent snacks. We included a bedtime snack because eating activates the parasympathetic nervous system that helps control those inner muscles. We also tried to prevent anxiety states by controlling anticipatory thoughts that produce anxiety and by a dosage of Effexor XR which helps control both depression and anxiety.

After using these methods for several weeks, Carol said, "Things are considerably better. For example, I'm sleeping much better at night, experience little or no pain when I awake at night, and after drinking some warm milk and eating a snack I go back to sleep for another three to four hours. I still have occasional pain but can live with it now."

Dr. Guillard had several opportunities to observe Carol's behavior as she went through all those diagnostic processes. He told me privately that her growing cognitive difficulties, like memory confusion, made it likely that Carol was in the early stages of late onset Alzheimer's disease. He recommended starting her on the only approved medicine, named Aricept.

I replied, "We both know there are a variety of ways dementia symptoms can be produced, so before acting I will talk with Carol and, with her approval, arrange for a thorough diagnostic appraisal." He agreed that was a sound decision.

On a lovely summer evening we sat on our deck listening to night sounds and enjoying a sky spread with stars and a full moon. I said, "Carol, Mother Nature is beckoning us to come enjoy her beauty. Could you join me for a picnic date on our bridge Monday noon?"

"I'd love to share my personal touch with a guy who appreciates all forms of beauty!"

For this date I took special pains to create a lovely, happy memory arousing setting on our bridge. I covered the card table with a grass green cloth and sat a shallow dish in the center with a single Kansas sunflower in it. I chose paper plates with tiny colorful fish printed on them and Carol's favorite pink crystal goblets. The picnic basket contained a thermos of minty Moscow Mules, tuna salad sandwiches, some crunchies, chunks of sweet watermelon and juicy sweet black grapes.

On a pleasantly warm day we strolled down to our bridge and sat shaded by a canopy of leaves, entertained by a musical gurgling of the stream flowing around us and an occasional butterfly. I poured our drinks and lifted my goblet, "Here's to our first picnic together sixty years ago today at Alcove Spring, and to our picnic today in this beautiful place."

Carol smiled and followed suit. "Here's to the man who makes my life beautiful with picnics like this." We clinked glasses and sipped our minty drinks.

"Carol, how long have we lived on this stream?"

"Must be 50 years now on both sides of Slab Cabin."

"I vividly remember the day you drove me over here, pointed to the woods and stream and said, 'Here's where we're going to build our home.'"

"And what did you say?"

Yes M'am!" and we both laughed. "Lots of memories here, Carol."

"You mean like the time the branch of bees fell on us and our babies!"

"And how about the time around midnight in the moonlight we tubed down the stream in the nude after one of our dates?"

"We *have* had some uninhibited fun, haven't we!"

I put a sandwich and some fruit on each plate. While eating we talked about the beauty around us and happy memories. Then I added a little beverage to our goblets and said, "Carol, we've talked periodically about your slowly increasing difficulties with memories and other kinds of thinking. Dr. Guillard thinks it has progressed enough that we should investigate possible causes to help guide us in knowing what to do about it."

"I know it's getting worse, and I'm worried and scared about it, remembering my mother's illness. Sometimes I try not to think about it – just deal with whatever happens. Other times I think that's stupid, that it's better to know so we can plan how to deal with it. You know more about this kind of stuff than I do, so what do you think?"

"Like you, I'm worried. I have two thoughts. First, there are different ways besides Alzheimer's that cognitive symptoms like yours can be caused, and some of those other ways might be fixable. Second, if it *is* Alzheimer's we might be able to figure out ways to control it somewhat as we did with your gut pain. If we don't know what's going on we can't do that. Is it better to try or not to try? I remember one of my father's sayings – 'Faint heart ne'er won fair lady.' I translated that to mean 'Don't let fear keep you from trying.'

There is one thing I'm sure of: Whatever you decide to do we will do as partners, and in our life together we've learned we're a damned good team. Throughout our life together we've both thought the song *You'll Never Walk Alone* applied to us and that will continue."

Carol reached across the table, took my hand and kissed it. "I don't know what the future holds for me, but I do know that you'll do everything you can to make it the best it can be. So, I say let's go find out what we have to deal with."

"You know Gerry McClearn, my good friend and colleague, who's an internationally respected scholar about aging. He's on a national commission with other distinguished experts. A friend of his on that commission, Dr. Guy McKhann, is director of the Mind/Brain Institute at Johns Hopkins University where Milton Eisenhower used to be president. McKhann is considered a top scholar in the world on these issues. Gerry will get us an appointment with him to help us if you want him to."

"He sounds like a person we can trust to give us accurate information and advice."

"OK, I'll work with Gerry to make the arrangements." I sipped at my drink, watching Carol's face for any sign of distress, then shifted to a happier topic, "Now, we can finish our picnic with some very good news. You remember that our friend, Fred Vondracek, interviewed Doug for a job here. Well, Fred offered Doug the job, and since he and Pam have an empty nest with all three of their kids in college, Doug has accepted an appointment as Assistant Dean for Undergraduate Studies in our college. They'll move down here as soon as possible, hopefully by October. Since the house we built for your Dad is available, they can move in there and be our neighbors."

"Oh Don, that's fantastic! That's another dream come true. I share and admire Pam's interests in art and having her to talk with will be wonderful. She's my kind of gal."

"You've often said that each time we needed something good to happen for us, it did at the last minute, and you thought 'someone up there' must be looking out for us. Well, it's happened again! Just when we need support and encouragement dealing with tough issues in our life, the best people possible are coming to be our neighbors. It will be special to have one of our sons help run the college you and I built together."

I helped Carol to her feet and we hugged each other close. "Thank you for our picnic, Don. As usual, our date has brightened my life when I greatly needed it." We stood together for a few moments, relishing that sweet embrace and the sounds of Slab Cabin Run singing its song as it flowed down stream past our home.

Finally, I kissed her and said, "Let's walk home – I'll pick this stuff up later." On the way home we stopped by our spring fed pond so Carol could pick flowers for the vase she always keeps by the kitchen sink. Then we went inside and took a nap.

Carol had an appointment with Dr. McKhann October 1st. He and his staff conducted extensive neurobehavioral exams and did a brain MRI. He personally reported to me, and later in writing to Dr. Guillard: "There is worsening impairment in multiple domains including memory, language and visuo-constructional abilities with some voice changes and motor slowing. The psychological and clinical appraisals 'are consistent with' an emerging Alzheimer's pattern and there is nothing in the MRI 'inconsistent with' that diagnosis. However Carol's well-preserved personality might argue somewhat against that diagnosis."

I explained the findings to Carol, "They suspect it might be late onset Alzheimer's but as you know they can't be sure. He says the fact you're actually functioning pretty normally – he called that 'a well preserved personality' – might raise a little doubt about that diagnosis.

He recommends playing it safe by starting two medications that research indicates might sometimes be helpful in slowing down Alzheimer's development and therefore might help your symptoms. Aricept is approved for use in the U.S. and Memantine is approved for use in Europe. It's expected to be approved for use in the U.S. within a year with the name Namenda. McKhaan's European colleagues report they get better effects by using both than using either separately. He recommends Guillard prescribe both if I can get Memantine through my personal contacts. Do you want to do that?"

"Are there any serious potential side effects?"

"No. Both have been widely researched and used clinically for several years."

"Then I suppose it's worth a try. What do you think?"

"I agree. You have nothing to lose and maybe lots to gain."

"OK, let's do it. Who can get it for you in Germany?"

"Penn State has a collaborative relationship with the University of Jena in Germany and Fred Vondracek can help us get it through his contacts there." Carol began using Aricept in October, 2002 and Memantine in January 2003. (Namenda became available in the U.S. later in 2003.)

We continued our usual fall activities including tailgating and football games. But a very special component was added to our daily life – Pam and Doug became our neighbors in October, 2002. We saw and talked by phone with one or both of them almost every day and frequently shared lunch or dinner.

Doug told me, "The only difference I notice in Mom compared to past years is some mobility limitation – some difficulty in moving around with her cane."

Pam added, "She still looks and acts pretty much the same – still physically active, still interested in doing things, still driving the car. She enjoys hearing us talk about our kids. I visited with her a couple mornings a week while you were teaching. She clearly enjoyed my visits, but was comfortable being alone, so after a while she sometimes said, 'I know you have other things to do so you don't need to stay here until Don gets home.' She loves pets and your dog Casey was gone, so she enjoyed seeing our dog Abby when we had her out for a walk."

During the Thanksgiving and Christmas holiday season Carol said, "Holidays are so much more fun now because we get to share them with Doug's family. They're a lively and fun bunch, and things get livelier when the boys and their families show up between Christmas and New Year's. Life is never dull with our gang around."

"Carol, you have your checkup with Dr. Guillard January 17th. I'm preparing written information for him to save interview time. Has your increased dosage of Effexor helped?"

"Oh yes! My episodes of anxiety are greatly reduced, and I'm eating well now and enjoying the taste of many foods again. I'm sleeping seven to nine hours a night and have less need for a long afternoon nap. Dr. Cherry's x-rays showed bursitis in my hip joint on the leg where that big muscle was removed. After his shot that pain is less frequent and severe."

"I think the hoarseness and high frequency sounds in your voice have increased a little while volume has decreased a little, but you're still easy to understand. With your soft voice and my poor hearing we make quite a pair!"

She laughed and said, "Maybe I should sing what I want to say to you."

"Do you want to take our traditional winter vacation trip to Florida?"

"Oh yes! Actually I feel pretty good and look forward to warm air and playing with our grandchildren."

We went to see Cam's family first this year instead of wandering along the coast. On a Friday morning, shortly after we arrived, Carol's gut pain began. By 3 p.m. it was severe; by 4 p.m. it was excruciating; and by 5 p.m. it was unbearable. Nothing we tried helped. Finally we called 911. The ambulance arrived about 5:30 p.m., the EMTs checked her vitals, put her on a heart monitor and IV, and headed for an emergency room. Around 6:30 p.m., shortly before arriving at the ER, the pain suddenly stopped. Triage postponed her case to deal with more urgent ones. Carol continued to feel OK, but during the wait she had to urinate frequently.

A doctor saw her about 11 p.m. All vitals were OK, no sign of infection, and no blood in the urine. Based on the severe pain location, and the relatively rapid onset and termination, he said the most likely cause was passage of kidney stones. Blood in the urine only occurs about half the time and she urinated so much while waiting four hours she might have eliminated any blood. A much less likely possibility was a very severe and persistent colon spasm or cramp.

The next morning, and for all our remaining time in Florida, there was no recurrence of that episode of pain, not even a mild version. And, the more painful aspects of the gut discomfort she'd been having the past two years were essentially gone. Carol said, "I'll bet my two years of severe gut pain was not from my gut but from my kidney. I remember my father had that kind of pain syndrome for a couple of years when he had kidney stones."

"Carol, you know I've passed kidney stones twice and my experience of increasingly severe and then sudden release of pain sounds like your description. In my episode at the shore we actually collected my urine for three days and saw the little stone when the pain suddenly stopped. This is the third time in your life the source of persistent pain has been misdiagnosed."

Later in the week, while our grandkids were making sleepover dinner waffles with our heart shaped waffle iron, Carol said, "I read in the paper about a show in town called *Muppets Live* starring Kermit, Fozzie and the whole gang. It sounds like fun – have you seen it?" Their answer was no but they sure would like to, so we took the whole family. On the way home, Carol and

Corin carried on an animated conversation about the show. Carol's favorite piece was Kermit the Frog singing *Bein' Green,* but Corin preferred Fozzie's *Veterinarian Hospital.*

We finished our winter vacation camping at a picturesque old fishing village on the gulf coast north of Tampa. They'd been trying to attract tourists by creating a venue for unusual arts and crafts. Many of the items on display were new to Carol so she loved the experience, and both of us enjoyed seeing what the historical fishing subculture had been like.

We returned home to welcome spring and summer back to Happy Valley and resumed our usual pattern of activities. Dr. McKhann had requested a one year follow up report on Carol's reactions to the medications he had prescribed. I wrote him on July 24:

"Carol began taking a daily 10 mg dose of Aricept in late October, 2002. After 3 months, no changes in cognitive or other behaviors were observed. Then, beginning January, 2003, we added Memantine, slowly building the dosage to 10 mg. taken twice daily. After 4 months, not only had further decline halted, but some clear recovery of functioning was observed, with no noticeable side effects.

Carol's **procedural memory** has significantly improved: e.g., planning and preparing meals; daily home management tasks are routinely accomplished; driving the car to anticipated destinations; playing her piano; and organizing large numbers of old photos to create picture albums with story lines. **Event memory** has improved: e.g., remembering that future commitments have been made and when they are to occur (anticipatory memory); remembering events of the recent past and being able to tell others about them (recall). **Name memory** has improved: e.g., names of and information about family members and friends (as well as things) are now more frequently recalled. The newspaper is read daily and commented on. Novels are read for leisure pleasure. Participation is more frequent in conversations at social occasions, and topics are occasionally initiated. Recovery is far from complete, but if functioning were to stabilize at current levels she could lead a reasonably satisfying effective life."

I reviewed the report with Carol and she said, "I think that's pretty accurate. I feel a lot better about things in general and I'm enjoying life more."

A setback in September disrupted our hopeful outlook. Carol drove to the dairy and couldn't remember how to start the car when she came out. Fright overwhelmed her and she asked the dairy employees to call me. As she waited, fear increased her confusion and that had escalated to sheer panic by the time I arrived to take her home. That episode of intense fear at being alone and helpless rapidly generalized, a process typical of such fear episodes in people's lives. She had previously been comfortable during my absences. Now she became quite anxious if I wasn't there, but felt secure when I was with her or she could see me. She stopped driving.

Pam gave two examples of Carol's change in behavior. I taught a graduate seminar two mornings a week each fall. Pam visited with Carol while I was gone. She said, "The previous fall, Carol was comfortable while you were gone, but this year she isn't. If you left before I got there, she'd be quite anxious when I arrived. She'd continue to be anxious waiting for your return and frequently asked when you'd be back. Or, if you were in the yard working she'd be anxious. I'd take her out on the deck so she could see you mowing. If your mowing took you out of sight, she'd get anxious, then be relieved when you mowed back into sight. By distracting her with positive thoughts or activities I can ease her anxiety."

Pam reported a statement Carol made that hit me in the heart! "When Don was building the college I did everything I could to help him. Now it's my turn – I need his help in dealing with my changes." I immediately quit teaching and devoted all my time to our relationship. I was angry that I hadn't made that decision sooner to prevent doubts her fears might generate.

It was now clear that Carol was experiencing late onset Alzheimer's. I reminded myself of the private commitment I'd made as we dealt with Winifred's Alzheimer's disease decades ago: *If Carol ever has Alzheimer's I'll invent ways of providing a meaningful and pleasurable life using capabilities she has left. I'll see to it that she's treated like a person, not as a patient!*

Chapter Thirty-Two
Carol's Magic Man Devises a Plan

Carol will be a person, still my talented, beautiful Carol, and not a patient. I was determined to fulfill that commitment. In quiet times, I concentrated on potential rationales and strategies to implement a plan that might benefit Carol's daily life experience. I'd created theories and applications in the past about health and human development, but now those theories had the added dimension of being personal.

An early reviewer of this book said, "Don, you must have felt sorrow and despair at times. You need to inject more of your personal feelings about Carol's illness. In my experience most readers faced with caring for loved ones with Alzheimer's surely must feel lost, hopeless, despairing and overwhelmed at times. They have to be able to relate to you on a personal level to find hope in your plan that you implemented despite your feelings." I understand her point; I lived Carol's distress as she watched and cared for her mother through Alzheimer's, and her pregnant daughter-in-law dying of cancer. So, I will give you a peek into my feelings.

Remember this book started with an episode in which Carol and I read to one another letters we wrote about our feelings. I wrote: "*Our limitations may grow in unpredictable ways. For example, since both your mother and aunt died in nursing homes with Alzheimers's disease, the fear it might eventually reach you has been present. Circulatory problems killed my father and could get me. We could be in an automobile accident. But let's not focus on the bad things that might happen. Let's savor the good possibilities that lie before us and make them happen.*"

Later Carol reacted to that part of my letter: "I do occasionally have anxious thoughts about my family tendency to

Alzheimer's. Of course, I hope it doesn't happen, but I know there is no cure if it does. What you said in your letter helps me immensely. I know that no matter what happens to me, if it can be fixed I can count on you to get it fixed, as you have throughout our lives. If it can't be fixed I know with your love and creative mind you'll find ways to help us continue to live a meaningful life together. So as you suggest, I'll join you in focusing on the good things our life offers, and try not to worry about the bad possibilities." She added "Grandma often said: 'Don't waste time crying over spilt milk.'"

Fortified by our deep love for each other, we daily found ways to live that positive view for the rest of our lives. Actually, that view was not new for us; from the beginning of our marriage our mutual commitment was to enrich one another's life despite any difficulties that might arise. The **developmental model of care** we developed was built on the idea that, regardless of limitations, there are always possible ways left for getting some pleasure and satisfaction out of life. That belief sustained both of us through the Alzheimer's ordeal.

Each time we talked, each time I heard her laugh, each time I took her into my arms to dance, each time she displayed joy in some episode, each beautification day she enjoyed, each time she greeted a son with love, each time she expressed love for me in words or acts, I felt a wave of pleasure and happiness. In the early stages we both occasionally had moments of anxiety, sadness and discouragement, but we had those before Carol's illness also. They were fleeting because we quickly shifted psychological gears and initiated episodes that produced feelings of accomplishment, satisfaction and pleasure. In the last few years such negative emotions seldom occurred. We had created and were living a pattern of daily life that brought to each day some pleasure, satisfaction, and happiness.

Developmental care focuses on "accentuating the positive" and "limiting the negative", and on making both the caregiver and care receiver feel like they accomplished some positive things each day. Read the comments of Carol's caregivers later to feel the power of feeling one has accomplished something worthwhile. I confess to one period of a deep sense of sadness, loss and a dark, lonely future. I was alone! Then I discovered I wasn't. Carol was still with me in meaningful ways. That discovery is what produced this book. (But, I still miss her terribly.)

To those of you who now, or may, face this kind of ordeal I suggest: Don't focus on what is being lost—identify positive possibilities that are potentially within reach. Then create daily activity patterns through which you, and your loved one, can gain some satisfaction from those remaining possibilities. Carol's story illustrates that is possible.

If you've stayed with me as I shared Carol's life history with you, now you'll see why knowing that history was essential to her plan of care.

One influential theory on the nature of human development is called *Developmental Living Systems Theory*. It provided the theoretical framework for Carol's daily care and will help readers understand how she lived the rest of her life as a contented person who just happened to have Alzheimer's, rather than a patient who was helplessly sick. (References provided in the epilogue.)

Preserving biological life, the core objective of the currently dominant **medical model of elder care,** is not the same thing as helping a person cultivate a satisfying life. I call the approach I created for Carol a **developmental model of elder care.** This kind of approach has long been used with children and adults who have to cope with limitations, but is too seldom used with senior citizens needing elder care. We assume too often that developing alternate ways of behaving is not possible for most old people. Extensive research on aging has proven that assumption incorrect. Here are key components to the **developmental model**:

The primary source of meaning in life comes from setting personal goals and accomplishing them with activities that yield pleasure and satisfaction in their achievement. Goals can range from small and short term to big and long term, but the way they operate is the same.

All of a person's behavior every day is organized into cohesive patterns of goal setting and implementation in a specific context. Each pattern is called a Behavior Episode (BE). Each episode starts with a decision about something one wants to accomplish, where and when. That activates thoughts about how to do it, which trigger and guide implementing actions. Thoughts and emotions evaluate the success of those actions. Producing desired consequences is the source of satisfaction and pleasure that leads a person to pursue similar BEs in the future. A life without goals and goal achievement yields a barren existence filled only with boredom, dissatisfaction, loneliness and feelings of anger, depression, helplessness and uselessness. Staying alive seems meaningless.

Behavior can only occur in the here and now; it can't occur tomorrow or yesterday. How then can the past and potential futures influence what a person does now? That is the role of thoughts with names like memories, expectations and goals. When such thoughts are disrupted, the nature and guidance of current behavior episodes occur primarily through perceptions of what is going on in the here and now. That is the nature of the mental life of an infant, and becomes evident in advanced Alzheimer's disease. *That is why a person with Alzheimer's disease can display organized patterns of behavior in the here and now, as long as they don't try to organize their actions with thoughts about the past or future.*

At any moment in life, the goals a person can successfully pursue are controlled by the possibilities and limitations provided by their current contexts, capabilities, and characteristics. Throughout each person's lifetime, those personal circumstances, possibilities and limitations change and evolve, requiring changes in goals and ways of achieving them. For example, consider the changes illustrated by a child's development, a permanently injured adult, a stroke or Alzheimer's victim, or an aging adult. But – and this is a critical point – **as limitations grow there are always options left for a person to use to gain satisfaction and pleasure out of life, if those possibilities can be freed by the person's current activities!**

How can you identify the behavior conditions needed to help a person (like an Alzheimer's or stroke victim) bypass their limitations and perform behavior episodes that might produce satisfaction and pleasure? The best source for that information lies in identifying the BE activity patterns that consistently produced pleasure and satisfaction for the person in many similar episodes throughout life. That knowledge can then be used to create current activity versions of their history within present abilities and limitations. I call that a person's *activity record*, similar to the medical record that follows a person into a nursing home.

In Carol's situation, I needed to develop forms of behavior episodes that would:

(1) *maximize positive thoughts and emotions* – success, satisfaction, affection and pleasure from accomplishing personal goals, and;

(2) *minimize negative thoughts and emotions* – loneliness, failure, incompetence, fear, discouragement and anger from faulty, unsuccessful or absent BEs. In modern psychological science this approach is called *positive psychology*.

Feelings are evolutionary products that have a powerful evaluative and regulatory influence on each person's behavior. They are conscious "desirable" or "undesirable" experiences. Desirable feelings automatically motivate activities aimed at producing or continuing those feelings. Undesirable feelings do the opposite – they motivate efforts to end or avoid such experiences.

The most primitive kinds of feelings are called **affects:** Biological states produce experiences like *sleepy, hot, fatigue, and pain;* Sensory-perceptual processes produce states like *smells or tastes good (or bad), sound is too loud, light is too bright.* **Emotions** are feelings linked to biological states activated to support some kind of action.

Instrumental emotions enable effective goal accomplishment: *Curiosity and interest* motivate goal directed exploration; *Satisfaction and pleasure* signal progress towards and accomplishment of goals and motivates continuation and repetition of that effective activity; *Disinterest and boredom* signals routine activities of no personal value and motivate stopping or avoiding such activity; *Anxiety and fear* signal events the person interprets as potentially harmful, unpredictable and uncontrollable and motivates avoiding or escaping from such events; *Annoyance and anger* signals interpretation of some events as obstructions to accomplishing goals and motivates actions to overcome such obstacles.

Social emotions enable cooperative group living: *Affection and love* signal a desire for interpersonal caring and sharing, and motivates commitment, comfort, and sacrifice; *Sexual arousal* signals a desire for sensual pleasure and facilitates courtship and mating activities; *Loneliness and sorrow* signals separation from others we care for and motivates efforts toward reunion; *Embarrassment, shame, guilt and humiliation* signal violation of group customs and values and motivates conformity and submission to group living.

Understanding the dynamics of different emotion patterns helps evaluate a person's current behavior. For example, Carol's smiling and laughing signals her satisfaction and pleasure at succeeding in current activities. Carol's distress when she forgot how to start her car at the dairy was fear triggered by facing a situation she was unable to control.

Memory processes help shape the content of every episode in a person's life. Memory disruption is a key symptom of Alzheimer's. So, understanding the nature of memory processes is a key to understanding how to work with people who have Alzheimer's disease.

What are memories? Every person's behavior is composed of different behavior patterns that I call episodes to indicate they are integrated patterns. Each episode provides a subjective experience pattern from which memory patterns are constructed.

When a person performs behavior episodes guided by similar goals in different settings on different occasions, the memory patterns they construct will be a combination of the experience patterns of each of those similar episodes. For example, think of the many times you drive your car to work or shop. Since these are generalized versions of similar episode experiences, we'll call them *meaning patterns or packages.* Thus, memories are organized packages or patterns of meanings. The process of remembering activates aspects of those meaning patterns, not just specific elements.

Where are memories (meaning packages) when you aren't using them? The old but incorrect answer was they were stored somewhere in the brain like a book in a library. Research has proven that memories are not stored as separate entities in separate neurones. They are *reconstructed* when a person's current experience pattern has similarities to a previous meaning package.

So, people don't actually "lose their memory", but they may lose the ability to reactivate specific meaning patterns with their usual retrieval cues. **Even with Alzheimer patients, many (perhaps most) of their meaning packages are still potentially available if you can find different ways of activating them.**

Any current experience that can activate reconstruction of a meaning pattern is called *a retrieval cue*. Each meaning pattern contains many kinds of experience – different sights, sounds, odors, emotions, contexts, words, and actions, any of which can function as retrieval cues for that pattern. For example, the delicious odor of freshly baked bread or reading a letter written by grandma may activate the same or similar childhood memories of grandma's kitchen (meaning patterns). An old maxim says, "Many roads lead to Rome." Even very old meaning packages can be reactivated with the right combination of retrieval cues. **For example, 80-year old Carol, while looking at and talking about pictures of herself dancing when she was seven, could reconstruct memories of those activities and contexts.**

Words are the most widely used retrieval cues. Words themselves have no basic meaning; they are only labels (or handles) for activating and using our memory meaning packages. For example, different kinds of meanings can be activated by the word 'drinking' (how many meanings does that word activate in you?).

The power of words is that if different people use the same word to activate the same meaning pattern, sharing meanings with others becomes possible. If a word typically used as a retrieval cue for a specific meaning package no longer activates those meanings, try alternate retrieval cues. For example, if saying the word 'drink' doesn't activate the desired behavior in a person, use gestures like pretending to drink something. **We think with meanings not words!**

So now you know most of the key ideas behind the **developmental model** used to enrich Carol's life with Alzheimer's. As I continue with her story, I'll describe in greater detail how we implemented my plan. My goal is to help you understand how the care model worked and provide supportive information for those who wish to use the ideas and methods that worked so well with Carol. You don't have to be a doctor, scholar, or medical professional to use this model of care. **All you need is a**

basic knowledge of a person's history and behavioral activities, the genuine desire to enrich their daily life, and the imagination to create daily activity patterns based on that knowledge that will enrich that person's daily life.

The emotional impact of the dairy episode on Carol's daily behavior faded fairly rapidly so we could comfortably resume our daily routines and enjoy our daily lives. As 2004 began, the beneficial effects of Carol's Alzheimer medications reported to Dr. McKhann in 2003 persisted. I wrote to Dr. Otto Witte at Jena University in Germany:

"I want to thank you for your kindness in making Memantine available for my wife. It is now available in the U.S. as Namenda so we will no longer need your help in obtaining it. Aricept alone had little impact, but the two together seem to have stopped further decline from her illness, and produced some recovery of function. If her current steady state continues, she will be able to enjoy her life in ways that your help has made possible."

Despite limitations Carol had developed in the early stages of Alzheimer's, she was still largely able to organize and guide her own activities. She could still walk, talk, manipulate objects, take care of herself, socialize with others, set and pursue personal goals, and accomplish a variety of tasks. She could still enjoy a day at the lake on her pontoon boat. Major changes in her patterns of daily living weren't yet necessary. In this phase of Alzheimer's development, it was important to treat Carol as a capable adult rather than an ill patient, and essential that she be helped to adapt daily activity patterns to accommodate emerging limitations.

My first step in making this phase of Carol's life satisfying was to focus on health promotion activities. Throughout our married life she'd focused on a sound diet as a key health promotion method, so that was already part of our daily routine. She also believed in regular exercise to keep her body fit and flexible, so I made sure that activity continued.

Her safety was a prime concern. I installed a walk in bathtub with a built in bench, added several grab bars in the bathroom and reversed the bathroom door to accommodate Carol's wheel chair. Wherever safety features were needed to provide protected mobility around the house, I added them. Such changes are typically simple and inexpensive.

Carol had been taking nine pills a day for several years. Were all of them still needed? Years ago her doctor had prescribed a small nightly dosage of Ativan (Lorazepam) to help her sleep. I asked, "Carol, you've been sleeping well for some time. Would you be willing to try getting along without Ativan now?"

"If that doesn't work could I go back on it?"

"Sure."

She agreed to discontinue Ativan and we were both surprised and pleased with the results, as I described it to our sons: "After about 4 weeks, there were some valuable changes in your mother's behavior. She began to stand more erect, and to walk more normally. The occasional muscle spasms and arm and hand tremors nearly disappeared. The ability to feed herself markedly improved, and not only did she begin to eat better but also had more enjoyment in eating. Her mood and emotions improved greatly, and occasional crying episodes stopped. She no longer becomes uncomfortable when we have visitors. There must have been some med interactions, but we have no idea what they might be. She still sleeps well.

She tries to read again. During the past year she was unable to cooperate during eye tests. Recently, they tried again. To our surprise she was able to read the charts, report what she saw, and her vision was 20/25 (better than mine)."

Then Carol began having frequent gut pains again and nothing we tried eliminated them. I said, "Carol, you take a lot of pills every day, all with your food at breakfast except one you take at bedtime. Do you think they might be interacting with each other in some way to produce your gut pains?"

"My only clue is I tend to have more gut distress in the morning than at any other time."

"I've been trying to find research that evaluates the behavioral, psychological and biological interaction of pills taken simultaneously and have found little information. It's hard to believe that when you mix a bunch of different chemicals together at the same time there aren't some interactions. Want to try an experiment? We could spread them out to reduce potential interactions and promote better health, such as breakfast – lunch – dinner – bedtime."

"I'd sure like to get rid of these gut pains so let's try it."

After a few weeks of the experiment, Carol joyfully reported, "My gut symptoms have nearly disappeared! It's almost too good to be true. I haven't felt this good in a long time."

My next focus was promoting dental health. Early in his career our dentist, Kevin Labosky, acquired specialized knowledge and competence by taking time from his regular practice to provide dental services to nursing home patients. He said, "Nursing home patients often have some tooth decay that doesn't hurt or interfere with eating. Because of behavioral limitations, doing dental procedures inside their mouth is often difficult and risky. Instead of trying to fix it, unless it starts hurting, I recommend focusing on prevention. Extensive research has demonstrated that a new form of low calorie sugar named Xylitol prevents cavity formations if used in sufficient amounts. For example, it's now included in some standard chewing gum but in such small amounts it provides no benefits. Research has revealed a minimum of 6 grams of xylitol a day produces significant cavity prevention."

We found Xylitol available as mints, gum, tooth paste, mouthwash, and granulated sweetener from internet sites (we used Epic). We used the tooth paste twice a day and one piece of gum or 2 mints after each meal. We used the granulated form for a sweetener and to make Carol's special strawberry-rhubarb jam. As a result of our experiment, Carol needed no dental repair work the rest of her life.

In her pre-Alzheimer's years, Carol believed physical movement essential for maintaining a healthy body. For example, it promotes healthy respiration, blood circulation, gastrointestinal functioning, muscle strength and coordination, and neural functioning. She used to begin every day with calisthenics and dancing exercises, swam a lot, took care of a big house, and used her arms and hands while working in her shop. She walked a lot while running errands around town.

Declines in motor skills made many of those forms of exercise difficult or impossible. For example, she was fearful of swimming because of limited control, despite wearing a life vest and having me with her. So, I focused on using other movement capabilities she had left. I used all the ways I could think of to cultivate coordinated physical movement of various parts of her body by involving her in goal directed behavior episodes that required movement patterns. I'll outline some exercises later. **Such exercises provided Carol with satisfying behavior episodes that also allowed her to successfully accomplish goals.**

Carol could still help prepare and set the table for a meal, walk around the kitchen to collect and put dirty dishes in the dishwasher, and take clean dishes from the dishwasher and put them away. Sitting down and standing up without help occurred at least twenty times a day. I planned shared activities and tasks such as doing laundry, putting clean clothes away, going downstairs to view our big TV, and walking outdoors to admire the flowers around our little spring fed pond. These activities involved walking and going up and down stairs six or more times a day with me beside, in front, or behind her for safety. We went shopping several times a week which required a good bit of walking and helping put groceries away when we got home. Occasionally we danced together in the evening. If someone came to the door we walked through our entry garden to greet them, walked them to the living room to visit, and back to the door when they left. All these everyday activities had been and continued to be part of the normal routine Carol enjoyed.

Next, I looked for alterations in her goal directed activities that could accommodate her current limitations. I felt it was essential that Carol experience activities she enjoyed and succeed in the activities she attempted rather than being upset because she failed. The next several pages will show examples of those alterations.

Her endurance and coordination limited how far and how long she could walk and stand, so she couldn't easily navigate crowded places (like stores) or uneven surfaces (like walking along our stream to enjoy nature's beauty). So, to continue the pleasure of shopping together, Carol learned to drive an electric cart in stores. By driving a cart she experienced the satisfaction of independence, rather than depending on others to control her agenda in a wheel chair. Driving a cart also enabled social interactions. Carol was well known and liked around town and frequently met a friend or former customer while shopping who wanted to visit awhile. Having a cart to sit in rather than standing made friendly gabfests possible.

Carol enjoyed frequent interactions with other people, but emerging limitations significantly reduced such opportunities.

Many friends had died or moved away, and she no longer participated in groups that provided such interactions, such as choral groups. I sought to create alternative ways of providing the daily socialization she relished. For years we'd enjoyed sharing a midmorning coffee break and some conversation. Throughout her life, a coffee break gabbing session with other women had been a frequent pleasure. Another of Carol's pleasures was eating a tasty (particularly sweet) snack. Her favorite treats with coffee were a raspberry Danish or a cinnamon roll. I decided to combine those sources of pleasure into a social occasion.

Because her motor skills were impaired, I cut her coffee break treat into smaller pieces for finger food she could manage on her own. And I passed the word that midmorning would be a good time to visit her. Daughter-in-law Pam frequently came for coffee break. Carol loved her and Pam was a favorite gabbing partner. Watching the closeness of their relationship was a joy for me. Sometimes Doug, his sons, or one of Carol's old friends dropped by. Our old friend Earl Elliott, now a widower, visited often at coffee break, bringing Carol a flower or tasty treat and his lap top to show pictures of his family or a recent trip. Carol and I had helped them get married, so Earl's visits triggered happy memories in Carol.

Carol had enjoyed a couple of soap operas on TV for decades. She jokingly called her favorite *The Young and the Useless.* I organized our lunch time to coincide with that show so we could watch it together while we ate. She often joked about familiar storylines or the actors who had played the same characters for decades.

From childhood, Carol had enjoyed being in the great outdoors with its natural beauty in every season. For decades she'd experienced hours of pleasure from what she called our "Slab Cabin Family Resort." She greatly missed that part of her life because of mobility limitations and I'd been wracking my brain for a solution. Carol's sons found an answer. Pam was the messenger. She came for a visit and said, "Mom, what's that thing sitting in your driveway?"

"What thing?"

"Come out and see for yourself." Waiting outside were Doug, Russ, and several grandchildren, standing around an electric golf cart with a big red bow tied to it and a pair of blue and white dice hanging from the windshield. They all applauded and sang a boisterous version of "Happy Birthday!" Carol was speechless, but obviously delighted. Pam walked her to the cart and helped her into it. Doug had convinced his brothers to buy a used golf cart for the mobility needed for Carol to enjoy her "Mother Nature paradise" and visit neighbors.

Doug and Russ showed her how to drive it. Then Carol, with sparkling eyes and a big smile, drove across the lawn and down to her Slab Cabin stream with Pam riding co-pilot and the others trailing behind. She drove along the stream to Pam and Doug's house, where they had a picnic table set up on a grassy spot near the stream. Looking one direction, Carol could see the stream and woods, complete with quacking ducks. In the other direction, she could see a glorious hillside flower garden with Pam and Doug's house above it. Tearfully, but with a broad, dimpled smile on her face, Carol said "I'm so happy!"

Anything that brought a smile to Carol's face warmed my heart. For the rest of her life, that cart brought Carol great pleasure. For both safety and companionship, someone always rode with her, or chauffeured her along the stream to Slab Cabin Park and its "suicide hill" – the site of exciting sledding in winter – and sometimes they drove around the neighborhood.

For example, Pam acted as chauffeur when driving Carol up and down neighborhood streets. They stopped periodically to enjoy someone's flower garden, often discussing the colors as artists do, and "gabbed" with neighbors who came to the cart to say hello. That gave Carol the pleasure of interesting camaraderie and helped her continue to feel a part of the community. The cart provided a great advantage over a motorized chair because two people could ride together and that made it a social outing while providing safety as well.

Marion Perryman had been helping Carol clean house for twenty five years. They became good friends. Marion described her view of what Carol's life was like before we needed a team of aides, and how Carol enjoyed her companionship. Marion modified her regular cleaning activities so Carol could participate in maintaining her own home within her limitations during which they had gab sessions:

"I've known Carol from the top of her capabilities to when she died. She was the nicest person I ever knew. She was wonderful to be around and talk to, even as Alzheimer's developed. Early in

the disease she would sometimes start to say something and then say, 'I forgot what I was going to say,' or she'd go into a room and then forget what she went to do – and I would say, 'That's ok – just relax and it will come back to you' and it usually would. She told me about her mother having Alzheimer's and I think she knew she was heading in that direction but she never complained about it.

When I first started coming, Carol's typical day was spent working in her craft shop. I remember one year she was making gifts for her daughters-in-law. About 11 a.m. she'd start lunch – she looked forward to Don coming home for lunch. Don asked me to keep her involved in daily activities as much as possible so I let her work with me when she wanted to. For example, she'd help me fold laundry and we'd talk. As time went by, that became more difficult for her so I modified the routine so that I folded all the big ones and she folded the smaller ones. Sometimes she'd have difficulty, so I'd show her how to do it and she picked up on it.

She loved talking about her grandchildren. When we worked in the same room she'd say 'I have some new pictures – would you like to see them?' I'd look at them and show her my newest pictures. I never saw Carol get mad!! I saw her worry. For example, even before her disease started and Don wasn't home she'd say things like, 'I don't know where he went,' or 'He should have been home by now.' That got worse as the disease developed. I'd reassure her and pretty soon Don would come. She'd often work on her picture albums – that was one thing she really wanted to accomplish – to get them all in good shape before she couldn't work on them anymore.

Carol seemed to realize she was changing. For example, she stopped going downstairs by herself and walked more slowly – I think she was afraid of falling. She always wanted to make her bed. She fell one day, Don helped her up and she was ok, so I told her I'd make the bed with her to make it easier and that's what we did.

I was so impressed with how much better Carol's life was compared to my sisters' two Alzheimer's patients. They were helpless, in bed all the time, always had bed sores, and had no activity or people around them. In contrast, when I was here, even to the last, I could hear and see Carol talking, laughing, doing things and enjoying life."

Warm interpersonal relationships, particularly with women, had always been a major source of pleasure and satisfaction, so this became a somewhat lonely period of life for Carol. Most of her old friends were gone. She had given friendship and support to many as they died of breast cancer, strokes or other diseases. Some had moved away. She no longer participated in organizations where personal interactions occurred naturally, like choral groups, and no longer had women coming to see her in the craft shop. Her list of frequent and affectionate interactions had shrunk to me, Pam, Doug, Earl and Marion, supplemented with occasional visits by family members living elsewhere and a couple of friends she had known since our early years at Penn State.

As had so often happened in Carol's life, a need was suddenly and unexpectedly met. Her contact list expanded when Doug and Pam's two sons came home to live while finishing BS degrees at Penn State. Matt (Carol's first grandchild) had been pursuing a career in the movie industry, decided he didn't want that as a long term career, and chose to shift his career pathway to journalism. Ryan was a talented musician and performer, but after a year in a professional school of music decided not to pursue a musical performance career. He chose to emphasize music's technical side. They were delightful, interesting and talented young men with the gift of gab and a lively sense of humor.

During their two years at Penn State, we had occasional "happy hours' and family dinners every week during which the boys kept everyone entertained with lively conversation and laughter. Being a lifelong movie buff and musician, Carol was fascinated with the experiences they shared with us. She loved Matt's stories of his adventures in the movie industry, and enjoyed sitting beside Ryan as he played her piano.

Once, Ryan got a bit too enthusiastic and loud for Carol's taste. She couldn't talk well enough to tell him to tone it down, so she chose another way of making her point. She took hold of the wooden key board cover and, to his surprise, flopped it down on his fingers. Everyone roared with laughter while she sat there grinning at him. When limitations grow, people can find alternate ways of accomplishing the same goal. This episode is the perfect example of what the neuro doctor meant when he said Carol had a strong personality. Despite Alzheimer's, she still demonstrated her sweet or sometimes mischievous personality.

I wanted to keep Carol involved with people as a natural part of our shared life, so instead of meeting with colleagues on campus or at a restaurant, I invited them to join Carol and me for a "professional lunch" in our home. She generally seemed to find them interesting, but let me know by her body language if she thought the visit was dragging on too long. She particularly liked it when our guest was a woman, like our talented Dean of Nursing, Paula Milone-Nuzzo. Carol told me, "She's a nice, down-home person – the kind I like. She's not afflicted by 'bigshotitis'."

I also wanted to keep Carol involved and enjoying a social life outside our home because that was a familiar pattern throughout our marriage. Sometimes we went to a friend's home for dinner or to a nice restaurant with friends or family members. She'd always loved getting her hair done and "gussying up" as she called it, so such events also triggered happy memories.

While living in Rochester, Pam and Doug had become widely admired for their scenic designs and construction in the theatre. Shortly after moving to State College, the local high school hired them to do scenic design work for their plays. When a play was in the advanced rehearsal stage, they sometimes invited Carol to watch rehearsal and Pam entertained her with a running commentary. Carol thought that was great fun, especially when the actors greeted and talked with her. She'd always loved theatre productions, and that enjoyment did not change in the Alzheimer's years.

Football season brought an influx of family and visitors to our home seven weekends in the fall. Despite her increasing limitations, Carol enjoyed those weekends. We had tailgated and attended games with friends for half a century. Now our tailgaters and football fans were mostly our children, grandchildren, their spouses and friends. We took our RV for tailgating, which Carol still enjoyed, especially seeing grandchildren 'duded' up for the game. When everyone left for the game, we napped in the RV.

Sunday mornings after games we hosted lively breakfasts with our guests where Carol watched, listened and sometimes participated with pleasure. If there was a piano player in the crowd they sometimes played for or with Carol. For example, our son

Martin (a rabid Penn State football fan) shared his mother's love of playing the piano. In earlier years they sometimes played duets. Now they sat on the bench together and Martin played with his left hand while guiding Carol's hand through the right hand part of the music. Seeing her sparkling eyes and joyous smiles while they played a 'duet' warmed the hearts of all of us listening to them perform.

As we had for decades, we moved from football season directly into the holiday season. Thanksgiving and Christmas had always been Carol's favorite time of year but her enthusiasm had faded a bit with the onset of Alzheimer's. With Doug, Pam, Matt, Ryan and their daughter, Lindsay, around for the holidays, Carol's joy was renewed. We drove Carol's cart down our private lane to their home for Thanksgiving dinner, Pam's favorite holiday. They have a long standing family tradition where each person is responsible for helping make some part of the dinner. It was a wonderful time, filled with great food and noisy fun. That night in bed we talked about how their entire family shared the fun of preparing the dinner and what wonderful cooks Pam and Doug are.

I said, "After preparing Thanksgiving dinners for half a century, I bet it's great to just watch, eat and enjoy the fun." She smiled and nodded a yes. Then as we had for more than fifty years, we kissed and drifted off to sleep.

A week after Thanksgiving, based on our long tradition, we tackled Christmas decorations using familiar items Carol had created in previous years. (Continuing to live in a familiar environment helps an elderly person feel secure and comfortable. Familiar traditions not only help them enjoy life but also provide "retrieval cues" for happy memories and remembering visitors.) We went with Doug and Pam to cut our 52nd Happy Valley seven foot blue spruce Christmas tree. Later, I played some of Carol's favorite choral Christmas music, got out our decorations and we decorated the tree together like always. (I made sure to give her ornaments she could successfully hang to avoid turning fun into frustration). Together, we arranged in our glass front china hutch the beautiful nativity scene she had displayed for years.

Carol supervised while I hung the various kinds of wreaths she'd made for our home in previous years. I knew from past experience that each decoration had to go in a specific place and was pleased to note that Carol hadn't forgotten. The first one up was a huge wreath of artificial fir branches with a big red bow hung over the fireplace. Two were made of wild grapevines from our private forest, one in a circle decorated with red silk poinsettias and green holly leaves with red berries, and the other in an oval with red cardinals sitting in fir branches. Finally I hung one made of different kinds of pine cones, nuts and fruit, and another of blue spruce branches with white poinsettias. All of these were hung on the pretty grey barn wood walls of our entry garden.

Looking at our festive decorations with Carol, I said, "Seeing all these beautiful things you made over the years makes me want to sing, *You're Back in the Saddle Again!*"

She laughed, "Too bad you can't sing good."

For decades, one of Carol's Christmas pleasures was to host a Slab Cabin Lane Christmas party for old friends and neighbors. Now we modified it into a Pam, Doug, Carol and Don party. Everyone was invited to bring a tasty treat, while we provided food and beverages and planned games for fun and frolic. That night in bed Carol said, "That was fun – I love Christmas with such nice people."

Christmas morning we snuggled together in front of our fireplace listening to the Mormon Tabernacle Choir (one of her favorites) sing Christmas music while enjoying the warmth of a fire and the beauty of our Christmas tree. I said, "May I have a Christmas kiss?"

Carol smiled as I took her in my arms for a lingering kiss. She gently touched my cheek while looking into my eyes and softly said, "Merry Christmas." We had our traditional Christmas morning breakfast of orange juice, coffee and warm homemade cinnamon rolls, and launched our 57th Christmas together. Later, we unwrapped our presents slowly, commenting on each gift and occasionally sharing a memory of Christmas past with a particular present providing the memory cue.

Then we showered and dressed. Carol wore the grey slacks and a soft, multicolored sweater I'd given her, and I wore the black slacks and green sweater she'd given me. We smiled at each other while admiring ourselves in the big mirrors on our sliding closet doors. Then we made our bed and started the rest of our day.

About 1 p.m. we drove Carol's golf cart down the lane to Pam and Doug's to enjoy an afternoon Christmas dinner with their family. They had the family custom of going together to an early movie after Christmas dinner. We went home to enjoy telephone Christmas greetings and conversations with our other sons' families in Hershey, Virginia, and Orlando. As we went to bed that night Carol looked into my eyes, placed both hands on my cheeks, and said, "A wonderful day. I love you!" You can probably imagine how happy that made me feel.

The next two years followed essentially the same pattern with small, slow progressive changes in Carol's limitations. One unique event occurred.

Our grandson Matt had to do a video news story for one of his classes. He decided to do a story about his grandma and her golf cart and what it meant in her life. When Matt asked her cooperation in his plan, Carol said to me with a delighted smile, "I'm gonna be in the movies, like Bette Davis!" (One of her favorite actresses.) In my favorite scene, Matt was on top of the hill above Doug and Pam's lovely flower gardens on a beautiful, sunny day, aiming his camera at Carol as she drove along the stream with a big smile, looking up and waving at him. I could see her delight and knew she was having fun. That night as we prepared for bed, I jokingly said, "I think you like being a movie star!"

With twinkling eyes and a big grin she replied, "You bet, Buster!" When Matt showed her his 'movie', she clapped her hands and laughed with delight, obviously tickled pink to star in his production.

Chapter Thirty-Three

Accentuate the Positive and Eliminate the Negative

As we began 2007, Carol was in good physical health. All vital signs were good, she had a good appetite and all body functions were working well (breathing, digestion, elimination). She could see, hear and taste things OK. She slept eight to ten hours a night, and took a one to two hour afternoon nap.

There had been a significant decline in her remembering processes. Occasionally she didn't recognize a person but often told them they looked very nice. As such declines occur in an Alzheimer's person they increasingly live in the here and now, so I encouraged everyone to respond to her questions or concerns in those terms, and to avoid responses that focused on her deficiency or may arouse uncomfortable emotions. Here are some examples:

When a different person entered Carol's current behavior episode (BE) setting, I would immediately identify them and the reason for their presence so she could deal with them in here and now terms in case she didn't remember them. That technique also provided memory cues that might be useful. For example, "Carol, our daughter-in-law, Pam, is here to join you for your coffee break and a gab session." "Carol, here's our old friend, Earl Elliott. He wants to show us some pictures of his trip to Oregon."

A few times she didn't recognize me. If she asked "Who are you?" I'd say something like, "I'm Don, and I'm here so we can do things together today." Or if she said, "Where's my husband?" I'd say, "He's around here somewhere – he'll show up soon." (NOT "Don't you remember I'm your husband?")

She occasionally asked, "Where are mom and dad?" She accepted the answer, "They don't live here now. Maybe we'll hear from them later." (NOT "Don't you remember, your parents are dead?") Infrequently she might say something like, "I want to go home." I might respond, "This is your home today so we can do things together." She almost always accepted these kinds of responses and went on with her activities.

The greatest changes had occurred in her action (behavioral) capabilities. She found it increasingly frustrating to feed herself, particularly with her right hand, because of declining control in arms and hands. She was still able to use a spoon. To accommodate that increasing limitation, where possible her food was presented in small pieces she could pick up with a spoon or fingers. It was often served in dishes with compartments to make it easier to scoop up soft or wet food with a spoon. To limit her frustration, someone always sat beside her and, if necessary, helped guide her hand with the spoon to her mouth, and to feed it to her if she was having too much difficulty. She accepted such help graciously if it was offered without fussing.

She could still walk without assistance, but walked slowly with a kind of shuffle rather than steps which made her balance unstable. Her walking endurance was more limited. She could still go up and down stairs by holding to the bannister, but her caution and slowness indicated she was unsure and a little afraid of that activity, so an adjustment was made where someone was always in front of or behind her on the stairs to prevent falling.

Carol's ability to communicate her needs or thoughts with words was slowly eroding. She still talked with words, but sometimes that was mixed with a kind of speech-sounding jargon she had created for herself. This same phenomenon frequently occurs with infants before they learn to talk with words. For example, our 1-2 year-old twins carried on lengthy conversations in their own jargon, accompanied with laughter, before they learned to talk with words. Remember, people think with meanings not words, so loss of word talk doesn't mean they no longer have personally meaningful thinking activity. Carol's jargon and body language slowly became her alternate way of trying to communicate what she was experiencing or thinking.

As communicative change evolved, it became necessary to develop ways of understanding her. Here are some examples:

Those of us who knew Carol well communicated an interpretation of some of her meanings with *questions about goals* like, "Do you want to go to the bathroom?" or "Do you want to look at those pictures?" or "Would you like your food warmed up?" Sometimes I simply tried to communicate that I understood her by using a method called *restatement of content:* "That baby is cute." or "That's hard to do." Sometimes through tone of voice or gestures she seemed to be communicating some emotion in a current behavioral episode. I used a method called *reflection of feelings* to try to convey my understanding: "That's frustrating and makes you angry." or "You enjoyed listening to the piano music." or "You feel bad because you can't do that." Carol's verbal and body language responses provided clues about the accuracy of my interpretations.

None of these methods are complicated or new. Most parents have used them while caring for their babies. It's <u>essential</u> for people who provide elder care to realize that care receivers are still capable of an active psychological life despite their communication limitations.

Because of Carol's increasing action limitations, her doctor recommended she see a neurologist to check out potential causes for those symptoms. He conducted an interview and clinical exam in his office, and then walked her down a hallway to observe her movement patterns. His written report to Carol's doctor included the following excerpt:

"All her biological systems appear to be working well. Reflexes are all present and equal. Carol is alert and cooperative. She responds to my questions with very short phrased but appropriate answers. She smiles occasionally. There is no gaze disturbance. She walks hesitantly and slowly with a shuffling gait. I have no question that this woman has Parkinsonism and may, indeed, have true Parkinson's disease. It would be tempting to put this all under a single category of Lewy body disease with dementia leading to Parkinson's. Dopamine might improve motor control a little, but pre-existing dementia makes me very worried about the effects of dopamine on behavior. I warned her husband about this."

I explained the report to Carol. "We now have three diagnoses: Alzheimer's, Lewy body disease, and Parkinson's. Distinguishing among them is very difficult because there is a lot of symptom overlap, no one knows what causes each symptom, and none can be halted or cured.

I suggest we stop thinking about all the diagnoses and *what you can't do*. Instead, let's focus our thinking and actions on *what you can do* and how you and I together can figure out ways you can use those capabilities to get some satisfaction and pleasure out of life. Remember Johnny Mercer's popular song during WWII, *Accentuate the Positive, Eliminate the Negative, Latch On to the Affirmative and Don't Mess with Mr. In-between.* Let's take his advice and accentuate the positive and stop worrying about the negative. What do you think of that idea?"

"I like it. I'm tired of doctors who do nothing but discourage us. My grandma said 'No point in crying over spilt milk!' I'm still healthy and enjoy doing some things."

Once again in our life our talk had cleared away the fog about our future. We hugged each other and continued as a team down the last of our pathways together in life.

Over breakfast on a sunny early fall morning a few days later I asked Carol for another of our dates: "Would my favorite artist and dance partner join me for a picnic lunch this noon in the beauty of Slab Cabin Run?"

"I like dates with you."

I set up a little picnic table on our Slab Cabin bridge, covered it with a grass green cloth, and placed a small crystal vase in the middle containing an Alpha Xi pink rose and a TKE sweetheart red carnation. Our picnic basket contained tuna salad sandwiches, black sweet grapes and chunks of bright red seedless watermelon, with minty Moscow Mules (with just a little taste of vodka). I hoped this familiar activity would spark happy memories and meaningful talk.

After driving to the bridge in Carol's golf cart, we stood with our arms around each other's waist, breathing in the fragrant air. The familiar scents of early fall along the stream washed over us as we took in the natural beauty. I helped Carol to a chair and filled her favorite pink goblets with minty Moscow Mules (the focus of our interaction is on the here and now).

Carol lifted her goblet and said, "Here's to us."

I replied, "Here's to the team that has filled our lives with love and fun!"

We touched our goblets, sipped our drinks and savored the minty taste. Carol said, "I love the feelings and colors of fall."

"Carol, of all your many paintings my favorite is the one of this stream with the trees around it wearing their early fall colors, as they are today."

I laid our sandwiches and fruit on cheery paper plates embossed with fall colored leaves. I'd cut Carol's lunch in small, bite sized pieces ahead of time. As we ate I said, "Being together like this in early September brings back a special memory of a date with you a long time ago. Can you guess what that memory is about?" (Long term memories, especially if those experiences contained strong emotions, are often easier to reactivate than short term memories for people with Alzheimer's.)

She thought a little and then, with a smile and teasing voice, she said, "The first time you met my parents?"

"That's a special memory alright, but that was a scary rather than a fun time, and besides I didn't have a date with them."

Carol laughed and said, "I was anxious about it too. I wanted them to like you." (Carol had started remembering that time so I tried to keep it going.)

"That was the first time in my life I went on a trip by myself, rode on a train, went to a 'big city' and a State Fair. I was pretty excited about being with you."

"My special memory of the fair is when you were home on leave and we fell head over heels in love. Those emotions were wonderful." (Now that positive feelings about us are activated I tried to bring her back to the present.)

"Carol, we have some surprising news. Penn State has decided to honor me by naming a building recently obtained for the College of Health and Human Development *The Donald H. Ford Building*. A public dedication ceremony is being planned."

Carol's eyes sparkled and her voice trembled with emotion, "Don, that's nice! I'm so proud!"

"I'm going to tell them it should be named the *Carol and Donald Ford Building* because you played a big role in helping created that new College!"

She smiled and said, "That makes me very happy."

Our entire family of children and grandchildren gathered for the ceremony. Carol was beautiful with her silvery hair, a pretty burgundy and gold dress with matching jewelry, a happy dimpled smile and sparkling eyes. Before the ceremony a steady stream of old friends, visitors and officials greeted Carol as she sat before "our building" like a queen in her wheel chair. With help, she was able to climb three small steps and sit on the platform facing the audience.

The Dean, Nan Crouter (a friend and colleague), opened the ceremony and said nice things, followed by the Board of Trustees Chairman. Then President Graham Spanier explained how he had started in our college as a newly minted assistant professor, and blamed me for encouraging him to consider the pathway that eventually led to his becoming Penn State's President. Suddenly, the ceremony was interrupted by a thundering rain storm that convinced people who were standing outside to squeeze into the tent. Nan introduced me. I expressed gratitude for the honor and then said, "Carol deserves this honor too. Recruiting people to work in our new college was challenging because they had to choose to come, not because of what we were but because of what we planned to become. Carol was my star recruiter. Her slogan was, 'You never just recruit a person; you are also recruiting a family and they must be happy with it too.' Carol organized her friends in the community and mates of current faculty and administrators to help convince visitors this would be a wonderful place to live and work.

If there were children, she harnessed our sons and their friends to make sure the children got a look at the schools through the eyes of friendly kids who were students in those schools, and showed them a good time. Our sons were good at it. For example, our oldest son Russ won the hearts of a young husband and wife candidate by getting his folk-rock group to play for them.

Despite the extra work involved, Carol entertained candidates informally in our home because she believed that made a warmer and more personal impression than taking them to some restaurant. Later she invited faculty wives, two or three at a time, for informal coffee talk and get acquainted sessions. For ten years she did everything she could to help our new college become successful and the faculty proud of it. Therefore, this should be called the Carol and Donald Ford Building."

As the crowd enthusiastically applauded her, I turned to help Carol stand, but the noisy storm blowing rain in frightened her so Pam had come to sit with and sooth her. I thanked the audience on her behalf, finished the occasion, and joined guests for refreshments in a nearby building. People again greeted and talked with Carol. I proudly watched her enjoy it, unashamed of her limitations, thinking of what we had accomplished together.

Throughout the rest of 2007, Carol's limitations in both speech and behavior control continued, but she could still talk some and walk a little with help. Her general health remained good. We gave up football tailgating, but family continued the tradition and Russ and Barb spent every game weekend with us. Russ noticed his mother's decline but said, "I can still have a conversation with Mom. It takes longer and words are more halting, but we can clearly exchange meanings." Once again we enjoyed Thanksgiving with Doug and Pam's family.

Then, we had a discouraging setback. As we prepared for bed one mid-December evening, Carol stepped away from the bathroom sink after brushing her teeth and fell backwards against the wall. I knelt beside her and asked, "Do you hurt anywhere?"

She shook her head and said, "No". So, I helped her up and into bed. Next morning I decided she should be checked and x-rays showed she had a broken hip!

Dr. Cherry, who had cared for Carol in previous years, did a surgical repair that afternoon, reported it went perfectly, and said,

"She's exceptionally healthy so should recover quickly." Because of her limitations in feeding herself, communicating, and anxiety over the suddenness of it all, I arranged to stay with her in her hospital room.

Cherry checked her the next day and said everything was great, and authorized beginning physical therapy. That afternoon, I followed Carol to her first therapy session and found our Dean, Nan Crouter, waiting for us with a Christmas arrangement in a lovely holiday ornament vase. That boosted our morale and, while we talked, we watched Carol try to walk holding onto exercise bars. Nan said, "Carol is a courageous woman! How's it going?"

"Good. Thank you for your thoughtfulness. She'll have two weeks of physical therapy before she goes home. She can do that in a nursing home only a half mile from our house."

Because of Carol's limitations, I paid for a private room I shared with her. I experienced 24/7 nursing home care for two weeks. It was nearly identical to Winifred's care several decades ago. Time had not led to improvements in the nursing home medical model of elder care.

The daily care program consisted of getting patients up in the morning, helping them toilet and dress, then parking them in the corridor (if they needed a wheel chair) until it was time to eat. They were taken to the dining room three times a day for meals. The rest of the day involved administering meds, providing nursing or personal care as needed – pressure sore care, catheter care, taking them to the bathroom as needed, checking vitals, etc. The comfort of bathing or showering in warm water was a rarity – Carol had only two baths in two weeks.

Each caregiver had twelve to twenty patients to care for, depending on the shift. The timing of care activities was shaped more by staff schedules than patient needs or desires. For example, each patient had a button to push for help. Carol was no longer capable of that simple act, nor was she capable of going to the bathroom by herself. Imagine yourself as Carol with an urgent need to go to the bathroom. I'd push the button and she'd typically wait from ten to thirty minutes before someone came to help her. For legal reasons, I was prohibited from helping her. When I asked staff why the delay, the typical answer was they were doing other tasks or were on break time. Would you feel angry, demeaned or embarrassed if you had to pee your pants or worse when it could have been avoided by prompt assistance? The people who worked with Carol were nice, caring, and capable but only trained to provide medical model care.

I ate three meals a day with Carol. Nursing home patients eat more slowly for a variety of reasons. So, a meal served hot often cooled off by the time it was half eaten. Most people don't like a hot meal turned cold, which may be why many plates were left with food on them.

Carol went to physical therapy once a day. There were usually three to five patients at any point in time (the nursing home subcontracted that service) with one or sometimes two staff. The result was that each patient got 15-30 minutes of personal attention a day. Any physical fitness expert will tell you that's too little for a strong, rapid recovery.

We often spent time exploring the building. During our explorations, we met patients and family members we knew. Sadly, they often expressed bitterness or frustrated anger. I knew the staff meant well, but they just didn't have the time or training for developmental care. We had a few pleasant times. Our offspring adorned Carol's room with Christmas decorations and lights. Another day, some of Doug and Pam's theater students came to music-lover Carol's room and sang Christmas songs. Carol smiled and tried to sing along with them.

As a surprise, I took Carol home Christmas morning to spend the day. We had decorated our home before her accident so being in our own home Christmas day was a delight and relief. A few days later she was discharged. Together again in our own bed that night I said, "Carol I <u>promise</u> you that you will never live in a place like that again. We've taken care of each other for decades and we'll spend the rest of our lives doing that here in our home."

Carol said, "I'll like that!"

I needed to do four things immediately to provide the context for our home care program: Refurnish our bedroom to fit Carol's needs; Arrange for home care medical support; Hire aides; Create plans for Carol's transportation when needed.

Medicare provided a good hospital type bed with electric controls. I bought another for myself, removed our king size bed, put the two hospital beds side by side and covered them both with a nice comforter so it ended up looking like our old king size bed. We continued to sleep side by side, and Carol didn't have to get used to something different.

Carol and I had agreed on a basic plan for home care while in nursing home rehab. We agreed to have a personal aide/companion for her every morning from 7 a.m. to noon who would be responsible for a morning program of activities. That would give me every morning for business, professional, scholarly, home and yard activities. I would be Carol's aide/companion every afternoon and evening responsible for creating pleasurable activities we could share. We arranged home health care services through a nursing service.

The need for home medical assistance was immediate because I discovered Carol came from the nursing home with pressure sores on her bottom and one heel. I was angry because I was with Carol 24/7 and knew that staff hadn't examined her for pressure sores or talked with me about the preventive care needed.

A pleasant surprise offset my anger. The head of Centre Home Care was Ellen Weaver. She had been born next door to us when we lived on the other side of Slab Cabin. As a little girl, she'd visited Carol's shop "to look at all the pretty things". They went to work on the pressure sores immediately. Our family physician provided medical backup as needed. Ellen also arranged for a physical therapist to continue home rehab of Carol's walking limitations.

Carol's home care nursing service was terminated after a year because Medicare rules support only medical model care. Despite the fact Alzheimer's disease had advanced to the point where Carol was unable to care for herself in any way, she wasn't "sick enough" to need it.

I explained to Ellen my home care program plan, outlined the aides needed, and said, "You've been in the home care business for a while. Do you have any suggestions about where I might find the kind of aides I want for Carol?"

"Would you be willing to have a man as one of Carol's aides?"

"Yes, if he's competent, nice and Carol likes him."

"I teach some classes training LPNs and recently had one young man who is very good. He just recently obtained a good paying, full time non-nursing job because he's a divorced father who needs the money to raise his two daughters. But, he liked nursing and might be interested in one of your weekend morning positions. Would you like me to check with him?"

"Yes, please. Our aides don't have to be licensed nurses, but that would be a nice bonus."

Carol and I interviewed him and really liked his pleasant, friendly manner. That's how Tim became part of our team. Tim had a good friend named Kelly who had worked for a decade as a caregiver for people with serious limitations served by the Association for Retarded Citizens (ARC). Tim told her about us and his new part time job. She expressed interest, he recommended her, and we interviewed her. Carol smiled and nodded her head, "Yes." She clearly liked Kelly and found her easy to talk with. That's how Kelly joined our weekend team.

Kelly worked with an LPN named Linda, a mother, grandmother and farmer's wife, whose competence and work style as an ARC nurse Kelly respected. They had become good friends so Kelly told her about us and her new weekend job. Linda expressed interest, Kelly recommended her, and we interviewed Linda. I told Carol Linda lived on a farm. She smiled and said, "So did I. She's nice." So Linda became our five mornings a week team member.

We needed to transport Carol to various places but she couldn't get into our car. We tried the public handicap transportation, but it turned out to be very time consuming, inconvenient, and often frustrating because of scheduling complications with multiple people, not to mention confusing for someone with Carol's limitations. Carol needed comfortable, convenient transportation for a diversity of reasons including leading a satisfying, relatively normal life.

Our son, Russ, surfed the internet and discovered many used handicap vans available. He found a minivan equipped with a mobility seat in the front passenger side. It was identical to a large, comfortable regular front seat, but mounted so that by pushing an electric switch the seat automatically rotated, slid out the front door, and lowered itself. Carol could easily be transferred from her wheel chair to the car seat. The switch then raised the seat, slid it back into the car, rotated into the proper position, and locked it into place. I traded our old Buick for it.

That different seat also played a health promotion role because sitting in different chairs during the day varied the skin pressure patterns and helped prevent bed sores. That advantage is not available when the person has to remain in their wheel chair while being transported. We could load her wheel chair in the back of the van, fasten her seat belt and be on our way. It was easy, safe, comfortable, and provided a great view through the front window. It enabled us to treat Carol like a person, not a patient. We could drive right up to the front door of most restaurants, unload Carol and then park the van. And the loading and unloading could be done in our garage, so we didn't have to struggle with the weather. After her first ride Carol said, "This is wonderful – I can see everything. Getting in is like my own carnival ride!"

Carol was now immobile without assistance 24/7. Each day she would be in her bed approximately twelve hours and in her wheel chair most of the other twelve hours. That greatly increased the likelihood of pressure sores. I went searching for a mattress and wheel chair cushion designed to help protect against pressure sores.

I learned from our wound clinic that once a person has a pressure sore, that area of their skin becomes more vulnerable to recurring breakdown. The recommended preventive procedure is to roll a patient from one side to the other every two hours to change the pressure pattern. A good night's sleep is a key factor in promoting good health, so waking someone up every two hours didn't make sense to me, and placed an extra burden on a caregiver twenty four hours a day (which is probably why that often isn't done in nursing home or home care).

I found, read and evaluated research from all over the world about bed sore prevention mattresses, many of which are very costly. I reported back to my helpful colleague in our school of Nursing, Ann Kolanowski, "A few individuals seemed to benefit from such expensive mattresses, but I found no reliable scientific evidence that any of the specialized mattresses actually made an important difference for most of the patients studied. Without scientific evidence, I looked for professional experience and talked to the highly regarded wound nurse at our local hospital who strongly recommended the EHOB waffle mattress overlay used at her hospital and widely used elsewhere. I decided to try it." It is an inflated plastic mattress with holes the size of tennis balls all over it, so when a person lies on it half of their body is lying on air. Carol's wheel chair cushion was composed of a gel that made a fairly firm seat. Our wound clinic's experts on pressure sores said a cushion by ROHO was most effective. Its' pressure points varied with movement and was much more comfortable.

We examined Carol's skin every morning. If signs of bed sore development appeared Carol's aides immediately began treatment to stop it. Over a four year period we had only occasional small sores and only in the already vulnerable areas of skin.

Other aspects of our home remained the same, including several of her own paintings and family pictures displayed on walls. That familiar setting provided many memory cues that helped guide daily activity patterns in the stable pleasurable context Carol needed.

Chapter Thirty-Four

Carol's Home Care Plan in Action

In this chapter I'll describe Carol's **Developmental Model of Elder Care** designed to fit her emerging limitations. Its purpose was to fill each day of her remaining life with people and behavior episode activities through which she could accomplish personal goals that yielded some form of satisfaction and pleasure while maintaining her health. A person's history of positive and pleasurable activities provides the possibilities for making their current life satisfying. The purpose of sharing Carol's life story has been to illustrate to readers how to obtain that kind of knowledge about a person's satisfying activity patterns. Stop and think for a moment: What kinds of activities repetitively yielded significant pleasure during Carol's life?

I will answer that question and then provide a detailed example of how to use that knowledge to create a developmental model of elder care for a specific person. I hope it will be useful for those who may wish to learn how to create such a program for their loved one. I understand not everyone can provide the sort of home care Carol had because each person's situation is different. **The important point made in this chapter is that everyone can provide, or see that nursing homes provide, the developmental model of care if they know their loved one's history of life satisfactions and have an understanding of how to use that knowledge in elder care.** The information provided here can be shaped to fit most situations.

Table 1 summarizes fourteen basic kinds of memory patterns representing different kinds of behavior episode experiences Carol created during her life, each of which produced satisfaction and pleasure over many years and through many BEs. It also summarizes the kinds of activities she used in the past to produce those experiences and therefore might be used in some form to effectively produce similar positive feelings in new behavior episodes.

The guiding theory is simple. A persons' daily life is organized in integrated activity patterns called behavior episodes (BEs). A BE begins when a person adopts a personal goal to be achieved. Others may suggest goals to a person, but it has to be committed to by the person or it won't function as a personal goal. Goal adoption produces activities intended to achieve that goal. Successful accomplishment ends that BE by producing positive thoughts and feelings; failure yields negative thoughts and feelings. Kinds of BEs that produce positive results are likely to be sought and repeated; those that produce negative results are likely to be avoided in the future. The size, scope and importance of goals vary, but the dynamics of each goal guided BE is fundamentally the same.

Table 1. Carol's Pleasurable Memory Patterns and Potential Elicitors for New BEs

Pleasurable Memory Patterns of Personal Care and Grooming

Potential Elicitors:

a. Bathroom and bathing activities – shower, bubble bath, fragrant lotion
b. Grooming herself attractively – getting hair washed, set, styled
c. Selection of clothing to wear

Pleasurable Memory Patterns of Personal Health Promotion and Rhythmic Activity

Potential Elicitors:

a. Swimming with husband, family and friends
b. Home calisthenics to promote health of different muscle groups

c.   Aerobic solo dancing in home for full body health and pleasurable exercise
d.   Walking in the great outdoors by self and with husband
e.   Diet and exercise to control weight

Pleasurable Memory Patterns of Eating

Potential Elicitors:

a.   Warm meals and tasty foods
b.   Sweet foods and ice cream
c.   Congenial eating companions

Pleasurable Memory Patterns of Piano Music – Especially Classical Music

Potential Elicitors:

a.   Playing a piano
b.   Listening to piano recordings – especially kinds she has played
c.   Listening to others play – especially in concerts, or by family or friends
d.   Watching movies/TV about or involving pianists
e.   Talking with others about piano music and performances

Pleasurable Memory Patterns of Choral Music – Especially Classical Music

Potential Elicitors:

a.   Singing in a large chorus of men and women – especially singing the *Messiah*
b.   Singing with a small chorus of women – especially popular and barbershop music
c.   Singing in church choirs
d.   Listening to recordings and watching/listening to choral groups in concerts, movies, TV

Pleasurable Memory Patterns of Dancing – Especially Social Dancing

Potential Elicitors:

a. Dancing with husband at formal dances, dance clubs, night clubs, parties and at home
b. Watching movies and TV programs involving dancing
c. Talking about, and watching others dancing

Pleasurable Memory Patterns of Friendships and Gabbing With Women

Potential Elicitors:

a. Talking with 1-3 friends over coffee or lunch
b. Talking with friends while sharing some creative or other activity
c. Talking with visitors/customers in her arts and crafts studio/shop
d. Entertaining friends and guests in her home
e. Looking at pictures of friends and of activities with them

Pleasurable Memory Patterns of Family and Home Life

Potential Elicitors:

a. Providing a supportive context for family members' personal development, life's problems
b. Shared activities fostering love, fun, competence, achievement, cooperation, sound values
c. Dates with husband
d. Loving and caring for babies
e. Family activities celebrating holidays, individual accomplishments, and travel adventures
f. Providing a welcoming context for all friends of family members, relatives and visitors
g. Looking at pictures of family members, their activities and accomplishments

Pleasurable Memory Patterns of Painting, Arts and Crafts

Potential Elicitors:

a. Sketching, painting, or creating arts and crafts by self or with others

b. Exhibiting or selling her creations in her studio or at arts festivals

c. Shopping for, and searching the great outdoors for, arts and crafts materials and ideas

d. Examining and admiring others' arts and crafts work in pictures, exhibits and other cultures

e. Creating special gifts for family and friends and decorative elements for home

f. Talking with and teaching others about how to make arts and crafts

Pleasurable Memory Patterns of Activities In the Great Outdoors and Mother Nature's Beauty

Potential Elicitors:

a. Camping, boating and exploring different natural phenomena – particularly with husband

b. Searching for driftwood, grasses, other objects and plant products for arts/crafts creations

c. Admiring, painting and photographing beautiful and meaningful scenes

d. Having fun and easing stress by herself, with husband, family or friends in natural settings

e. Beautifying and preserving the natural environment around and within her home

f. Talking about and looking at pictures, movies and TV about aspects of the natural world

Pleasurable Memory Patterns of Watching Movies, TV and Internet Programs

Potential Elicitors:

a. Going to movies with family and friends for pleasure and relief of loneliness, stress

b. Looking at recorded movies and internet programs on home TV

Pleasurable Memory Patterns of Social Life

Potential elicitors:

a. Sharing activities and parties with close friends and families

b. Entertaining friends and acquaintances at her home

Pleasurable Memory Patterns of Travel Activities and Adventures

Potential Elicitors:

a. Trips by auto, in RV, or with commercial travel to explore different parts of the U.S. and the world, and experiencing different cultures

b. Looking at pictures of different places and of different travel activities

Pleasurable Memory Patterns of Caring for the Needs of Others

Potential Elicitors:

a. Volunteer service and fund raising activities to benefit others

b. Contributing resources and personal assistance to help individuals and families

c. Contributing resources to create and support community health and human services programs d. Being helpful to family members and friends.

Each person's history of satisfying and pleasurable experiences is different so the kinds of behavior episodes and elicitors that worked for Carol might not work for someone else; the BEs must be designed to fit each person. For a person with advanced Alzheimer's, every day is a new day, so to enrich her life the guiding goals should be achievable in that day. Creating effective actions, requires a clear understanding of the goal to be achieved, and feedback about what has been achieved. Every day in a person's life is composed of many different BEs.

People with other limitations (e.g., a stroke) can still gain pleasure from anticipations of future BEs (e.g., anticipating a visit by a loved one or a shopping trip).

To help you understand how this process was used in Carol's care, I'll describe one day of her activities so you can see it in the form Carol experienced and lived it – as we've done in describing her earlier life – rather than in broad generalizations. I will often use the words of a caregiver to describe their work with Carol. Different parts of each day were focused on different kinds of goals and activities. I'll use the categories in Table 1 to organize the presentation and start with Linda's description of one morning which is typical of all Carol's mornings for the rest of her life:

"Around 6:30 each morning, Don would start the day by playing a recording of some of Carol's favorite piano, choral, popular or big band music for her to wake up to. The first goals of the day focused on *personal care and grooming.* He would help Carol sit on the edge of the bed as she woke up, and help her drink a glass of about 6 oz. of water. That was the first step towards the goal of 30-50 oz. of fluid every day to keep her well hydrated. Her swallowing reflex had begun weakening (as it often does in older people) so a substance called *Thicket* was added to make swallowing easier. While doing that, he spoke to her about simple topics. About 7 a.m. I would walk into the bedroom and Don would loudly say some version of, 'Carol, here's Linda to have fun with us today!' to remind her of who I was and why I was there.

I would sit beside her, put my arm around her and talk with her. Don would briefly describe to Carol what we were going to do that day, and who might drop by for a visit. That was his first step towards setting goals we would help her accomplish that day. I transferred her from the bed to her wheel chair, took her into the bathroom, and stated two goals 'First you can go to the pot and then I'll give you a basin bath.' I put her hands on a grab bar, helped her stand, turn, and sit on the stool. After she emptied her 'tanks' I put a small tub of warm water beside her and used a cloth to wash all of her body. That was when we checked for pressure sores.

Twice a week we gave Carol a shower in her walk-in tub rather than a basin bath. That transfer required two of us. I would get in the tub, Don would position the wheel chair with Carol's feet through the tub door on a nonskid surface. Then, I helped her stand in the tub, turn and sit on the bench. I got out, Don squirted her, I washed her with soap, and then he squirted off the soap. We tried to make it fun, singing songs about raining, joking with her, and squirting the plastic hat on her head so that it made a rain on the roof noise. When we finished, Don got in the tub, helped Carol stand, turn and sit down in her wheel chair which I had positioned at the tub opening. Carol enjoyed her shower, knew what to do, and would follow instructions, (e.g., 'Close your eyes because I'm going to squirt your face.' or 'Turn so you can sit in the chair.')

I covered Carol's skin over her entire body with a special moisturizing cream called VaniCream to hydrate it, protect it and keep it healthy – it made her skin soft and supple. You couldn't see any dry, old or wrinkled looking skin on her anywhere. Our wound clinic recommended it because Carol had sensitive skin and it was free of additives that irritate some people's skin. Carol had a tendency to get a rash under her breasts (called contact dermatitis), and after trying several preventive measures we found that Desenex used for athlete's foot was a very effective prevention. I dressed her in disposable undergarments.

I would then bring in two outfits from her closet, hold them before her, and ask which one she'd like to wear. Sometimes she pointed and said something, or reached to touch one, or simply looked at one more than the other. That procedure was designed to give her another small goal to accomplish, and to help her feel like she had some control over her life. I would interpret her action to be her choice and help her dress. I would groom her beautiful silver hair. Through all of this I talked about things with her, sometimes asked her a question, and sometimes she commented, usually in her own lingo. If I didn't understand her answer I acted like I did and proceeded with the conversation. We no longer used cosmetics – her skin was still lovely and she didn't need them to look nice.

I confirmed that she had accomplished that set of goals by saying something like 'We're all done, good job, you look very nice.'

The next goal pattern was *Eating*. I would set the next goal by saying, 'Let's go have breakfast now.' While I was grooming and dressing Carol, Don prepared breakfast. Before eating, Carol's meds were crushed to avoid swallowing difficulties and added to a spoonful of apple sauce topped with a dab of strawberry rhubarb jam (her own creation).

Carol loved the beauty of the natural world, so she had their small breakfast/lunch area designed so the small table faced an indoor entry garden with growing plants, and big windows where Carol could look outdoors and see trees, sun, rain or snow, and birds and squirrels performing on their feeders. During breakfast we sometimes commented on what could be seen (e.g., 'Look at the pretty cardinals!' or 'That squirrel is hanging upside down.')

Because chewing and swallowing food had become a little more difficult, Carol's breakfast was a bowl of hot oatmeal flavored with apples and cinnamon, and half a banana cut in small pieces. Her fluid intake was increased with 6-8 oz. of orange juice and milk on her cereal. It took about an hour to help Carol eat, stopping sometimes to reheat her food in the microwave because hot food that has become cold isn't very tasty. If we kept her food warm, she typically ate everything.

Don read things from the morning paper that might interest Carol and me while she ate, and showed her pictures she might like, e.g., cute babies or animals; beautiful scenes. He planned their breakfast activities to be as similar as possible to the way it was before Carol's illness to treat her as, and make her feel as, a person with interests and capabilities, and as an interactive part of a social group. This familiar routine provided a sense of continuity and security, and of having accomplished something.

After breakfast I took Carol to the bathroom and then helped her brush her teeth. One night Carol had a lot of congestion and it took several hours for Don to get it straightened out. It wasn't from a cold. He discovered she was having trouble rinsing her mouth thoroughly after brushing her teeth, so particles of food sometimes remained in her mouth. We adopted the practice of swabbing around her teeth and cheeks to remove any pieces of food, either using some gauze around a finger or a throw away vinyl glove.

This procedure was important, both because her mouth was and felt cleaner and because it prevented serious night time problems. For example, if there were food particles in her mouth when she went to bed they could accidentally get into her 'windpipe' and cause serious and dangerous congestion.

I then took Carol to the dining/living area to pursue the next goal pattern of *personal health development through physical exercise.* Before her illness Carol was a very active person and every part of her body got lots of exercise. Those patterns of activity could no longer occur so we worked with her physical therapist to design a set of exercises for the goal of keeping each of the muscle groups in various parts of her body flexible and healthy. They also served to maintain strength and coordination of full body activities."

Table 2. Personal Health Promoting Physical Activities

A goal of number of repetitions was set for each activity episode and the repetitions were counted out loud until the goal was reached (if Carol couldn't do it herself the aide helped); then Carol was congratulated on her success after each activity.

Arm Lifts: Separately, lift each arm vertical over head; hold 2-3 seconds; repeat 10 times.

Arm Stretches: Separately, hold each arm horizontal from body; hold 2-3 seconds; repeat 5 times.

Hand Flex: Separately hold each hand flat on a surface; hold wrist down with one hand; lift front of hand up and down; repeat 15 times. (Carol's right hand began to spasm rigidly closed. The physical therapist provided a brace to be fastened to that arm to keep the hand open. It was awkward and uncomfortable and prevented self control. We decided to help her control it herself. We rolled an ordinary face cloth into a tube, wrapped a tape around it and put it in her hand. She had to close her hand to hold it and open it to drop it. She could do both. Soon the rigid spasms stopped and did not return, even when she wasn't holding anything. Sometime a soft ball or toy football was used.)

Shoulder Shrugs: Carol seated; hold elbows close to body; put hands under both elbow; push up 5 times.

Neck Exercises: Put heating pad on neck for 10 minutes; move head side to side to stretch muscles; or neck and shoulder massage to relax muscles; repeat 10 times.

Leg Lifts: Seated; put one hand on knee and other hand on ankle; lift leg horizontal; hold 10 seconds; stretches and strengthens ham strings; repeat 3 times each leg.

Toe Raises: Seated with shoes on; feet flat on floor; hold heel on floor and pull front of foot up; hold 10 seconds; repeat 3 times for each foot.

Sit/Stand: Seated, place hands underneath arms and help stand; hold for 10 seconds and sit; repeat five times; have her do by self if she can do so safely.

Walk /Stand: Hold her arm; walk until she stops follow with wheel chair for safety.

Balloon Ball: Inflated heavy duty party balloon larger than a basketball; tell Carol to catch and throw back or hit back when tossed to her; continue as long as she wants to; (she found it more fun to hit it back and try to hit aide who jumped and yelled if she got hit – record, 40 times).

Pulleys: Pulleys hang from door; with Carol's back to door raise hands above head and grasp pulley handle with each hand; pull down with one hand and then other; repeat 10 pulls with each hand; help Carol pull down if necessary. One day, after watching Carol play balloon ball, Russell said, "I was astonished at Mom's ability to play your game of balloon ball in the last couple of years. To follow the trajectory of a big ball coming towards her, to judge its speed, to coordinate her arms and her timing to hit it back or to catch it is a very complicated action pattern that requires a good bit of concentration and thought. She did it through a series of exchanges, clearly she was having fun, wanted to continue and a lot was still going on in her mind!" As each exercise was completed, Carol had a short rest break, was warmly praised for her success (goal achievement), and asked to take a sip of water. Because one of our goals was to help Carol feel that she had some control over her life, we never insisted if she resisted any activity. I would say, "That's ok – you don't have to do that now if you don't want to. Maybe you'll feel like it later." When we came back to it later she usually accepted. We all believed our effectiveness in helping Carol depended on creating relationships that were more like a close friendship than a caregiver. It was a joy to each of us to see her laugh and smile and to see that twinkle in her eye. All those activities took about 1½ hours including the rest pauses and drinks. I congratulated Carol profusely for completing everything (providing success and satisfaction) and said "Let's go to the bathroom and then have a coffee break!"

I typically tried to join Carol and her aide for coffee break. The break served three purposes: the tasty snacks and companionship functioned as a kind of reward for her morning accomplishments (*eating pleasure*); it enabled us to get a little more nutrition and fluids into her diet (*health promotion)*; it provided a happy time interacting with people she liked (*gabbing pleasure)*. Initially, Carol would have a 6-8 oz. glass of milk with bite sized pieces of Danish or cinnamon roll she could pick up with her fingers and eat. When her hand skills declined, we shifted to a glass of cranberry juice to serve health promotion purposes, and a small container of yogurt with fruit in it which was tasty, easier for her to eat and helped insure she got enough protein in her diet. Frequently Pam, Doug or a friend would join us for coffee break, making it a pleasant period of social interaction with occasional laughter. Carol liked these episodes a lot, and was sometimes quite talkative, combining ordinary words and her own lingo.

The rest of Carol's morning was devoted to creating some of the kinds of activities that had brought her satisfaction and pleasure in the past (see Table 1). For example, from the time she was a little girl on the family farm she loved *the great outdoors and Mother Nature's beauty.* Linda and Kelly would take Carol out on our deck where they could sit, look at the stream and wooded slope behind it, and see a walking and bike path at the top of the slope on which people might be seen riding their bike or taking their dog for a walk. They could also admire the flowers growing around our small spring fed pond, and enjoy the smells and sounds. If I was mowing the grass I would drive the mower up to the deck and gab a little. Carol found it pleasant to feel the sun and breezes on her face. Even in the spring and fall coolness Carol could be dressed warmly and enjoy being outdoors.

A three-foot wide deck with railing connects the living deck to a covered dining deck on the other end of the house. Tim and

Carol liked being outdoors and walking together on that narrow deck while Carol held on to the railing.

Everyone liked taking Carol "golf cart cruising." She loved going on rides through the neighborhood, looking at the houses, their flowers and landscaping, pets, cars and sometimes "talking" with neighbors who came out to visit with them, which added the pleasure of gabbing with other women. That kind of experience seemed to give Carol a sense of being free and living in a bigger world, instead of just being trapped in her house. Tim described one occasion that illustrated the depth of Carol's thinking capabilities despite her verbal limitations:

"My daughters were given some baby ducks for Easter. The ducks grew up and we had no place to keep them. Since there were ducks on Slab Cabin Run, we decided to release those young ducks there. We took them down to Doug and Pam's place because they had a nice shallow piece of stream with a flat bank. While Carol watched from her golf cart my daughters released their ducks. Suddenly Abby, Pam and Doug's dog, saw them, got excited and chased them around in the water trying to catch them. Carol got very distressed and yelled in fear for the young ducks. Carol clearly understood what was going on. Fortunately, the ducks escaped but we never saw them again."

That example clearly illustrates that you should <u>never underestimate</u> the thinking capabilities and kinds of psychological states of Alzheimer's patients just because of their limited verbal, physical or memory capabilities.

Piano playing was another lifelong source of pleasure for Carol. Linda described one such experience:

"I parked Carol's chair at her piano and put her hands on the keys. Earlier in her illness she could press on the keys and 'make some music' and she and I would 'sing along.' Later, she needed more help so I might play some notes while her hands were on the keyboard, or hold her hand and press her fingers on different keys to play simple tunes. One day I (who couldn't play the piano) was trying to make some music. Carol suddenly surprised me by smiling at me and saying, 'You don't know how to play the piano, do you?' I laughed and said, 'You caught me.' She gave me a big grin. Carol's son, Russ, gave her a child's electric key board on which she could make music with a light touch. Sometimes she'd sit and play it for 30 minutes or more."

Another source of pleasure was looking at photo albums she had created, particularly about *family and home life*, and talking about memories they activated. Over the years, Kelly, Linda and Tim all took many memory trips with Carol through her albums. Tim particularly enjoyed looking at albums of Carol's early years and gave an example of how enduring were the memories they represented:

"One morning, Carol pointed to pictures where she and a friend were in childhood dance costumes around 7-8 years old, and launched into an enthusiastic commentary about 75 year old memories." That is a good illustration that people don't necessarily "lose their memory", but may have to find different ways of activating them.

Russell described well the nature of "album trips" with his mother: "Through the years her illness was progressing I found that looking through old albums representing her earlier life brought her pleasure and stimulated memories. She would point to people, smile and sometimes say their names or tell a story in her lingo. She had an album of movie stars of her youth, like Ronald Reagan, which could bring smiles and sometimes talking, usually in her own lingo. Looking at her albums provided a kind of episode within which we could personally interact. I always tried to respond as I would with a normal person, even if I didn't understand her, with words to convey my understanding that she remembered them with pleasure. Clearly, some of the old Carol was still active inside her and could bring pleasure in her current experience by sharing it with me and others. I would always try to gaze into her eyes as we interacted, and as I did that it often increased her interaction with me."

Carol could still walk somewhat, with a little assistance, when we began our developmental model of home care. Walking became increasingly difficult for her as her motor skills declined. Her physical therapist taught me how to support her while walking beside her. That worked for a few months, and then she started giving up after 6-7 steps.

One morning during coffee break, I said, "Linda, trying to walk with someone beside her holding her up is a new and awkward way of walking for Carol. I've been trying to think of other possibilities. There is a movement pattern that Carol has loved using since she was 16 years old – social dancing with me. People think of the process of remembering as a cognitive thing, but there is another form sometimes called 'motor memory'. Highly practiced elaborate movement patterns come to function as an integrated unit without requiring thoughtful control. Dancing is like that. Carol and I have danced together a lot for over 60 years and she loves dancing. That kind of movement pattern must have deep roots in her nervous system. I wonder if that might enable us to substitute dancing for walking?"

"That's an interesting idea, why don't you try it!"

Here's the description Linda wrote to inform Kelly and Tim of our experiment: "Don put on a Glenn Miller big band recording (music to which Carol loved to dance), asked Carol to dance with him, took her in a dancing embrace, and off they went. They danced past her piano, through the dining and living rooms, past the fireplace, onto and across the entry garden walkway, took a small step down onto a flagstone walkway, danced across that to 2 small steps up, danced to the breakfast/lunch dining area and Don sat Carol down on a chair. Don and I cheered and applauded her accomplishment while she beamed with pleasure and pride. I followed them with Carol's wheel chair in case she got tired, but she danced that 80' distance without stopping for a rest.

The actual dancing wasn't Carol's only source of pleasure. Think how seldom, if ever, a woman in Carol's condition is held in an intimate, loving embrace with her husband (or anyone else) as they move as one to the music, and how they may miss it when it no longer occurs!"

Carol and I both loved it, and from there on we danced before lunch almost every day for several years! Watching her deal with those small steps produced other interesting information. Carol concentrated hard to organize her body to step down or up those steps. If, after trying a while, the stepping leg she was trying to use wasn't working, she would shift and try the other leg. Sometimes I'd suggest she try such a change and she'd implement my suggestion. <u>People mistakenly don't expect that kind of problem solving thinking from advanced Alzheimer's cases.</u>

These examples illustrate the power of using knowledge about a person's past sources of satisfaction and pleasure to guide creation of behavior episode experiences in their current lives that can yield daily pleasures and satisfaction. There are a great diversity of possibilities with this method, illustrated by ways I used it with Carol over the last six years of her life.

Now I'll return to Linda's description of a typical morning with Carol: "After all the morning activities, I took Carol to the bathroom to prepare her for lunch. Then she sat in the kitchen watching me, and sometimes 'talking' with me as I prepared lunch. The menu included finely chopped tuna, ham, chicken or turkey salad, soup, or an omelet, with a glass of milk. Eating tasty food is an important source of pleasure in most peoples' life so I included in Carol's salads things she liked, such as sweet pickle relish or fresh fruit like grapes or melon. I served the lunch on their breakfast table and left as Don and Carol ate lunch together while they enjoyed their pretty entry garden and sometimes talked.

One day a week was different, we called it *beautification day,* which Carol loved. After the morning coffee break, I took Carol to the bathroom. Then, the three of us got into the van and drove to Carol Patterson's beauty parlor where our Carol had been a customer for decades. Don and I transferred Carol from her wheel chair to the beautician's chair. Carol's hair was washed and set while 'beauty parlor' conversation flowed around her. Don then helped her walk/dance to a drying chair where I sat showing her magazine pictures while she dried. After a few weeks, Carol began complaining as if her bottom hurt as she sat in those chairs. When we transferred Carol's special RoHo cushion from her wheel chair to the harder beauty shop chairs, her complaining stopped. After hair drying, the beautician gave Carol a new beautifying hair do. Then we took her to a restaurant for lunch to show off her beauty. (Thousands of times in her life Carol had enjoyed the treat of getting beautified before she went for lunch with friends or to other special occasions, so beautification day renewed those pleasures.)

We varied where we ate to add variety to Carol's life and ours. After a few trips, staff at each restaurant recognized Carol and seated us where she could watch other customers, especially those who had small children. Because it was easier to eat, Carol usually had some kind of soup, e.g., favorites like tomato bisque, asparagus, potato, chili, or vegetable. We mashed chunky soups with a fork to make them easier to eat. Both Carol and I liked chocolate milk shakes so we shared one if it was on the menu. Pam and/or Doug sometimes joined us for that special lunch and conversation, and occasionally a friend stopped at our table for a brief visit. Carol never seemed to be self-conscious about her limitations during these public outings. She acted, and seemed to feel, as if she was just another ordinary person. As soon as we got home I took Carol to the bathroom because it had been several hours since she last went. Surprisingly, she was usually still dry. Of course, she had youthful training to 'hold it' until she got home. We guessed being in public activated that heavily learned habit since she seldom held it that long when at home. I left for home while Don put Carol to bed for her afternoon nap."

Carol's mornings were full of activity with another person so she had no time to be bored and was ready for a nap by 1 p.m. I lay down with her to reassure her with my presence and read until she was sound asleep. Then, I would do small chores like paying bills or starting a load of laundry before returning to read or nap with her. She typically slept until around 2:30 p.m.

Carol had been a movie lover since her grade school years, so after a bathroom visit we watched a movie. Our old large screen TV was downstairs and Carol was no longer mobile enough to go down there, so we used the smaller TV in our breakfast area. I was surprised Carol's interest in the movies wasn't stronger, given her history. Doug suggested the problem was the small screen. So, he helped me create an entertainment center by covering our fireplace with a 47 inch flat screen TV.

After we'd watched the big TV for a couple weeks, Doug said, "I was blown away with the dramatic difference your big screen made for Mom. With the little screen she often seemed disinterested, but being close to the big screen was more like being in a movie theater. She became very involved and stayed interested until the end of a movie. It was obvious she was following the plot because she laughed when the movie was funny, cried when it was appropriate, and reacted emotionally to the sad ending of the movie, *Where the Red Fern Grows*."

Cam came to visit a few weeks after we installed the big screen. He immediately installed technology so we could pick up programs off the internet and show them to Carol on the big screen. That opened up a new door for her pleasure. She could watch her old soap operas, could watch and hear choirs sing her favorites like *The Messiah,* and could see beautiful scenery. Carol and Cam spent a lot of pleasurable time together looking at internet programs during his visit. One evening Cam put a dog show on the screen. The dog was given subtraction problems to solve. The first was 8 – 2 = ? and Carol immediately said, "Six!" before the dog could even bark.

One internet Christmas episode she loved illustrates how the internet was a rich source of experiences that provide many different sources of pleasure. The episode begins with a large, self-serve cafeteria room with lots of people eating lunch – e.g., individuals, couples, parents with kids. Suddenly a woman stood and started singing; then another woman in another part of the room stood and joined her; then a man in a different part of the room stood and joined them. That process continued until there was a choral group of about 50 people standing all over the cafeteria, among the diners, singing a beautiful choral piece together. The diners were delighted, and so was Carol. Perhaps it reminded her of the joy she experienced singing opera songs with other customers at Asti's in New York City.

We bought movies, got them from the library, rented movies, and taped old movies off TV channels. We looked for movies linked to her interests such as classical music, dancing, children, pets, family, art, and Mother Nature, and of favorite actors like Bette Davis. As a young woman Carol went to a piano concert by Jose Iturbi, loved his playing and met him personally. He performed in several movies and eventually I was able to find and show all of them to Carol, to her delight. When we watched South Pacific, Carol quite clearly said, "That reminds me of when we were in Hawaii."

When kids went to the movies during the depression years, taking popcorn and Kool Aid was a kid tradition because we couldn't afford to buy refreshments. We renewed that tradition with our home movies with a nutritious drink (like ensure) and snacks (which helped serve our diet and fluid intake goals). We only interrupted movies when a bathroom visit was necessary. During Carol's last four years we enjoyed hundreds of movies together.

We ate dinner around 6 p.m. Pam and Doug both enjoyed cooking, were good at it, and emphasized good nutrition. Several times a week they prepared our dinner, ate with us, and one of them fed Carol. Occasionally, when weather permitted, I rolled Carol down our private lane in her wheel chair so we could eat dinner outdoors on Pam and Doug's upstairs deck where we could look down on their hillside gardens and Slab Cabin Run.

Pam's older sister, Kim, had severe limitations since young adulthood, so Pam and Doug had lots of experience helping a person with limitations. They used all their experience to be helpful to us. They strongly believe eating should be a pleasurable experience, both in terms of tastes and appearance of food and the companionship it provided. Here are examples:

Doug said, "It's important to enable a person to feed themselves as much as possible and as long as possible because it helps them feel they have some control over their life. They're sometimes embarrassed to have to be fed, so you shouldn't focus attention on the feeding process but on other things, like what they're eating or how it tastes. When possible, focus on their eyes – that produces a much more personal relationship. I finally realized I was always feeding Mom from the side. I changed and started facing and feeding her so she could see what was on the spoon and that improved her eating behavior."

Pam said, "It's important to feed a person with limitations the way you'd like to eat. Feed them the same food as other members of the family and keep their food tasty and warm. Sometimes serve things you know were 'comfort foods' in the past for them. For example, both Doug and Mom have always liked her tuna noodle casserole. Don't shift to something like 'baby food' when a person's limitations make it harder to chew and swallow. It's demeaning to be treated like a baby, and there is little pleasure for an adult's taste. Any food can be made easier to eat by cutting it up with a little electric food chopper. Keep foods you're serving separate. For example, this evening we had barbecued ribs, green beans and mashed potatoes. I chopped up the rib meat and then the green beans and put them and mashed potatoes on Mom's plate separate from each other so when Mom ate she could enjoy the tastes of each."

Doug said, "Keeping the food warm is very important – none of us like a good hot meal when it gets cold. Often a person stops eating, not because they're full or don't like the food but because it has become cold. It typically takes a person with limitations longer to eat, so usually their food is cold before they finish. I've found that if we start with a warm plate and later warm it up in the microwave, Mom would continue or renew eating when the food was warm. I wish someone would invent a plate that would keep a meal warm while eating. None of the ones we tried have worked."

Sometimes other family members ate with us and it was an even livelier table. Throughout our married life Carol made our home a kind of 'entertainment center' for family and friends. Our children and grandchildren had fun joking around during dinner and produced a lot of laughter. Carol still enjoyed that. However if conversation got too serious, loud or involved, she would try to divert it by saying something like "Yackity – yackity - yackity!"

Carol enjoyed infectious laughter and often laughed along. Pam said, "Mom liked jokes. I can't remember her losing her sense of humor. One could joke with Mom and tell when she thought something was funny." For example, Pam was a high school band majorette. One evening she brought her baton to dinner and started dancing around and twirling it. Carol thought that was hilarious. Sometimes, when Doug and Pam were leaving for home, they'd stop in the entry garden and do a little goodbye dance which produced a big grin from Carol. Tim told me that one time during coffee break, he caught Carol trying to sneak a cookie from his plate and she laughed.

Sometimes after dinner, Pam, Doug and Carol gathered at the piano while I put dirty dishes in the dish washer. Like his mother, Doug has a very good singing voice, could harmonize with anyone, and had a lot of experience singing from high school on. Pam would play some melody while Doug and Carol sang. Doug told me later, "I was blown away singing with Mom because she was always on key, always, up to the last days of her life. When she couldn't sing the words she sang the notes, even the very high ones. It was amazing."

Sometimes we went out to dinner in the evening with some of our family, and all knew how to treat Carol as 'an ordinary person', as friends who occasionally stopped by our table put it. Carol never acted as if she was self-conscious about her limitations. I think that was at least partly because those of us around her never treated her as if she was sick. *We always treated her as a person, not a patient!* One evening when son Cam was visiting from Florida, we took him to dinner at one of Carol's favorite restaurants. She was in high spirits that night, looked at Cam with a big smile and said, "*You're pretty!*"

I said, "That's a big compliment, Cam. She only calls me and her aides *'Cute'*."

One of our family traditions for decades has been to have a *happy hour* before dinner to relax, forget our work, and to share news, interests or funny anecdotes. Sometimes it was only Carol and me, but often it would be a gathering of family, friends or an opportunity to get to know someone new. For example, one afternoon our granddaughter, Jennifer, brought her boss, a distinguished member of our college faculty, so we could become acquainted. Pam and Doug shared with us the latest stories about their offspring's antics and adventures. Happy hour might be the aftermath of a football game with three sons and their wives before a victory dinner. Or, it might include grandchildren, their spouses and/or great grandchildren. We gathered around a big coffee table flanked by two sofas and a couple comfy chairs, with Carol presiding in her wheel chair. Even during her Alzheimer's years, Carol was very much a part of the group, and family members included her in their conversations and stories. They were free-wheeling, fun and somewhat unpredictable 'mini parties'.

Russ described three occasions that illustrated Carol's involvement:

"In the last year of Mom's life, Barb and I and you and Mom were sitting in the living room having a happy hour when our youngest son, Jordan, and his girlfriend Dara came in and announced with great excitement and joy that they were engaged. Mom displayed delight! She smiled, she laughed, she clapped her hands together and watched them intently with sparkling eyes. Clearly she understood what was going on and enjoyed it immensely. It was a wonderful example that just because someone isn't able to verbally communicate doesn't mean there isn't a lot going on in their head and that they can't enjoy events of life with others.

Another example that year involved our very young granddaughter, Riley. We were visiting and having some family interaction among us and with Mom. Riley decided to become a part of that. She went over and stood beside Mom (her great grandmother), took her hand and began gently caressing it. Mom beamed with pleasure! It was such a sweet scene that it brought warmth to our hearts and tears to our eyes.

Once we were visiting with our granddaughter, baby Alyssa. She was given to Mom to hold and Mom responded with warmth and pleasure. Clearly the part of her previous life that involved pleasure with babies or little girls (Mom had only boy babies) was still capable of bringing pleasure to her life."

Happy hours weren't the only time family dropped in. For example, one afternoon Russ and Barb's daughters, Jennifer and Lisa, and Lisa's two little girls stopped by. It was a special treat for Carol to interact with females she loved.

Evenings when we ate by ourselves, Carol and I sometimes delayed dinner to go for a golf cart ride. Carol loved her golf cart. Unfortunately, her mobility skills declined so much she was no longer able to climb in her cart and its design made it impossible to lift her in. She couldn't use it for several months. Then our good friend, Mike Green, the creative architect, builder and master craftsman who had designed and built our home, figured out a way to rebuild the seat on her cart so we could slide it out to the side. Carol could then be transferred from her wheel chair to that seat, I slid the seat back into the cart, fastened the seat belt we'd created, and once again she could go for a ride. Boy, was she glad to be "back in the saddle again"!

After that, someone took Carol cart cruising almost every day in warm weather. Some evenings, Pam and Doug hosted a picnic by the stream at their house. I'd drive Carol to that lovely spot to enjoy their garden's beauty, the delicious food and pleasant companionship. For over fifty years she'd loved picnics by our stream and eating the tasty food and I was determined that Alzheimer's would not end that pleasure.

Some evenings after dinner we might diddle around with her piano, look at photo albums, go on the internet to watch something, or sit on our deck listening to music and watching fire flies float through the night. Whatever the familiar activity might be, Carol participated with either animated joy or quiet pleasure.

Each night I took Carol to the bathroom, prepared and dressed her for bed, brushed her teeth, cleared left over food from her mouth, put her to bed, gave her a kiss goodnight, and turned out the light around 8 p.m. I lay beside her and read until she slept. That didn't take long because after her typical busy day she was always comfortably tired. Then I went to sleep.

One night I conducted a "memory experiment". We had found security and pleasure sleeping together almost every night for two-thirds of a century. She had never slept with another man nor I with another woman, so talking of 'sleeping together' should reconstruct only one memory. I kissed her goodnight and said, "Carol, it makes me happy to sleep with you!"

She smiled and said in a sleepy voice, "I know, Don. Me too!" My dreams were especially sweet that night!

Carol's developmental elder care pattern I've described was essentially the same, with minor variations, every day for the four years before she died. Further decline during that period was slow and limited. As Kelly put it:

"I didn't see much decline over the years. Carol was pretty much the same from visit to visit. She always did good for me and we enjoyed each other. Near the end, she didn't care much for the exercises but would do them – I just made them shorter."

During those four years she was continually healthy (no illnesses of any kind), physically and mentally active, socially involved, and happy. For four years we kept a daily log of Carol's bathroom accomplishments, how much fluid she drank, what she ate, everything she did, people she interacted with, and meds taken. One column recorded communication and mood throughout the day. I considered that an indicator of the success we were having with trying to fill her daily life with pleasure and satisfaction. Here are examples of what over 80% of those written comments were like:

alert-pleasant; alert-talkative; very talkative; smiling-laughing; talked a lot-laughed some; talkative-smiled; reaching-smiling; some talking-laughing, mostly quiet, very talkative during a.m. care; very verbal today; smiling; concentrating on activities; laughed a lot.

Clearly, our developmental care program succeeded. Every day of her life was filled with episodes of activity and warm hearted interactions with other people that consistently filled her life with pleasure, satisfaction, healthy living, and affectionate, interesting companionship.

On Saturday, August 15, 2011, Doug, Pam and Ryan brought dinner to our dining room to celebrate my 85th birthday. Ryan said goodbye because he was moving to Chicago to a job to finance his life, while he got training in improv comedy. He could always make Carol laugh. On Sunday afternoon Pam took Carol on a leisurely cart ride and then parked by our butterfly garden where Carol could watch butterflies and Pam pulling weeds.

The following week Russ joined us for a delicious lasagna dinner cooked by our Italian daughter-in-law, Pam. Russ fed his Mom lasagna and some Heath bar ice cream Carol loved. Wednesday Linda noted in the log that Carol seemed a little tired and had her eyes shut part of the time. Thursday was *beautification day*. Carol was alert, pleasant and more talkative as she did all her activities. She seemed to be looking forward to getting her hair done. We had lunch at one of Carol's favorite restaurants where Carol had tomato soup, half a chocolate shake, and smiled watching two babies. After her afternoon nap we watched *The Glenn Miller Story,* one of her favorite movies because of the big band dance music.

The next morning Carol seemed more rested. Linda said Carol was alert, pleasant and talking a little as she did her activities. After a bathroom break, Carol and I enjoyed our daily dance through the house and garden and then sat down to a leisurely lunch of tomato soup with a glass of milk. After another bathroom stop, I tucked Carol in for her afternoon nap. I lay down with her and read until she was asleep and then went to start a load of wash.

About a half hour later I came to join Carol in our nap and immediately saw she wasn't breathing. I gasped "Oh, Darling!" and grabbed the phone, called 911, and began chest compressions in an effort to restart her heart. The EMS headquarters is only a few blocks away, so they arrived quickly and took emergency steps to try to bring Carol back, which were continued at the hospital without success. They could find nothing wrong. There was nothing in her throat to block her breathing. The diagnosis was that her heart just decided to stop. We had our last dance together about three hours before she died.

The next week was a blurred whirl for me. All of our family came to honor her and to share in the public ceremonies. Carol was buried in a small historic church cemetery within walking distance of our home. Carol's resting place overlooked a spectacular view of Mt. Nittany. Her life was celebrated with a release of butterflies by her great granddaughters.

That evening, the family and Carol's aides gathered in our home to celebrate her life rather than to mourn her death. Everyone told funny and loving stories about their experiences with Mom, Grandma and Carol. It was an evening full of pleasure, love and laughter, and strengthening of family ties. Then they left and I began my new life in an empty home.

Carol no longer lay beside me at night, but in a way we renewed the kind of fantasy partnership we had lots of practice with while separated during WWII. Then, too, we were physically separated but shared life through an imagined relationship fed by our letters. In my loneliness, as I lay alone in our bed in the dark, I began again to imagine conversations with Carol. In one of them, as I described in the beginning of this story, we agreed to write this book.

During our life together we successfully helped one another with issues bothering us and, in accomplishing shared goals, leading us to describe ourselves as a terrific team. One night, lying in our bed looking into the darkness, I said, "Carol, our book is finished but I don't like the way we ended it with a story of loss and sadness. Somehow I would like to end it by 'accentuating the positive' but I haven't been able to find a way of doing that."

Out of the darkness came Carol's suggestion, "Tell them about our talks."

I lay in the dark puzzling over that suggestion and went to sleep wondering what it meant. The next morning I woke up with the answer. That's why our book ends this way.

During the year spent drafting *Carols' Alzheimer's Story* I sometimes got stuck trying to decide what the next step should be. Three times I lay awake in the dark at night and in my imagination talked with Carol about the difficulty I was having. Each time I woke up in the morning with an answer.

Our imagined talks are a symbol of the partnership we forged, in letters and in person, and used to envision and implement solutions to our problems and ways of accomplishing our goals. For example, our "team" cooperated in building our first house, in building a new counseling program and a new college, in building a creatively successful arts and crafts studio and shop, and in producing four wonderful boys/men.

Now, our team has written a book together aimed at trying to help enrich the lives of others. Through her many letters and greeting cards to me and her parents, and my memories of our conversations, Carol has written as much of this book as I have. So, our partnership continues to produce creative accomplishments. To symbolize that, *Carols' Alzheimer's Story* is published with co-authorship:

Donald H. Ford and Carol C. Ford

Note to Readers: We want to get these ideas to as many people as possible who may have to deal with Alzheimer's disease. Therefore, if you like this book, Carol and I hope you will encourage others, in person or through blogs and comments on the internet, to read it and join the effort to develop elder care to focus on treating them like a person, not a patient. We have established a web site, www.Carols-journey.com, where ideas and examples about developmental elder care, and "how to do it" questions, can be proposed and discussed.

The objective of this book is to try to stimulate improvements in the quality of eldercare for seniors with permanent limitations. Therefore, all royalties from this book will go into a special fund to support research, development, and demonstration projects aimed at that objective.

Epilogue

This book illustrates using the developmental model of care to create a home care plan for a specific person. However, it also has potential for enabling a satisfying life for senior citizens with any kind of serious limitation as they age, such as strokes. It would take another book to describe those possibilities in detail. I'll give some information and a few examples here to stimulate your thinking about other possibilities.

In October, 2011, MetLife published a survey of nursing homes in the United States. Women were 66% of the residents. The average annual rate for a semi-private room was $78,110; for a private room it was $87,235. In the description of Carol's mother, you read about the kind of life that bought for her. In contrast, the annual cost of Carol's home care was a little over one third of typical nursing home care. That bought for Carol a healthy life filled every day with companionship, sharing pleasurable activities and frequent intimate social occasions with family and friends in her own familiar home and neighborhood.

We hear considerable commentary about caregiver "stress and burnout" in Alzheimer's care. I suggest those results, at least in part, stem from the medical model's primary emphasis on dealing with what is wrong with the person. Caregivers gain little gratification from focusing on the negative, loss of competence and pleasure in life, and watching a person die when you can't fix it. The focus on helping people have a good life with what they have left, i.e., accentuating the positive, produced a different reaction from Carol's caregivers. For example:

Kelley said, "Seeing how happy Carol was as a result of the way you had us care for her made me happy and feel good about myself, and look forward to coming to work with her. It brought a lot of joy into my life."

Linda said, "I grew to care for Carol deeply, not just as a caregiver, but as a grafted in member of the Ford family. Carol was a beautiful, artistic, special lady, whom I've had the privilege to know and who will always have a place in my heart. I've never had so much fun and pleasure on a job in my life."

Tim said, "I cannot begin to express my gratitude for all you do. Spending time with Carol and you over the last few years has been some of the most rewarding experiences for me. I look forward to every weekend I work with you. I've learned so much about love, life and family from my experiences here."

With a little understanding and ingenuity the developmental model of home care can be used with anyone, anywhere, as illustrated by the following examples provided by caregivers of nursing home patients:

"I'd been a Registered Nurse for decades when the Administrator of a long term care facility hired me as a 'trouble shooter' of sorts. My first assignment was evaluating Mr. M. He had plagued the nursing home staff with difficult behaviors since his admission following a stroke. He argued with other residents, cussed at staff members, and refused medications and treatments. His children wouldn't visit him because any contact ended in a loud free-for-all. He insisted on eating in his room and avoided most human contact. Management allowed this isolation because of his tendency for physical violence. Mr. M. had great dexterity when it came to bashing people with his cane.

A brief glance around his room revealed the life of Mr. M. I saw piles of Atlases, classic novels, books about famous military leaders, newspapers, and current magazines. His mind was unraveling, but he struggled to hold onto the man he'd been through TV and reading. Until his stroke, he'd been a successful businessman, world traveler, and respected member of his community. Stuck in an institutional setting, Mr. M. was losing himself.

His health had been failing. He became bedfast and seemed uncharacteristically quiet. I asked if I could do anything that might make him feel better. He produced a dog-eared manuscript from beneath his blanket and said, 'Yes, read this and we can talk about it tomorrow.' The manuscript was poetry, *wonderful* poetry about the foreign cities he'd visited, his wife who died years ago, his children, wars and veterans he'd known. That poetry was his life put to paper, his legacy. The next day I begged him not to let his legacy slip away.

From that point on, he was a different person. I typed his hand written poetry and put a nice cover on it. He proudly showed his book to everyone who entered the room. He called his children and arranged a pleasant lunch so he could share his poetry with them. We discussed finding a publisher for his writing. Mr. M. died before that could happen, but he died a contented man. I never forgot him, and wished caregivers had known more about him sooner."

(Remember, anger occurs when some goal a person wants to accomplish is obstructed. Mr. M. discarded his anger when that nurse honored his accomplishments and the goal of sharing his poetry with others was achieved.)

"Ms. V. was a client for whom I was responsible in a group home. She had 'severe intellectual disabilities'. She couldn't verbally communicate when she wanted something or to do something, so she behaved in an agitated way. I decided I could help her get some pleasure out of life if I could understand what she wanted. So, I created a book for her that contained pictures symbolizing some need or goal (e.g., a telephone; a glass of water; a bathroom; musical notes; a TV) When she became agitated, I gave her the picture book. She leafed through it until she pointed to a picture. I knew what the picture meant to the girl. For example, pointing to the phone meant she wanted to talk with her parents. I called a parent who talked while the girl listened. All she wanted was to hear her parent's voice."

(She couldn't use words to convey the meanings she was thinking; pictures provided an alternate way of doing that)

"Mrs. L. was an Alzheimer's patient in a local nursing home. She was still mobile and could communicate some but had severe memory problems, seldom had visitors, and was often depressed. She was a widow and her children lived elsewhere.

For years she had loved working as a preschool teacher and caregiver, and the little kids loved her. Parents whose children she had cared for admired her and were grateful for her help. The current preschool teacher had been one of those kids. She enlisted the cooperation of the nursing home and a few other women to brighten Mrs. L.'s life. Twice a week one of them would pick up Mrs. L. and take her to the preschool for the morning. She sat watching and listening to the children, occasionally talked with the teacher, and sometimes had children come play or visit with her. Sometimes they came to hug her when they had to leave or when she left. She was delighted with their occasional little gifts.

She eagerly looked forward to being picked up for a visit. Her depressive episodes ceased. She told other patients about 'her children'. Their parents sometimes came to visit her. She enjoyed movies about children and looking at pictures of children."

These examples illustrate that it is possible to significantly enrich the lives of residents in traditional nursing home settings by applying a developmental approach. It's time we modernize and humanize the way we treat elderly people with limitations.

There has been growing recognition of this need, illustrated by three proposals: Selective Optimization With Compensation; The Green House Concept; The Moral Philosophy Guiding Person Centered Care. Each fits within the broad, theoretically based developmental model of elder care.

These references provide the scientific and professional knowledge base for our Developmental Model of Elder Care.

Ford, D.H. (1987; 1994). Humans as Self-Constructing Living Systems. Lawrence Erlbaum Associates.

Ford M.E. (1992). Motivating Humans: Goals, Emotions and Personal Agency Beliefs. SAGE Publications.

Ford, D.H. & Urban, H.B. (1998). Contemporary Models of Psychotherapy. John Wiley & Sons.

Ford, D.H. & Lerner, R.M. (1999) Developmental Systems Theory. SAGE Publications.